MOBILE SUIT

GUNDAM

THE ORIGIN

I

—ACTIVATION—

YOSHIKAZU YASUHIKO

ORIGINAL STORY BY:
YOSHIYUKI TOMINO • HAJIME YATATE

MECHANICAL DESIGN BY:
KUNIO OKAWARA

Collector's Edition

Mobile Suit Gundam
THE ORIGIN

I

—ACTIVATION—

CONTENTS

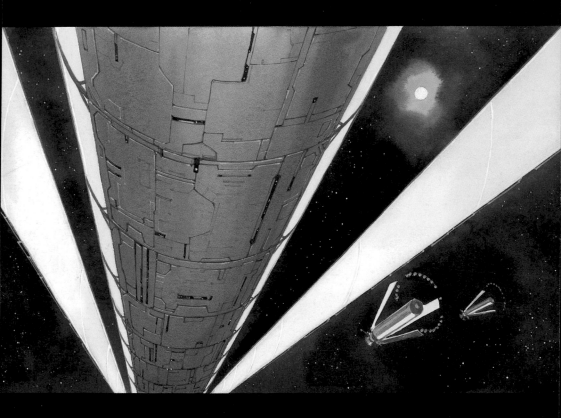

excess populations to space
for over half
a century.

Hundreds of enormous space
colonies floated in orbit around
the Earth.

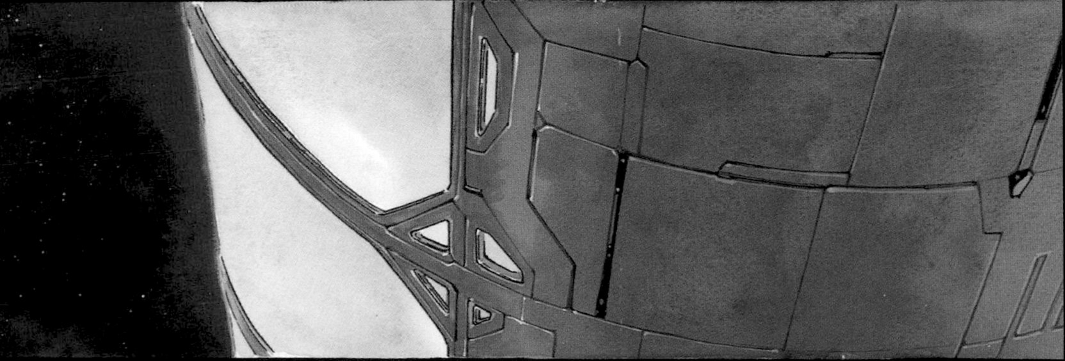

On the terraformed inner walls of the great cylinders,

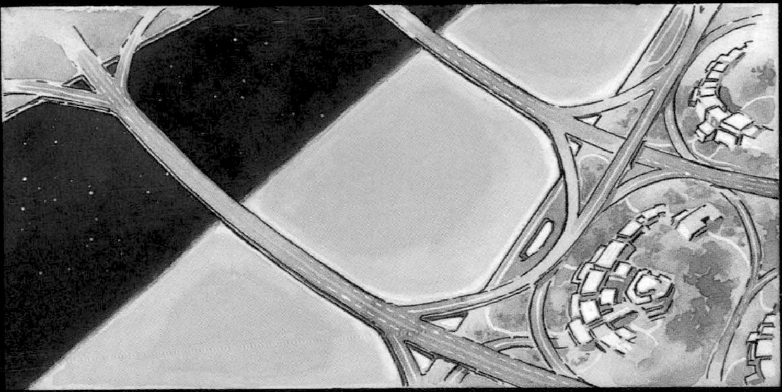

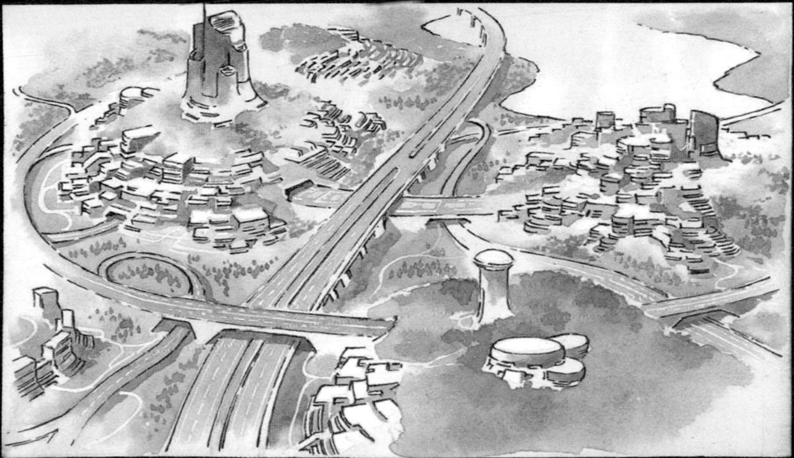

people found new homes.

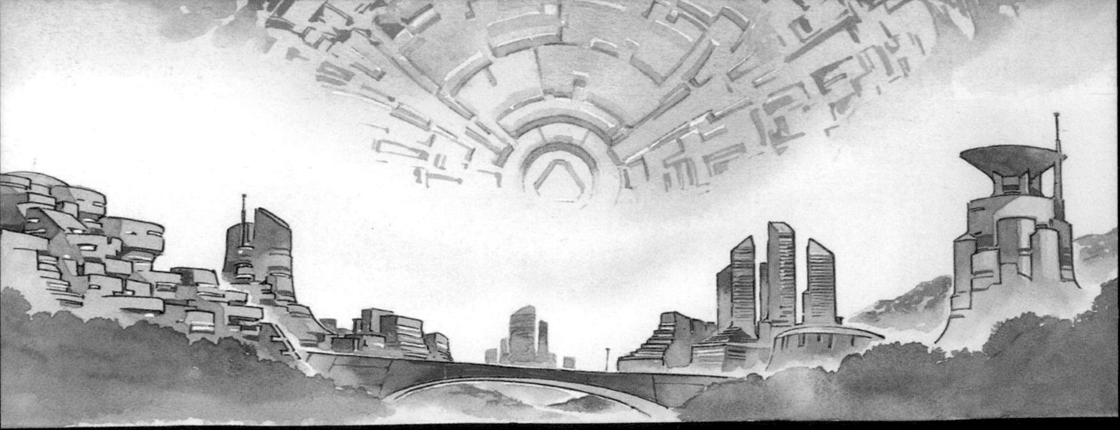

Millions of space colonists lived there, had children, and

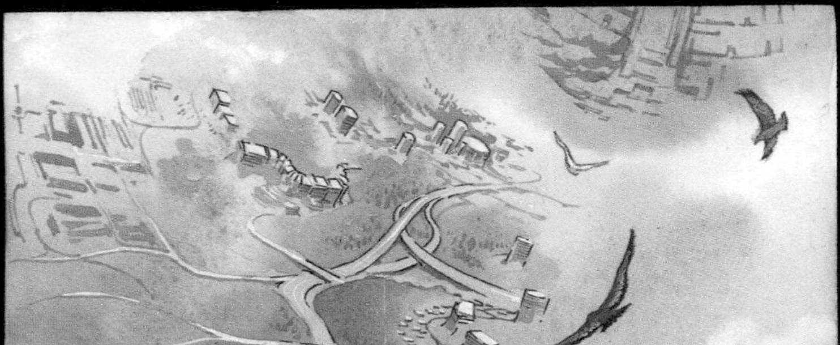

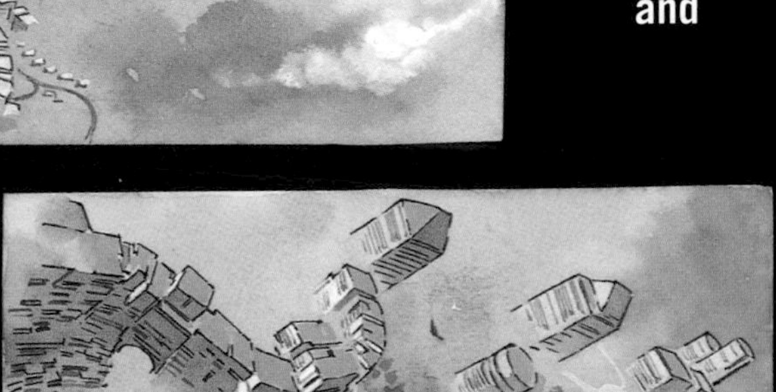

passed on.

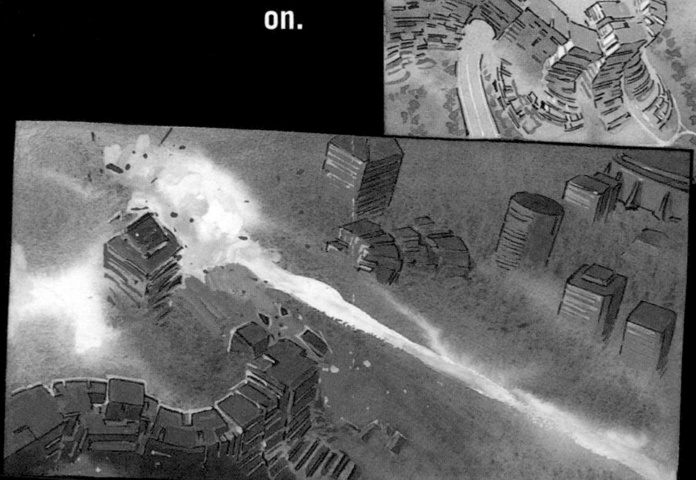

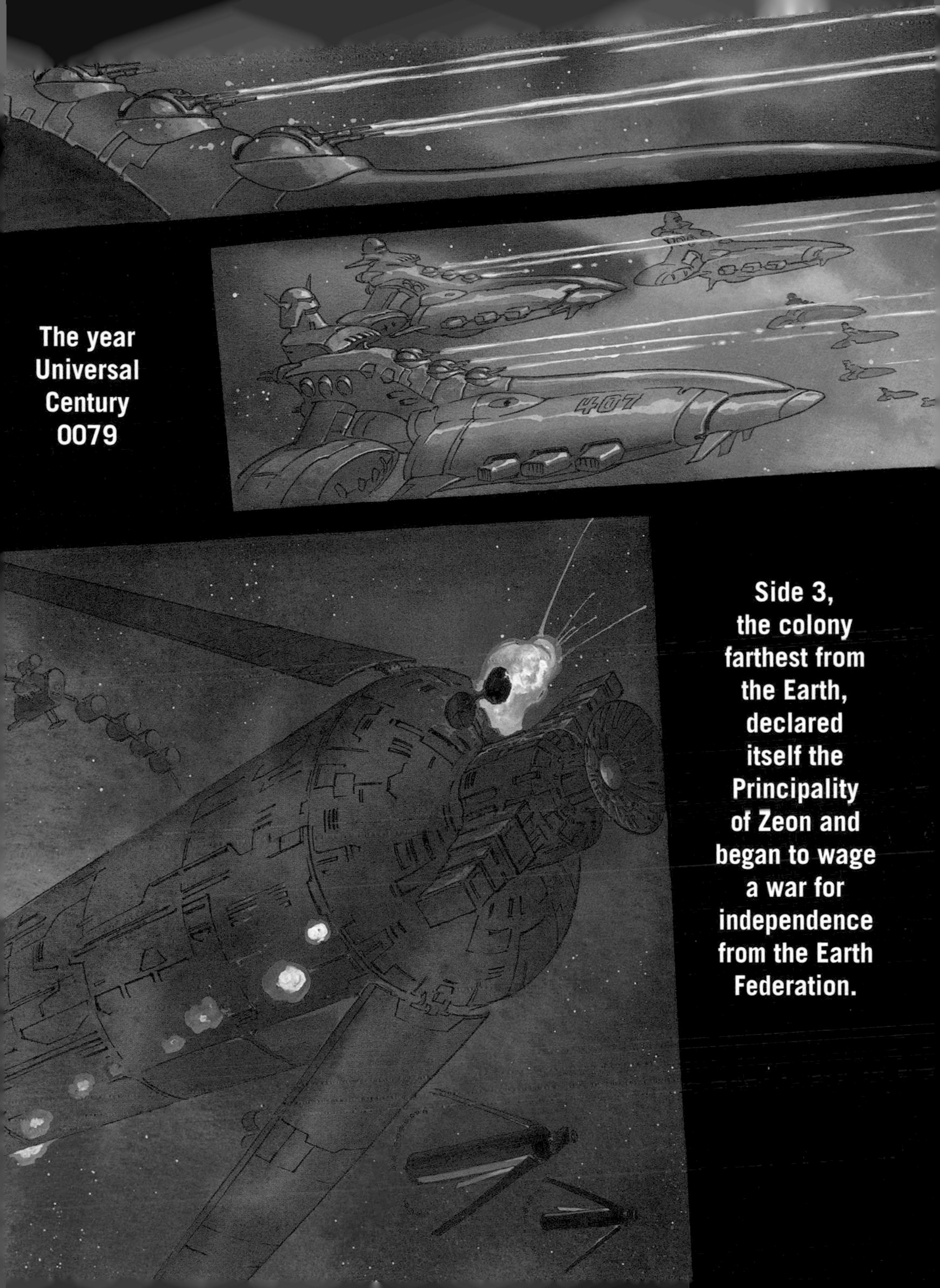
407
The year Universal Century 0079
Side 3, the colony farthest from the Earth, declared itself the Principality of Zeon and began to wage a war for independence from the Earth Federation.

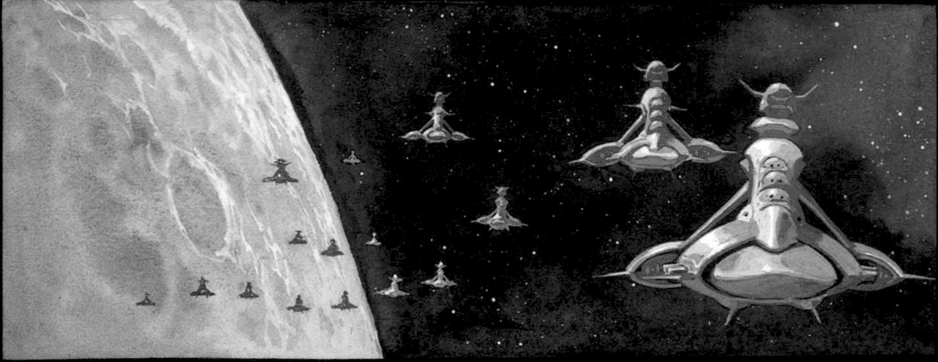

In scarcely
over a month
of fighting,
Principality
and
Federation
together
slaughtered

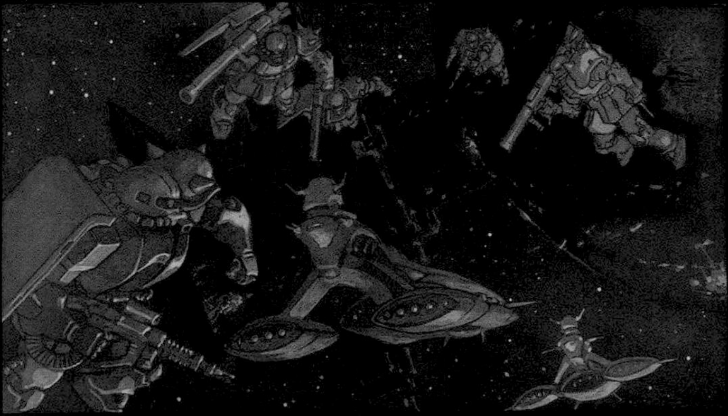

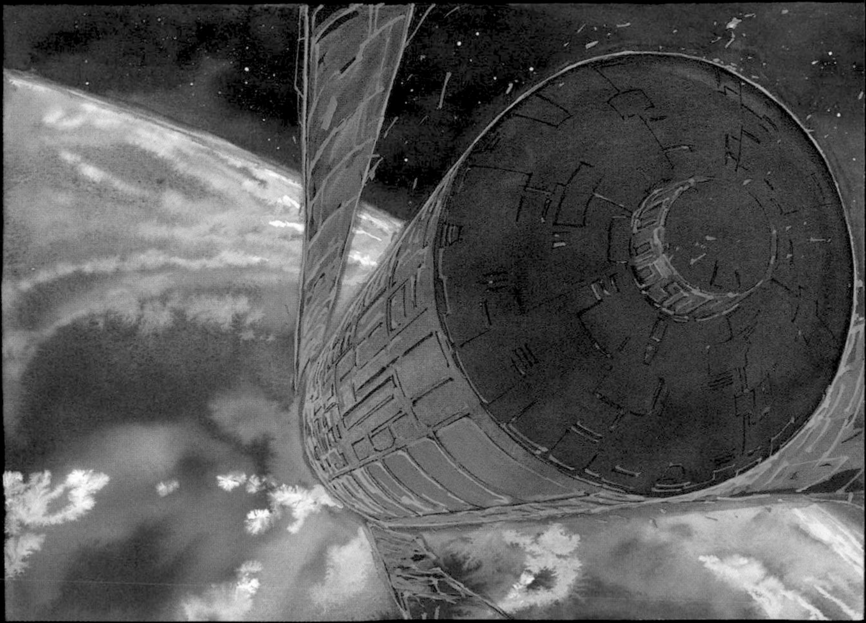

half of
humanity's
total
population.

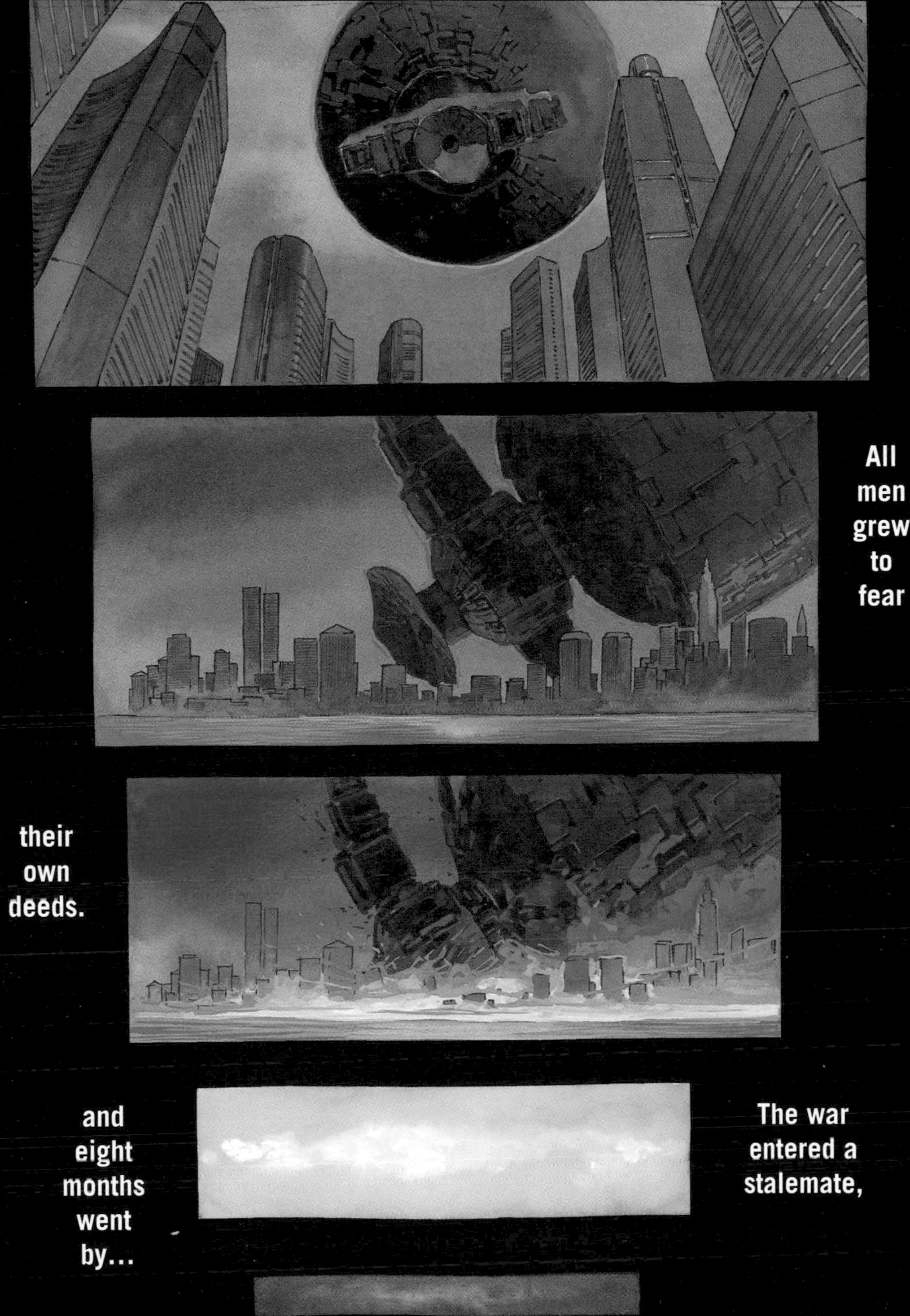
All men grew to fear
their own deeds.
The war entered a stalemate,
and eight months went by...

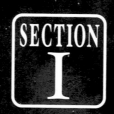

SECTION
I

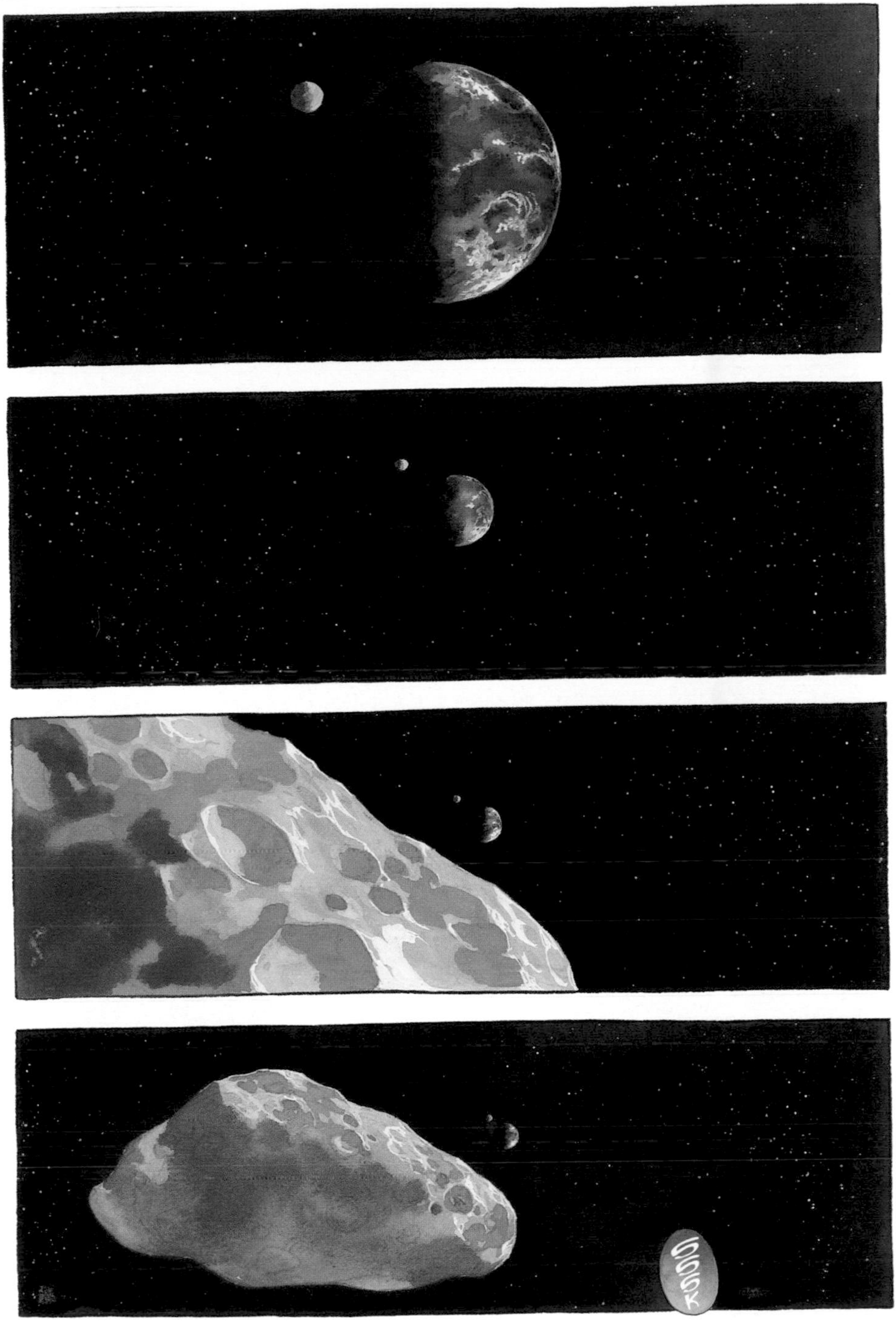
SSSK

SSSK
SSSK
SSSK
SSSK
SSSK
SSSK

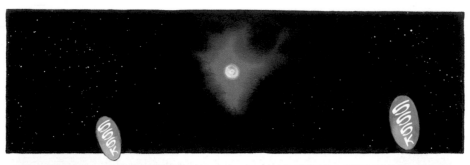

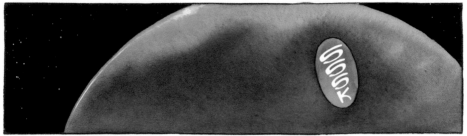

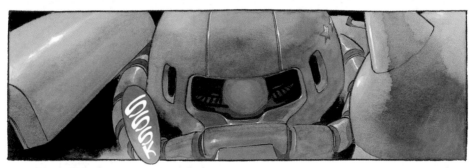

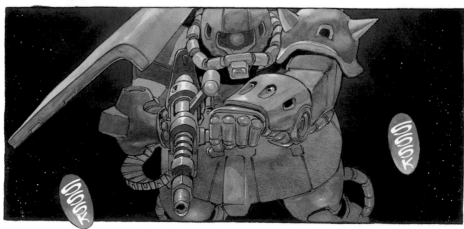

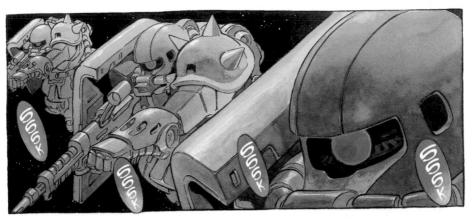

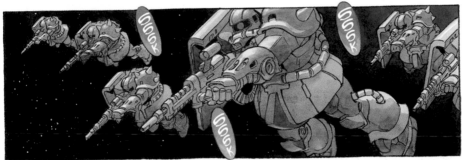

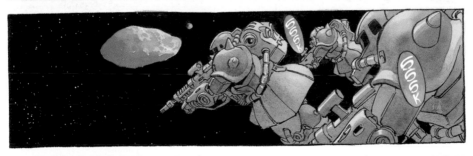

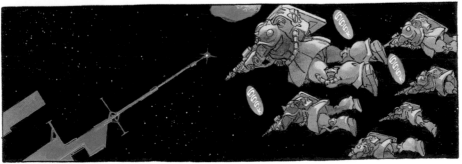

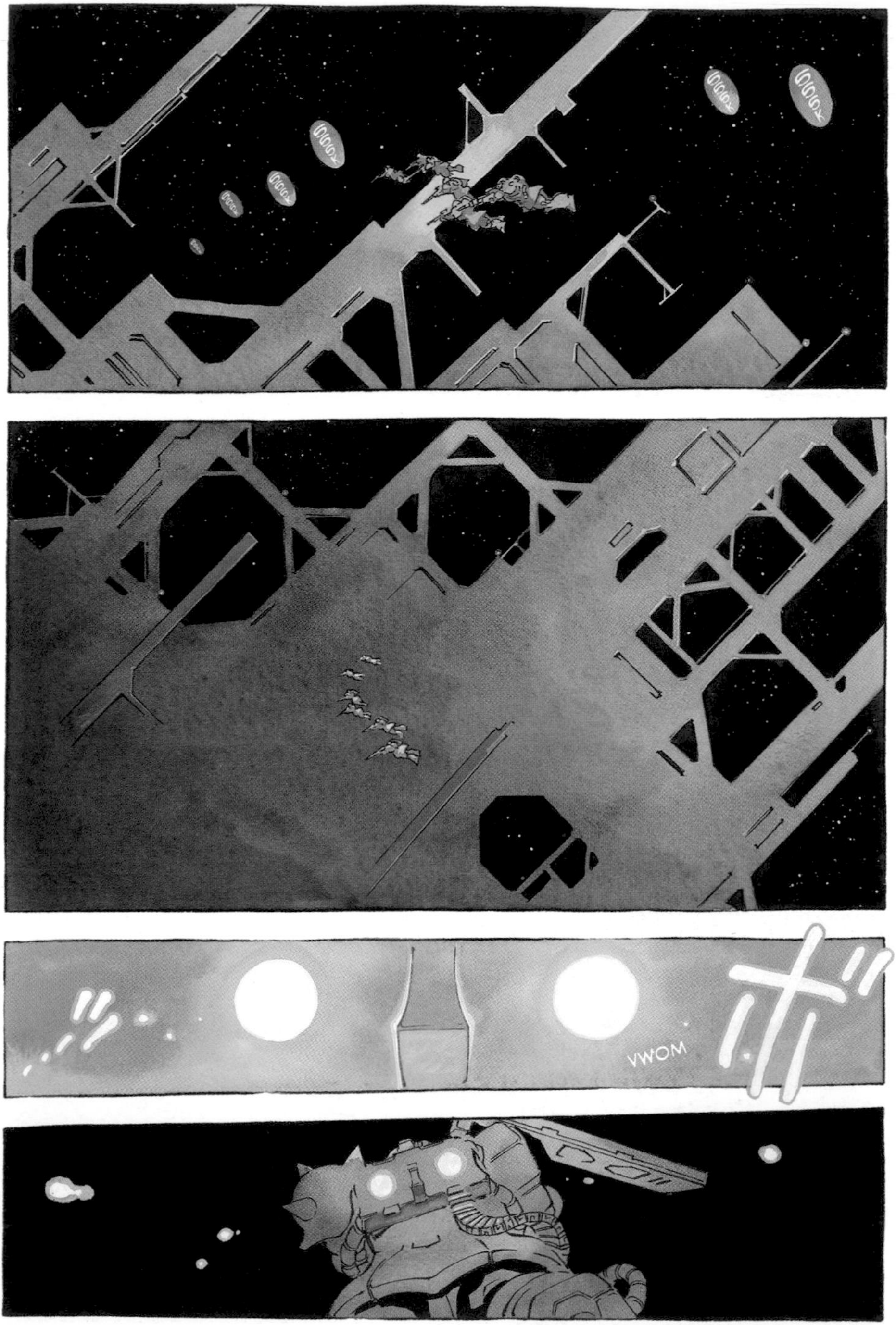
VWOM

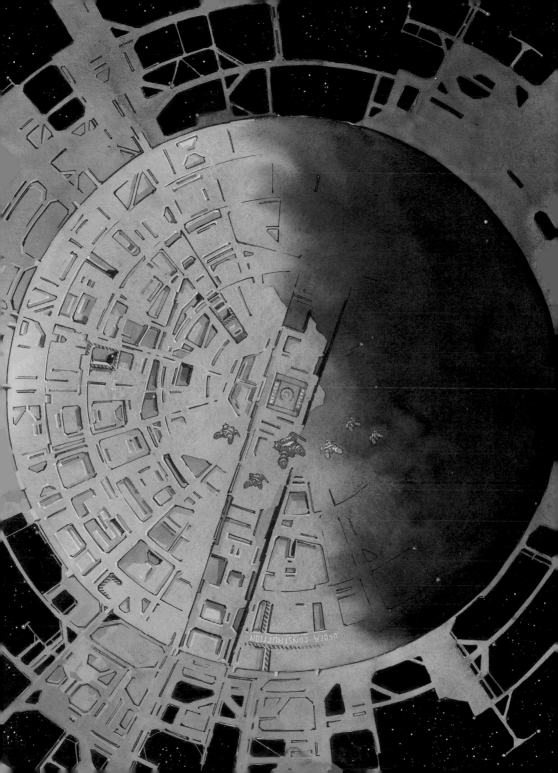

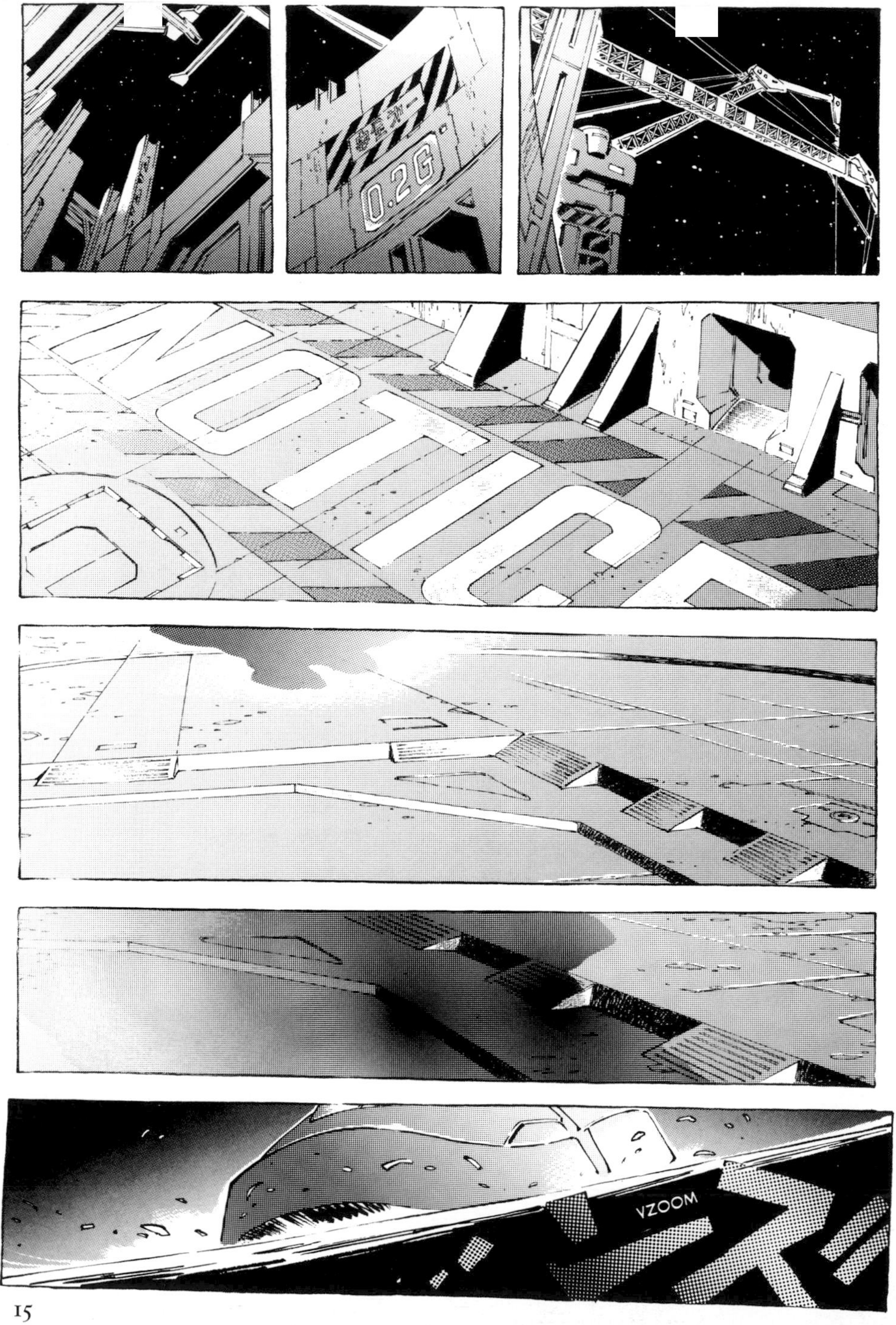
0.2G
NOTIC
VZOOM

ZZK
ZZK
FZZT
POMF

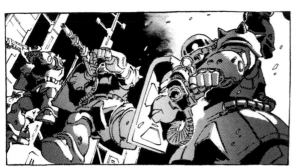

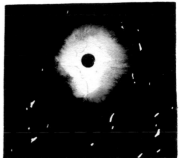

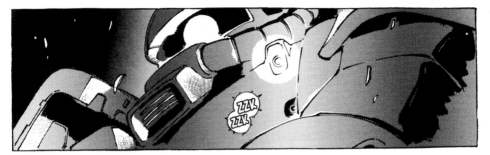

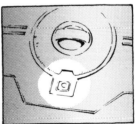

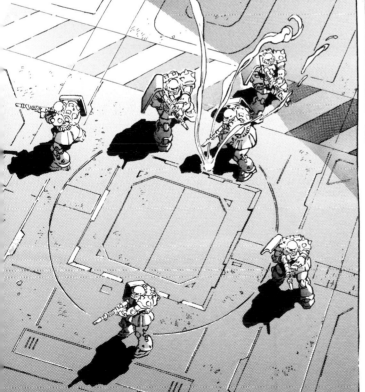

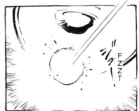

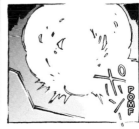

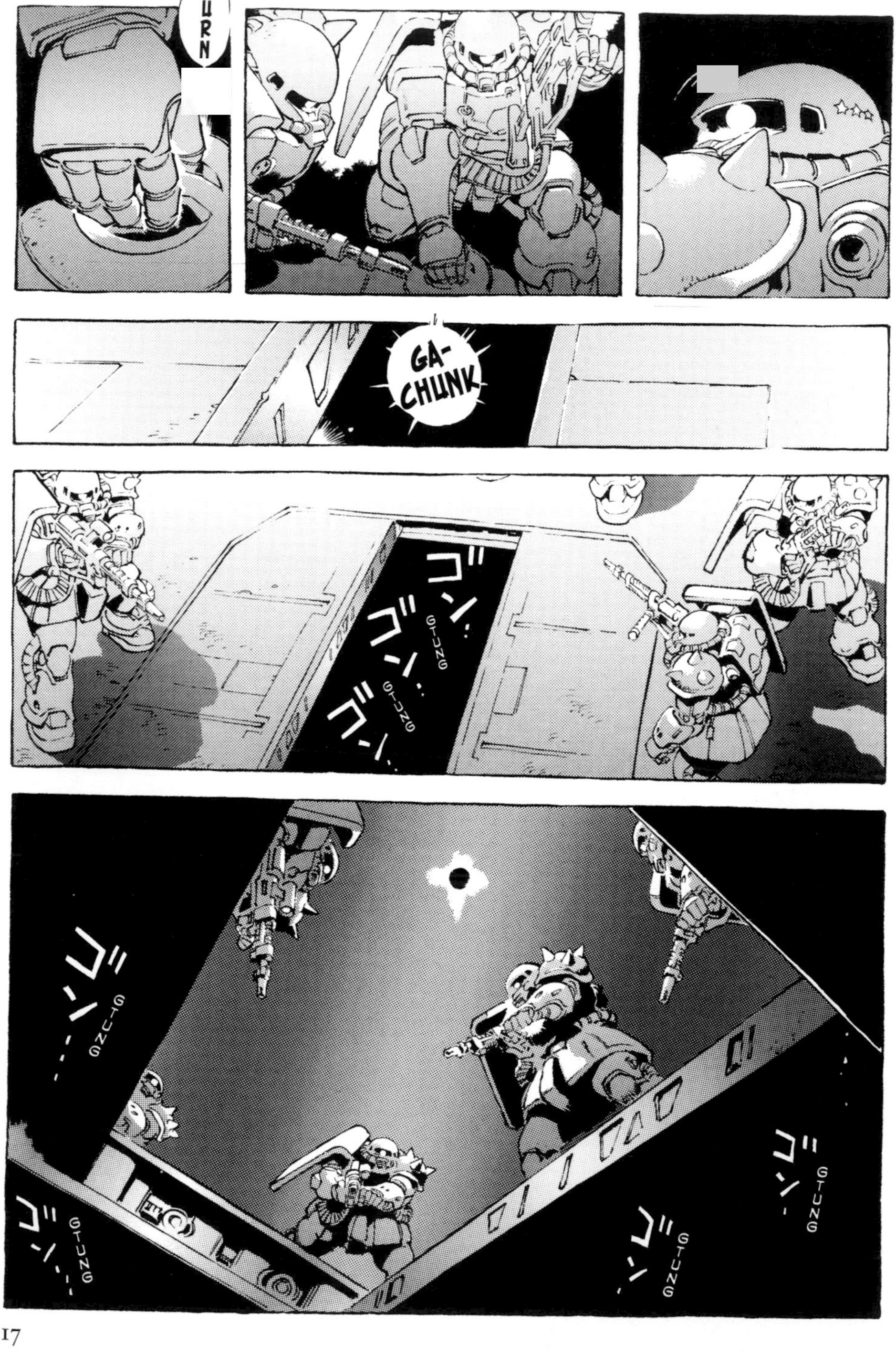

TURN
GA-CHUNK
ゴン‥
GTUNG
ゴン‥
GTUNG
ゴン‥
ゴン
GTUNG
ゴン
GTUNG
ゴン
GTUNG
ゴン‥
GTUNG

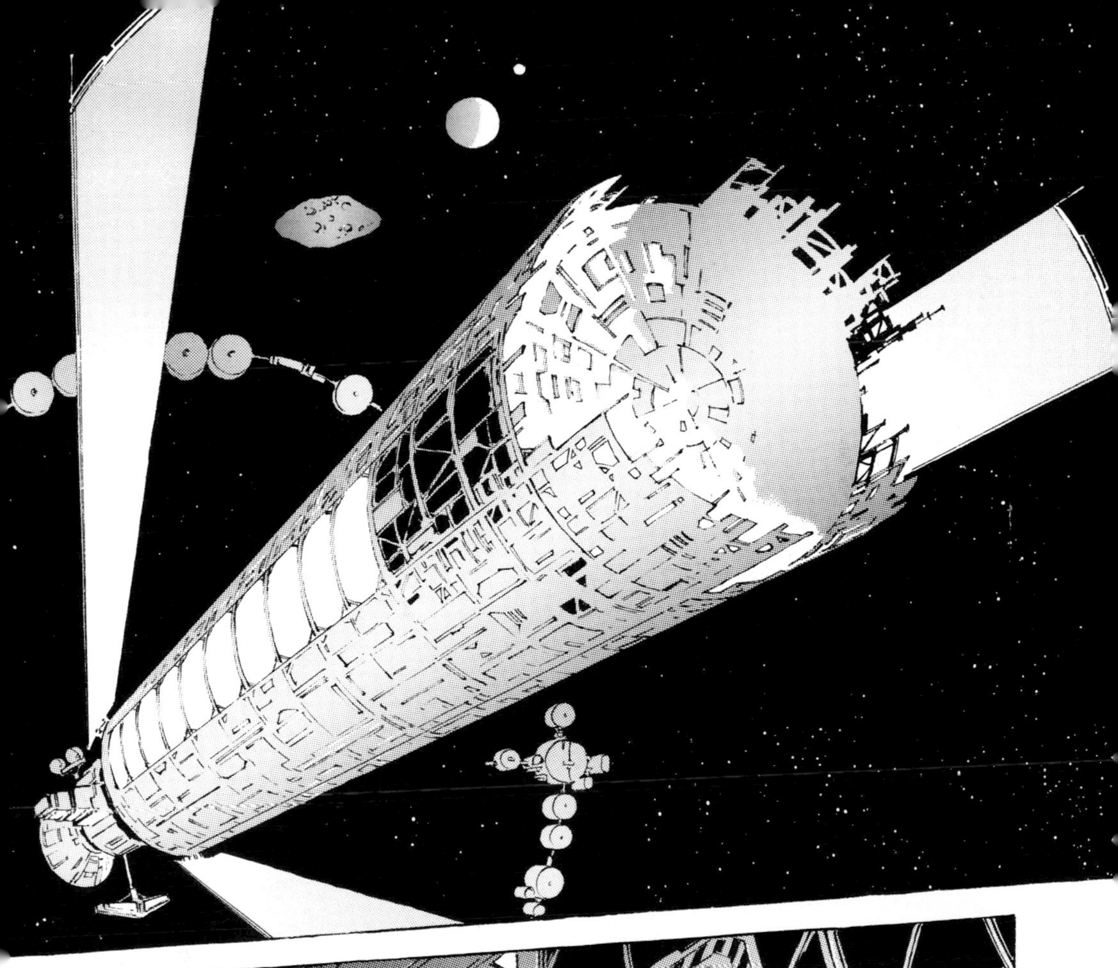

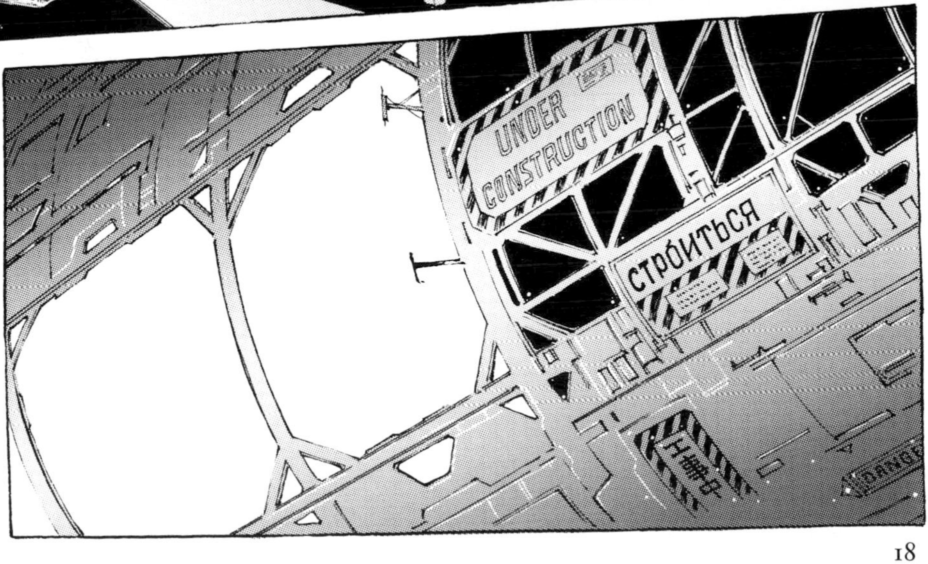
UNDER CONSTRUCTION
СТРÓИТЬСЯ

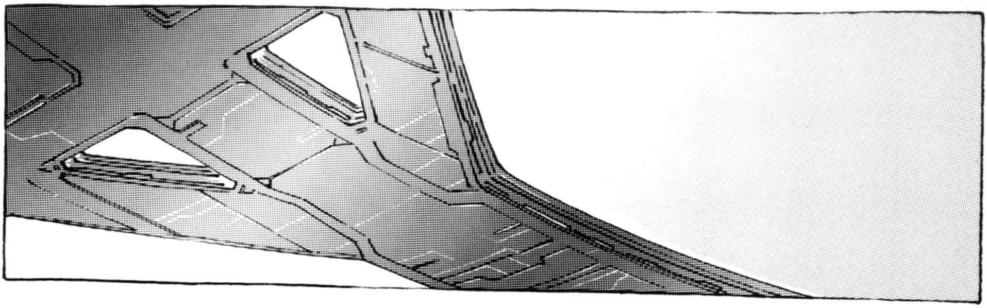

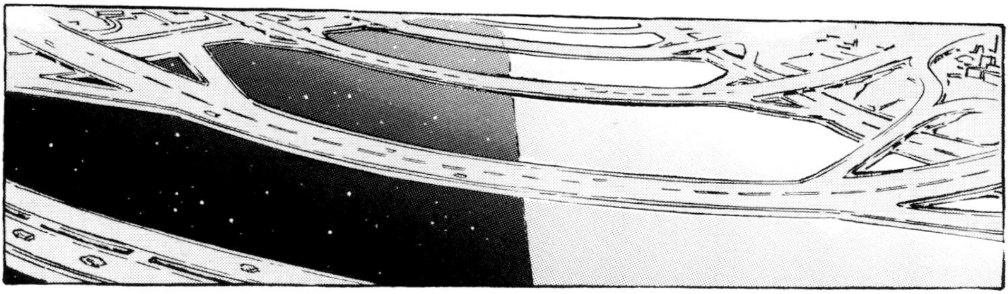

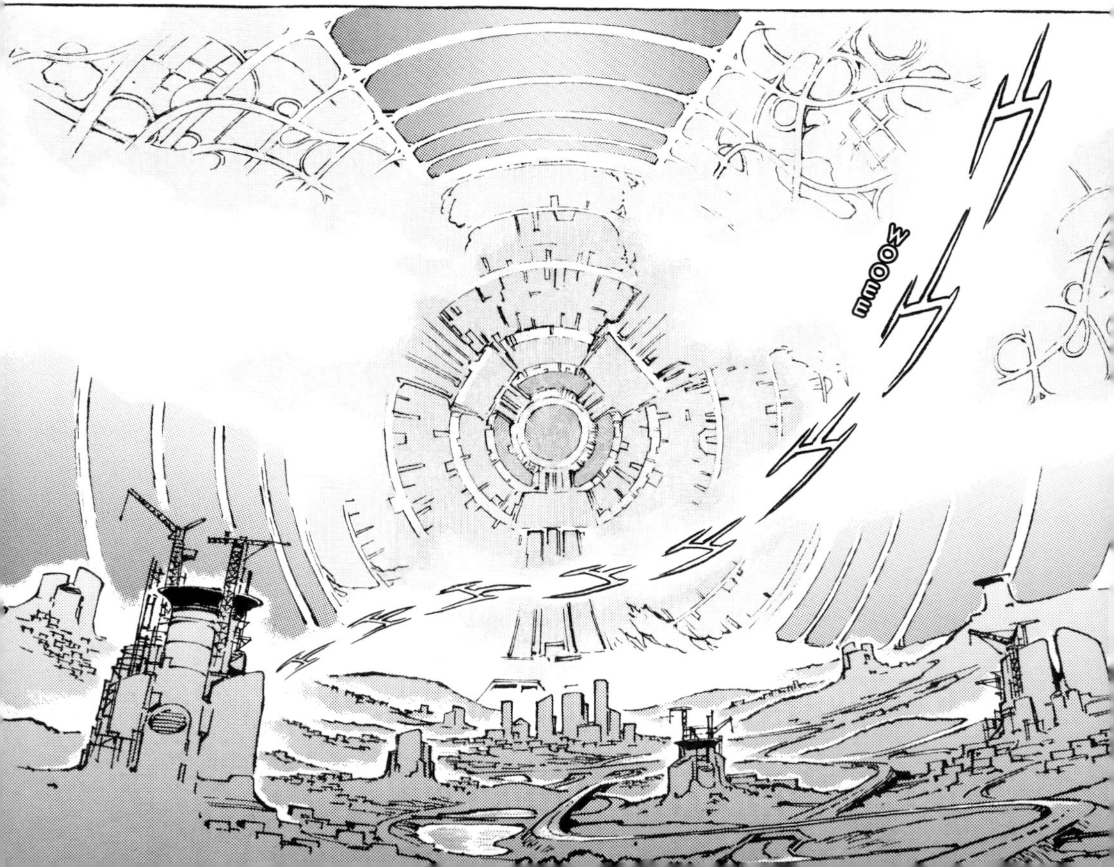
WOOmm

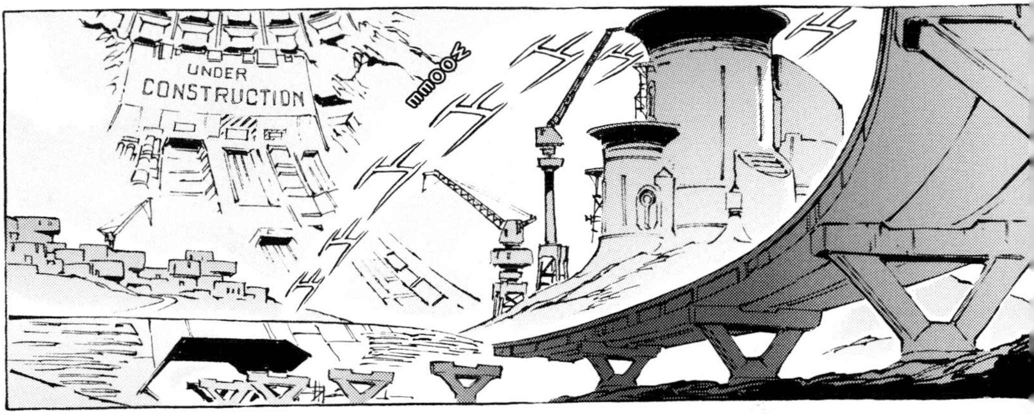
UNDER
CONSTRUCTION
WOOMM

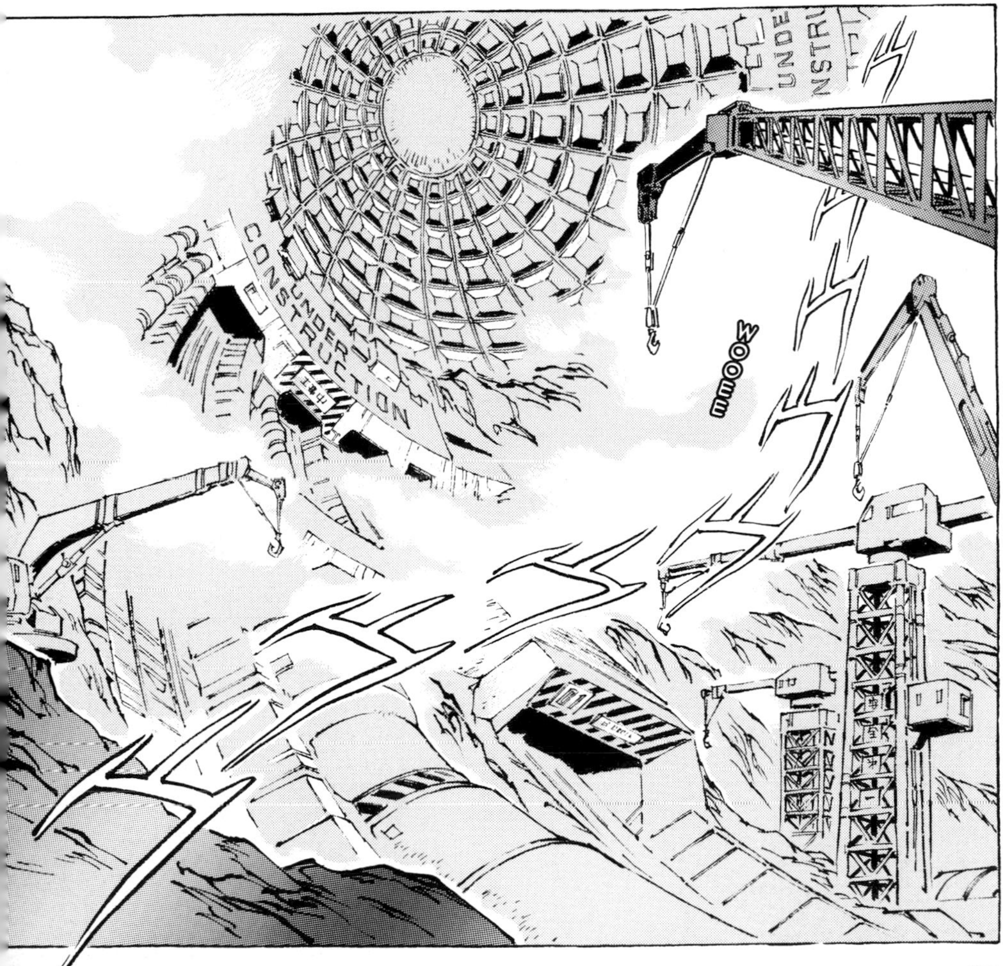
UNDER
CONSTRUCTION
WOOMM

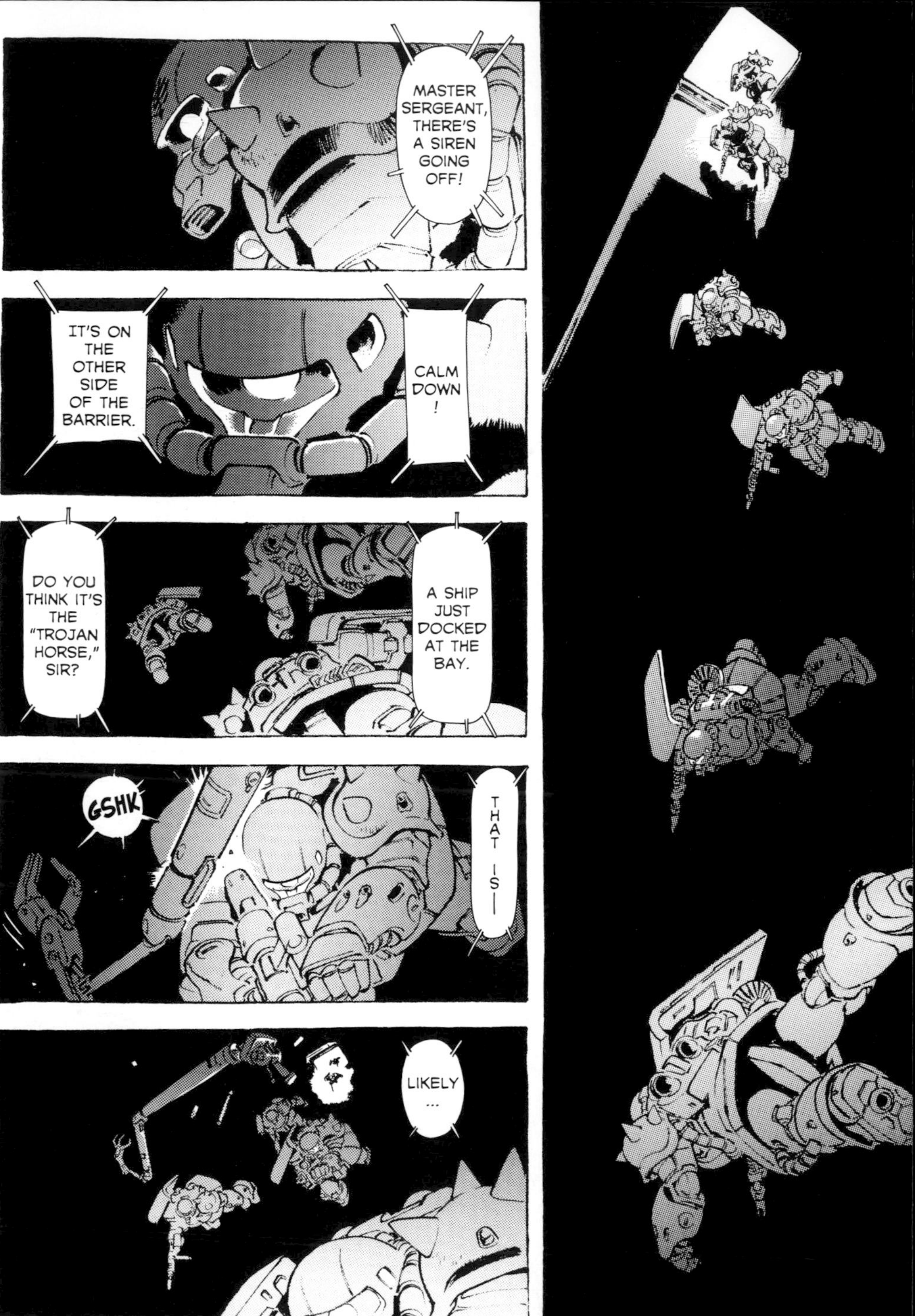
MASTER SERGEANT, THERE'S A SIREN GOING OFF!
CALM DOWN!
IT'S ON THE OTHER SIDE OF THE BARRIER.
A SHIP JUST DOCKED AT THE BAY.
DO YOU THINK IT'S THE "TROJAN HORSE," SIR?
THAT IS—
GSHK
LIKELY...

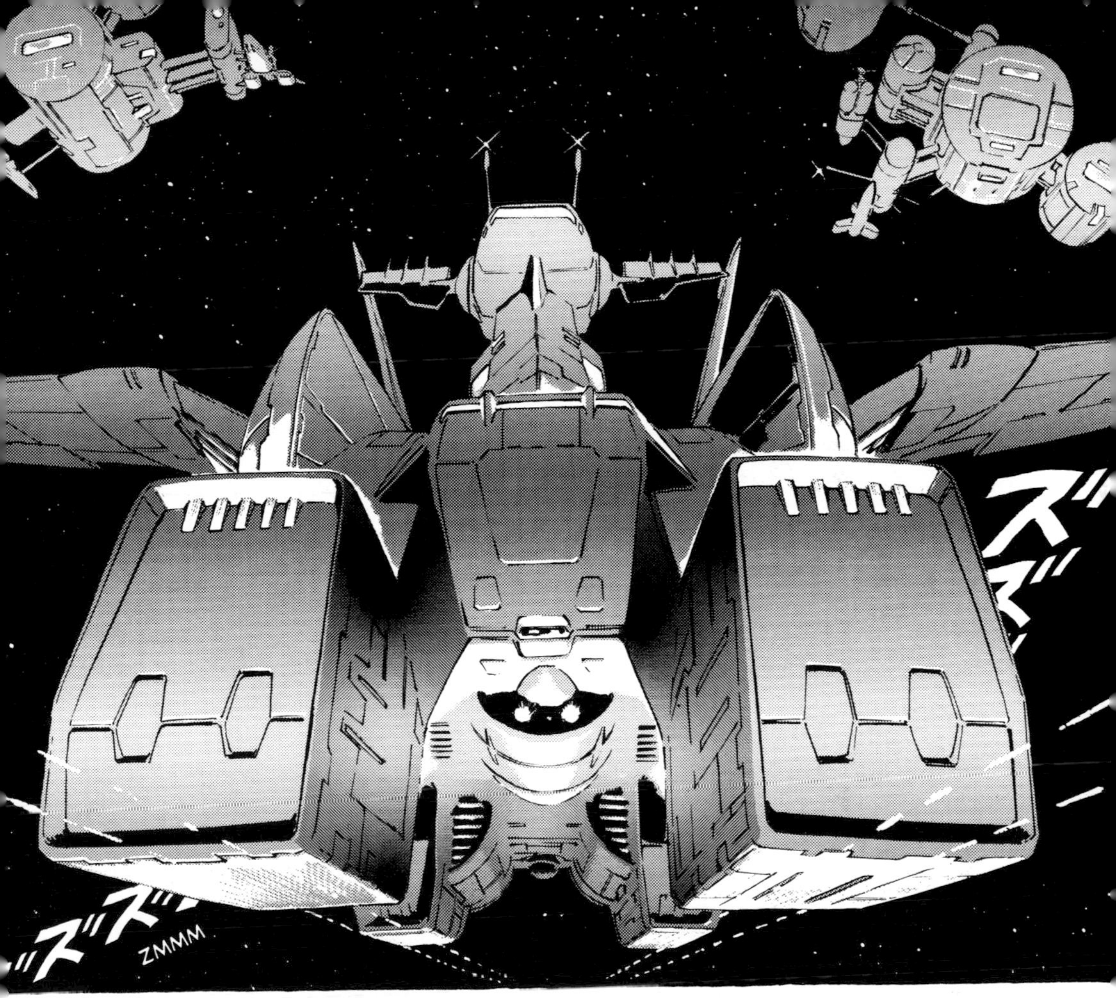
ズズ
ズズズ
ZMMM

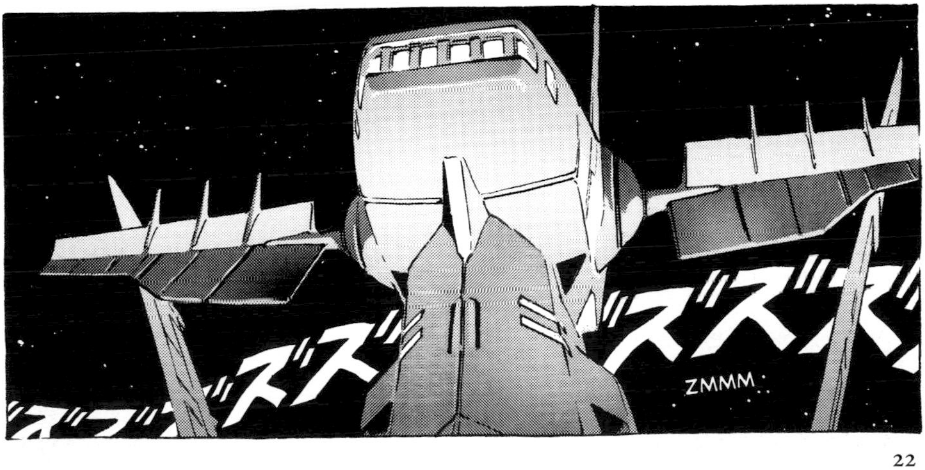
ズズズ
ズズズ
ZMMM

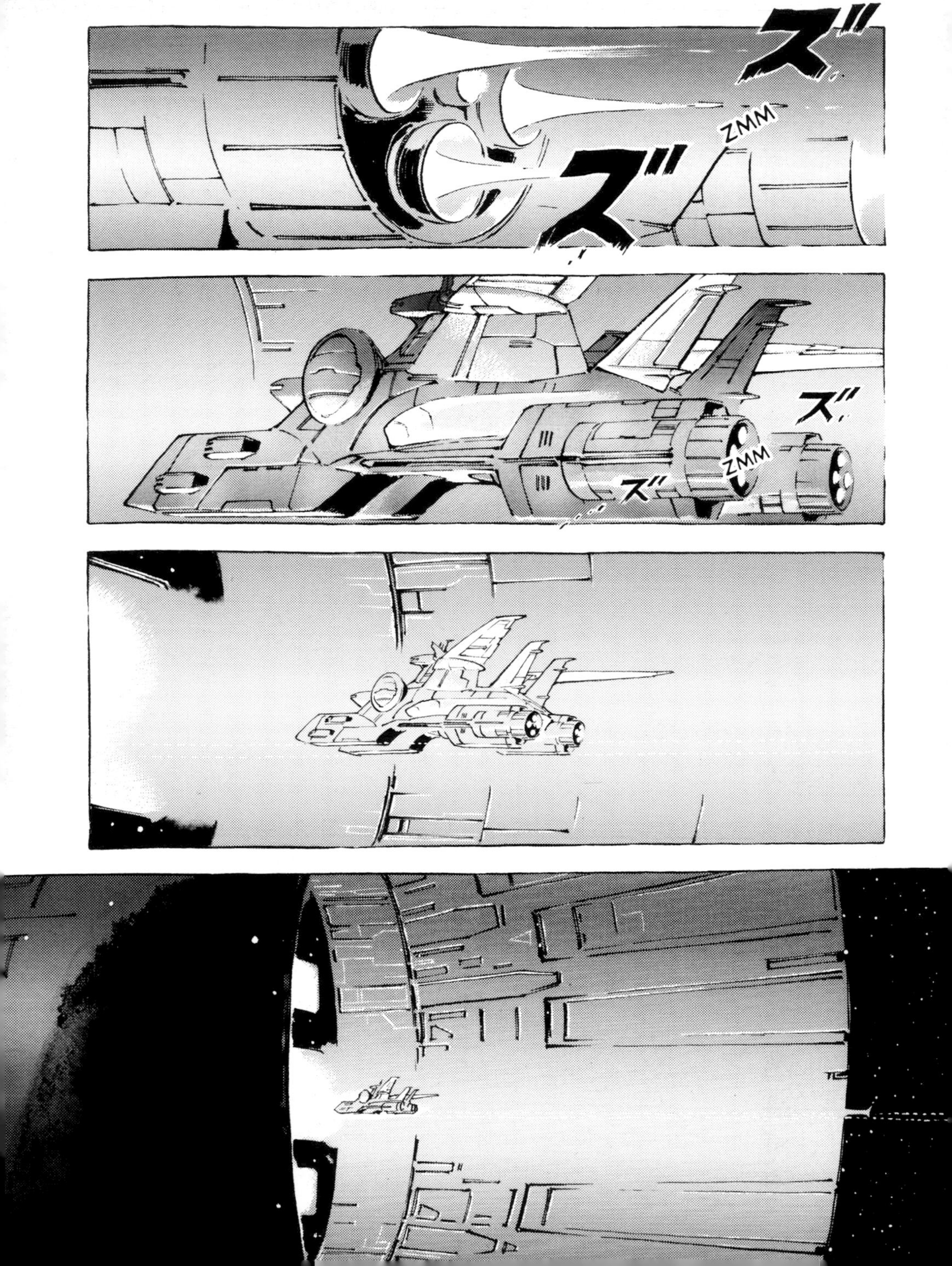
ズ
ZMM
ズ
ズ
ZMM
ズ

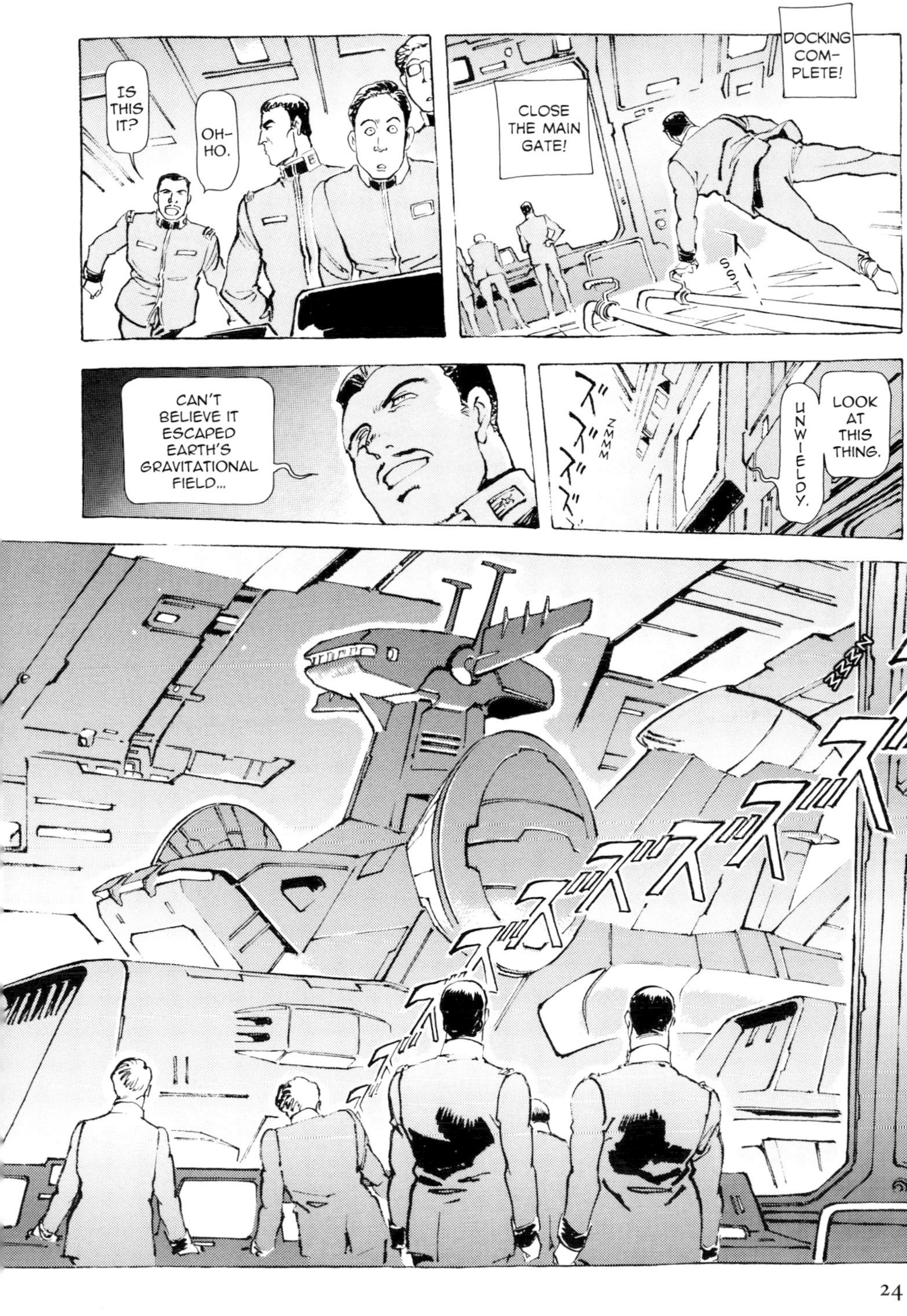
DOCKING COMPLETE!
CLOSE THE MAIN GATE!
SST
IS THIS IT?
OH-HO.
LOOK AT THIS THING.
UNWIELDY.
ZMMM
CAN'T BELIEVE IT ESCAPED EARTH'S GRAVITATIONAL FIELD...

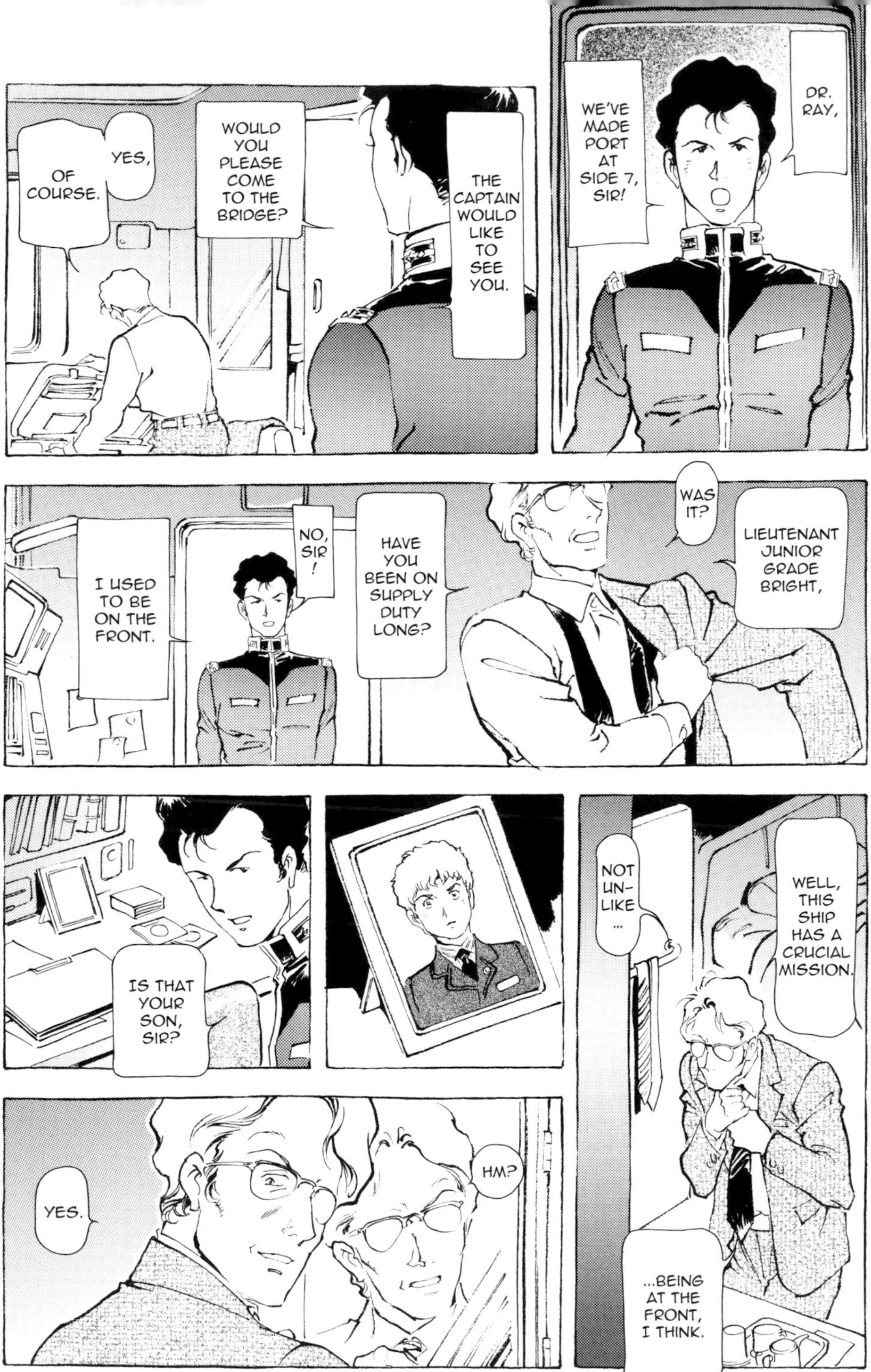
DR. RAY,
WE'VE MADE PORT AT SIDE 7, SIR!
THE CAPTAIN WOULD LIKE TO SEE YOU.
WOULD YOU PLEASE COME TO THE BRIDGE?
YES,
OF COURSE.
LIEUTENANT JUNIOR GRADE BRIGHT,
HAVE YOU BEEN ON SUPPLY DUTY LONG?
NO, SIR!
I USED TO BE ON THE FRONT.
WAS IT?
WELL, THIS SHIP HAS A CRUCIAL MISSION.
NOT UNLIKE ...
...BEING AT THE FRONT, I THINK.
IS THAT YOUR SON, SIR?
HM?
YES.

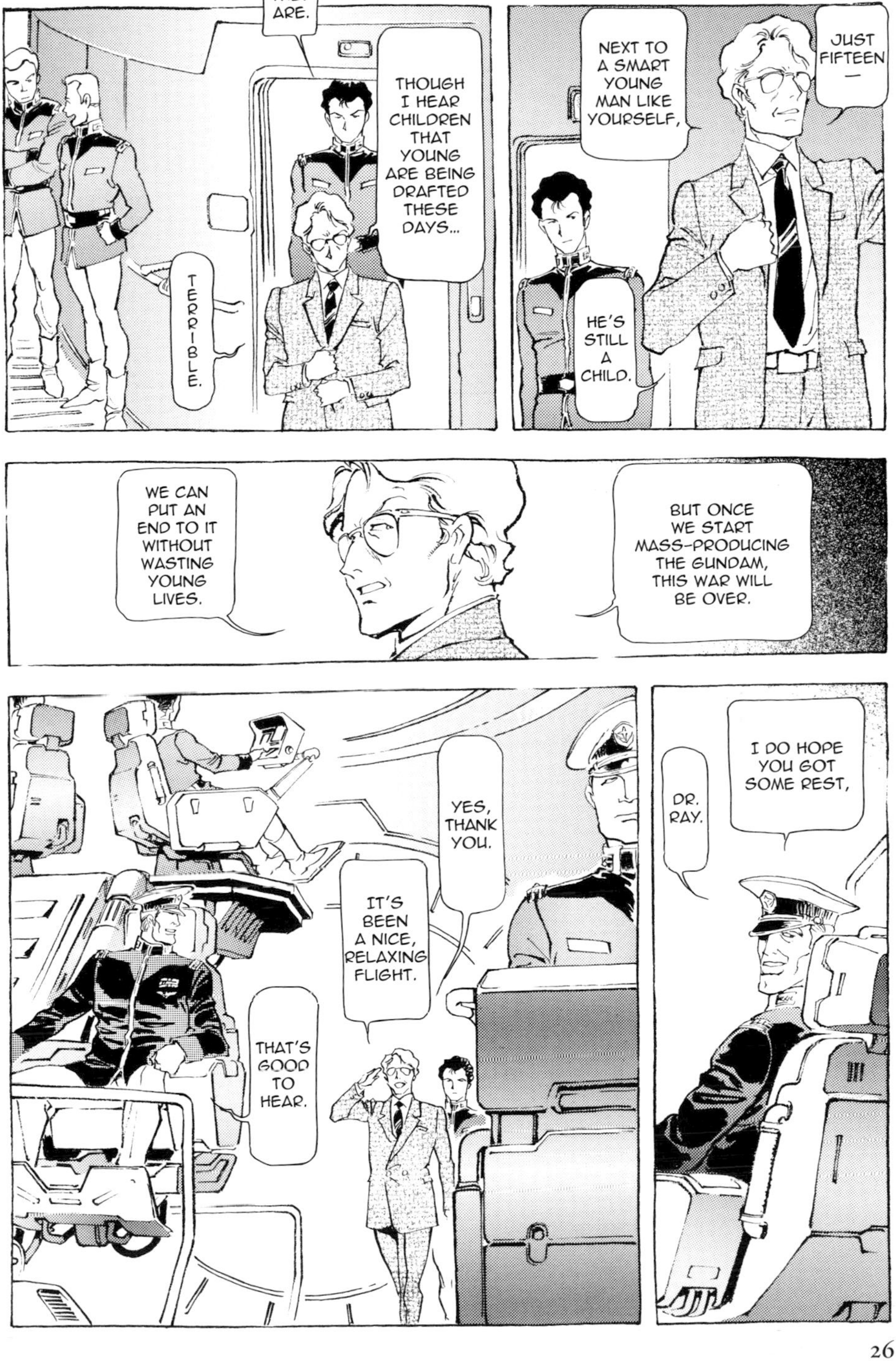
JUST FIFTEEN —
NEXT TO A SMART YOUNG MAN LIKE YOURSELF,
HE'S STILL A CHILD.
THEY ARE.
THOUGH I HEAR CHILDREN THAT YOUNG ARE BEING DRAFTED THESE DAYS...
TERRIBLE.
BUT ONCE WE START MASS-PRODUCING THE GUNDAM, THIS WAR WILL BE OVER.
WE CAN PUT AN END TO IT WITHOUT WASTING YOUNG LIVES.
I DO HOPE YOU GOT SOME REST,
DR. RAY.
YES, THANK YOU.
IT'S BEEN A NICE, RELAXING FLIGHT.
THAT'S GOOD TO HEAR.

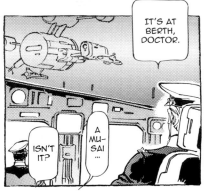

AND WHAT ABOUT THE ZEON SHIP
THAT TAILED US HERE?
SO YOU DID NOTICE.
IT'S AT BERTH, DOCTOR.
A MU-SAI ...
ISN'T IT?
BY TREATY, MILITARY SHIPS ARE NOT ALLOWED TO DOCK AT SIDE 7.
SO THE PROBLEM IS OUR RETURN FLIGHT...
DO YOU THINK
THEY'LL TRY ANYTHING?
...
HM ...
THIS IS A CIVILIAN *SUPPLY SHIP.*
IF THEY ARE SHAME-LESS ENOUGH TO ATTACK US...

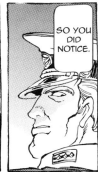

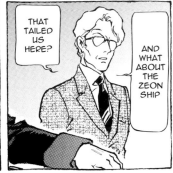

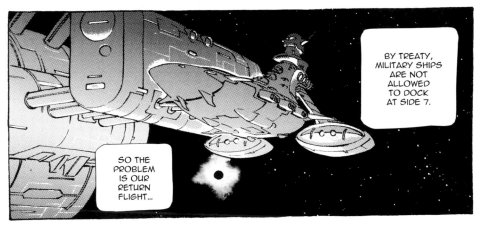

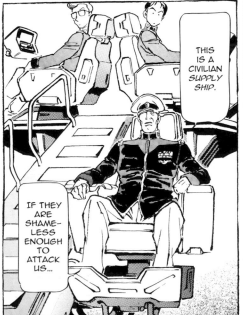

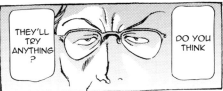

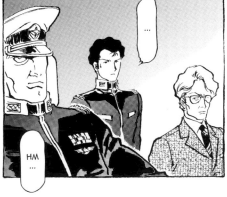

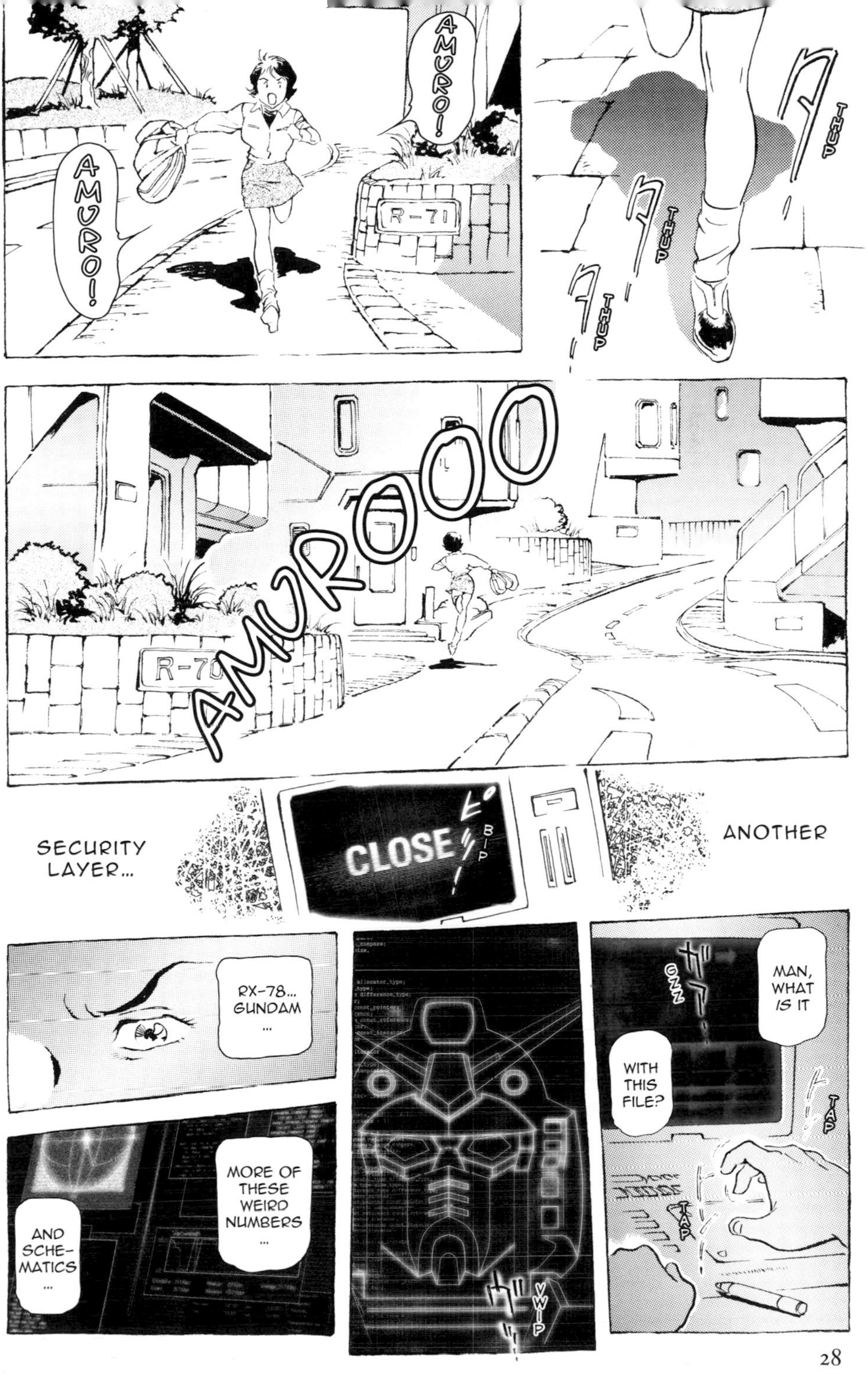
THUP
THUP
THUP
AMURO!
AMURO!
AMUROOO
ANOTHER
CLOSE
BIP
SECURITY LAYER...
MAN, WHAT IS IT
WITH THIS FILE?
GZZ
TAP
TAP
VWIP
RX-78... GUNDAM ...
MORE OF THESE WEIRD NUMBERS ...
AND SCHEMATICS ...

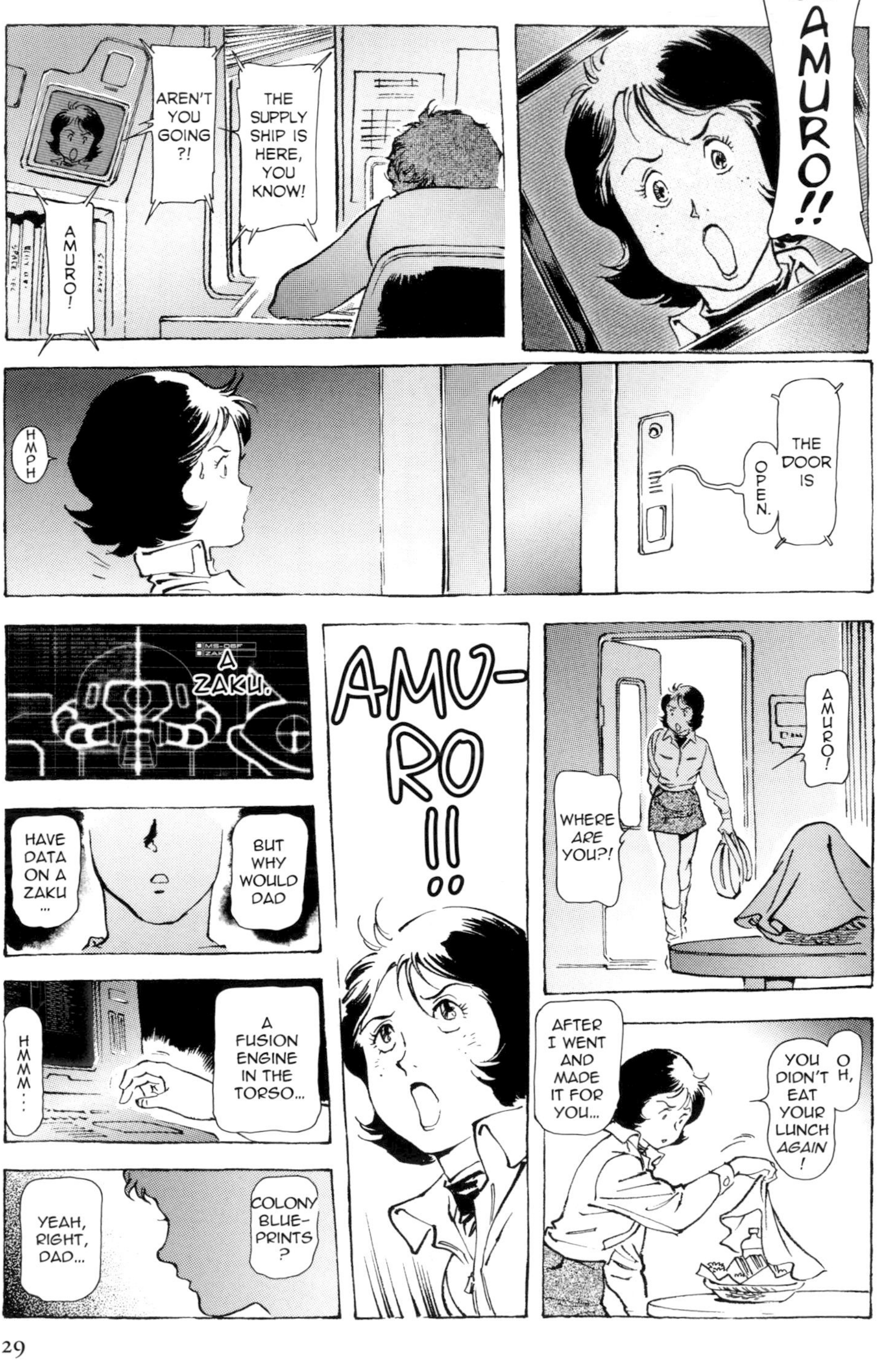
AMURO!!
THE SUPPLY SHIP IS HERE, YOU KNOW!
AREN'T YOU GOING ?!
AMURO!
THE DOOR IS OPEN.
HMPH
AMURO!
WHERE ARE YOU?!
OH, YOU DIDN'T EAT YOUR LUNCH AGAIN!
AFTER I WENT AND MADE IT FOR YOU...
AMU-RO!!
A ZAKU.
BUT WHY WOULD DAD
HAVE DATA ON A ZAKU ...
A FUSION ENGINE IN THE TORSO...
HMMM...
COLONY BLUE-PRINTS?
YEAH, RIGHT, DAD...

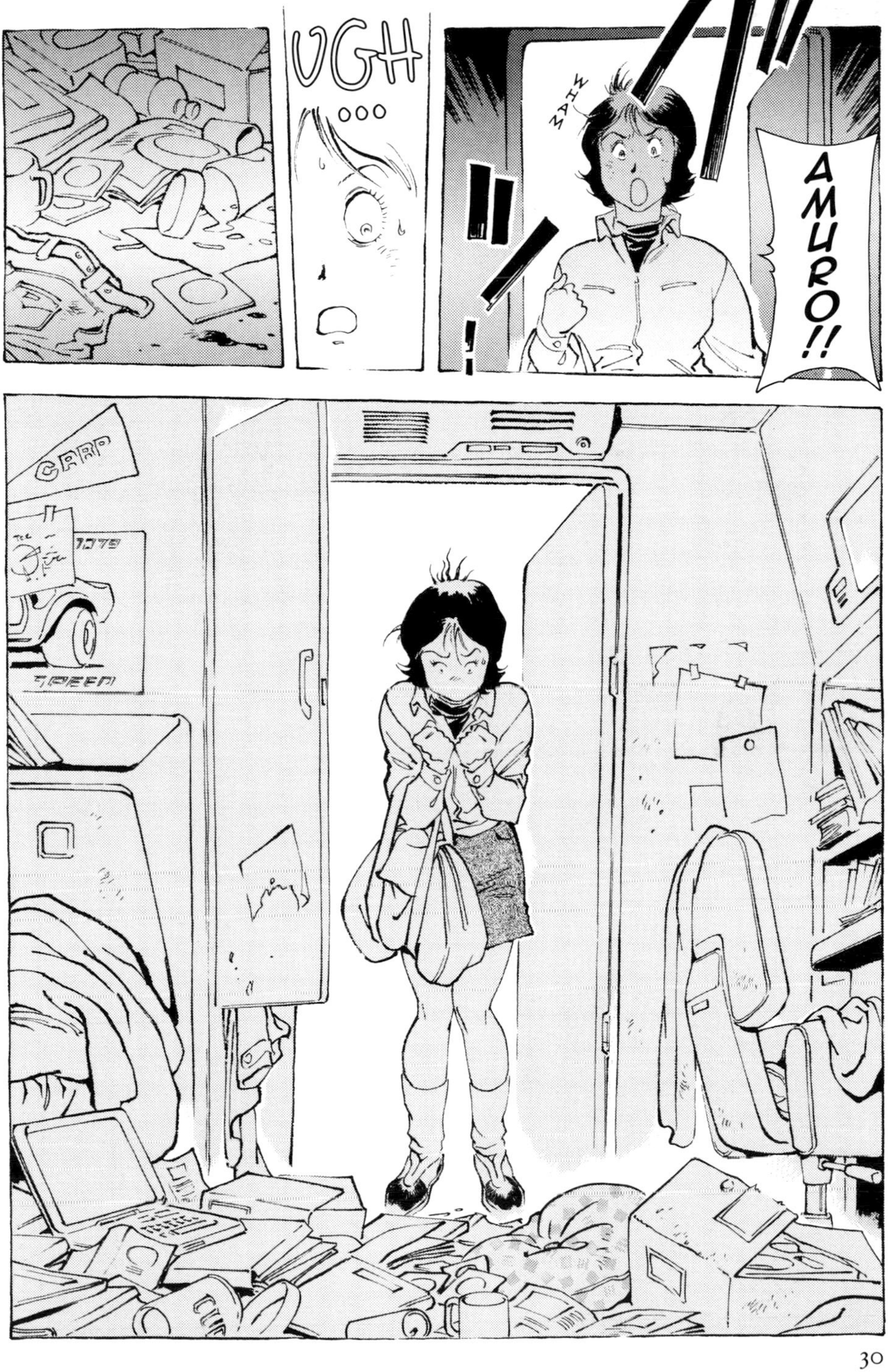
AMURO!!
WHAM
UGH
...

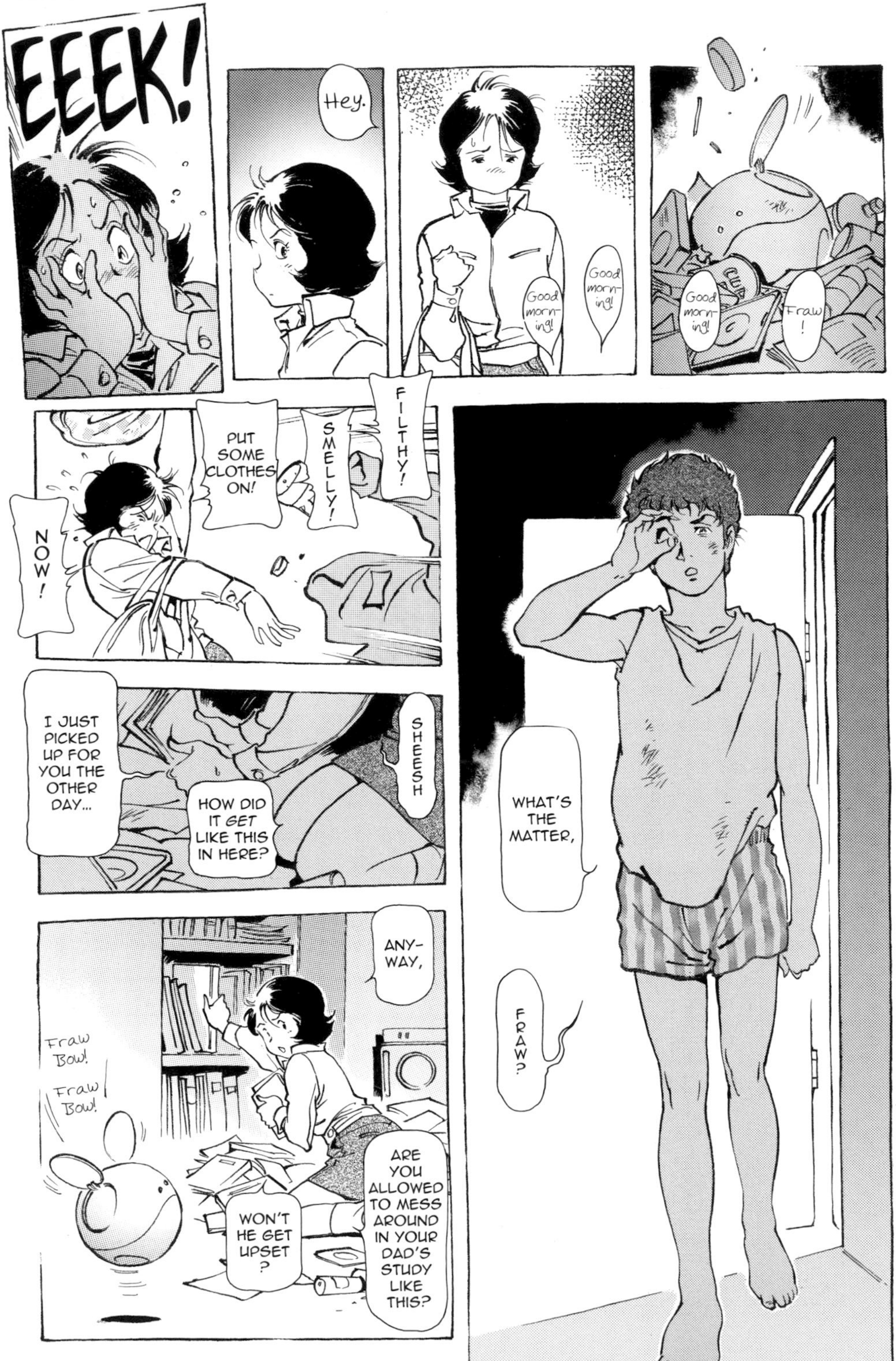

Fraw!
Good morning!
Good morning!
Good morning!
Hey.
EEEK!
WHAT'S THE MATTER,
FRAW?
FILTHY!
SMELLY!
PUT SOME CLOTHES ON!
NOW!
SHEESH
HOW DID IT GET LIKE THIS IN HERE?
I JUST PICKED UP FOR YOU THE OTHER DAY...
ANY-WAY,
ARE YOU ALLOWED TO MESS AROUND IN YOUR DAD'S STUDY LIKE THIS?
WON'T HE GET UPSET?
Fraw Bow!
Fraw Bow!

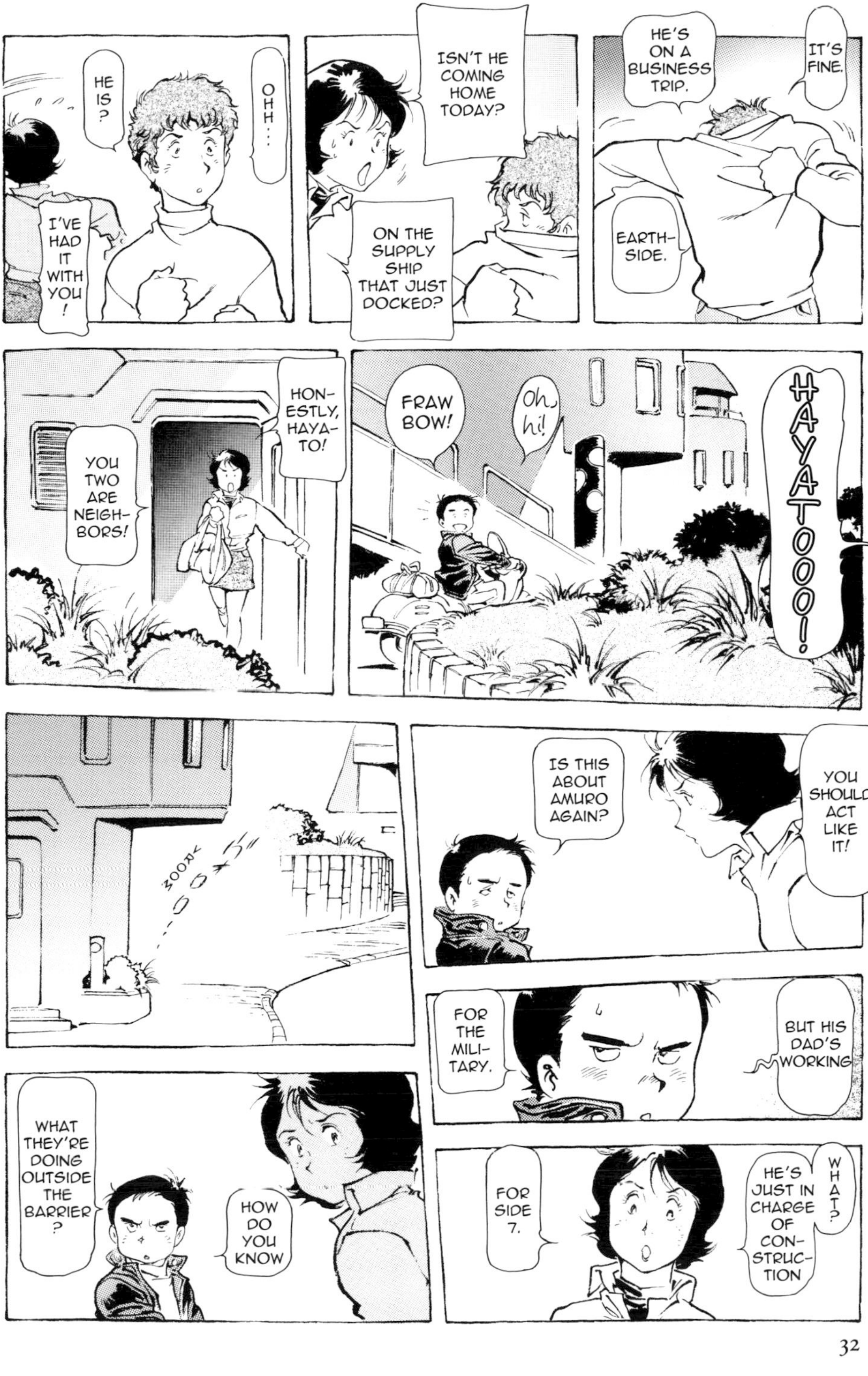
IT'S FINE.
HE'S ON A BUSINESS TRIP.
EARTH-SIDE.
ISN'T HE COMING HOME TODAY?
ON THE SUPPLY SHIP THAT JUST DOCKED?
OHH...
HE IS?
I'VE HAD IT WITH YOU!
HAYATOOOO!
Oh, hi!
FRAW BOW!
HON-ESTLY, HAYA-TO!
YOU TWO ARE NEIGH-BORS!
YOU SHOULD ACT LIKE IT!
IS THIS ABOUT AMURO AGAIN?
BUT HIS DAD'S WORKING
FOR THE MILI-TARY.
WHAT?
HE'S JUST IN CHARGE OF CON-STRUC-TION
FOR SIDE 7.
HOW DO YOU KNOW
WHAT THEY'RE DOING OUTSIDE THE BARRIER?

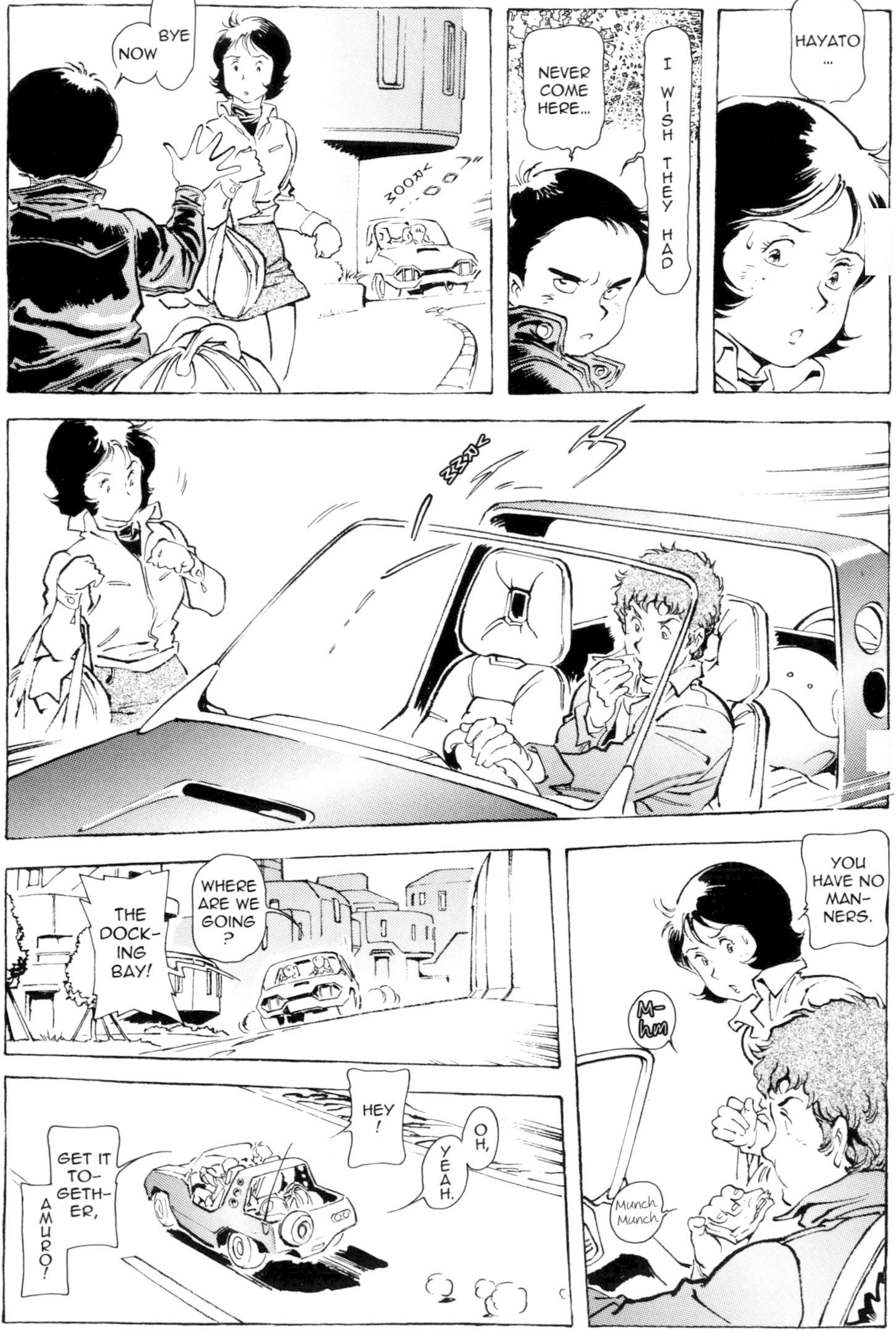
HAYATO ...
I WISH THEY HAD
NEVER COME HERE...
BYE NOW
YOU HAVE NO MAN-NERS.
M-hm
Munch Munch
WHERE ARE WE GOING?
THE DOCK-ING BAY!
HEY!
OH, YEAH.
GET IT TO-GETH-ER, AMURO!

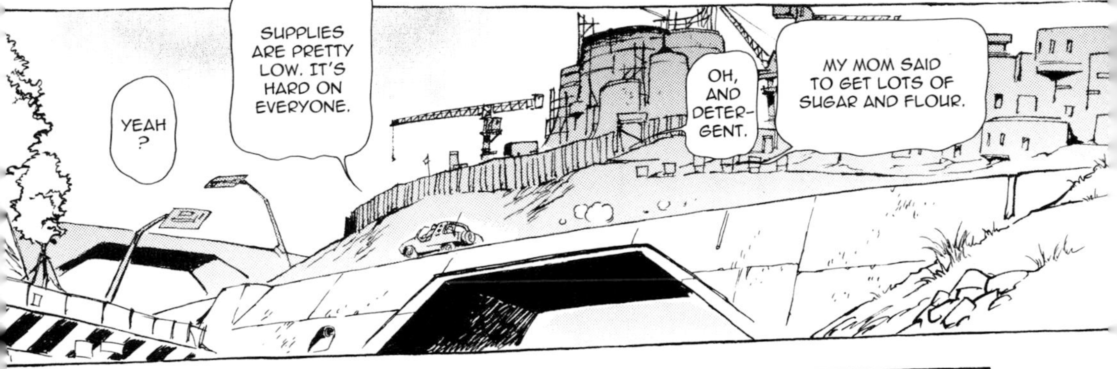
MY MOM SAID TO GET LOTS OF SUGAR AND FLOUR.
OH, AND DETERGENT.
SUPPLIES ARE PRETTY LOW. IT'S HARD ON EVERYONE.
YEAH?

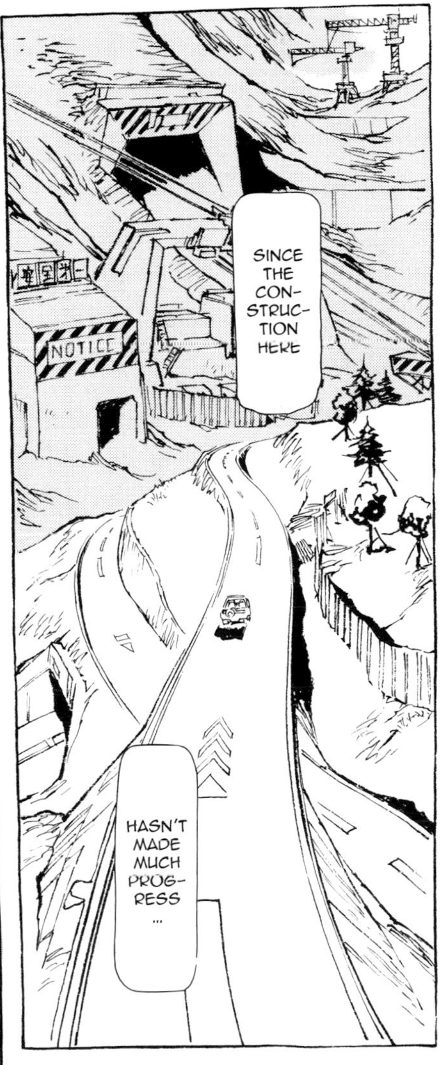
SINCE THE CONSTRUCTION HERE
NOTICE
HASN'T MADE MUCH PROGRESS ...

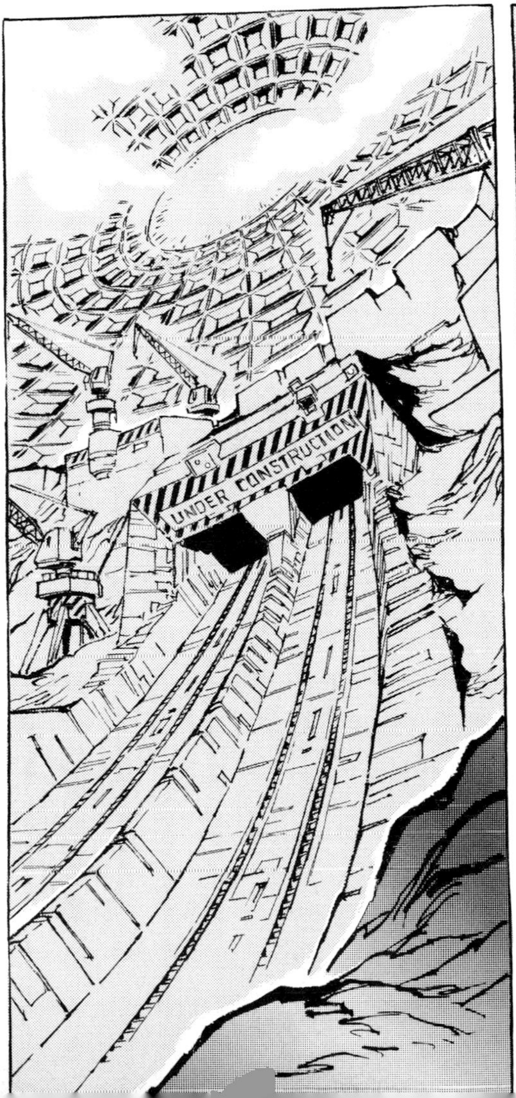
UNDER CONSTRUCTION

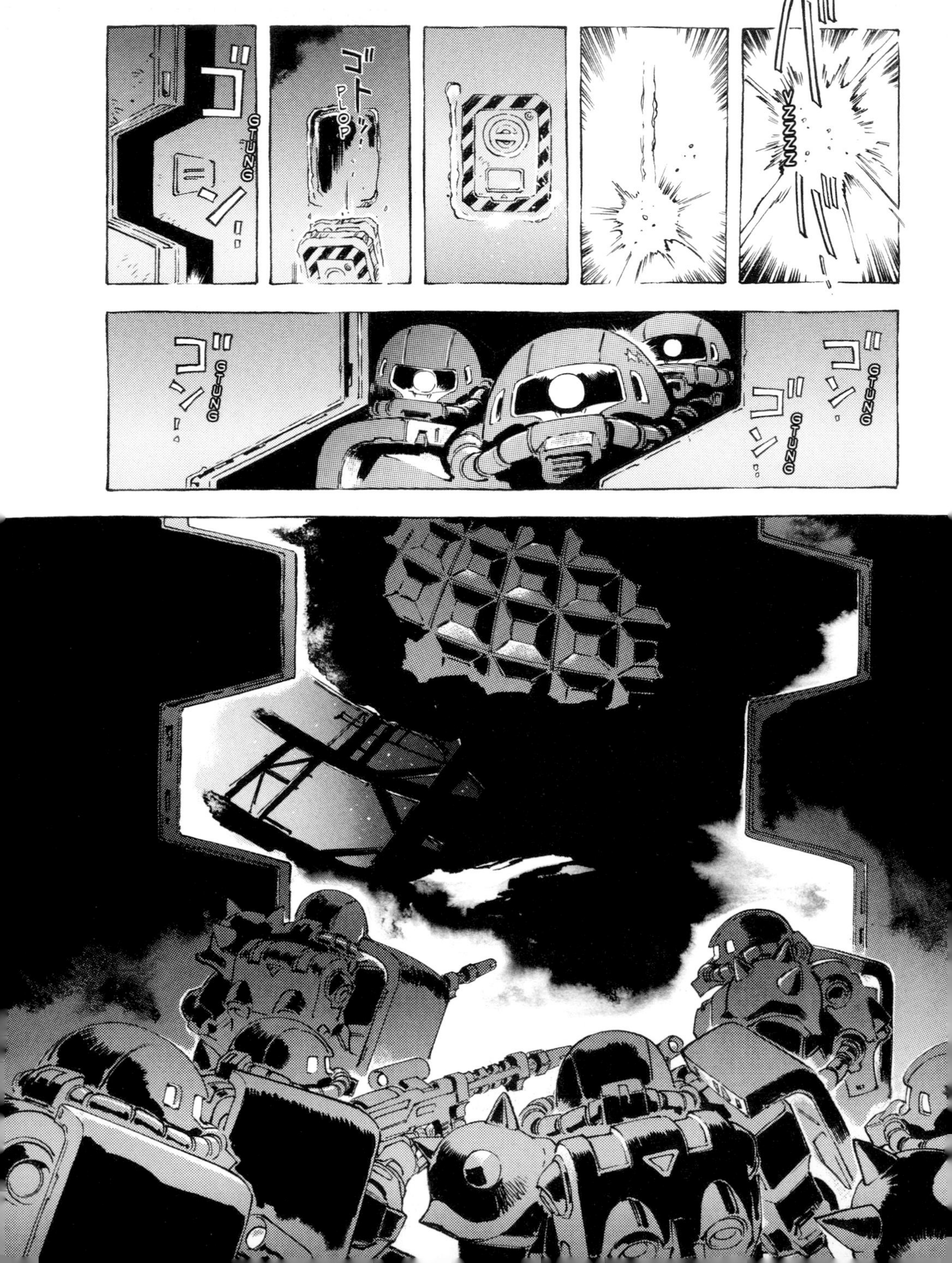
VZZZZ
ゴトッ
PLOP
GTUNG
GTUNG
GTUNG
GTUNG

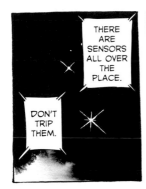

THIS AREA'S PRES-SURIZED.
OXYGEN CONCENTRATION IS OPTIMAL.
HOW FAR TO THE BARRIER?
ABOUT 5 KM.
THERE ARE SENSORS ALL OVER THE PLACE.
DON'T TRIP THEM.
SLENDER, YOU STAY BEHIND.
IF THIS TAKES A BAD TURN, MAKE A RUN FOR IT AND PUT A MAYDAY OUT TO LT. COMMANDER CHAR ON THE SHIP.
GENE, YOU'RE WITH ME.
YES, SIR!
ASH SQUAD, YOU'LL SCOUT ON THE LEFT!
MASTER SERGEANT
WHAT?
IF WE COME ACROSS THE *THING*
SHOULD WE DESTROY IT?

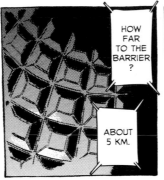

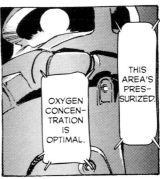

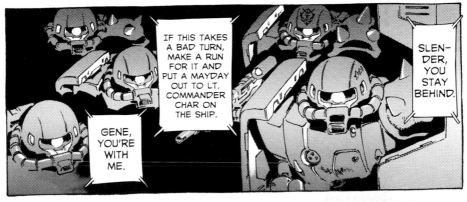

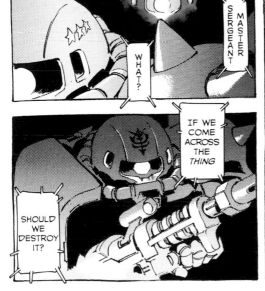

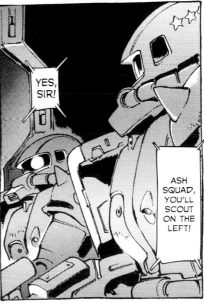

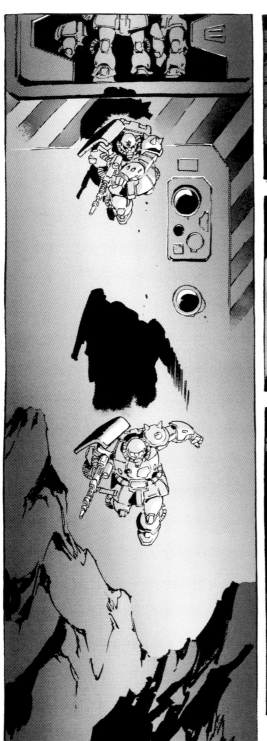

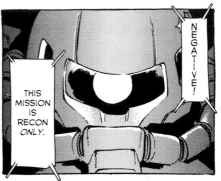

NEGATIVE!

THIS MISSION IS RECON *ONLY*.

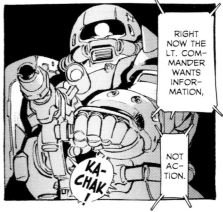

RIGHT NOW THE LT. COMMANDER WANTS INFORMATION,

NOT ACTION.

KACHAK!

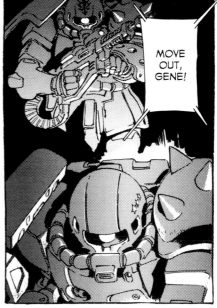

MOVE OUT, GENE!

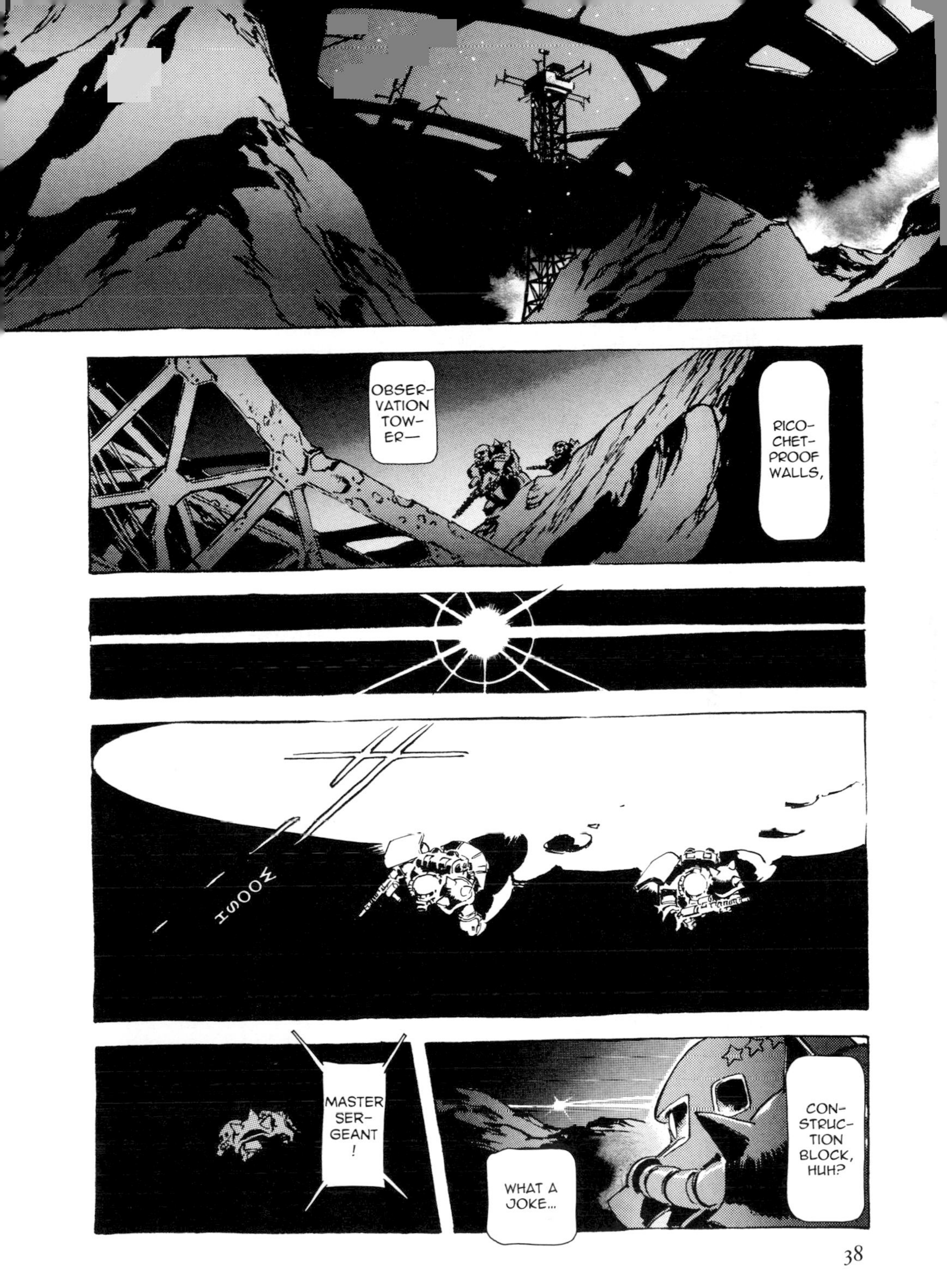
RICO-CHET-PROOF WALLS,
OBSER-VATION TOW-ER—
CON-STRUC-TION BLOCK, HUH?
WHAT A JOKE...
MASTER SER-GEANT!

IT'S AN OLD-MODEL MOBILE SUIT.
LOOKS LIKE IT WAS DESTROYED BY A HEAT-RAY WEAPON.
GET SOME PHOTOS OF THE IMPACT PLANE.
THERE'S MORE.
THAT'S—
CODE-NAME "GUN TANK."
I THINK.

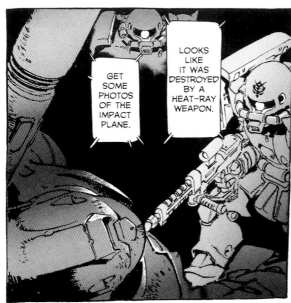

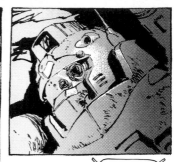

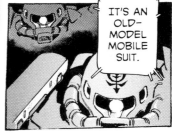

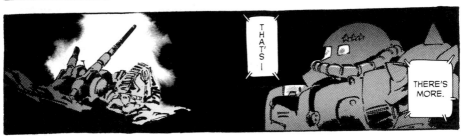

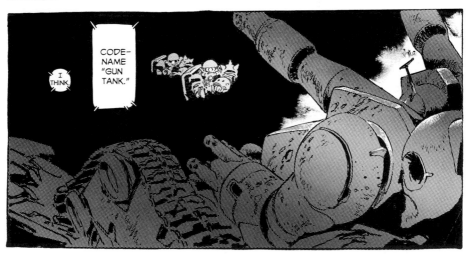

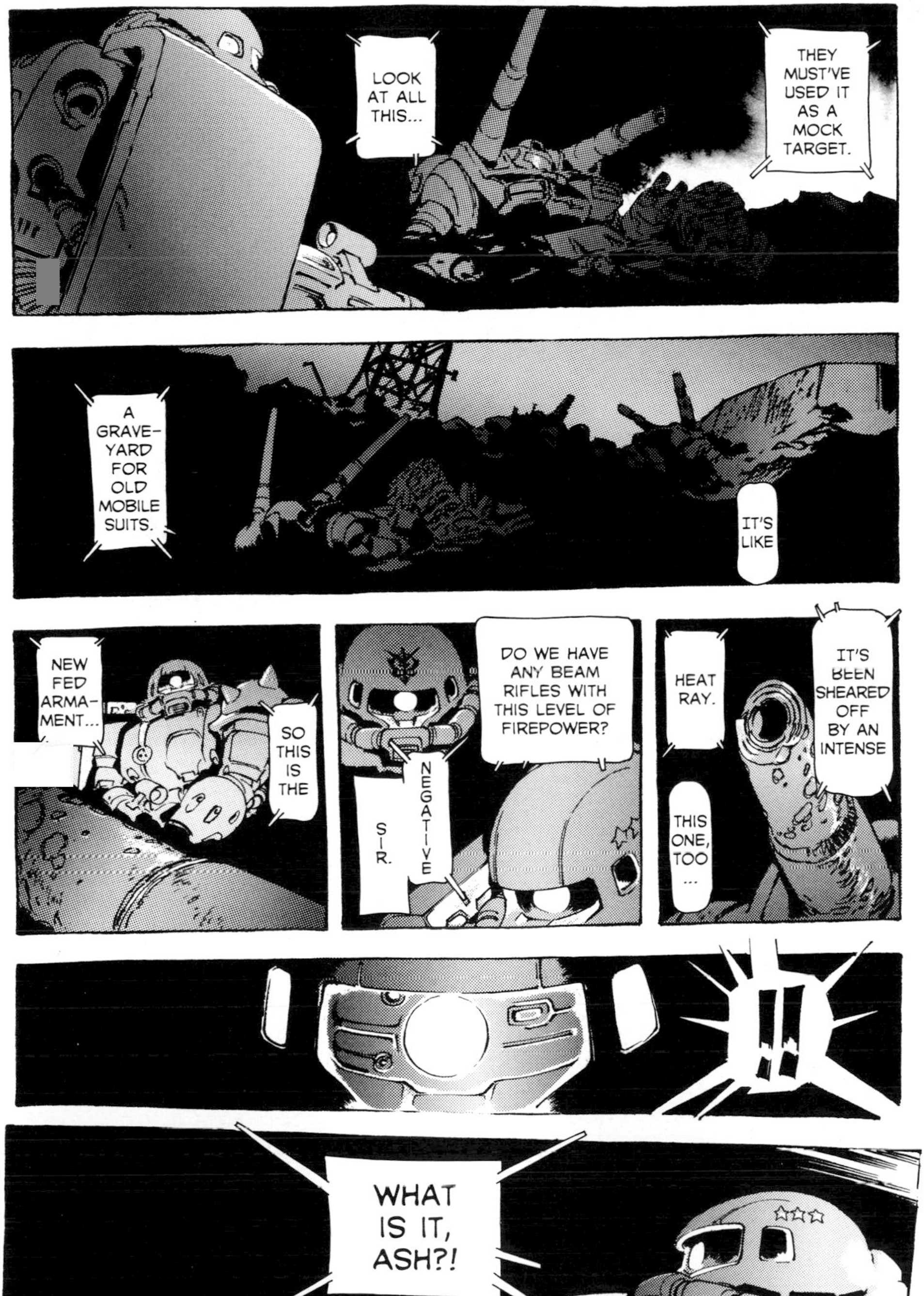
THEY MUST'VE USED IT AS A MOCK TARGET.
LOOK AT ALL THIS...
IT'S LIKE
A GRAVEYARD FOR OLD MOBILE SUITS.
IT'S BEEN SHEARED OFF BY AN INTENSE
HEAT RAY.
THIS ONE, TOO ...
DO WE HAVE ANY BEAM RIFLES WITH THIS LEVEL OF FIREPOWER?
NEGATIVE
SIR.
SO THIS IS THE
NEW FED ARMAMENT...
WHAT IS IT, ASH?!

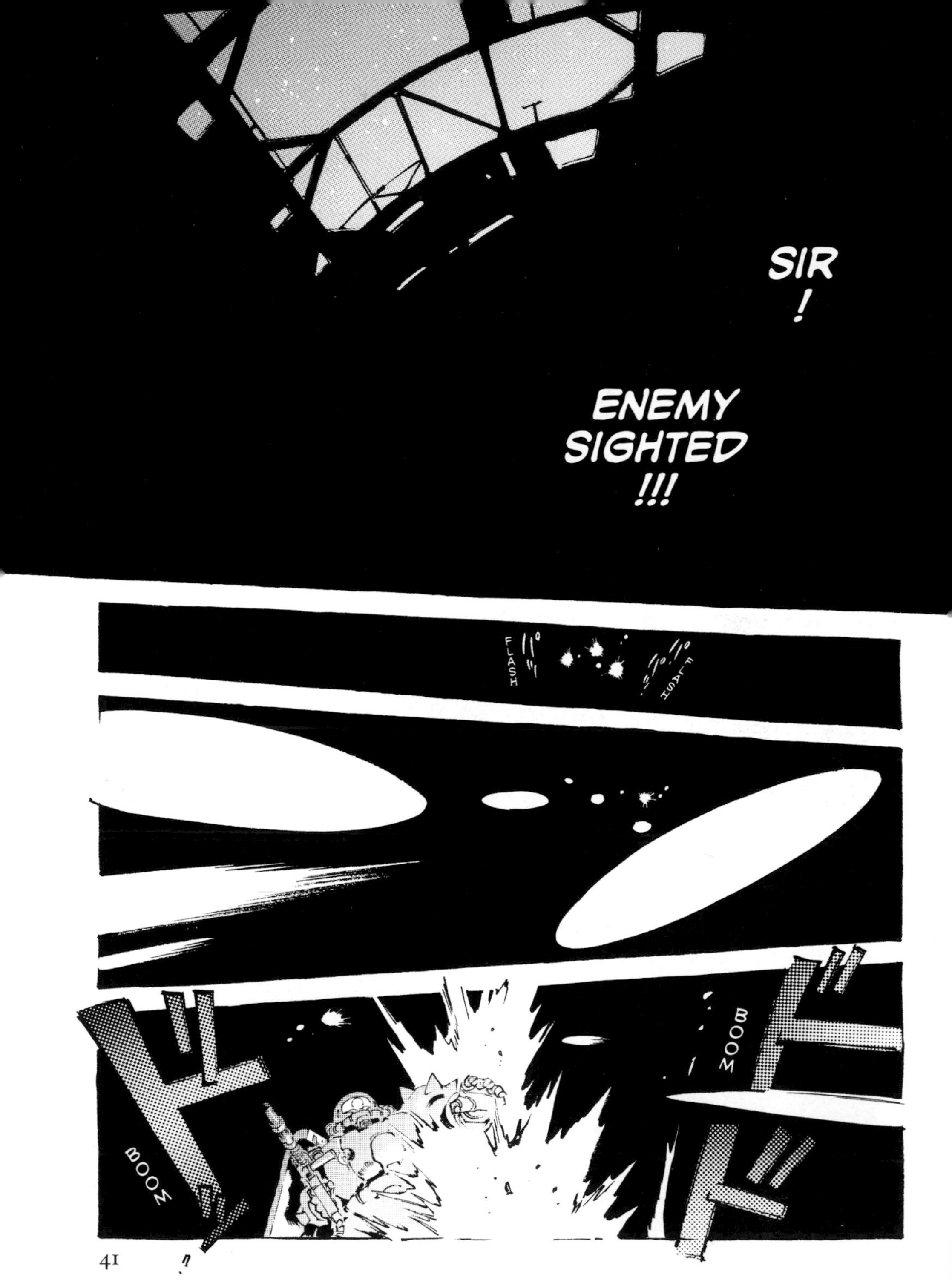
SIR!
ENEMY SIGHTED!!!
FLASH
FLASH
BOOM
BOOM

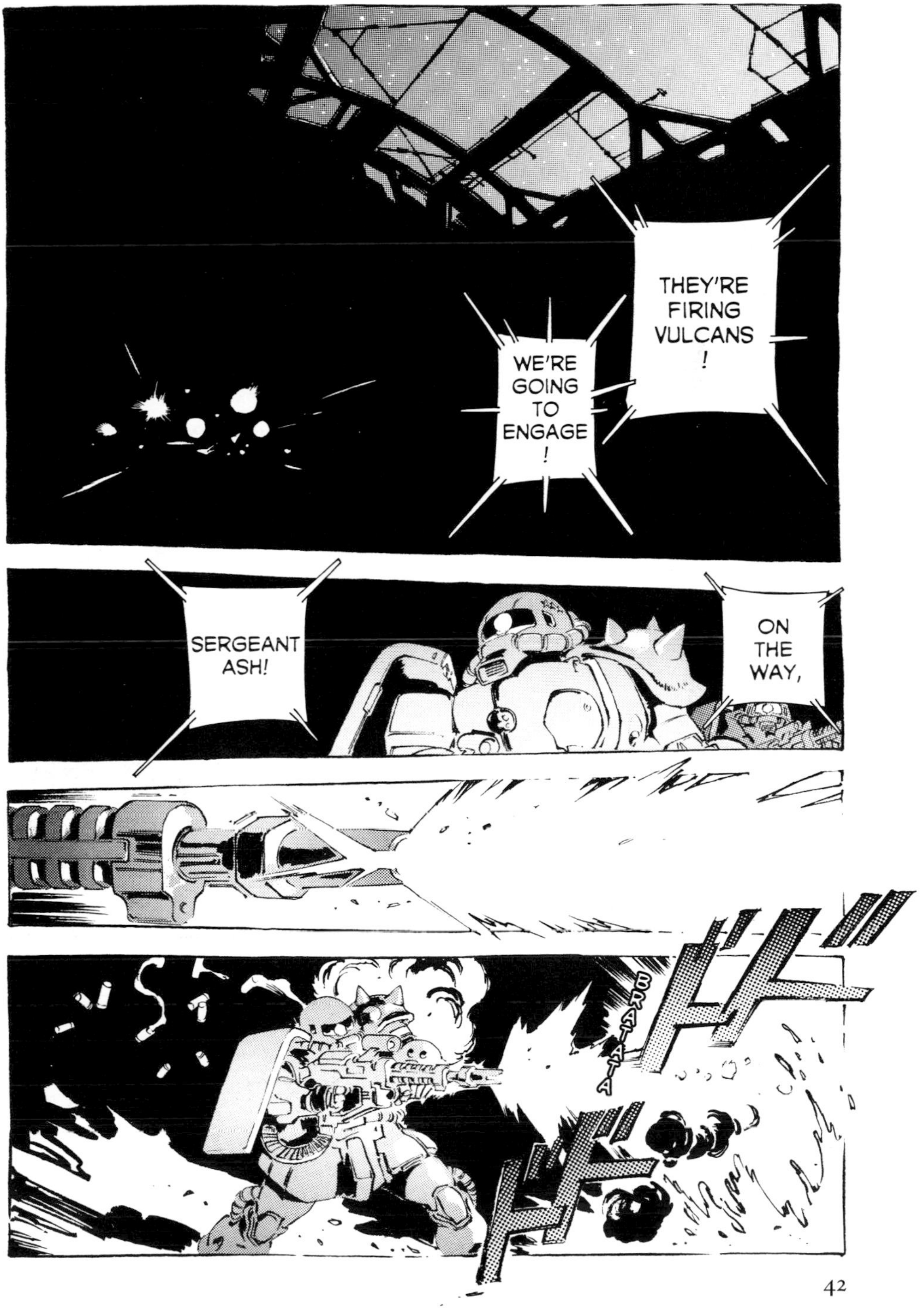
THEY'RE FIRING VULCANS!
WE'RE GOING TO ENGAGE!
ON THE WAY,
SERGEANT ASH!
BRA-TA-TA-TA

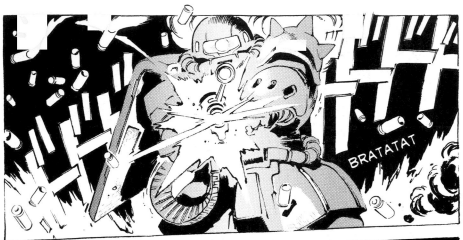

BRATATAT

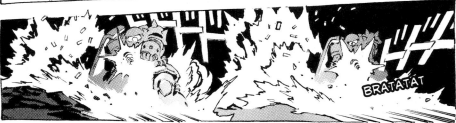

BRATATAT

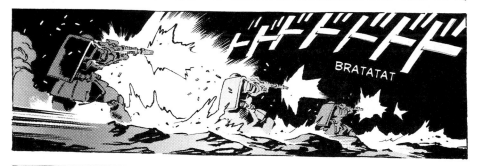

BRATATAT

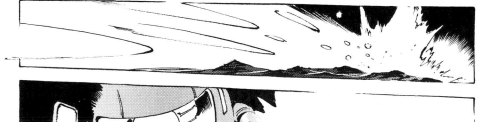

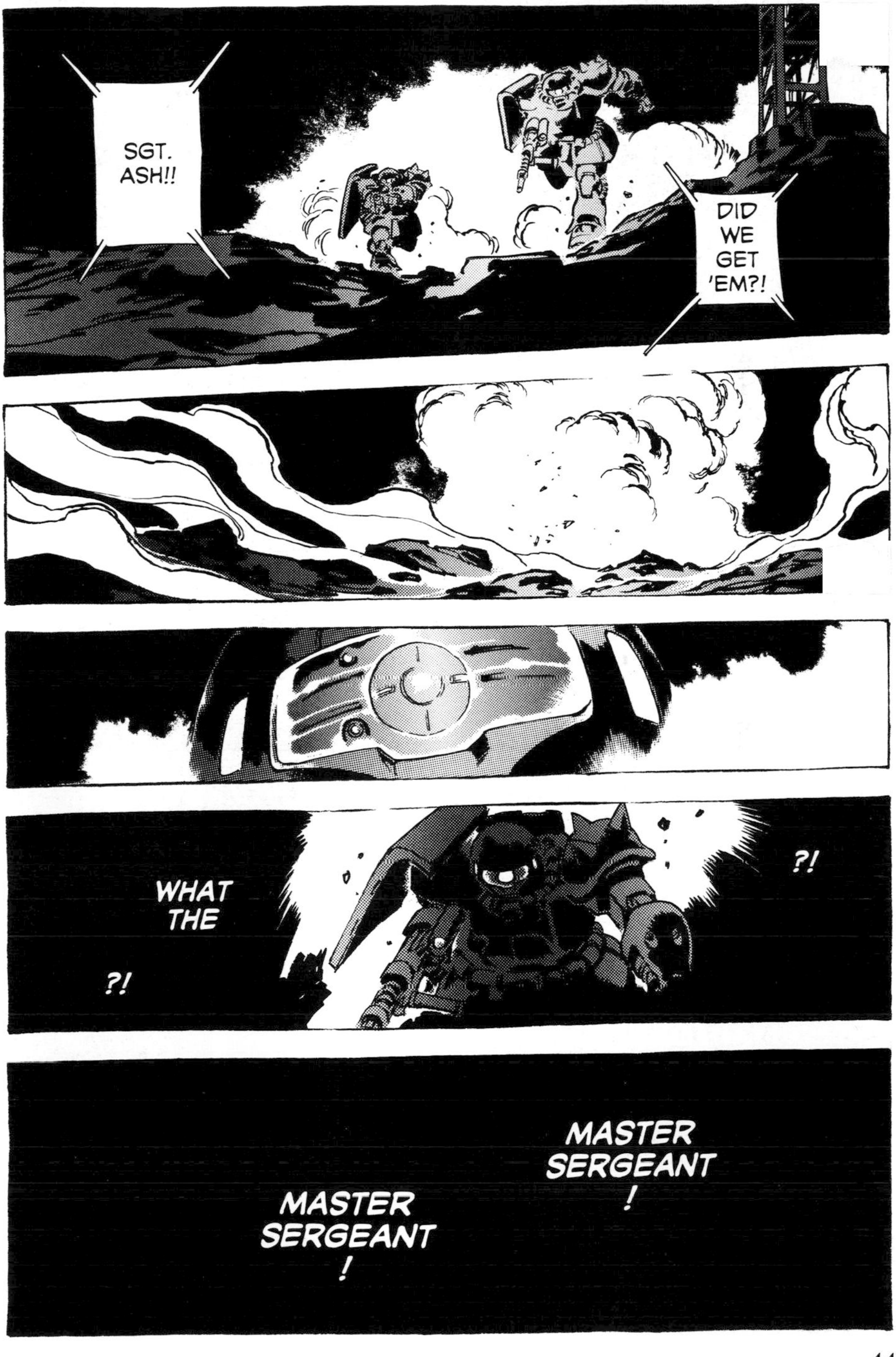
DID WE GET 'EM?!
SGT. ASH!!
?!
WHAT THE
?!
MASTER SERGEANT
!
MASTER SERGEANT
!

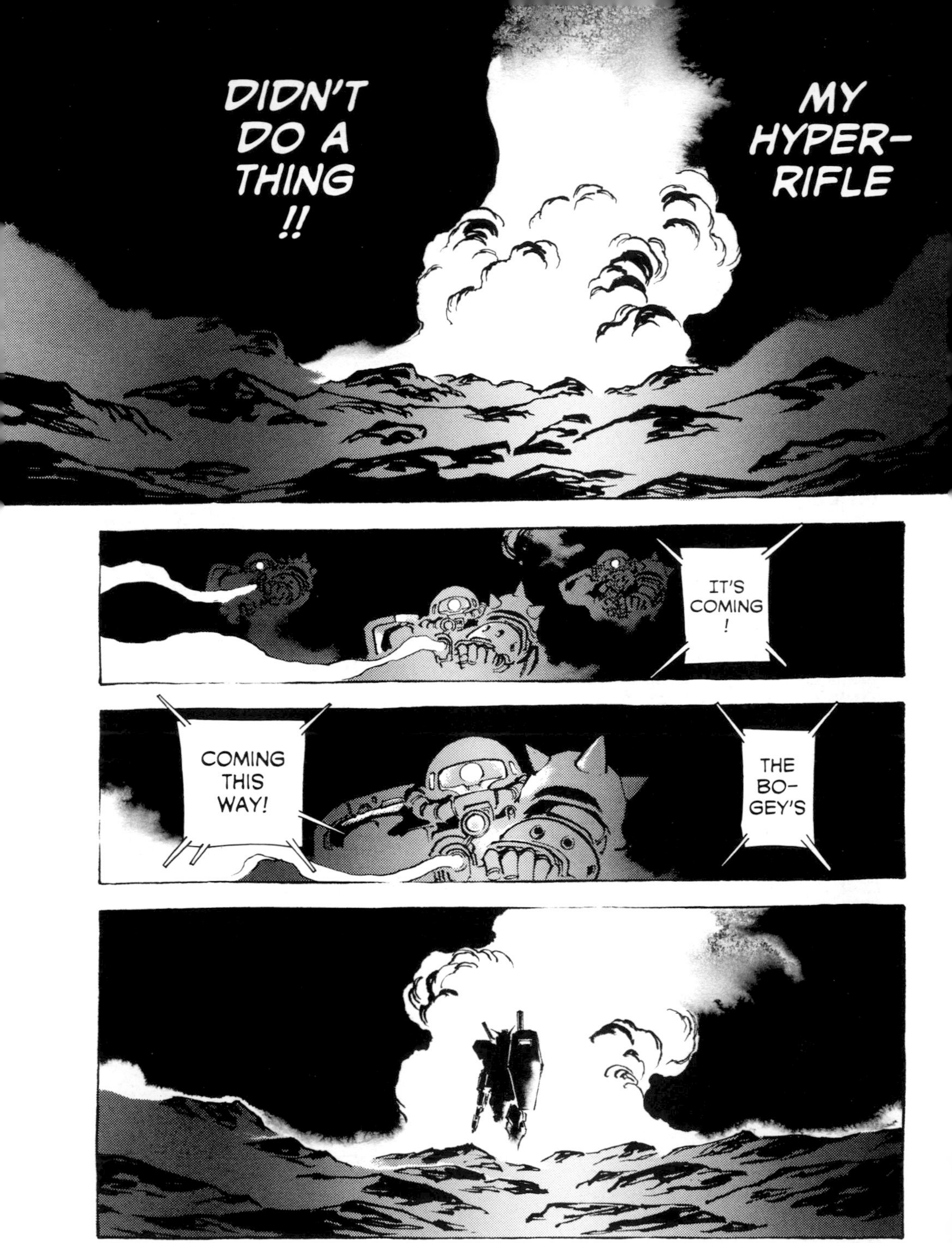
MY HYPER-RIFLE
DIDN'T DO A THING!!
IT'S COMING!
THE BO-GEY'S
COMING THIS WAY!

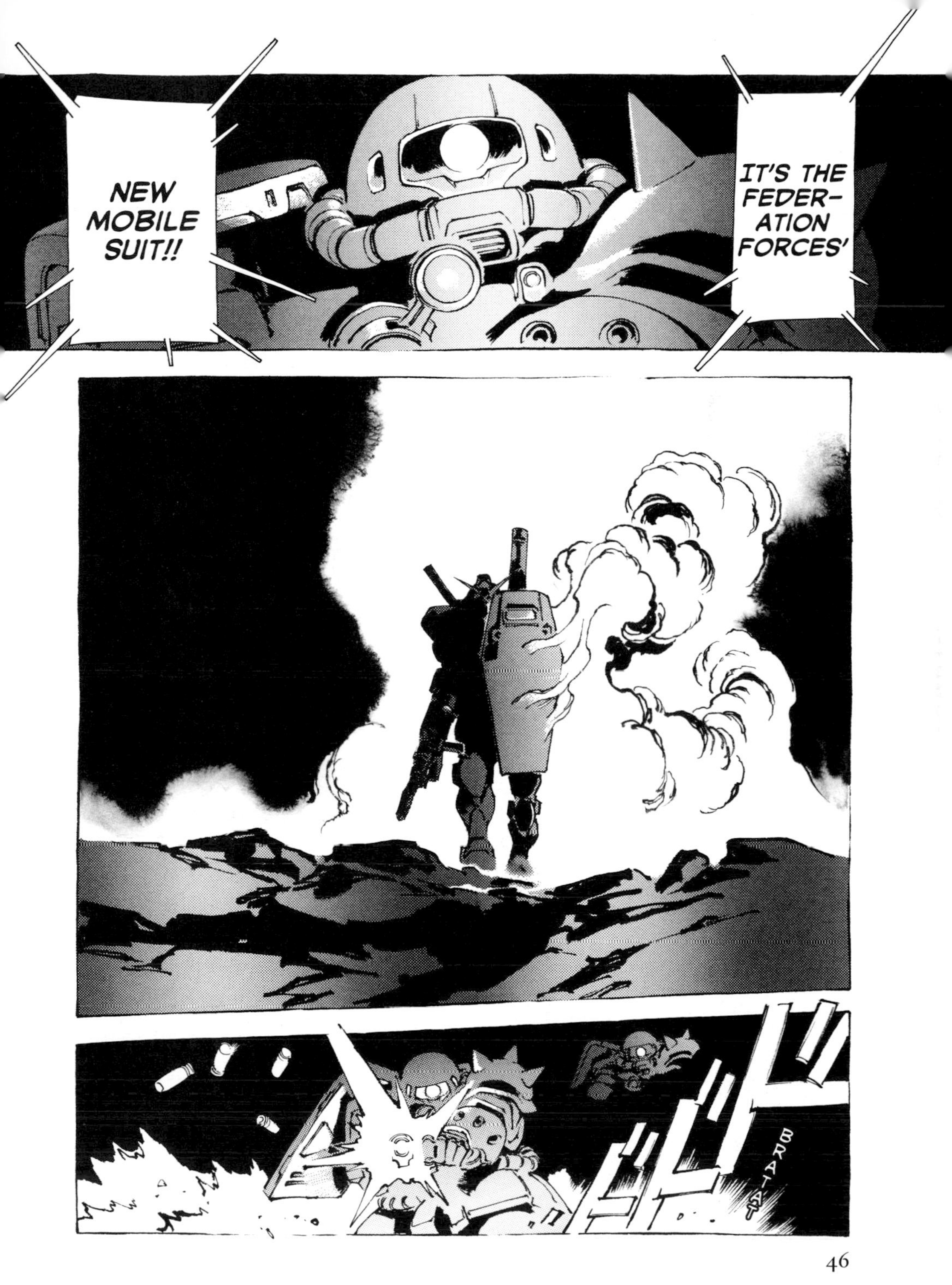
IT'S THE FEDER-ATION FORCES'
NEW MOBILE SUIT!!
BRATATAT

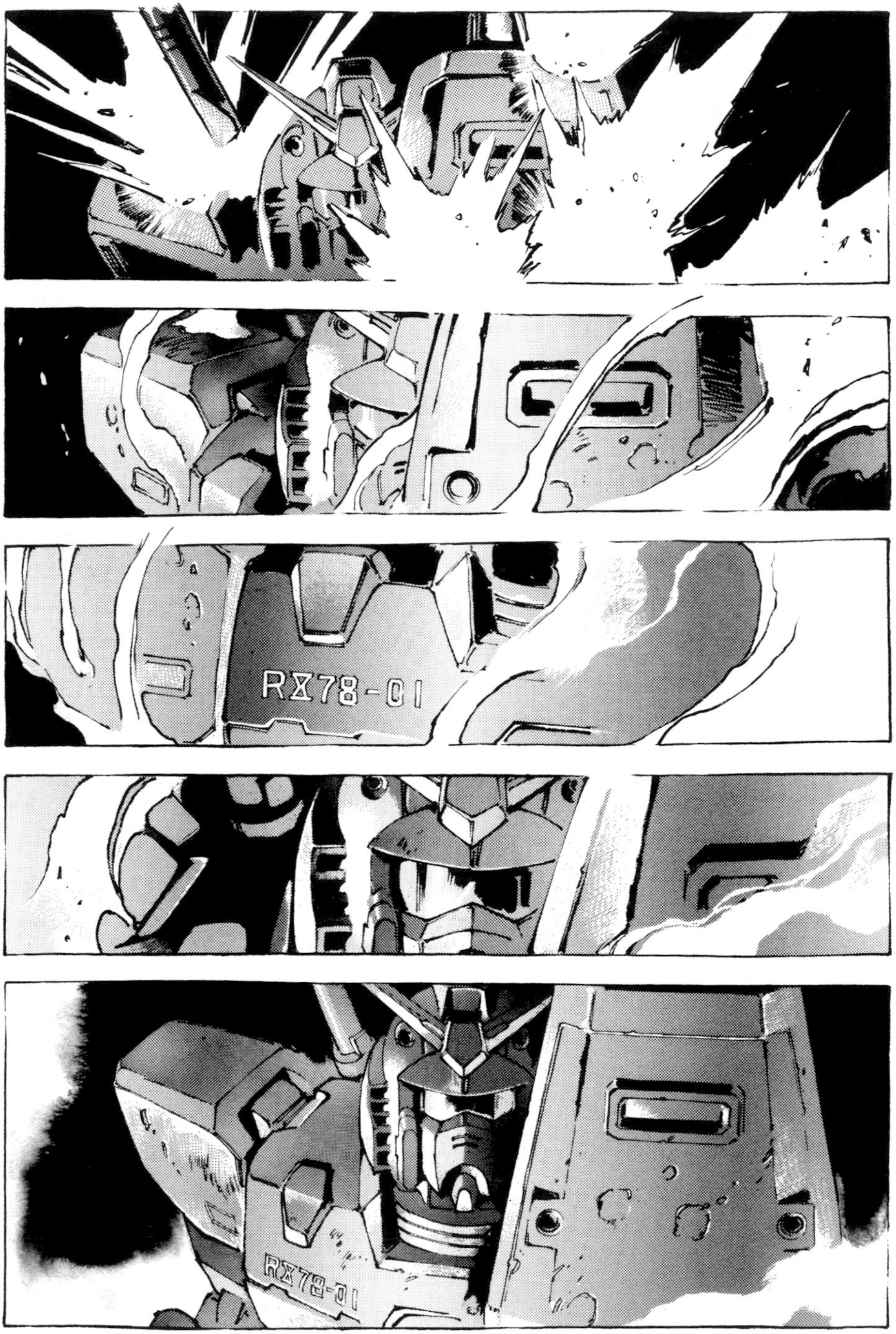
RX78-01
RX78-01

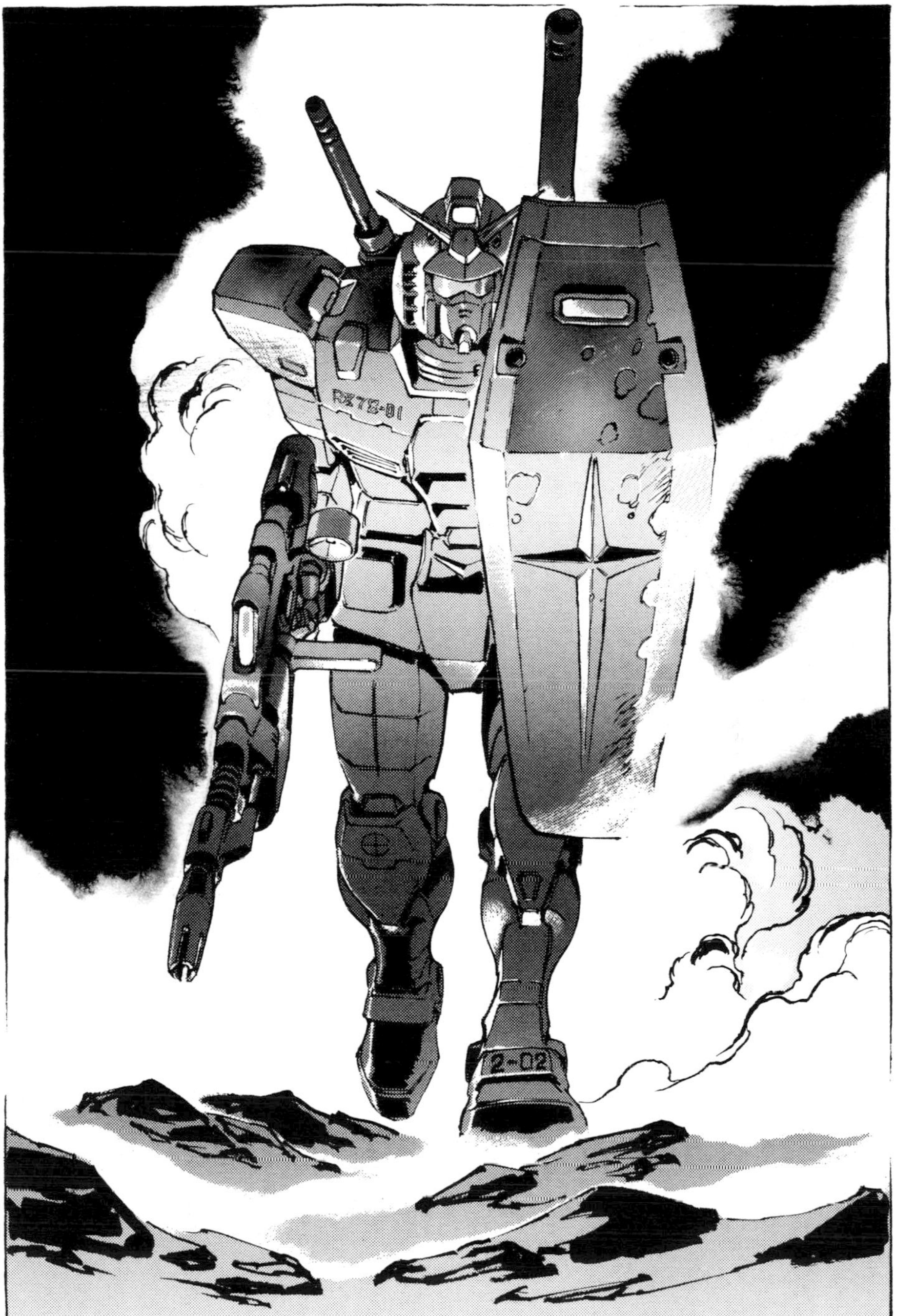
RX78-01
2-02

SECTION II

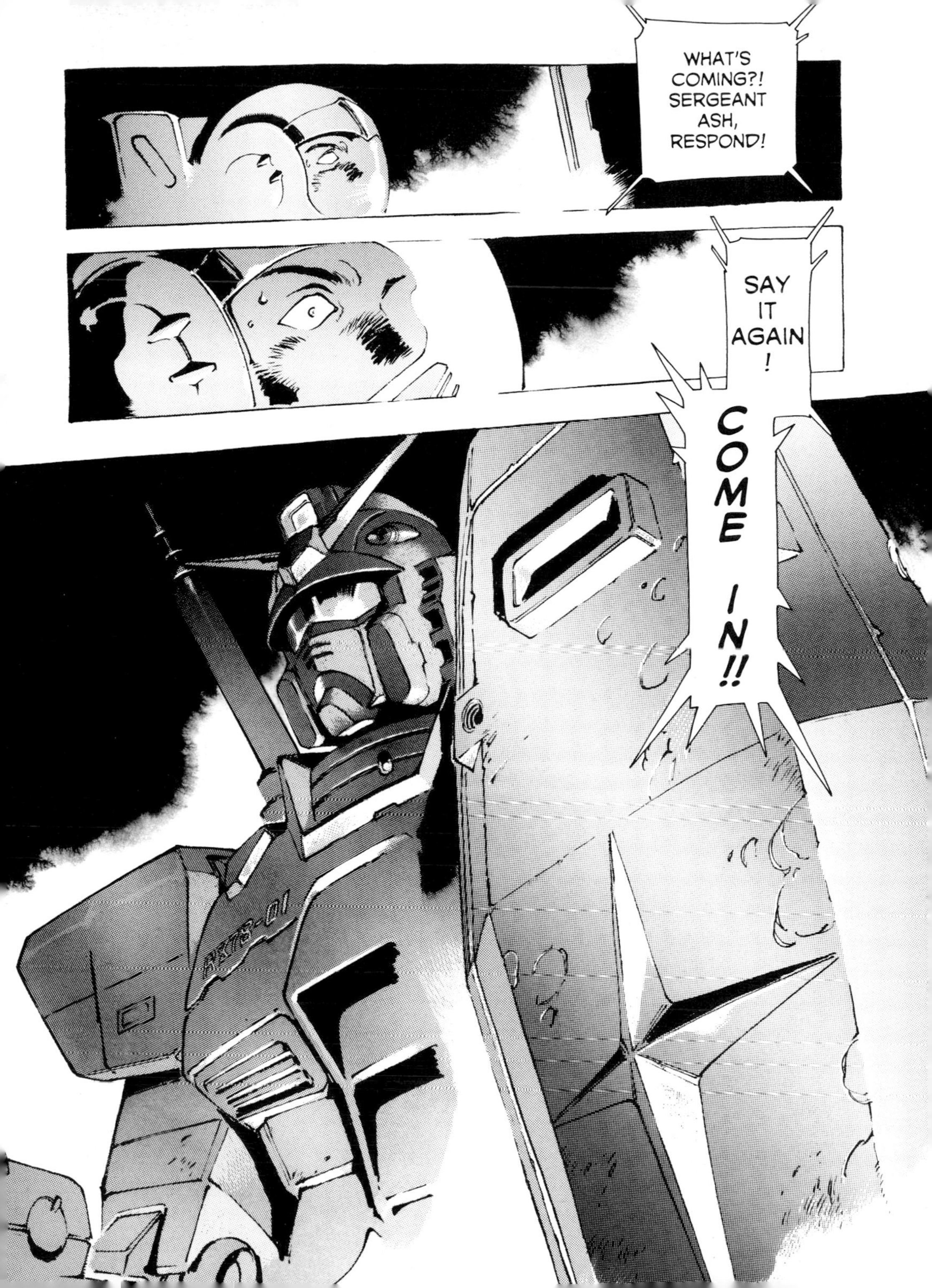
WHAT'S COMING?! SERGEANT ASH, RESPOND!
SAY IT AGAIN!
COME IN!!

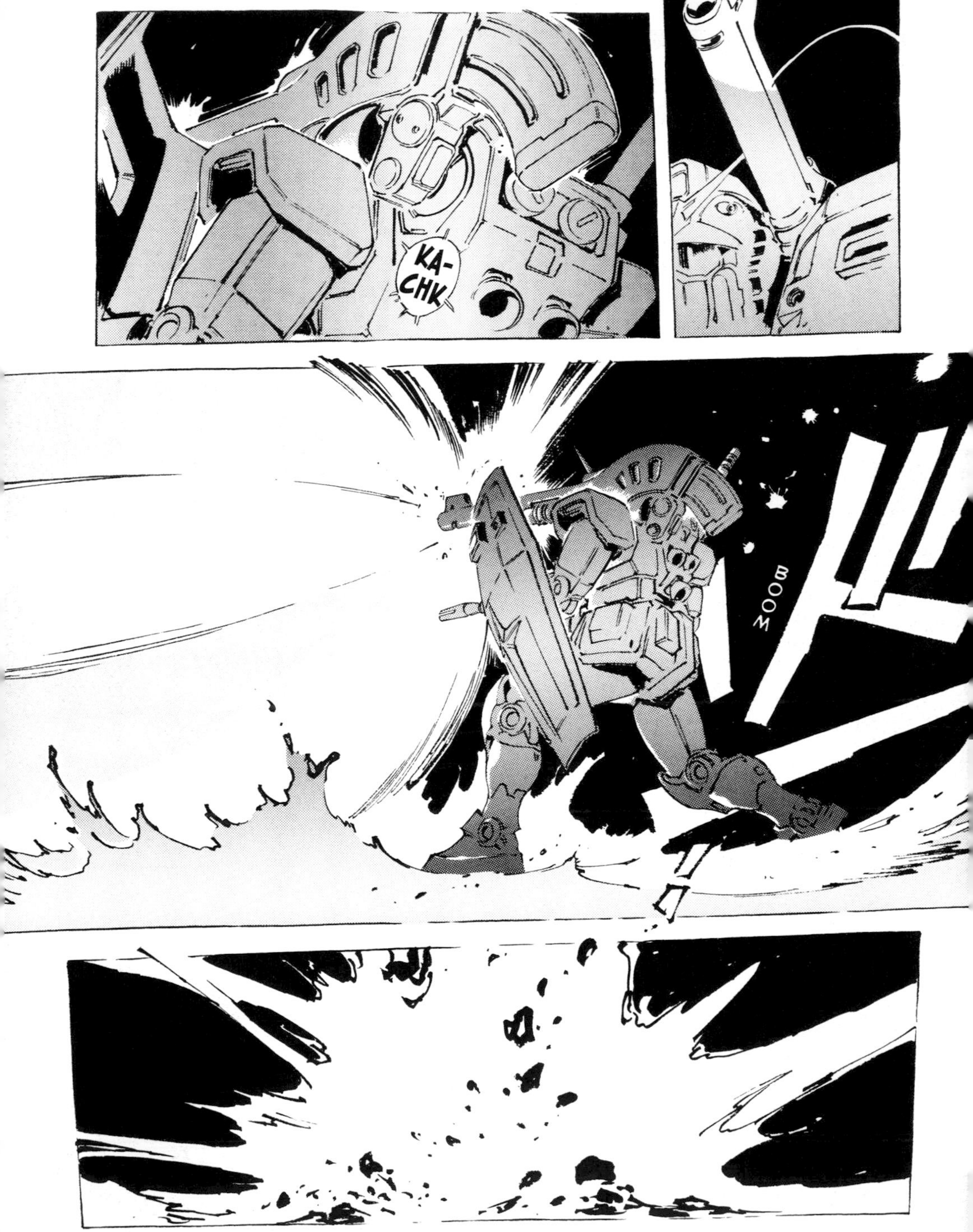
KA-CHK
BOOM

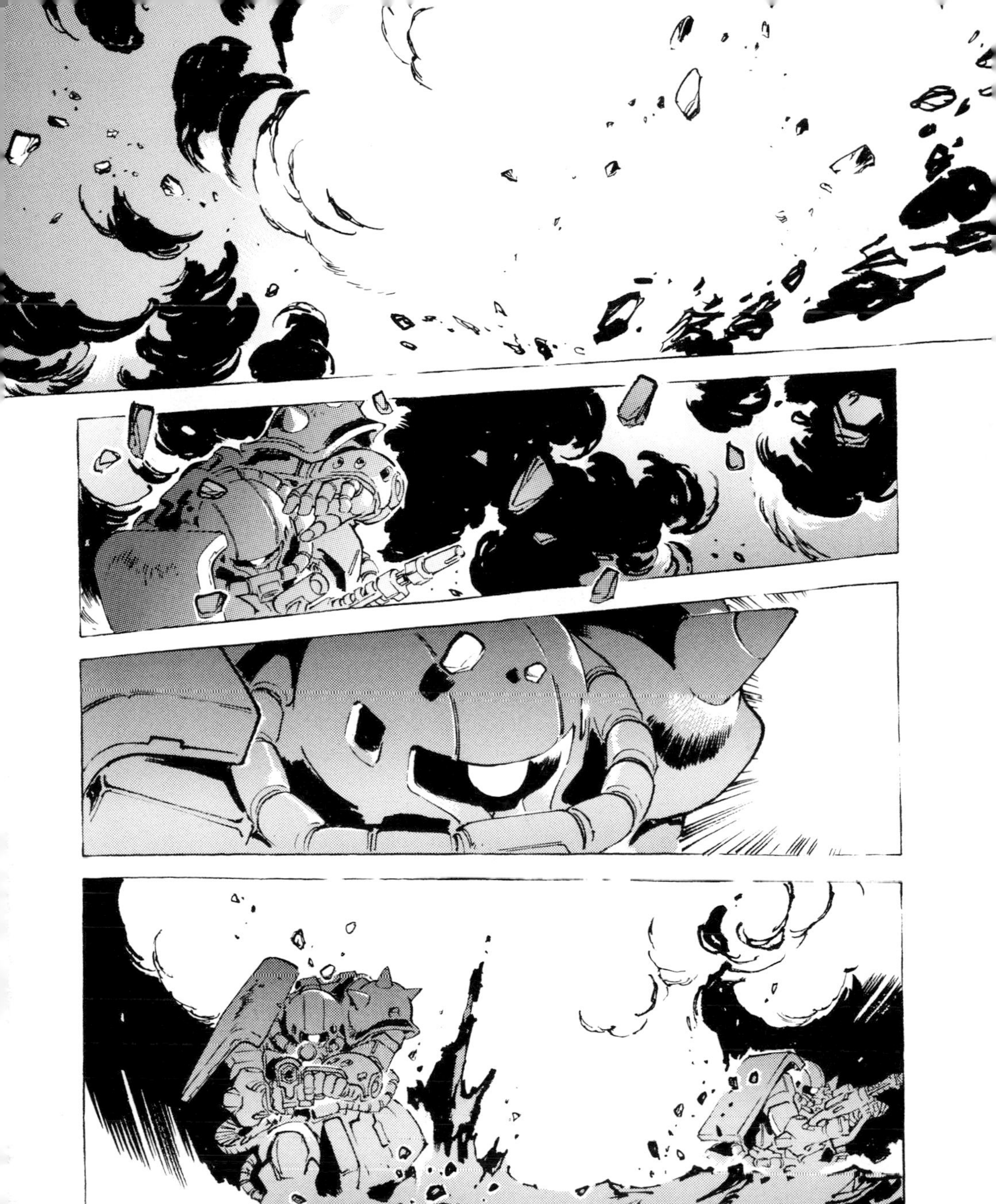

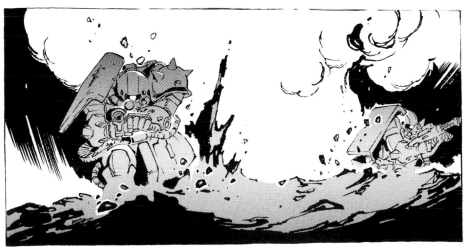

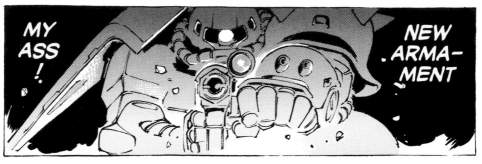

MY ASS!

NEW ARMAMENT

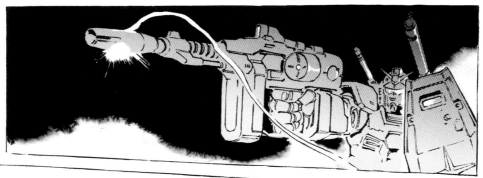

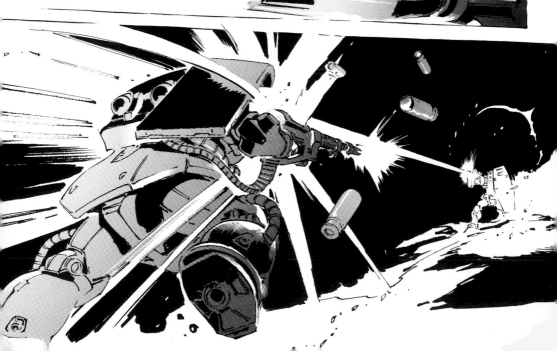

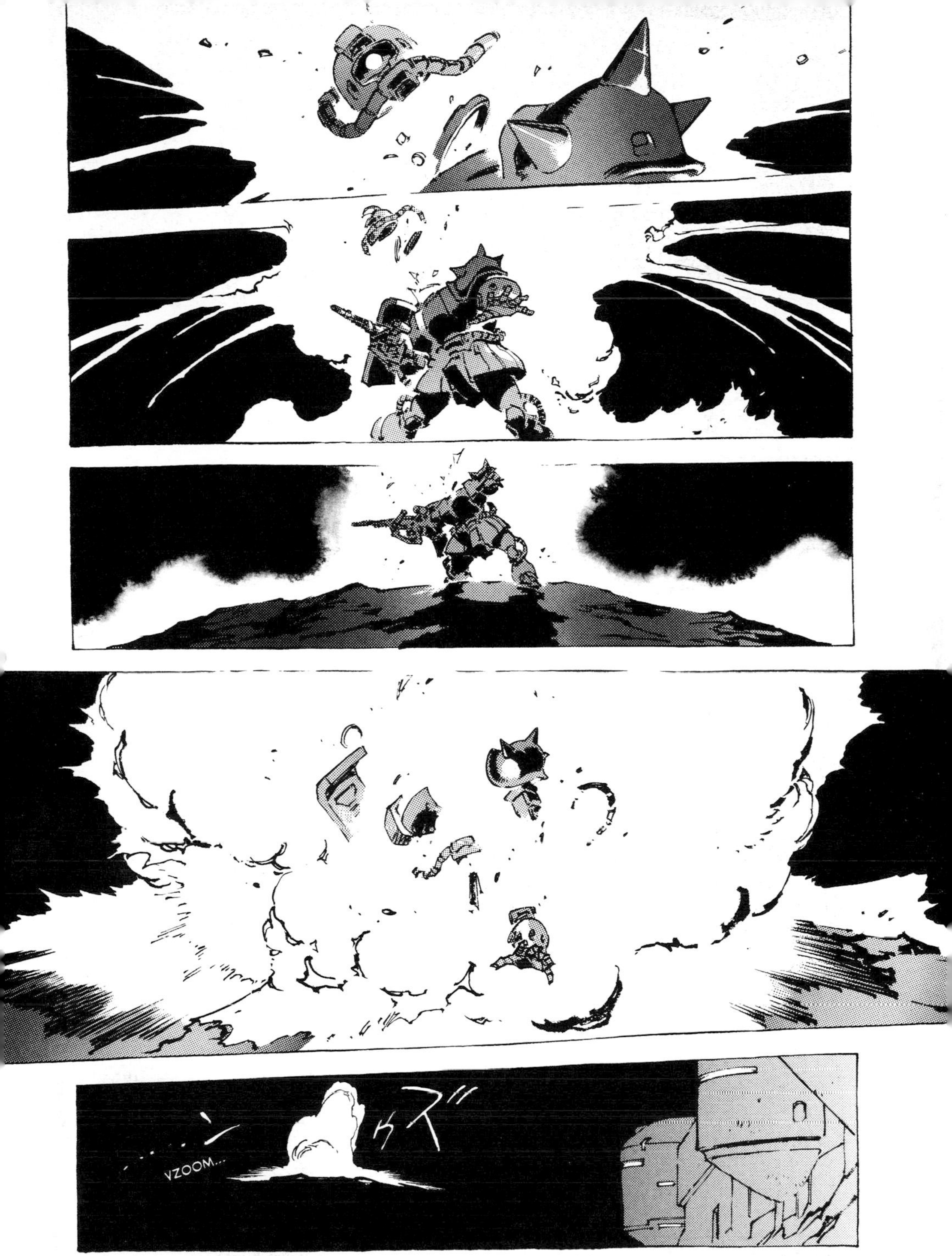
VZOOM...

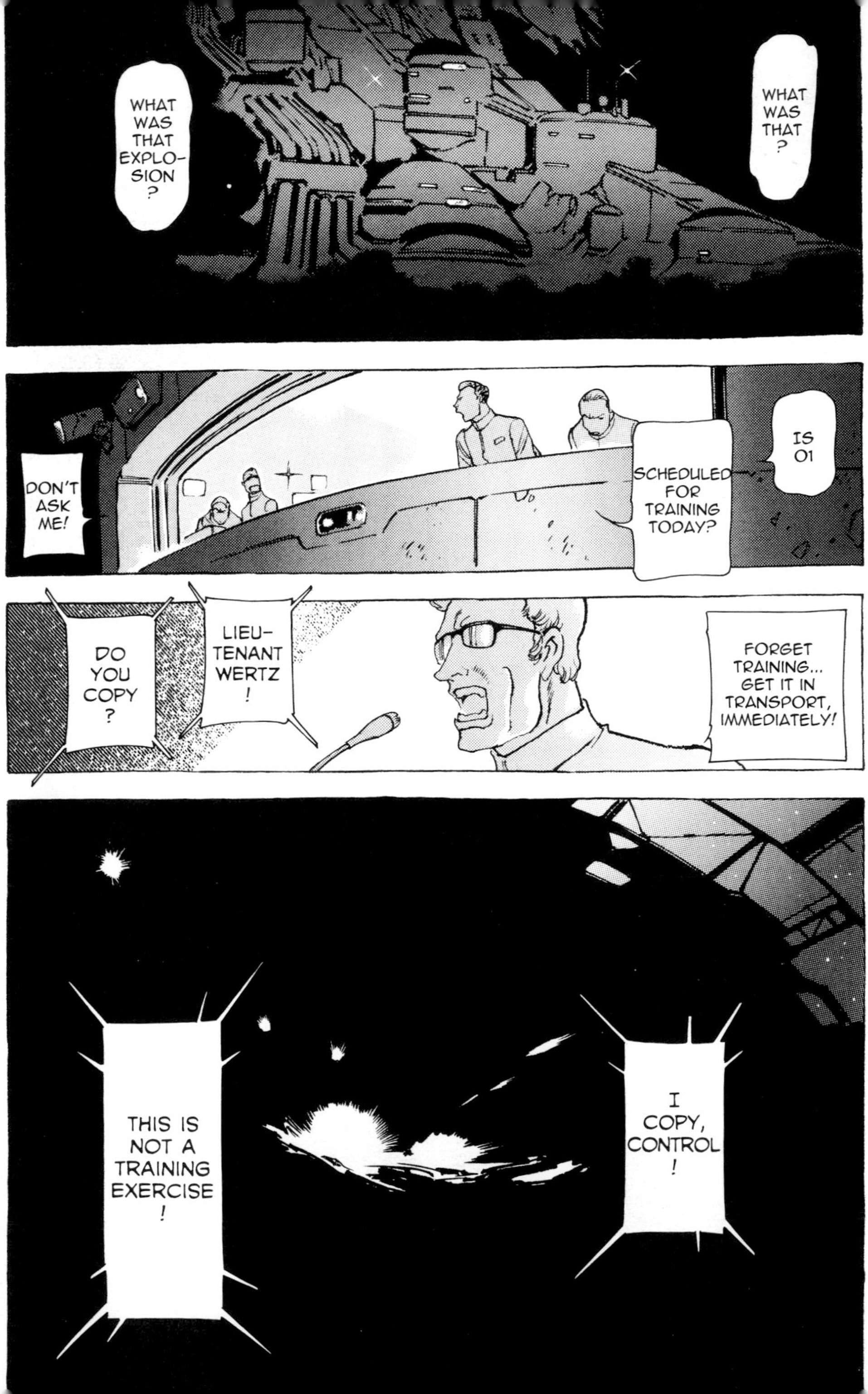
WHAT WAS THAT?
WHAT WAS THAT EXPLOSION?
IS 01
SCHEDULED FOR TRAINING TODAY?
DON'T ASK ME!
FORGET TRAINING... GET IT IN TRANSPORT, IMMEDIATELY!
LIEUTENANT WERTZ!
DO YOU COPY?
I COPY, CONTROL!
THIS IS NOT A TRAINING EXERCISE!

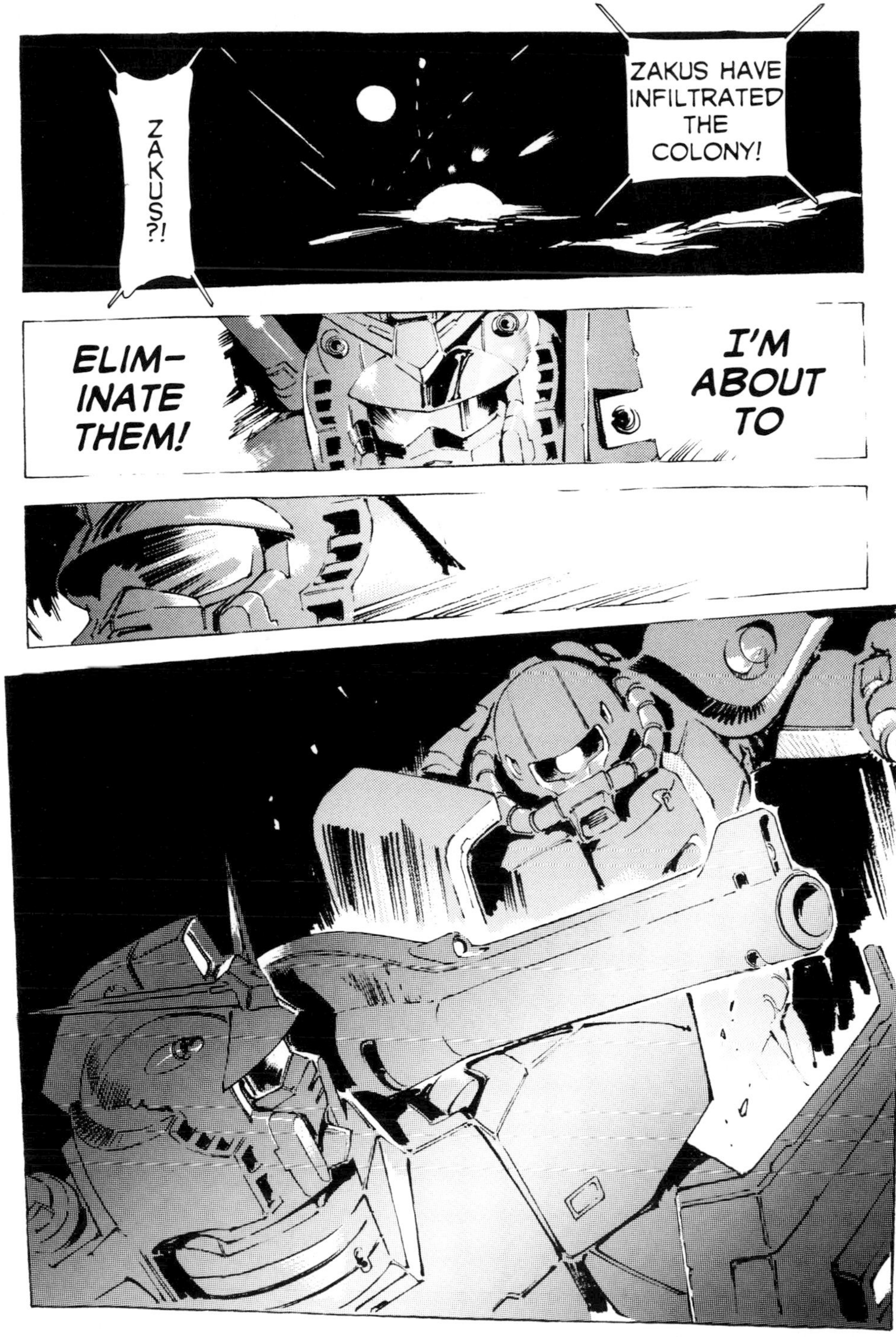
ZAKUS HAVE INFILTRATED THE COLONY!
ZAKUS?!
I'M ABOUT TO
ELIM- INATE THEM!

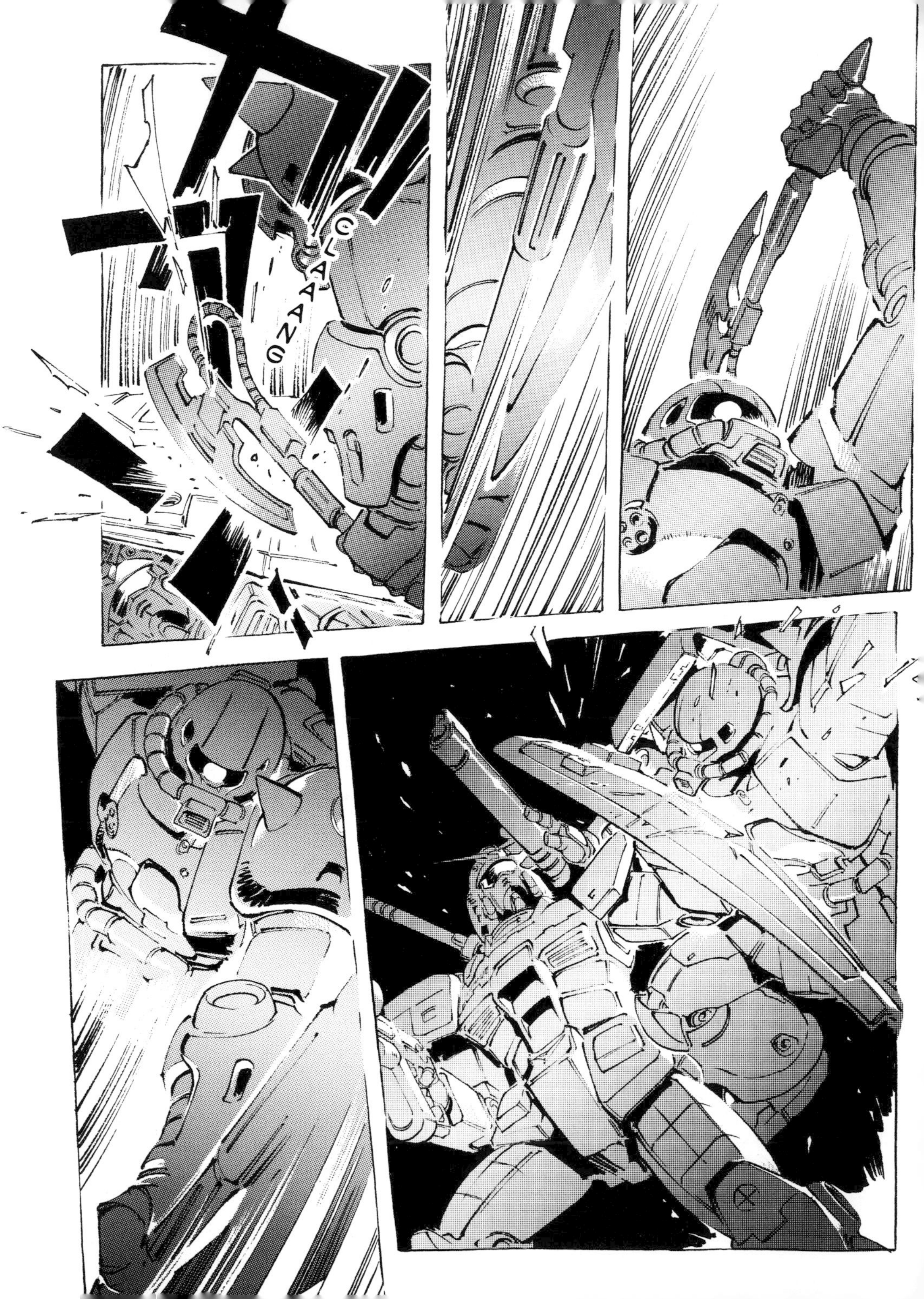
CLAAAANG

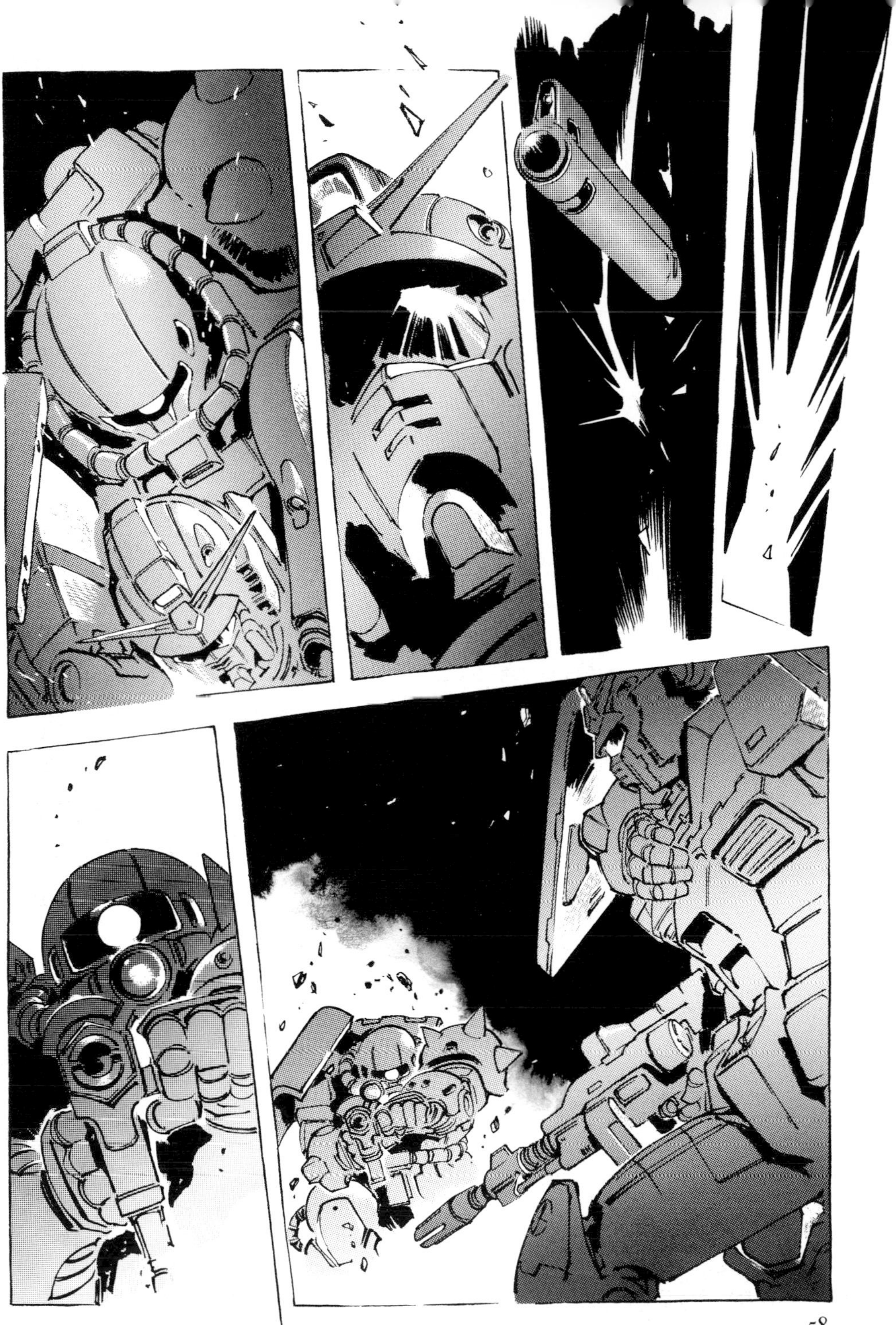

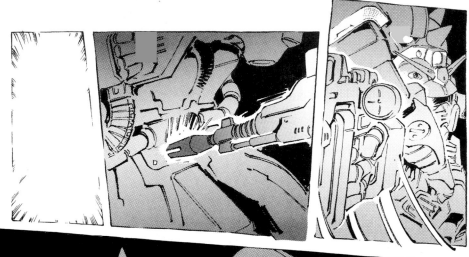
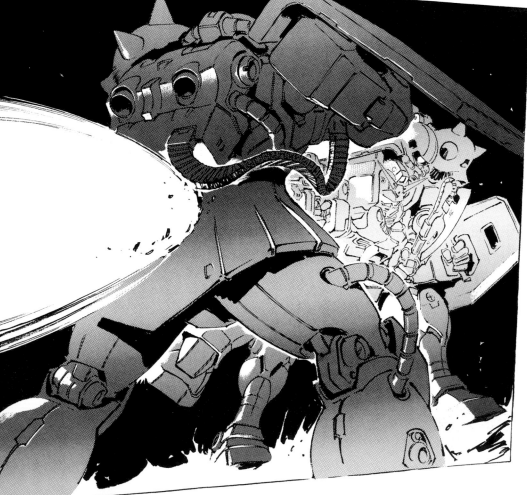

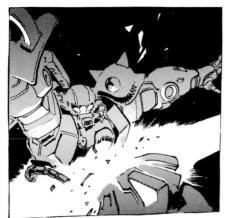
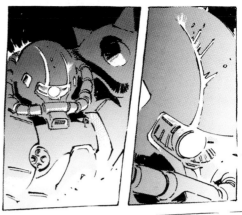
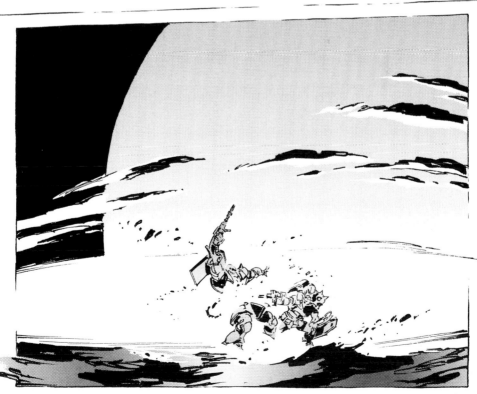

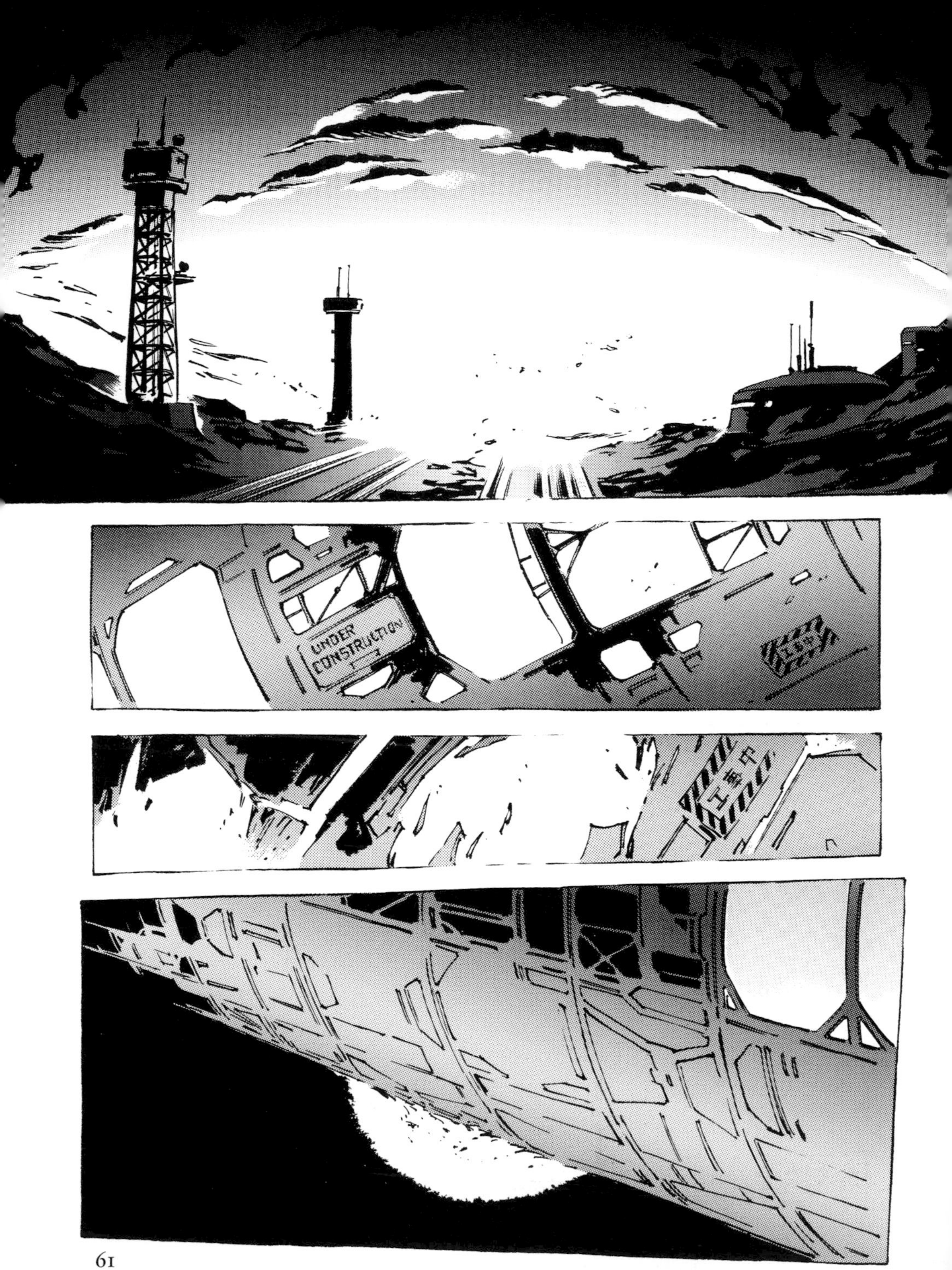
UNDER CONSTRUCTION

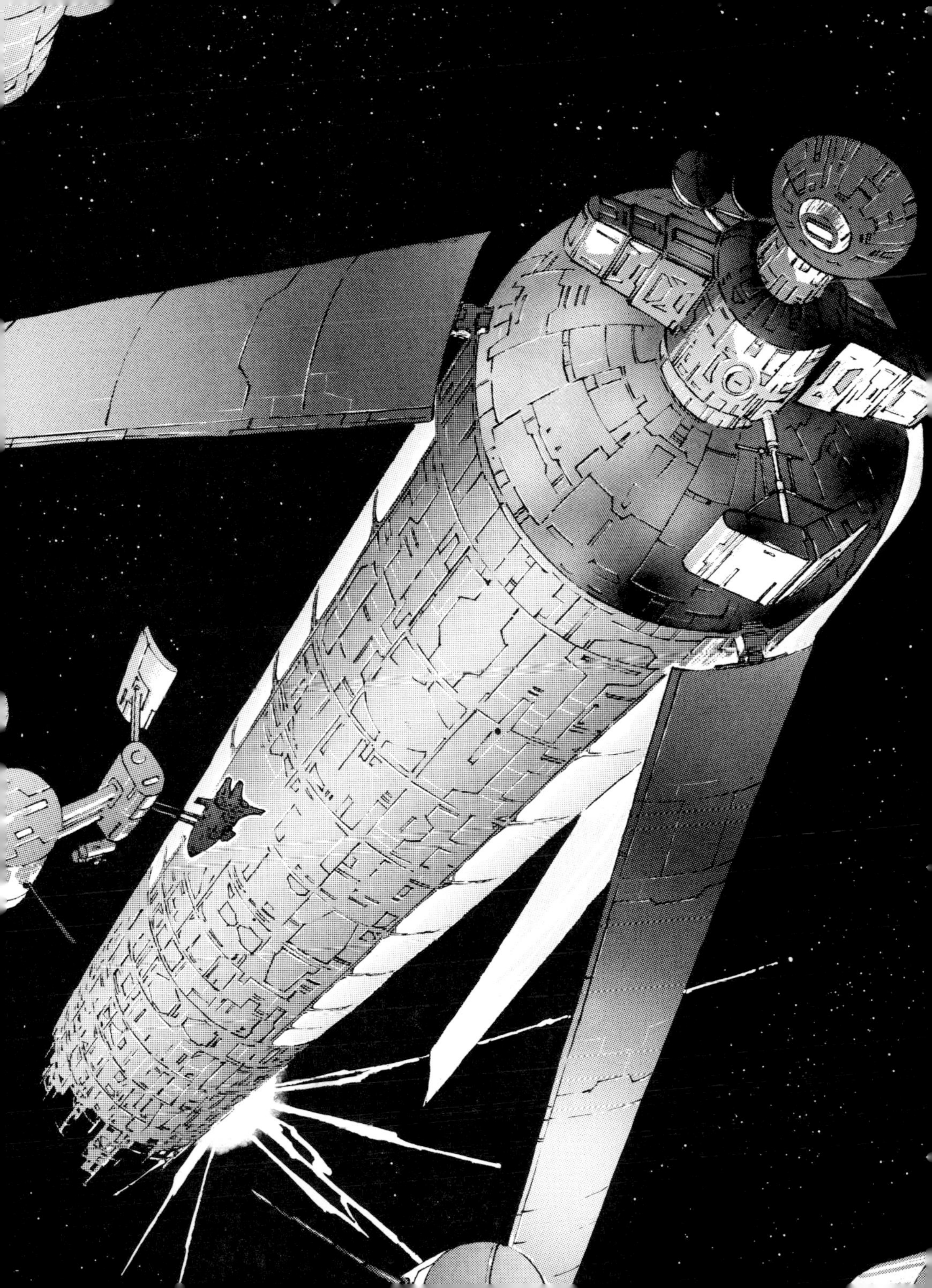

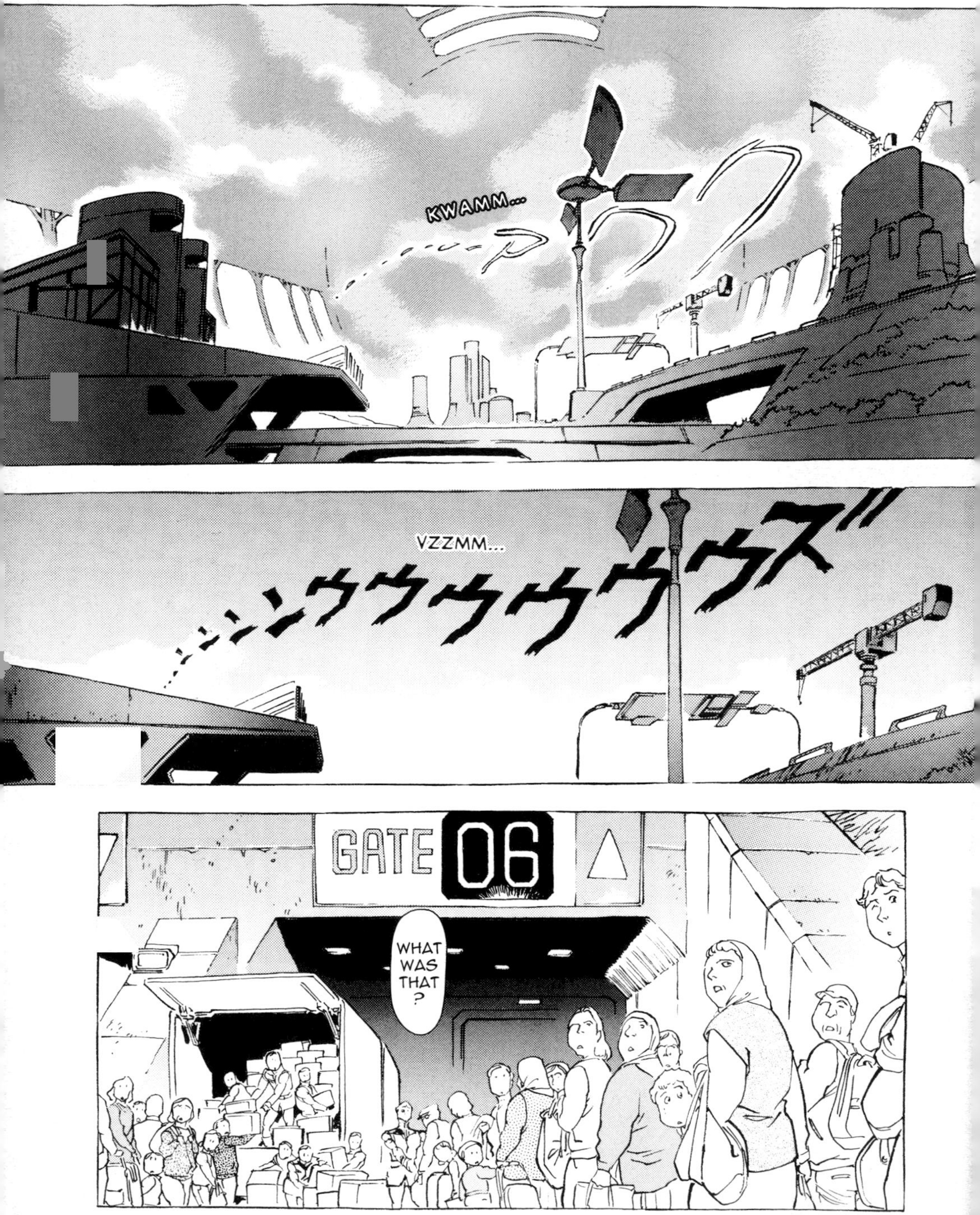
KWAMM...
VZZMM...
GATE 06
WHAT WAS THAT?

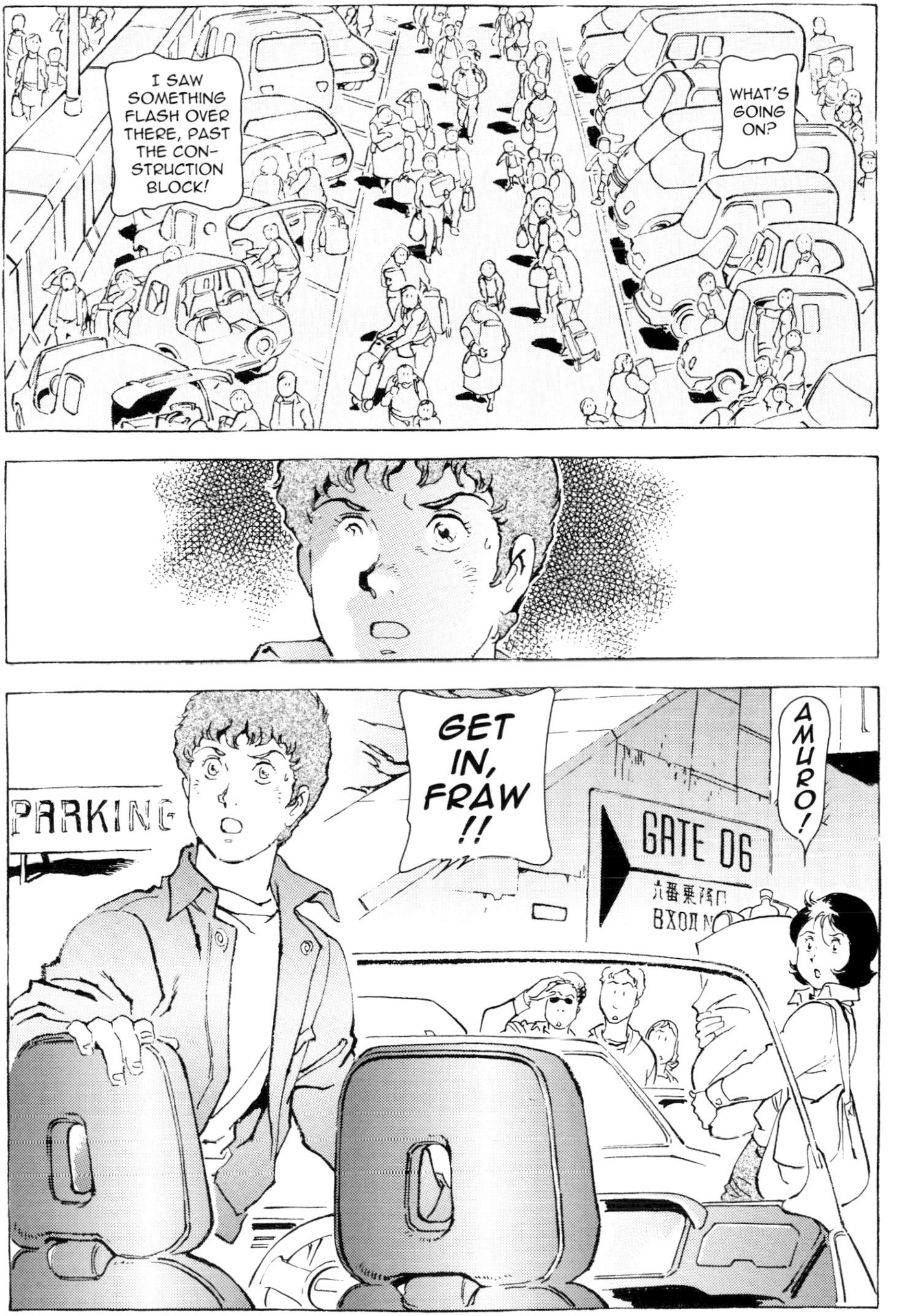
WHAT'S GOING ON?
I SAW SOMETHING FLASH OVER THERE, PAST THE CON-STRUCTION BLOCK!
AMURO!
GATE 06
GET IN, FRAW!!
PARKING

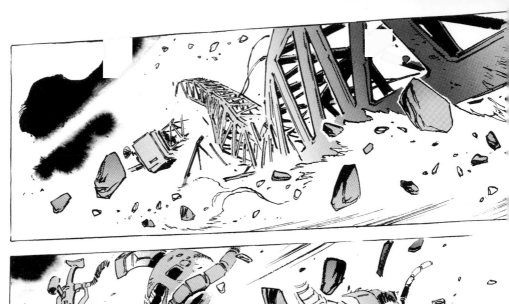

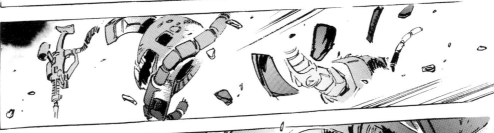

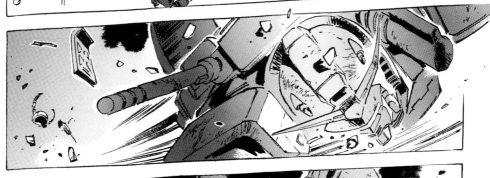

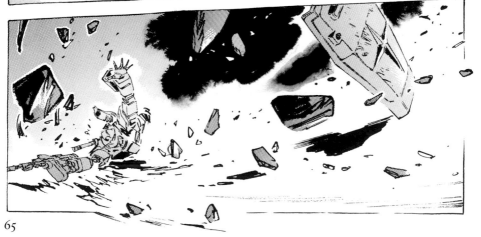

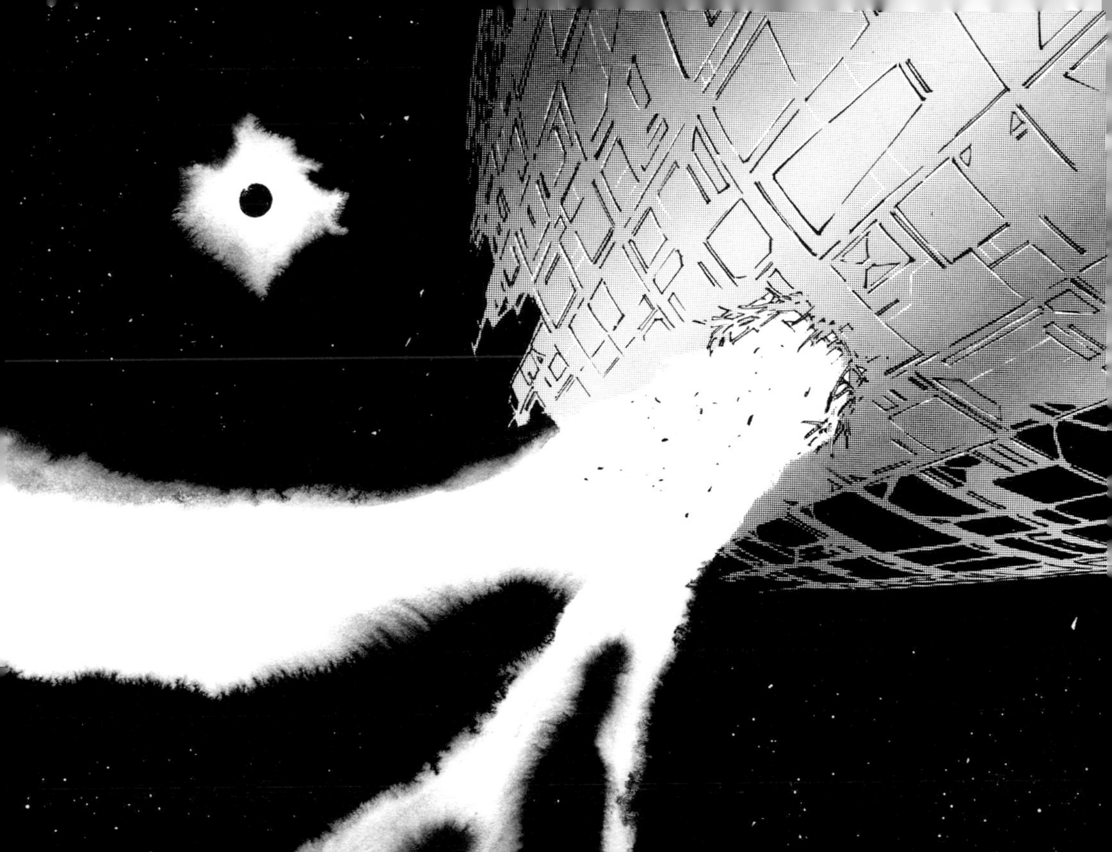

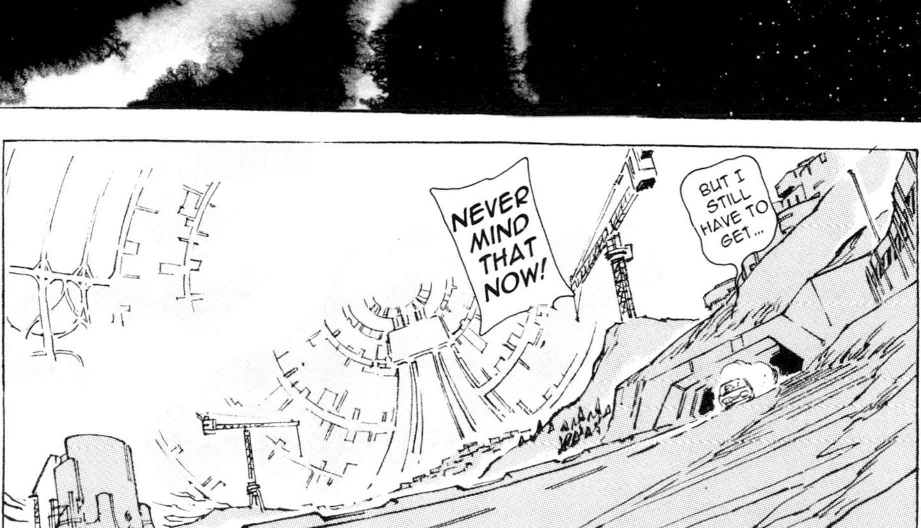
BUT I STILL HAVE TO GET...
NEVER MIND THAT NOW!

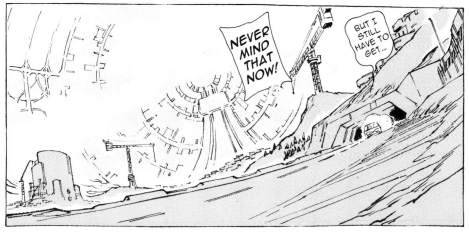

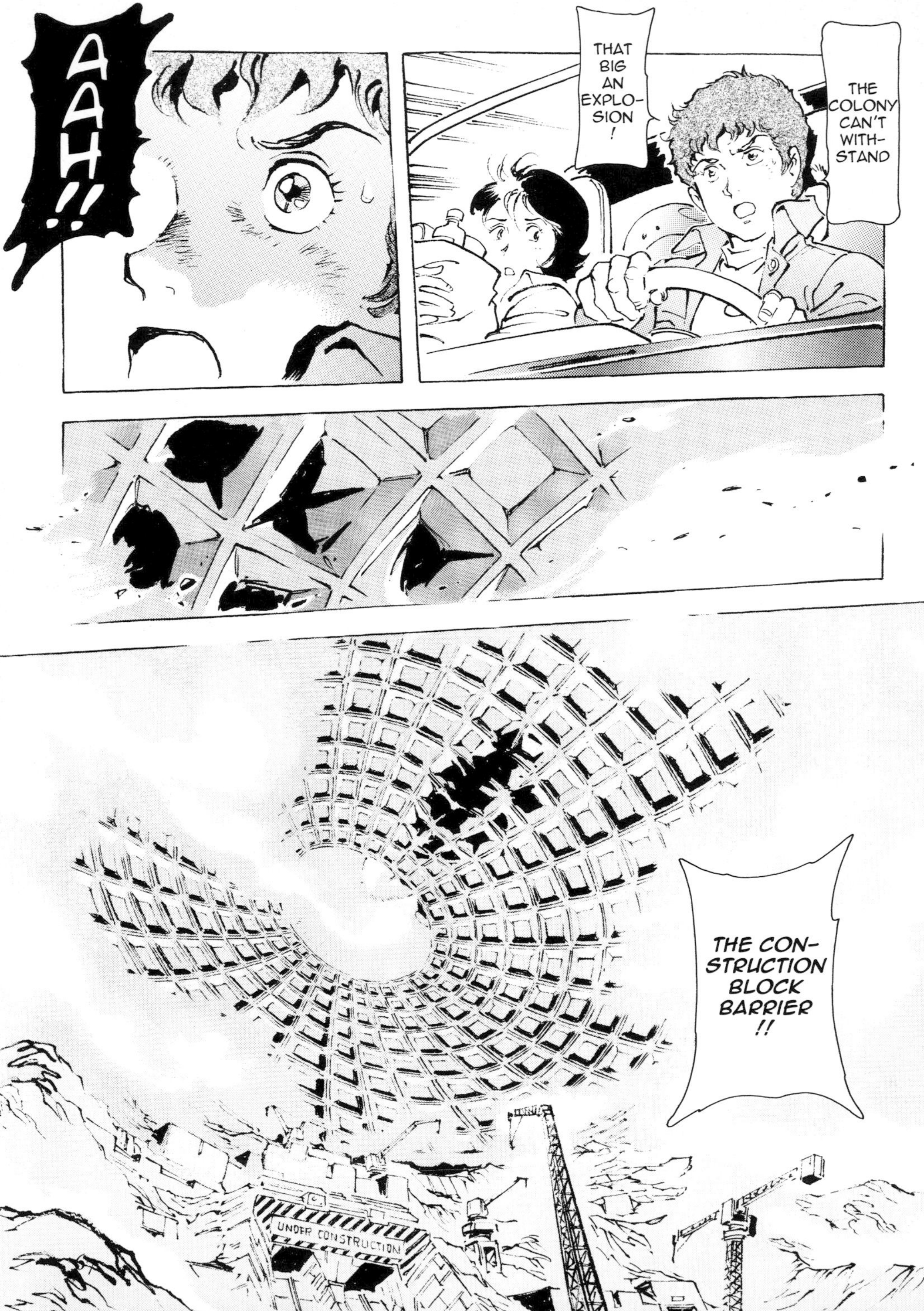
THE COLONY CAN'T WITH-STAND
THAT BIG AN EXPLO-SION!
AAH!!
THE CON-STRUCTION BLOCK BARRIER!!
UNDER CONSTRUCTION

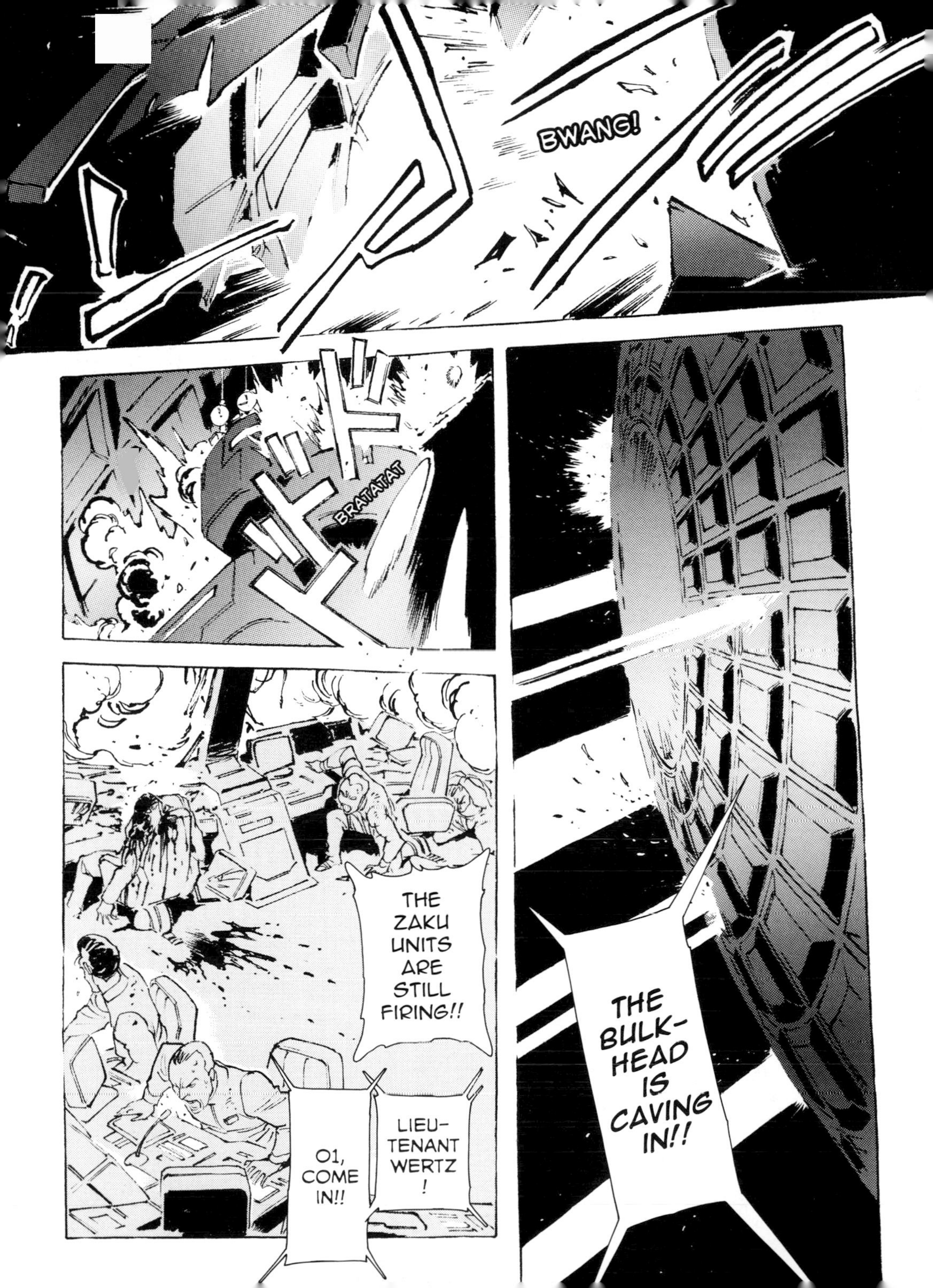
BWANG!
THE BULK-HEAD IS CAVING IN!!
BRATATAT
THE ZAKU UNITS ARE STILL FIRING!!
LIEU-TENANT WERTZ!
01, COME IN!!

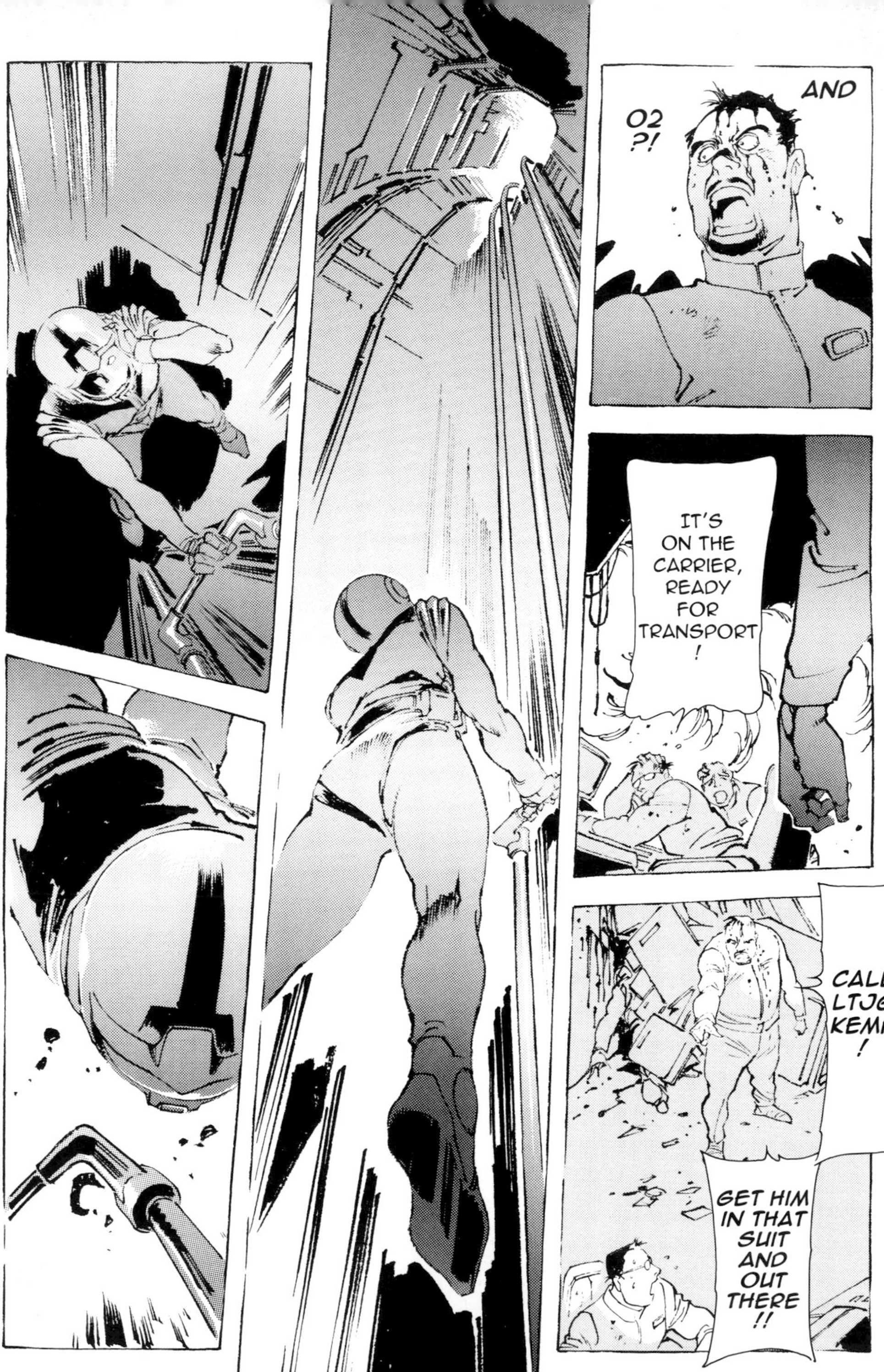
AND
O2 ?!
IT'S ON THE CARRIER, READY FOR TRANSPORT!
CALL LTJG KEMP!
GET HIM IN THAT SUIT AND OUT THERE!!

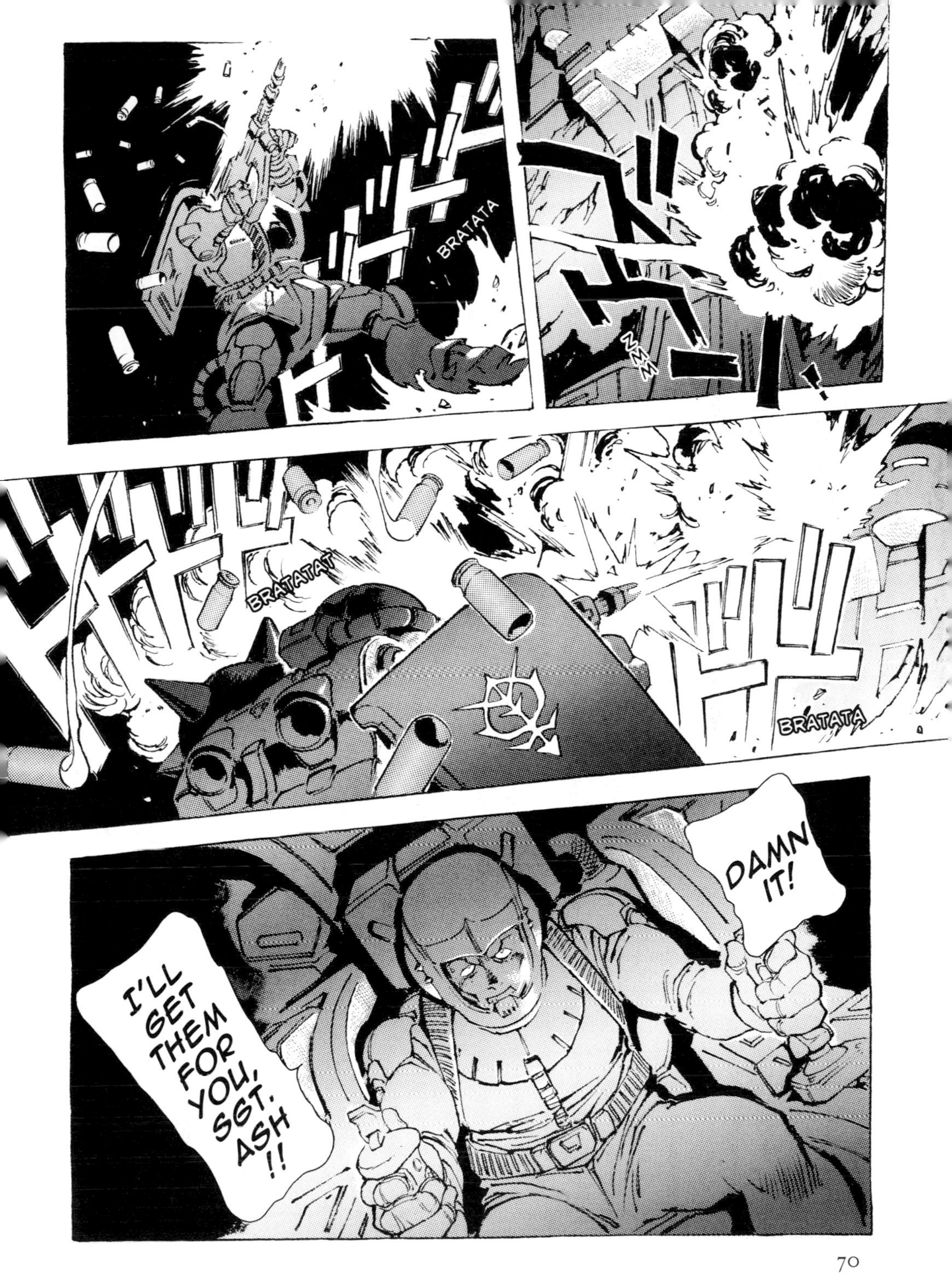
BRATATA
BRATATA
BRATATAT
DAMN IT!
I'LL GET THEM FOR YOU, SGT. ASH!!

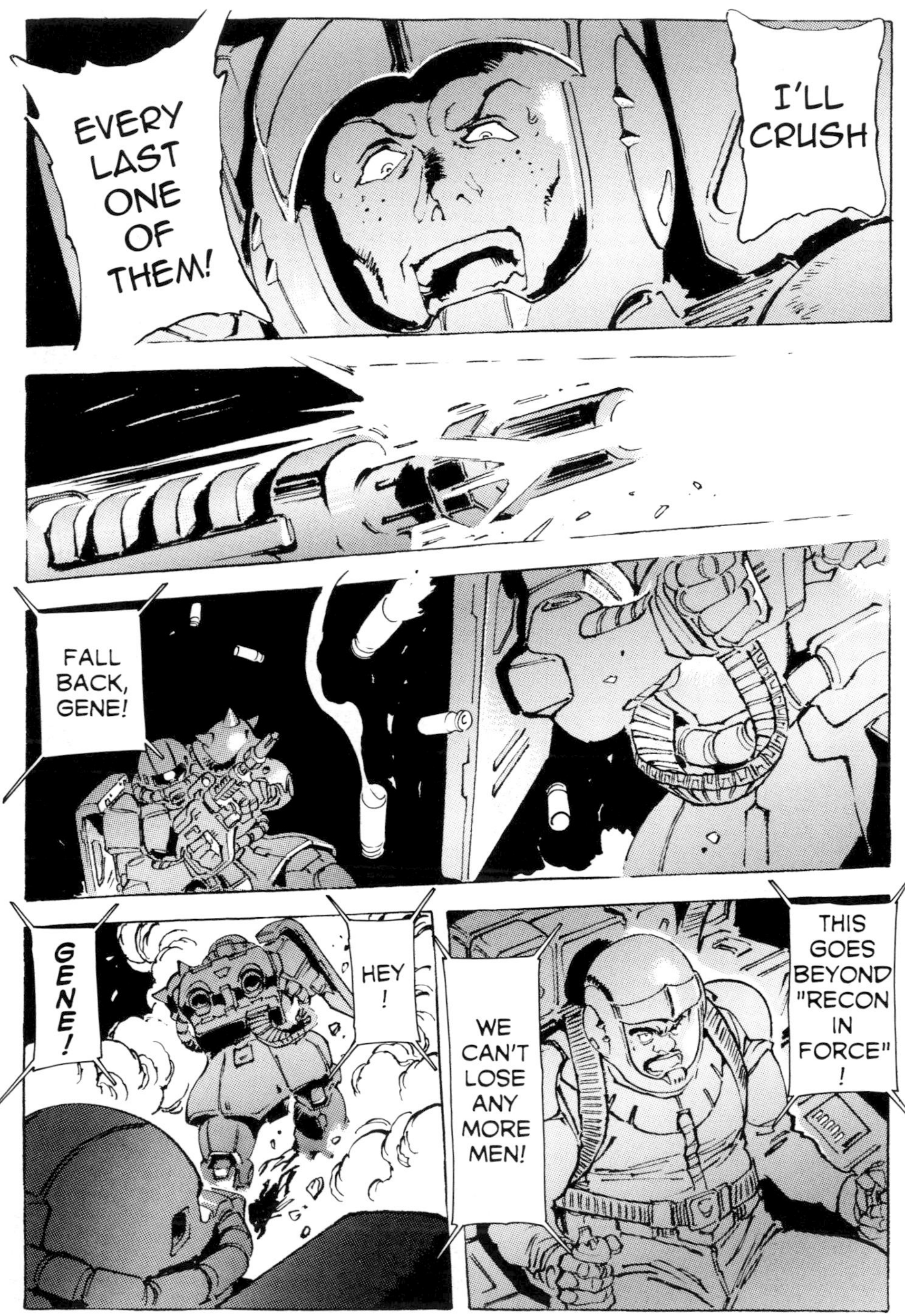
I'LL CRUSH
EVERY LAST ONE OF THEM!
FALL BACK, GENE!
THIS GOES BEYOND "RECON IN FORCE"!
WE CAN'T LOSE ANY MORE MEN!
HEY!
GENE!

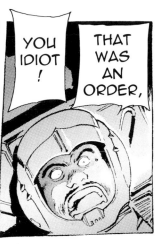

THAT WAS AN ORDER,

YOU IDIOT!

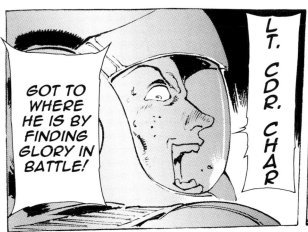

GOT TO WHERE HE IS BY FINDING GLORY IN BATTLE!

LT. CDR. CHAR

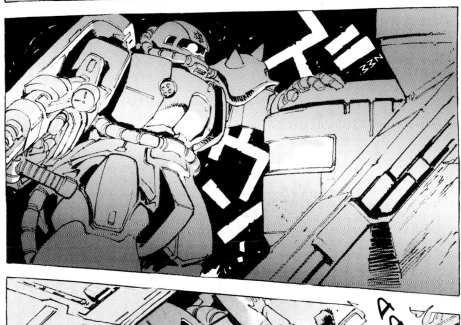

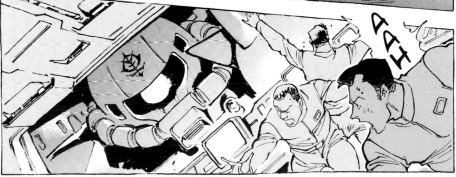

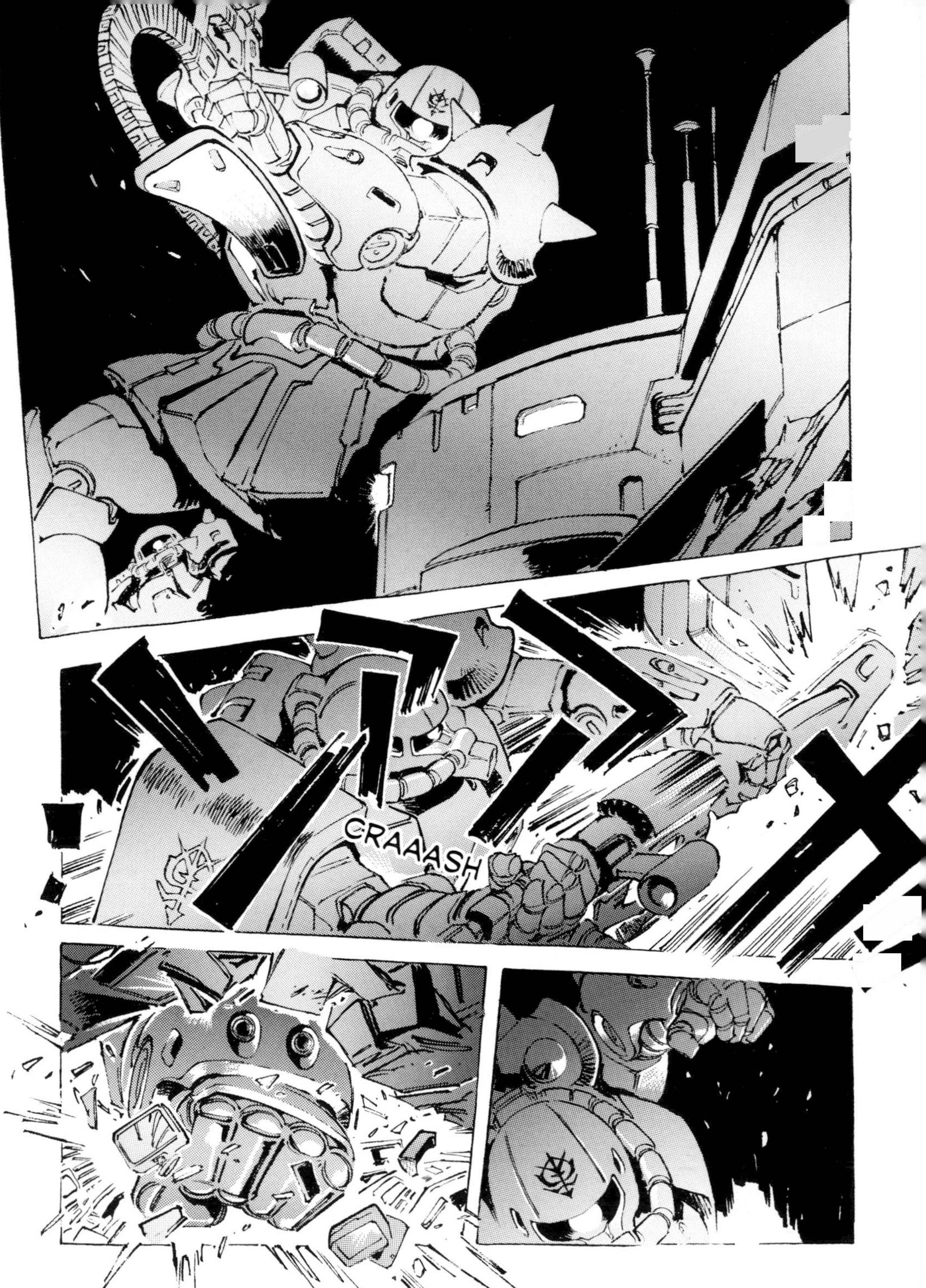
CRAAASH

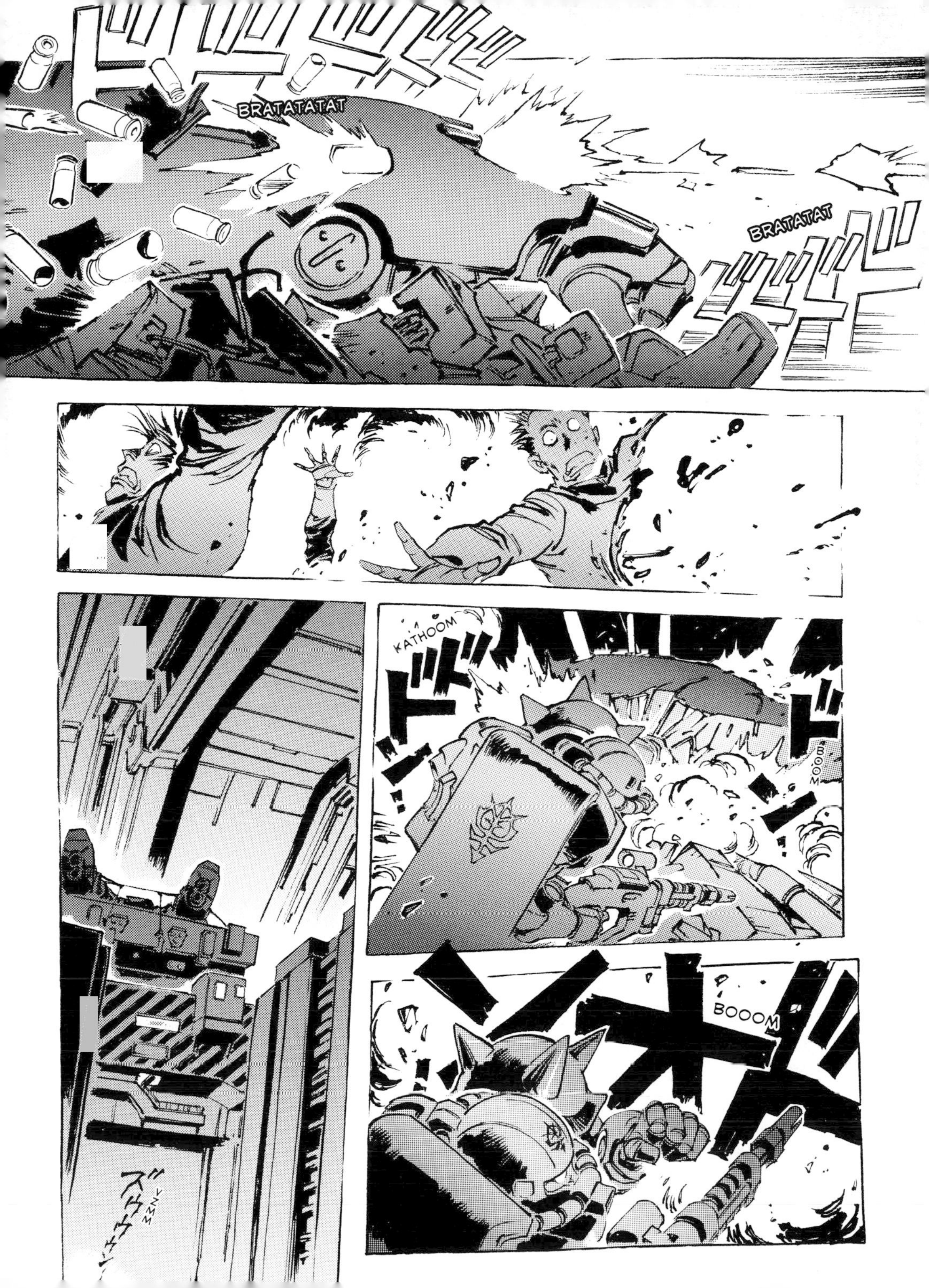
BRATATATAT
BRATATAT
KATHOOM
BOOM
BOOOM
VMMM

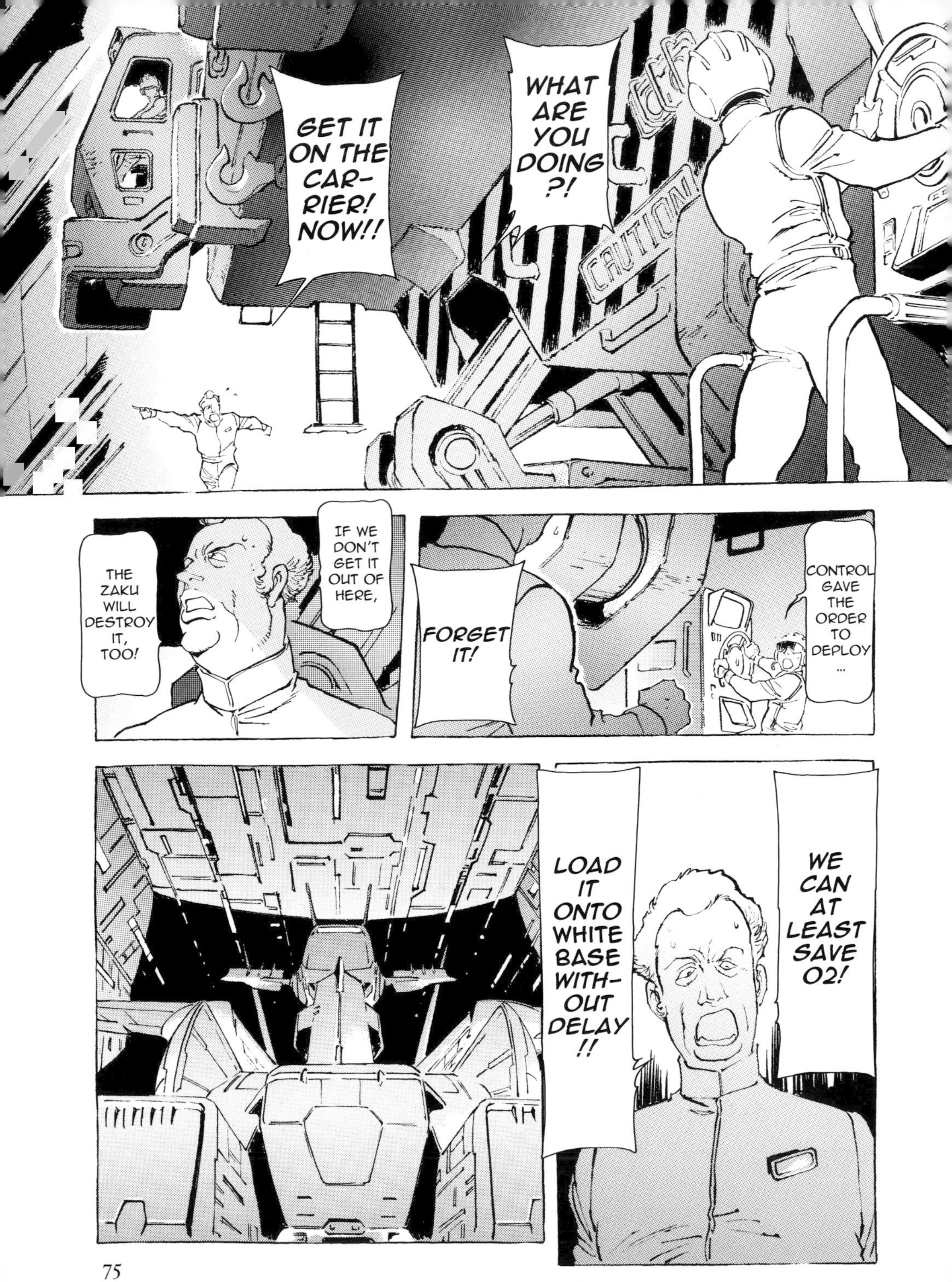
WHAT ARE YOU DOING?!
GET IT ON THE CAR-RIER! NOW!!
CONTROL GAVE THE ORDER TO DEPLOY ...
FORGET IT!
IF WE DON'T GET IT OUT OF HERE,
THE ZAKU WILL DESTROY IT, TOO!
WE CAN AT LEAST SAVE 02!
LOAD IT ONTO WHITE BASE WITH-OUT DELAY!!

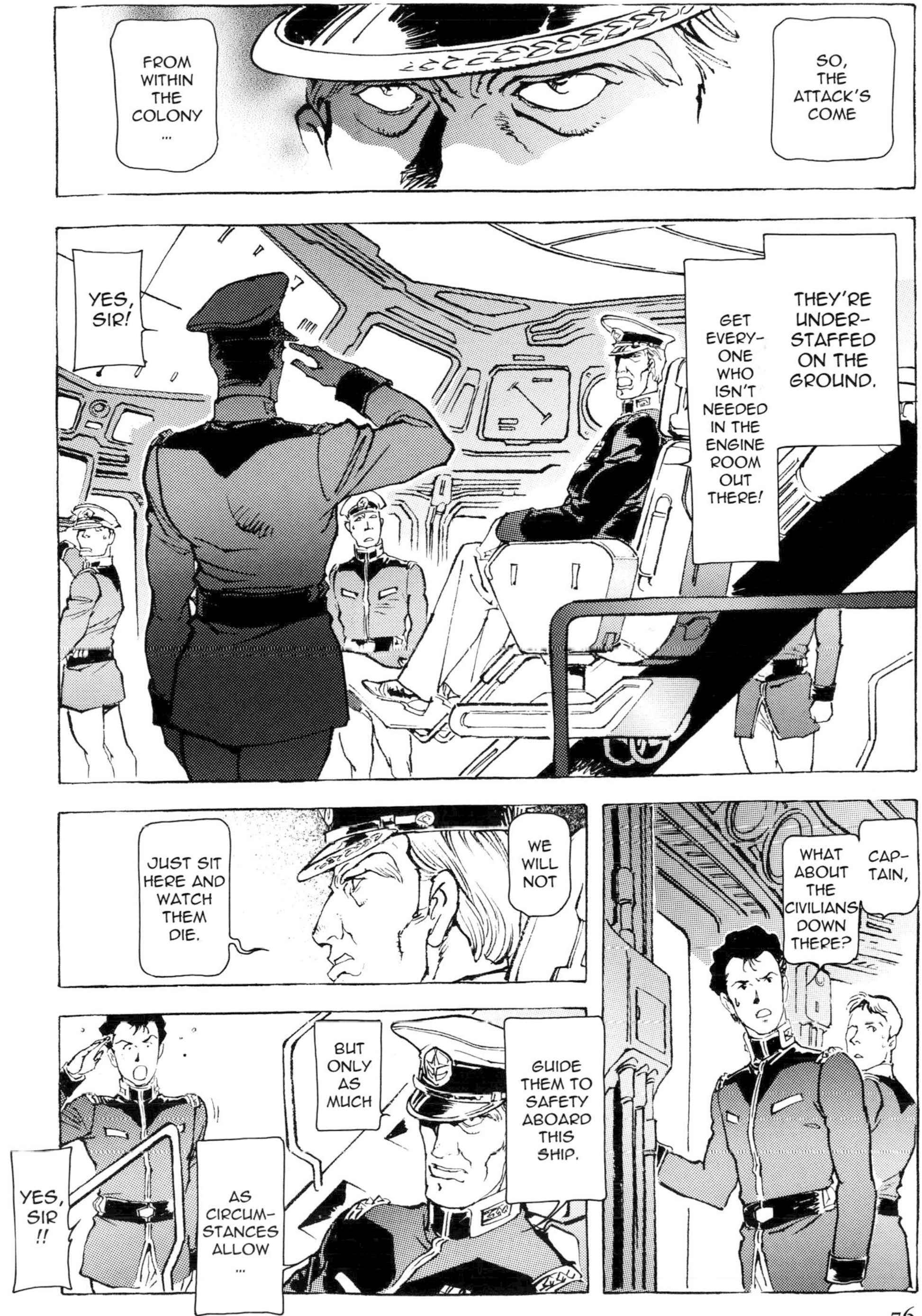
SO, THE ATTACK'S COME
FROM WITHIN THE COLONY ...
THEY'RE UNDER-STAFFED ON THE GROUND.
GET EVERY-ONE WHO ISN'T NEEDED IN THE ENGINE ROOM OUT THERE!
YES, SIR!
CAP-TAIN,
WHAT ABOUT THE CIVILIANS DOWN THERE?
WE WILL NOT
JUST SIT HERE AND WATCH THEM DIE.
GUIDE THEM TO SAFETY ABOARD THIS SHIP.
BUT ONLY AS MUCH
AS CIRCUM-STANCES ALLOW ...
YES, SIR !!

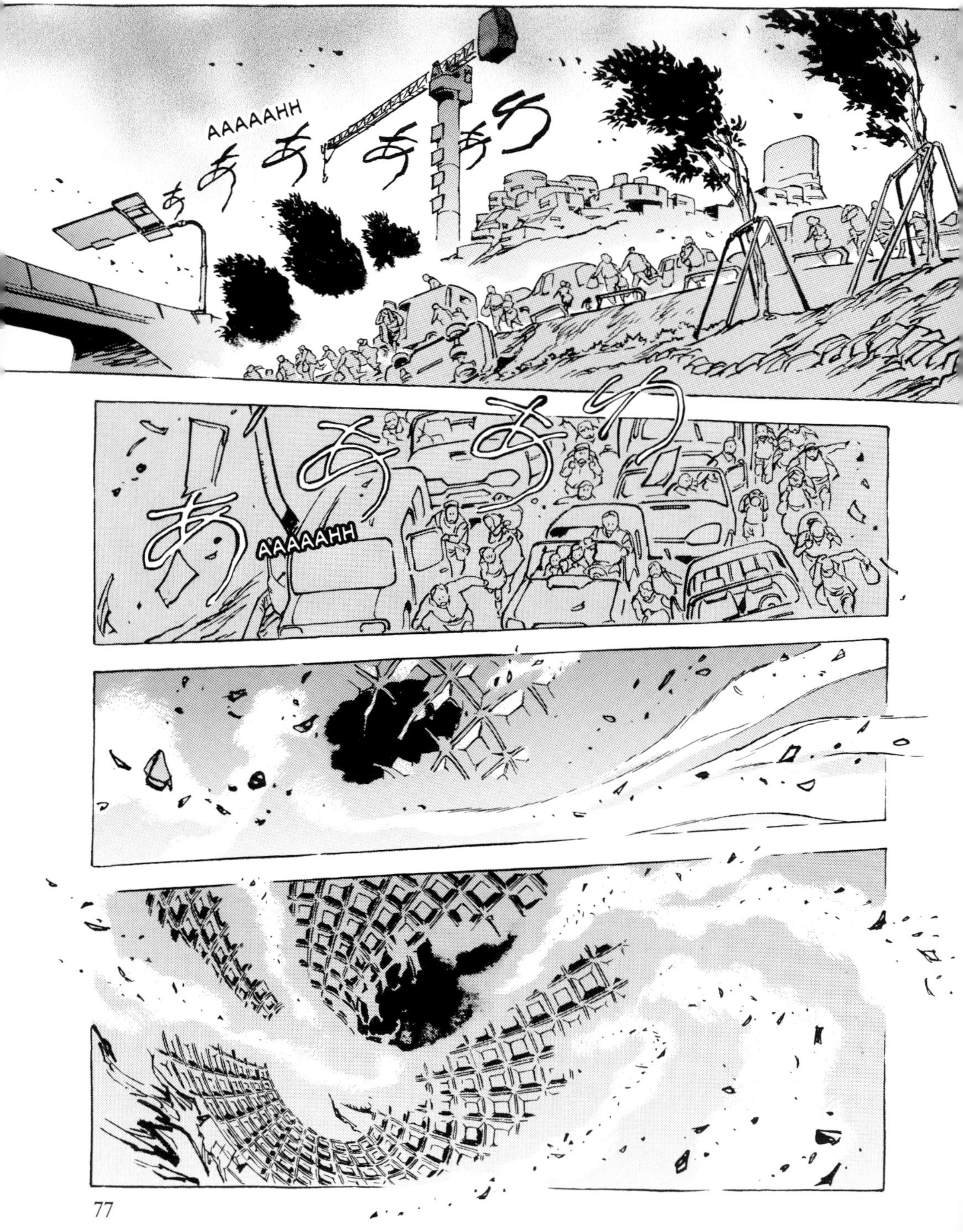
AAAAAHH
AAAAAHH

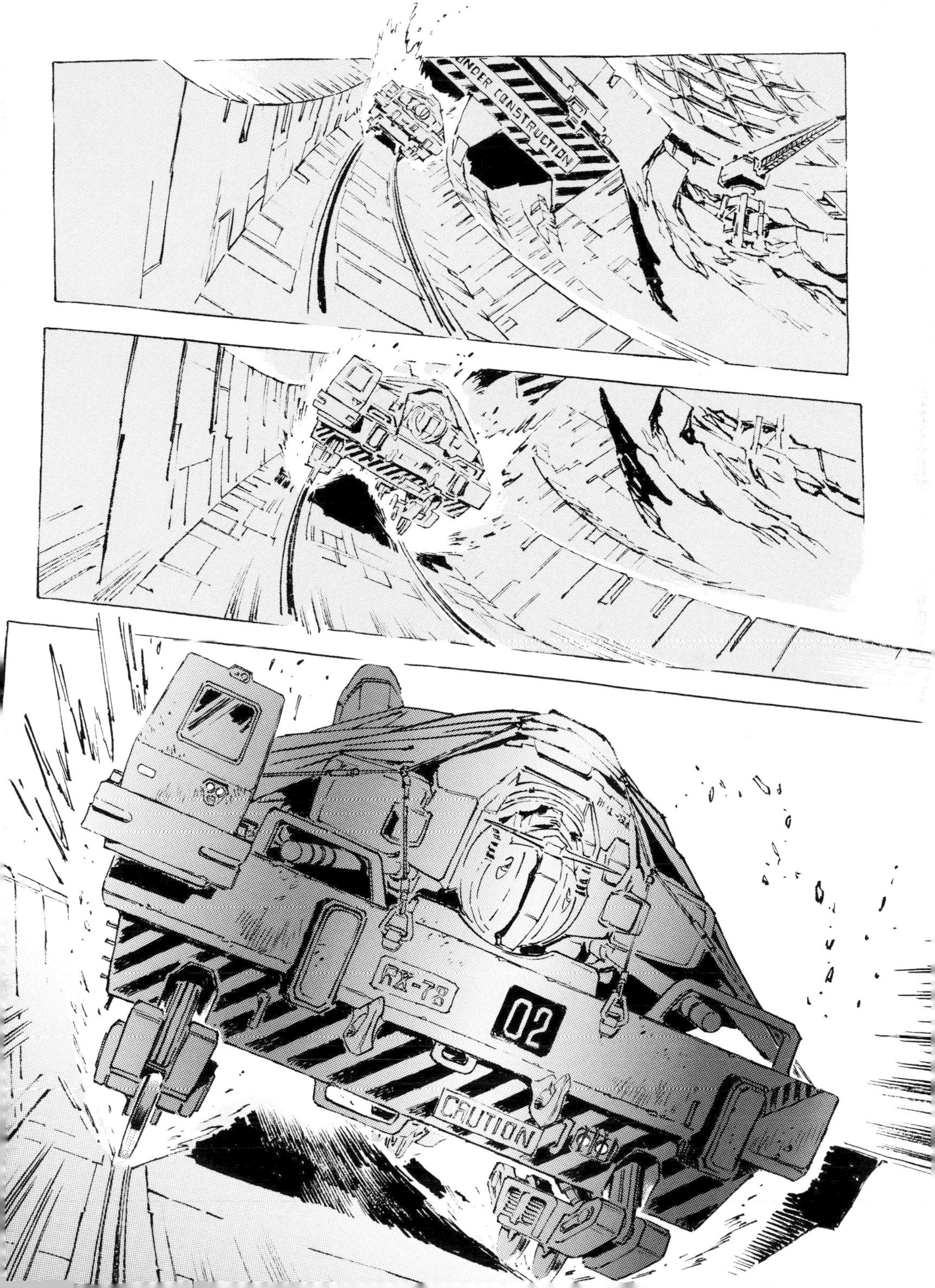
UNDER CONSTRUCTION
RX-78
02
CAUTION

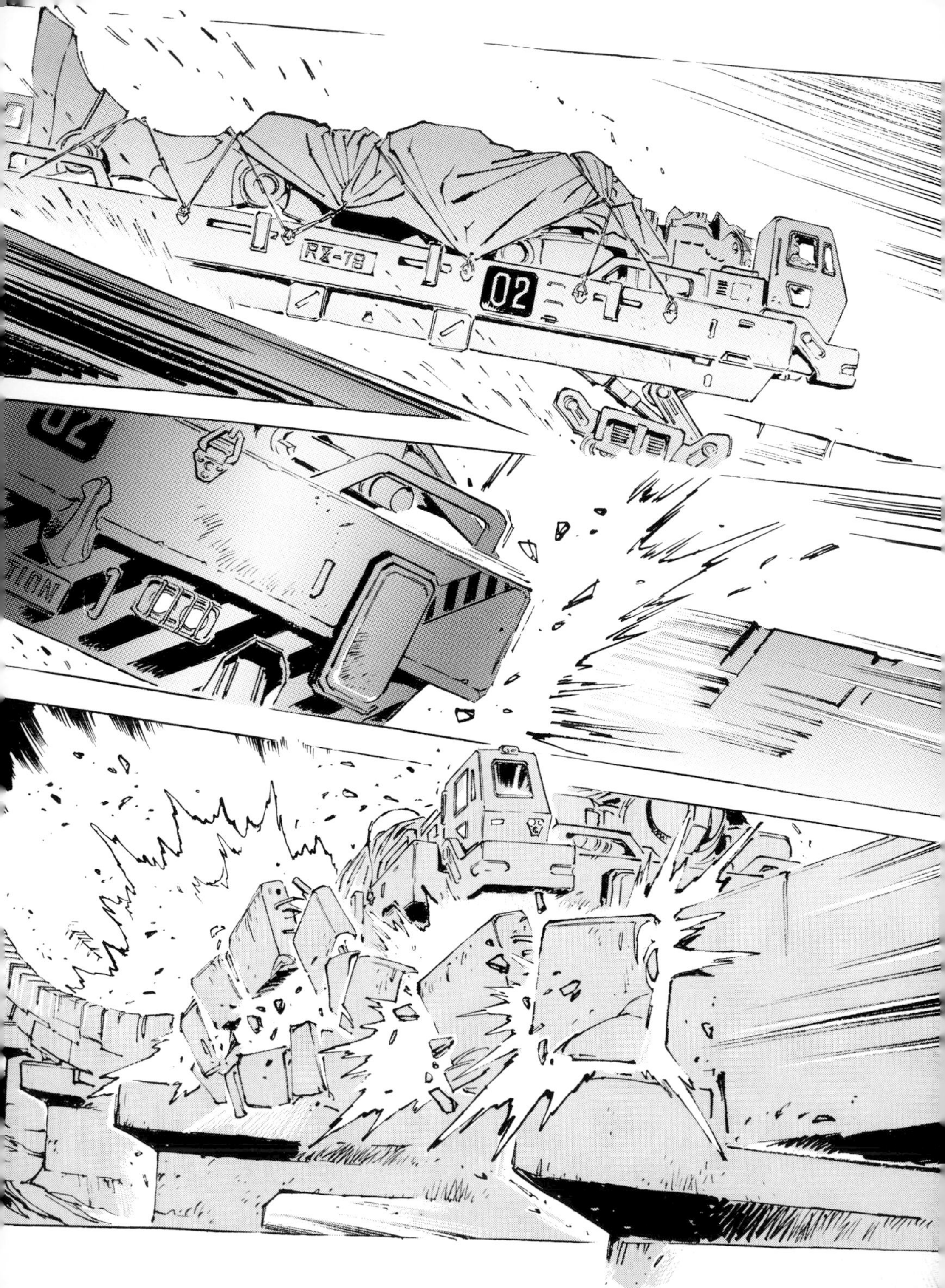
RX-78
02

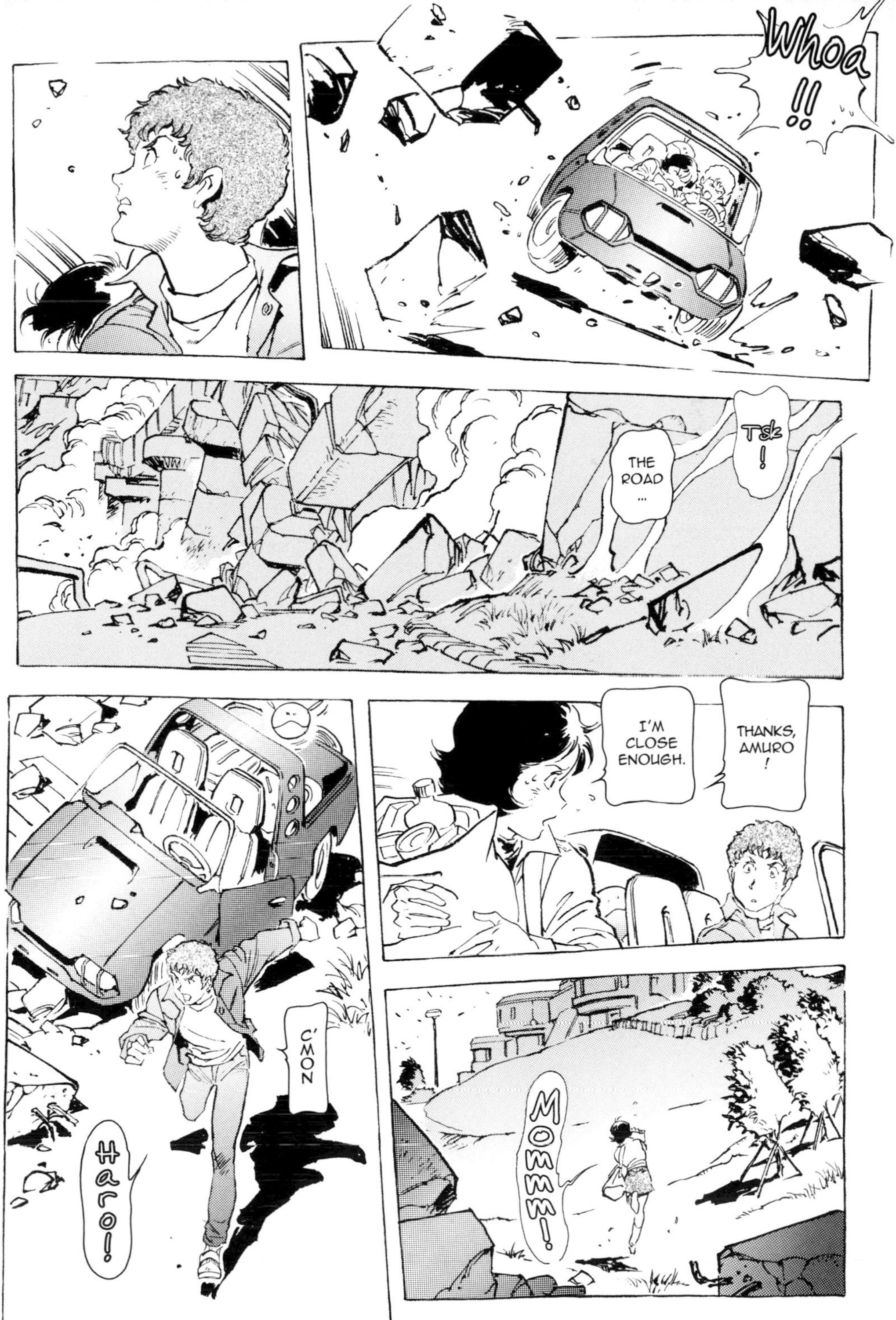
Whoa!!
Tsk!
THE ROAD...
THANKS, AMURO!
I'M CLOSE ENOUGH.
Mommm!
C'MON
Haro!

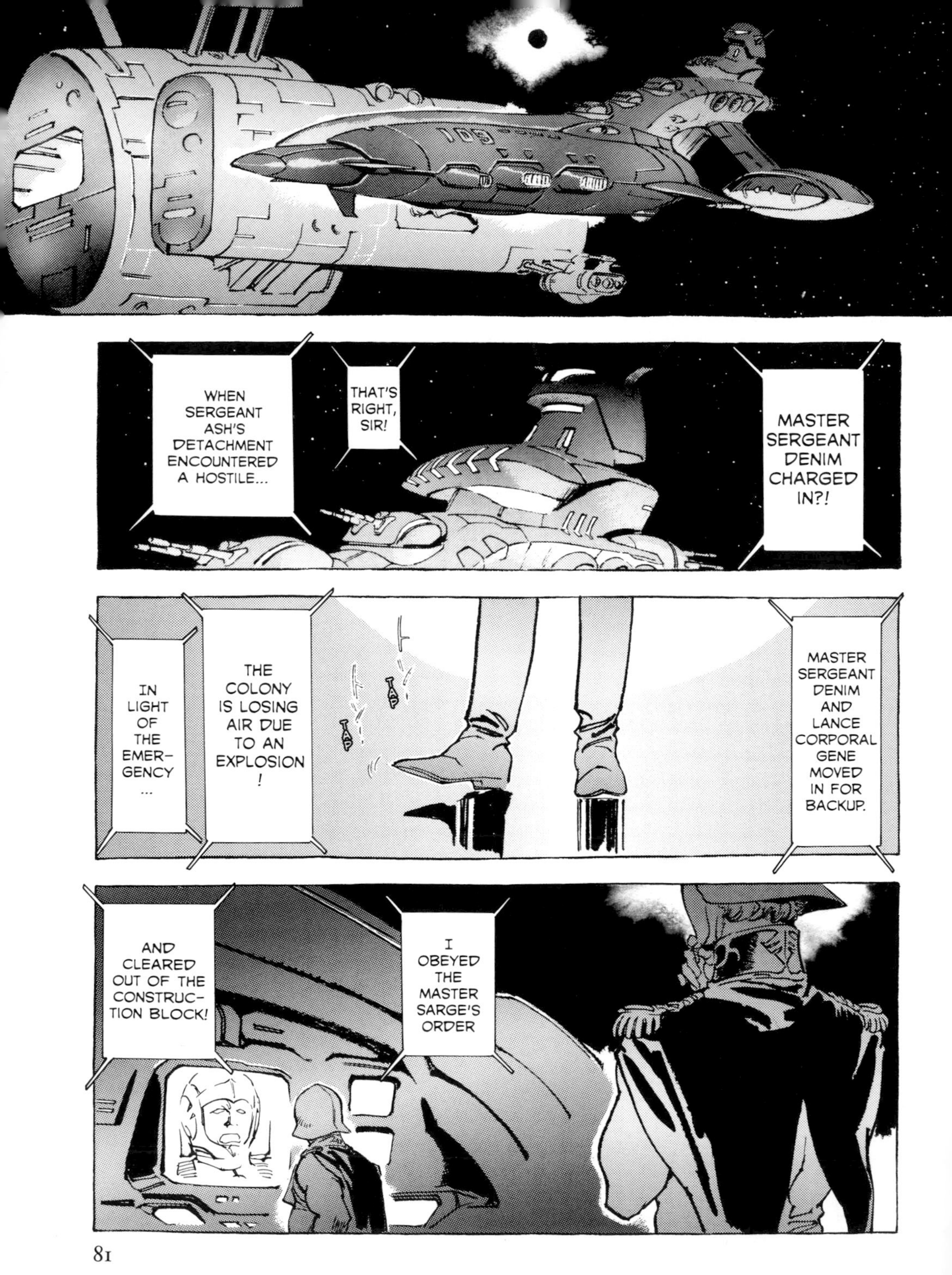
MASTER SERGEANT DENIM CHARGED IN?!
THAT'S RIGHT, SIR!
WHEN SERGEANT ASH'S DETACHMENT ENCOUNTERED A HOSTILE...
MASTER SERGEANT DENIM AND LANCE CORPORAL GENE MOVED IN FOR BACKUP.
TAP
TAP
THE COLONY IS LOSING AIR DUE TO AN EXPLOSION!
IN LIGHT OF THE EMER-GENCY...
I OBEYED THE MASTER SARGE'S ORDER
AND CLEARED OUT OF THE CONSTRUC-TION BLOCK!

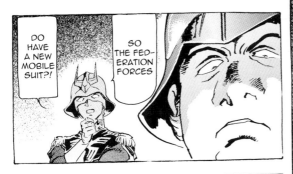

WELL DONE
CPL. SLENDER.
SO THE FEDERATION FORCES
DO HAVE A NEW MOBILE SUIT?!
THAT WILL DO, NOW RETURN TO SHIP!
YOU'LL BE DEBRIEFED LATER!
COLOR ME SURPRISED.
TO THINK DENIM COULDN'T KEEP HIS MEN IN LINE...
DREN,
DETACH THE SHIP AND APPROACH THE COLONY.

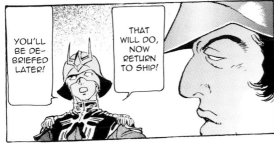

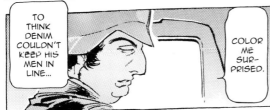

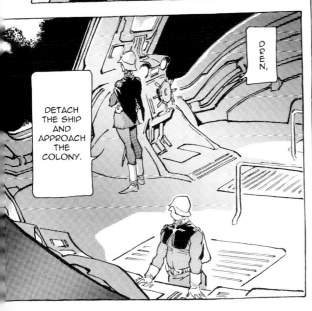

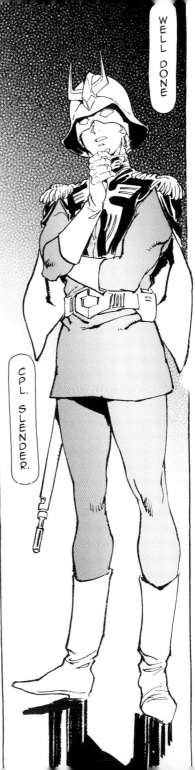

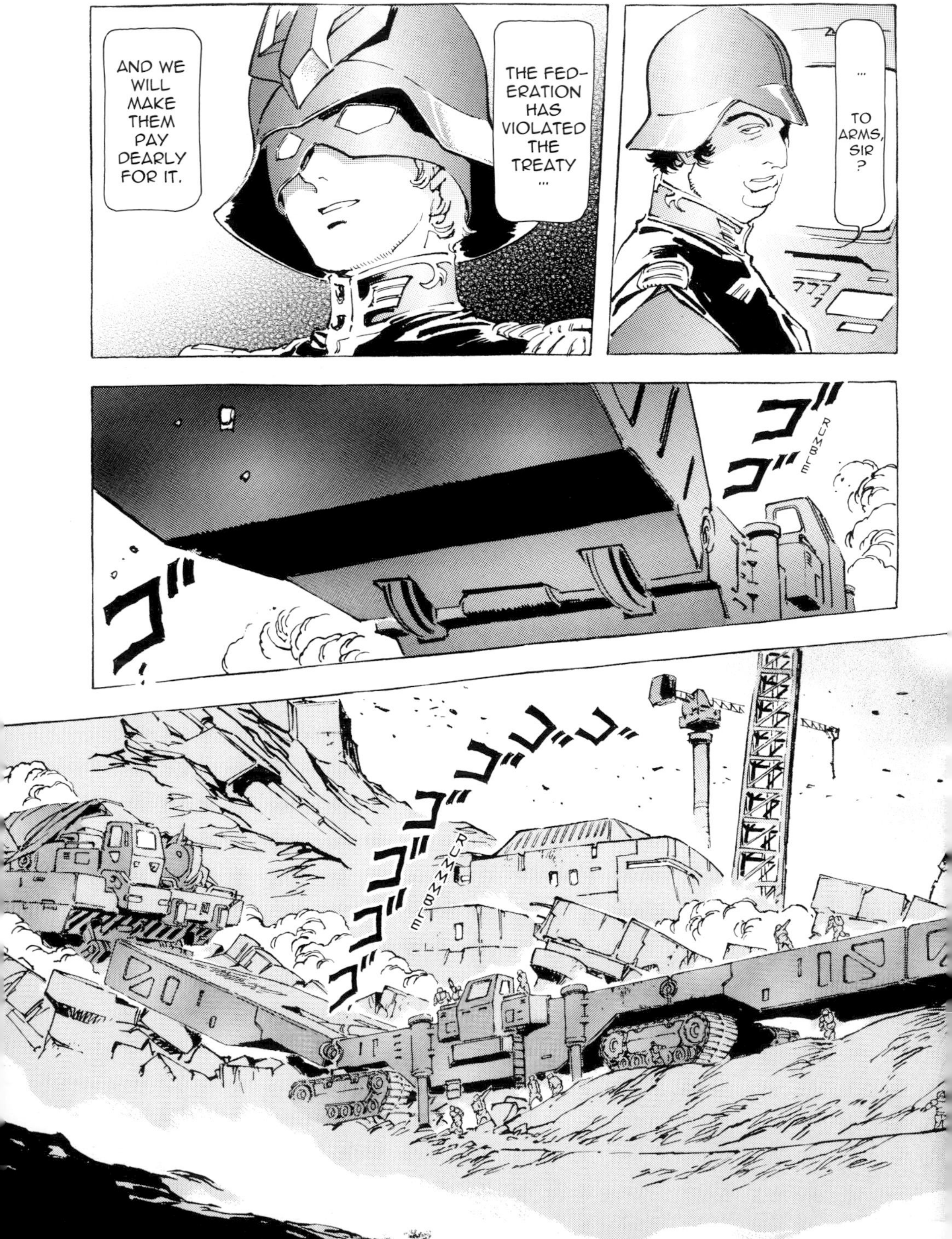
... TO ARMS, SIR?
THE FED-ERATION HAS VIOLATED THE TREATY ...
AND WE WILL MAKE THEM PAY DEARLY FOR IT.
ゴゴ
RUMBLE
ゴ
ゴゴゴゴゴゴゴ
RUMMBLE

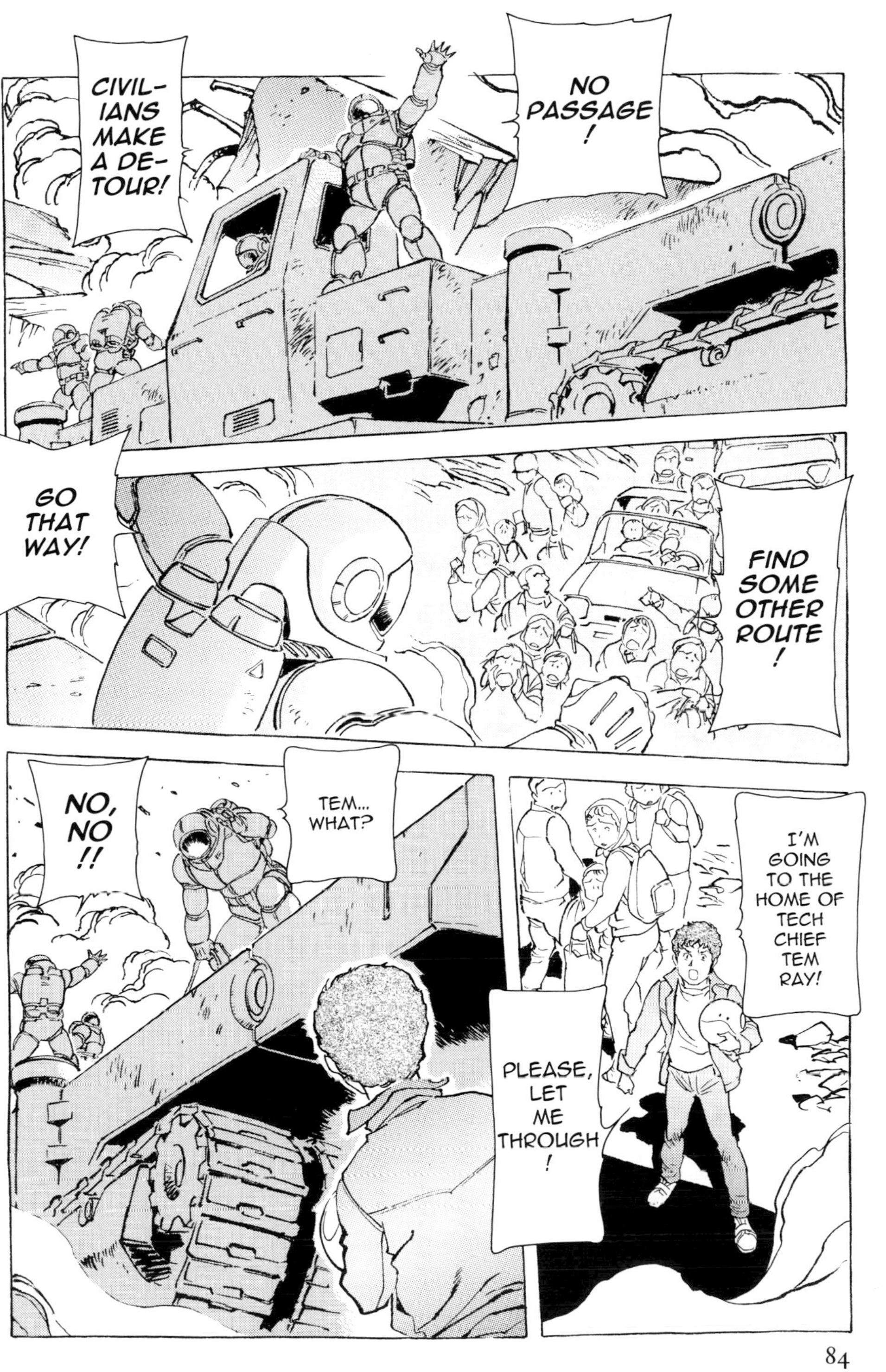
NO PASSAGE!
CIVILIANS MAKE A DETOUR!
FIND SOME OTHER ROUTE!
GO THAT WAY!
I'M GOING TO THE HOME OF TECH CHIEF TEM RAY!
PLEASE, LET ME THROUGH!
TEM... WHAT?
NO, NO!!

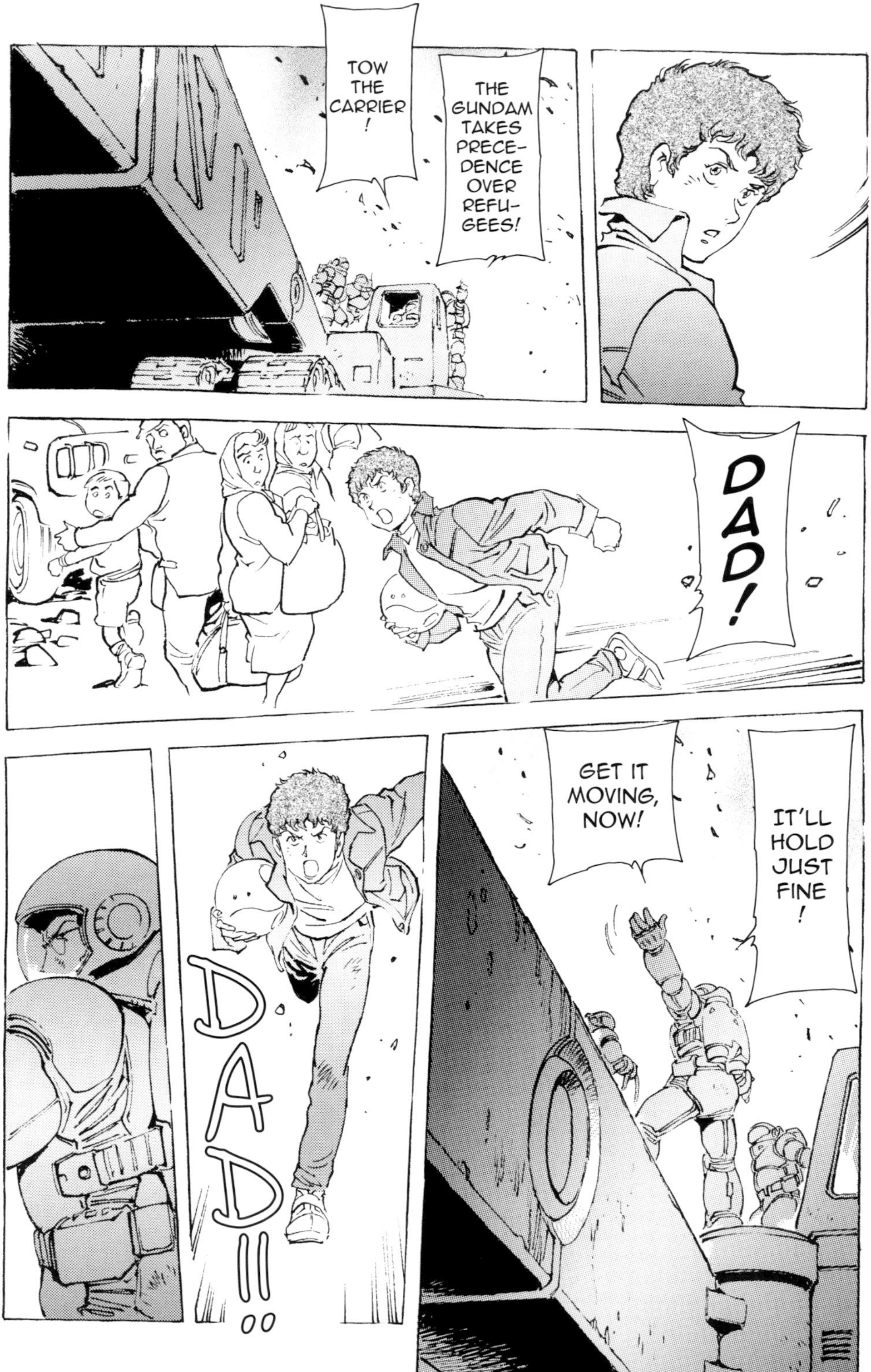
THE GUNDAM TAKES PRECE-DENCE OVER REFU-GEES!
TOW THE CARRIER!
DAD!
IT'LL HOLD JUST FINE!
GET IT MOVING, NOW!
DAD!!

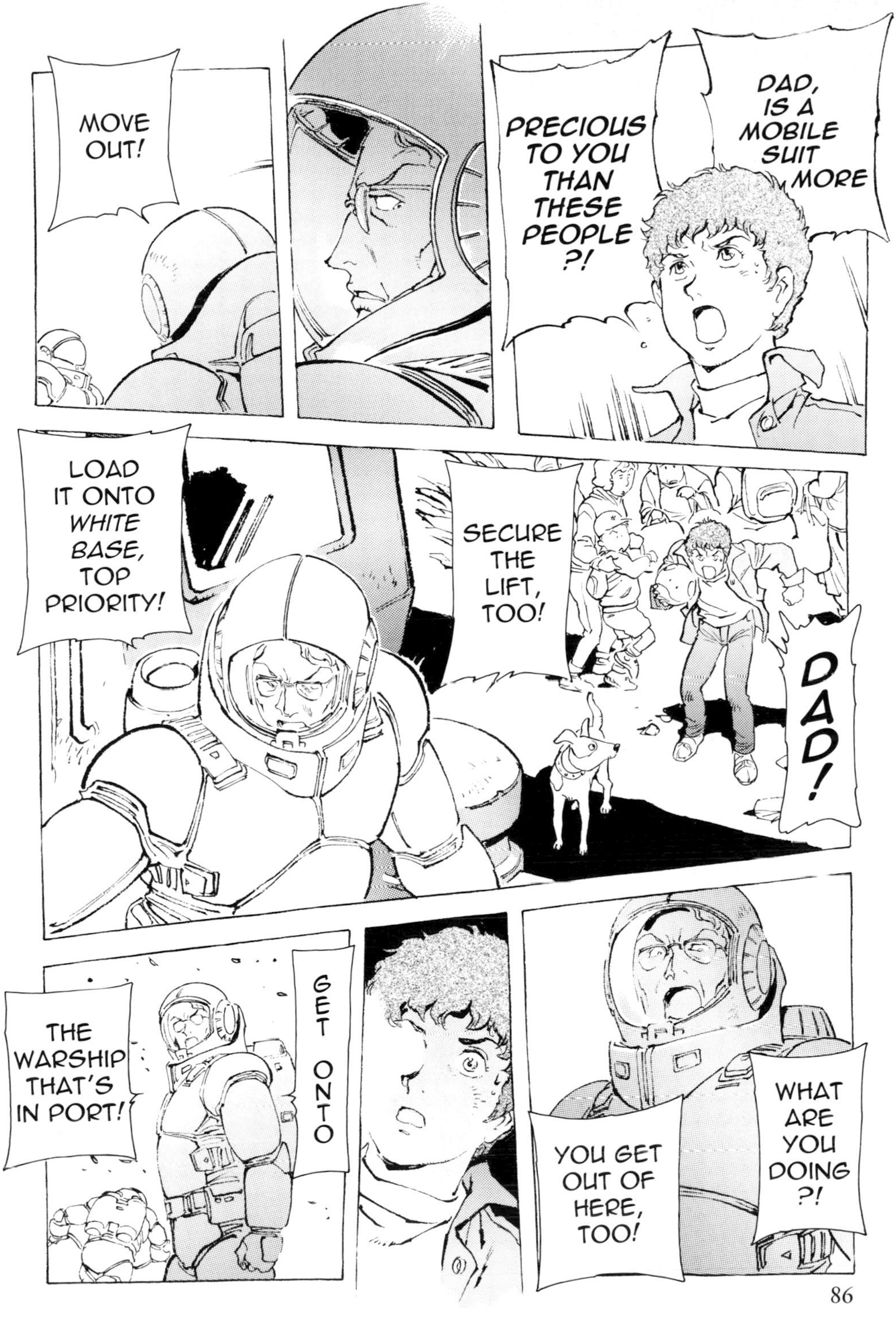
DAD, IS A MOBILE SUIT MORE
PRECIOUS TO YOU THAN THESE PEOPLE ?!
MOVE OUT!
DAD!
SECURE THE LIFT, TOO!
LOAD IT ONTO WHITE BASE, TOP PRIORITY!
WHAT ARE YOU DOING ?!
YOU GET OUT OF HERE, TOO!
GET ONTO
THE WARSHIP THAT'S IN PORT!

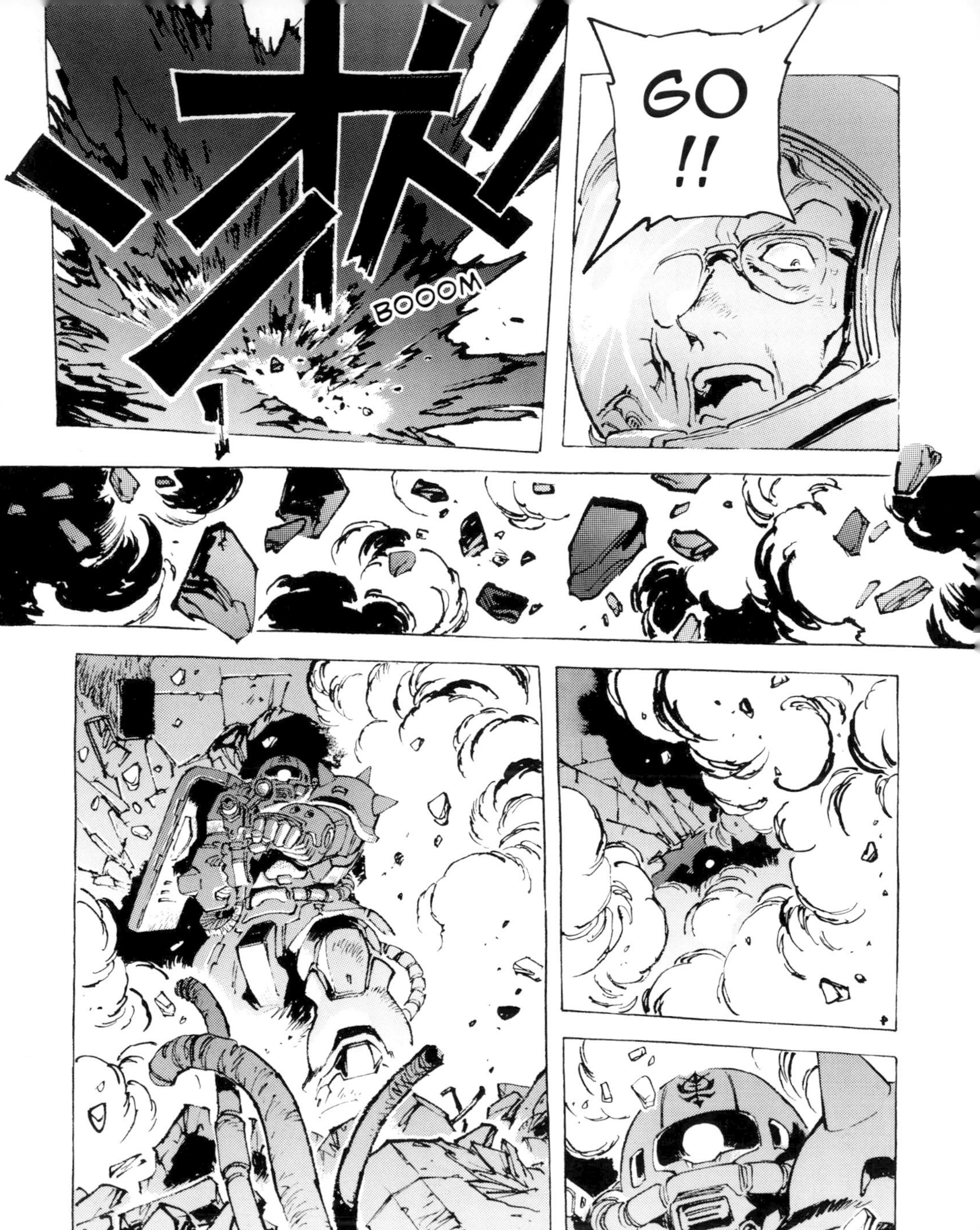
GO !!
BOOOM

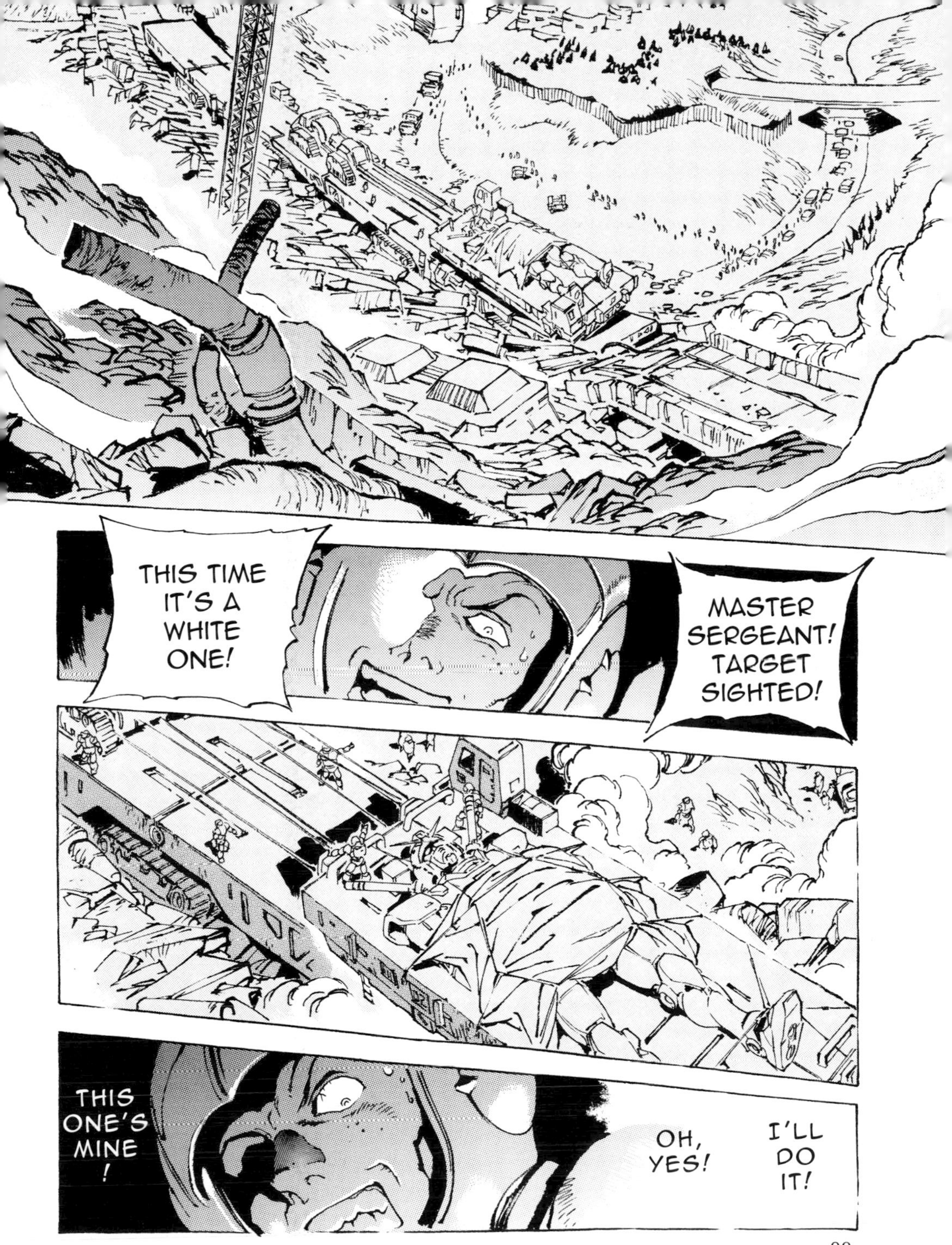
MASTER SERGEANT! TARGET SIGHTED!
THIS TIME IT'S A WHITE ONE!
I'LL DO IT!
OH, YES!
THIS ONE'S MINE!

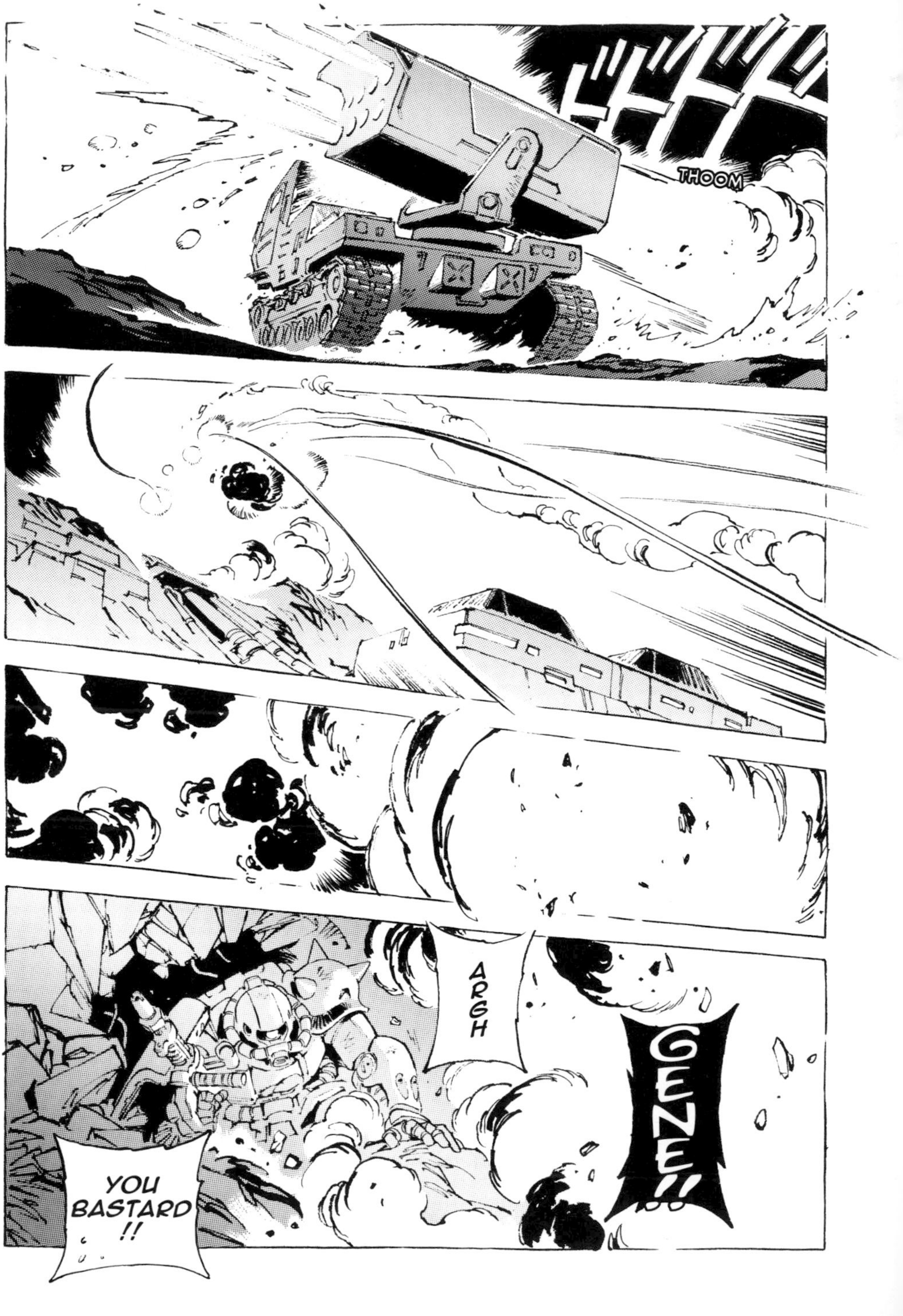
THOOM
GENE!!
ARGH
YOU BASTARD!!

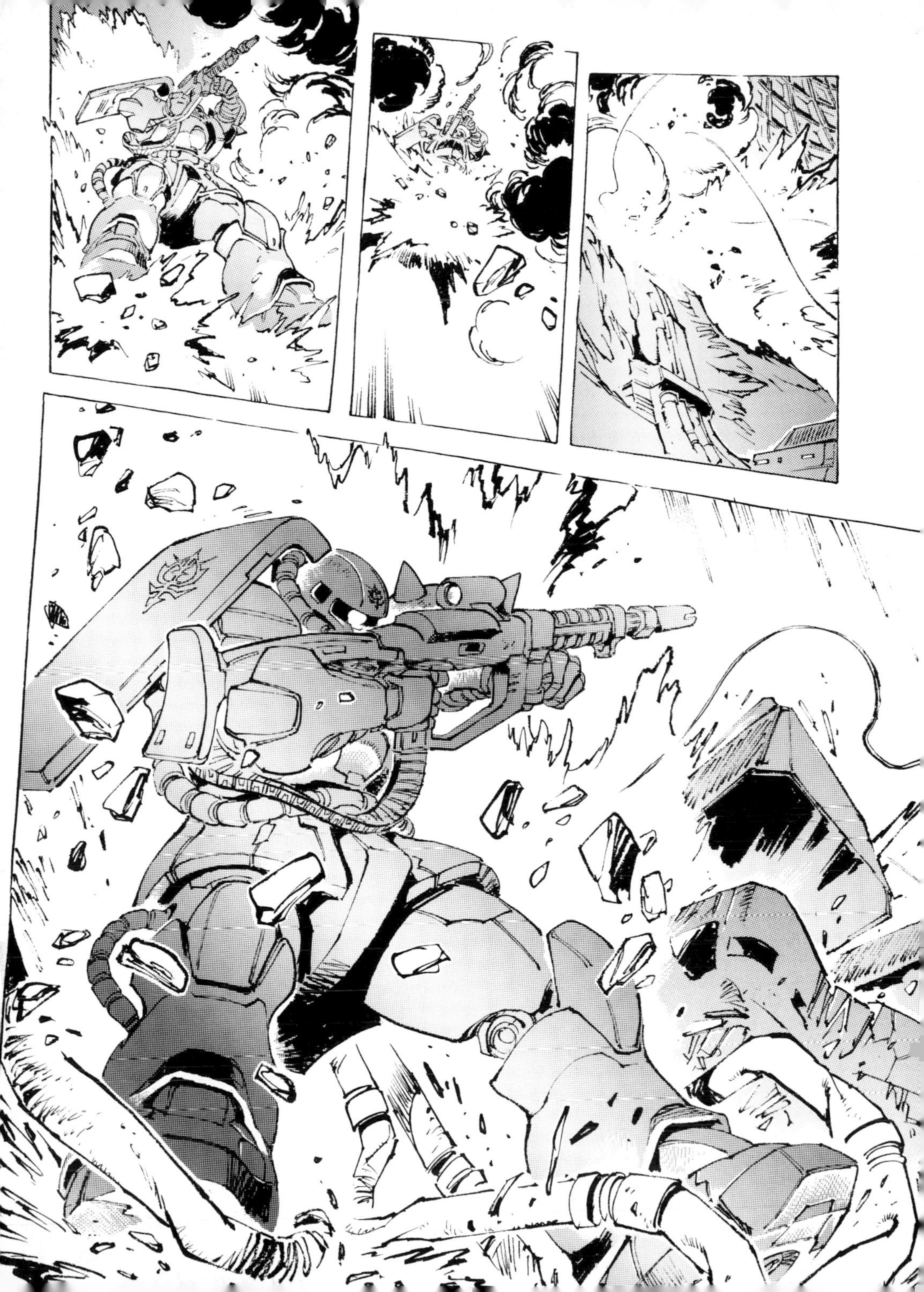

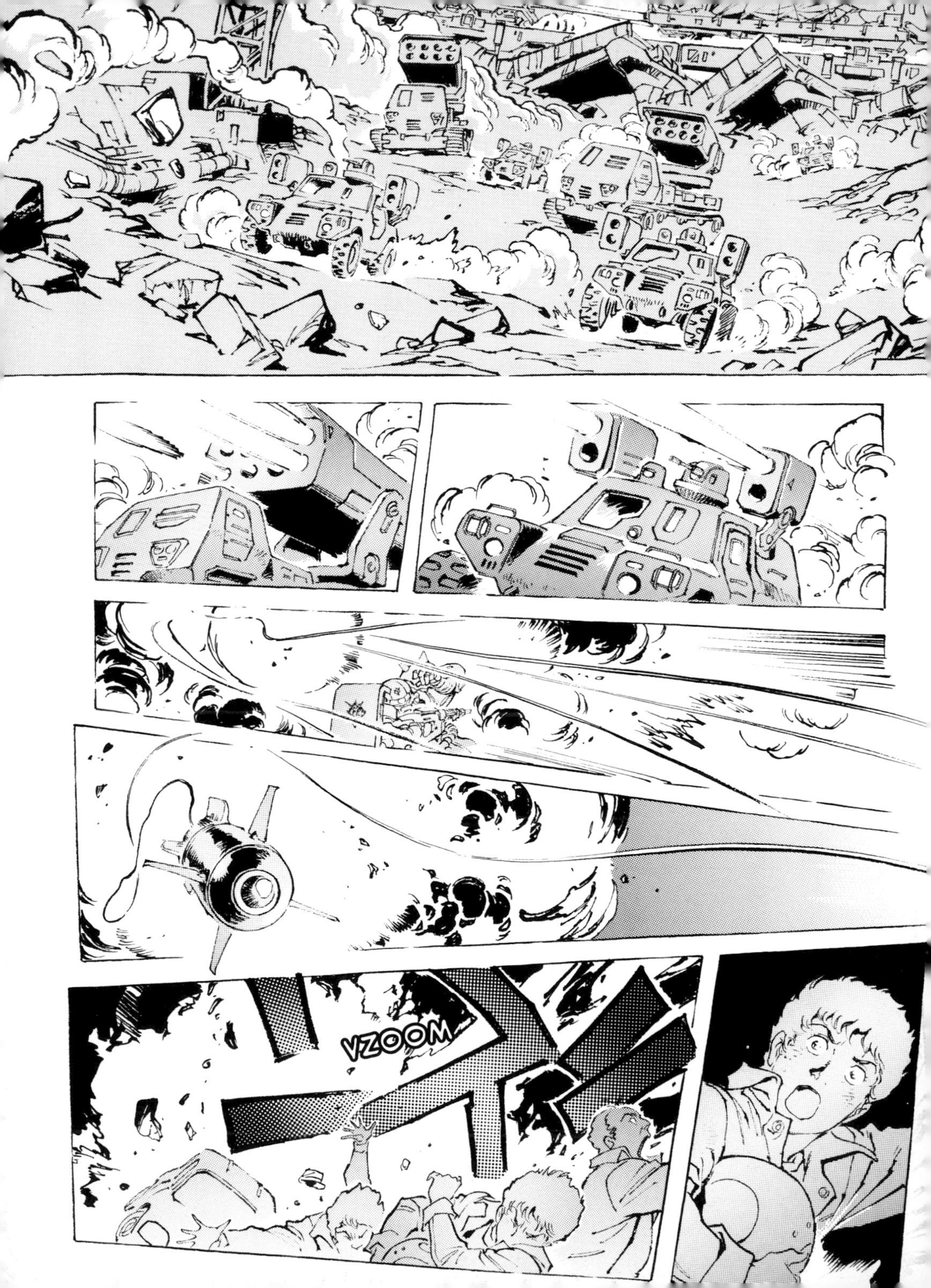
VZOOM

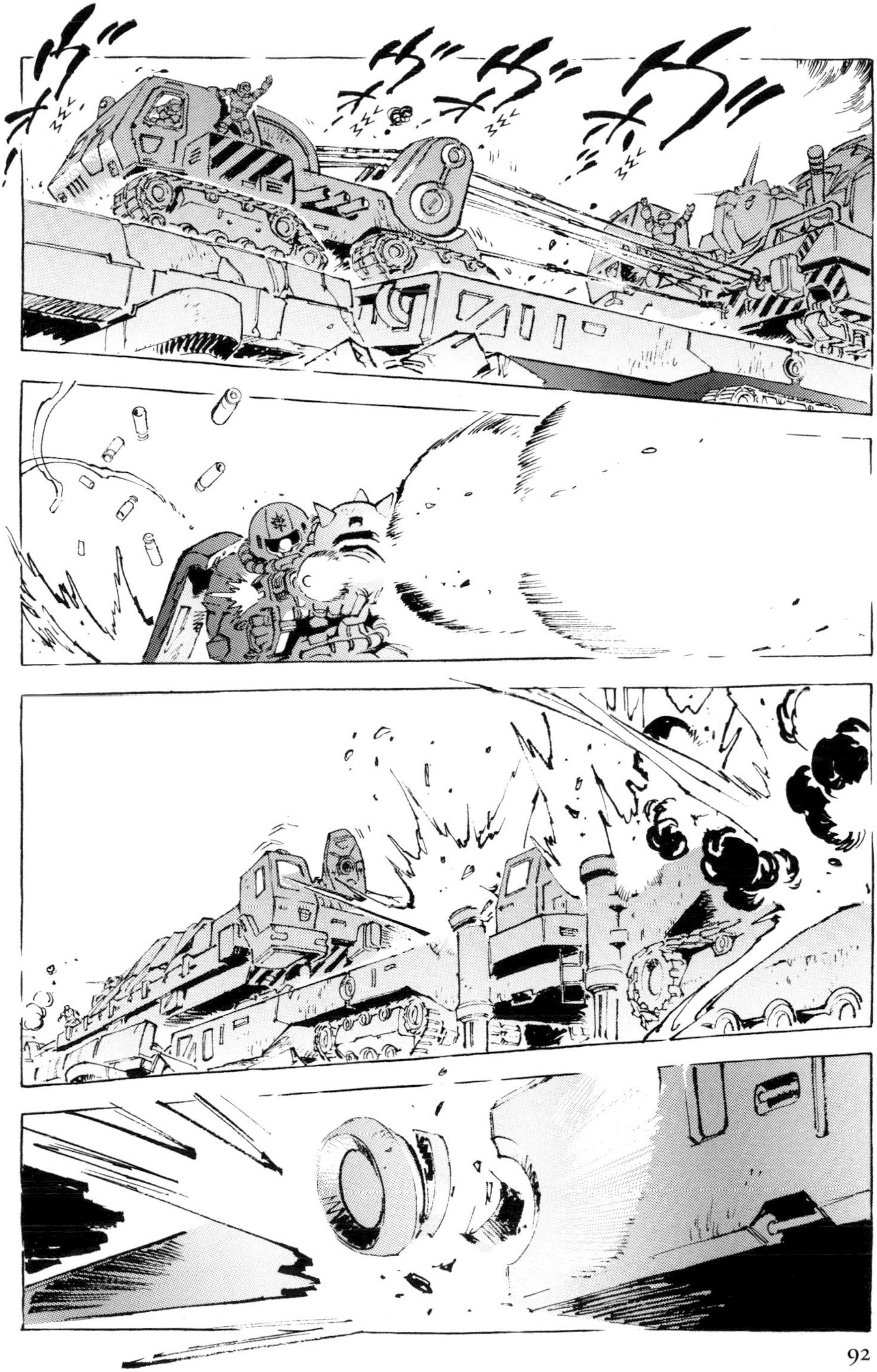

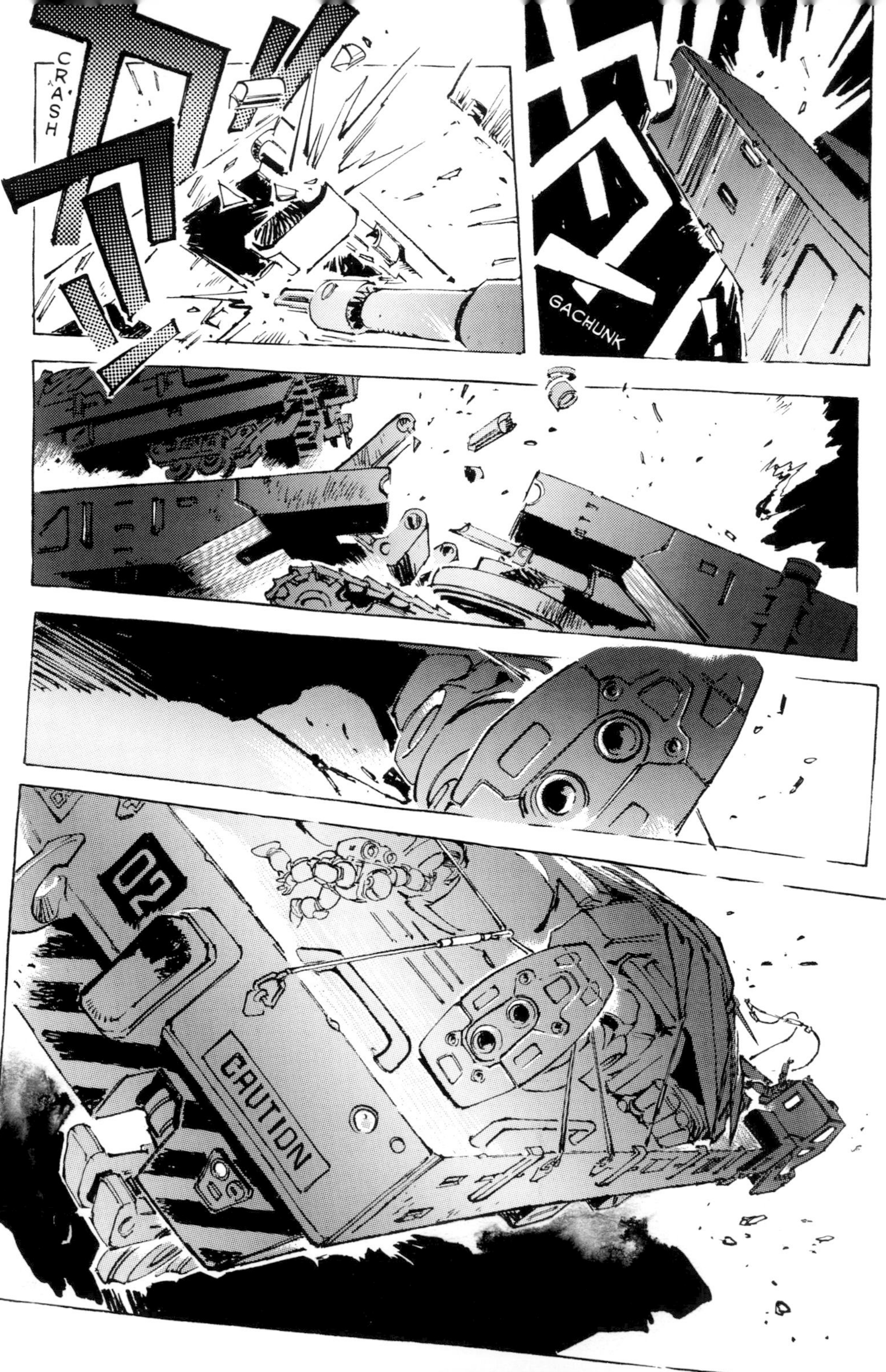
GACHUNK
CRASH
02
CAUTION

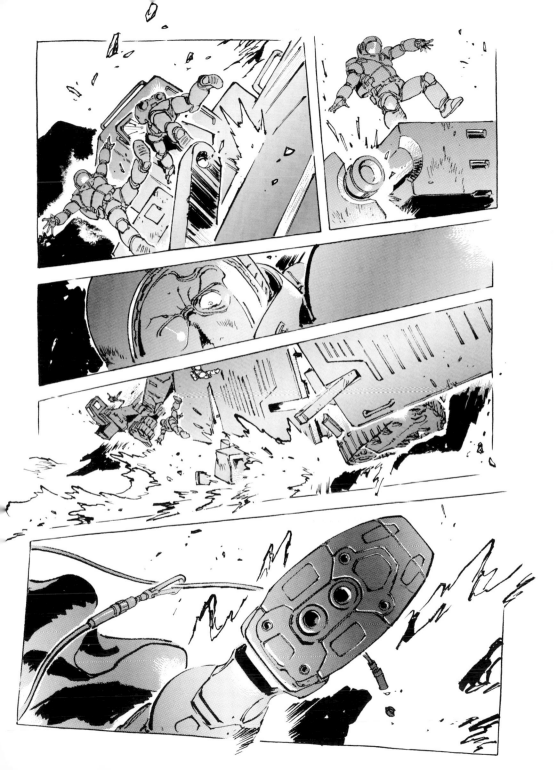

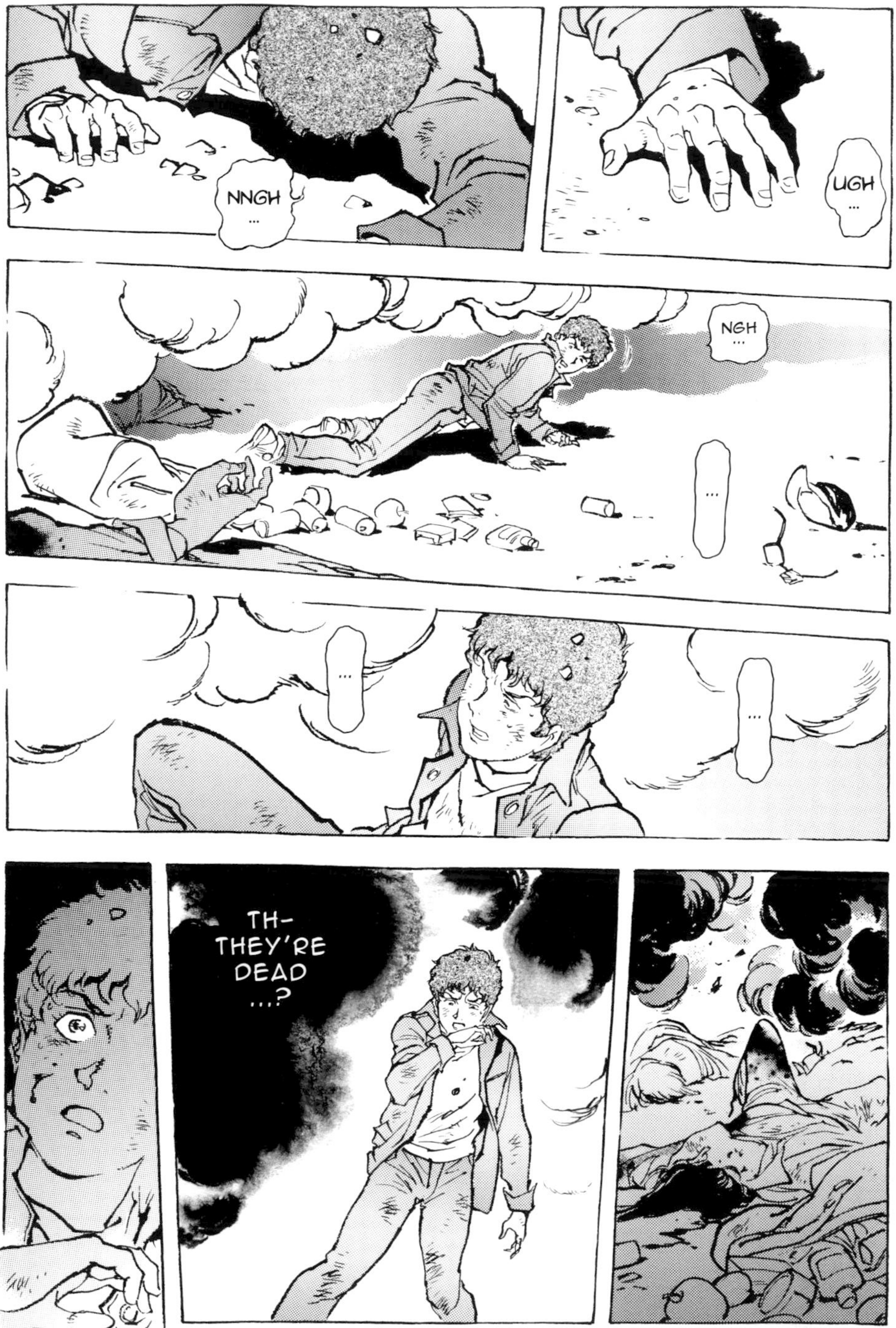
UGH ...
NNGH ...
NGH ...
...
...
...
TH- THEY'RE DEAD ...?

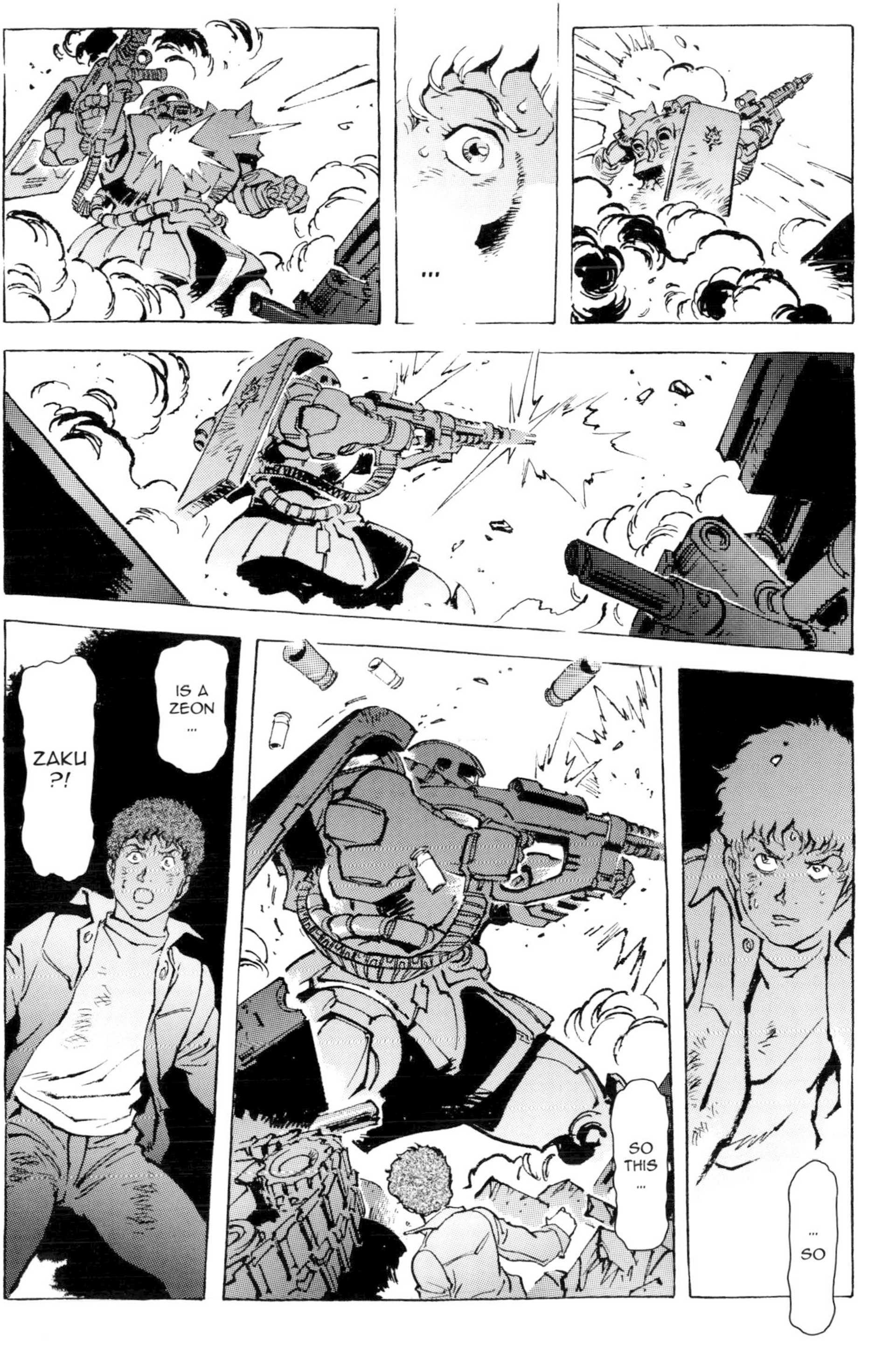
...
... SO
SO THIS ...
IS A ZEON ...
ZAKU ?!

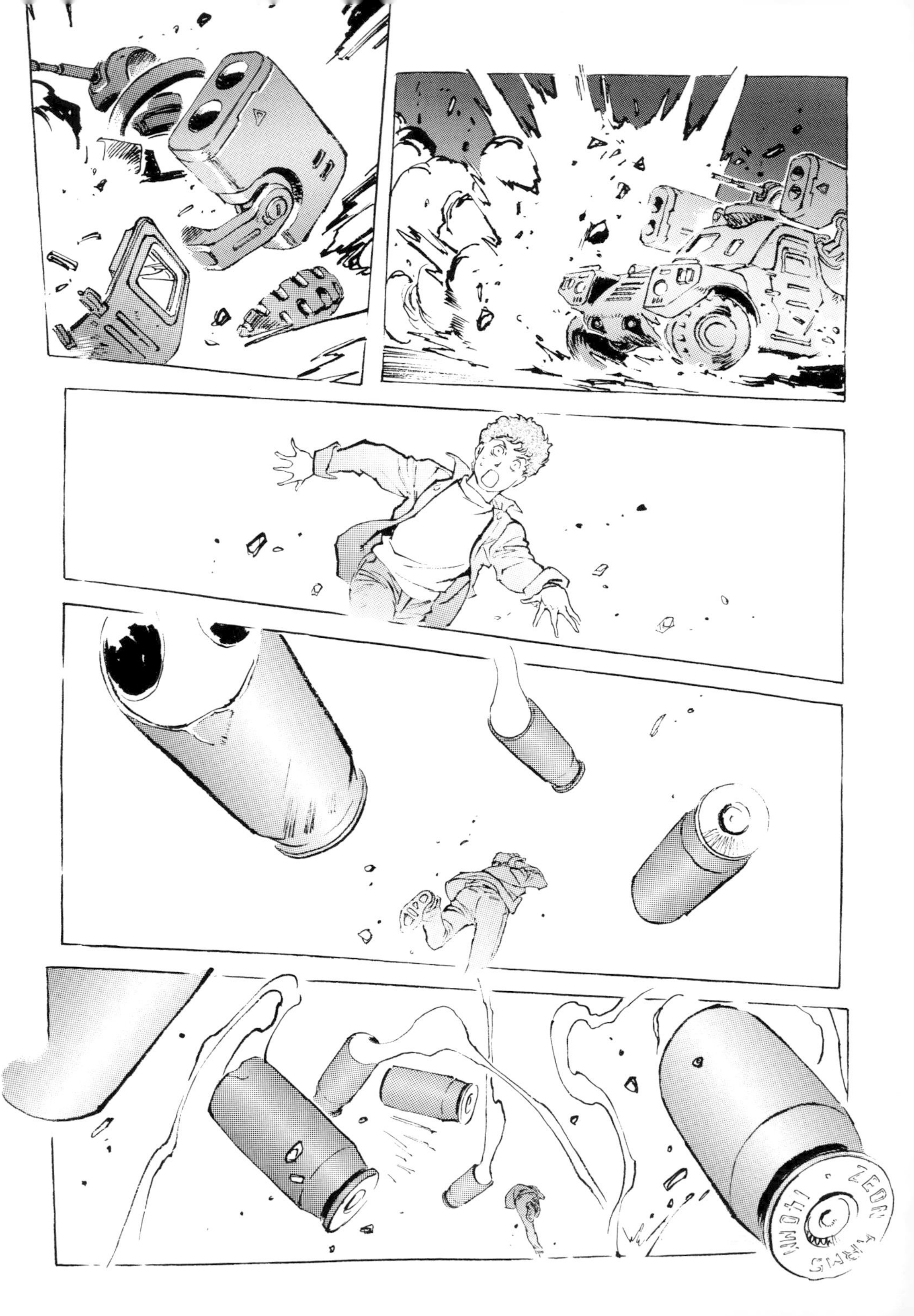
ZEON ARMS
140MM

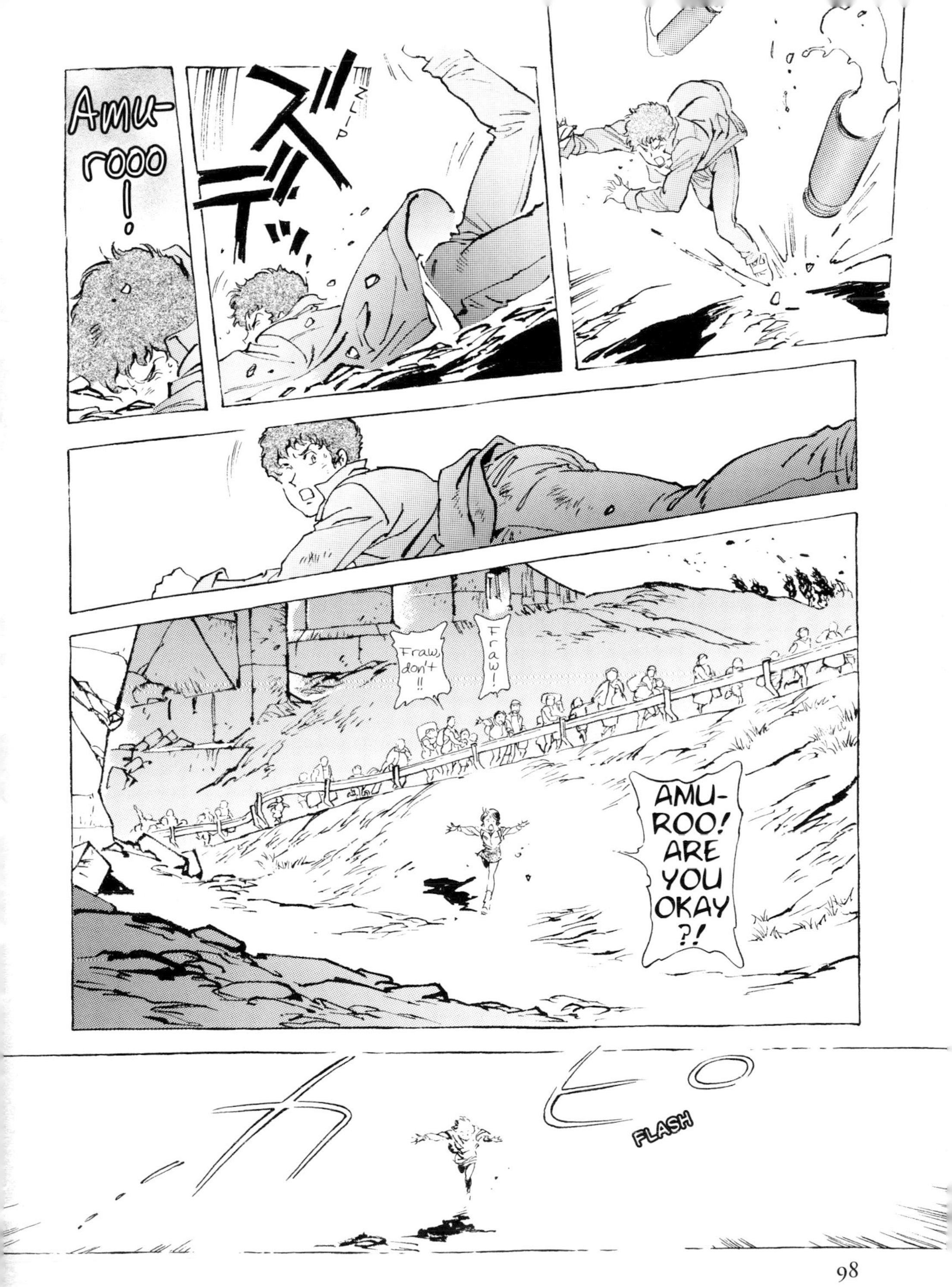
ZLIP
Amu-rooo!
Fraw!
Fraw, don't!!
AMU-ROO! ARE YOU OKAY?!
FLASH

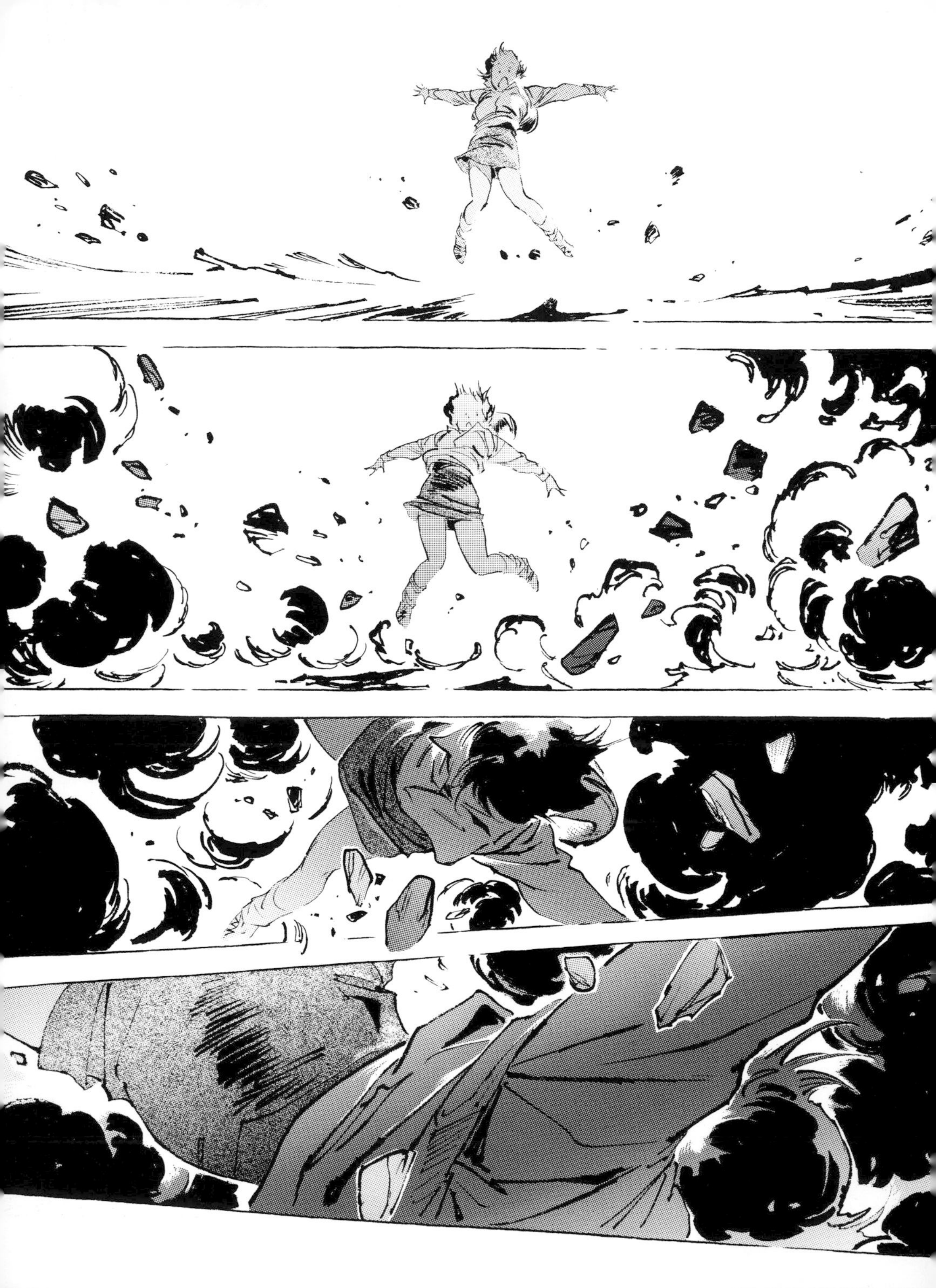

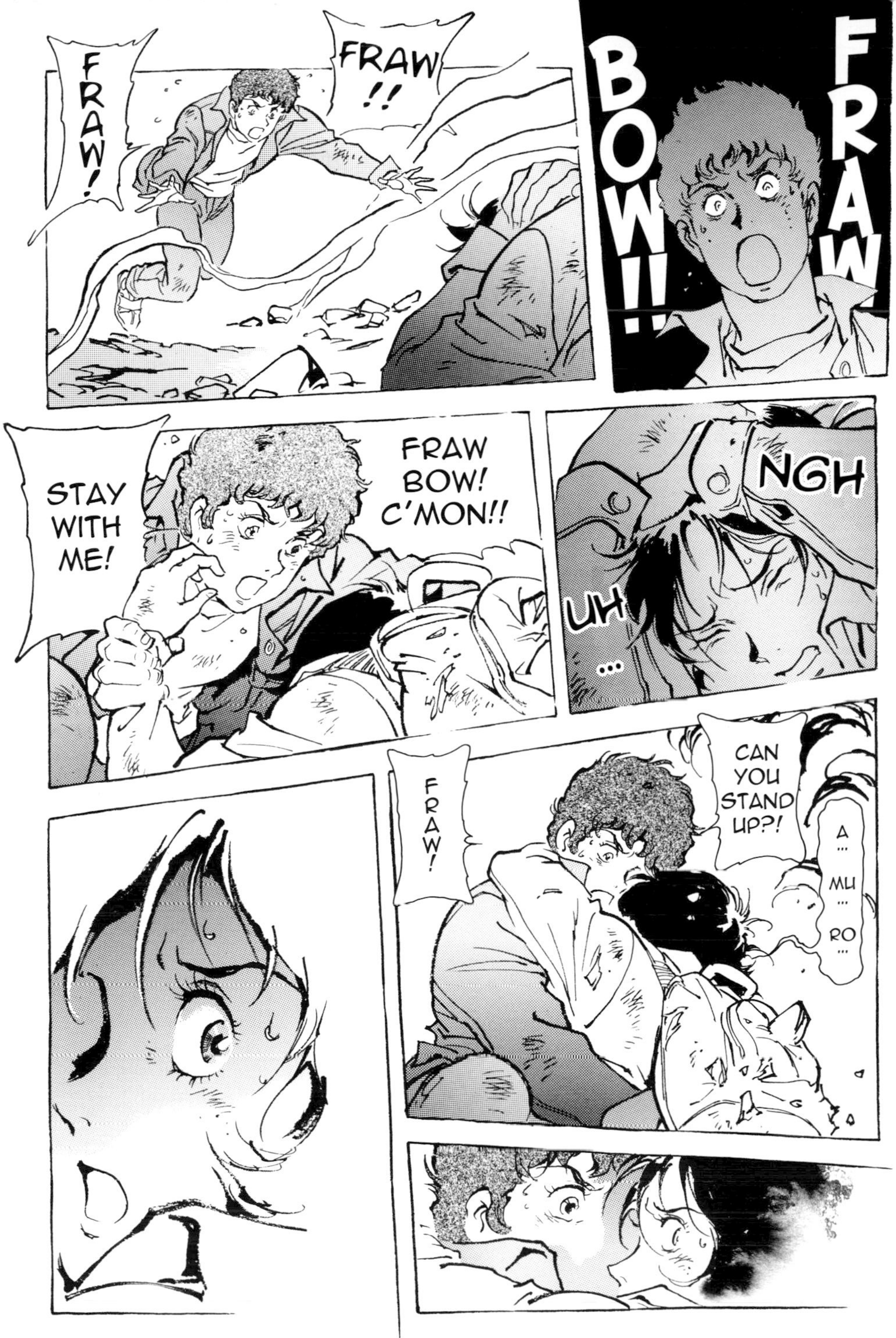
FRAW
BOW!!
FRAW !!
FRAW!
NGH
UH ...
FRAW BOW! C'MON!!
STAY WITH ME!
A... MU... RO...
CAN YOU STAND UP?!
FRAW!

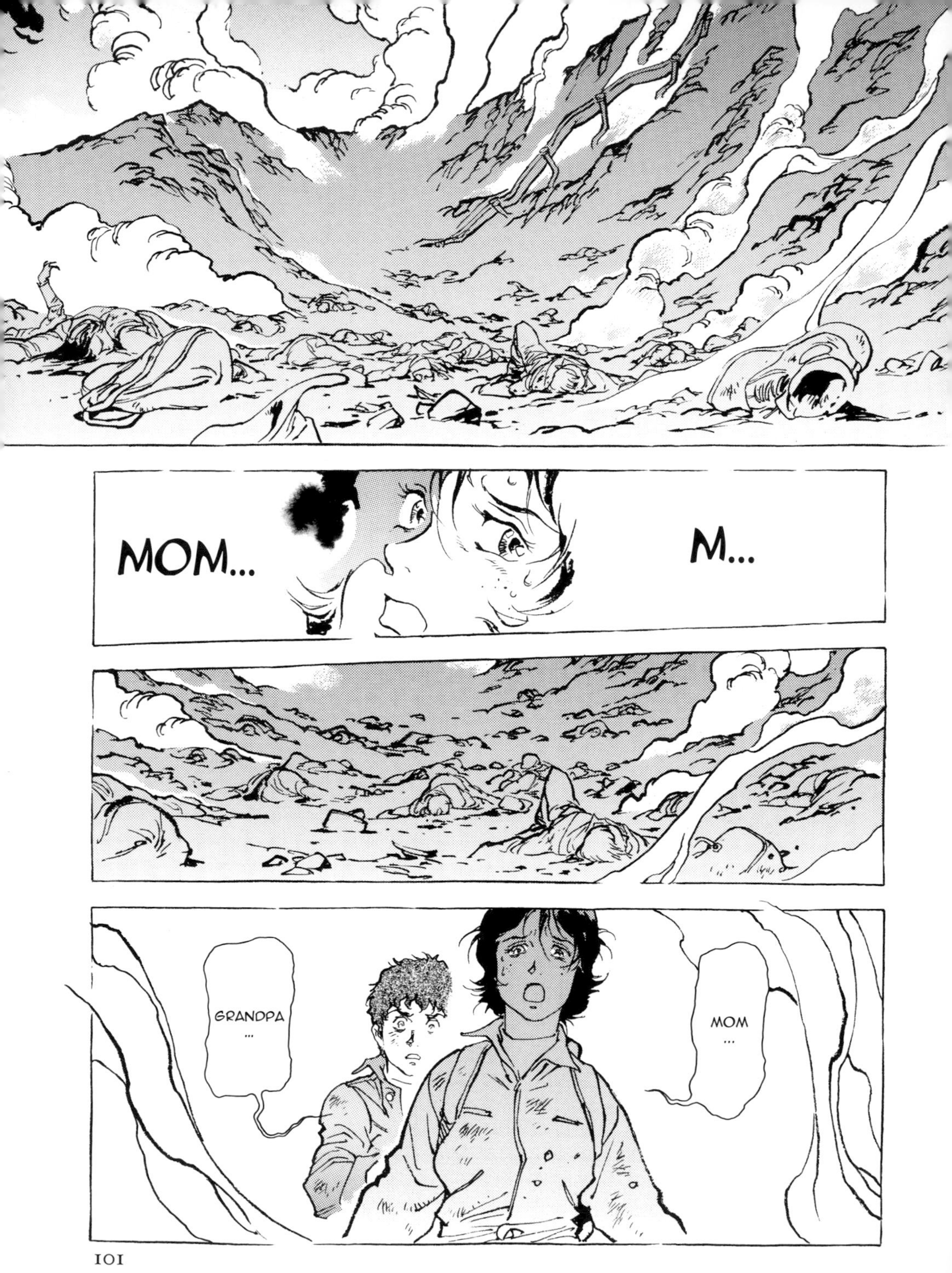
M...
MOM...
MOM ...
GRANDPA ...

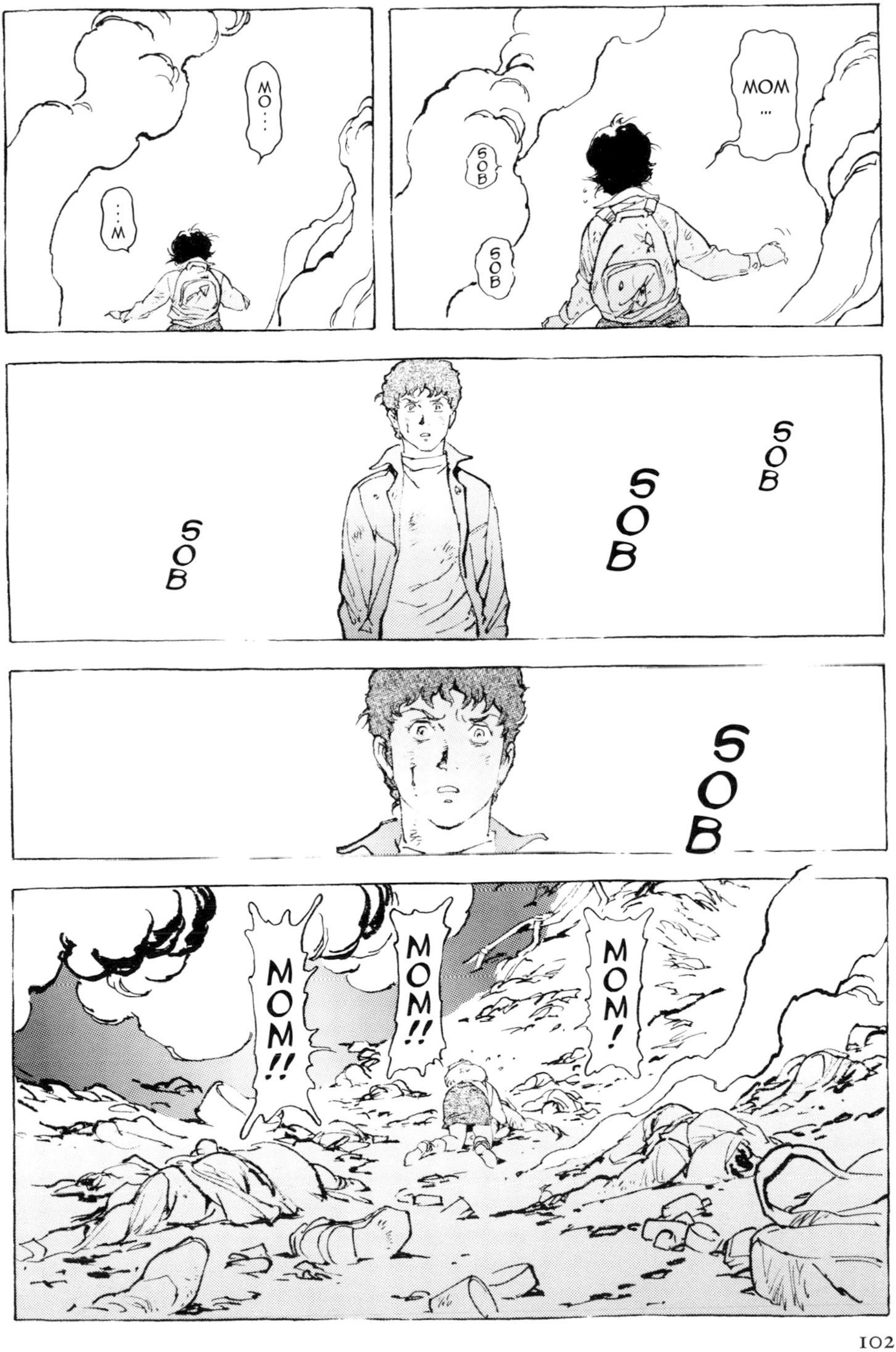
MOM ...
SOB
SOB
MO....
...M
SOB
SOB
SOB
SOB
MOM!
MOM!!
MOM!!

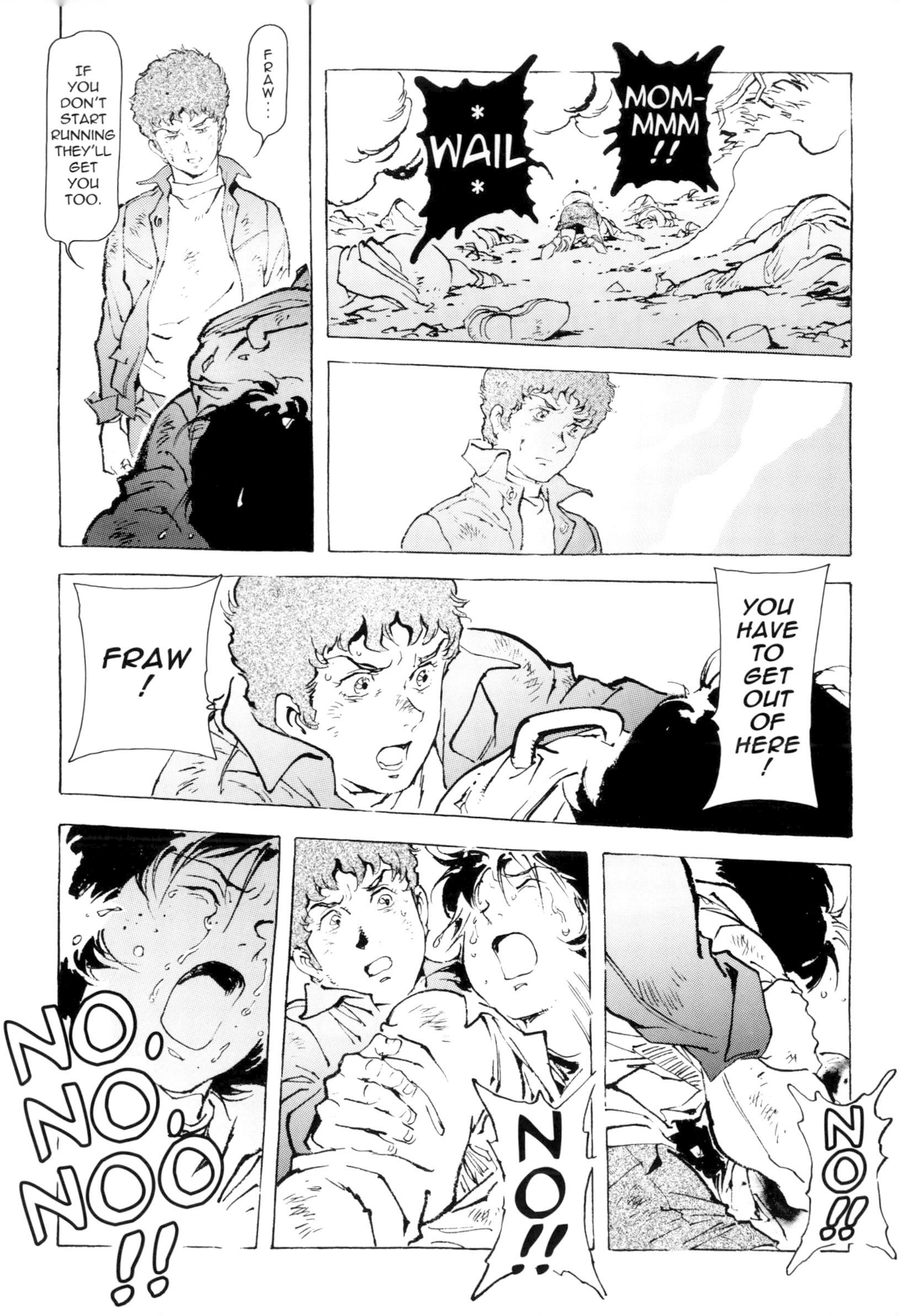
MOM-MMM!!
* WAIL *
FRAW...
IF YOU DON'T START RUNNING THEY'LL GET YOU TOO.
YOU HAVE TO GET OUT OF HERE!
FRAW!
NO!!
NO!!
NO, NO, NOO!!

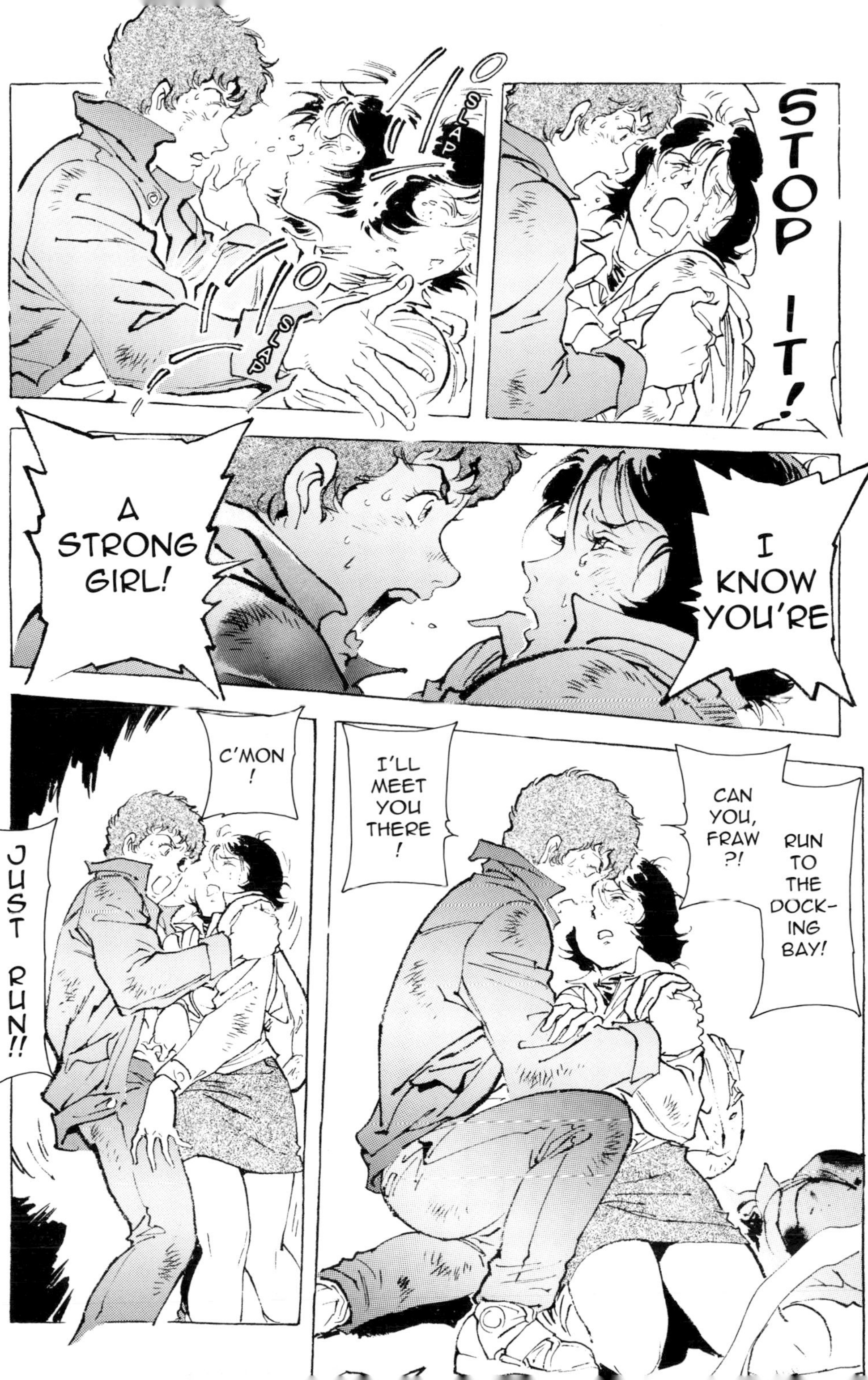
STOP IT!
SLAP
SLAP
I KNOW YOU'RE
A STRONG GIRL!
RUN TO THE DOCK-ING BAY!
CAN YOU, FRAW?!
I'LL MEET YOU THERE!
C'MON!
JUST RUN!!

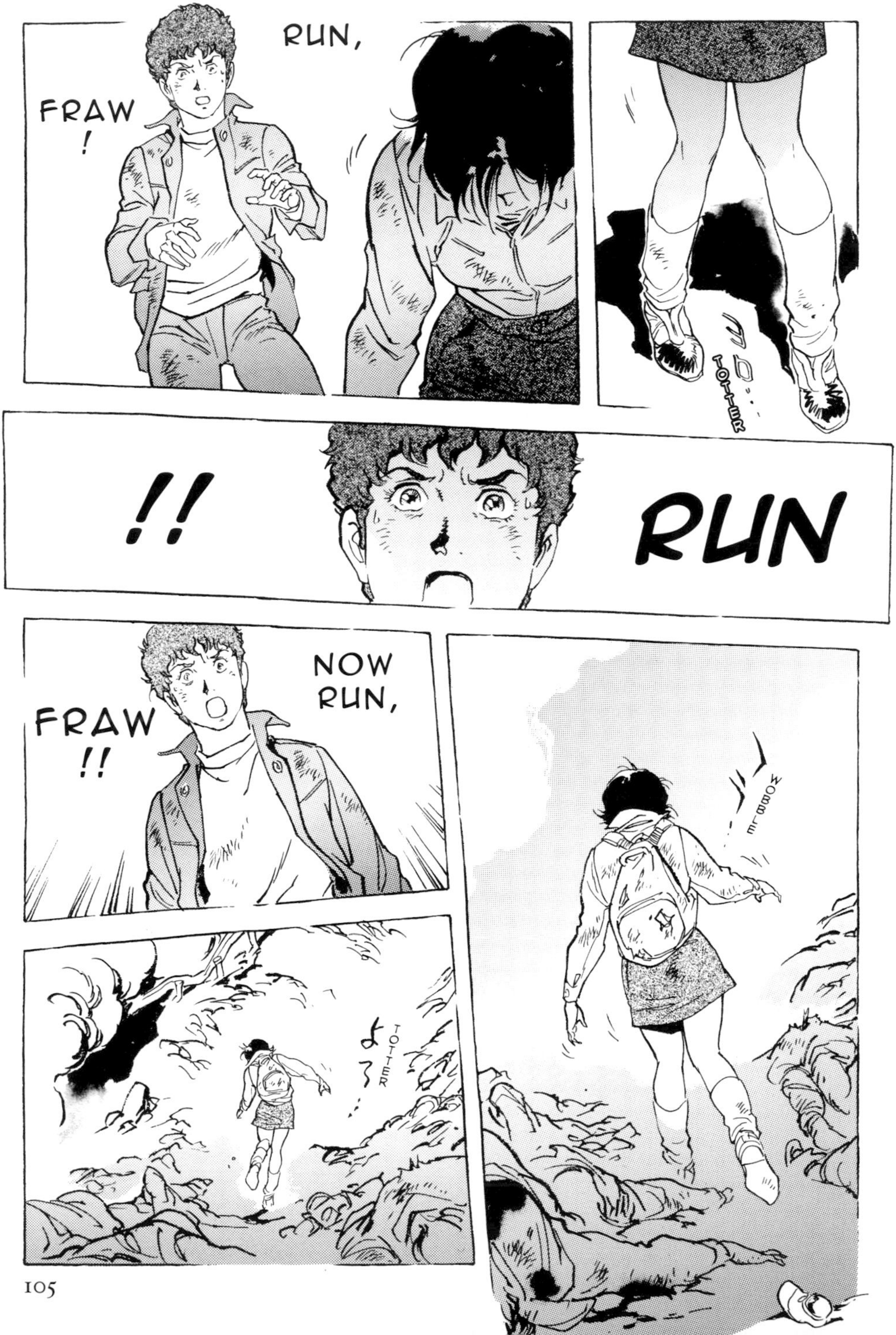
TOTTER
RUN,
FRAW
!
RUN
!!
WOBBLE
NOW RUN,
FRAW
!!
TOTTER

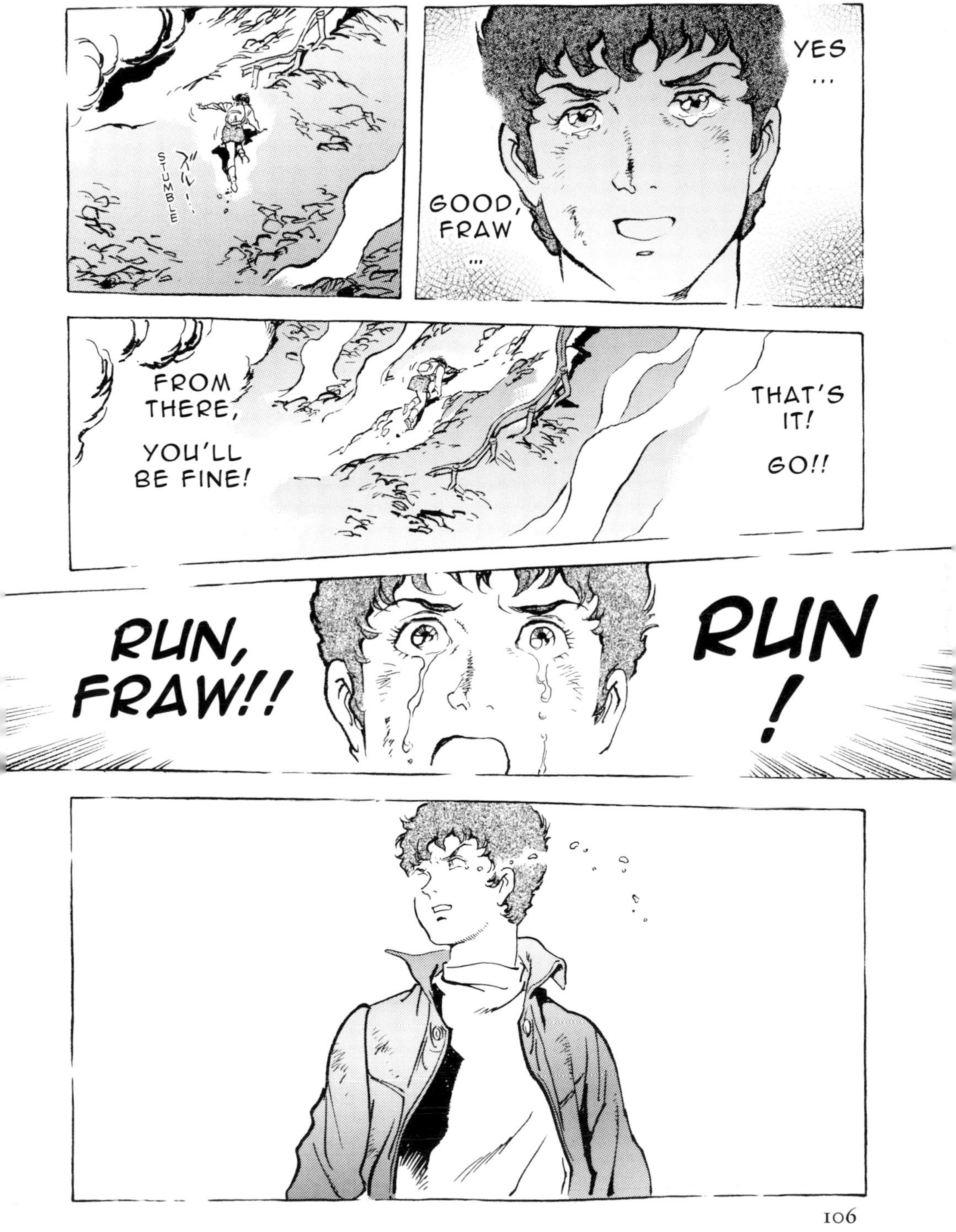
YES ...
GOOD, FRAW ...
ズルー…
STUMBLE
THAT'S IT!
GO!!
FROM THERE,
YOU'LL BE FINE!
RUN !
RUN, FRAW!!

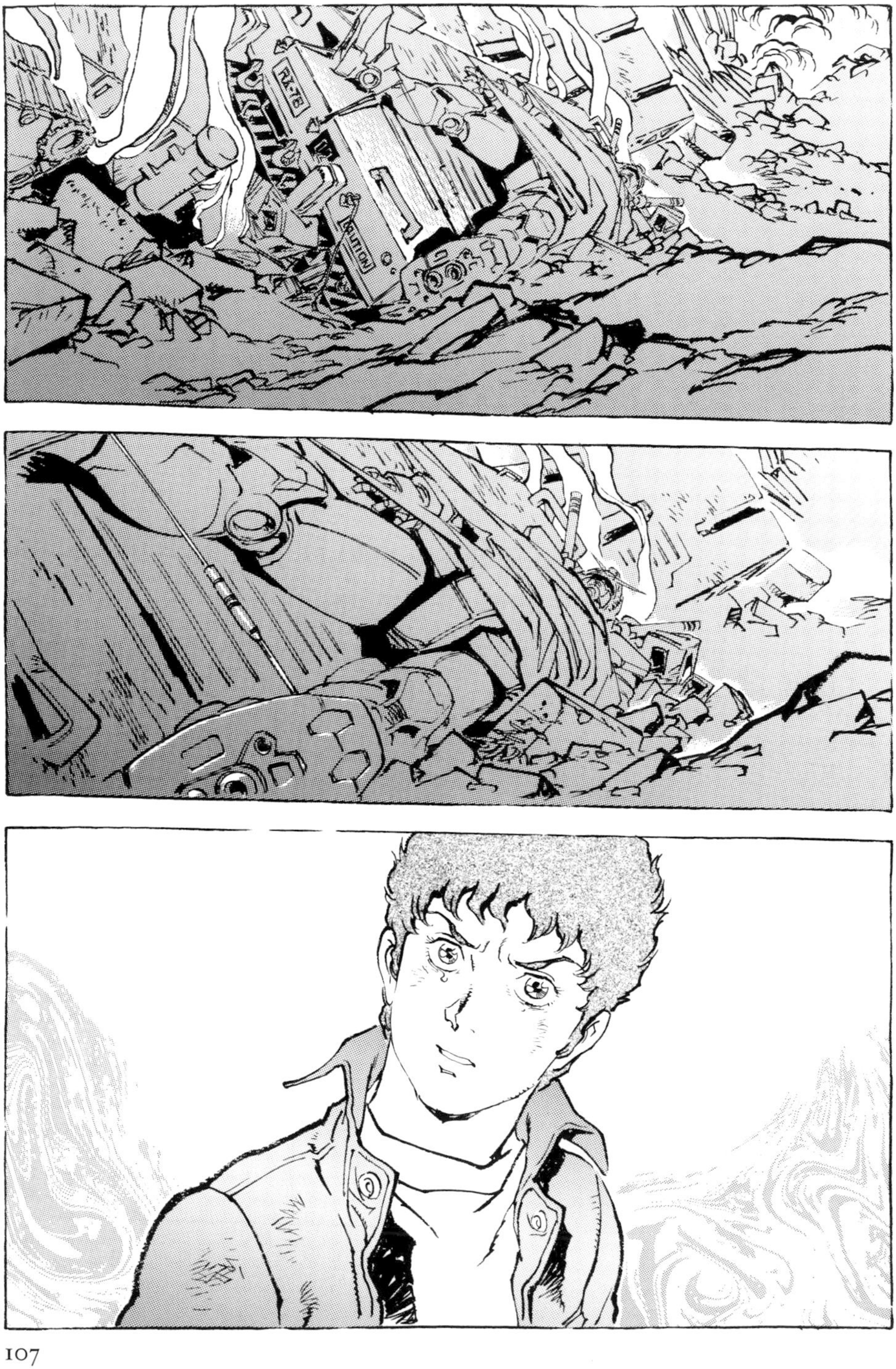
RX-78

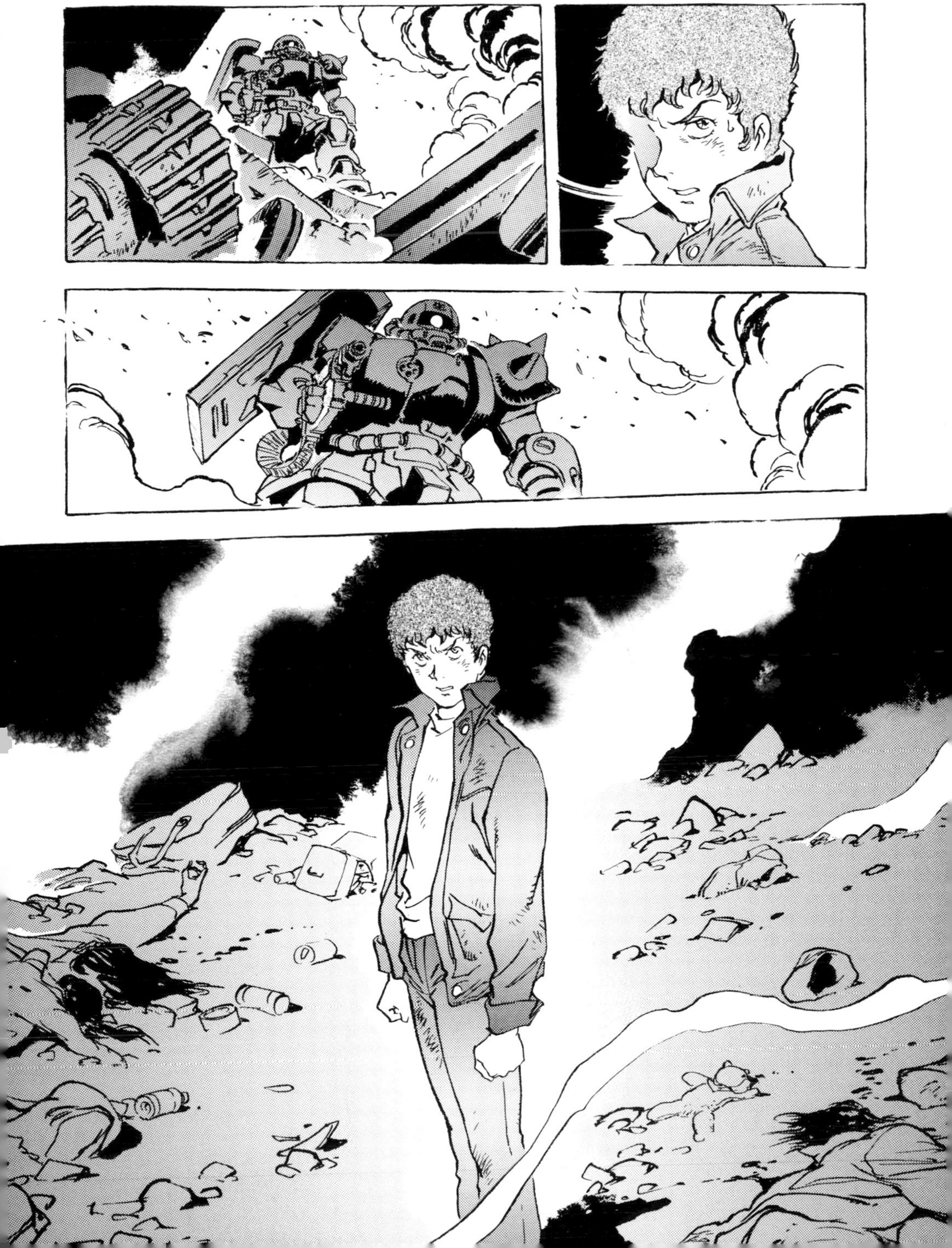

SECTION III

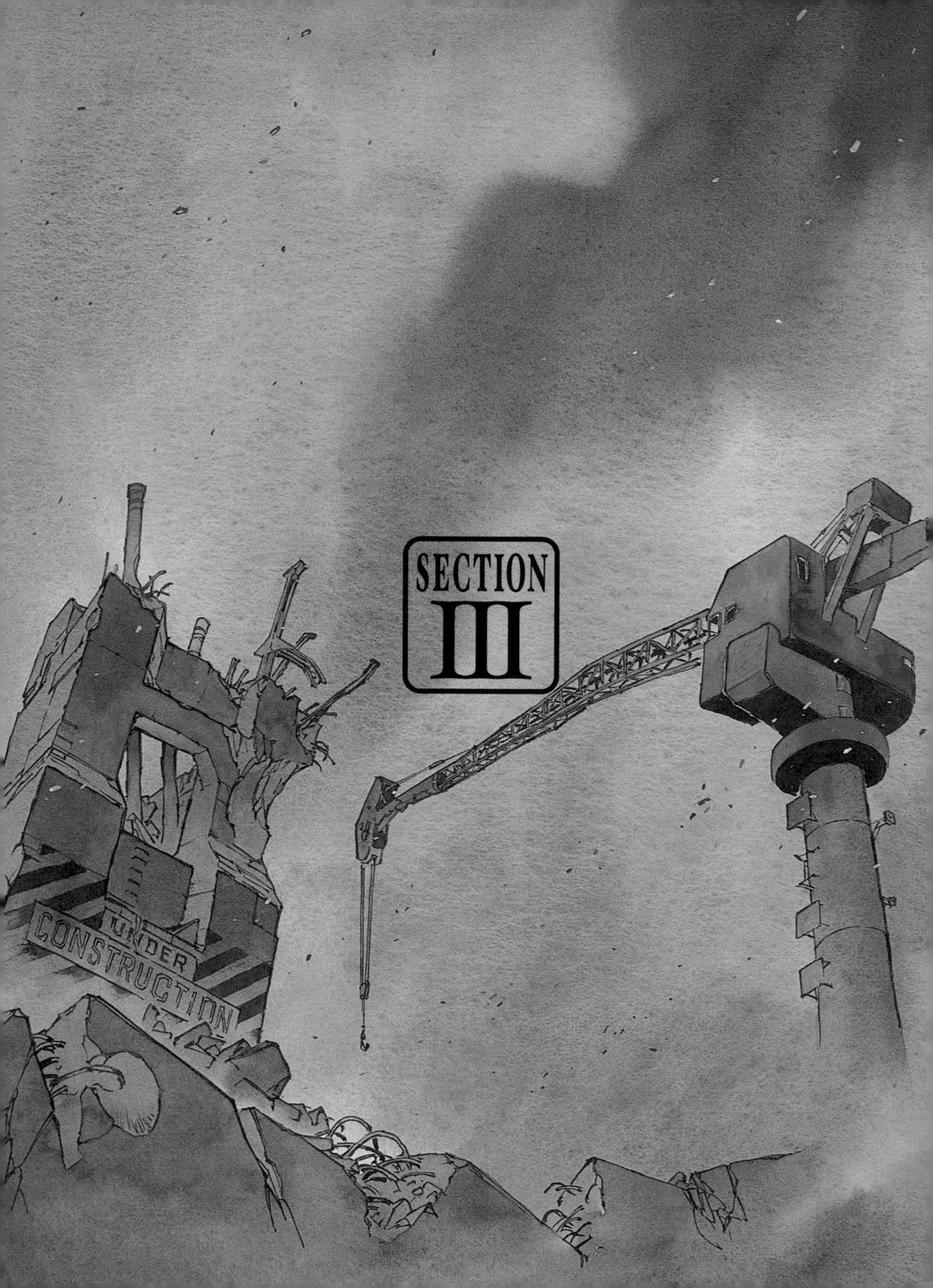
UNDER
CONSTRUCTION

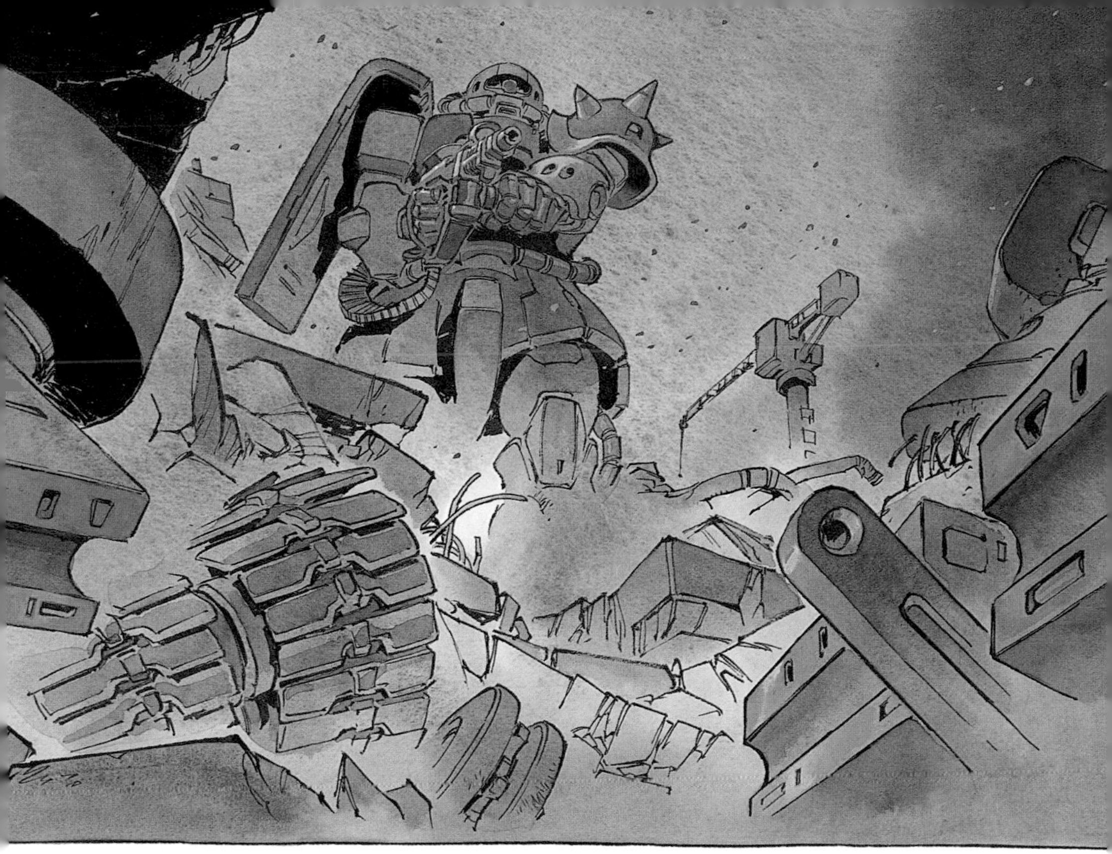
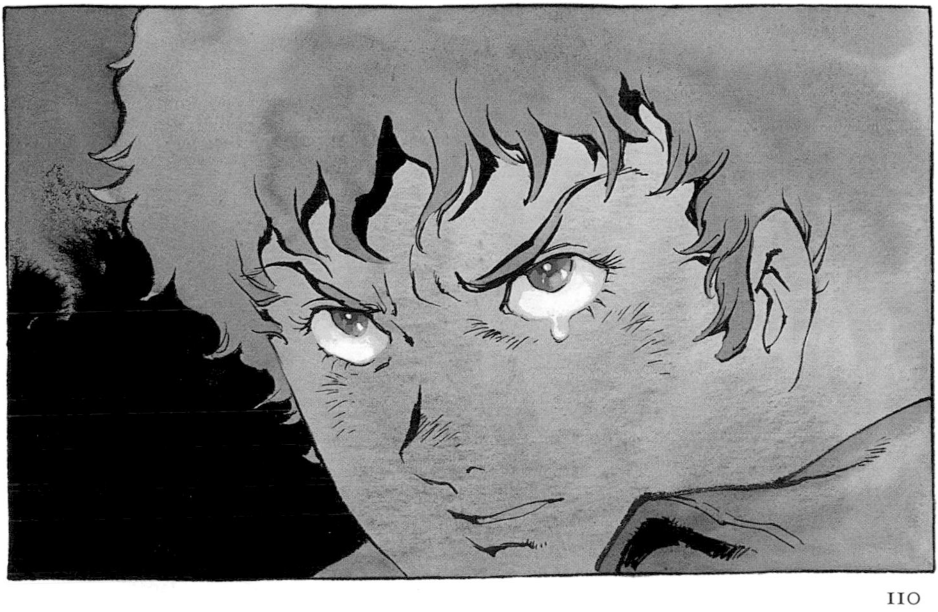

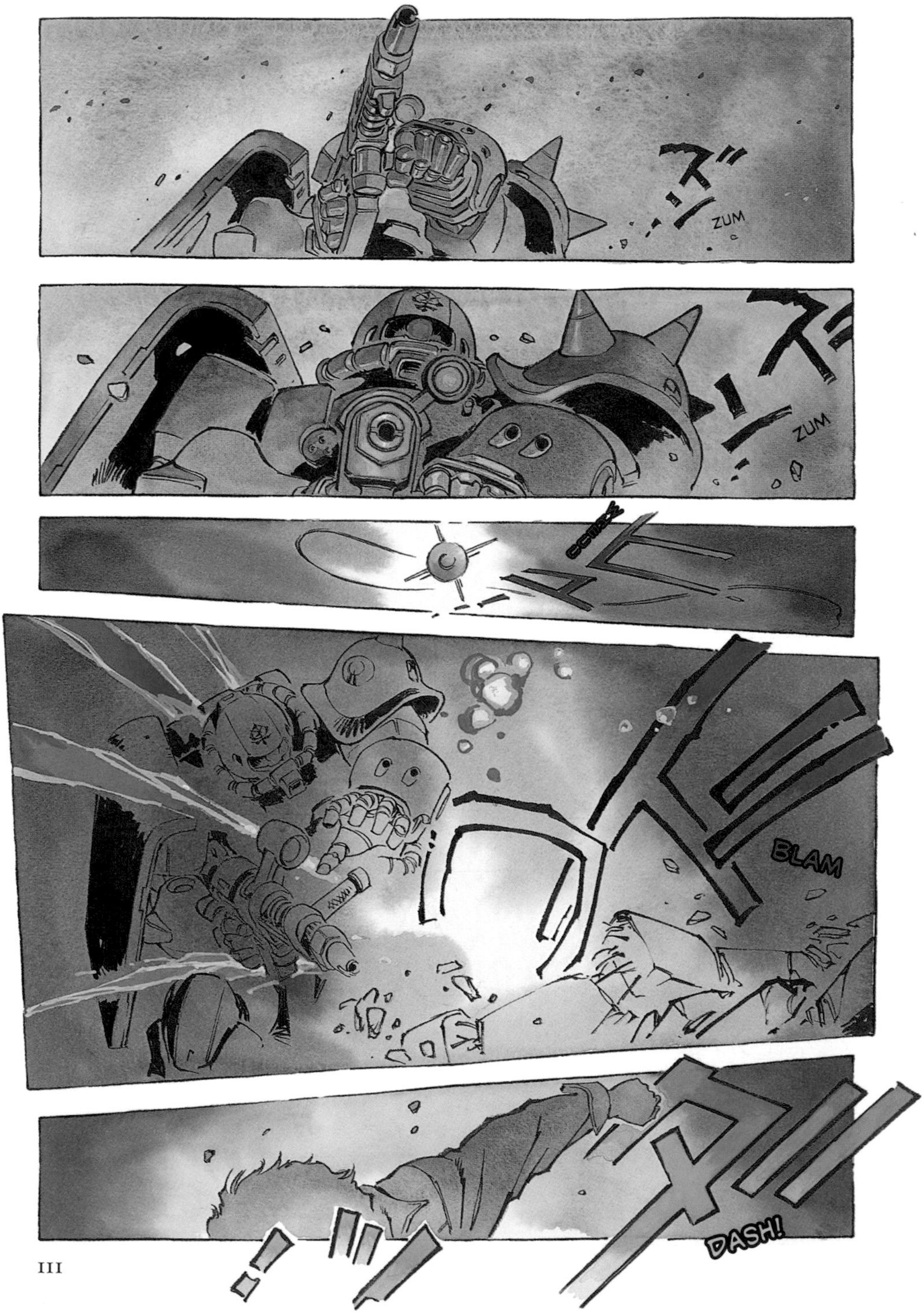
ZUM
ZUM
BLAM
DASH!

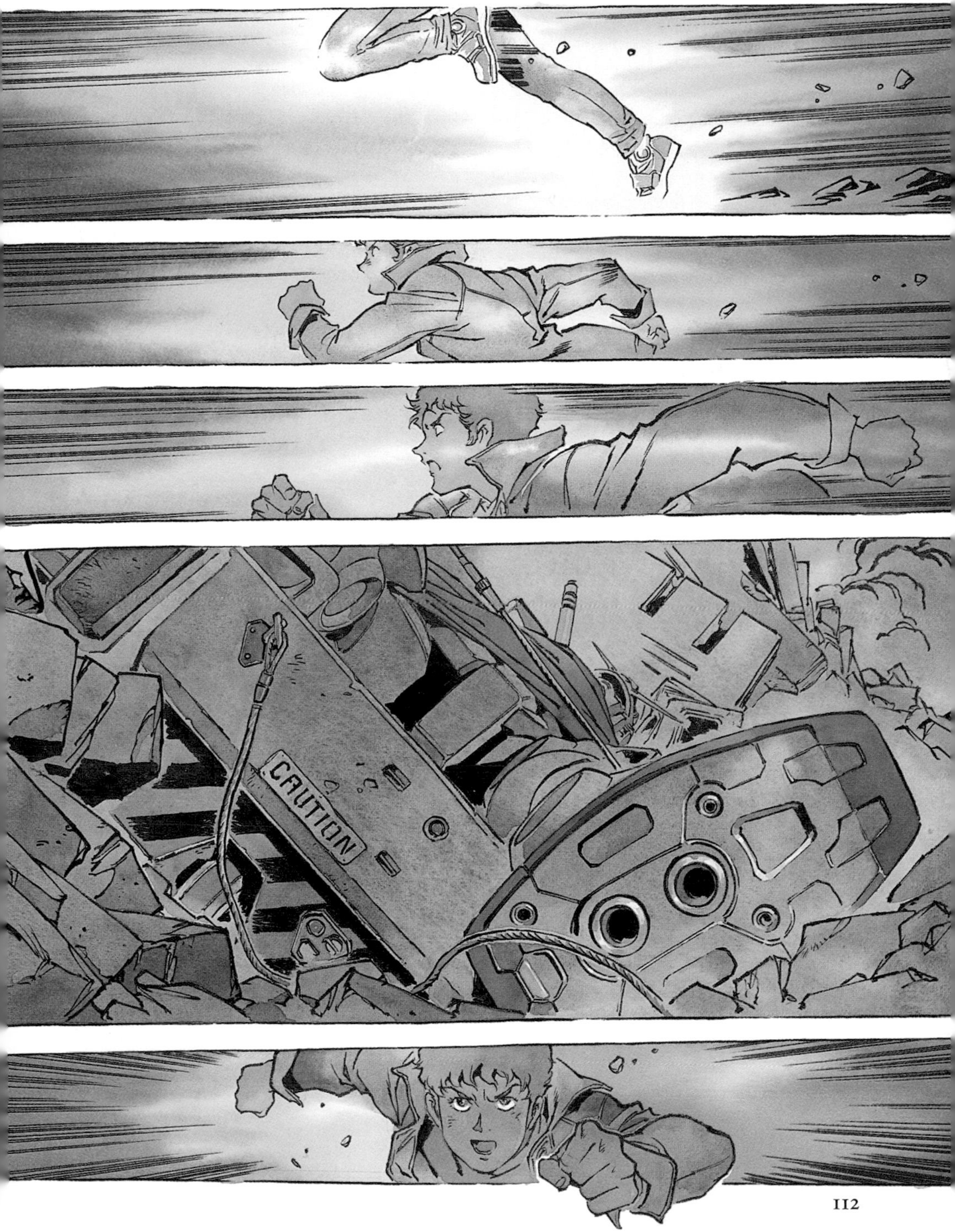
CAUTION

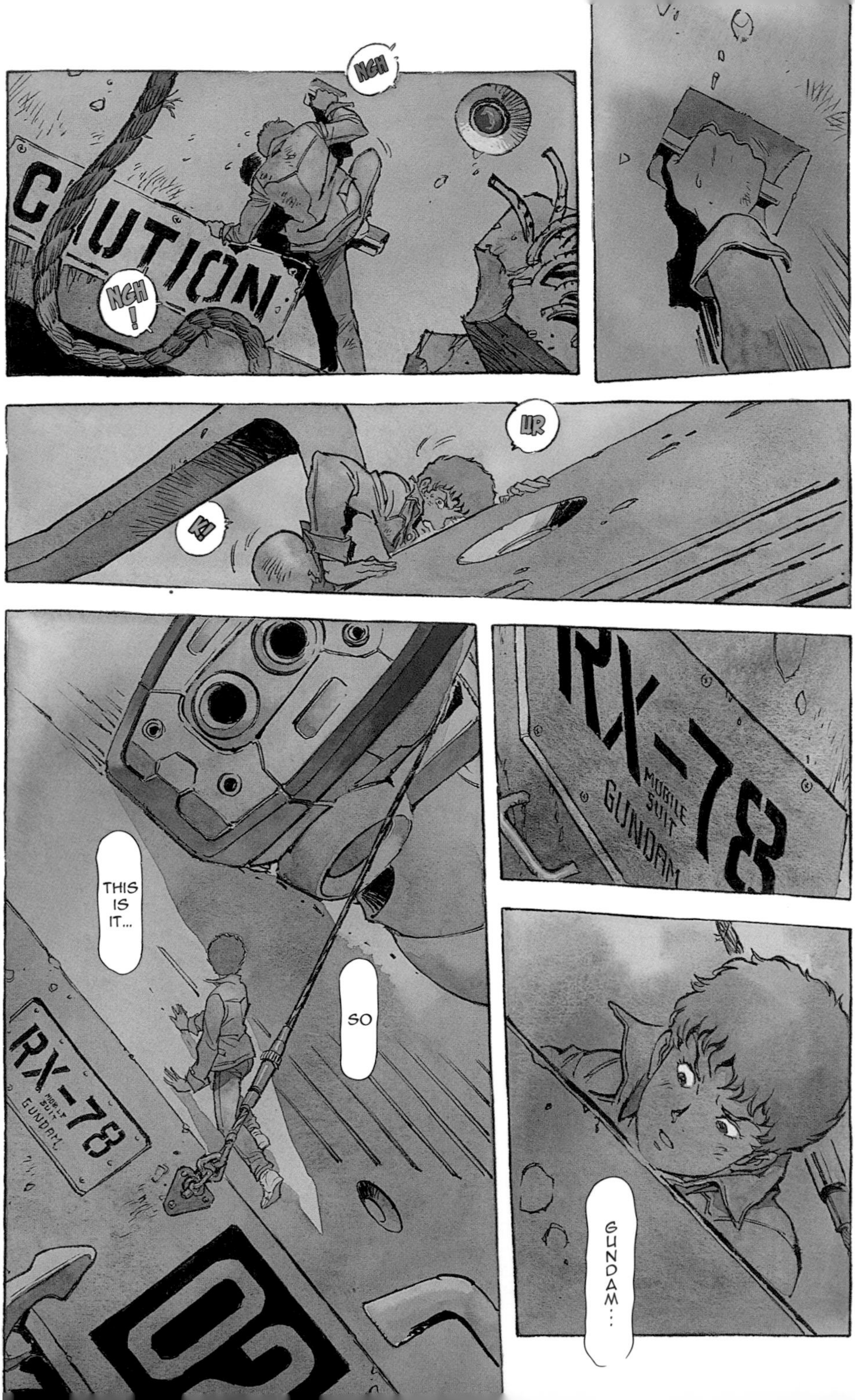
NGH
CAUTION
NGH!
UR
K!
RX-78
MOBILE SUIT
GUNDAM
GUNDAM...
THIS IS IT...
SO
RX-78
MOBILE SUIT
GUNDAM

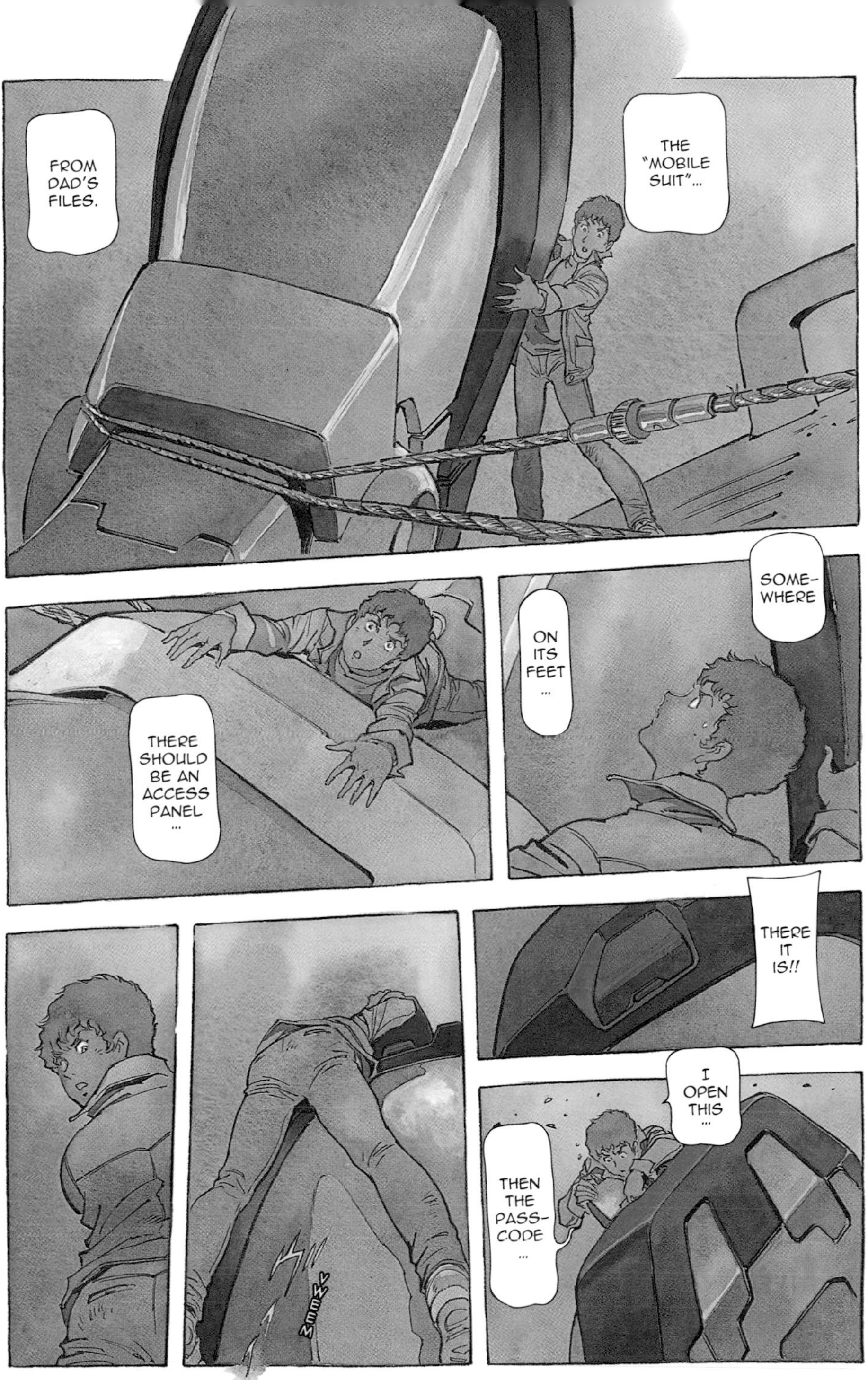
THE "MOBILE SUIT"...
FROM DAD'S FILES.
SOMEWHERE
ON ITS FEET ...
THERE SHOULD BE AN ACCESS PANEL ...
THERE IT IS!!
I OPEN THIS ...
THEN THE PASS-CODE ...
VWEEM

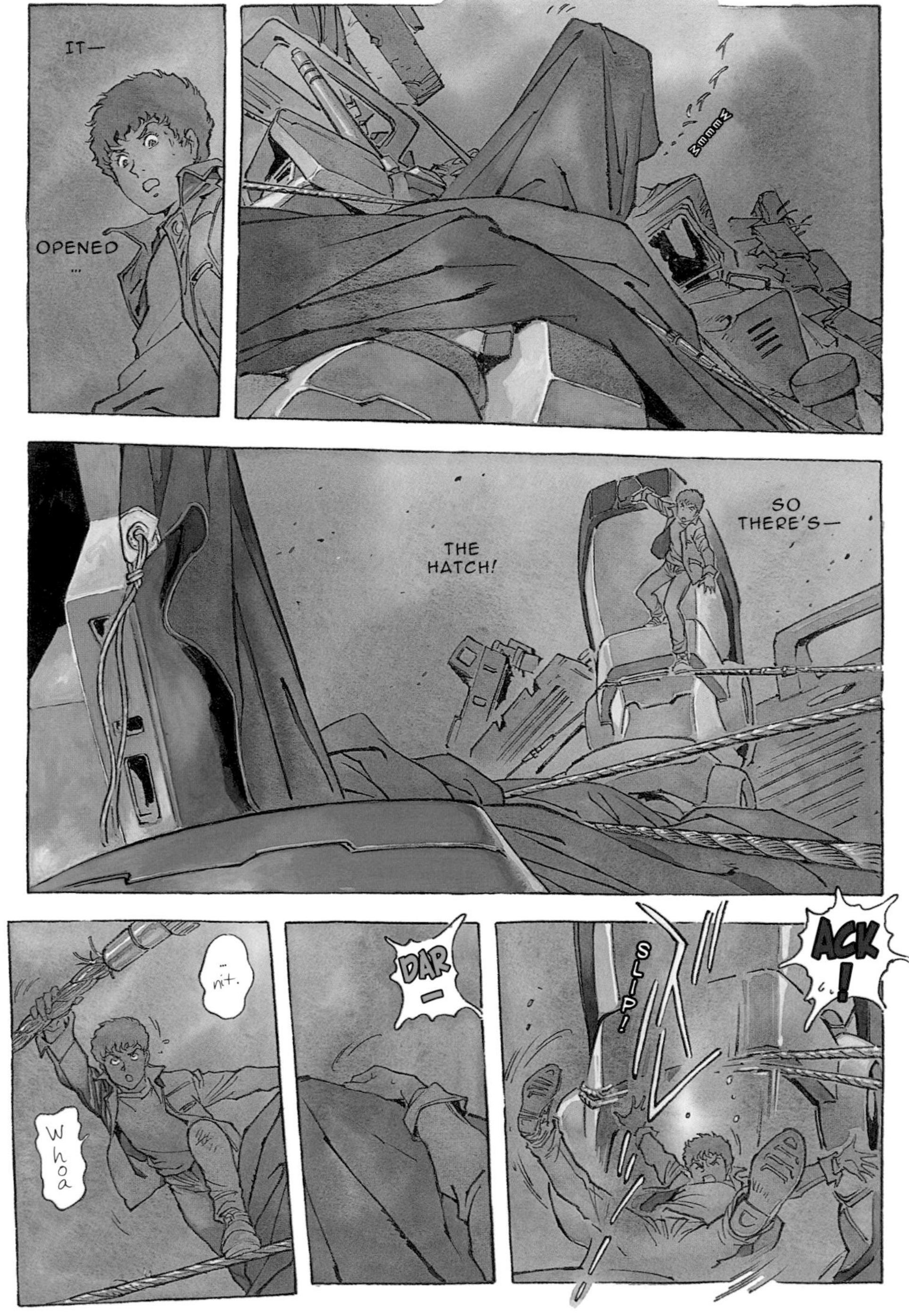
Zmmmm
IT—
OPENED ...
SO THERE'S—
THE HATCH!
ACK!
SLIP!
DAR—
... nit.
Whoa

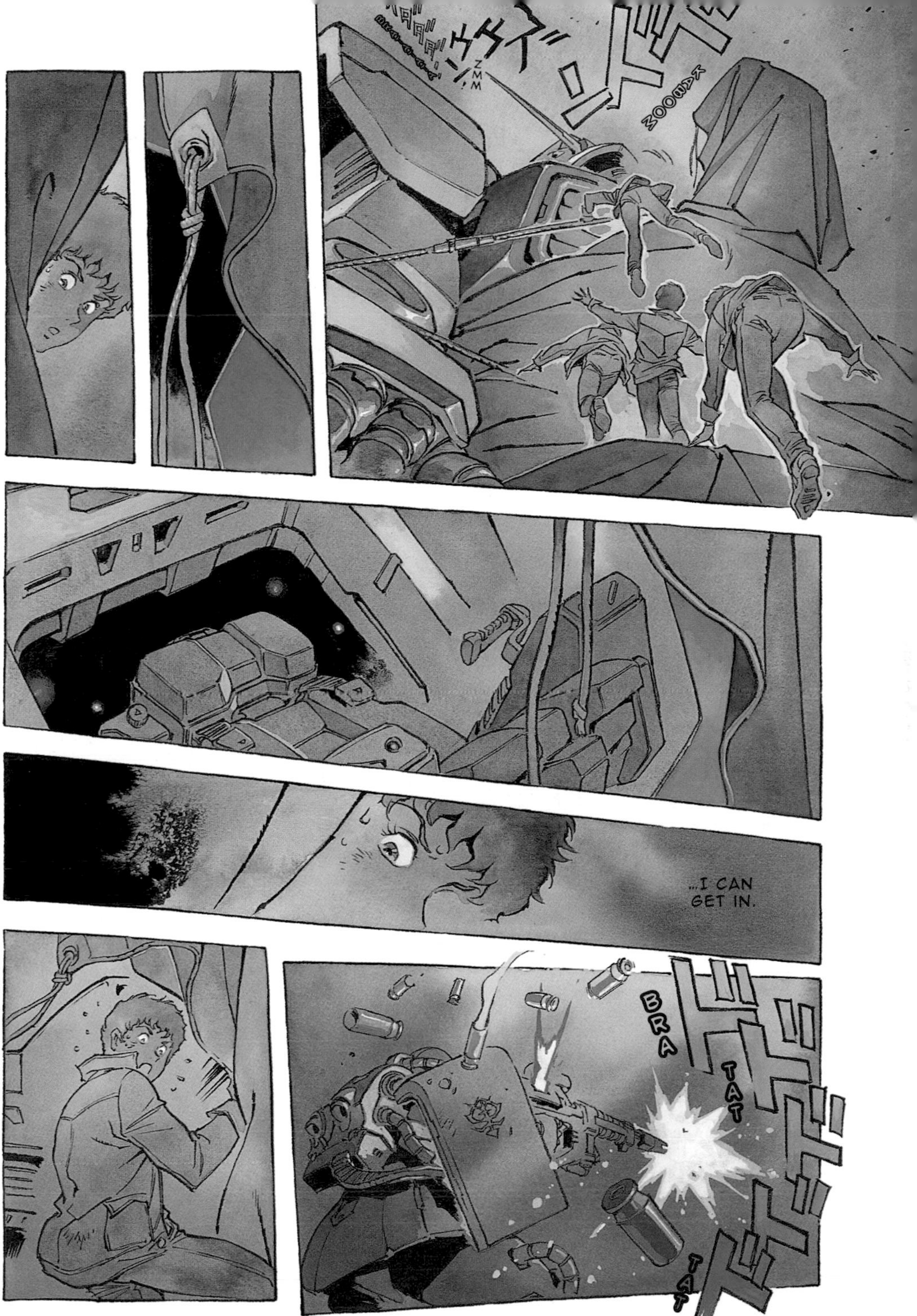
ZMM
...I CAN
GET IN.
BRA
TAT
TAT

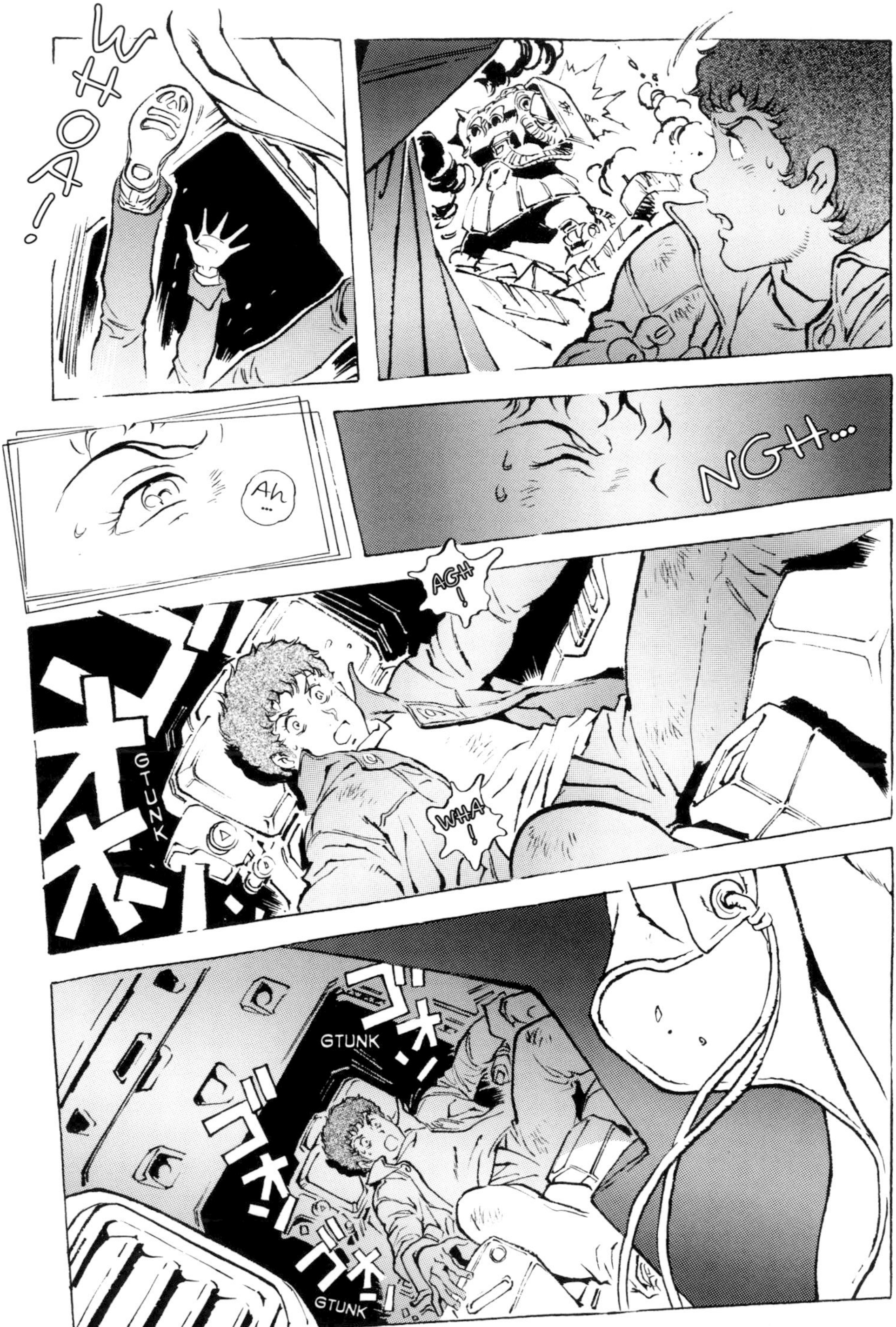
WHOA!
NGH...
Ah...
AGH!
WHA!
GTUNK
GTUNK
GTUNK

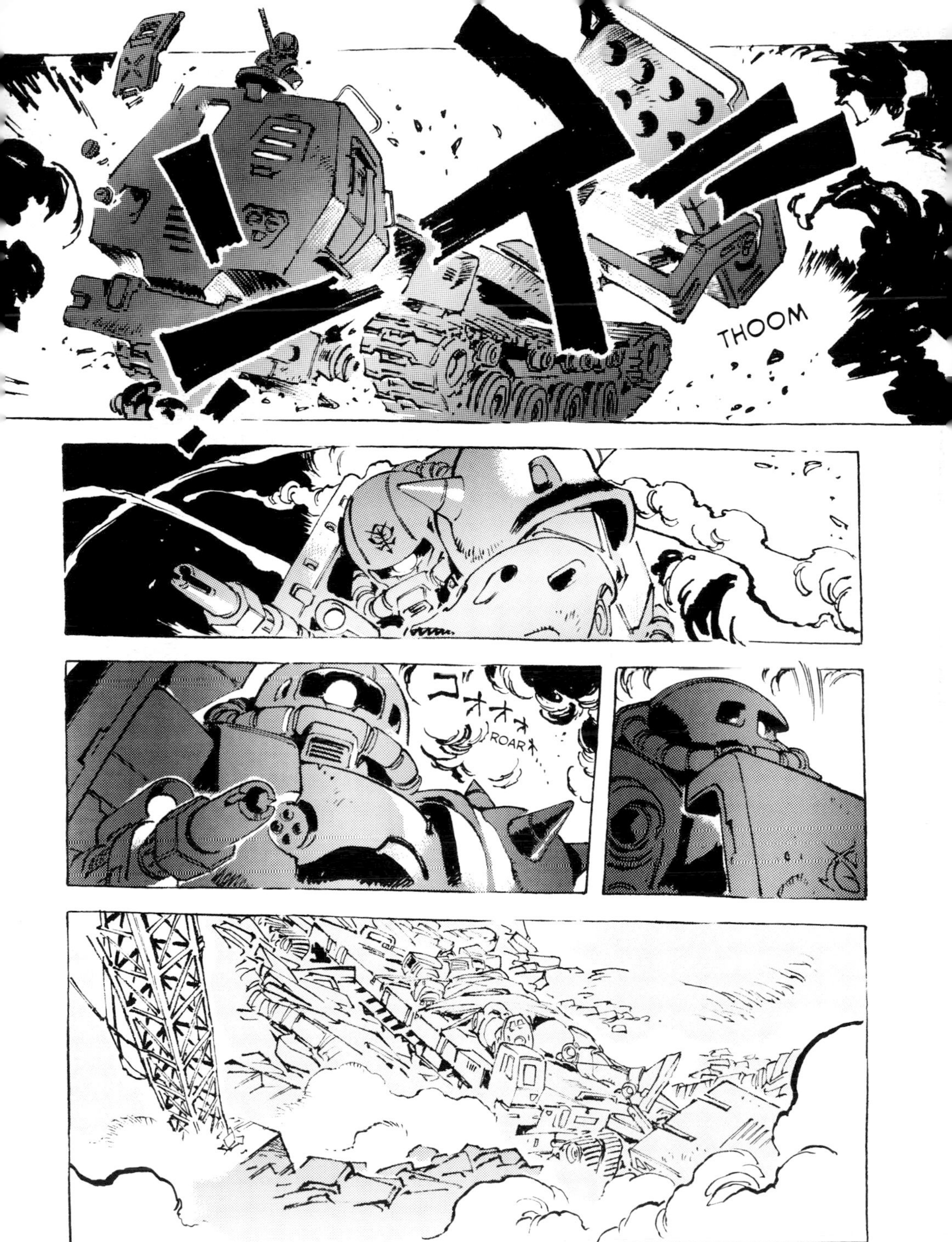
THOOM
ゴオオオ
ROAR

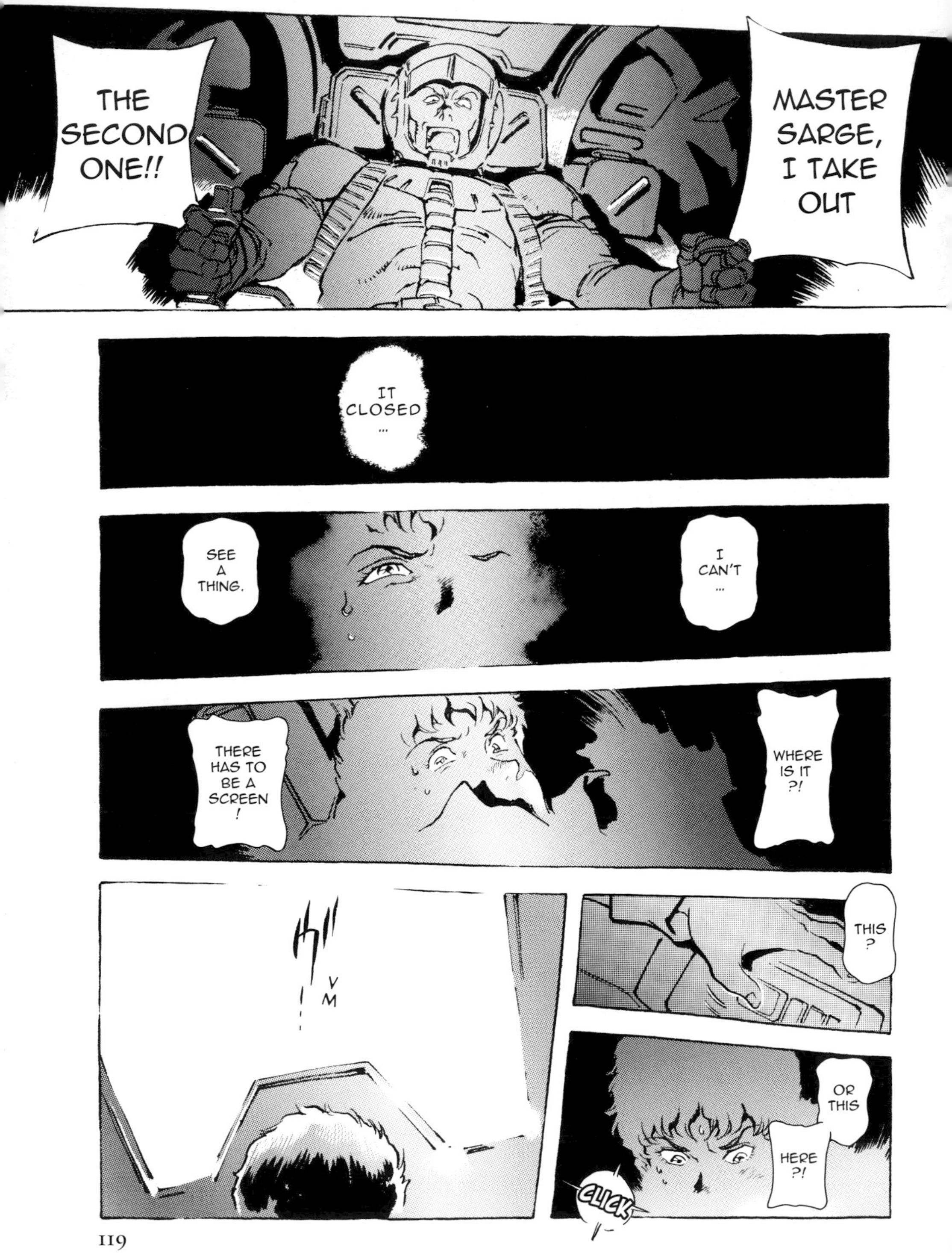
MASTER SARGE, I TAKE OUT
THE SECOND ONE!!
IT CLOSED ...
I CAN'T ...
SEE A THING.
WHERE IS IT ?!
THERE HAS TO BE A SCREEN !
THIS ?
OR THIS
HERE ?!
CLICK
VM

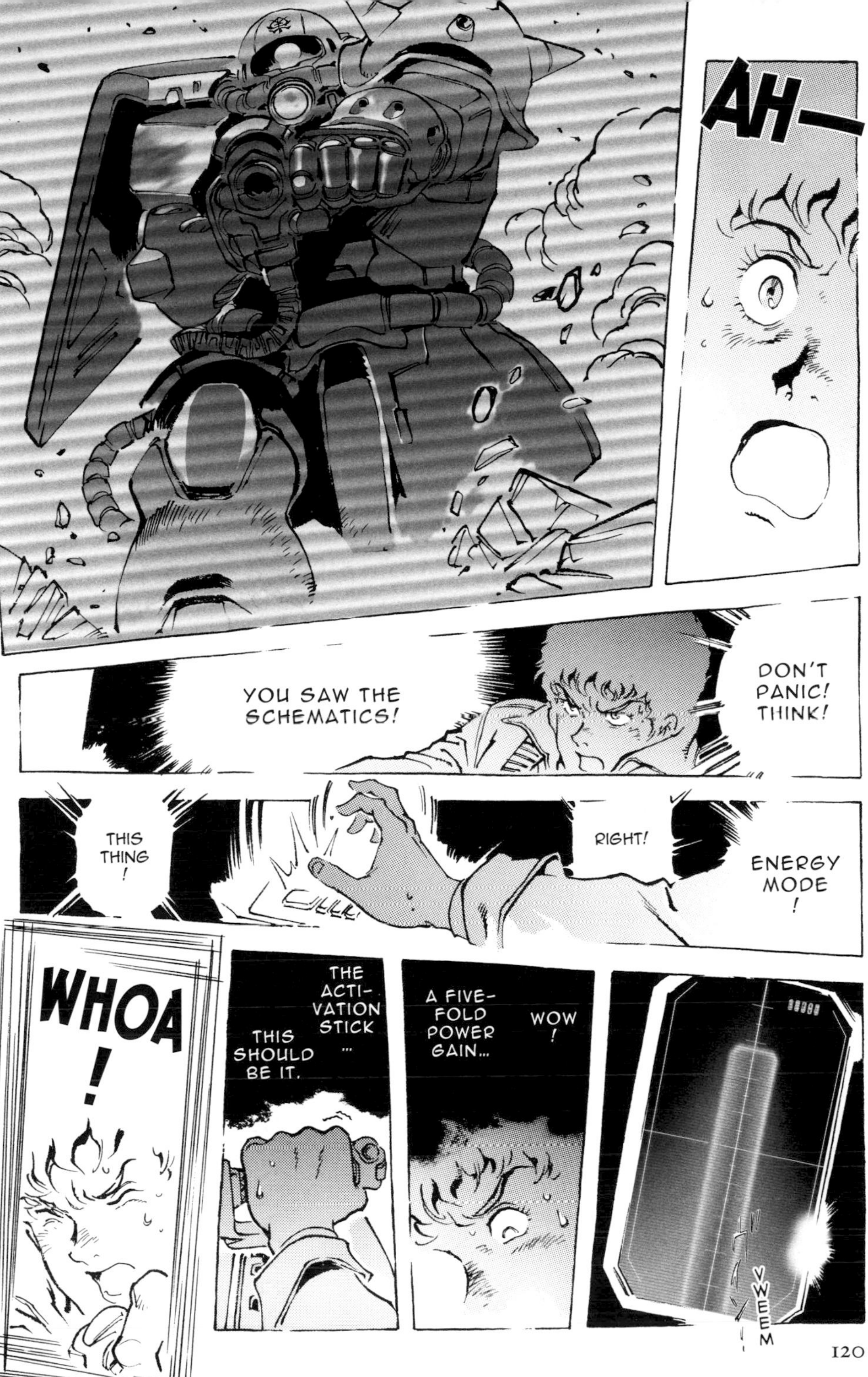

AH—
DON'T PANIC! THINK!
YOU SAW THE SCHEMATICS!
ENERGY MODE!
RIGHT!
THIS THING!
VWEEM
WOW!
A FIVE-FOLD POWER GAIN...
THE ACTIVATION STICK...
THIS SHOULD BE IT.
WHOA!

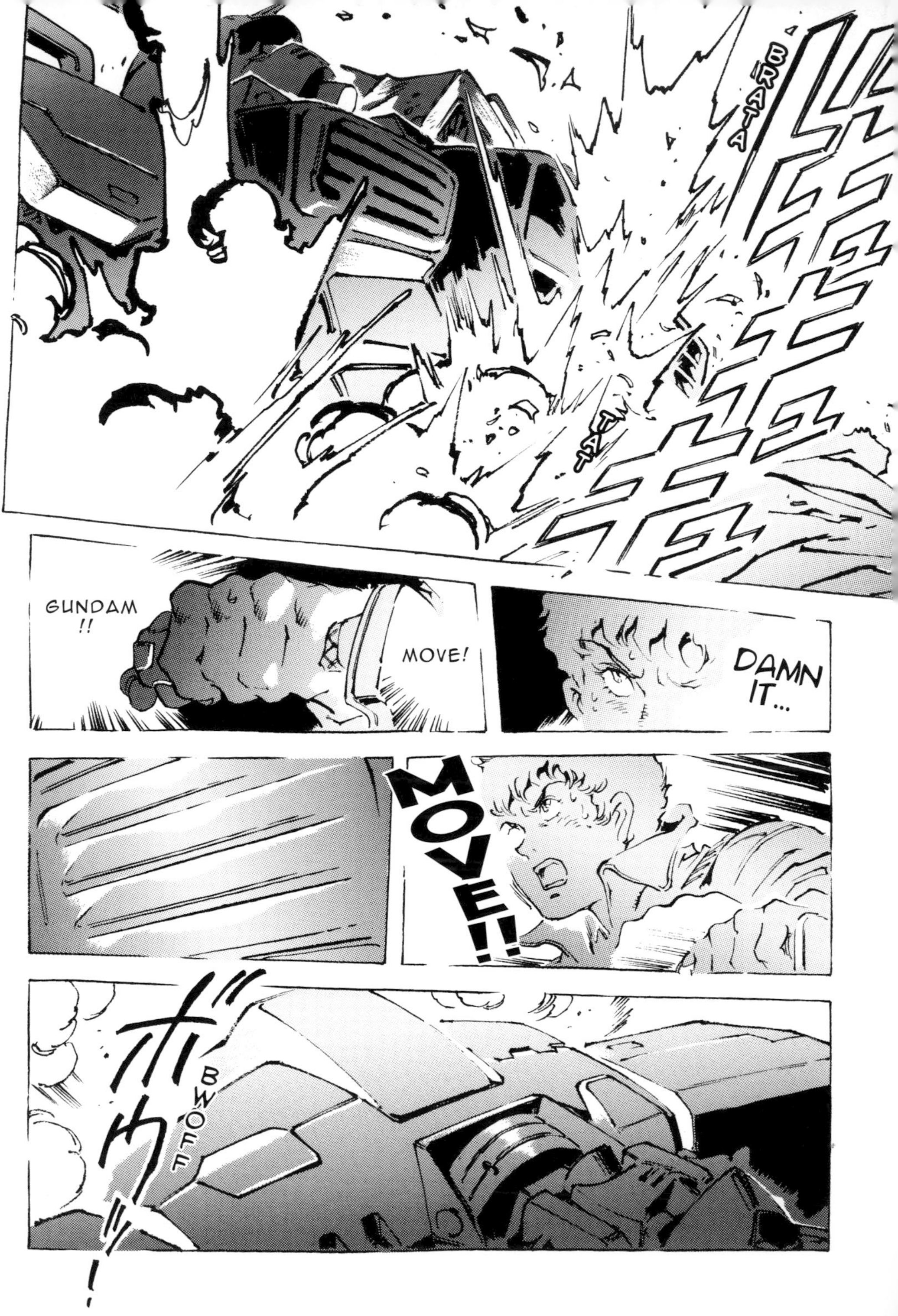
BRATATA
TAT
DAMN IT...
MOVE!
GUNDAM !!
MOVE!!
BWOFF

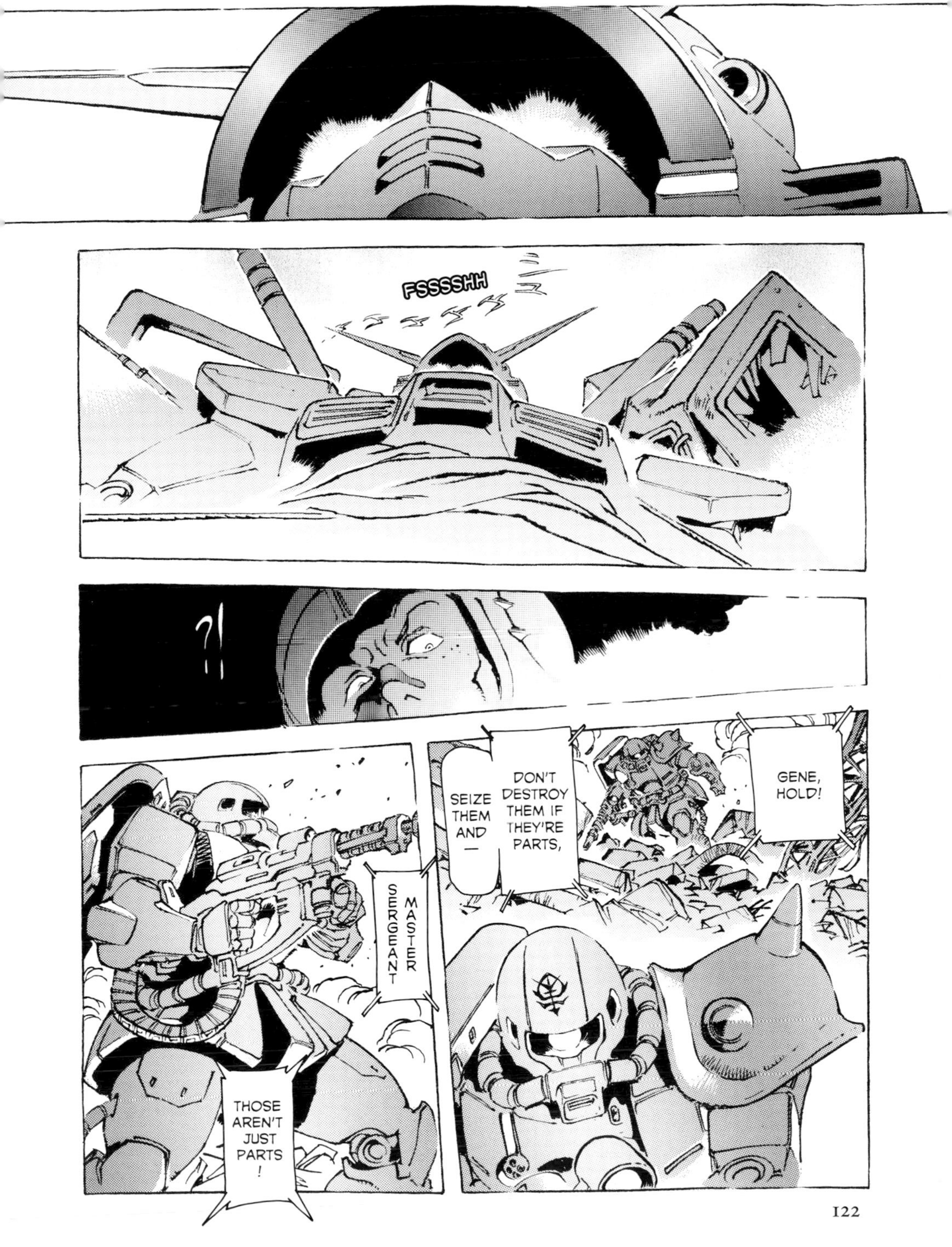
FSSSSHH
?!
GENE, HOLD!
DON'T DESTROY THEM IF THEY'RE PARTS,
SEIZE THEM AND —
MASTER SERGEANT
THOSE AREN'T JUST PARTS!

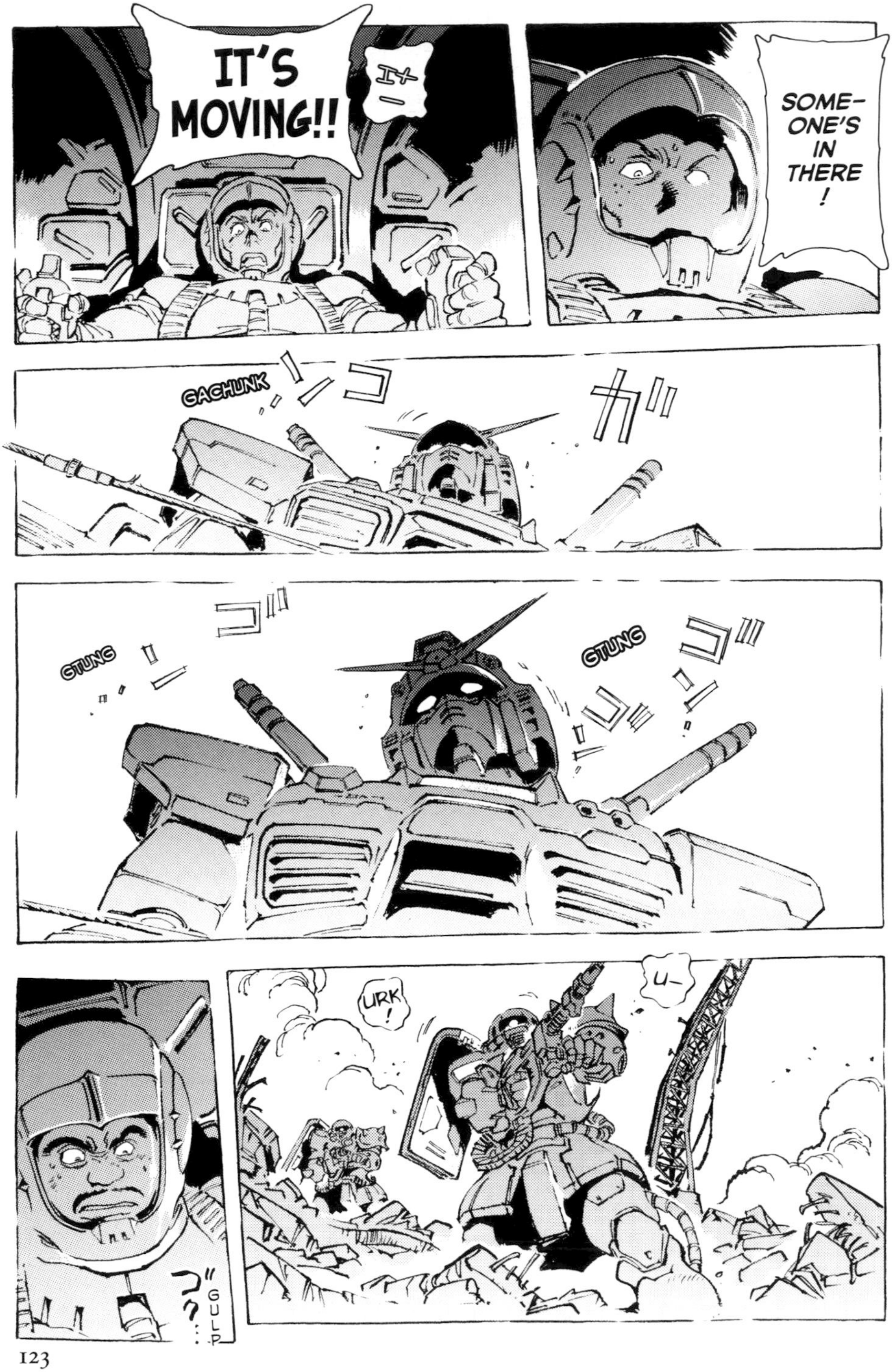

SOME-ONE'S IN THERE!
IT'S MOVING!!
GACHUNK
GTUNG
GTUNG
U–
URK!
GULP

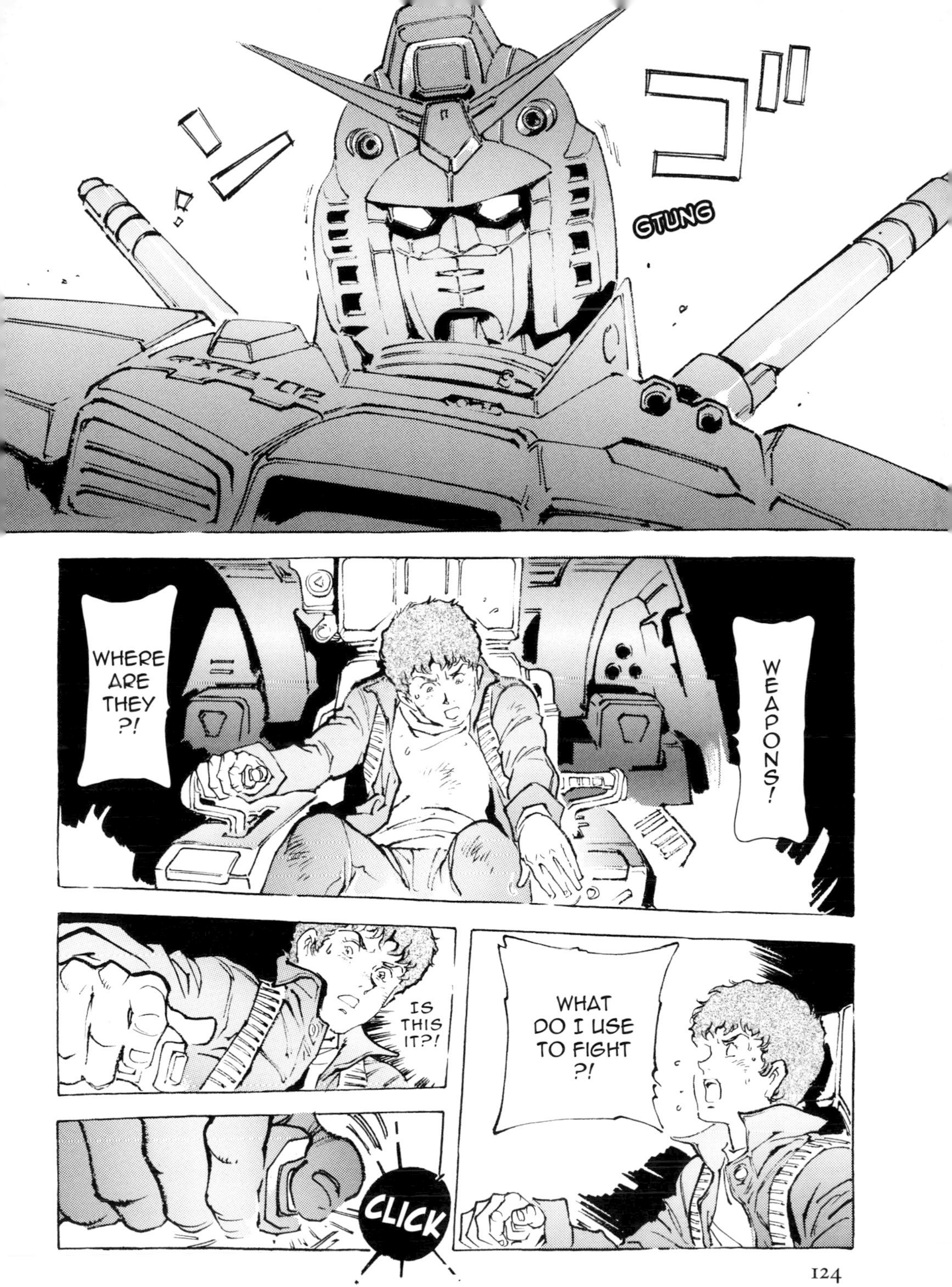
GTUNG
WEAPONS!
WHERE ARE THEY?!
WHAT DO I USE TO FIGHT?!
IS THIS IT?!
CLICK

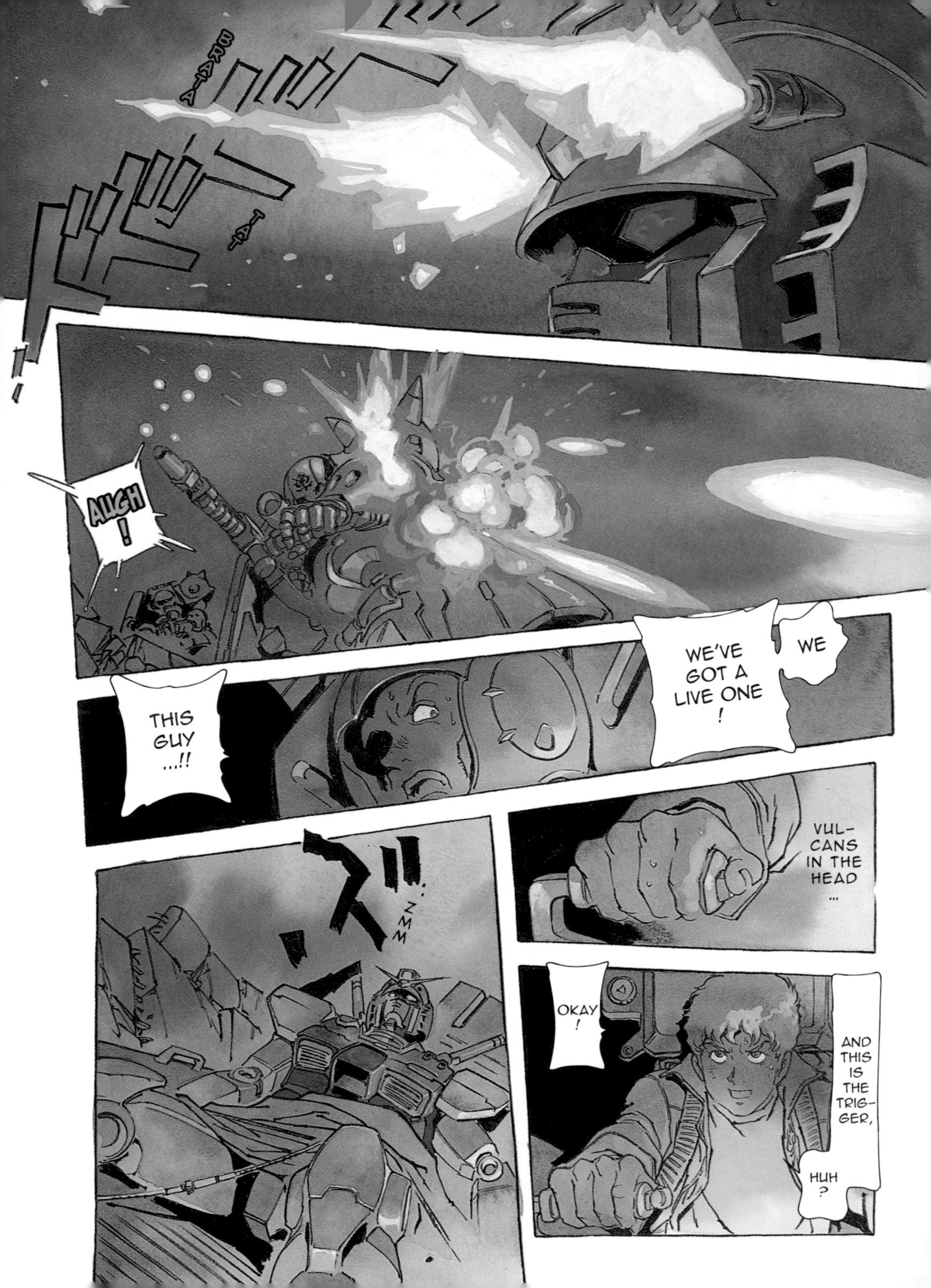
BRAATA
TAT
AUGH!
WE
WE'VE GOT A LIVE ONE!
THIS GUY ...!!
VUL-CANS IN THE HEAD ...
AND THIS IS THE TRIG-GER,
HUH?
OKAY!
ZMM

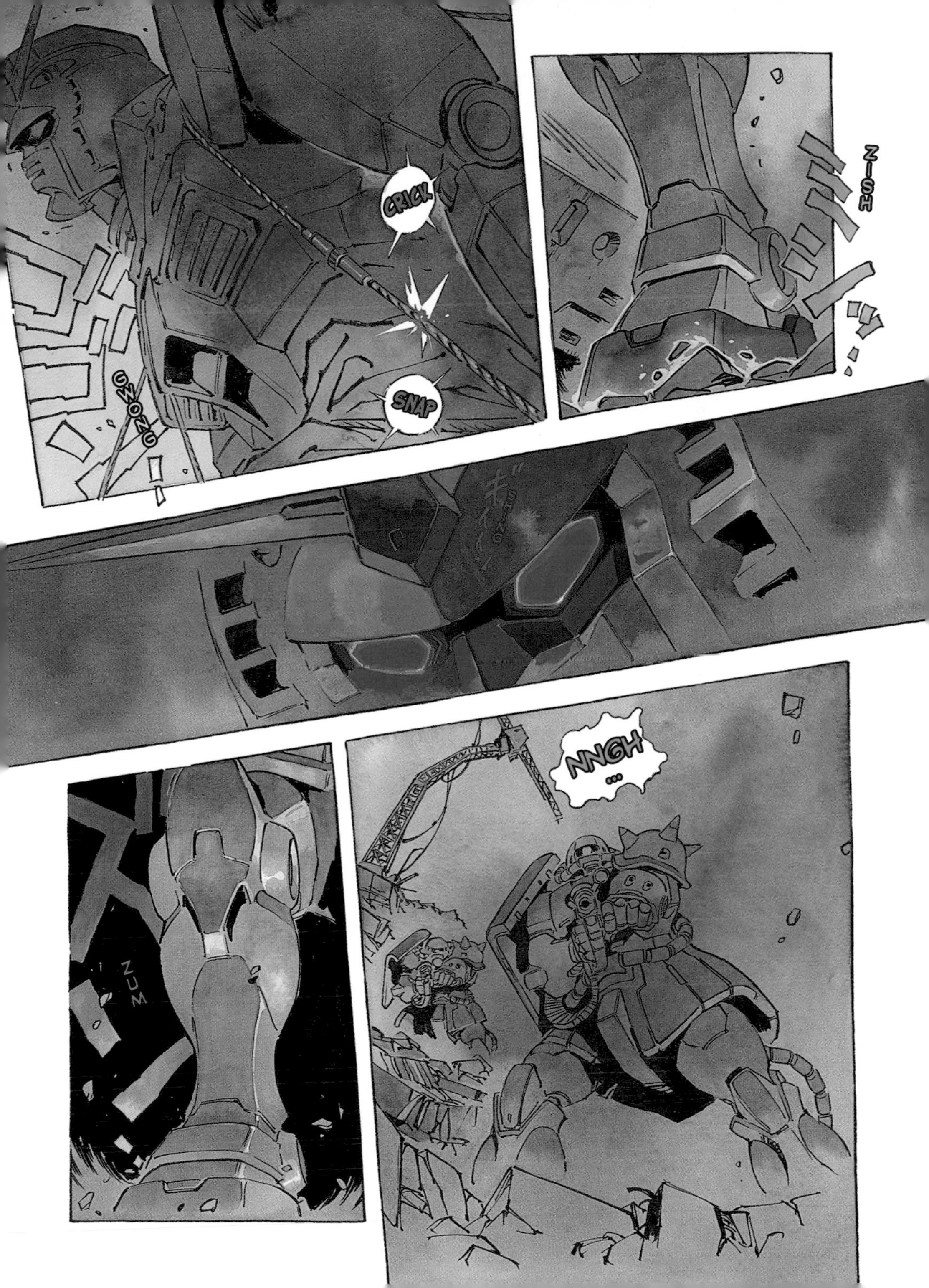
ZISH
CRICK
SNAP
GWONG
NNGH
...
ZUM

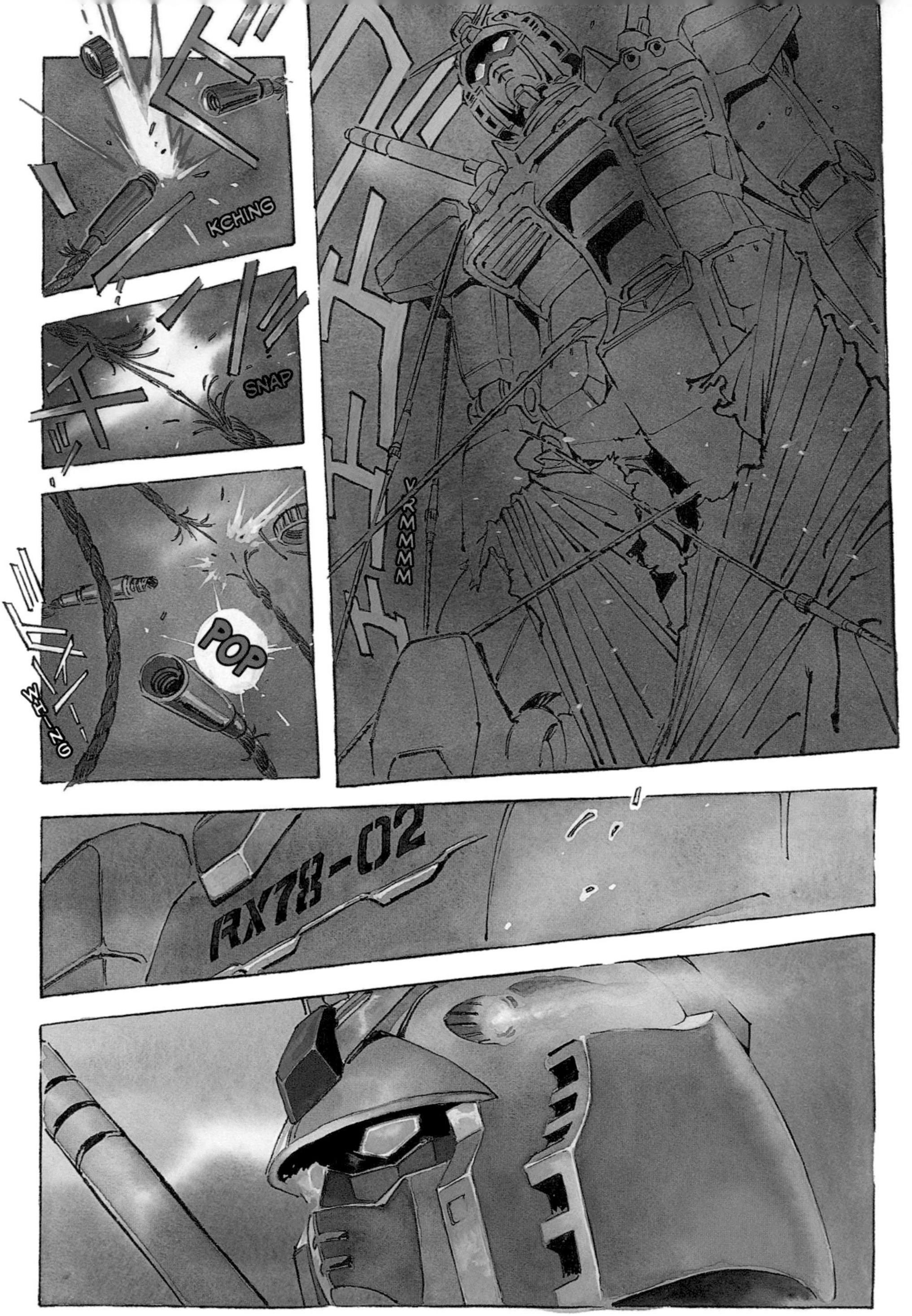
VRMMMM
KCHING
SNAP
POP
RX78-02

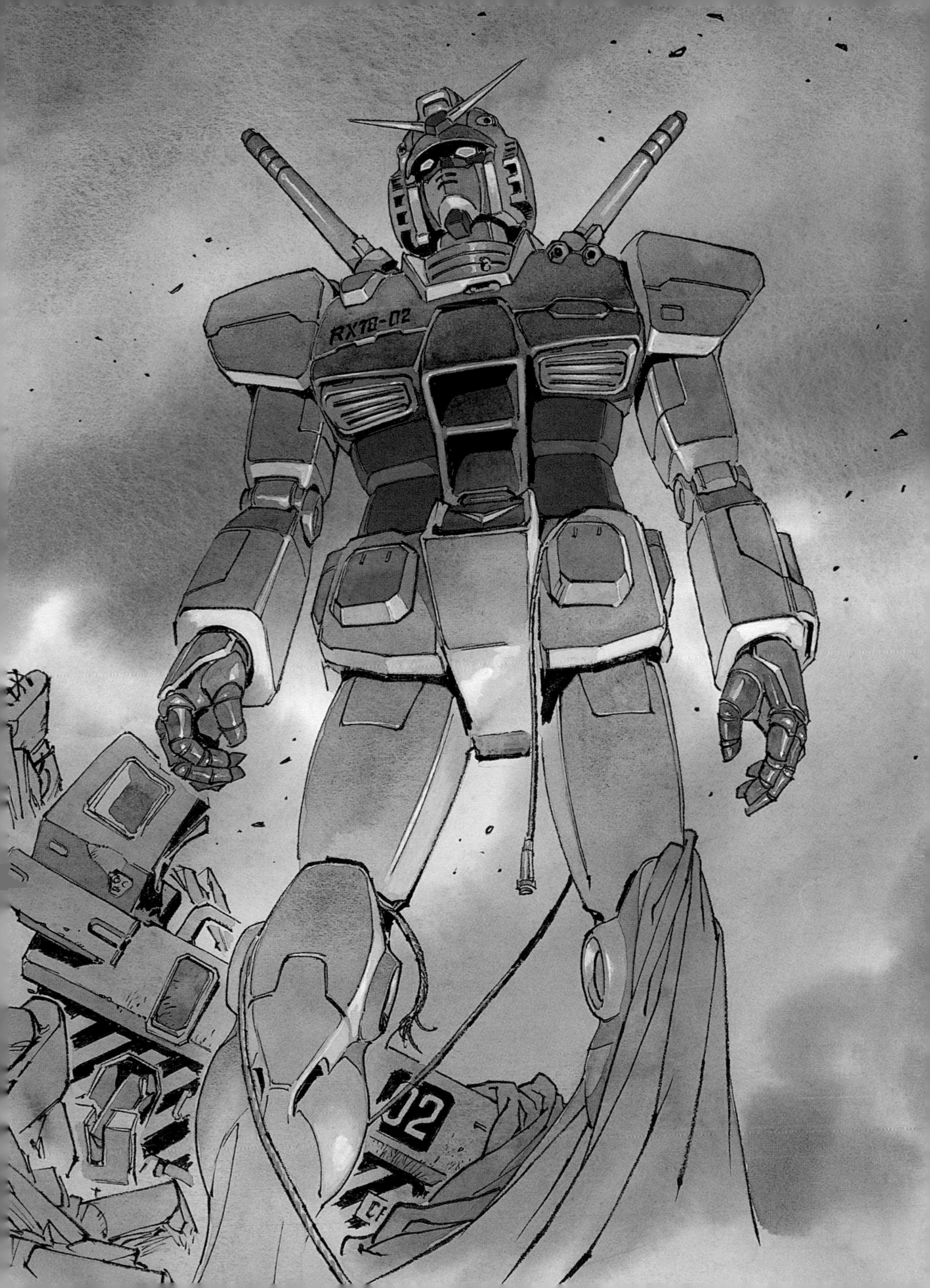
RX78-02
02

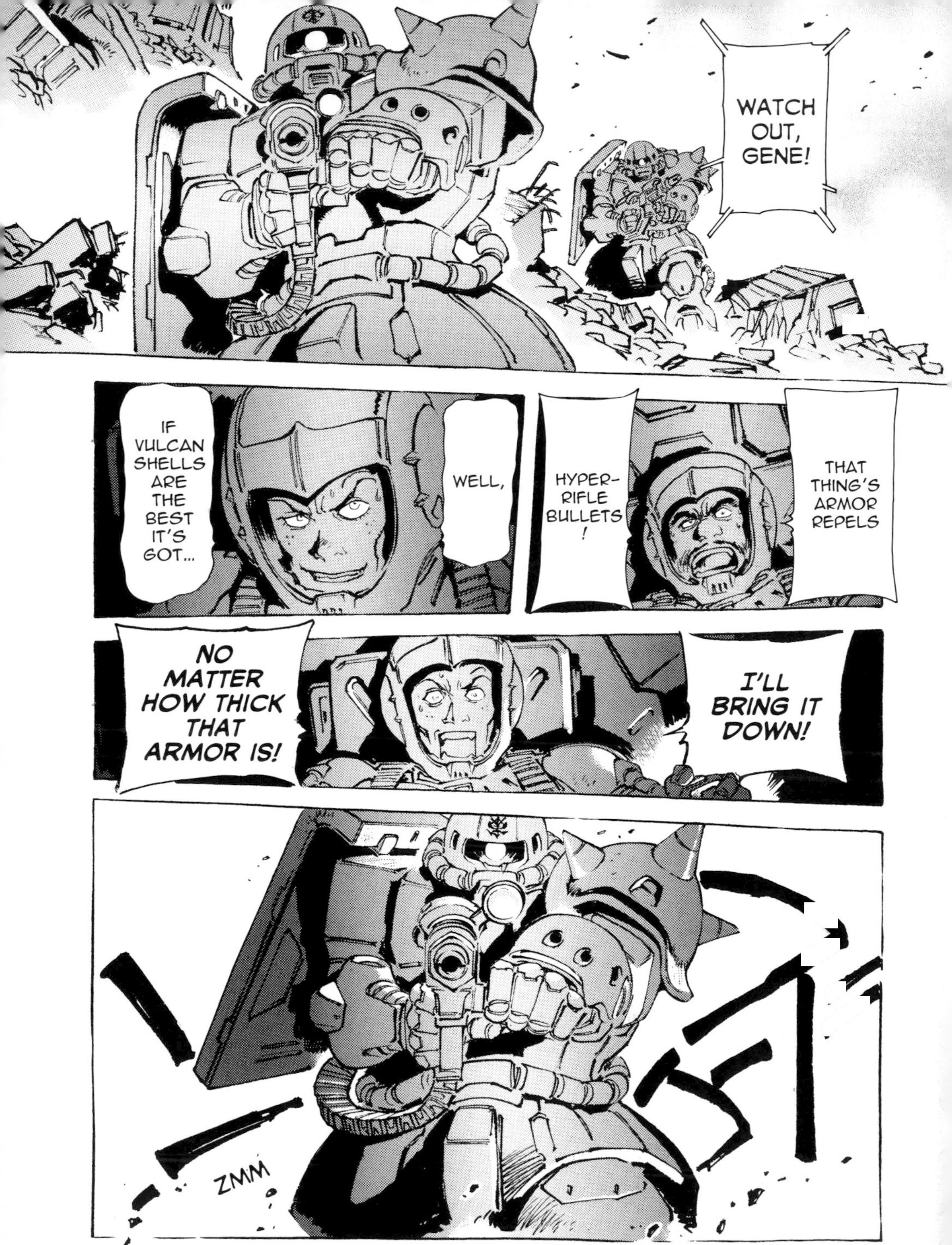
WATCH OUT, GENE!
THAT THING'S ARMOR REPELS
HYPER-RIFLE BULLETS!
WELL,
IF VULCAN SHELLS ARE THE BEST IT'S GOT...
I'LL BRING IT DOWN!
NO MATTER HOW THICK THAT ARMOR IS!
ZMM

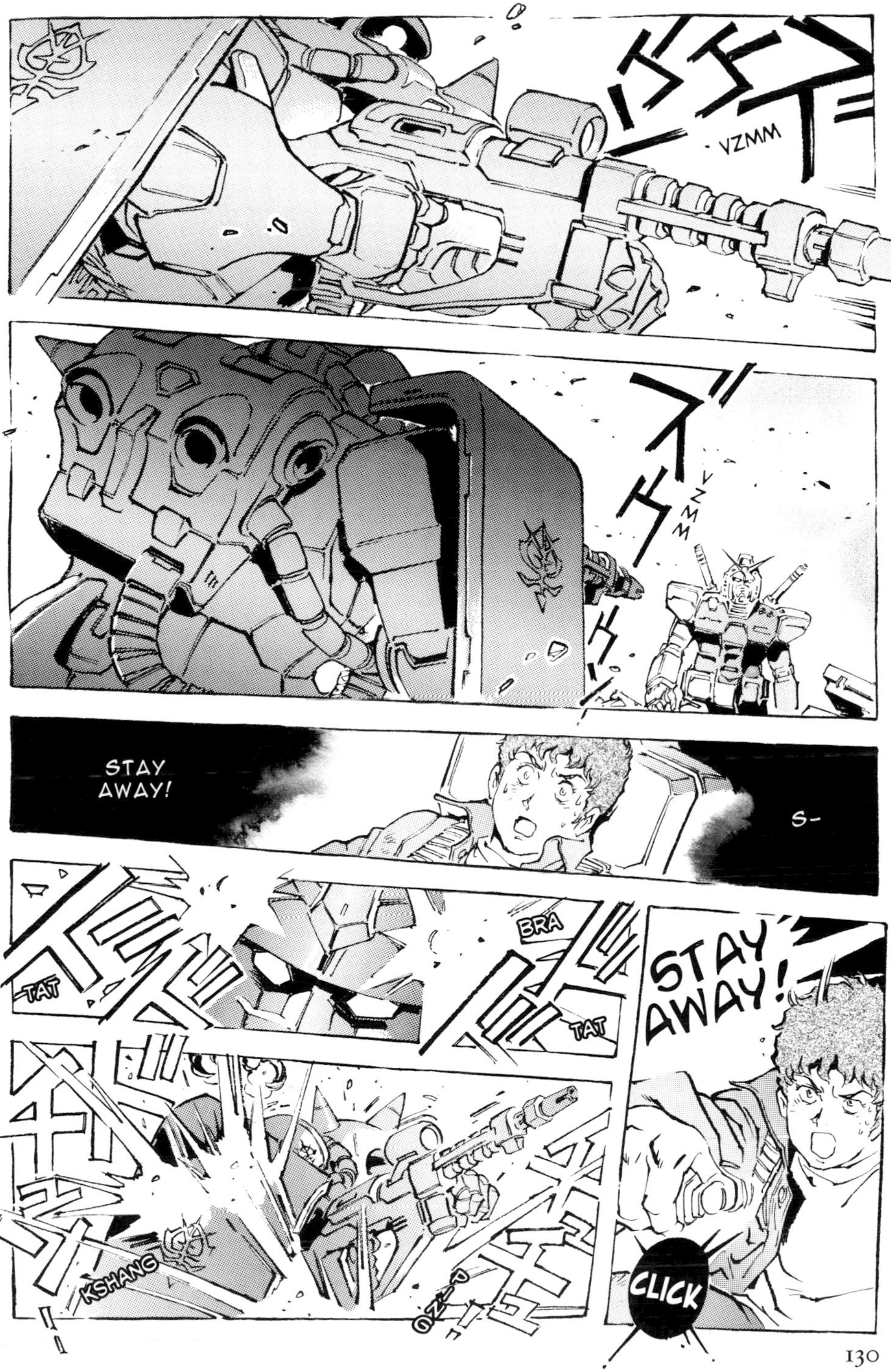
VZMM
VZMM
S-
STAY AWAY!
STAY AWAY!
CLICK
BRA
TAT
TAT
KSHANG

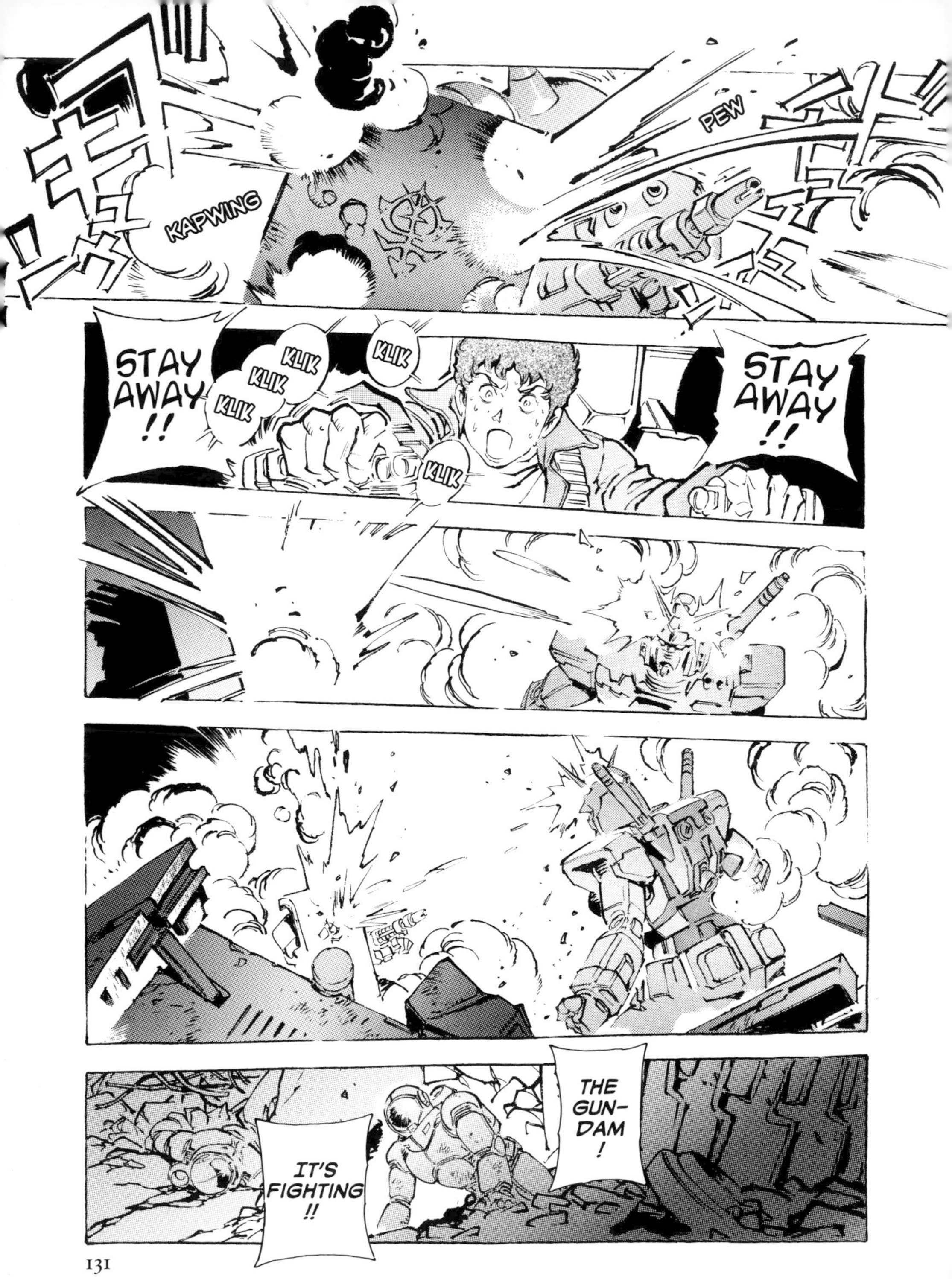
PEW
KAPWING
STAY AWAY!!
KLIK
KLIK
KLIK
KLIK
KLIK
STAY AWAY!!
THE GUN-DAM!
IT'S FIGHTING!!

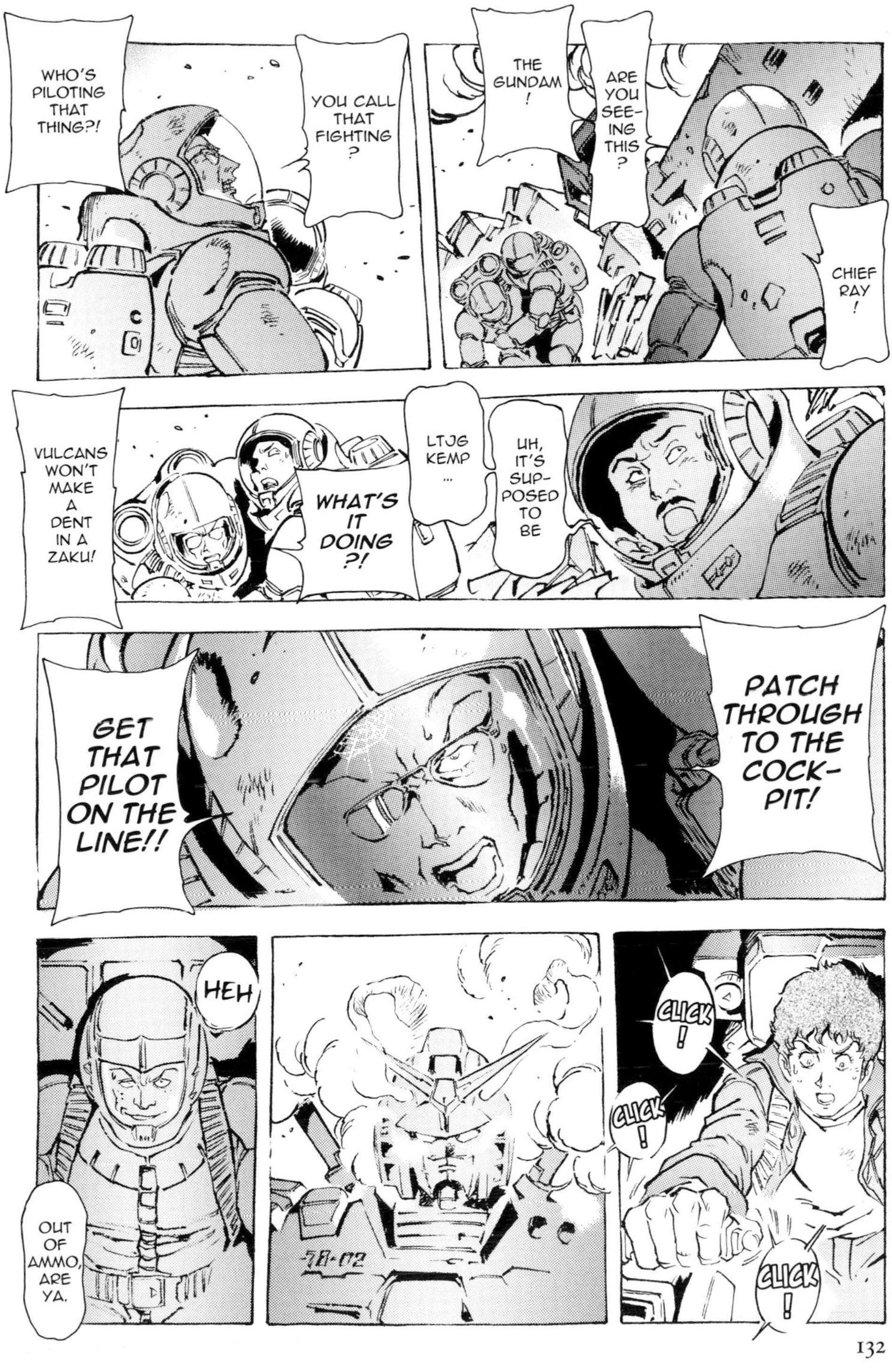
ARE YOU SEEING THIS?
THE GUNDAM!
CHIEF RAY!
YOU CALL THAT FIGHTING?
WHO'S PILOTING THAT THING?!
UH, IT'S SUPPOSED TO BE
LTJG KEMP...
WHAT'S IT DOING?!
VULCANS WON'T MAKE A DENT IN A ZAKU!
PATCH THROUGH TO THE COCKPIT!
GET THAT PILOT ON THE LINE!!
CLICK!
CLICK!
CLICK!
HEH
OUT OF AMMO, ARE YA.

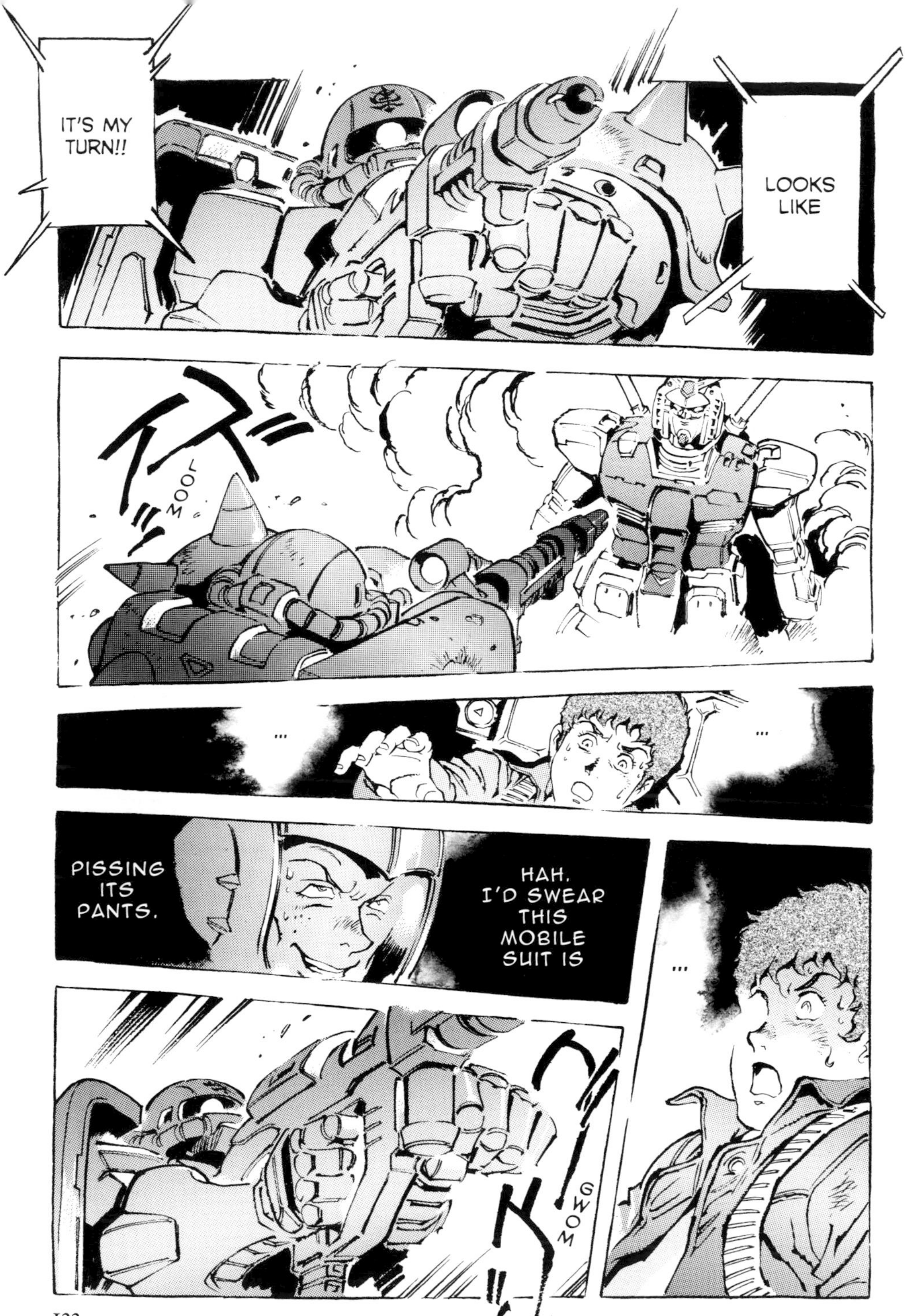
LOOKS LIKE
IT'S MY TURN!!
LOOM
...
...
...
HAH. I'D SWEAR THIS MOBILE SUIT IS
PISSING ITS PANTS.
GWOM

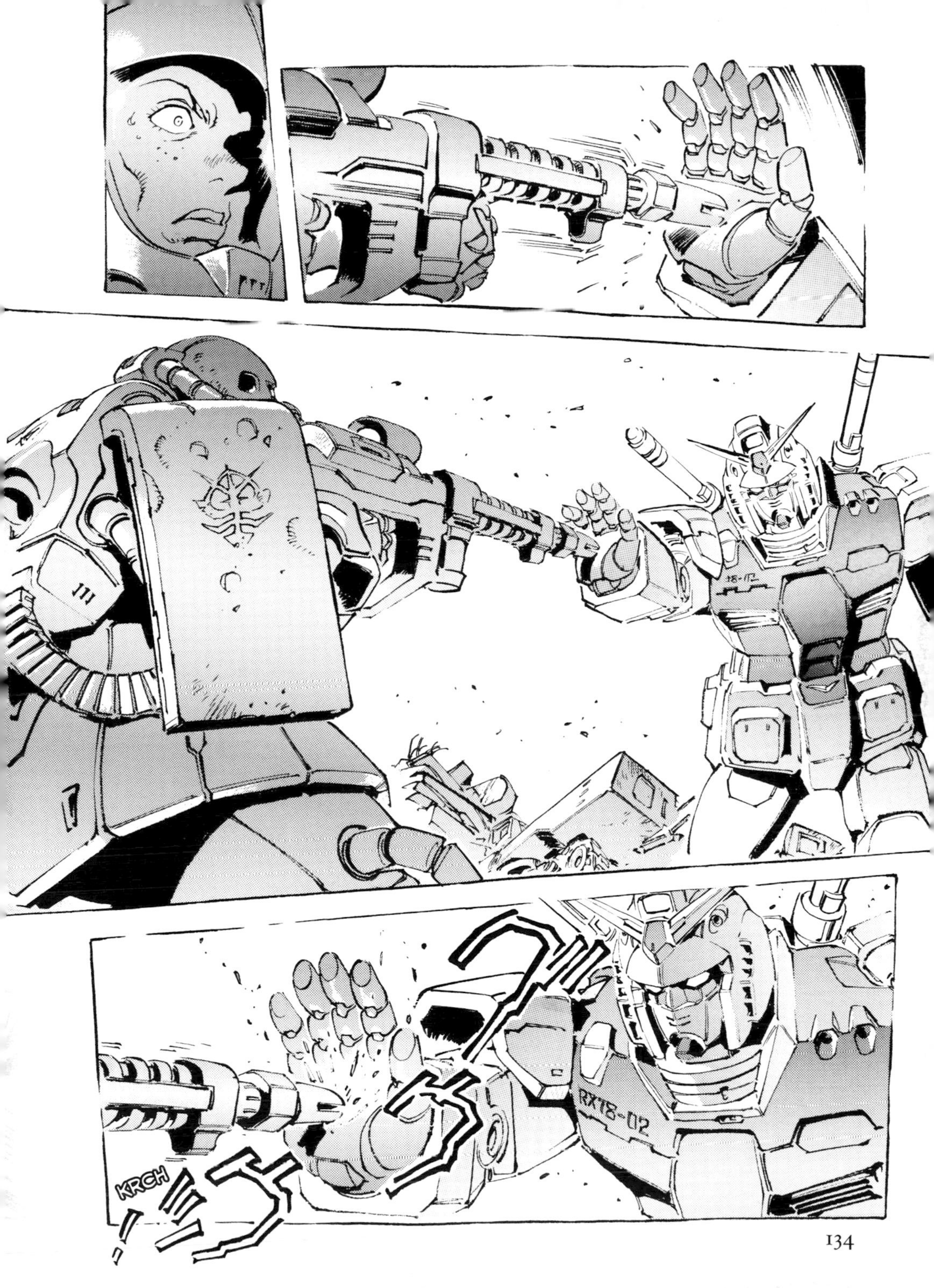
RX78-02
KRCH

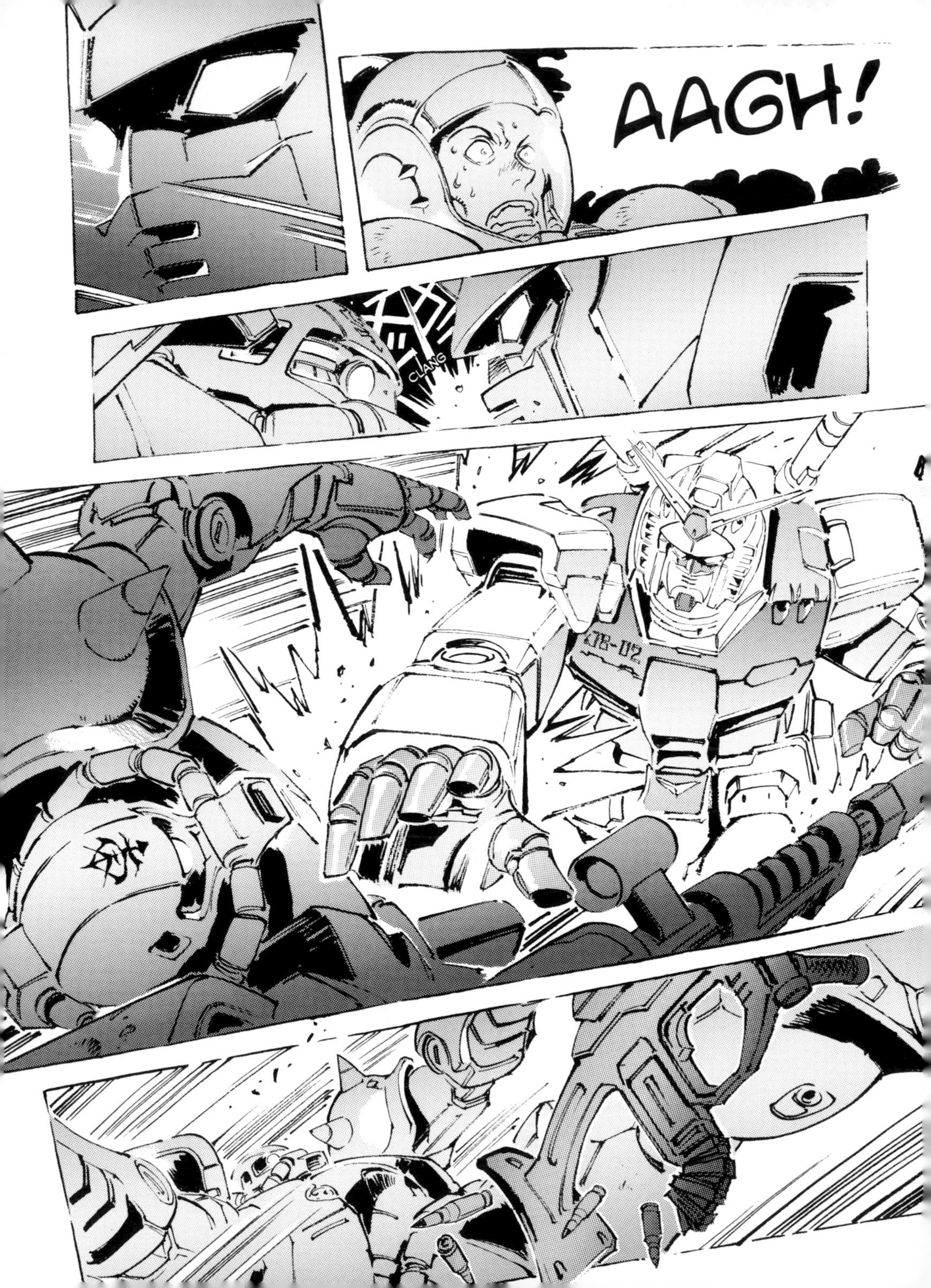
AAGH!
CLANG

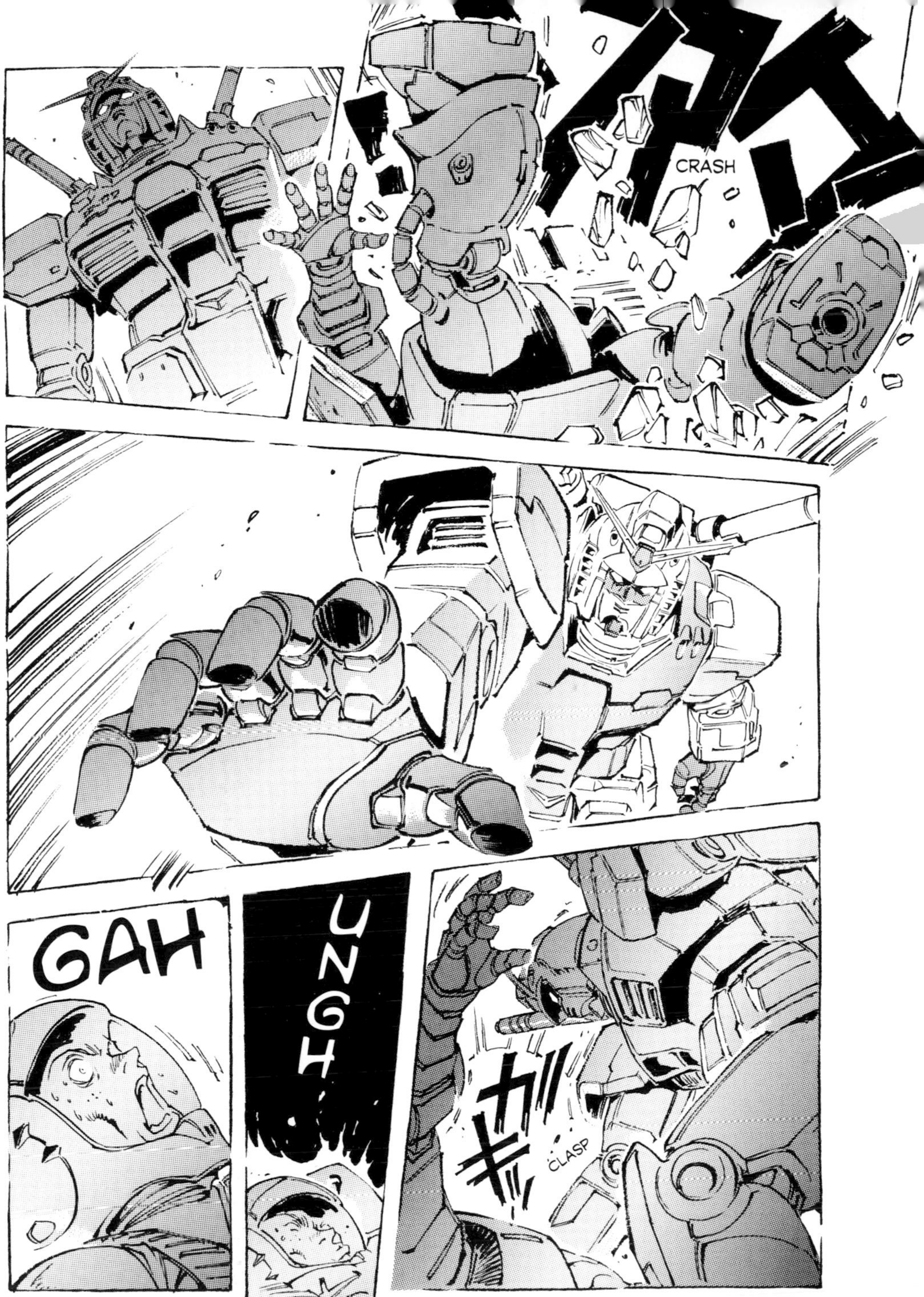
CRASH
ガギ
CLASP
UNGH
GAH

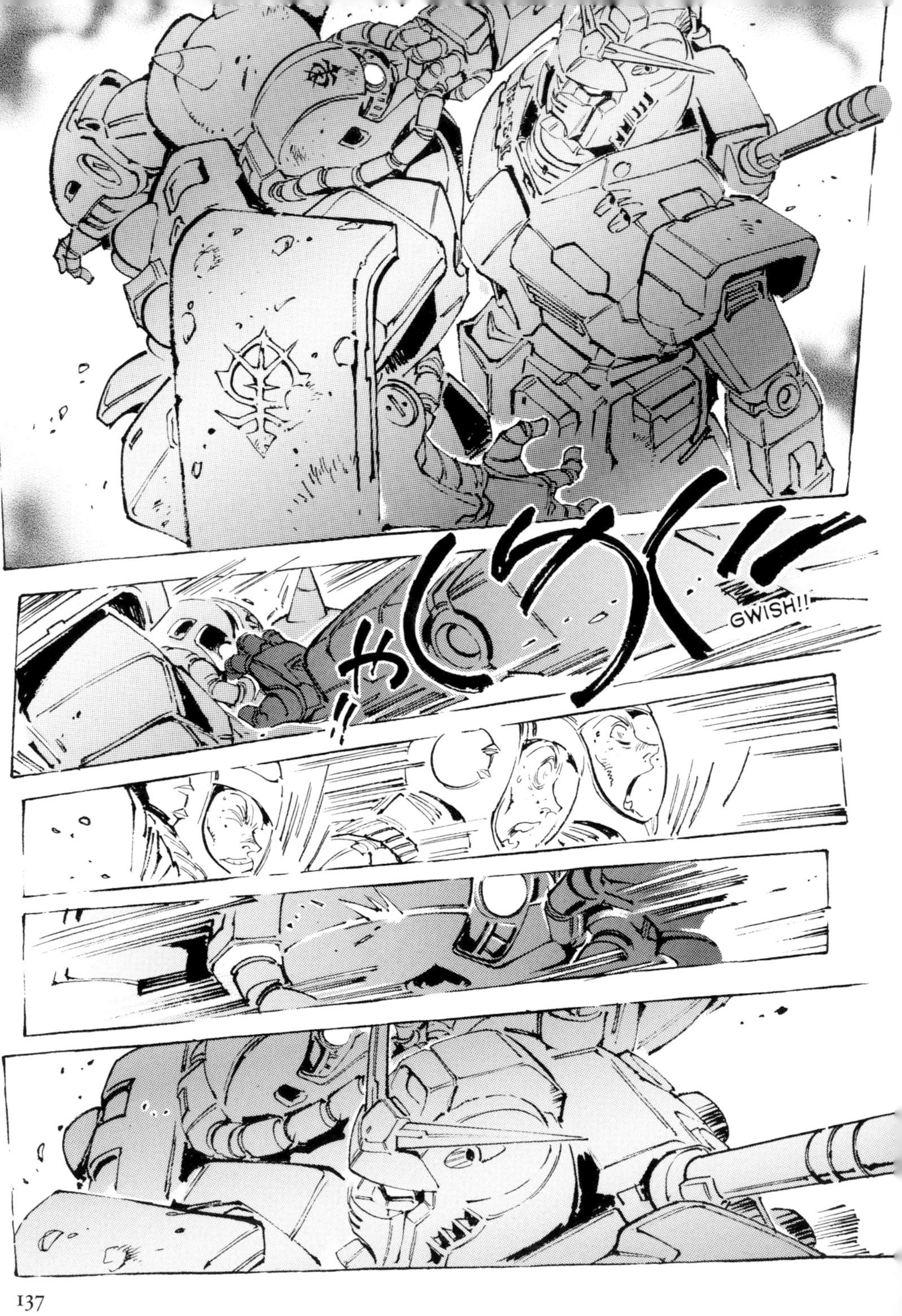

GWISH!!

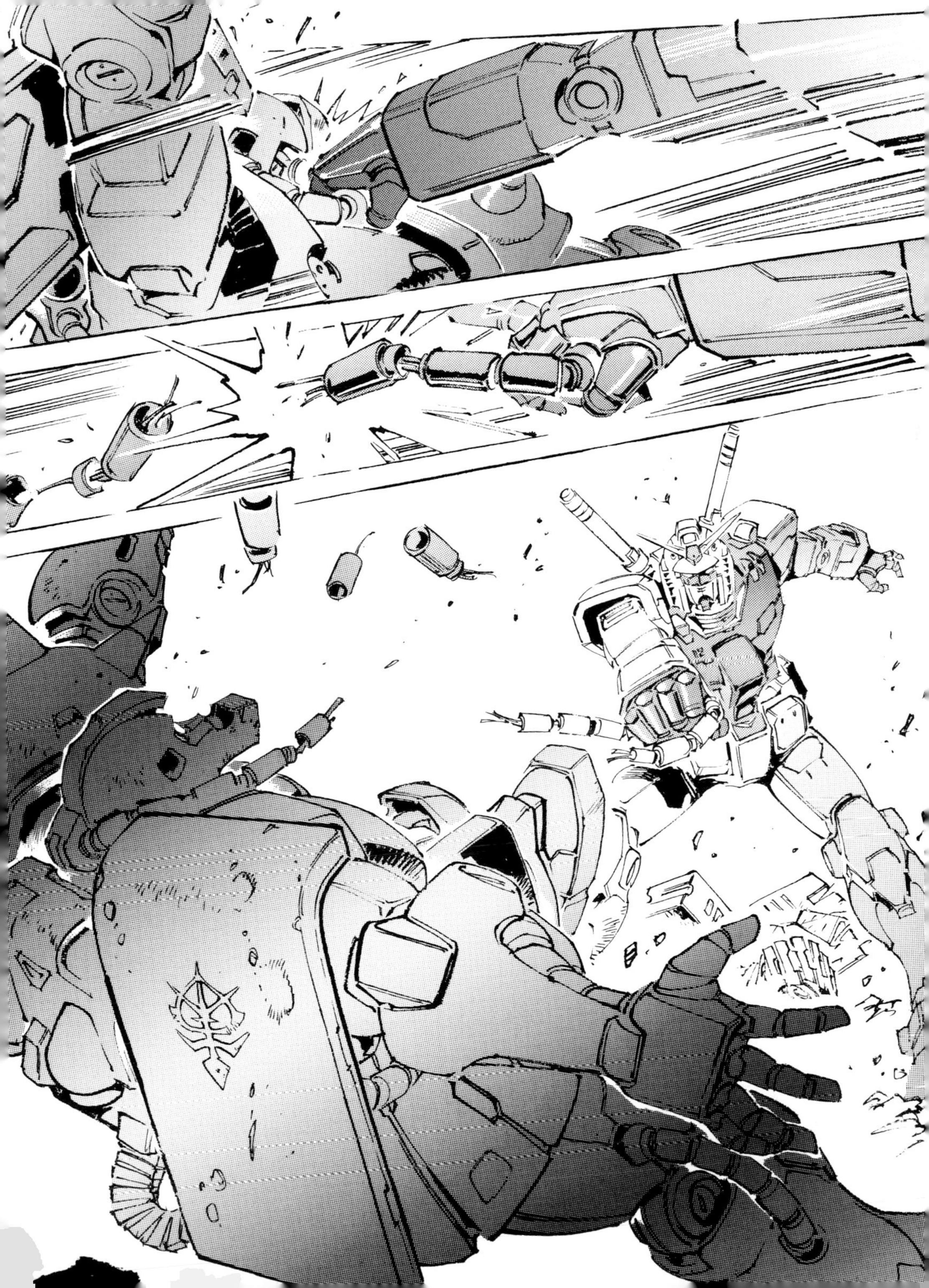

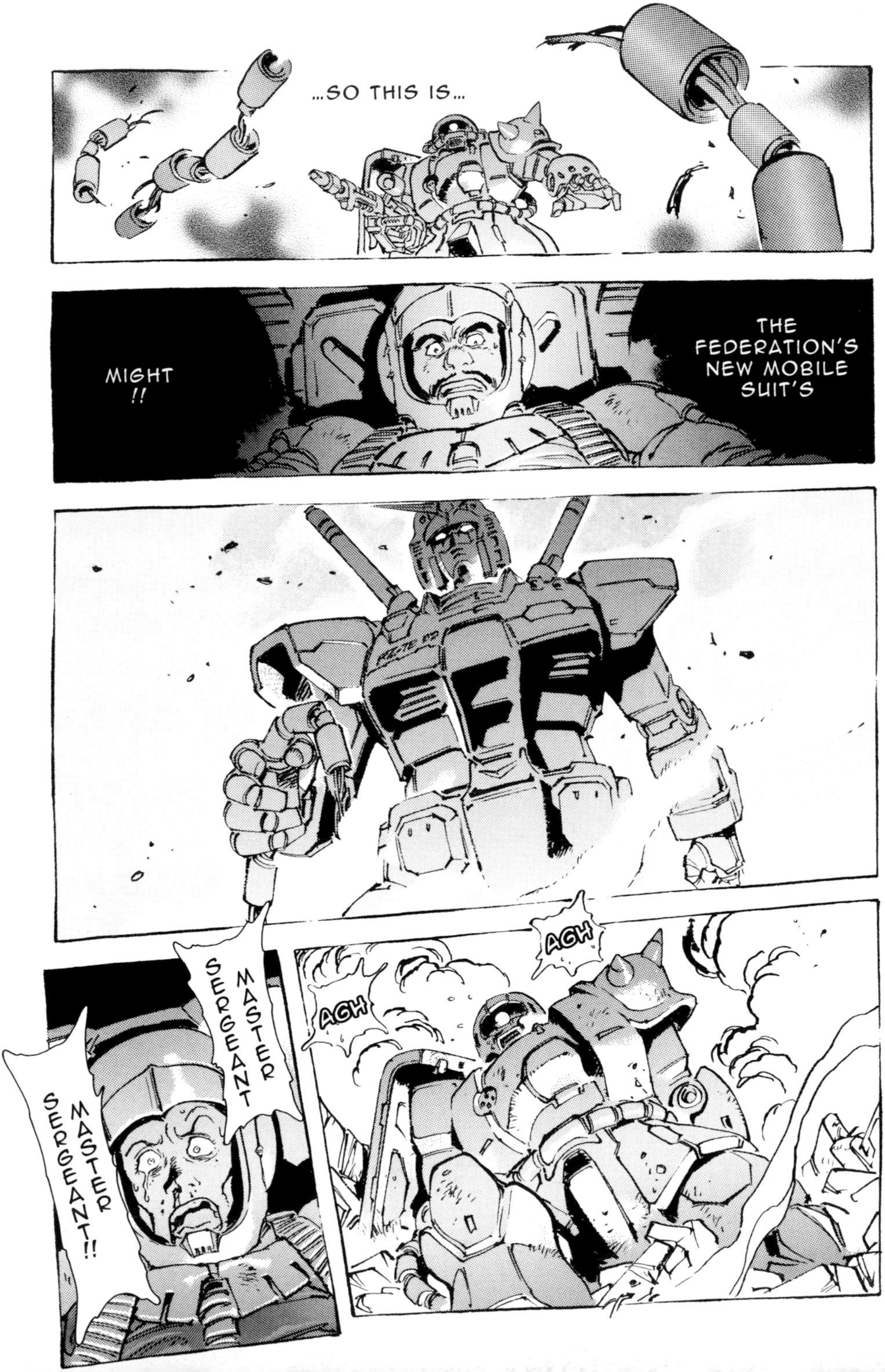
...SO THIS IS...
THE FEDERATION'S NEW MOBILE SUIT'S
MIGHT !!
AGH
AGH
MASTER SERGEANT
MASTER SERGEANT!!

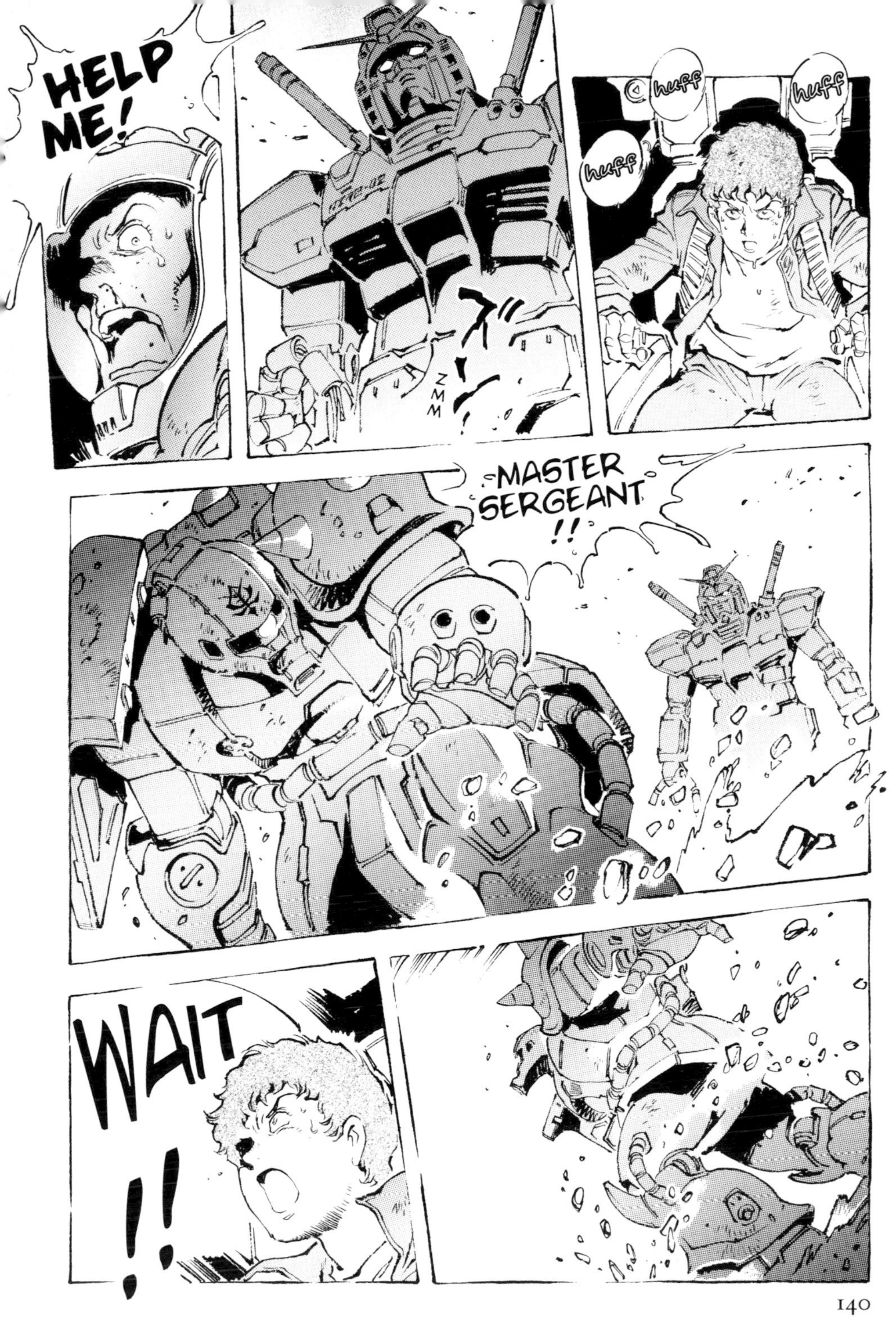
huff
huff
huff
ZMM
HELP ME!
MASTER SERGEANT!!
WAIT!!

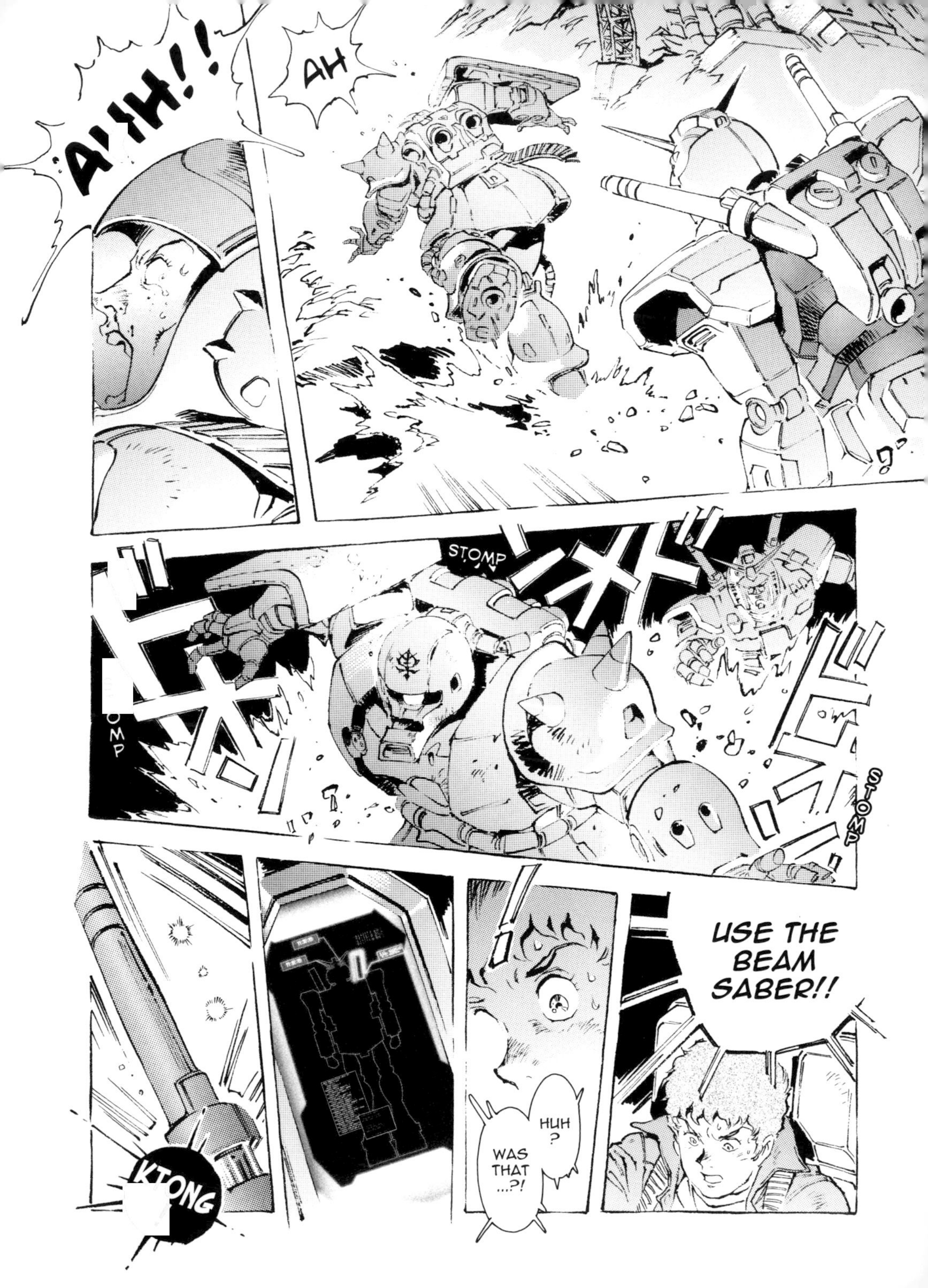
AH
AHH!!
STOMP
STOMP
OMP
USE THE BEAM SABER!!
HUH?
WAS THAT ...?!
KTONG

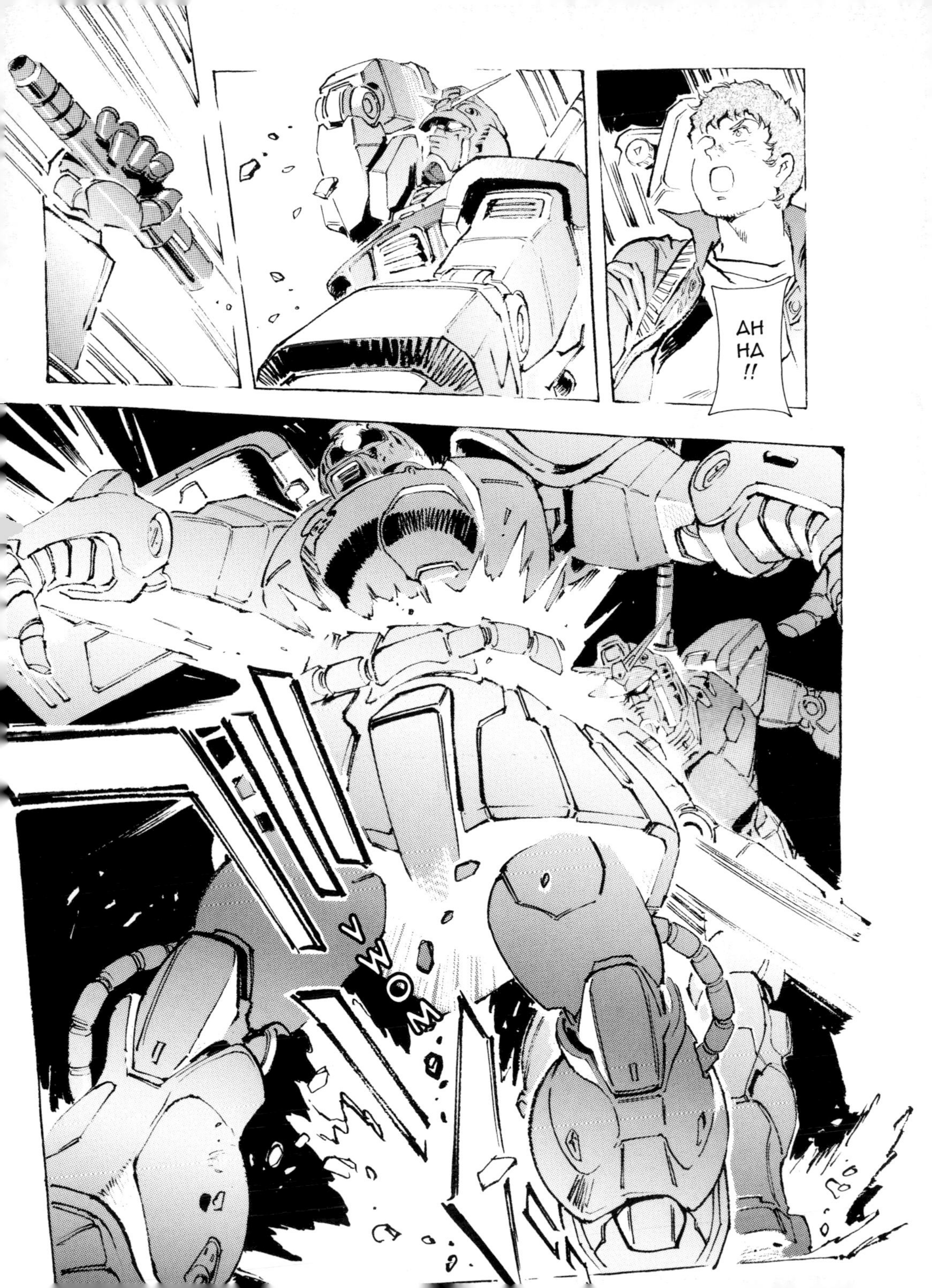
AH HA !!
VWOM

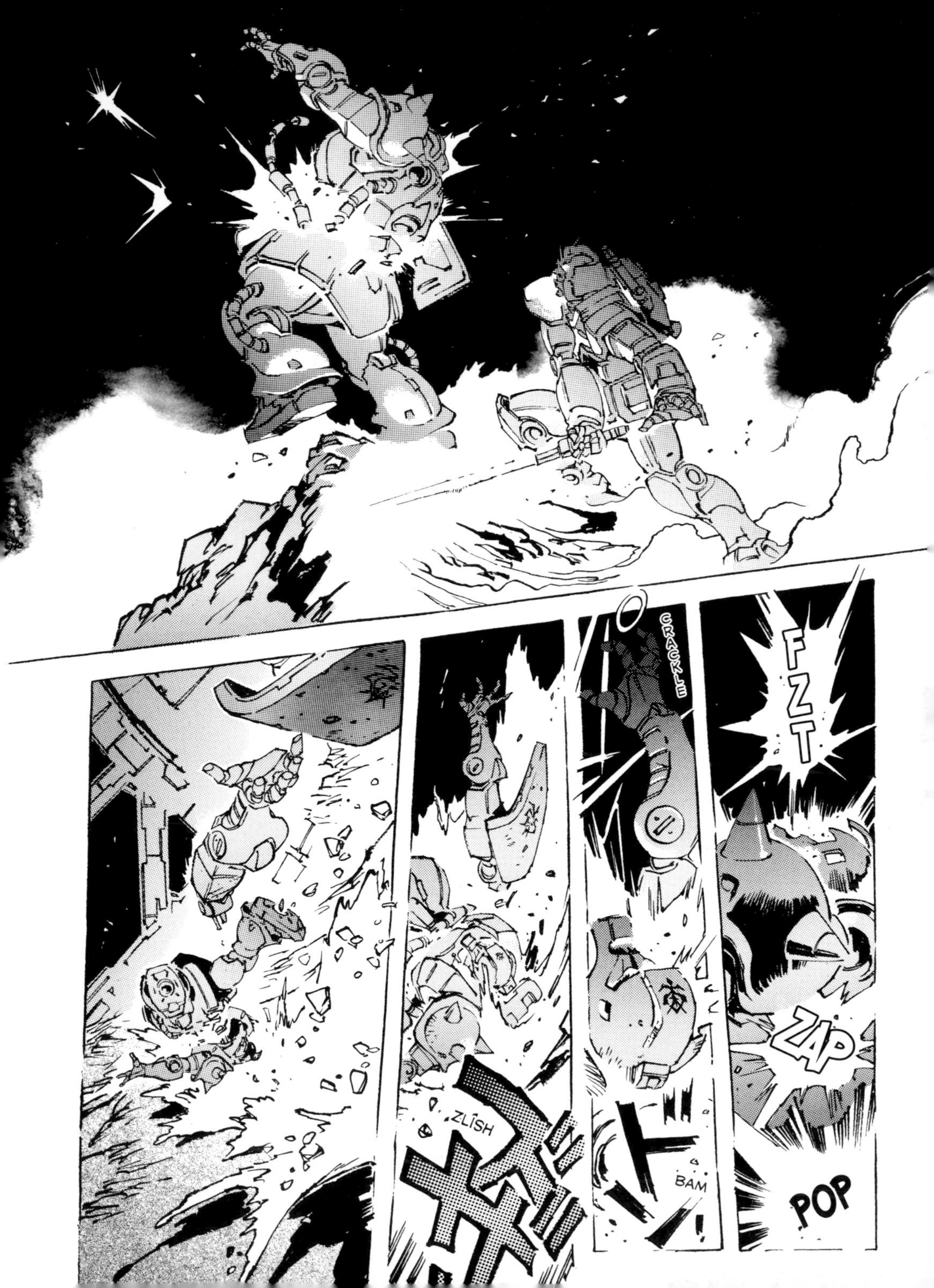
FZT
ZAP
POP
CRACKLE
BAM
ZLISH

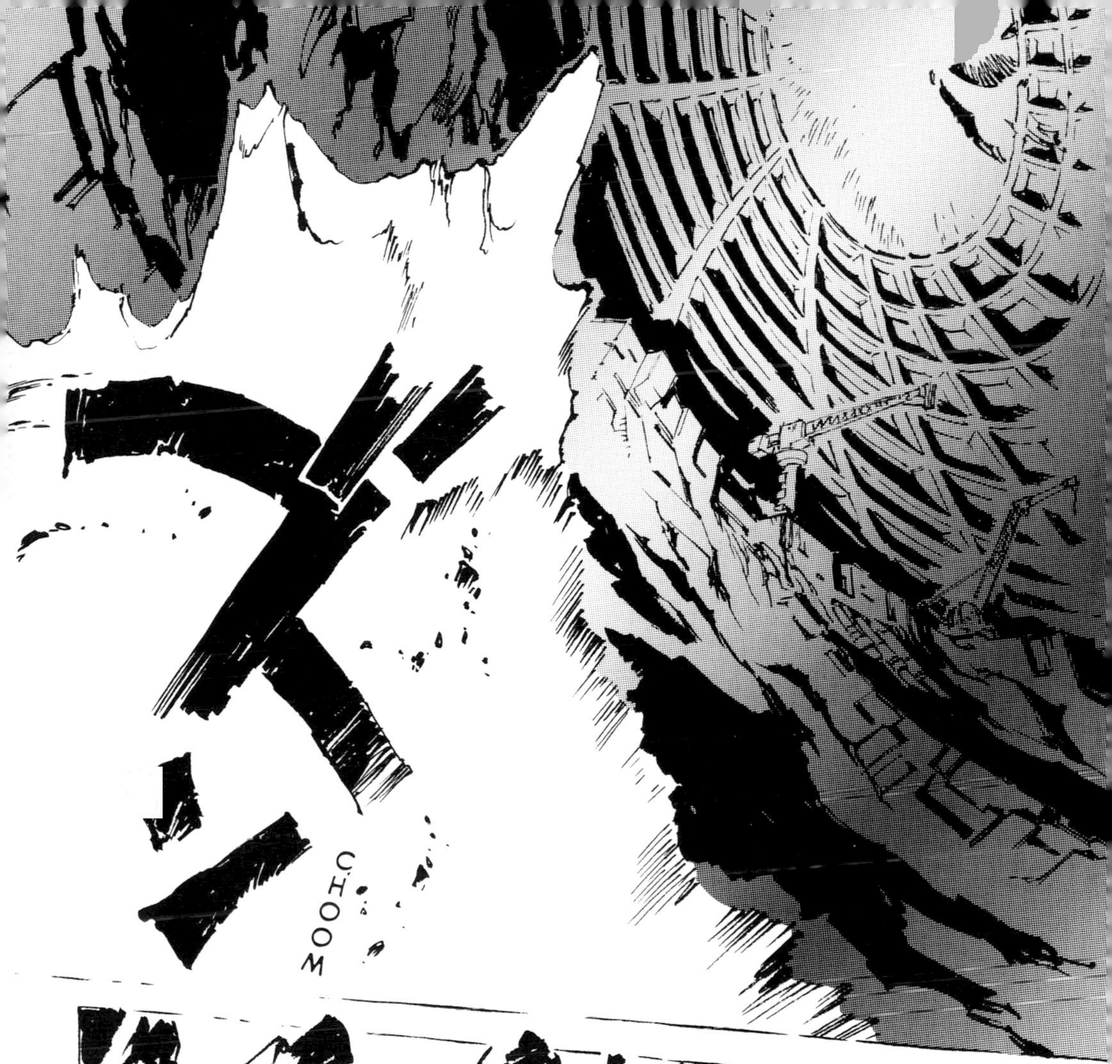
CHOOM
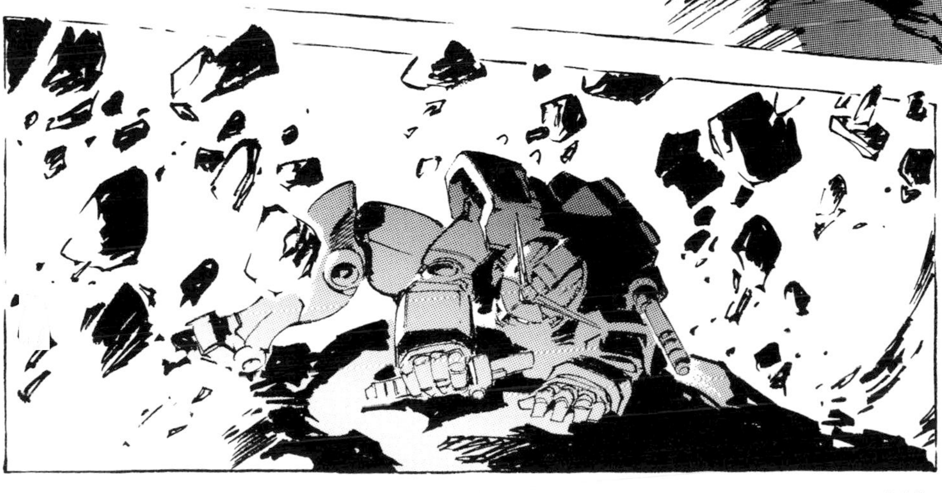

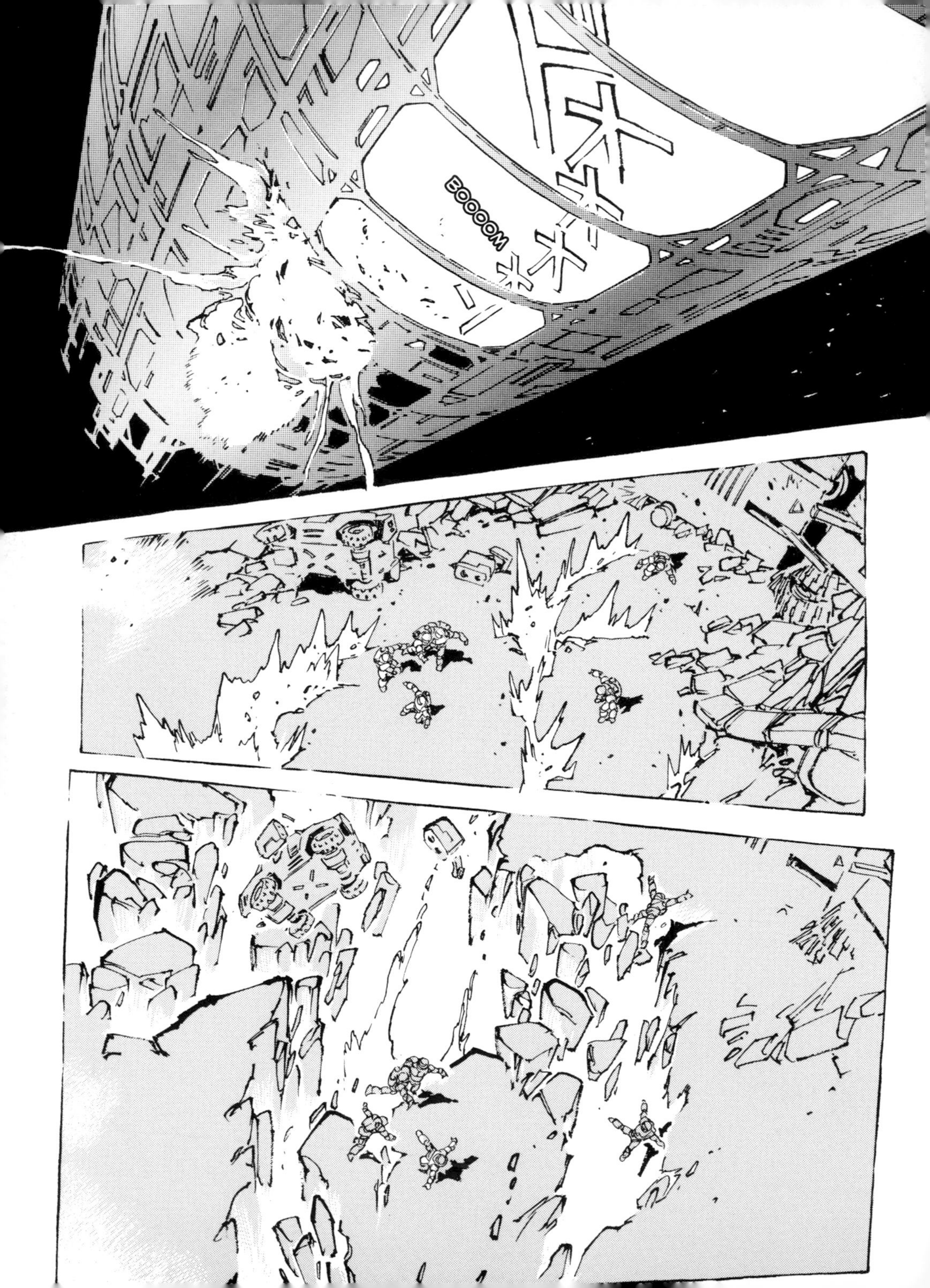
BOOOOM

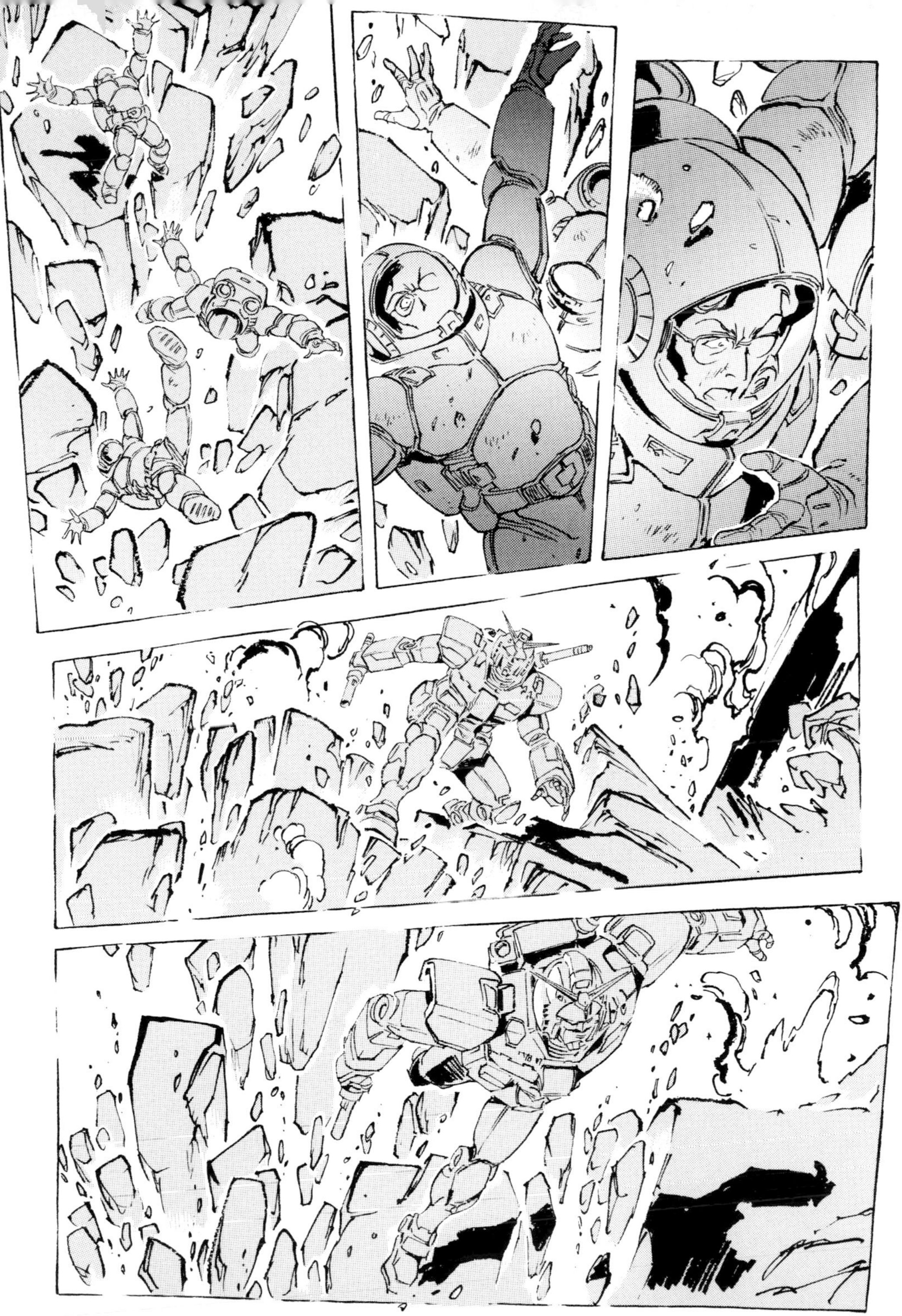

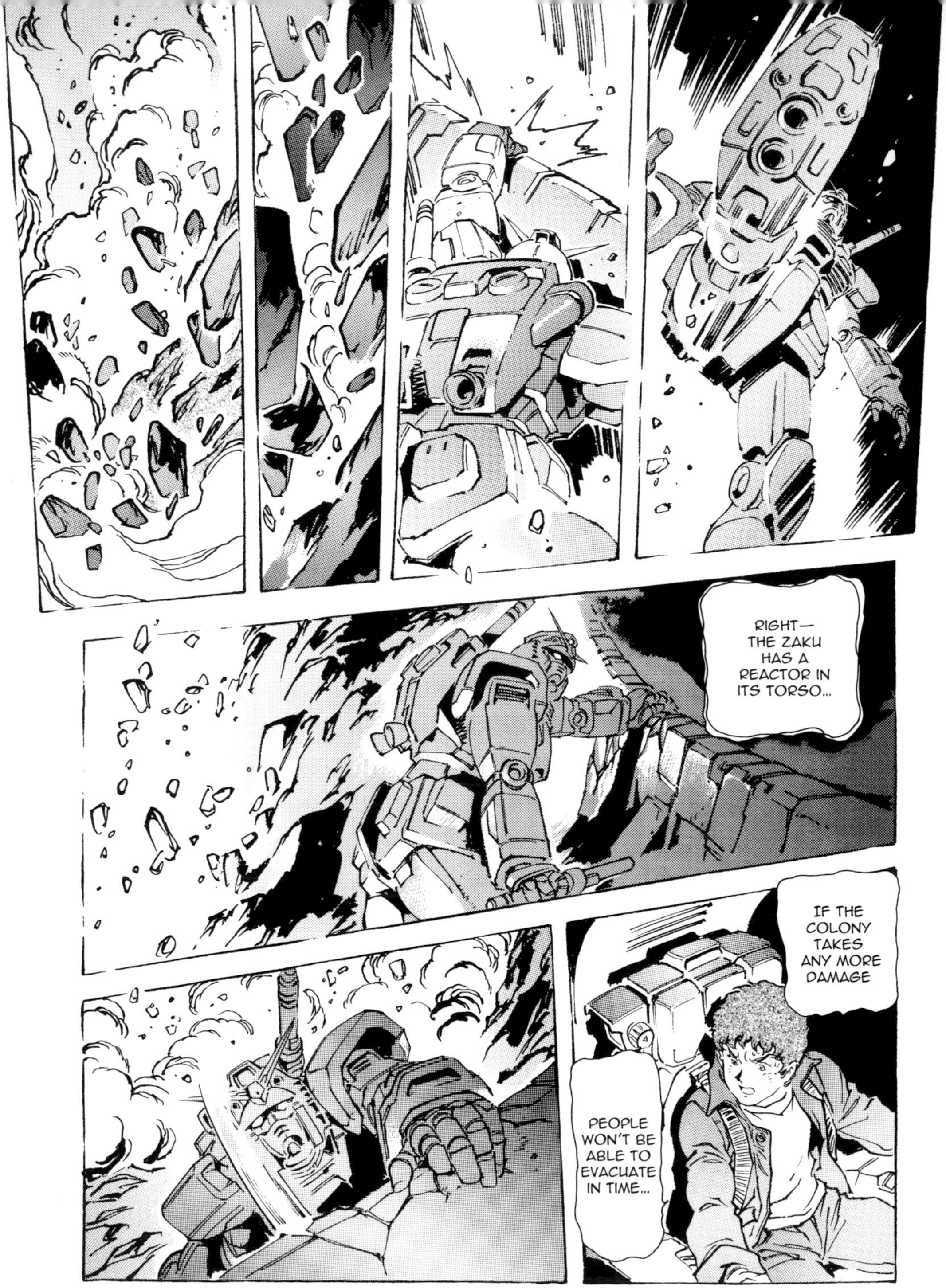
RIGHT— THE ZAKU HAS A REACTOR IN ITS TORSO...
IF THE COLONY TAKES ANY MORE DAMAGE
PEOPLE WON'T BE ABLE TO EVACUATE IN TIME...

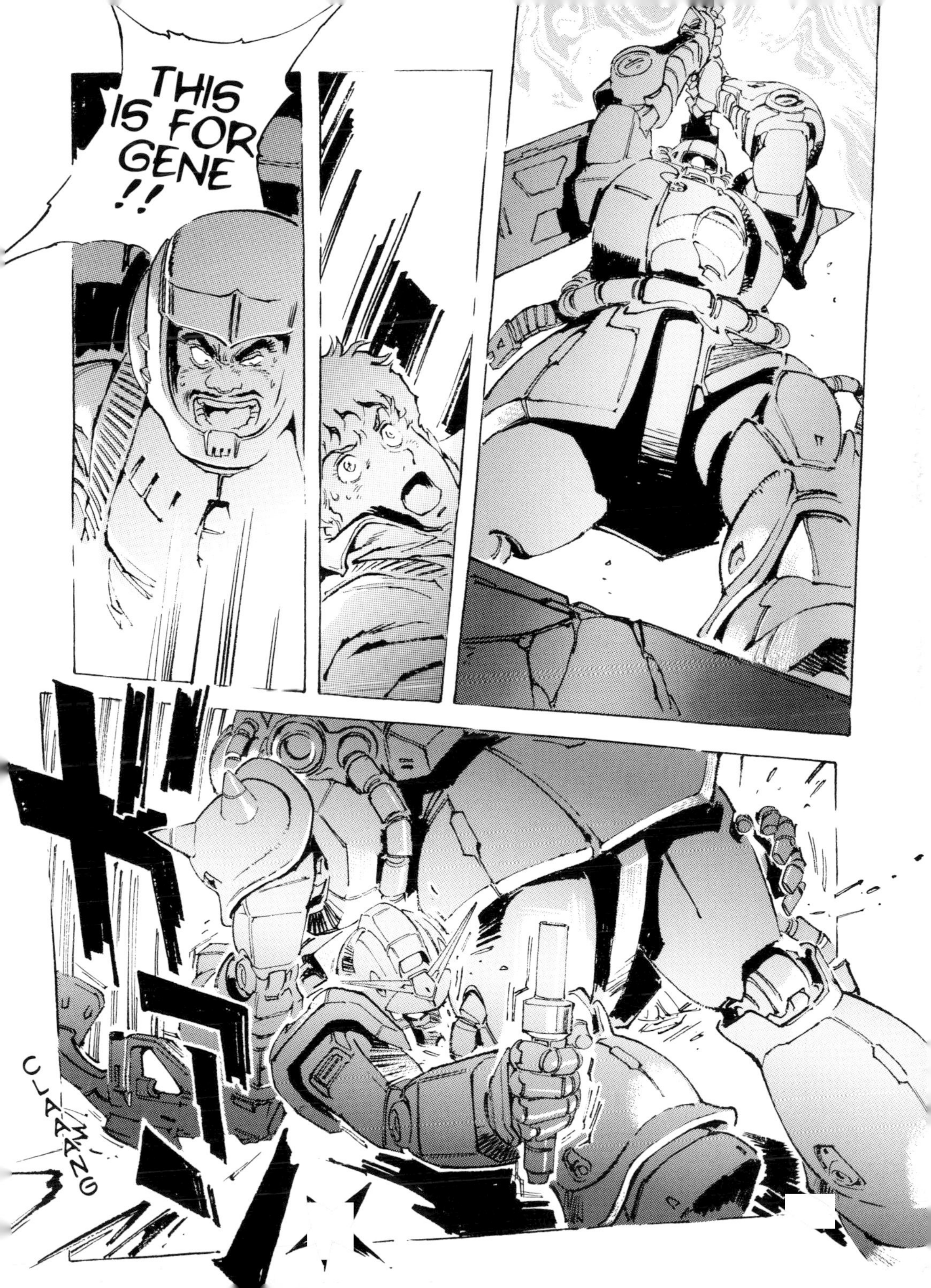
THIS IS FOR GENE !!
CLAAANG

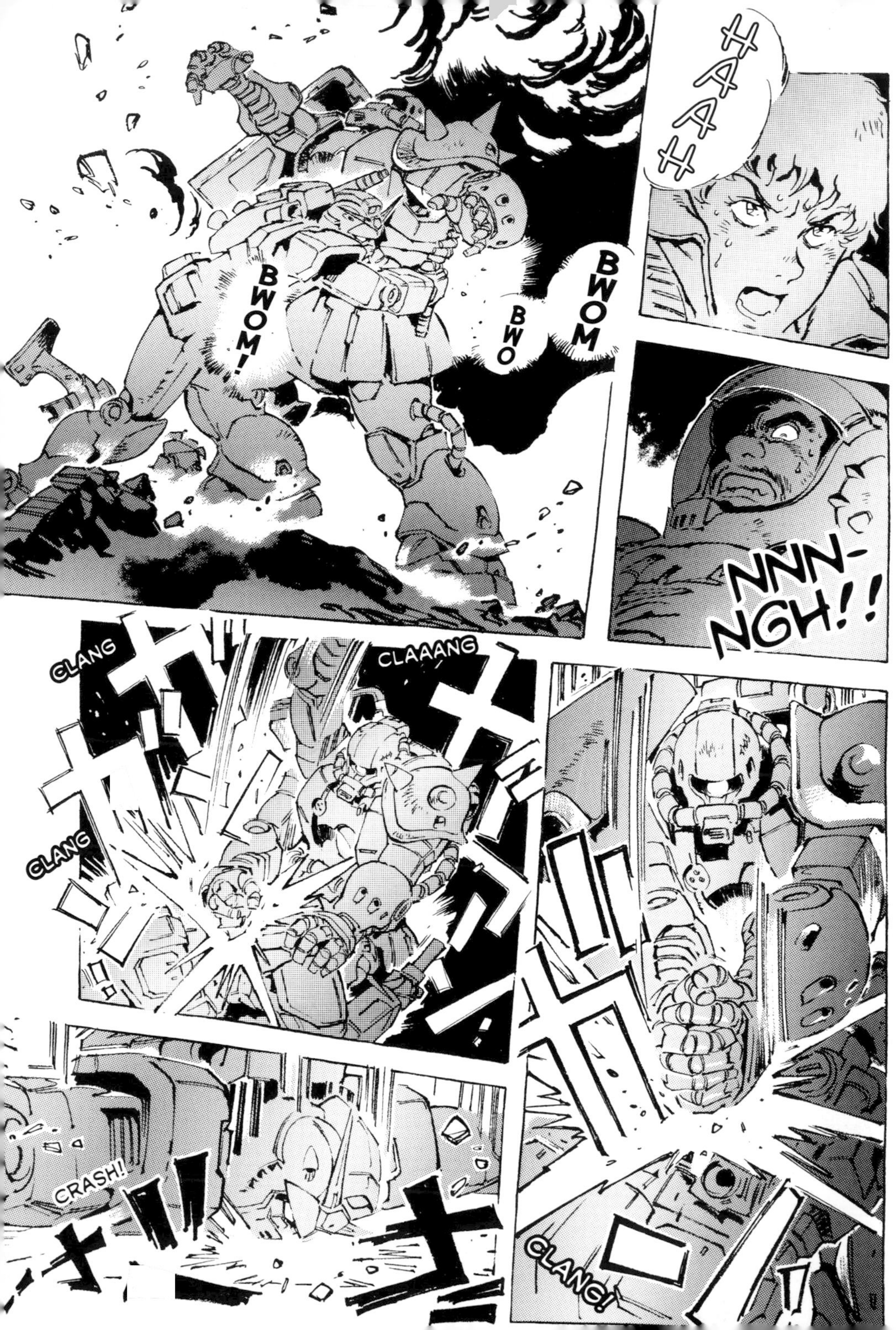
HAAAH
NNNN-NGH!!
BWOM
BWO
BWOM!
CLANG!
CLAAANG
CLANG
CLANG
CRASH!

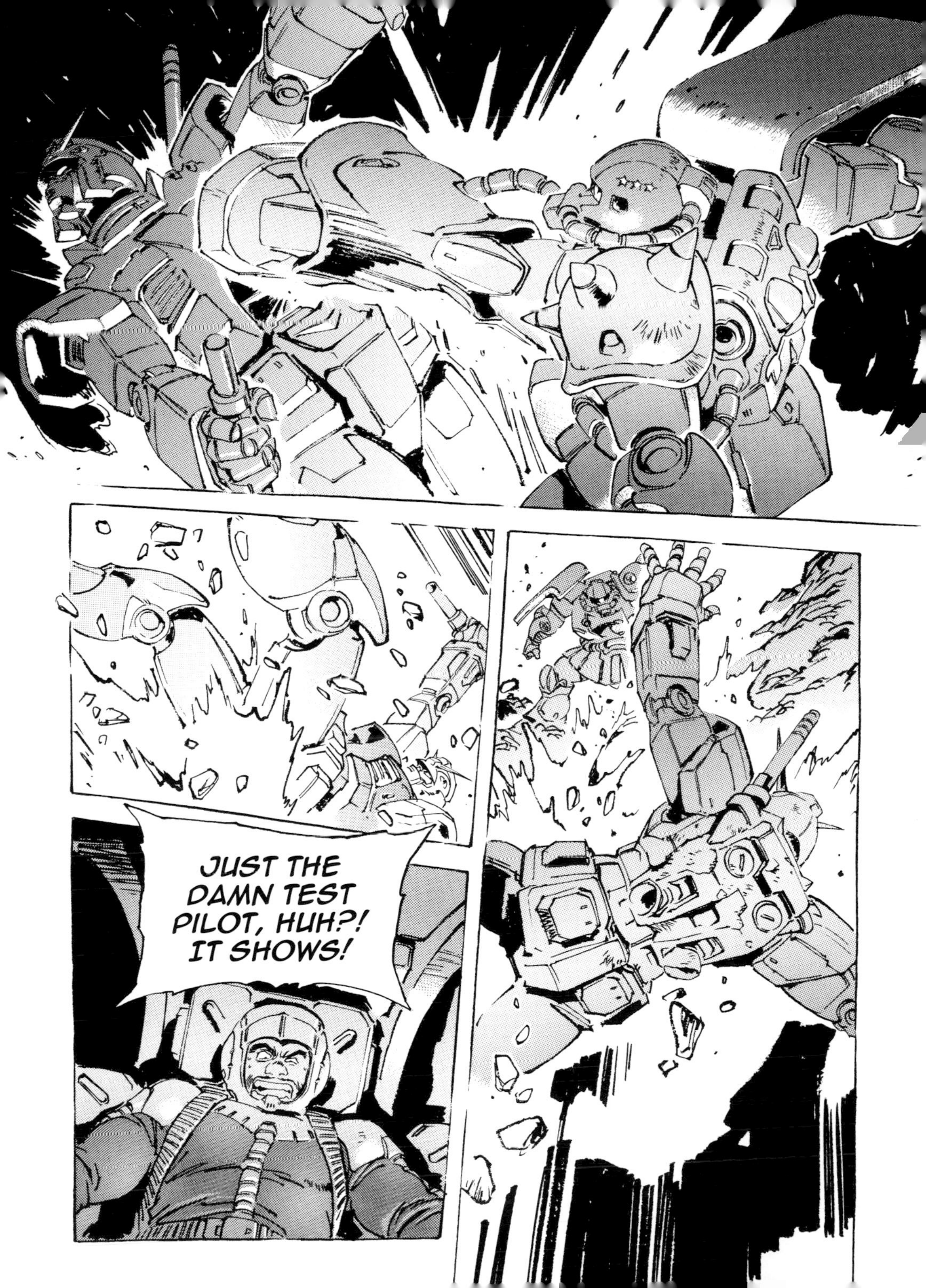
JUST THE DAMN TEST PILOT, HUH?! IT SHOWS!

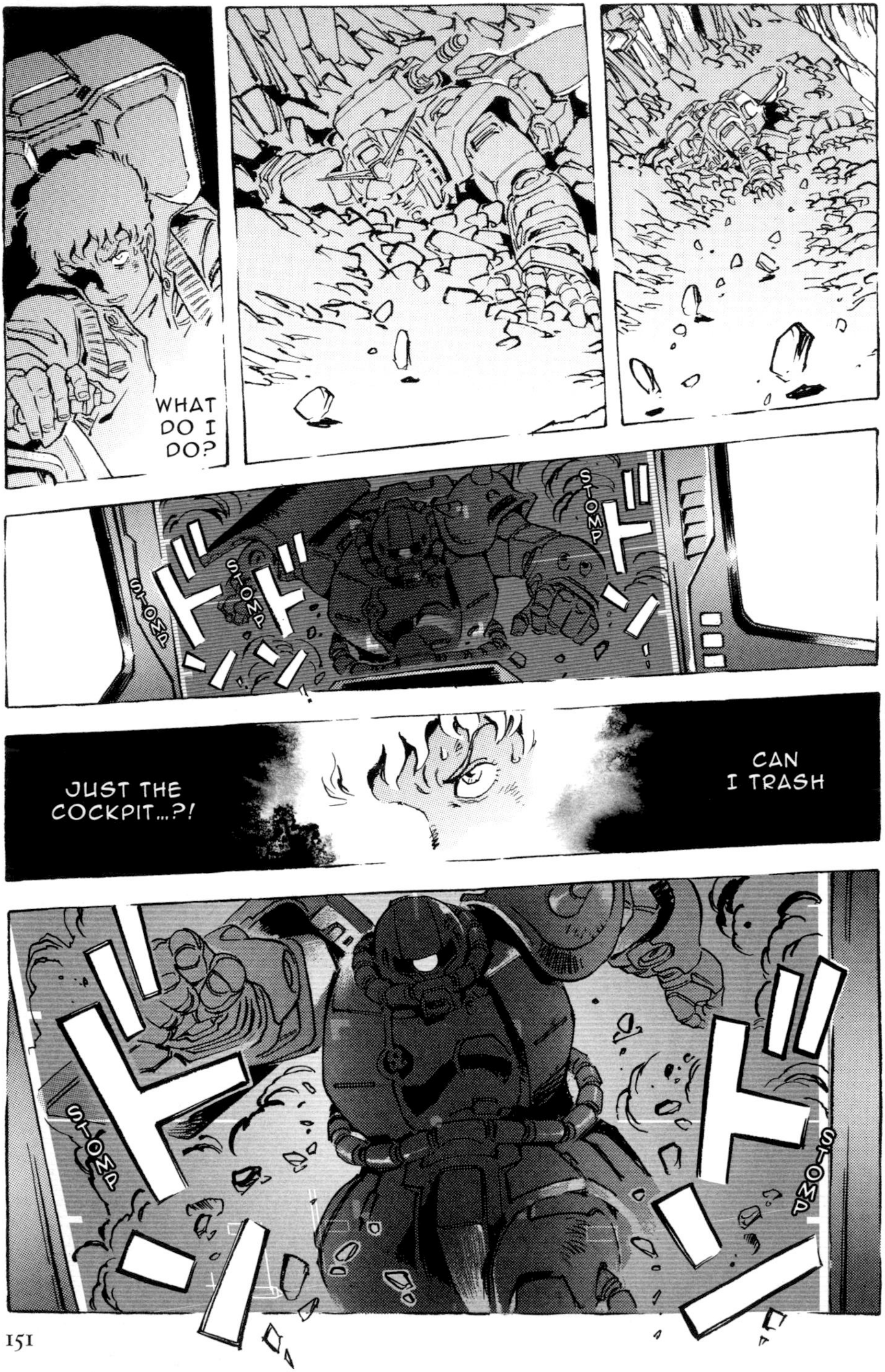
WHAT DO I DO?
STOMP
STOMP
STOMP
CAN I TRASH
JUST THE COCKPIT...?!
STOMP
STOMP

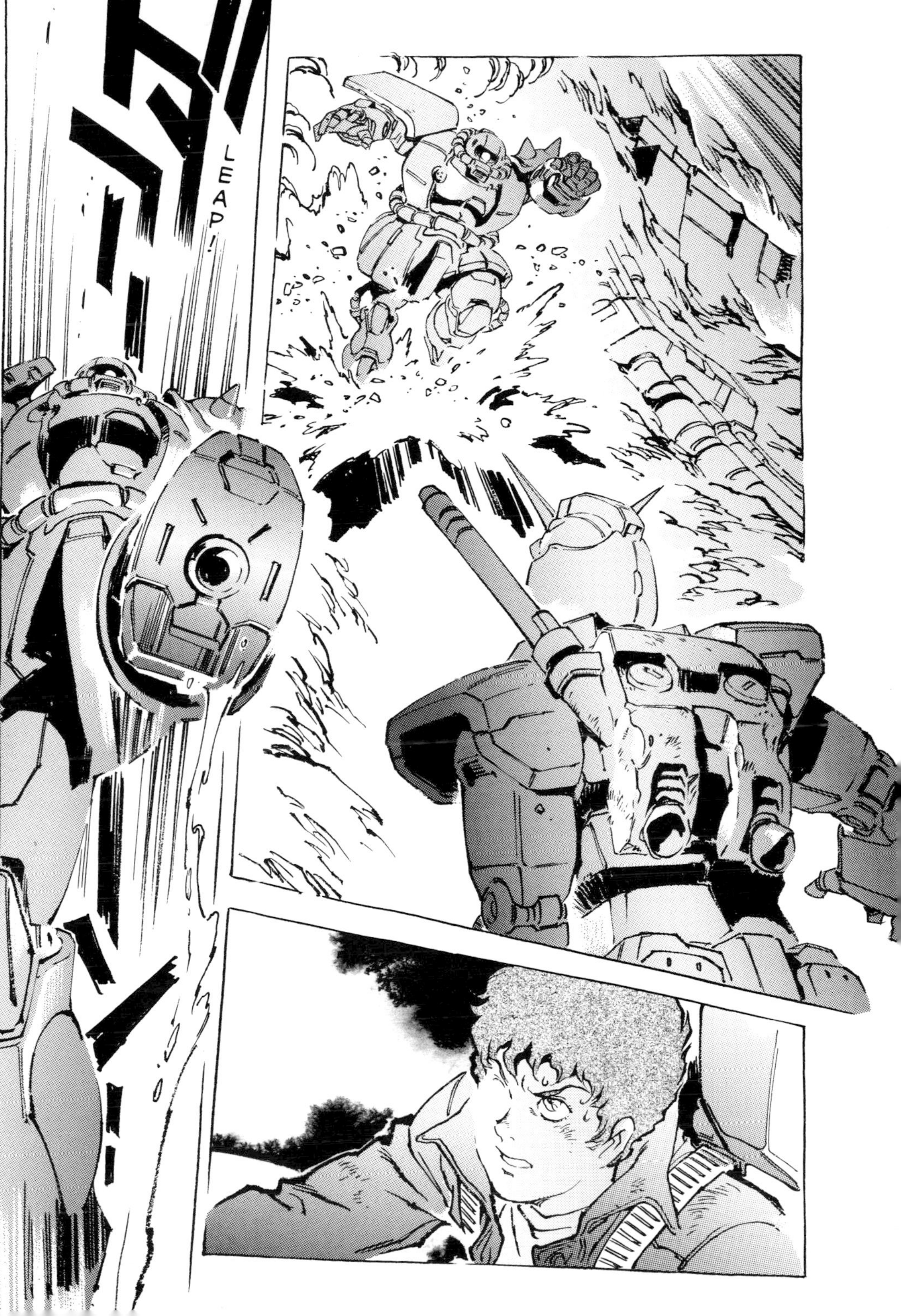
LEAP!

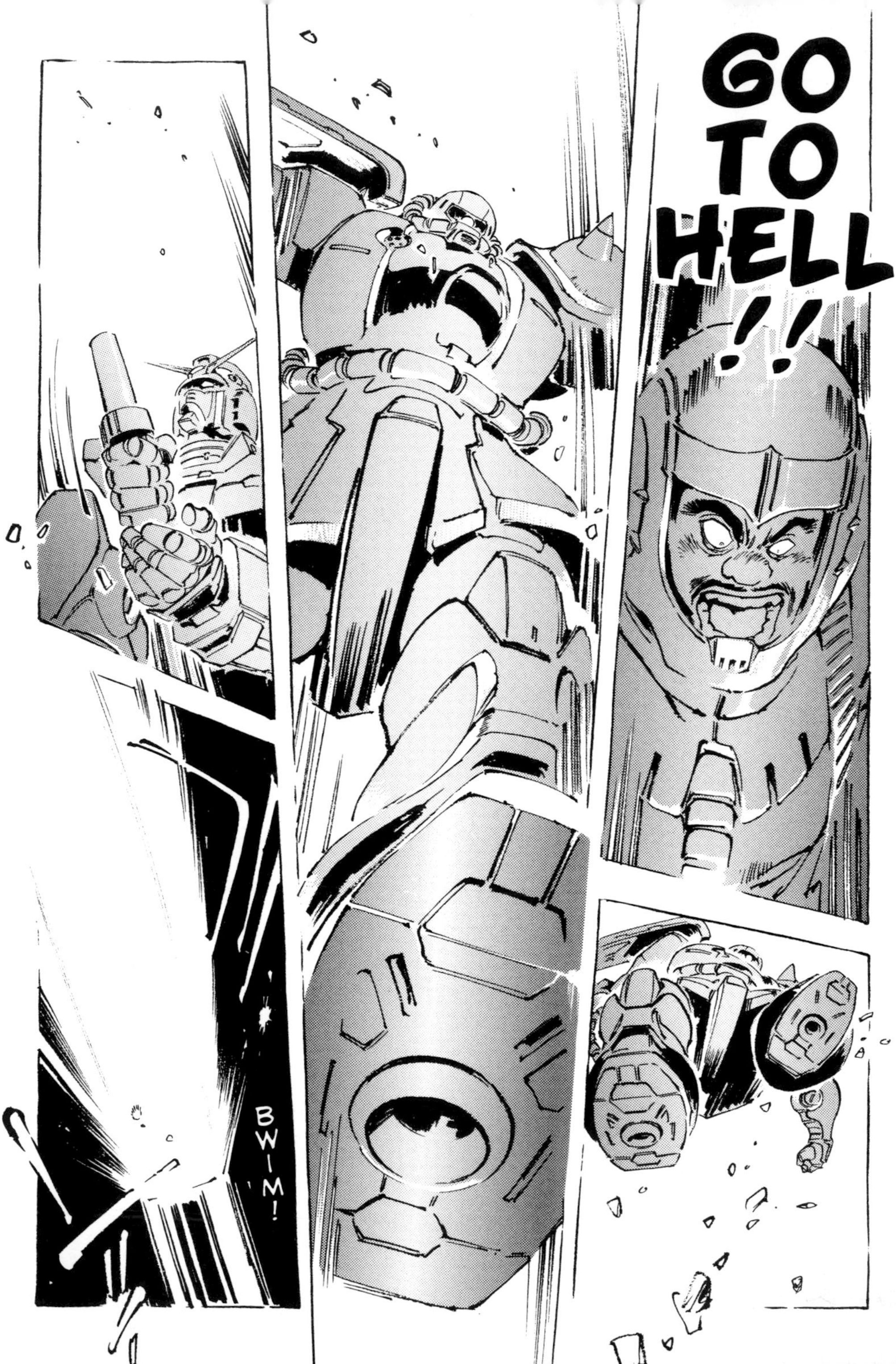
GO TO HELL!!
BWIM!

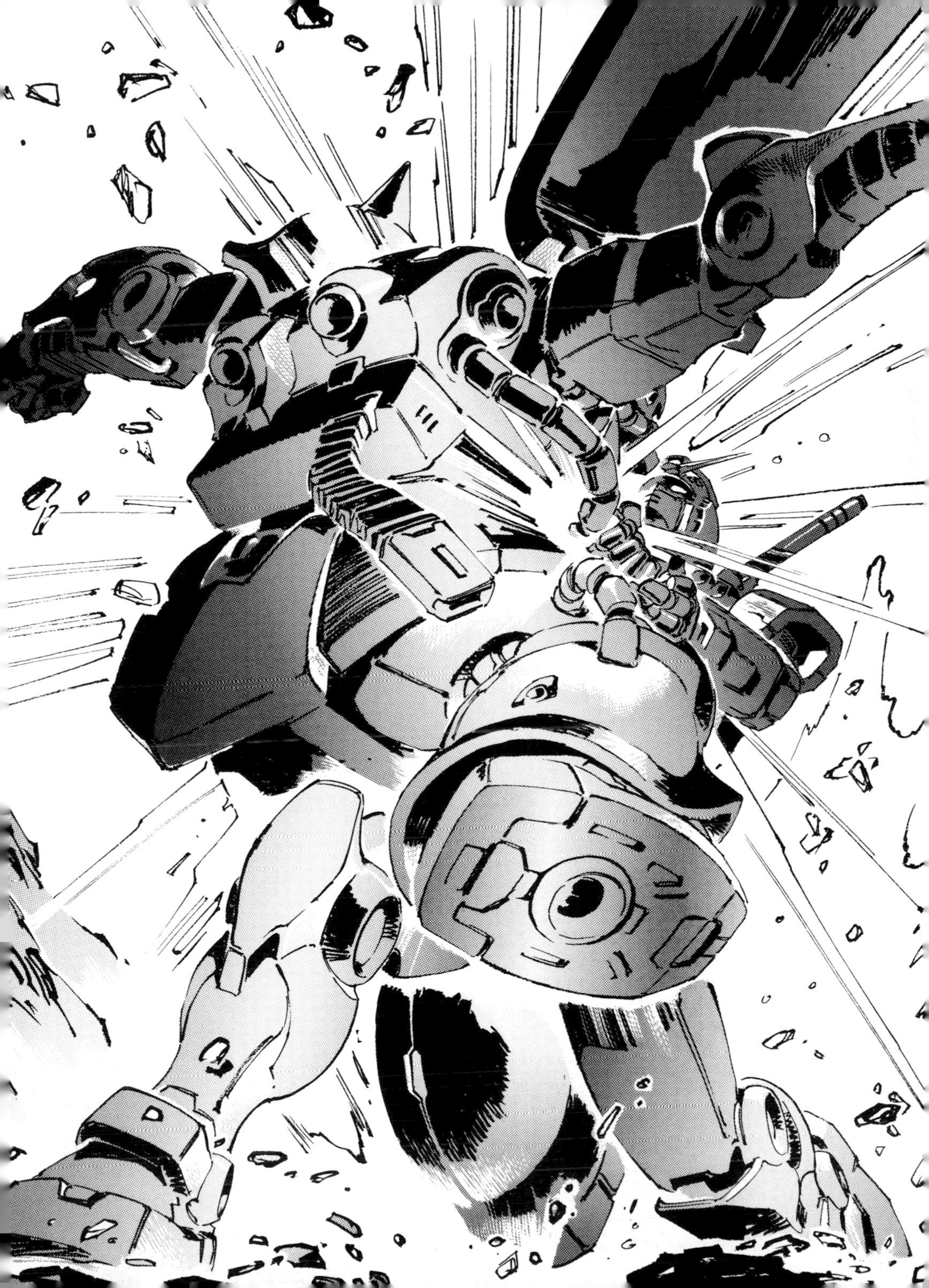

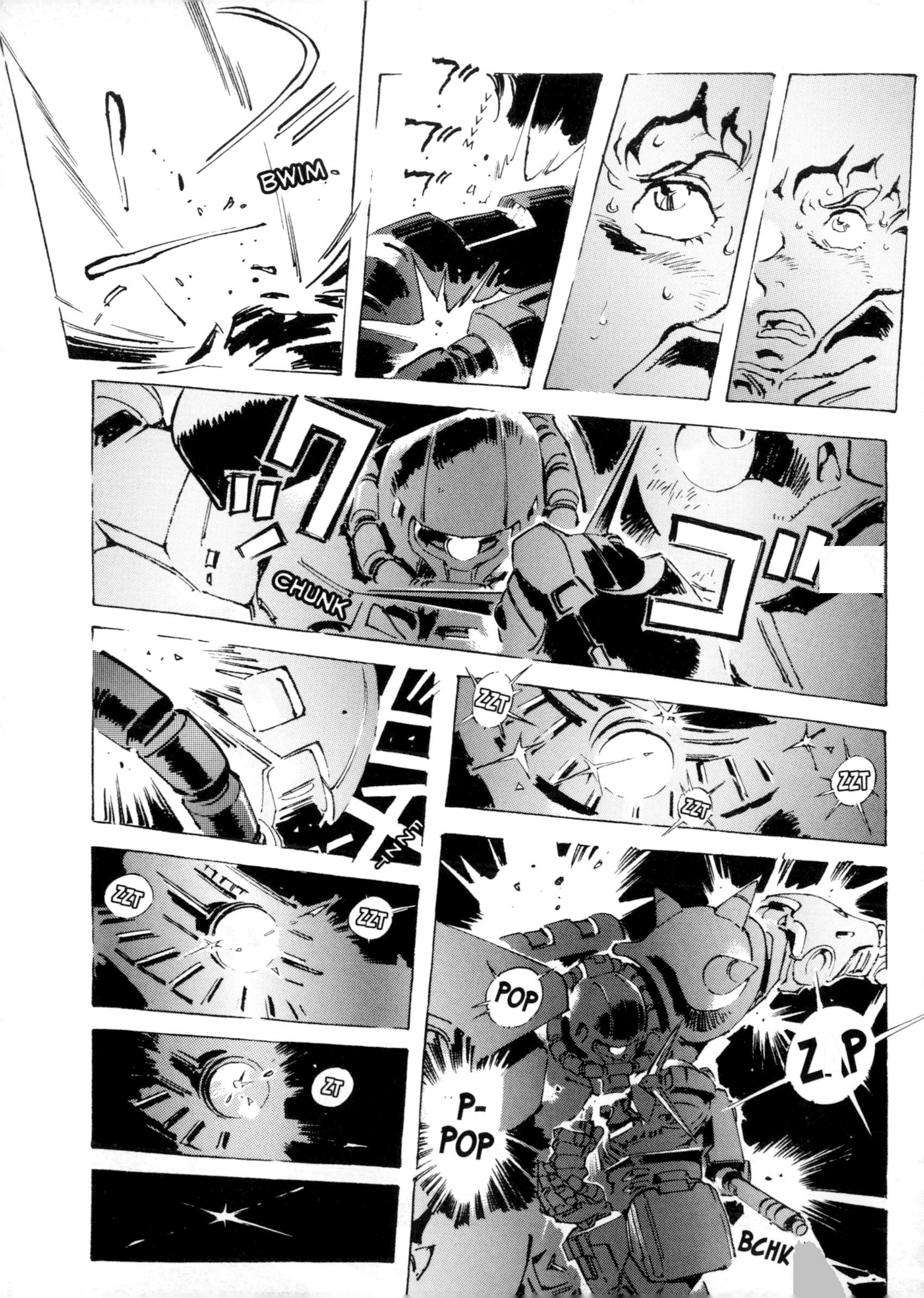
BWIM
CHUNK
ZZT
ZZT
ZZT
POP
Z P
P-POP
BCHK
ZZT
ZZT
ZT

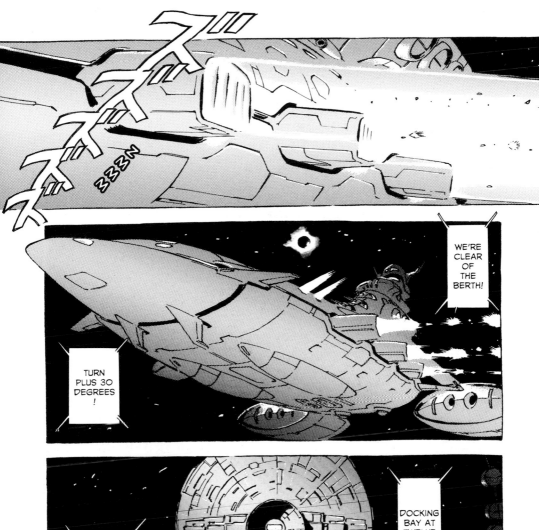

WE'RE CLEAR OF THE BERTH!

TURN PLUS 30 DEGREES !

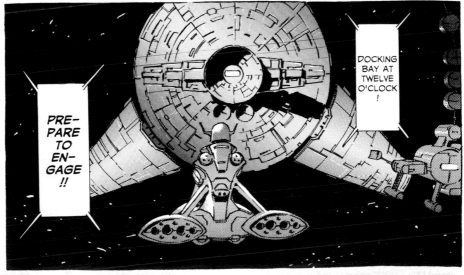

DOCKING BAY AT TWELVE O'CLOCK !

PRE-PARE TO EN-GAGE !!

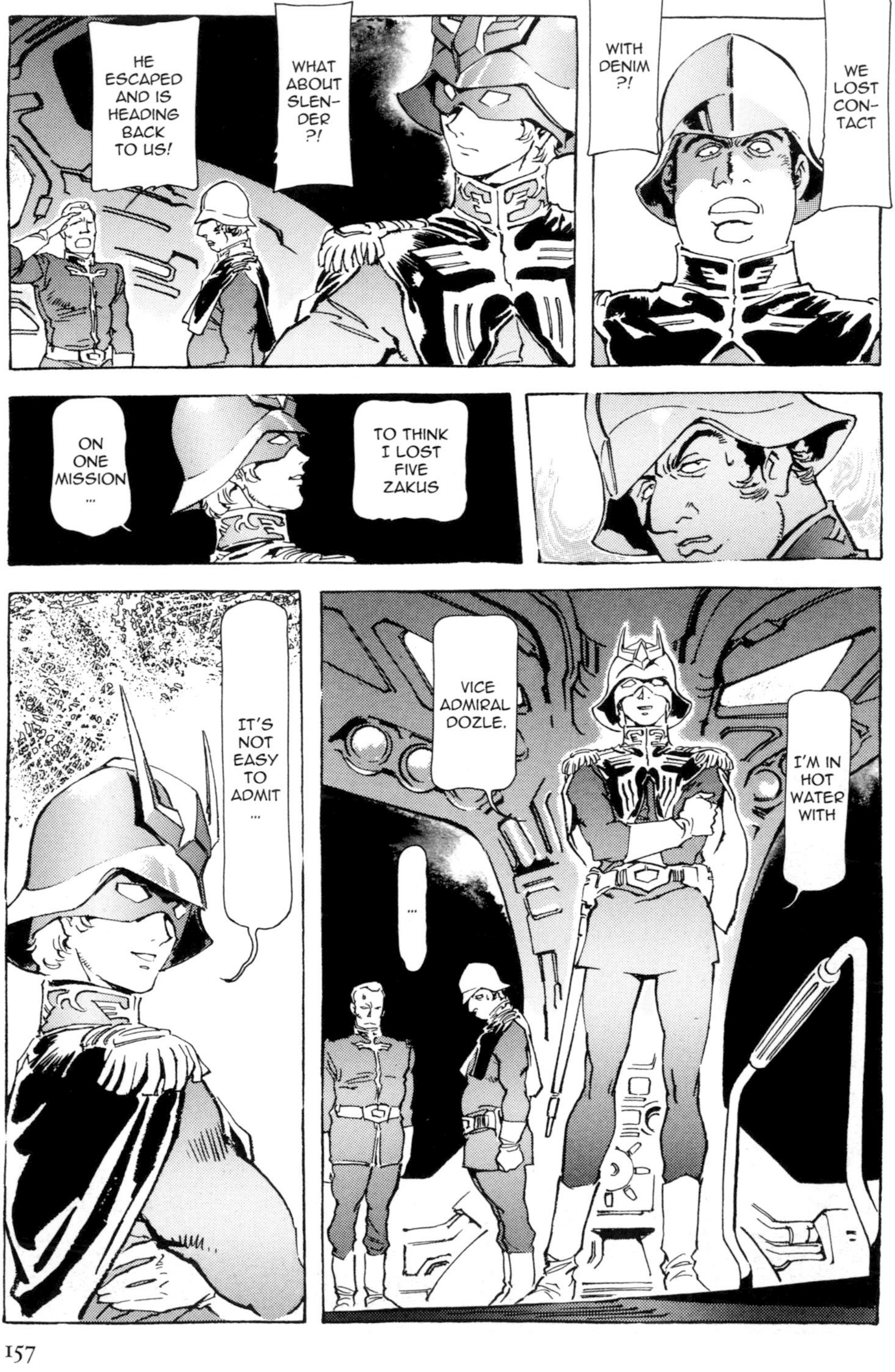
WE LOST CONTACT
WITH DENIM ?!
WHAT ABOUT SLENDER ?!
HE ESCAPED AND IS HEADING BACK TO US!
TO THINK I LOST FIVE ZAKUS
ON ONE MISSION ...
I'M IN HOT WATER WITH
VICE ADMIRAL DOZLE.
...
IT'S NOT EASY TO ADMIT ...

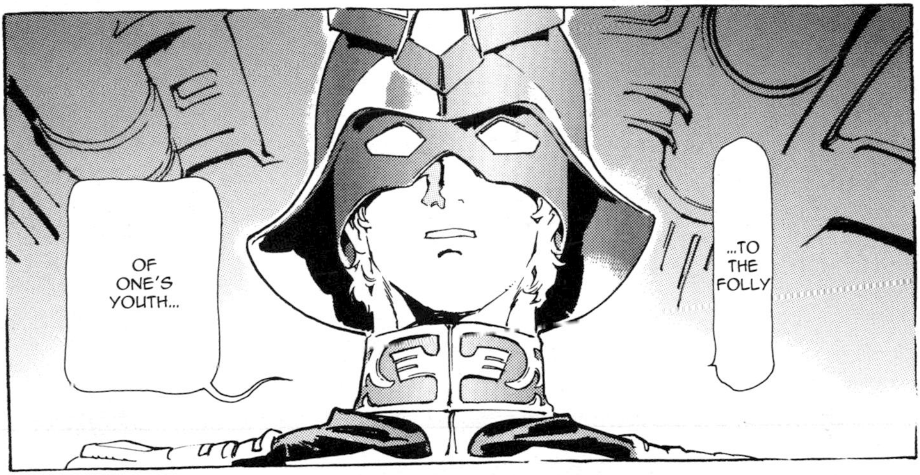
...TO THE FOLLY
OF ONE'S YOUTH...

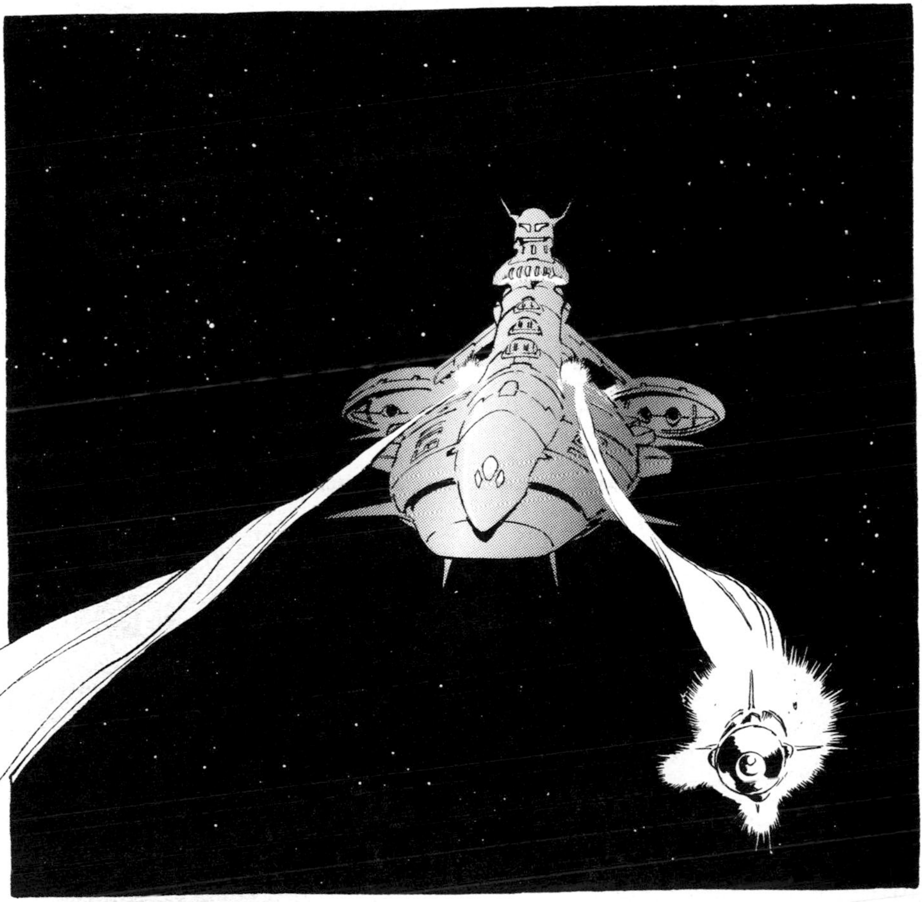

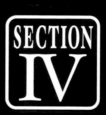

SECTION IV

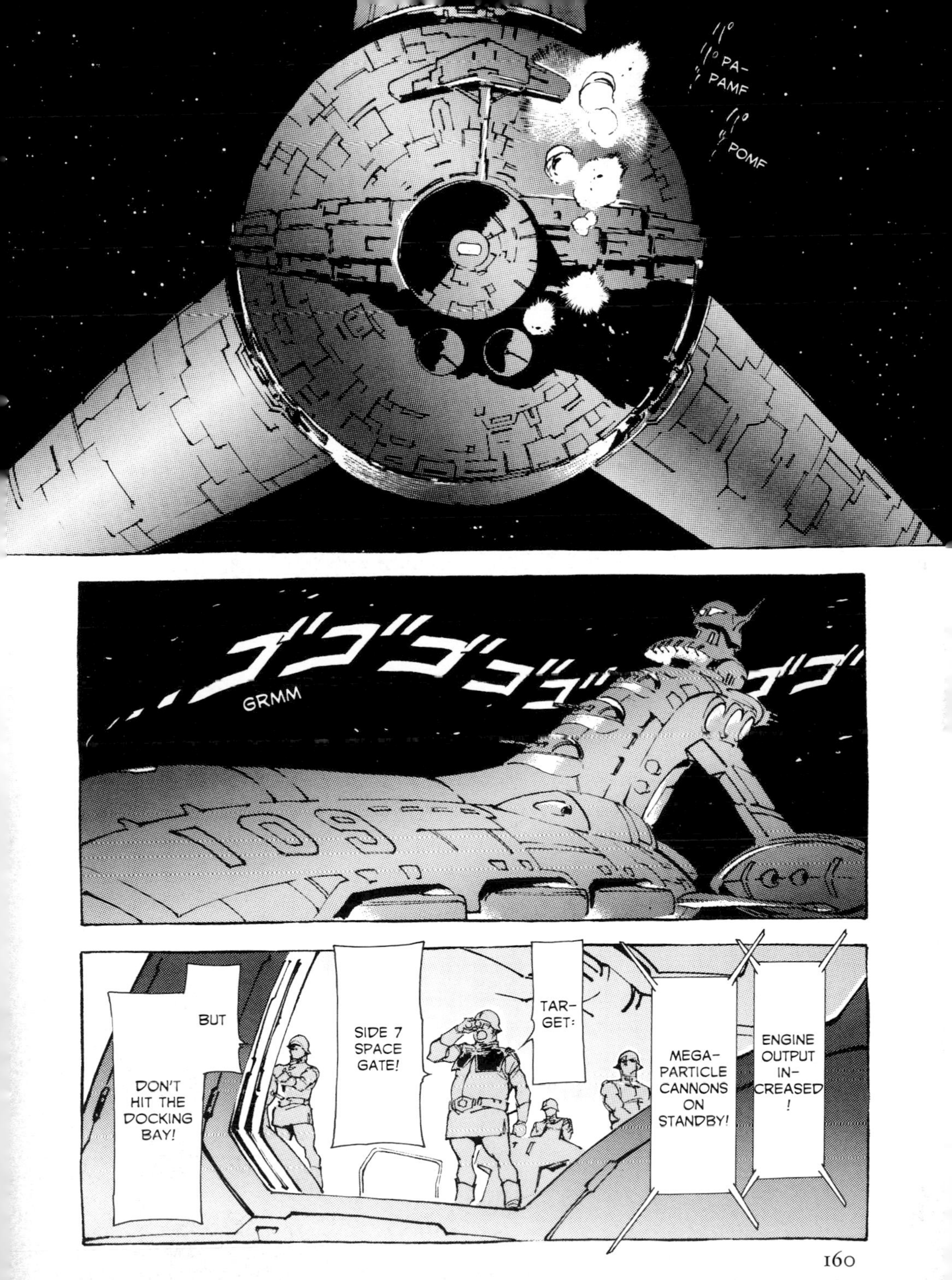
PA-
PAMF
POMF
GRMM
ENGINE OUTPUT IN-CREASED!
MEGA-PARTICLE CANNONS ON STANDBY!
TARGET:
SIDE 7 SPACE GATE!
BUT
DON'T HIT THE DOCKING BAY!

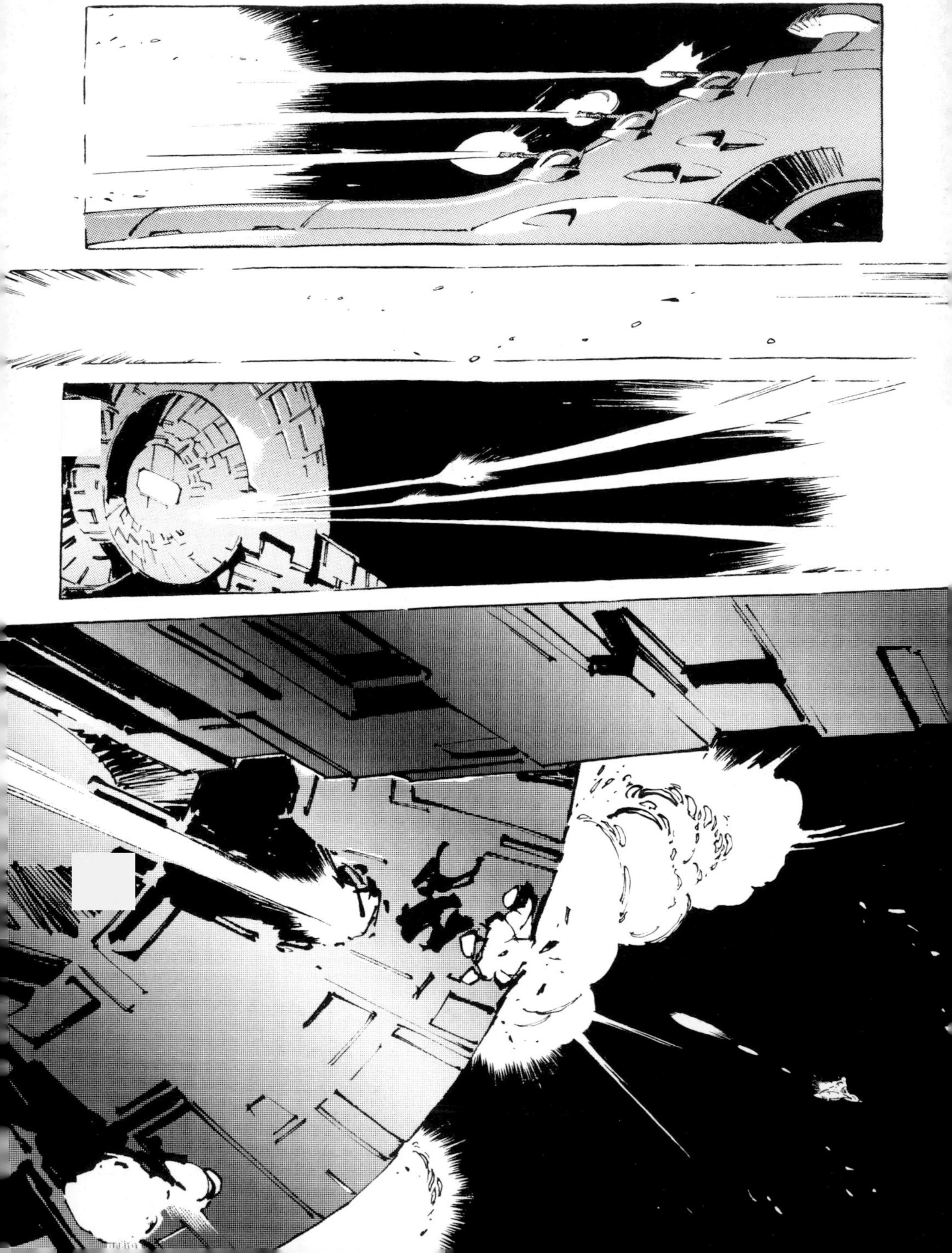

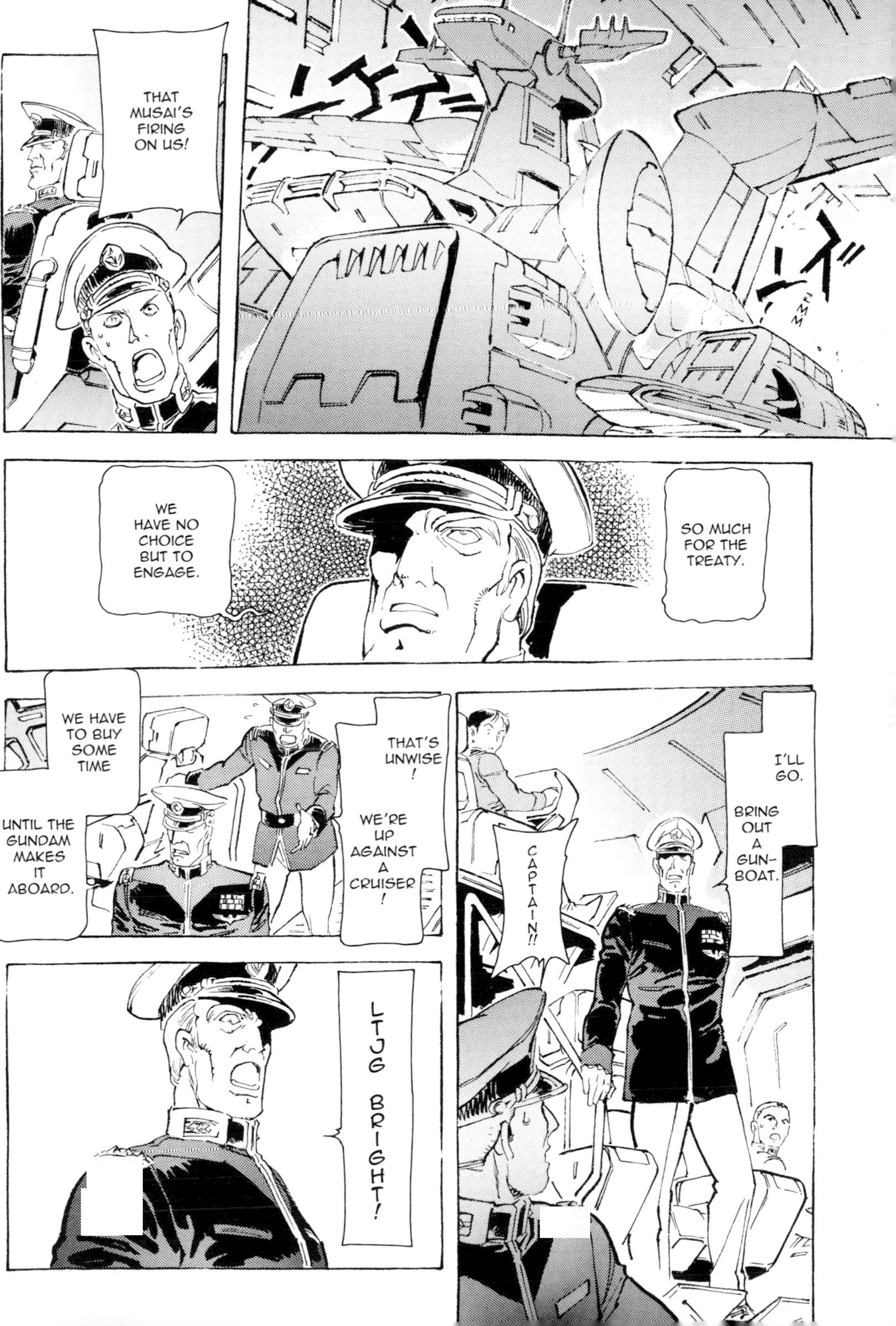
THAT MUSAI'S FIRING ON US!
SO MUCH FOR THE TREATY.
WE HAVE NO CHOICE BUT TO ENGAGE.
I'LL GO.
BRING OUT A GUN-BOAT.
CAPTAIN!!
THAT'S UNWISE!
WE'RE UP AGAINST A CRUISER!
WE HAVE TO BUY SOME TIME
UNTIL THE GUNDAM MAKES IT ABOARD.
LTJG BRIGHT!

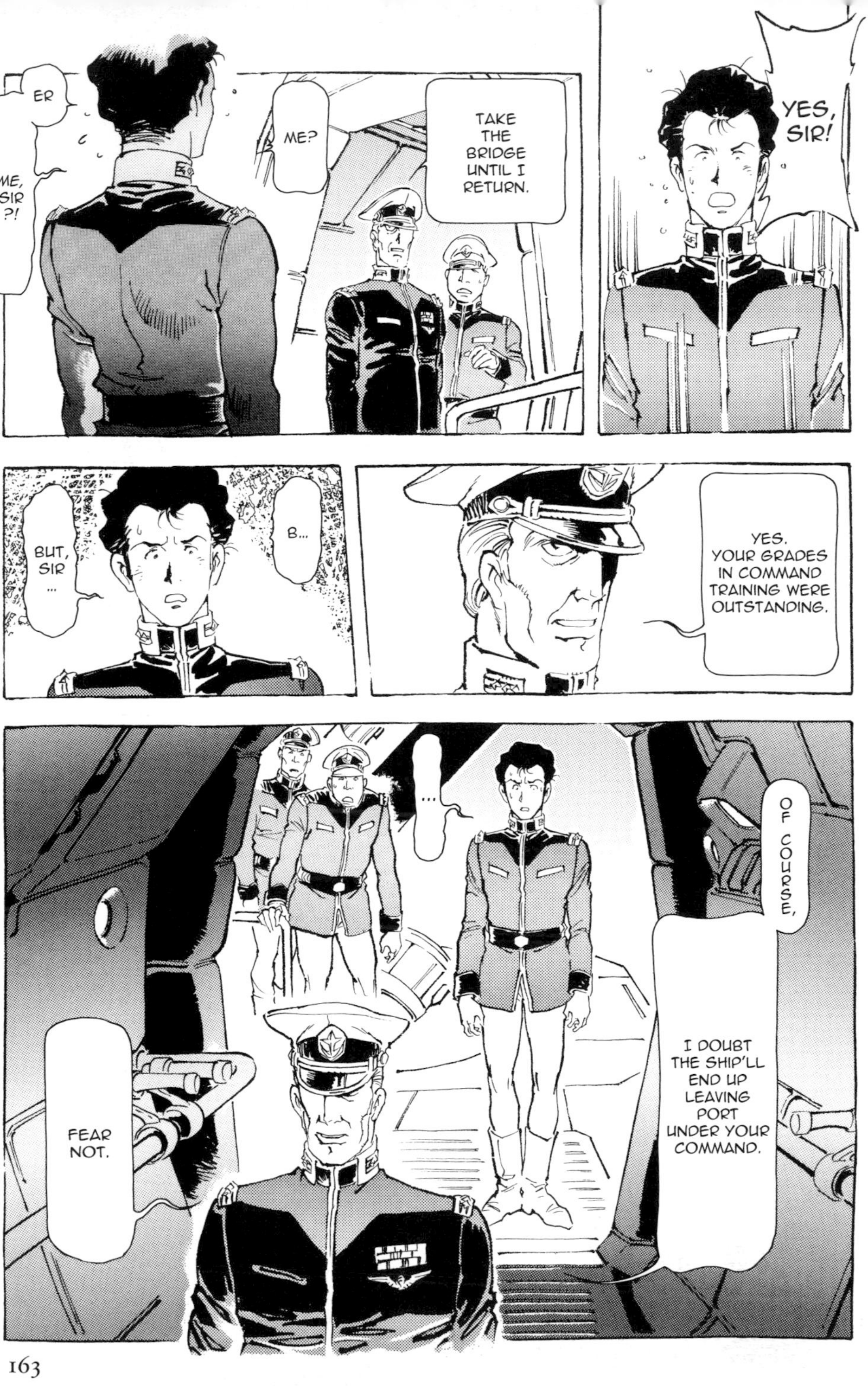
YES, SIR!
TAKE THE BRIDGE UNTIL I RETURN.
ME?
ER
ME, SIR ?!
YES. YOUR GRADES IN COMMAND TRAINING WERE OUTSTANDING.
B...
BUT, SIR ...
OF COURSE,
...
I DOUBT THE SHIP'LL END UP LEAVING PORT UNDER YOUR COMMAND.
FEAR NOT.

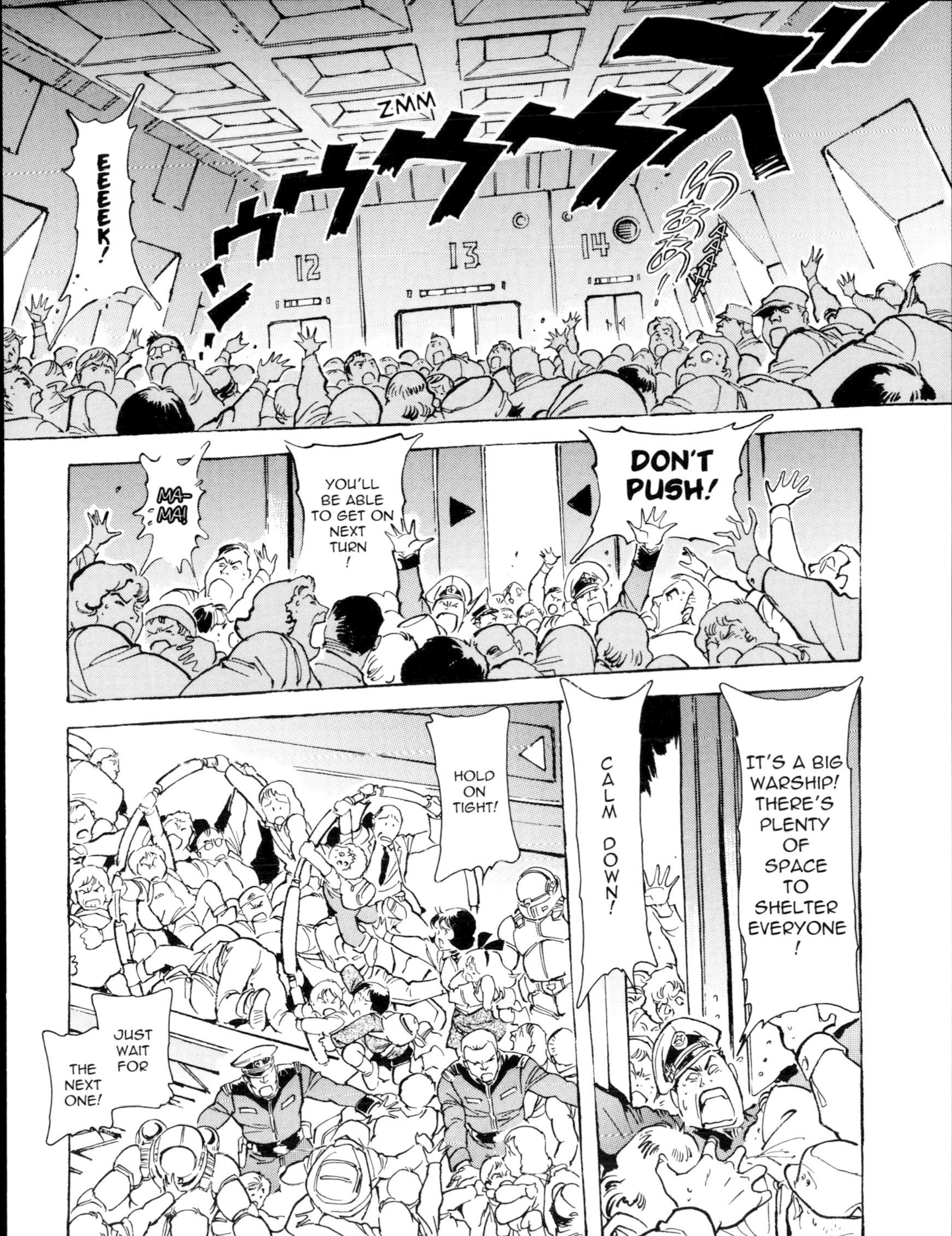
ズウウウウン
ZMM
わあああ!
AAAAH!
EEEEK!
DON'T PUSH!
YOU'LL BE ABLE TO GET ON NEXT TURN!
MA-MA!
IT'S A BIG WARSHIP! THERE'S PLENTY OF SPACE TO SHELTER EVERYONE!
CALM DOWN!
HOLD ON TIGHT!
JUST WAIT FOR THE NEXT ONE!

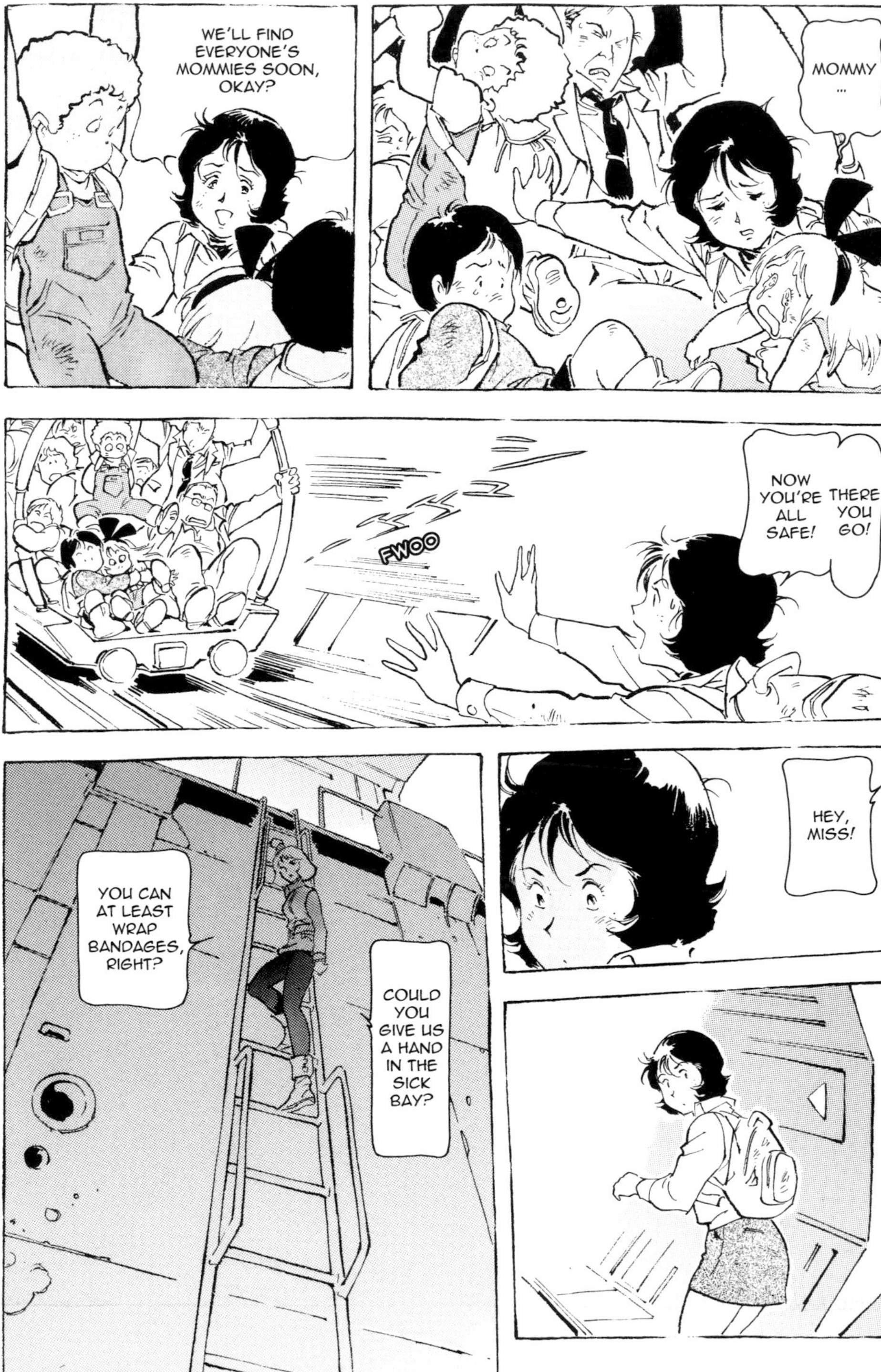
MOMMY ...
WE'LL FIND EVERYONE'S MOMMIES SOON, OKAY?
NOW YOU'RE ALL SAFE! THERE YOU GO!
FWOO
HEY, MISS!
COULD YOU GIVE US A HAND IN THE SICK BAY?
YOU CAN AT LEAST WRAP BANDAGES, RIGHT?

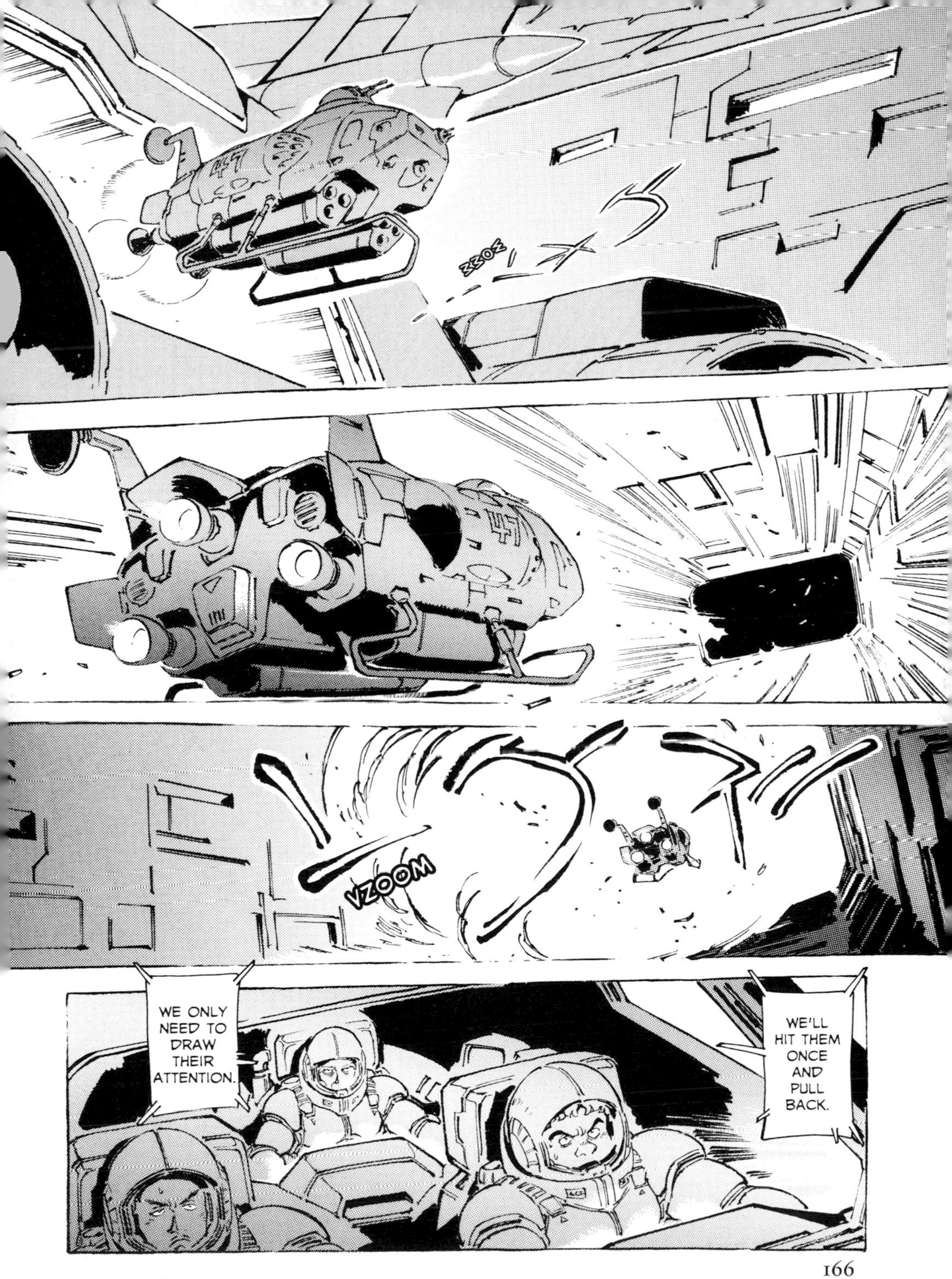
VZOOM
WE'LL HIT THEM ONCE AND PULL BACK.
WE ONLY NEED TO DRAW THEIR ATTENTION.

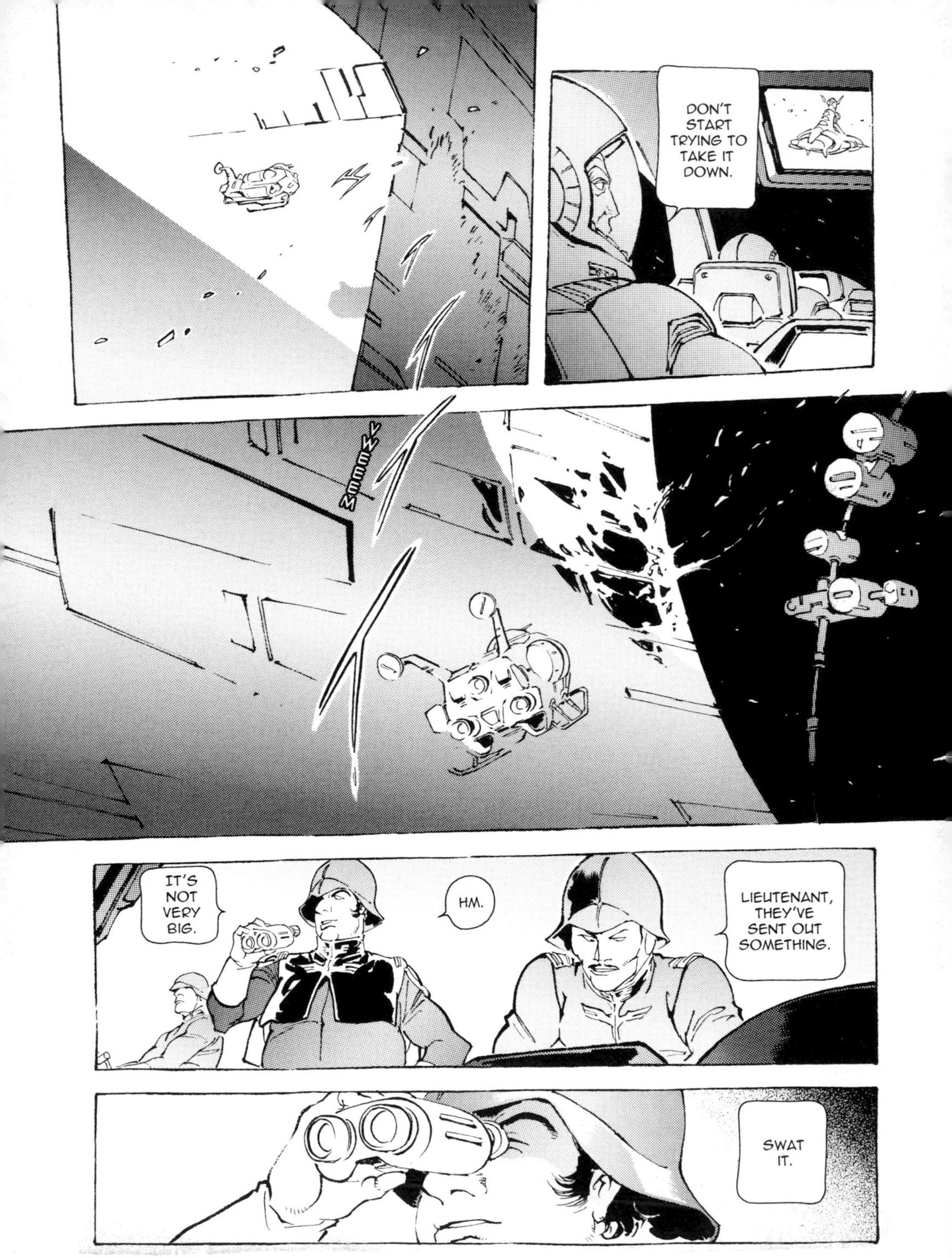
DON'T START TRYING TO TAKE IT DOWN.
VWEEEM
LIEUTENANT, THEY'VE SENT OUT SOMETHING.
HM.
IT'S NOT VERY BIG.
SWAT IT.

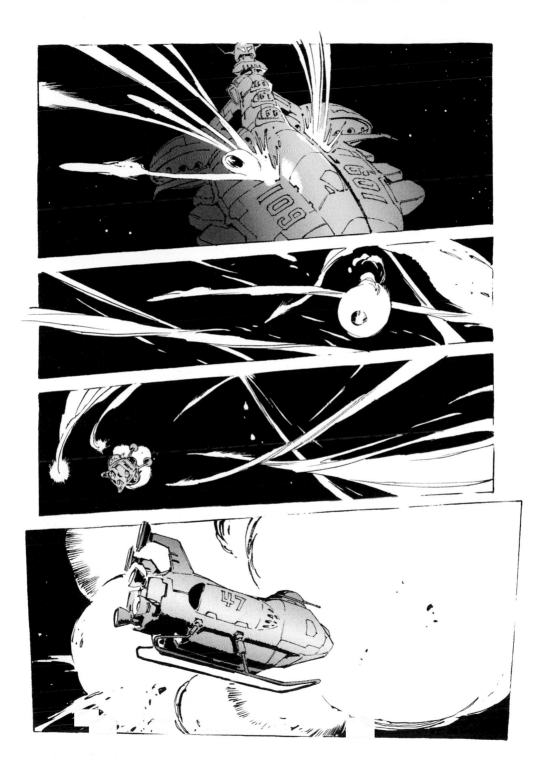

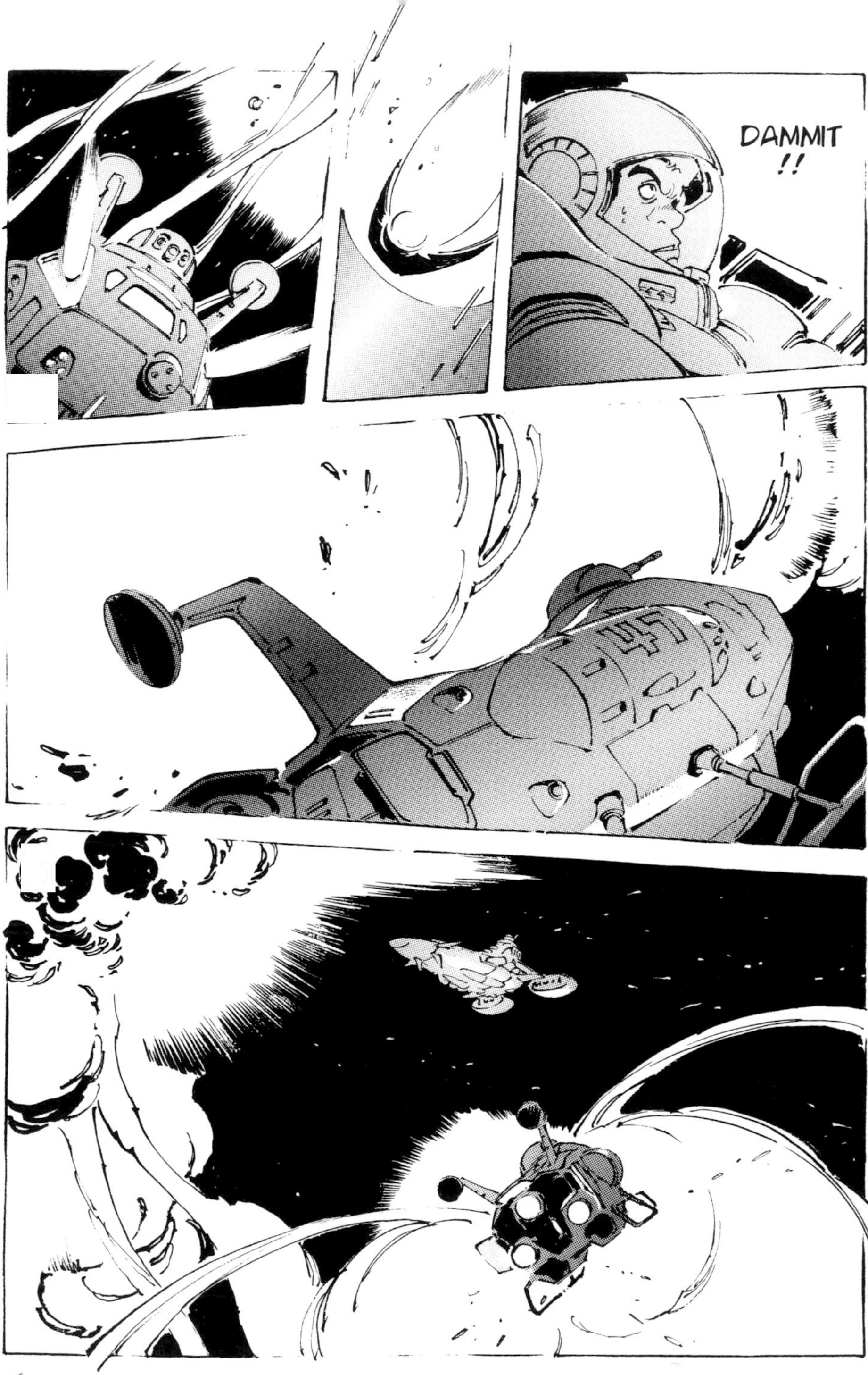
DAMMIT !!

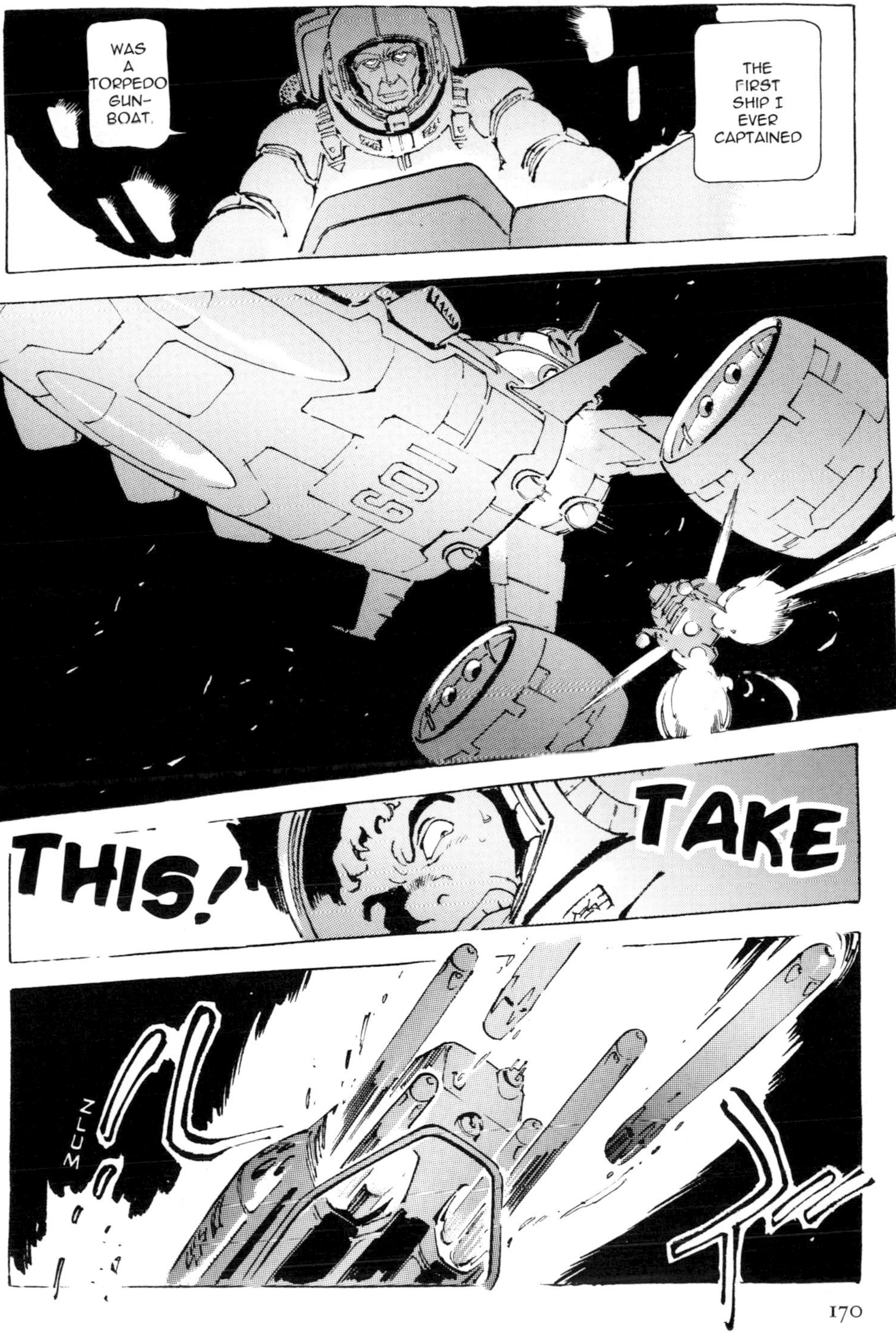
THE FIRST SHIP I EVER CAPTAINED
WAS A TORPEDO GUN-BOAT.
TAKE THIS!
ZLUM

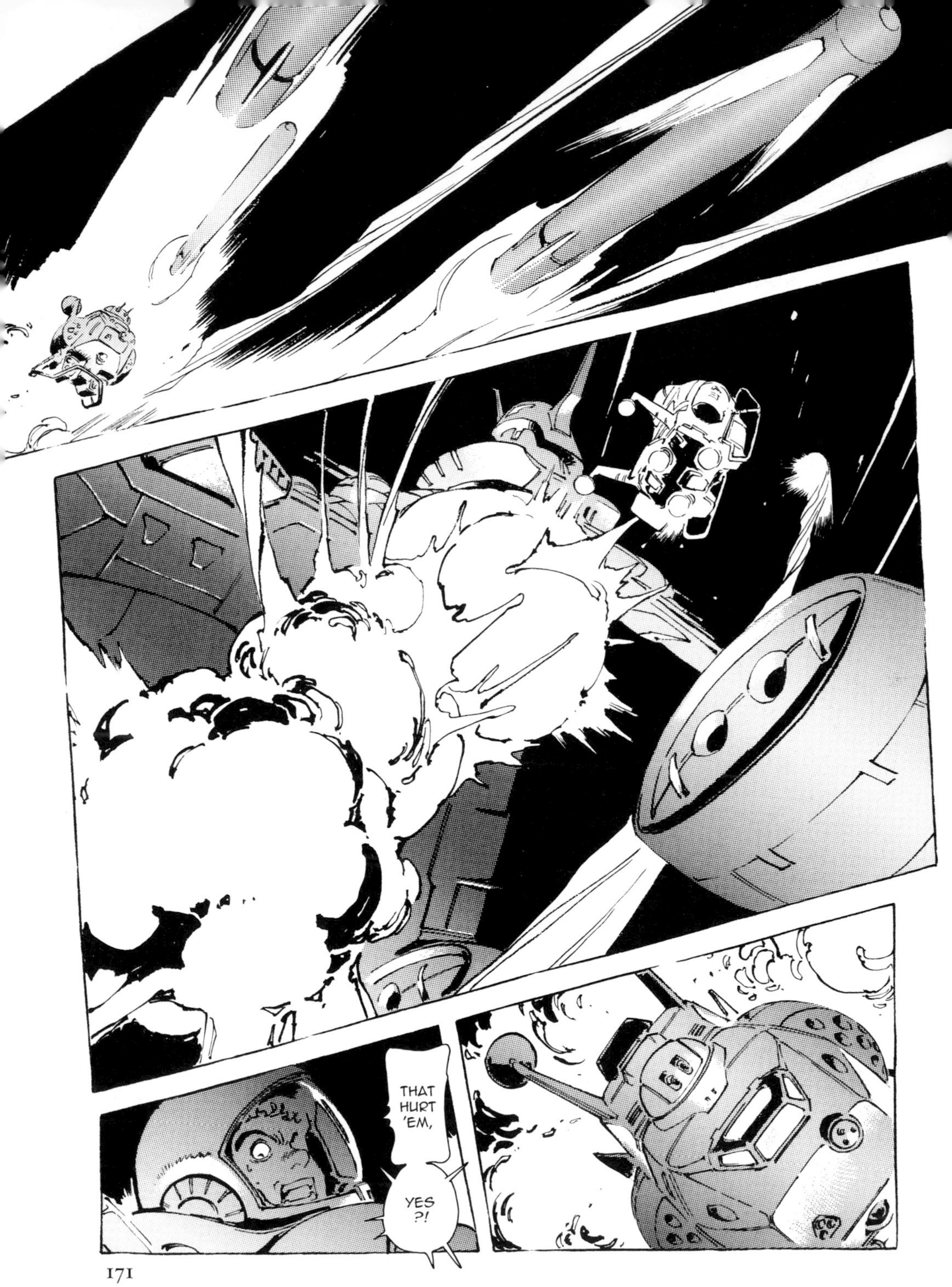
THAT HURT 'EM,
YES ?!

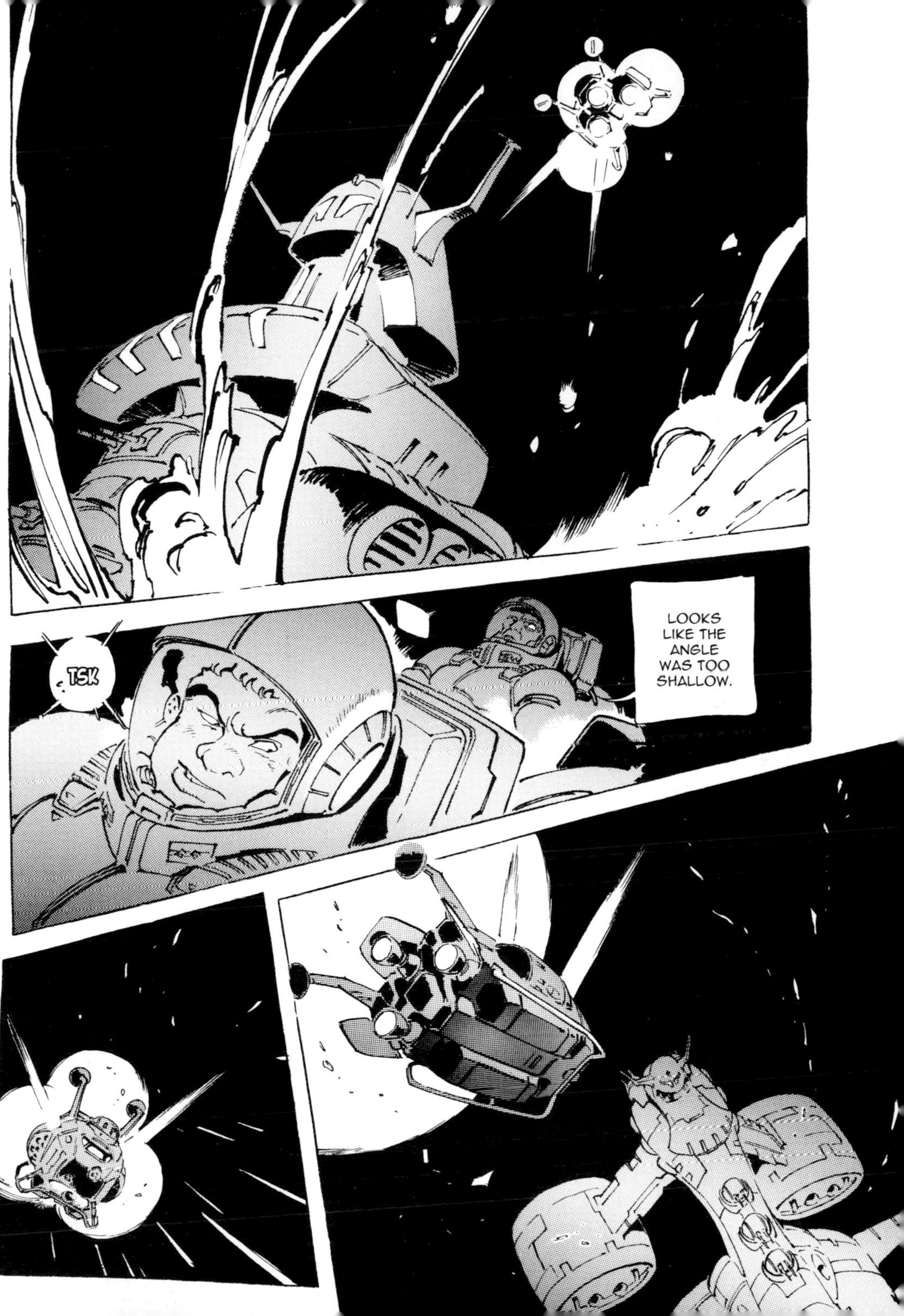
LOOKS LIKE THE ANGLE WAS TOO SHALLOW.
TSK

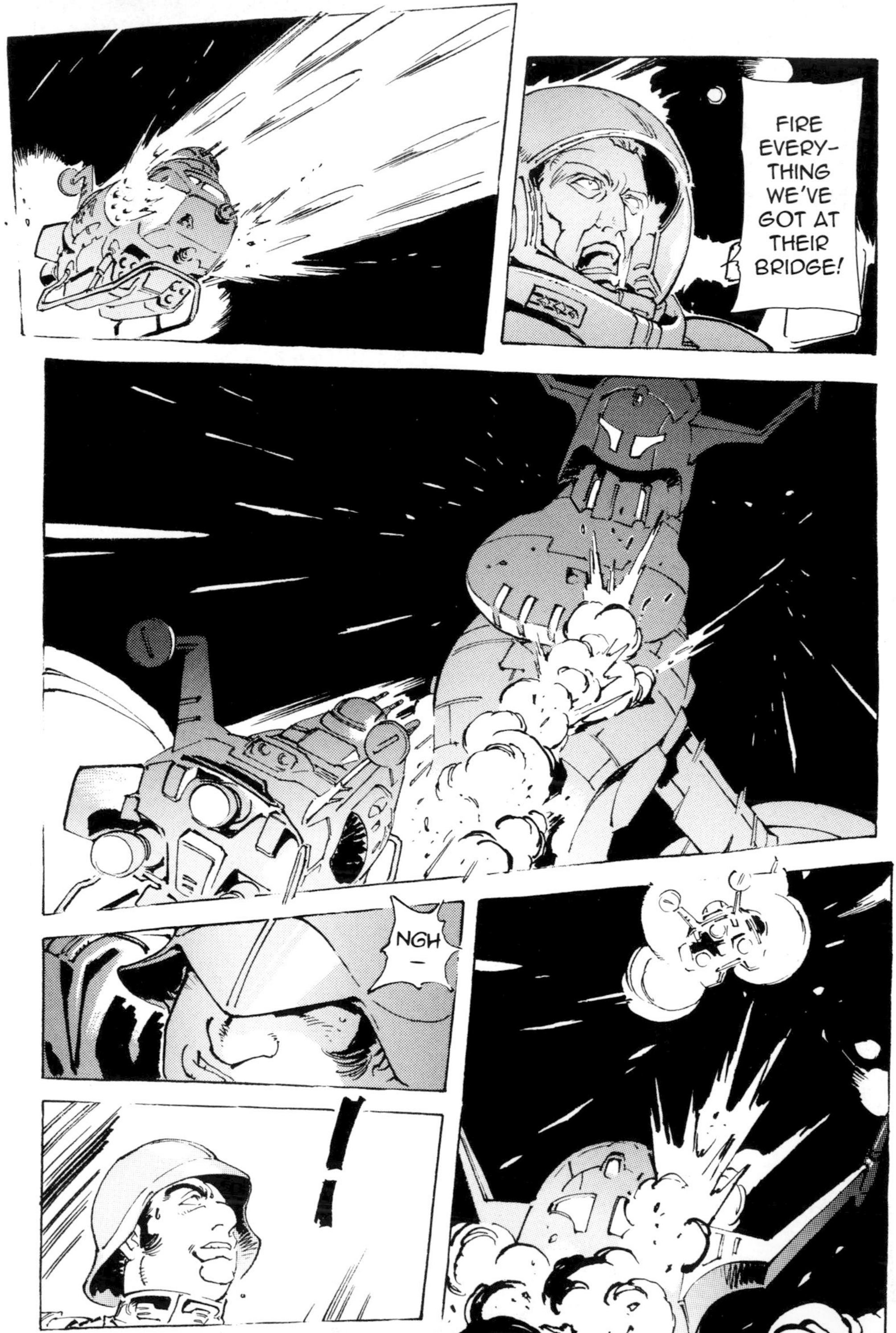
FIRE EVERY-THING WE'VE GOT AT THEIR BRIDGE!
NGH—

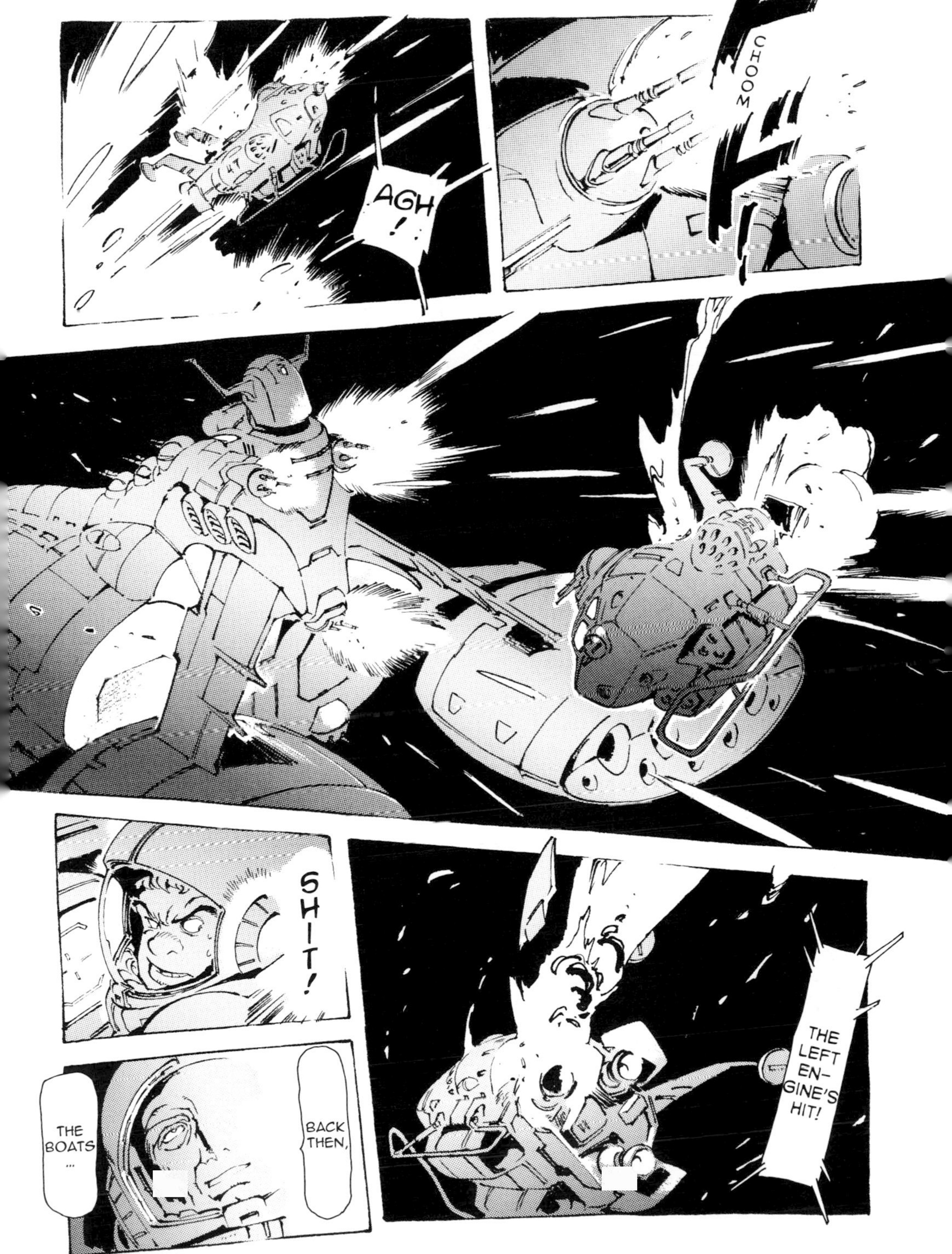
CHOOM
AGH!
THE LEFT EN-GINE'S HIT!
SHIT!
BACK THEN,
THE BOATS ...

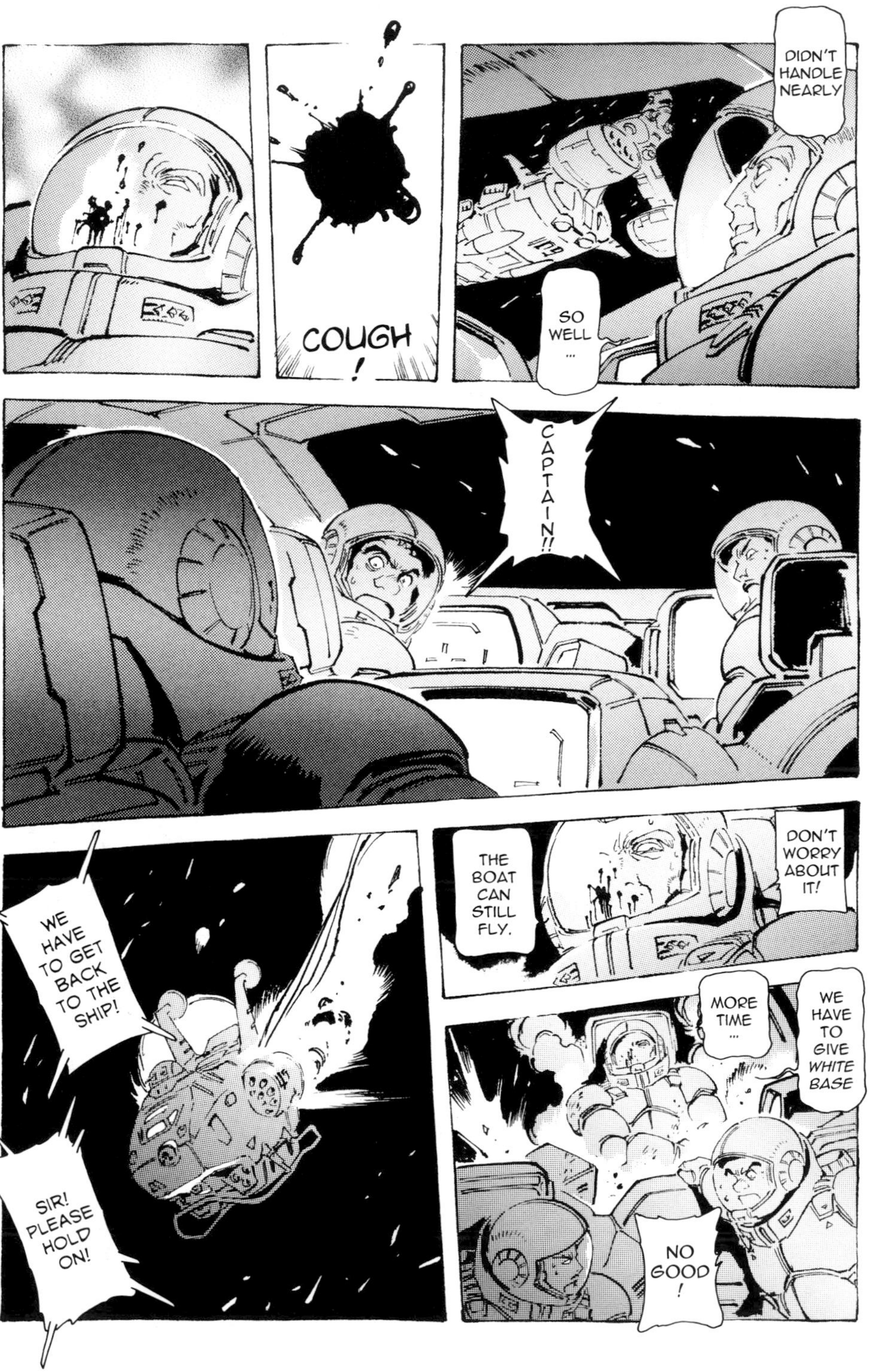
DIDN'T HANDLE NEARLY
SO WELL ...
COUGH!
CAPTAIN!!
DON'T WORRY ABOUT IT!
THE BOAT CAN STILL FLY.
WE HAVE TO GIVE WHITE BASE
MORE TIME ...
NO GOOD!
WE HAVE TO GET BACK TO THE SHIP!
SIR! PLEASE HOLD ON!

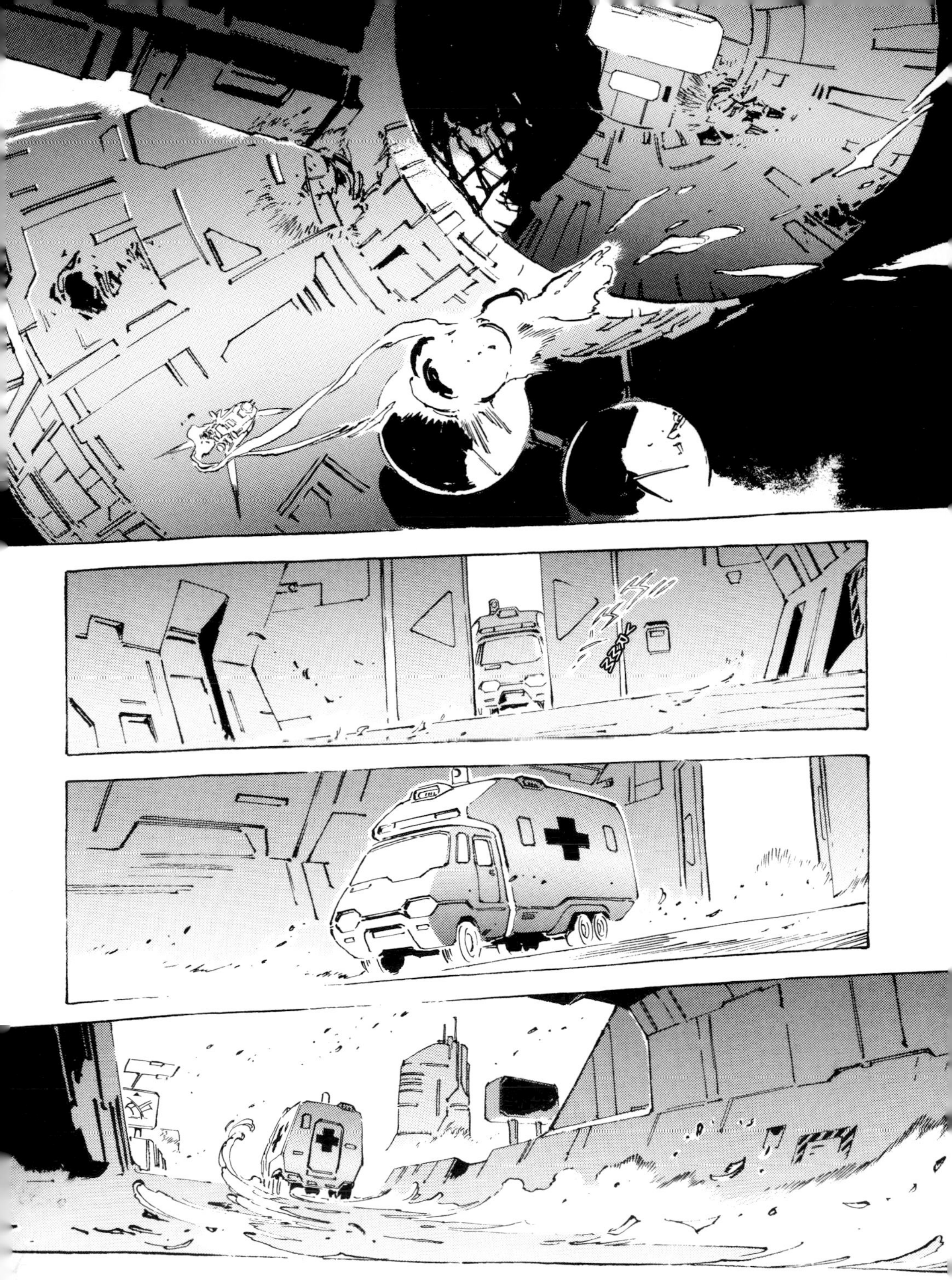

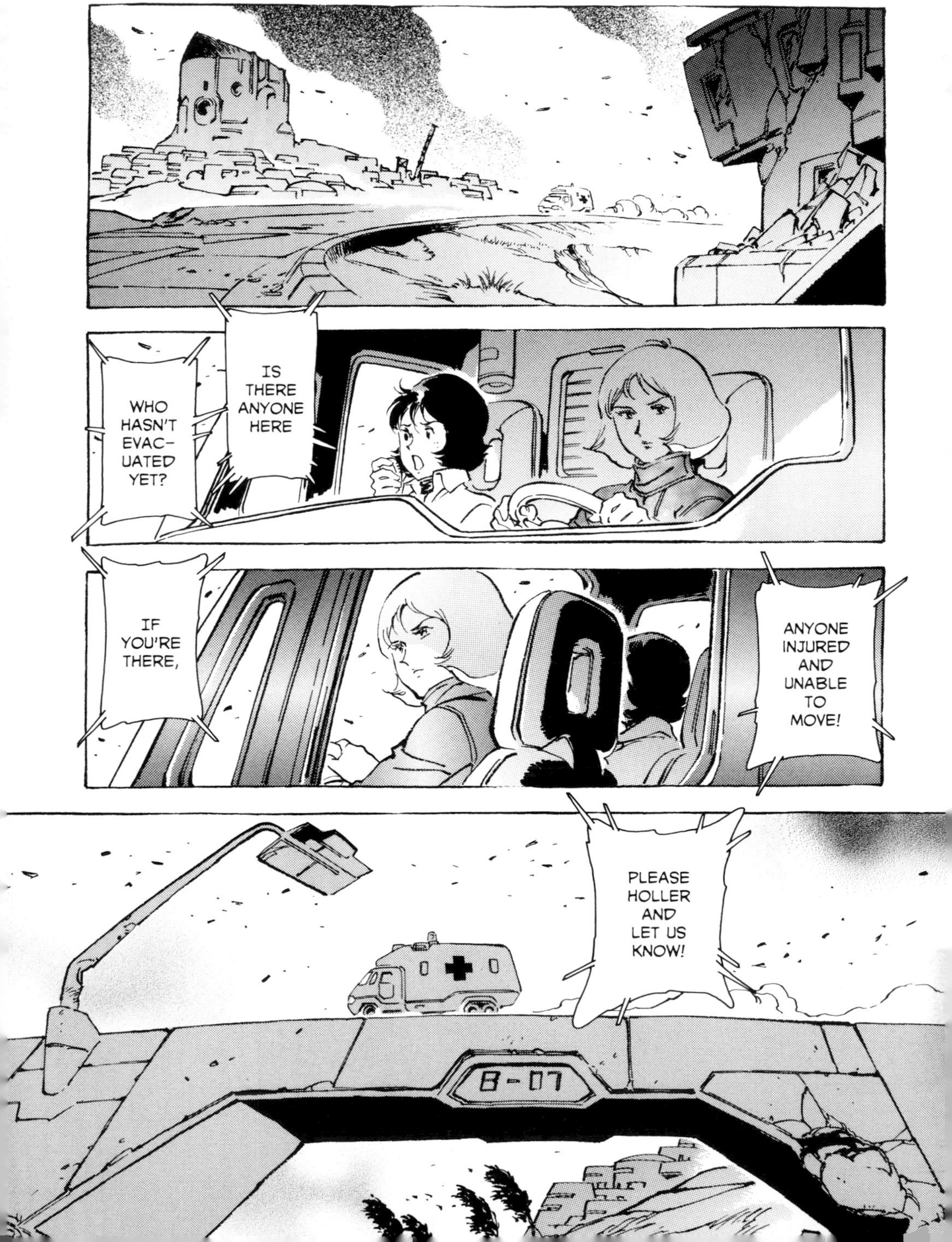
IS THERE ANYONE HERE
WHO HASN'T EVAC-UATED YET?
ANYONE INJURED AND UNABLE TO MOVE!
IF YOU'RE THERE,
PLEASE HOLLER AND LET US KNOW!
B-07

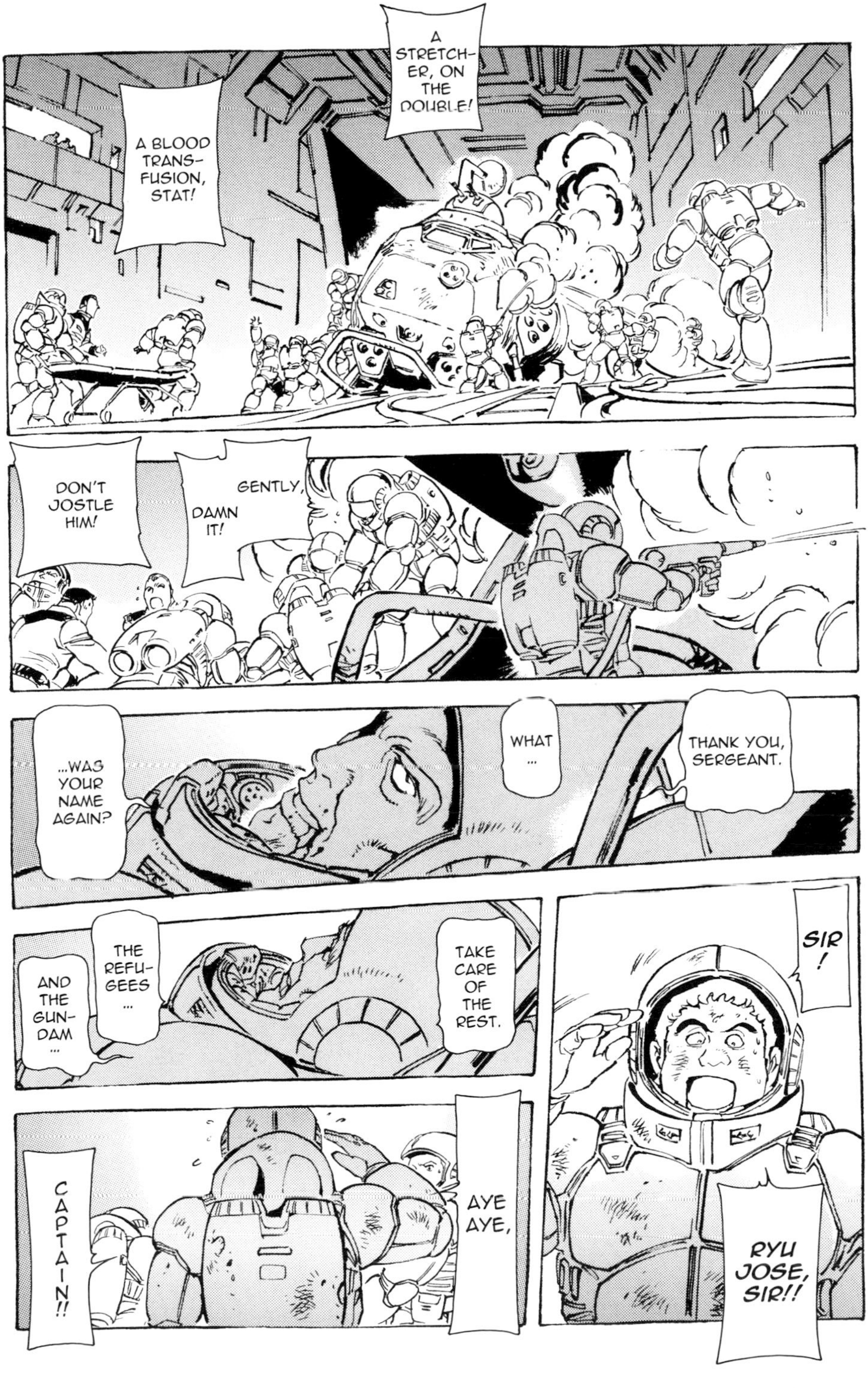
A STRETCHER, ON THE DOUBLE!
A BLOOD TRANSFUSION, STAT!
GENTLY, DAMN IT!
DON'T JOSTLE HIM!
THANK YOU, SERGEANT.
WHAT ...
...WAS YOUR NAME AGAIN?
SIR!
RYU JOSE, SIR!!
TAKE CARE OF THE REST.
THE REFUGEES ...
AND THE GUNDAM ...
AYE AYE,
CAPTAIN!!

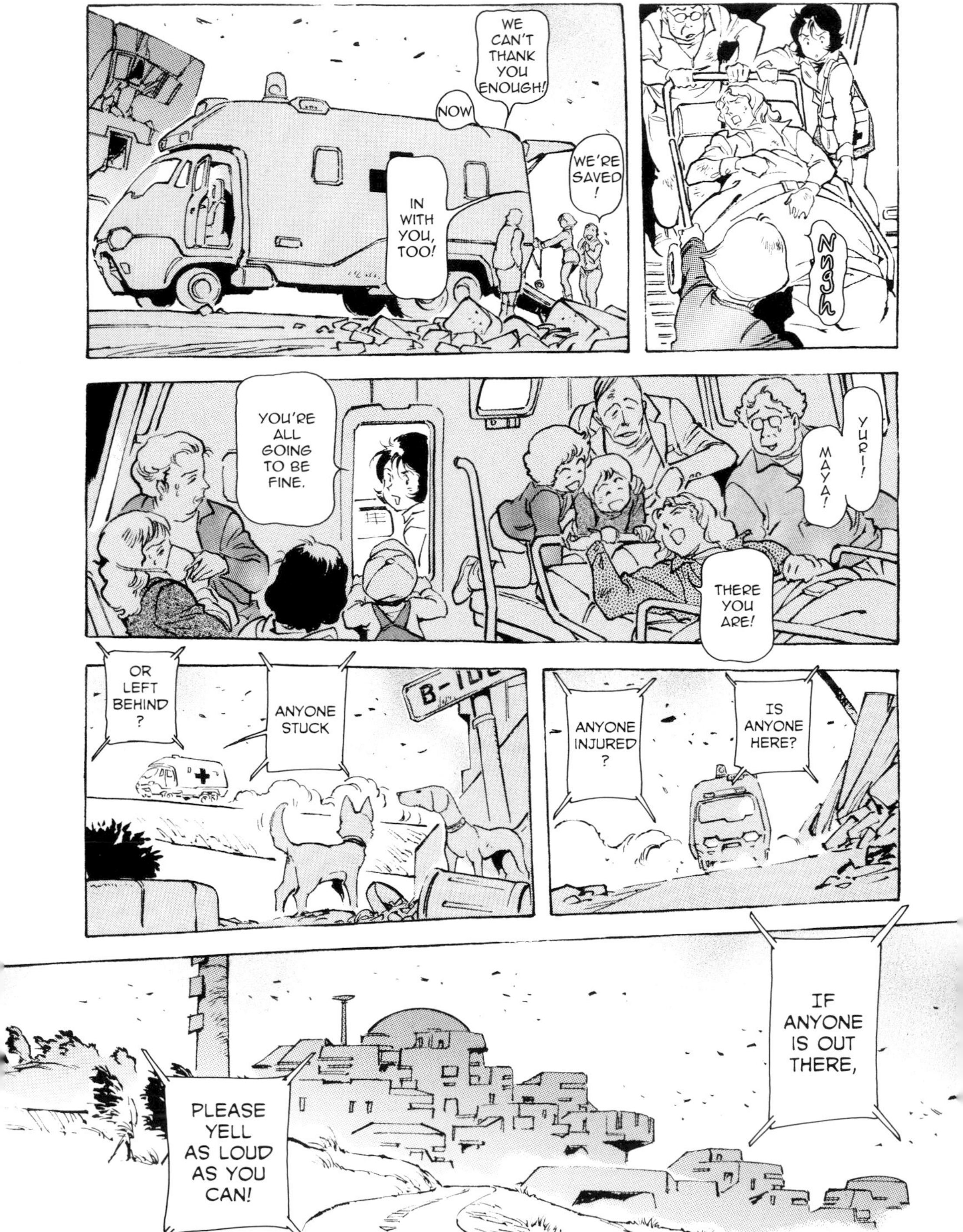
Nngh
WE'RE SAVED!
WE CAN'T THANK YOU ENOUGH!
NOW
IN WITH YOU, TOO!
YURI!
MAYA!
THERE YOU ARE!
YOU'RE ALL GOING TO BE FINE.
IS ANYONE HERE?
ANYONE INJURED?
ANYONE STUCK
OR LEFT BEHIND?
IF ANYONE IS OUT THERE,
PLEASE YELL AS LOUD AS YOU CAN!

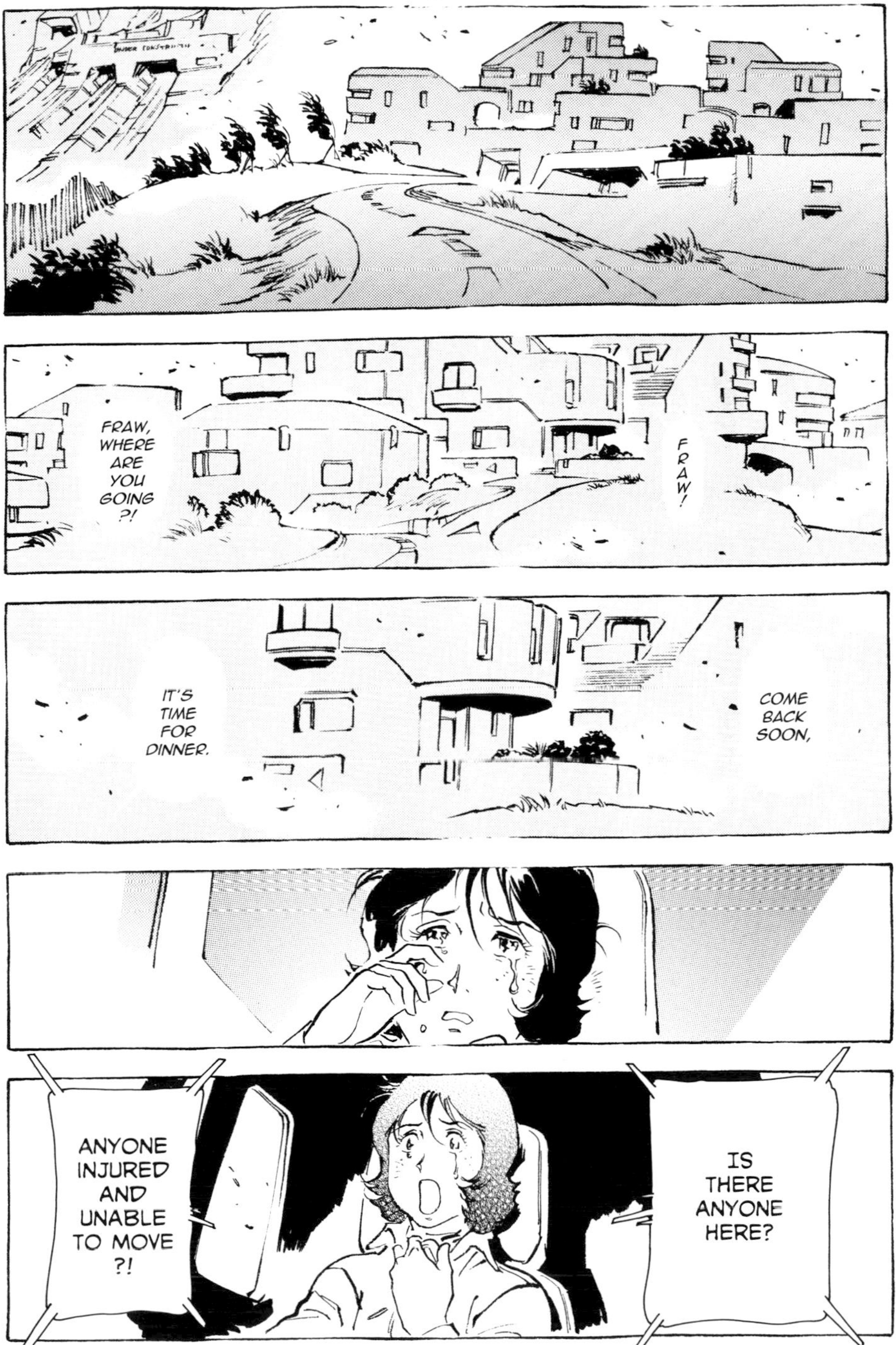
FRAW!
FRAW, WHERE ARE YOU GOING?!
COME BACK SOON,
IT'S TIME FOR DINNER.
IS THERE ANYONE HERE?
ANYONE INJURED AND UNABLE TO MOVE?!

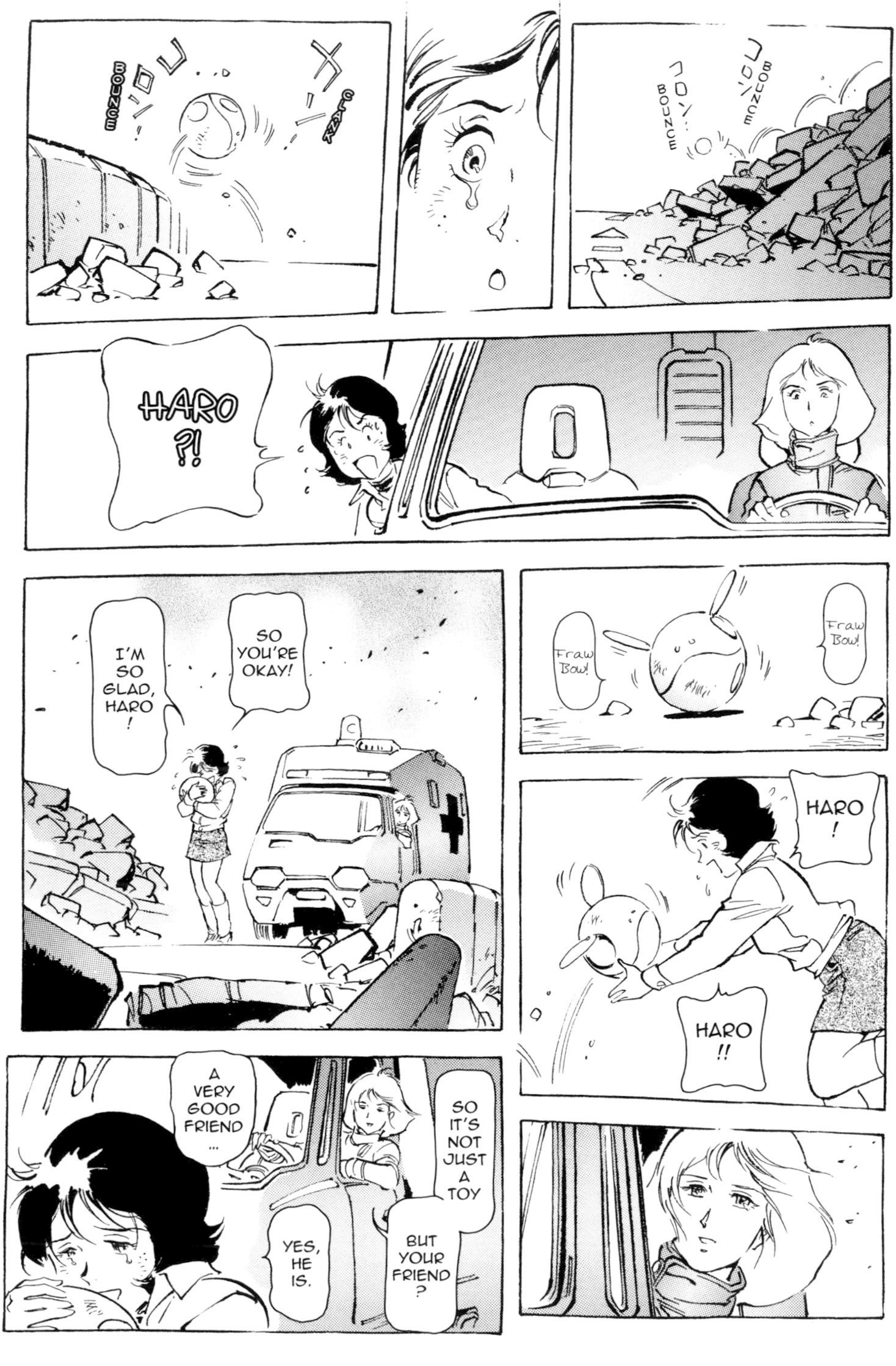
BOUNCE
BOUNCE
CLANK
BOUNCE
HARO ?!
Fraw Bow!
Fraw Bow!
HARO !
HARO !!
SO YOU'RE OKAY!
I'M SO GLAD, HARO !
SO IT'S NOT JUST A TOY
A VERY GOOD FRIEND ...
BUT YOUR FRIEND ?
YES, HE IS.

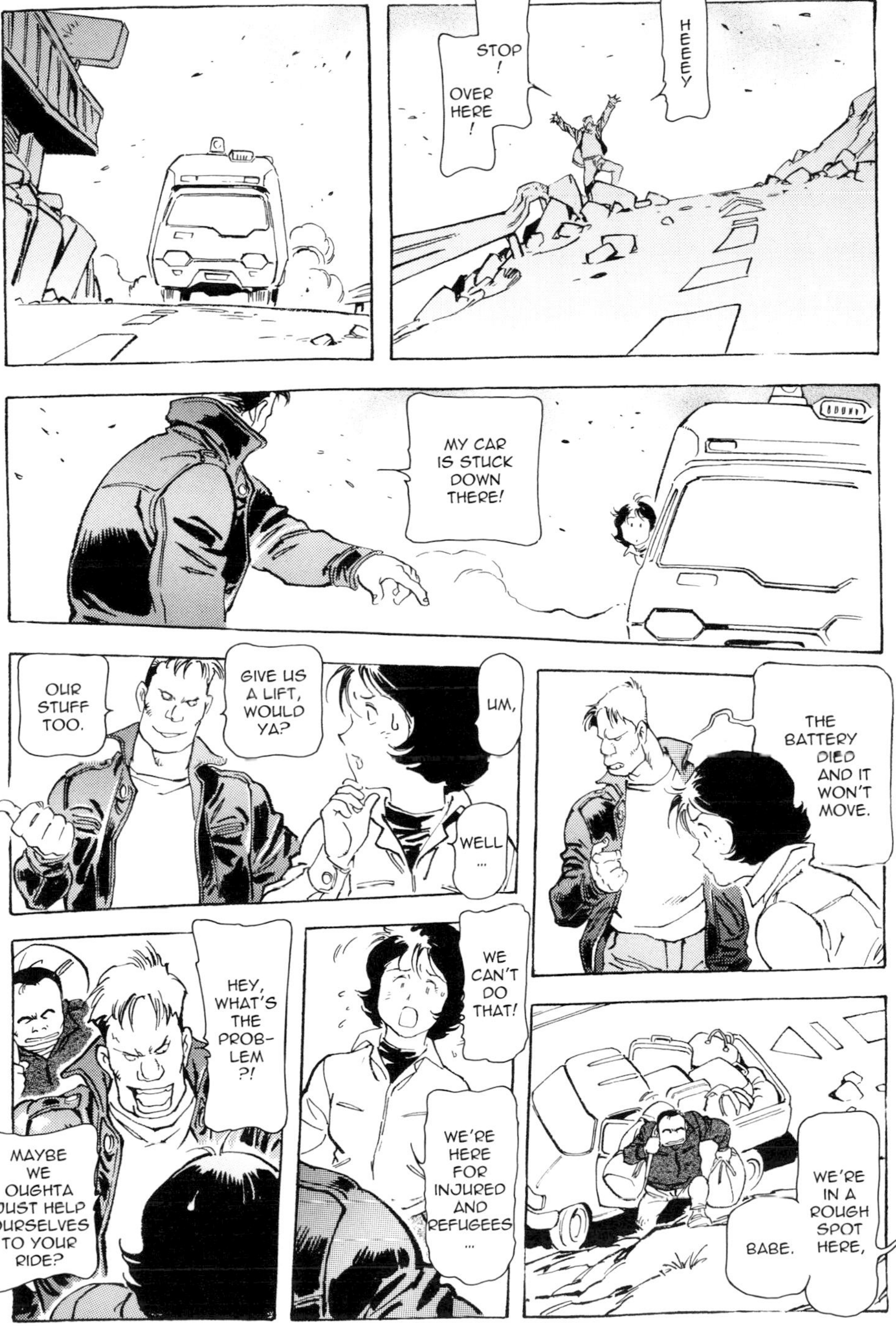
HEEEY
STOP! OVER HERE!
MY CAR IS STUCK DOWN THERE!
THE BATTERY DIED AND IT WON'T MOVE.
UM,
GIVE US A LIFT, WOULD YA?
OUR STUFF TOO.
WELL...
WE'RE IN A ROUGH SPOT HERE,
BABE.
WE CAN'T DO THAT!
WE'RE HERE FOR INJURED AND REFUGEES...
HEY, WHAT'S THE PROB-LEM?!
MAYBE WE OUGHTA JUST HELP OURSELVES TO YOUR RIDE?

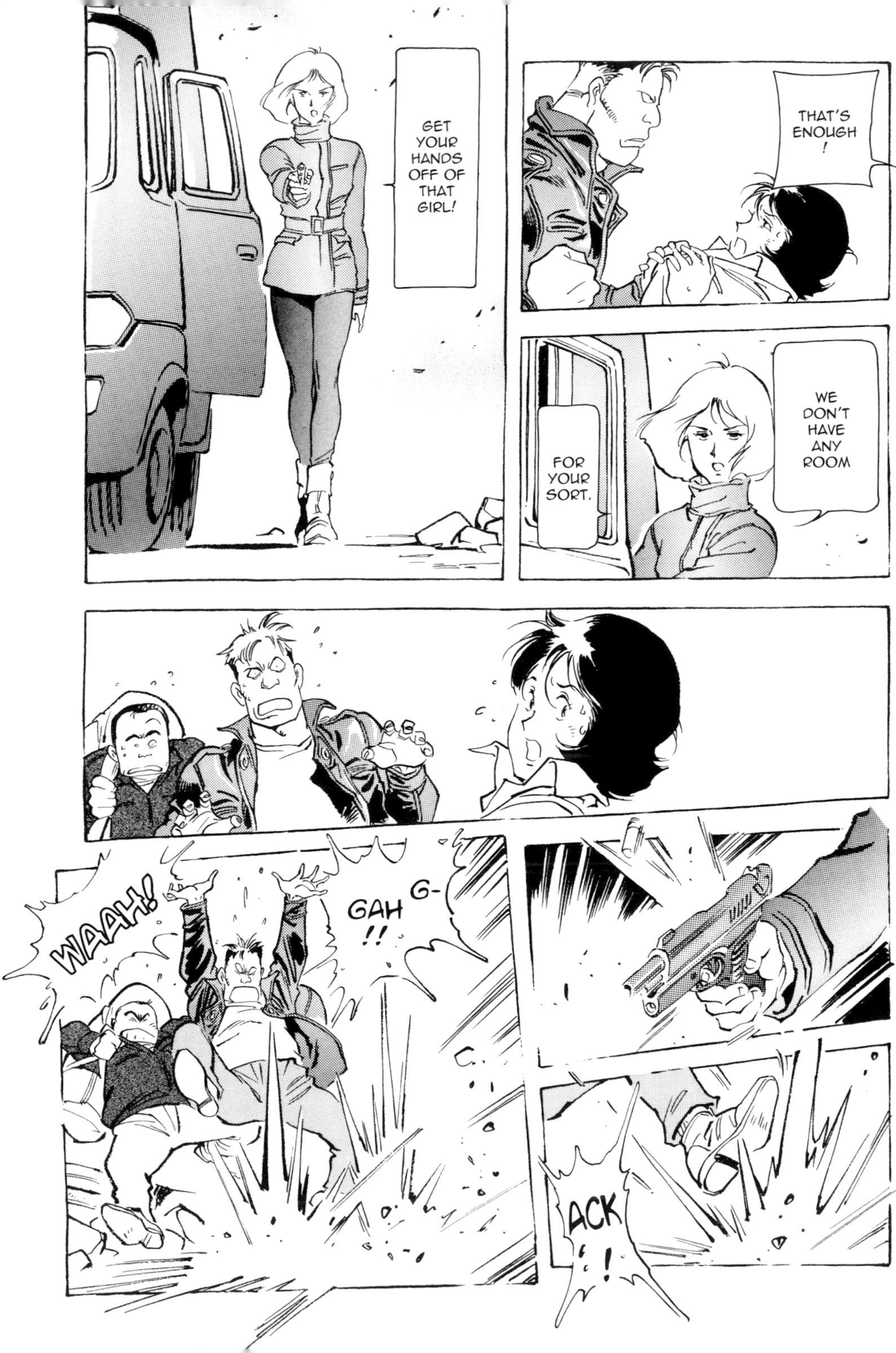
THAT'S ENOUGH!
WE DON'T HAVE ANY ROOM
FOR YOUR SORT.
GET YOUR HANDS OFF OF THAT GIRL!
ACK!
G- GAH!!
WAAH!

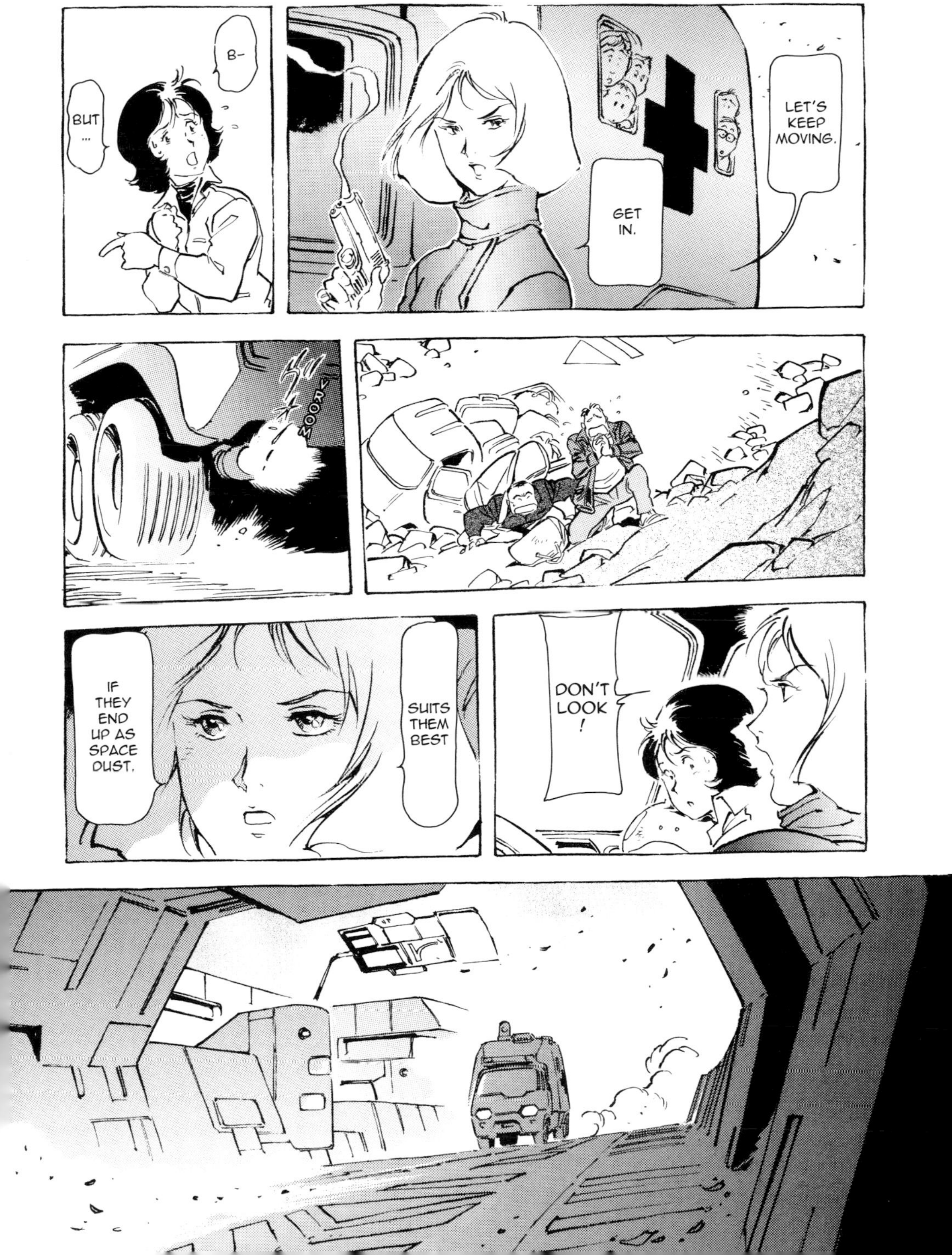
LET'S KEEP MOVING.
GET IN.
B-
BUT ...
VROOM
DON'T LOOK!
SUITS THEM BEST
IF THEY END UP AS SPACE DUST.

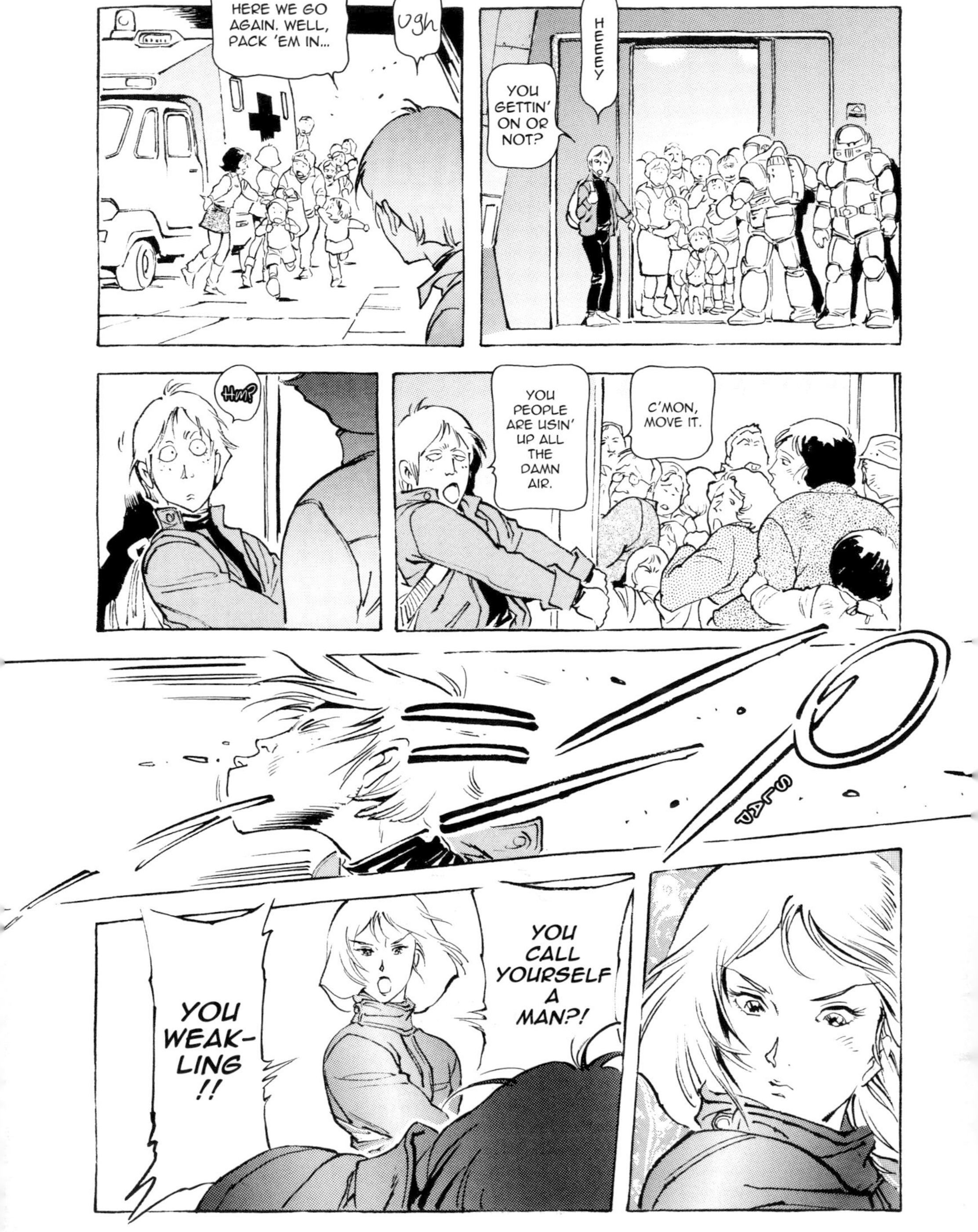
HEEEY
YOU GETTIN' ON OR NOT?
Ugh
HERE WE GO AGAIN. WELL, PACK 'EM IN...
C'MON, MOVE IT.
YOU PEOPLE ARE USIN' UP ALL THE DAMN AIR.
Hm?
SLAP
YOU CALL YOURSELF A MAN?!
YOU WEAK-LING!!

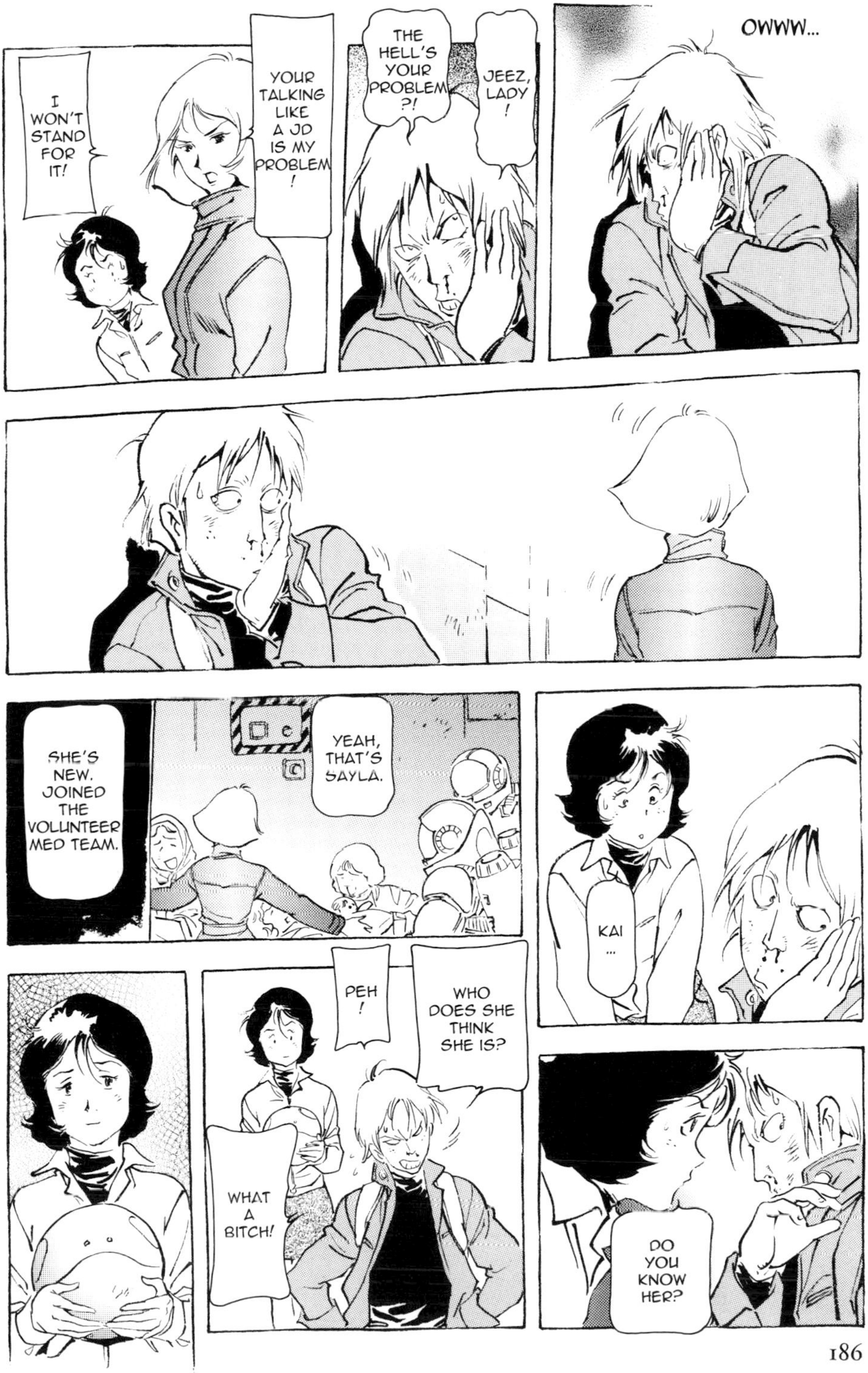
OWWW...
JEEZ, LADY!
THE HELL'S YOUR PROBLEM?!
YOUR TALKING LIKE A JD IS MY PROBLEM!
I WON'T STAND FOR IT!
KAI...
DO YOU KNOW HER?
YEAH, THAT'S SAYLA.
SHE'S NEW. JOINED THE VOLUNTEER MED TEAM.
WHO DOES SHE THINK SHE IS?
PEH!
WHAT A BITCH!

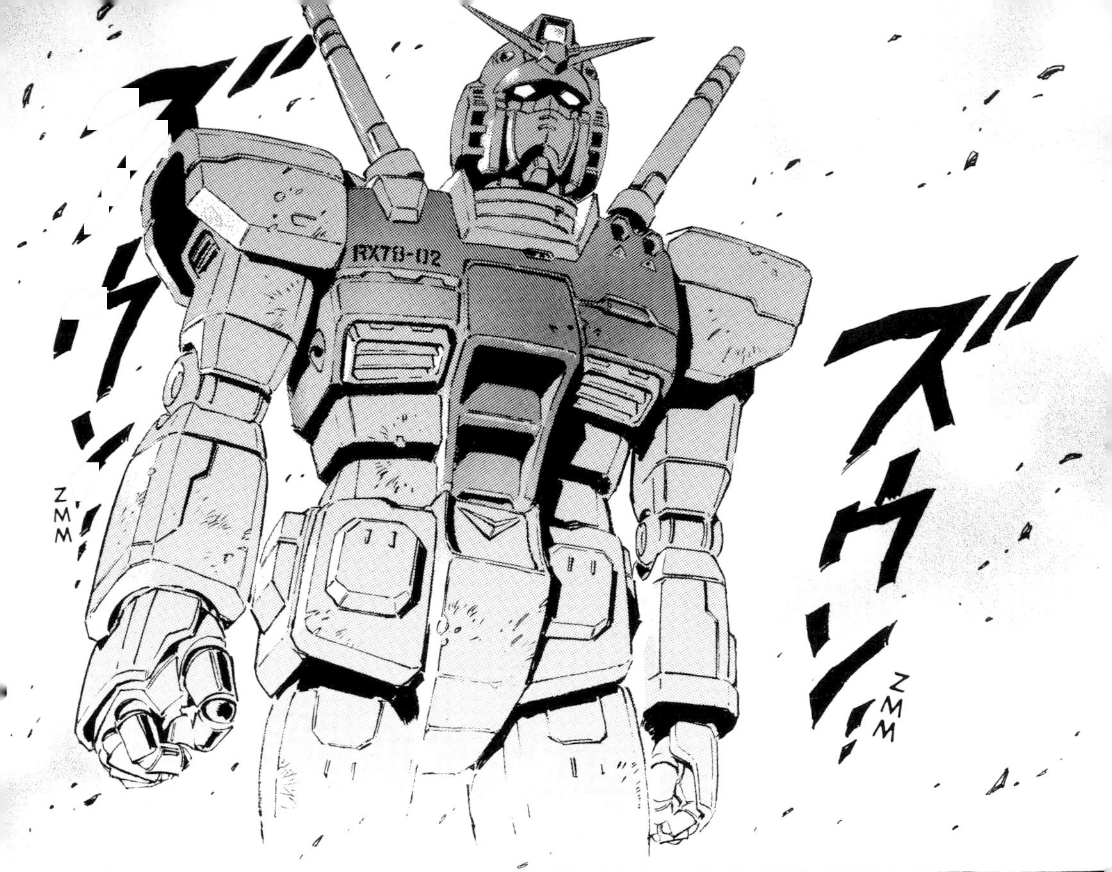
ZMM
ZMM

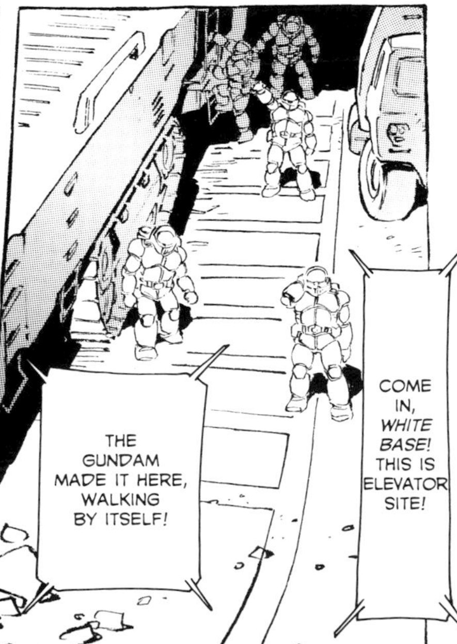
COME IN, *WHITE BASE!* THIS IS ELEVATOR SITE!
THE GUNDAM MADE IT HERE, WALKING BY ITSELF!

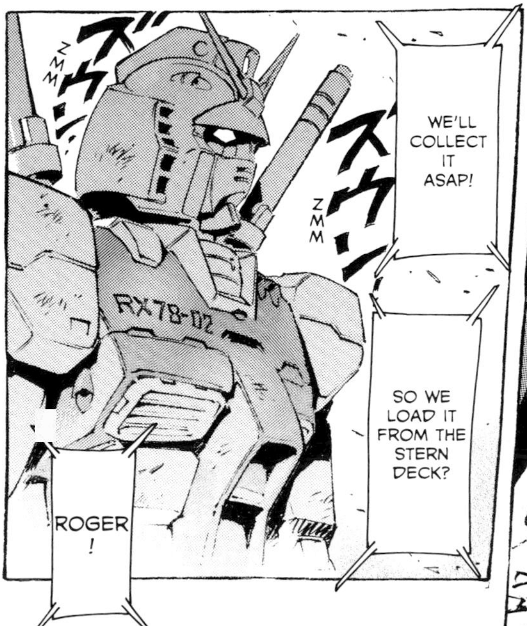
ZMM
ZMM
WE'LL COLLECT IT ASAP!
SO WE LOAD IT FROM THE STERN DECK?
ROGER!

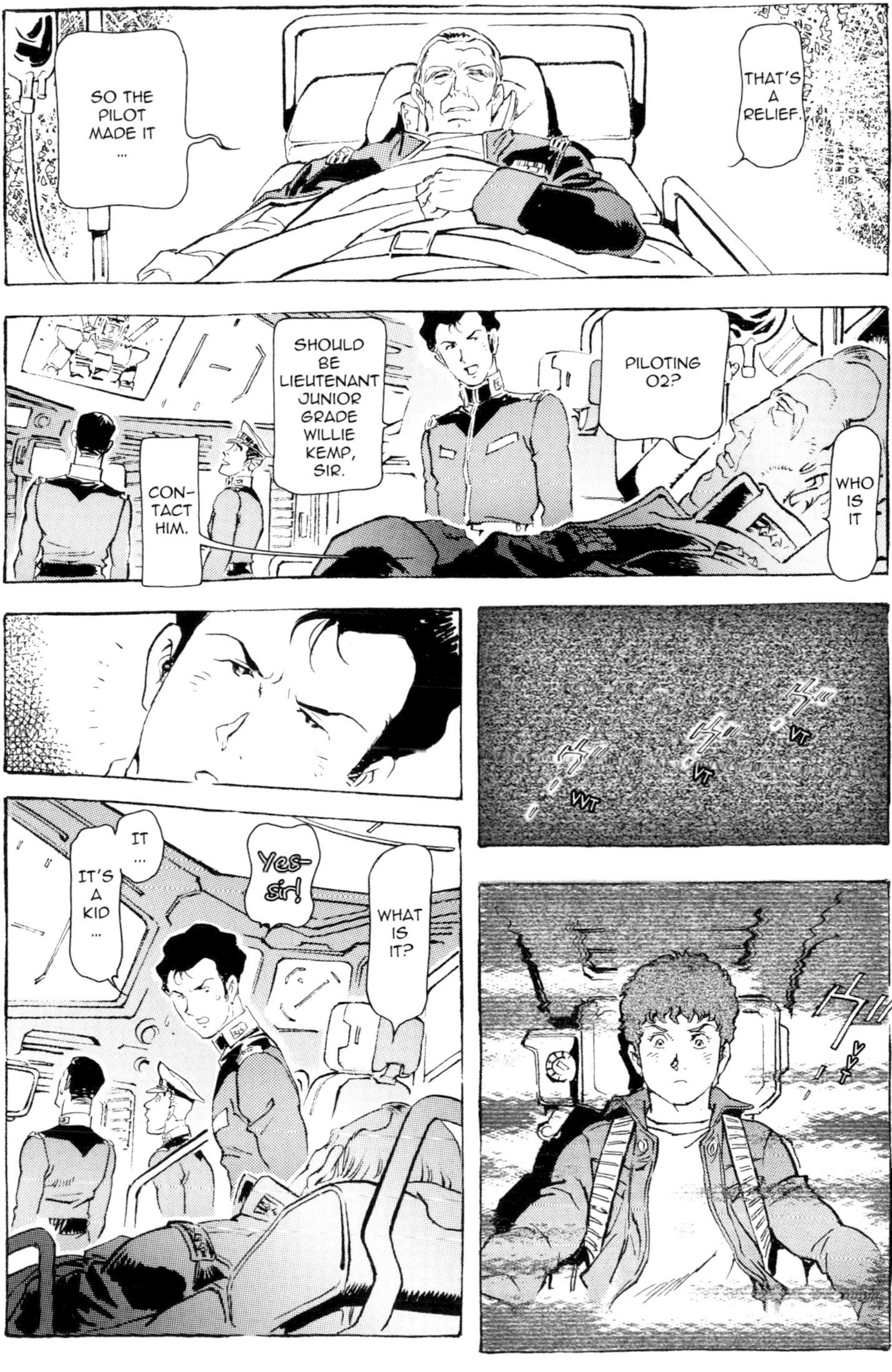
THAT'S A RELIEF.
SO THE PILOT MADE IT ...
WHO IS IT
PILOTING 02?
SHOULD BE LIEUTENANT JUNIOR GRADE WILLIE KEMP, SIR.
CON-TACT HIM.
VT
VT
VVT
WHAT IS IT?
Yes-sir!
IT ... IT'S A KID ...

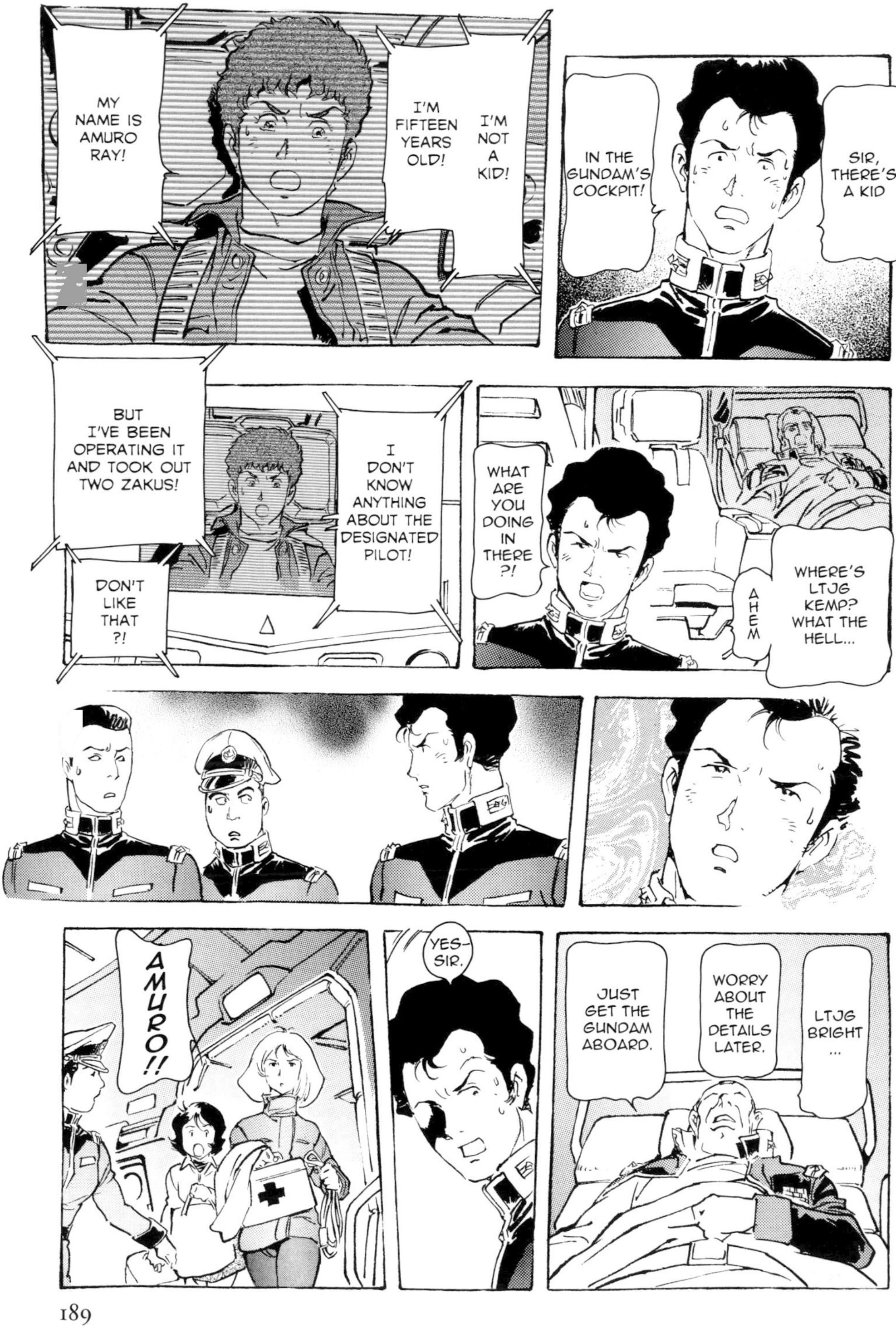
SIR, THERE'S A KID
IN THE GUNDAM'S COCKPIT!
I'M NOT A KID!
I'M FIFTEEN YEARS OLD!
MY NAME IS AMURO RAY!
WHERE'S LTJG KEMP? WHAT THE HELL...
AHEM
WHAT ARE YOU DOING IN THERE?!
I DON'T KNOW ANYTHING ABOUT THE DESIGNATED PILOT!
BUT I'VE BEEN OPERATING IT AND TOOK OUT TWO ZAKUS!
DON'T LIKE THAT?!
LTJG BRIGHT ...
WORRY ABOUT THE DETAILS LATER.
JUST GET THE GUNDAM ABOARD.
YES-SIR.
AMURO!!

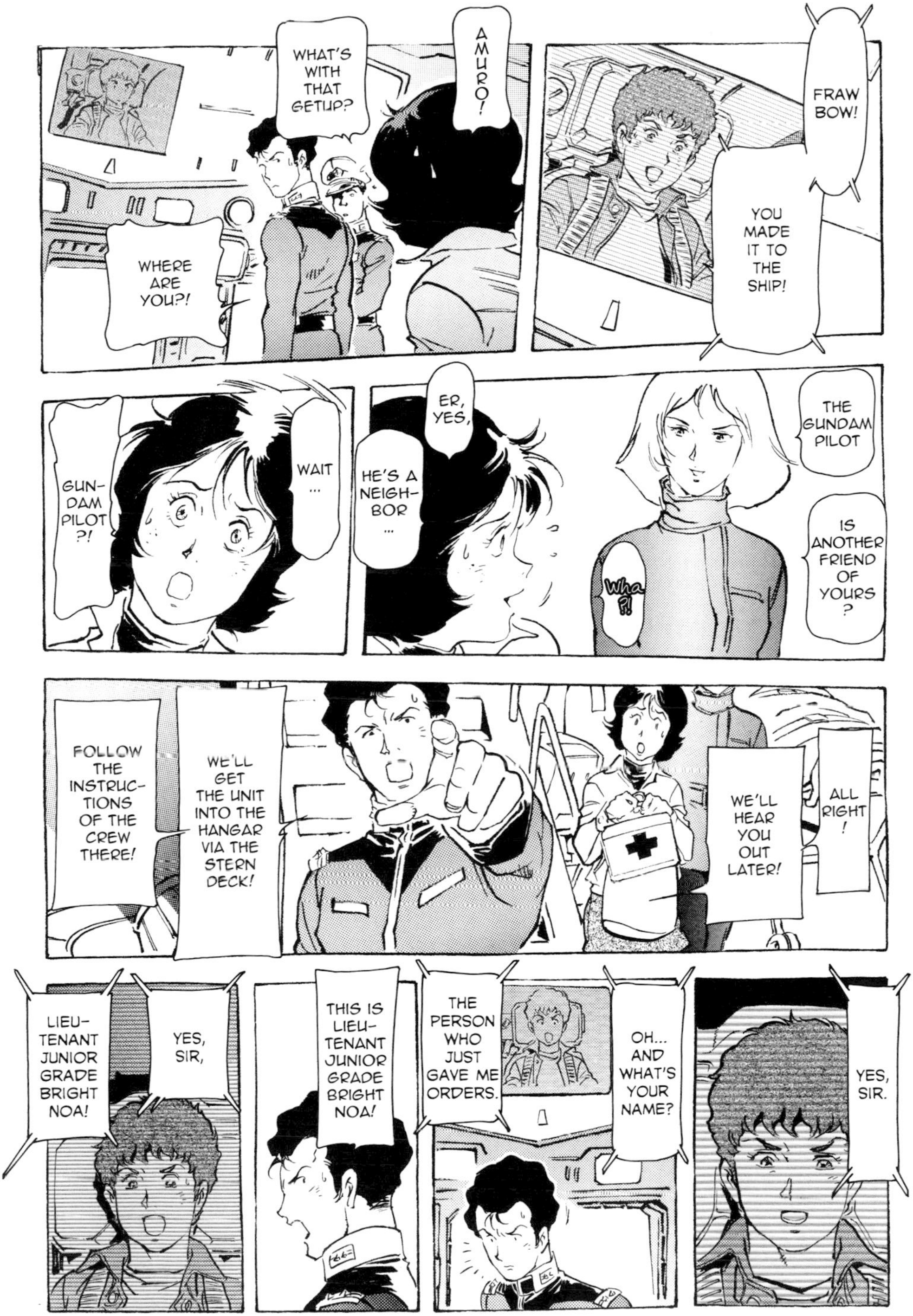
FRAW BOW!
YOU MADE IT TO THE SHIP!
AMURO!
WHAT'S WITH THAT GETUP?
WHERE ARE YOU?!
THE GUNDAM PILOT
IS ANOTHER FRIEND OF YOURS?
Wha?!
ER, YES,
HE'S A NEIGHBOR...
WAIT...
GUN-DAM PILOT?!
ALL RIGHT!
WE'LL HEAR YOU OUT LATER!
WE'LL GET THE UNIT INTO THE HANGAR VIA THE STERN DECK!
FOLLOW THE INSTRUCTIONS OF THE CREW THERE!
YES, SIR.
OH... AND WHAT'S YOUR NAME?
THE PERSON WHO JUST GAVE ME ORDERS.
THIS IS LIEUTENANT JUNIOR GRADE BRIGHT NOA!
YES, SIR,
LIEUTENANT JUNIOR GRADE BRIGHT NOA!

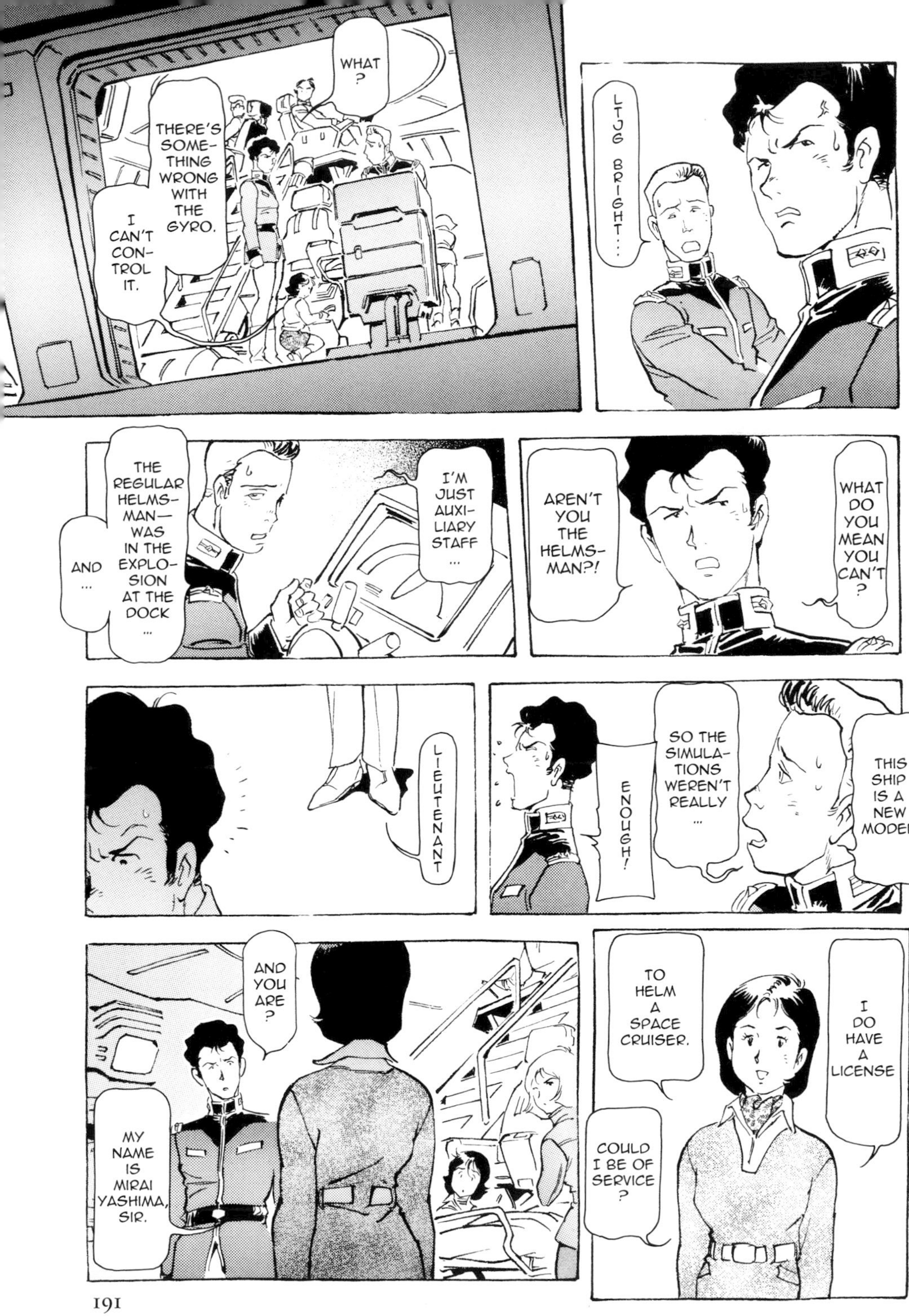
LTJG BRIGHT...
WHAT ?
THERE'S SOMETHING WRONG WITH THE GYRO.
I CAN'T CONTROL IT.
WHAT DO YOU MEAN YOU CAN'T ?
AREN'T YOU THE HELMSMAN?!
I'M JUST AUXILIARY STAFF ...
THE REGULAR HELMSMAN—WAS IN THE EXPLOSION AT THE DOCK ...
AND ...
THIS SHIP IS A NEW MODEL,
SO THE SIMULATIONS WEREN'T REALLY ...
ENOUGH!
LIEUTENANT
I DO HAVE A LICENSE
TO HELM A SPACE CRUISER.
COULD I BE OF SERVICE ?
AND YOU ARE ?
MY NAME IS MIRAI YASHIMA, SIR.

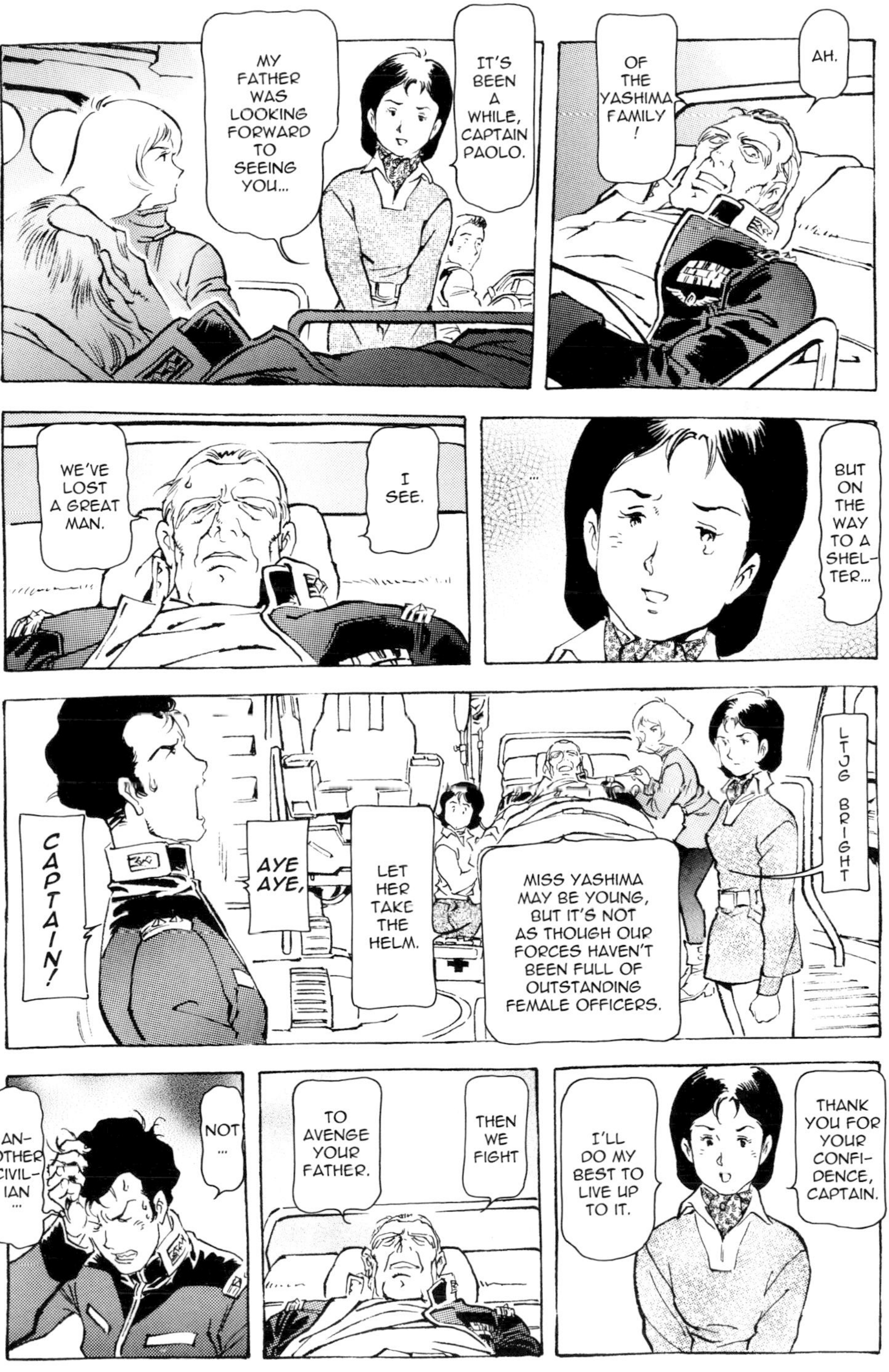
AH.
OF THE YASHIMA FAMILY!
IT'S BEEN A WHILE, CAPTAIN PAOLO.
MY FATHER WAS LOOKING FORWARD TO SEEING YOU...
BUT ON THE WAY TO A SHELTER...
...
I SEE.
WE'VE LOST A GREAT MAN.
LTJG BRIGHT
MISS YASHIMA MAY BE YOUNG, BUT IT'S NOT AS THOUGH OUR FORCES HAVEN'T BEEN FULL OF OUTSTANDING FEMALE OFFICERS.
LET HER TAKE THE HELM.
AYE AYE,
CAPTAIN!
THANK YOU FOR YOUR CONFIDENCE, CAPTAIN.
I'LL DO MY BEST TO LIVE UP TO IT.
THEN WE FIGHT
TO AVENGE YOUR FATHER.
NOT...
ANOTHER CIVILIAN...

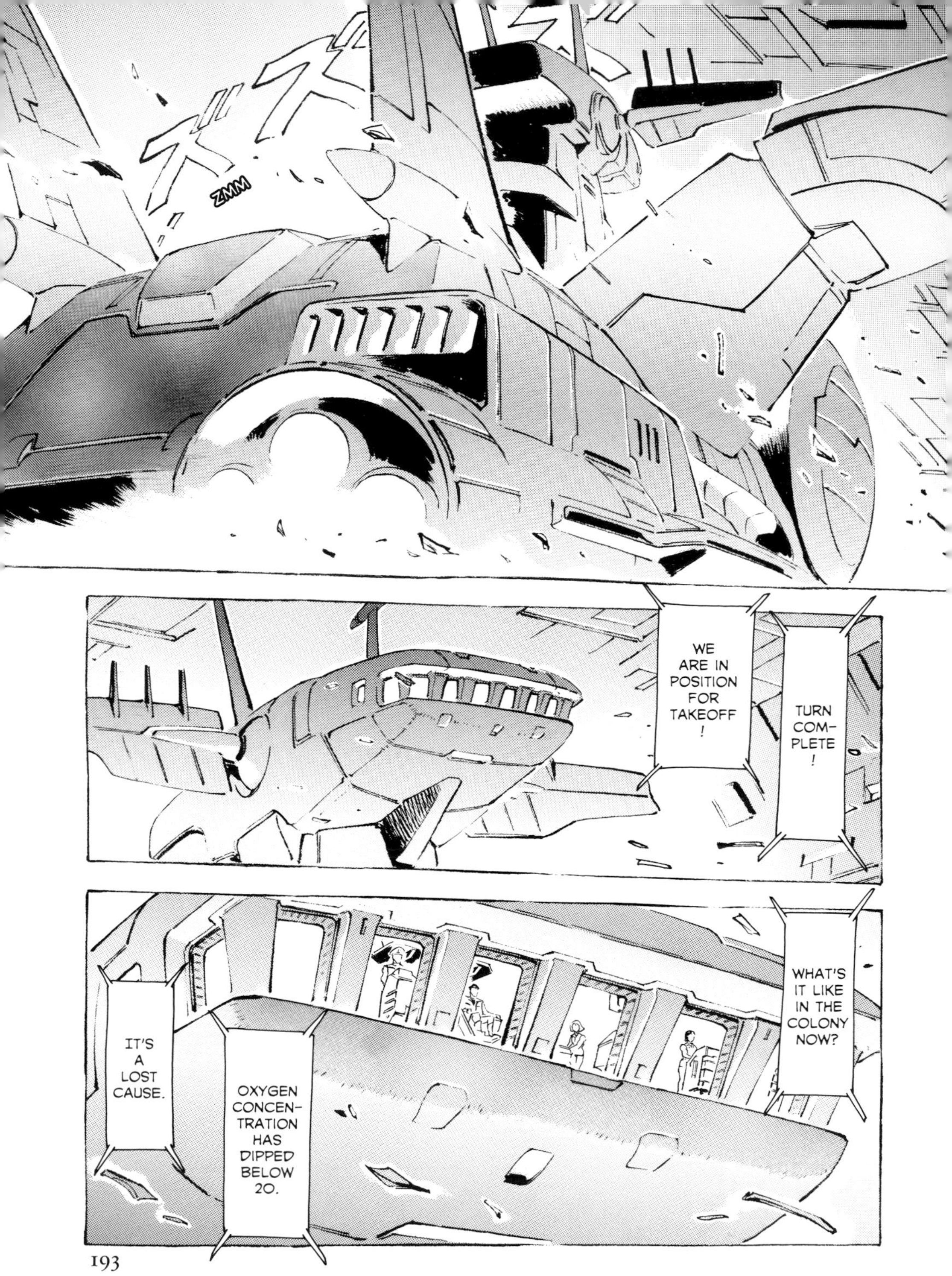
ズズズ
ZMM
TURN COMPLETE!
WE ARE IN POSITION FOR TAKEOFF!
WHAT'S IT LIKE IN THE COLONY NOW?
OXYGEN CONCENTRATION HAS DIPPED BELOW 20.
IT'S A LOST CAUSE.

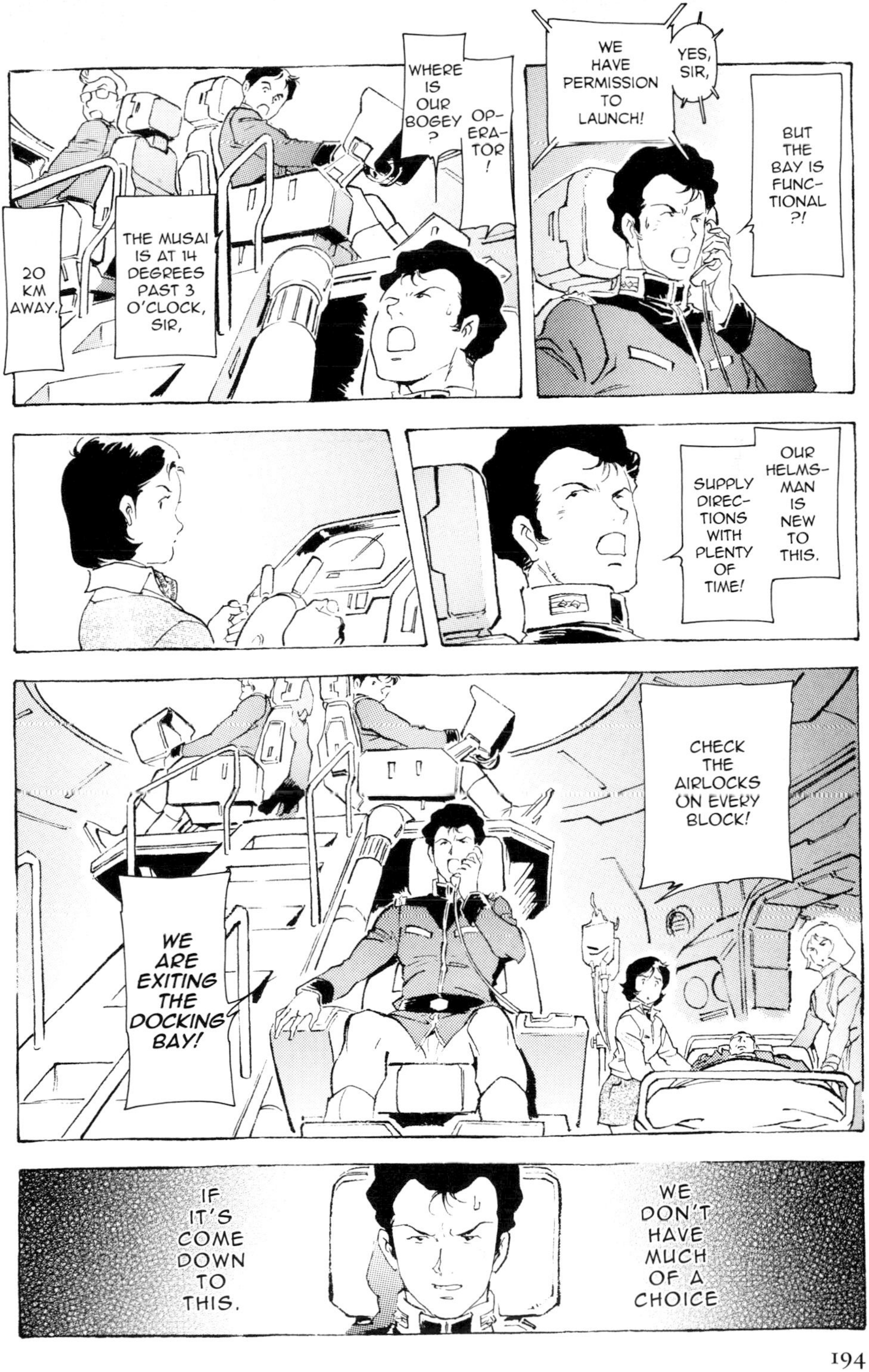
YES, SIR,
WE HAVE PERMISSION TO LAUNCH!
BUT THE BAY IS FUNCTIONAL?!
OPERATOR!
WHERE IS OUR BOGEY?
THE MUSAI IS AT 14 DEGREES PAST 3 O'CLOCK, SIR,
20 KM AWAY.
OUR HELMSMAN IS NEW TO THIS.
SUPPLY DIRECTIONS WITH PLENTY OF TIME!
CHECK THE AIRLOCKS ON EVERY BLOCK!
WE ARE EXITING THE DOCKING BAY!
WE DON'T HAVE MUCH OF A CHOICE
IF IT'S COME DOWN TO THIS.

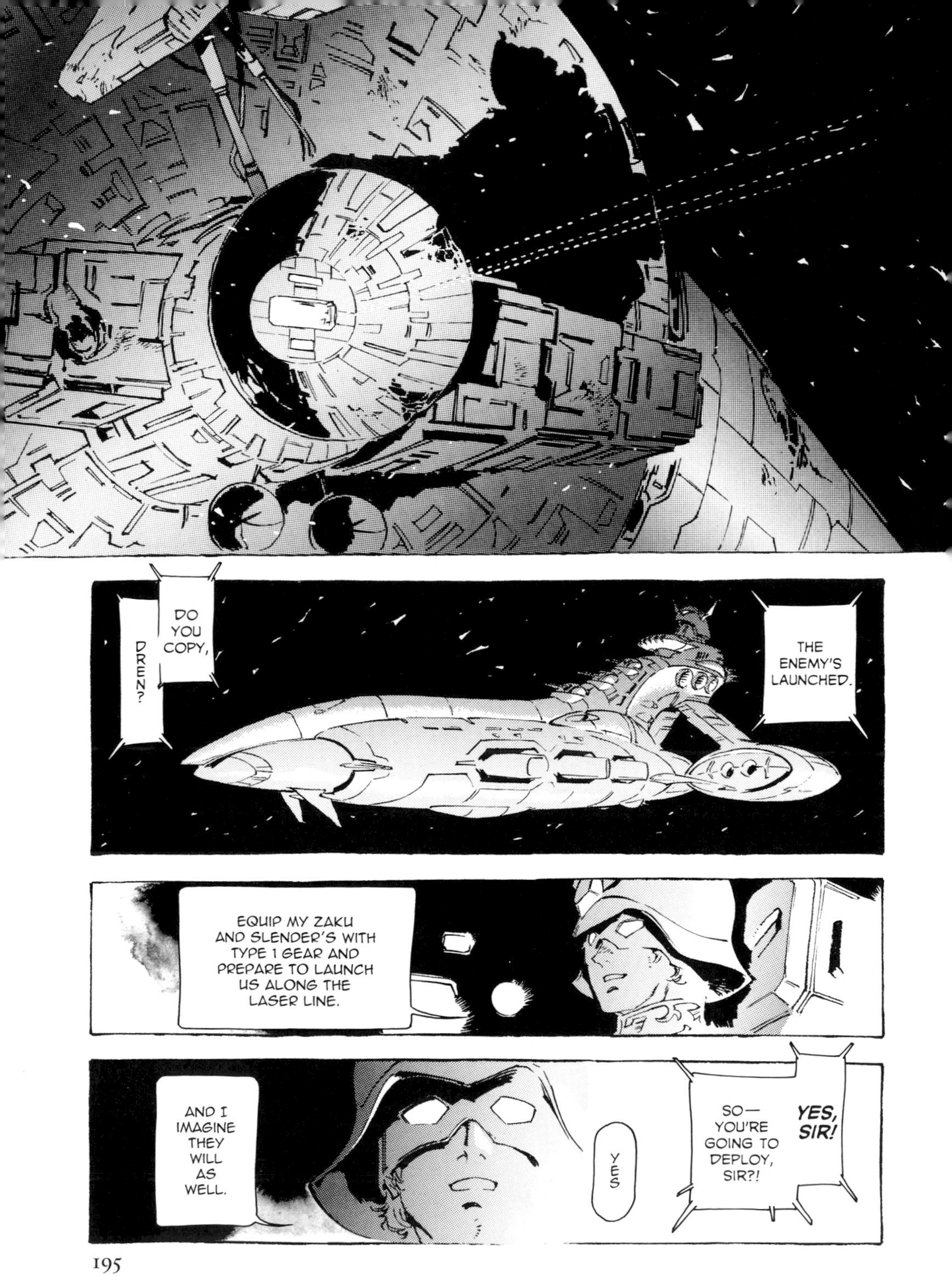
THE ENEMY'S LAUNCHED.
DO YOU COPY,
DREN?
EQUIP MY ZAKU AND SLENDER'S WITH TYPE 1 GEAR AND PREPARE TO LAUNCH US ALONG THE LASER LINE.
YES, SIR!
SO— YOU'RE GOING TO DEPLOY, SIR?!
YES
AND I IMAGINE THEY WILL AS WELL.

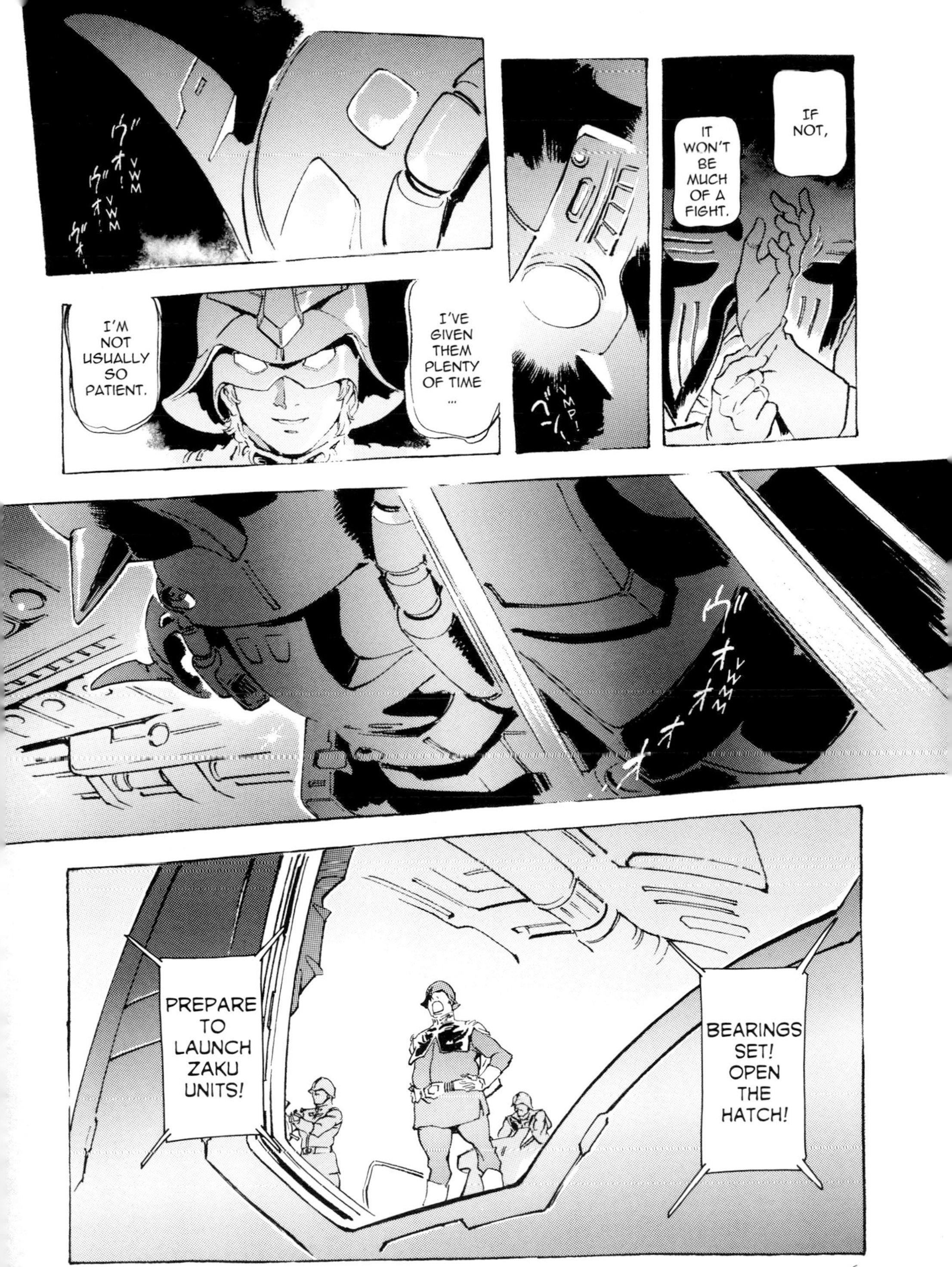
IF NOT,
IT WON'T BE MUCH OF A FIGHT.
VMP!
VWM! VWM! VWM
I'VE GIVEN THEM PLENTY OF TIME ...
I'M NOT USUALLY SO PATIENT.
VWMMM
BEARINGS SET! OPEN THE HATCH!
PREPARE TO LAUNCH ZAKU UNITS!

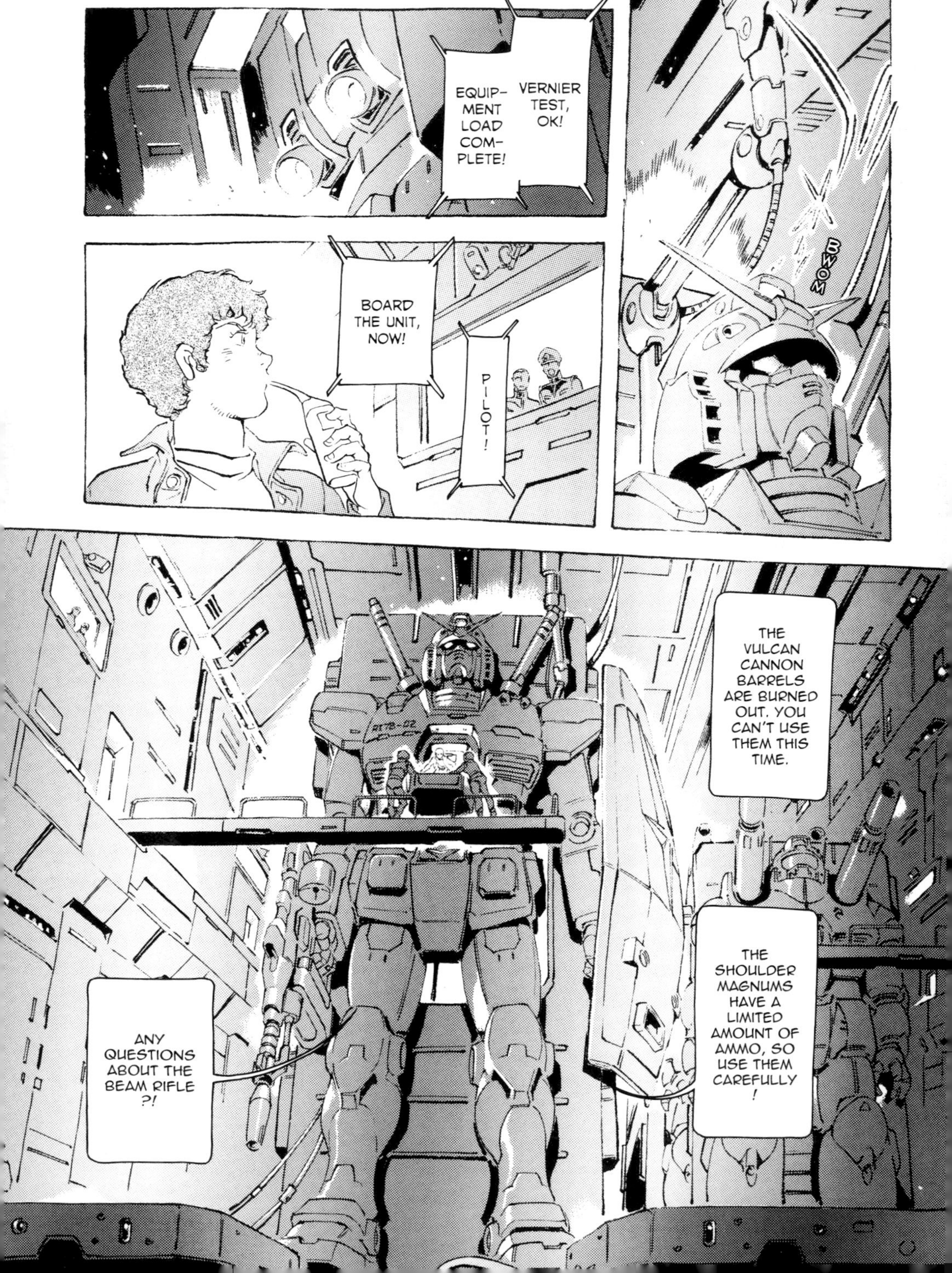
BWOM
VERNIER TEST, OK!
EQUIP-MENT LOAD COM-PLETE!
PILOT!
BOARD THE UNIT, NOW!
THE VULCAN CANNON BARRELS ARE BURNED OUT. YOU CAN'T USE THEM THIS TIME.
THE SHOULDER MAGNUMS HAVE A LIMITED AMOUNT OF AMMO, SO USE THEM CAREFULLY!
ANY QUESTIONS ABOUT THE BEAM RIFLE?!

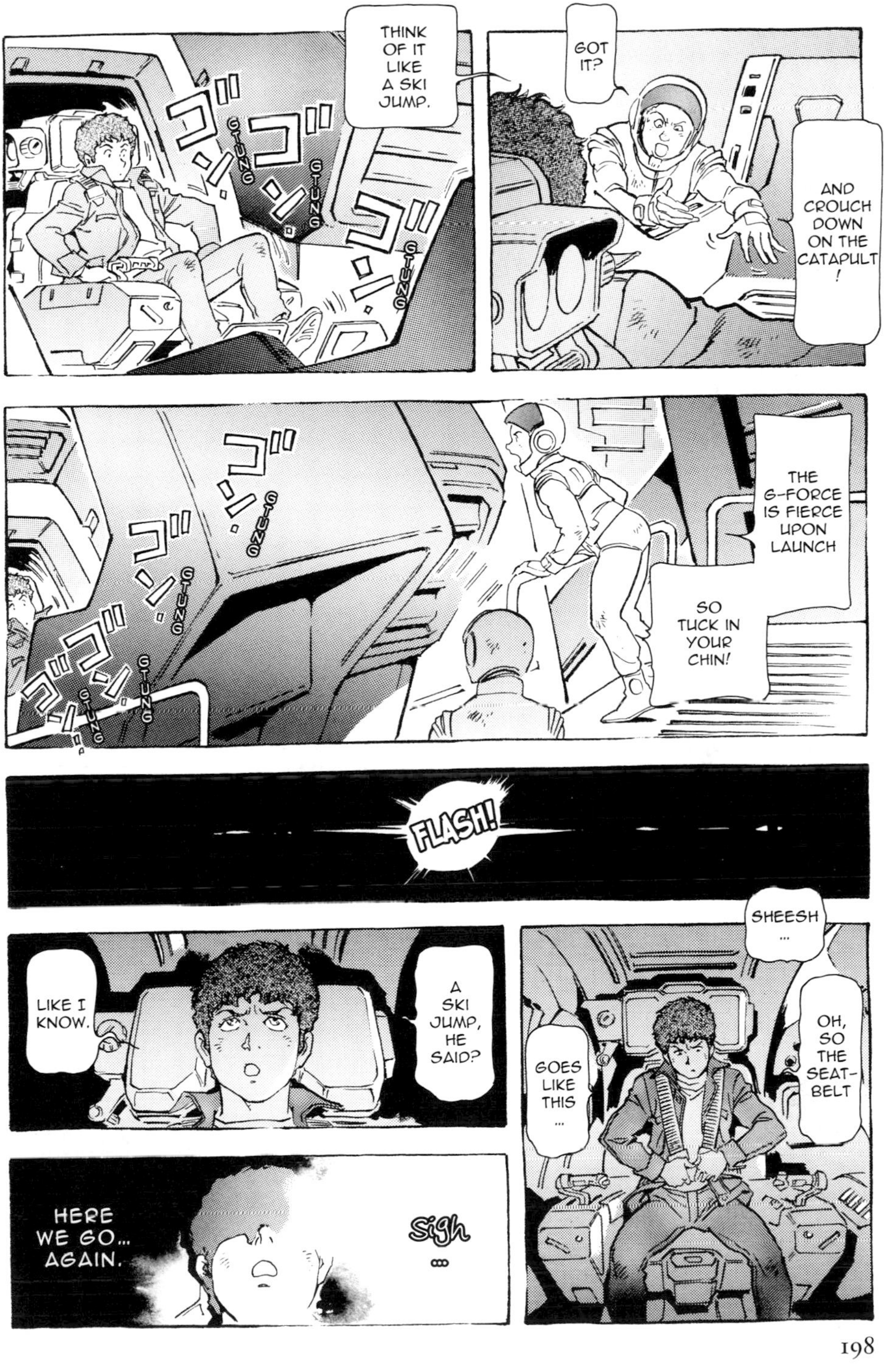
AND CROUCH DOWN ON THE CATAPULT!
GOT IT?
THINK OF IT LIKE A SKI JUMP.
GTUNG
GTUNG
GTUNG
THE G-FORCE IS FIERCE UPON LAUNCH
SO TUCK IN YOUR CHIN!
GTUNG
GTUNG
GTUNG
GTUNG
FLASH!
SHEESH ...
OH, SO THE SEAT-BELT
GOES LIKE THIS ...
A SKI JUMP, HE SAID?
LIKE I KNOW.
HERE WE GO... AGAIN.
Sigh ...

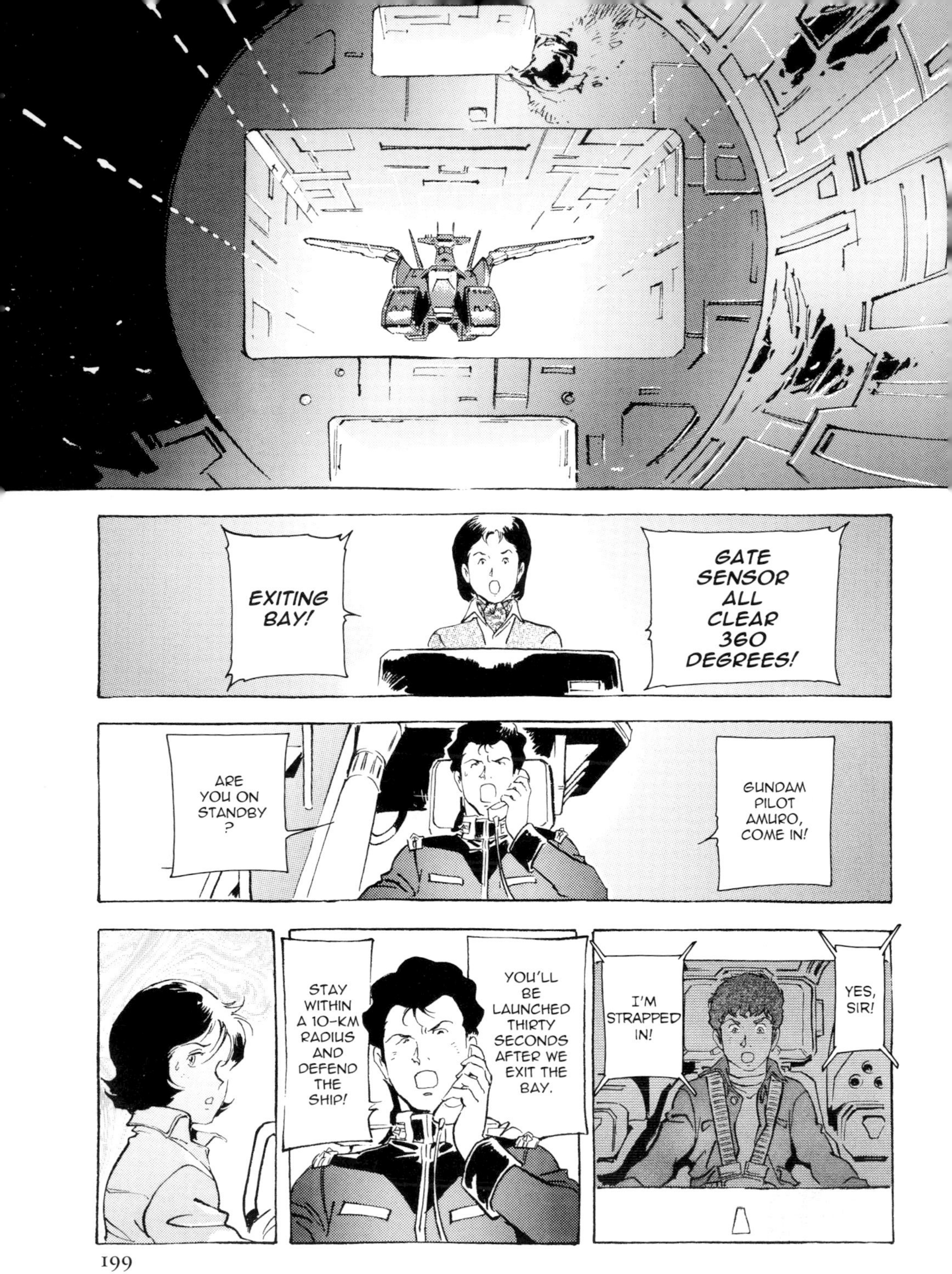
GATE SENSOR ALL CLEAR 360 DEGREES!
EXITING BAY!
GUNDAM PILOT AMURO, COME IN!
ARE YOU ON STANDBY?
YES, SIR!
I'M STRAPPED IN!
YOU'LL BE LAUNCHED THIRTY SECONDS AFTER WE EXIT THE BAY.
STAY WITHIN A 10-KM RADIUS AND DEFEND THE SHIP!

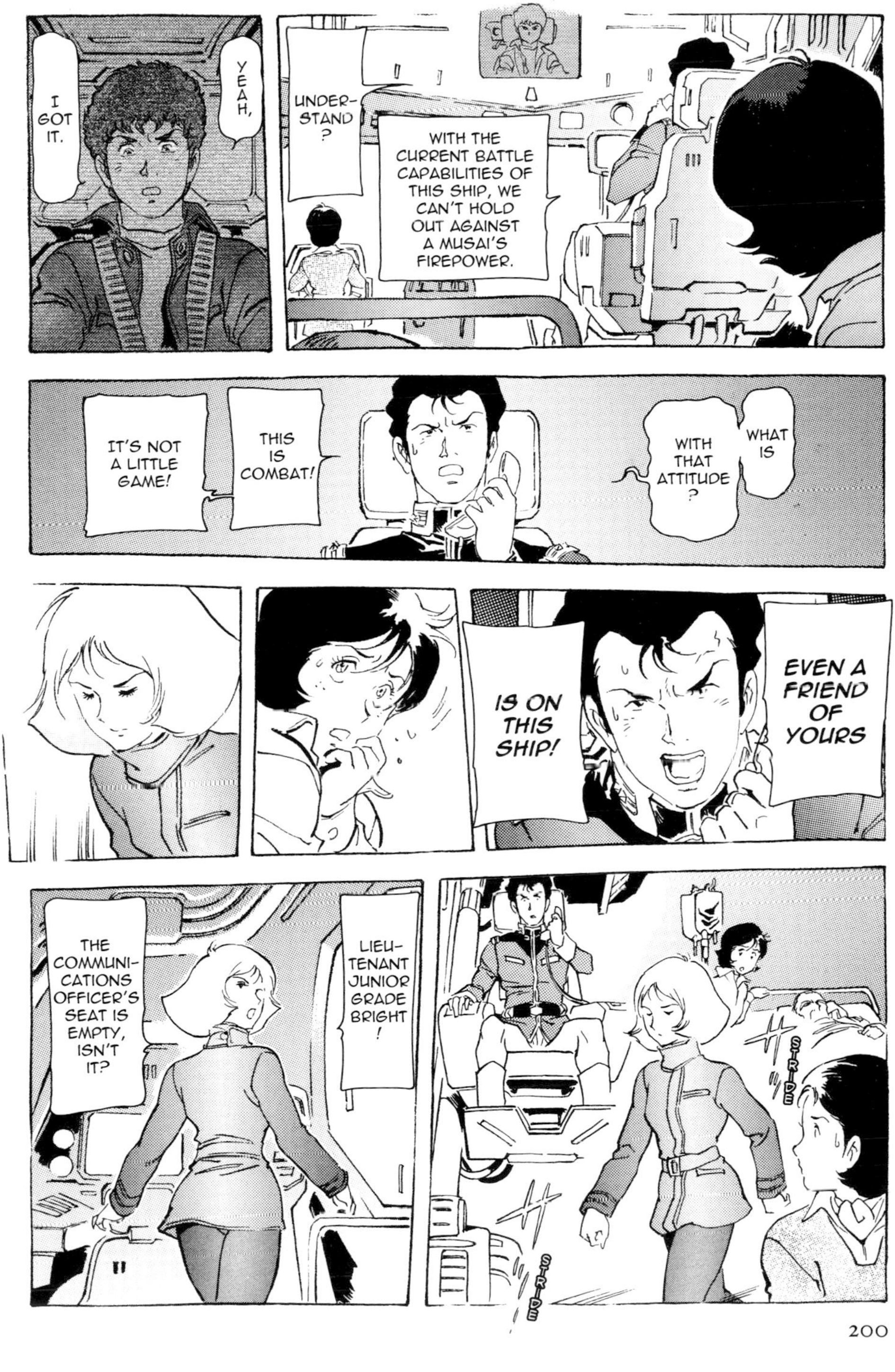
WITH THE CURRENT BATTLE CAPABILITIES OF THIS SHIP, WE CAN'T HOLD OUT AGAINST A MUSAI'S FIREPOWER.
UNDER-STAND?
YEAH,
I GOT IT.
WHAT IS
WITH THAT ATTITUDE?
THIS IS COMBAT!
IT'S NOT A LITTLE GAME!
EVEN A FRIEND OF YOURS
IS ON THIS SHIP!
STRIDE
STRIDE
LIEUTENANT JUNIOR GRADE BRIGHT!
THE COMMUNICATIONS OFFICER'S SEAT IS EMPTY, ISN'T IT?

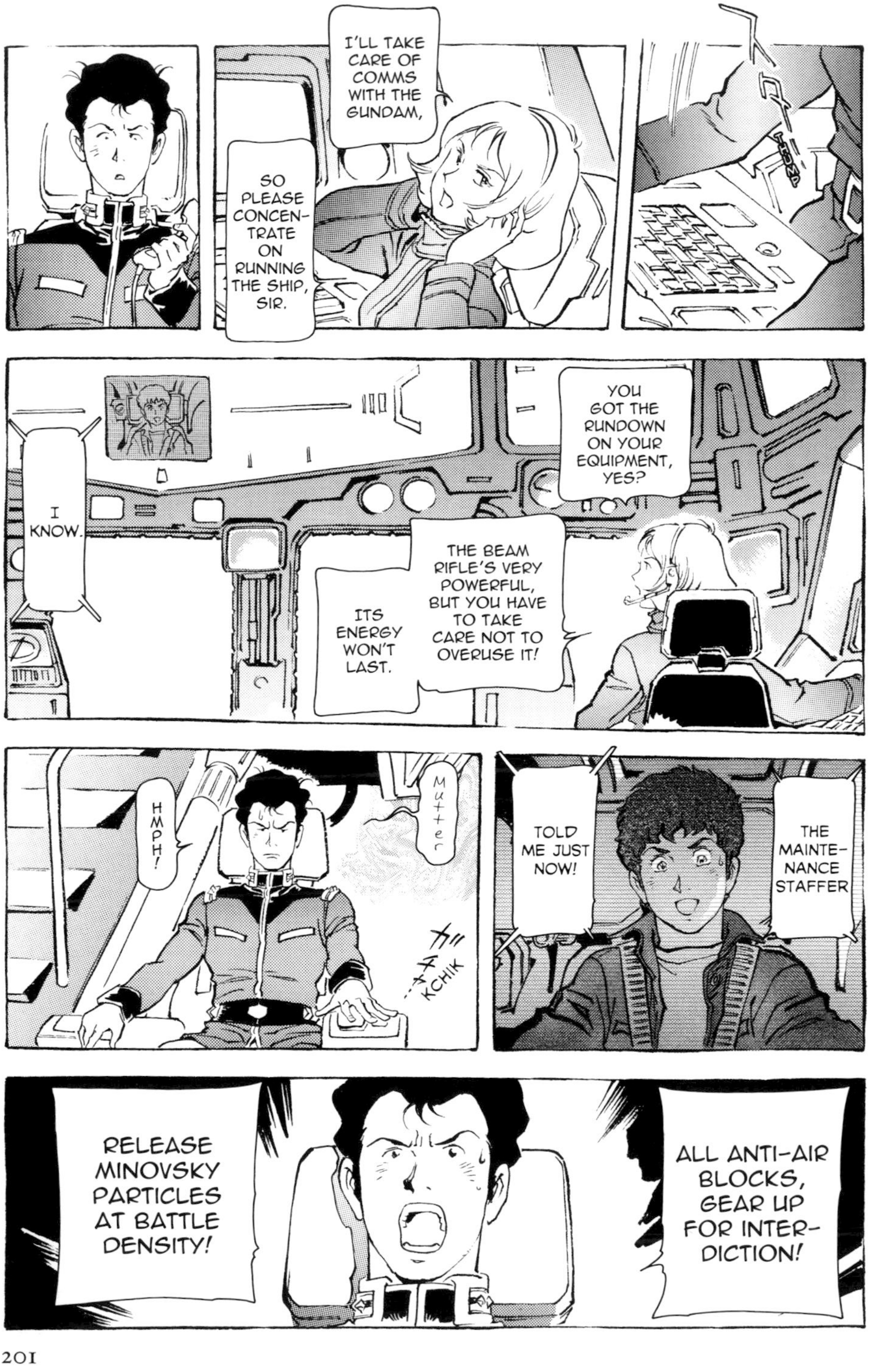
THOMP
I'LL TAKE CARE OF COMMS WITH THE GUNDAM,
SO PLEASE CONCENTRATE ON RUNNING THE SHIP, SIR.
YOU GOT THE RUNDOWN ON YOUR EQUIPMENT, YES?
THE BEAM RIFLE'S VERY POWERFUL, BUT YOU HAVE TO TAKE CARE NOT TO OVERUSE IT!
ITS ENERGY WON'T LAST.
I KNOW.
THE MAINTENANCE STAFFER
TOLD ME JUST NOW!
Mutter
KCHIK
HMPH!
ALL ANTI-AIR BLOCKS, GEAR UP FOR INTERDICTION!
RELEASE MINOVSKY PARTICLES AT BATTLE DENSITY!

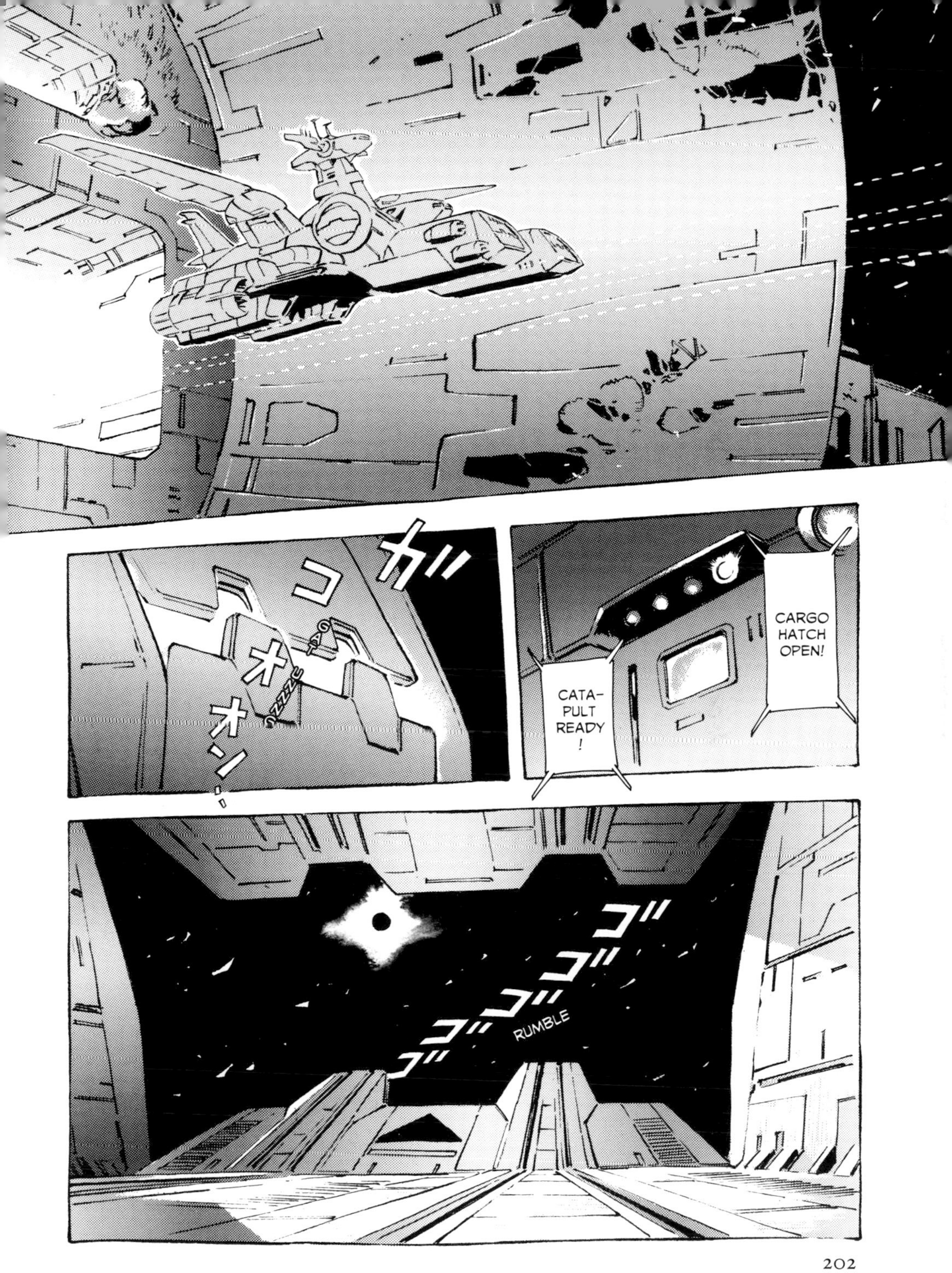
CARGO HATCH OPEN!
CATA-PULT READY!
RUMBLE

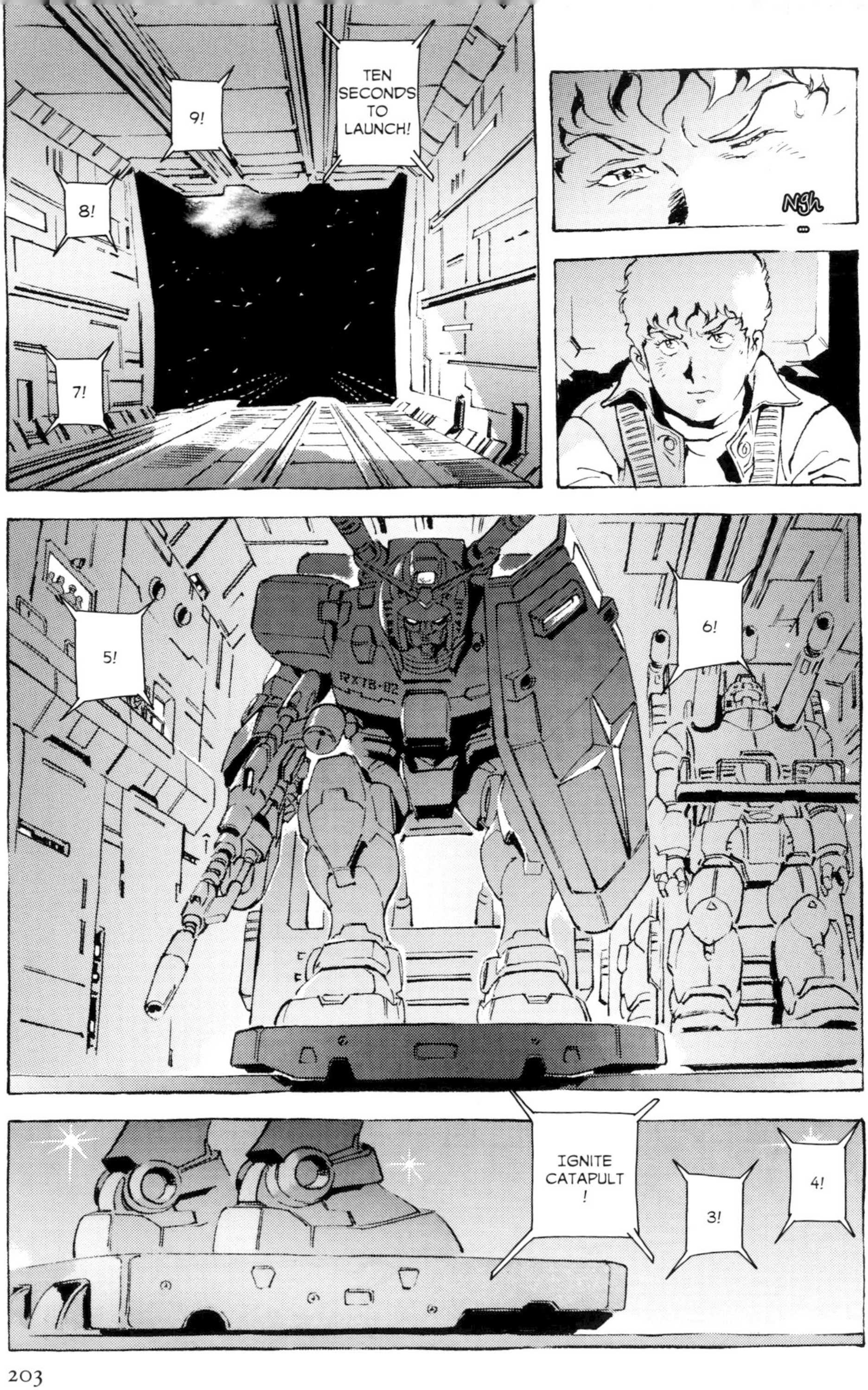
Ngh...
TEN SECONDS TO LAUNCH!
9!
8!
7!
6!
5!
IGNITE CATAPULT!
4!
3!

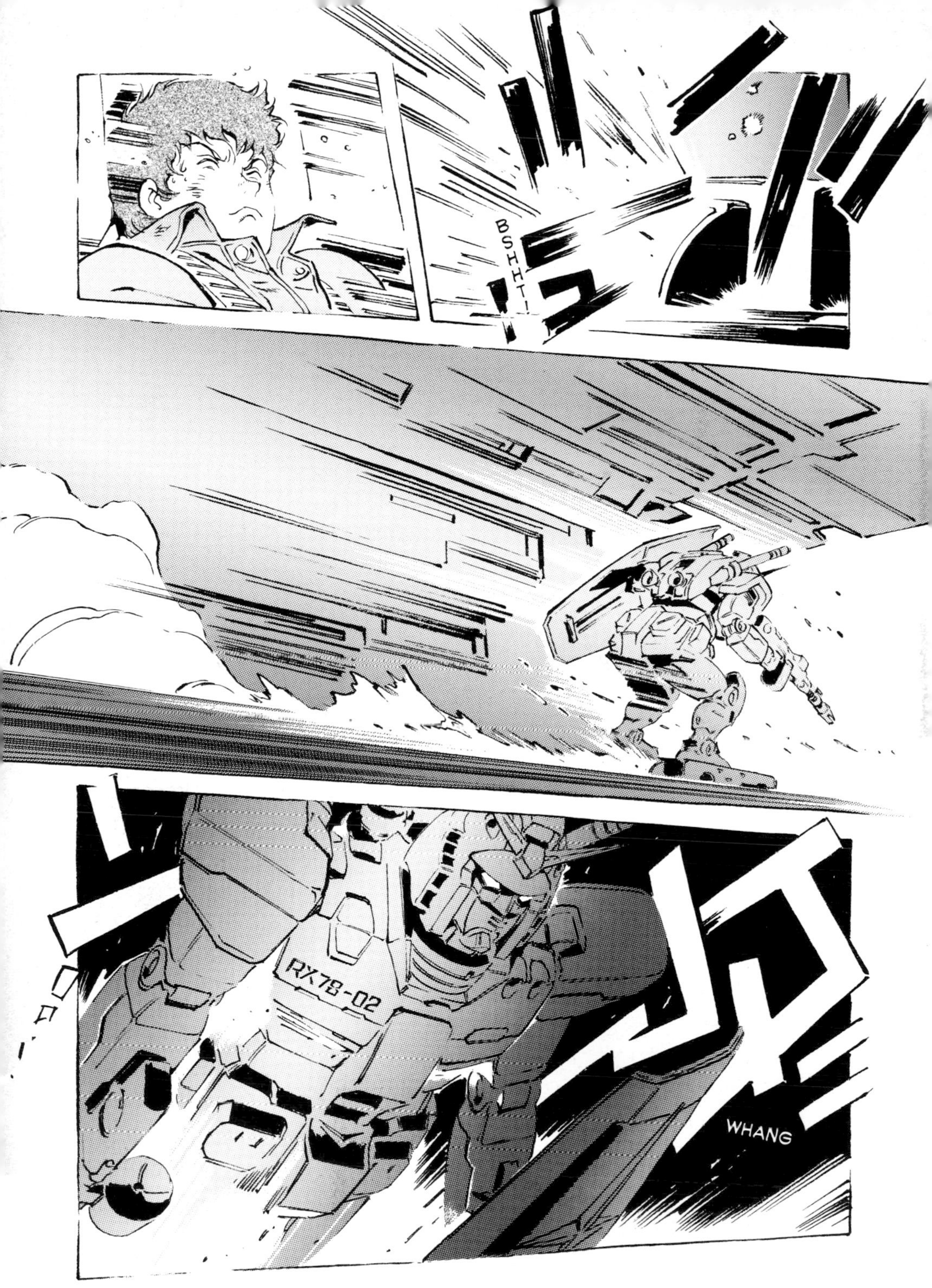
BSHHT!
RX78-02
WHANG

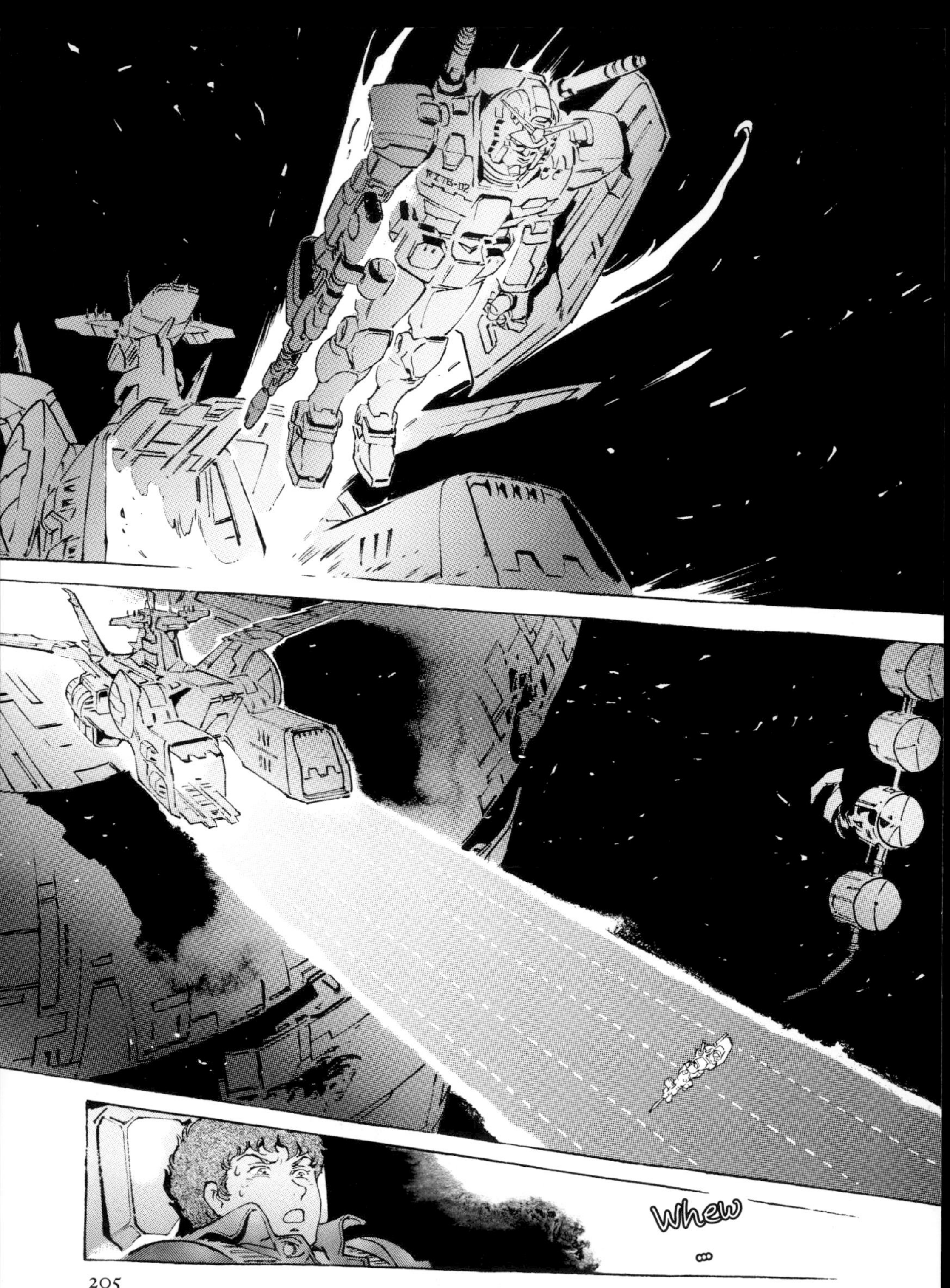
Whew
...

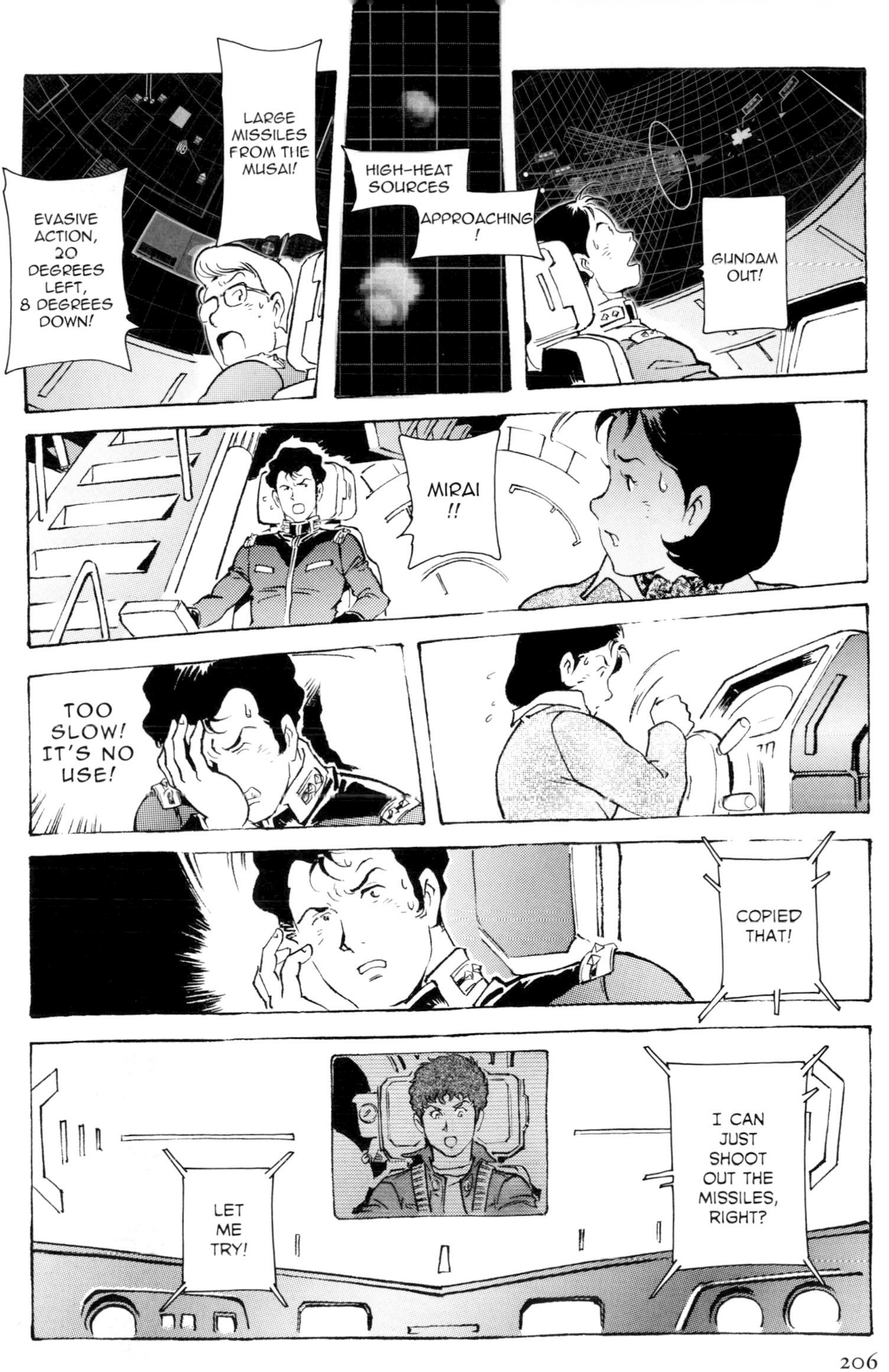
GUNDAM OUT!
HIGH-HEAT SOURCES
APPROACHING!
LARGE MISSILES FROM THE MUSAI!
EVASIVE ACTION, 20 DEGREES LEFT, 8 DEGREES DOWN!
MIRAI!!
TOO SLOW! IT'S NO USE!
COPIED THAT!
I CAN JUST SHOOT OUT THE MISSILES, RIGHT?
LET ME TRY!

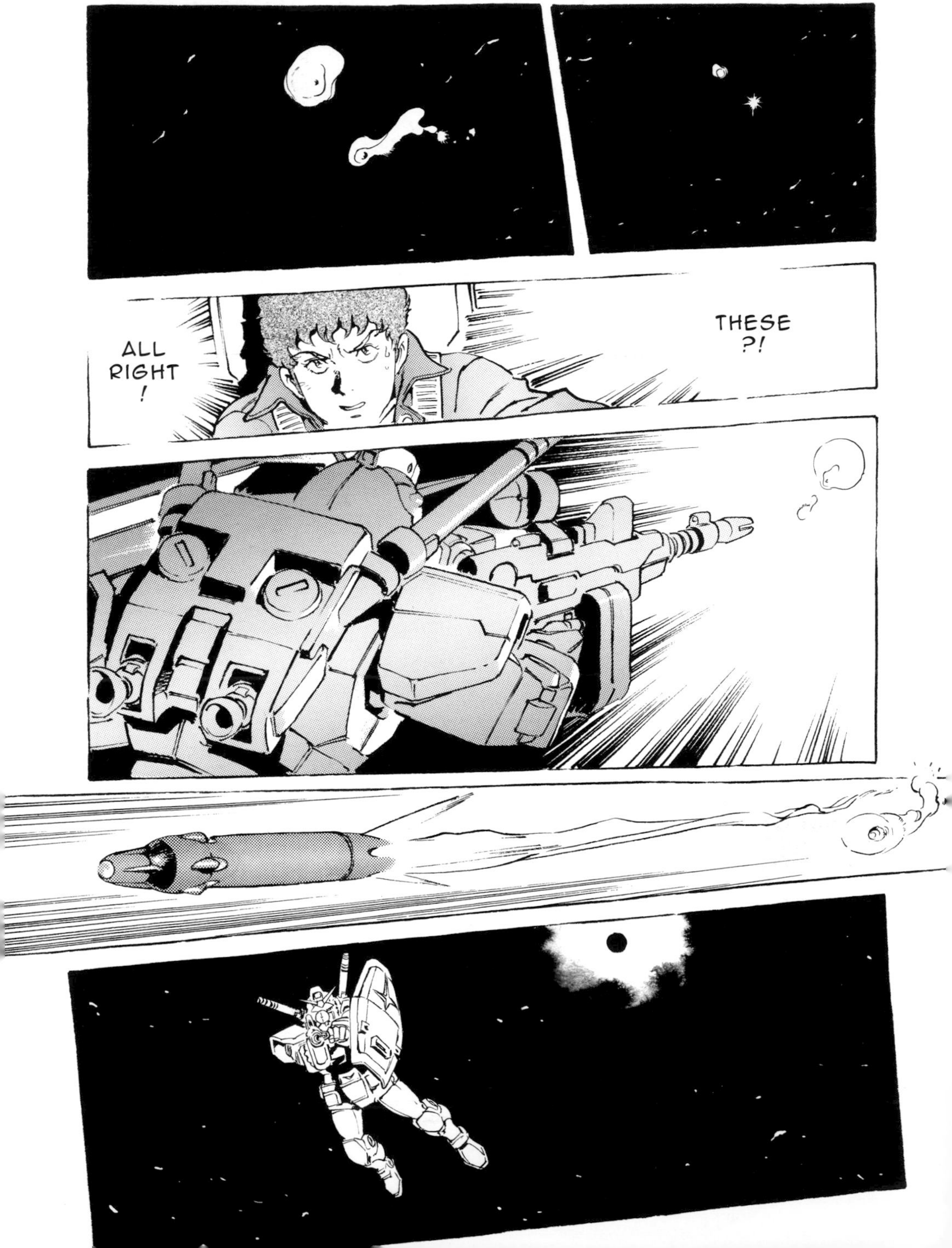
THESE ?!
ALL RIGHT !

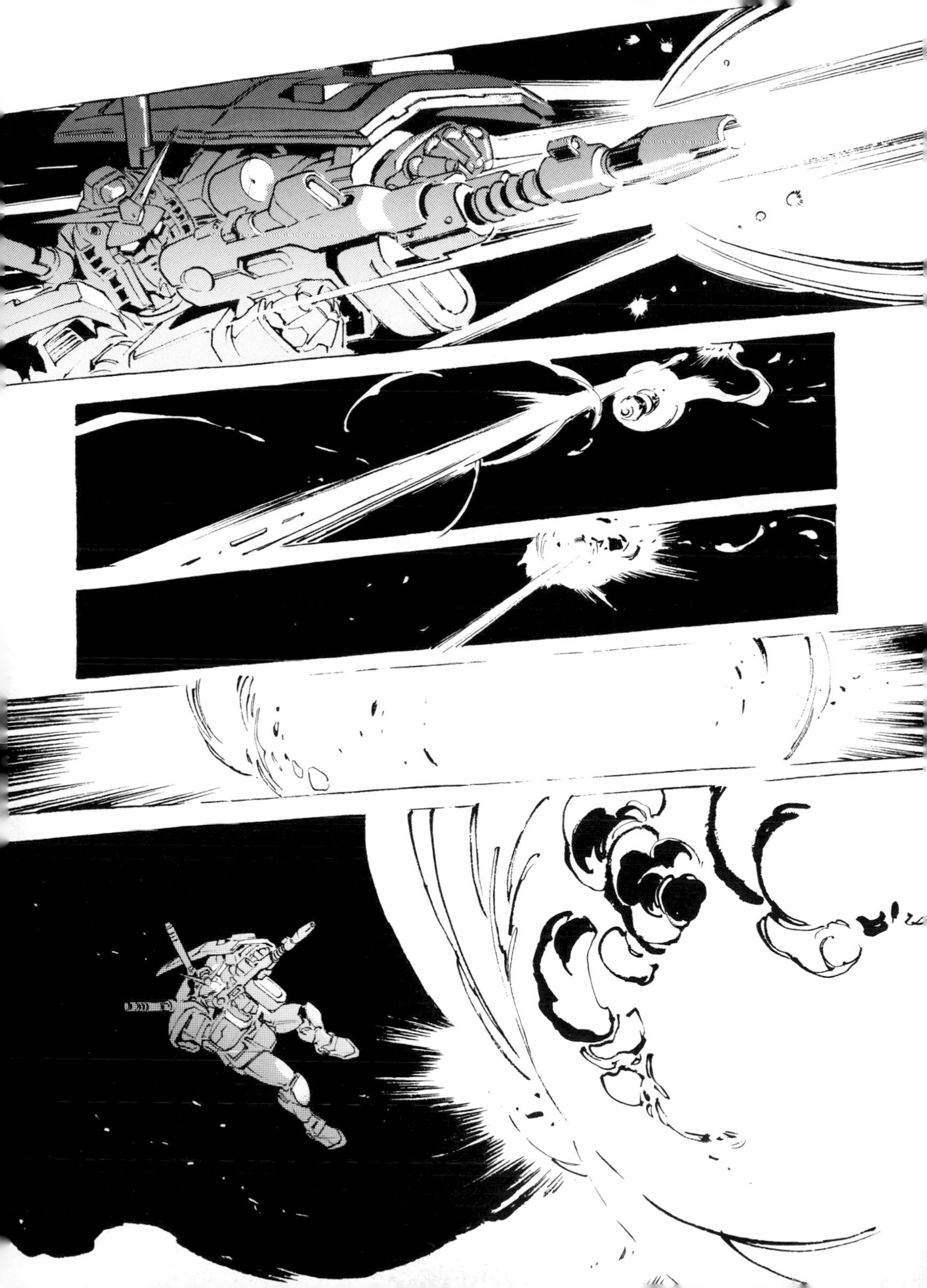

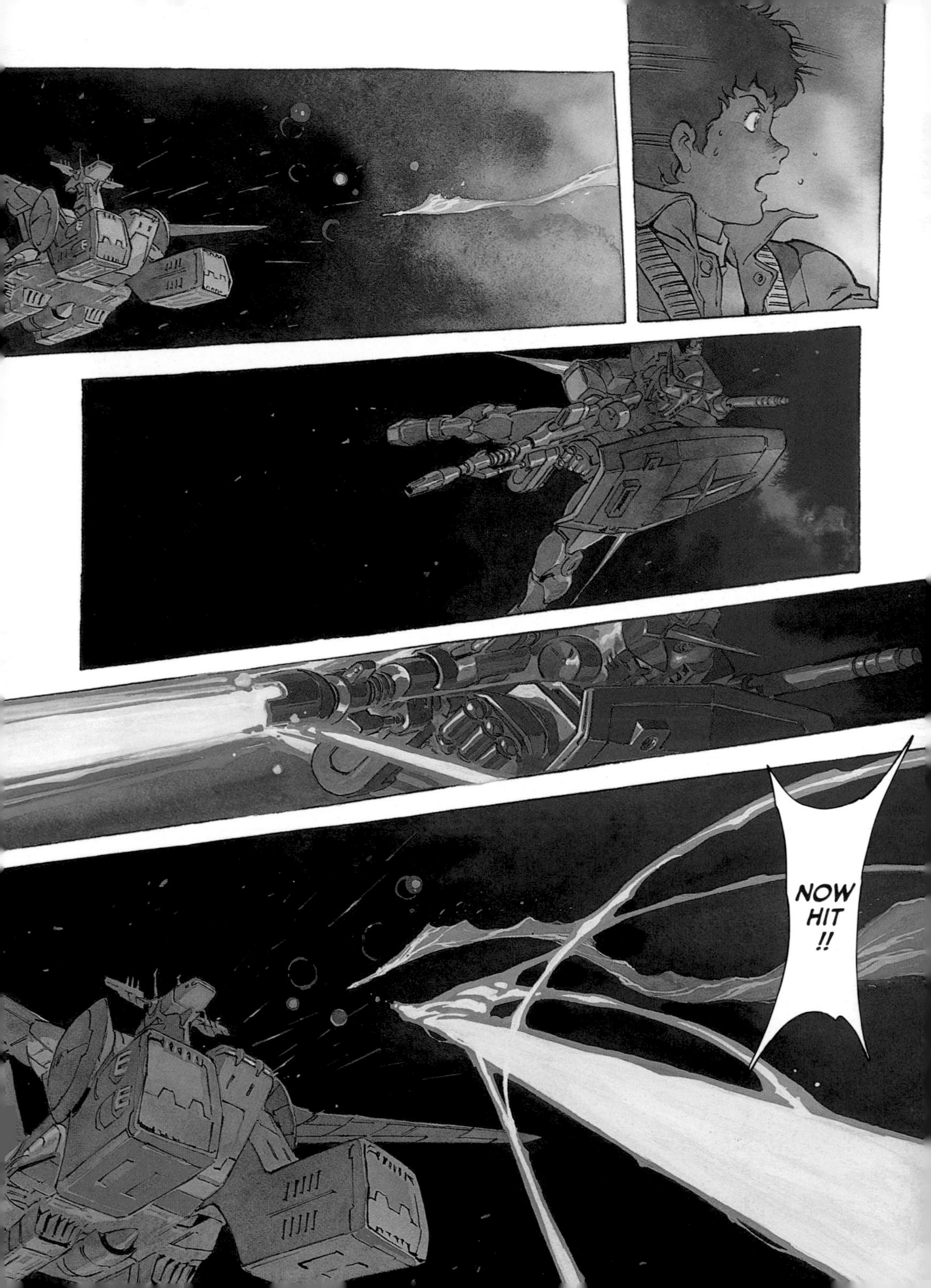
NOW HIT !!

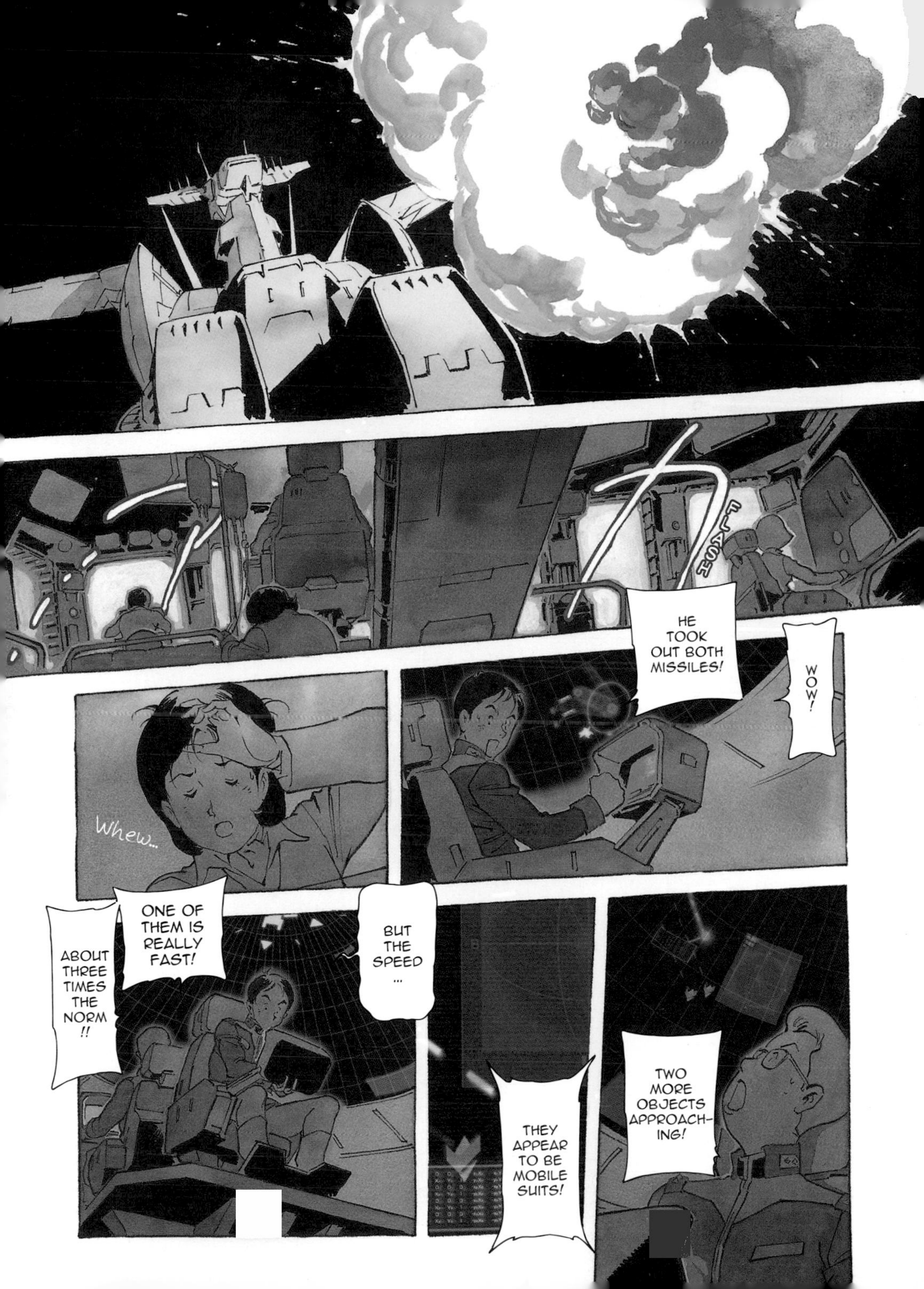
FLASH
HE TOOK OUT BOTH MISSILES!
WOW!
Whew...
TWO MORE OBJECTS APPROACHING!
THEY APPEAR TO BE MOBILE SUITS!
BUT THE SPEED...
ONE OF THEM IS REALLY FAST!
ABOUT THREE TIMES THE NORM!!

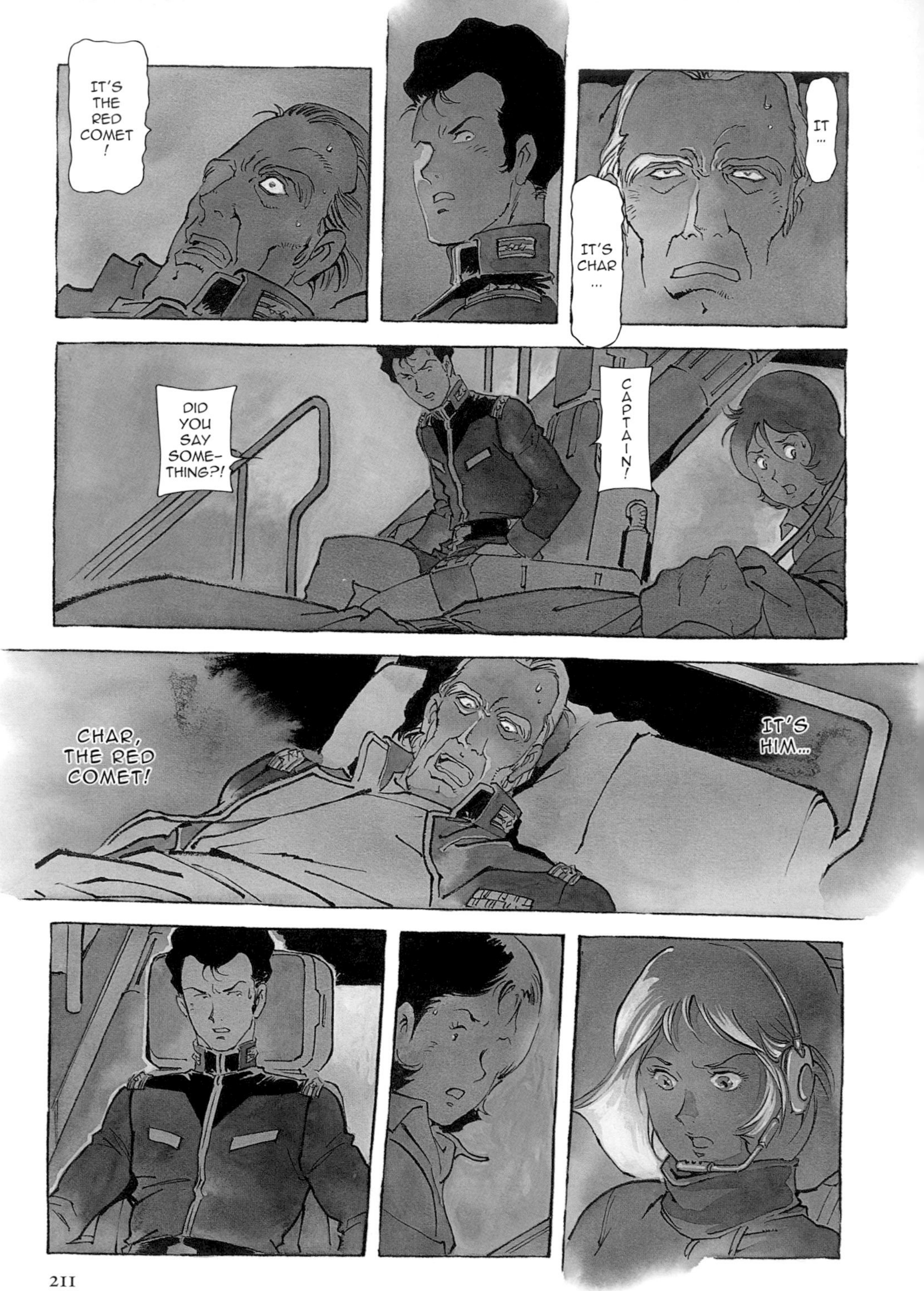
IT ...
IT'S CHAR ...
IT'S THE RED COMET!
CAPTAIN!
DID YOU SAY SOMETHING?!
IT'S HIM...
CHAR, THE RED COMET!

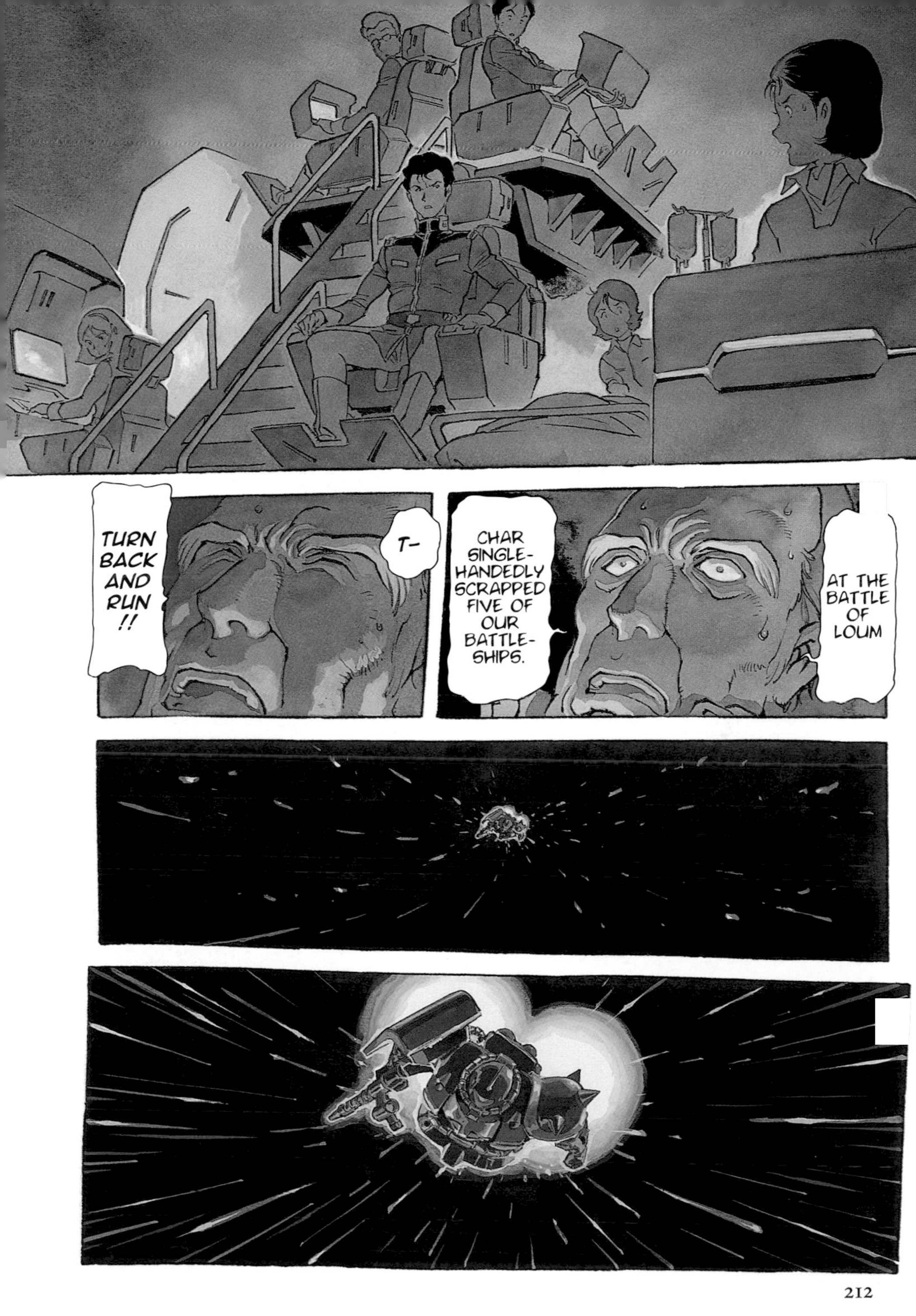
AT THE BATTLE OF LOUM
CHAR SINGLE-HANDEDLY SCRAPPED FIVE OF OUR BATTLESHIPS.
T-
TURN BACK AND RUN!!

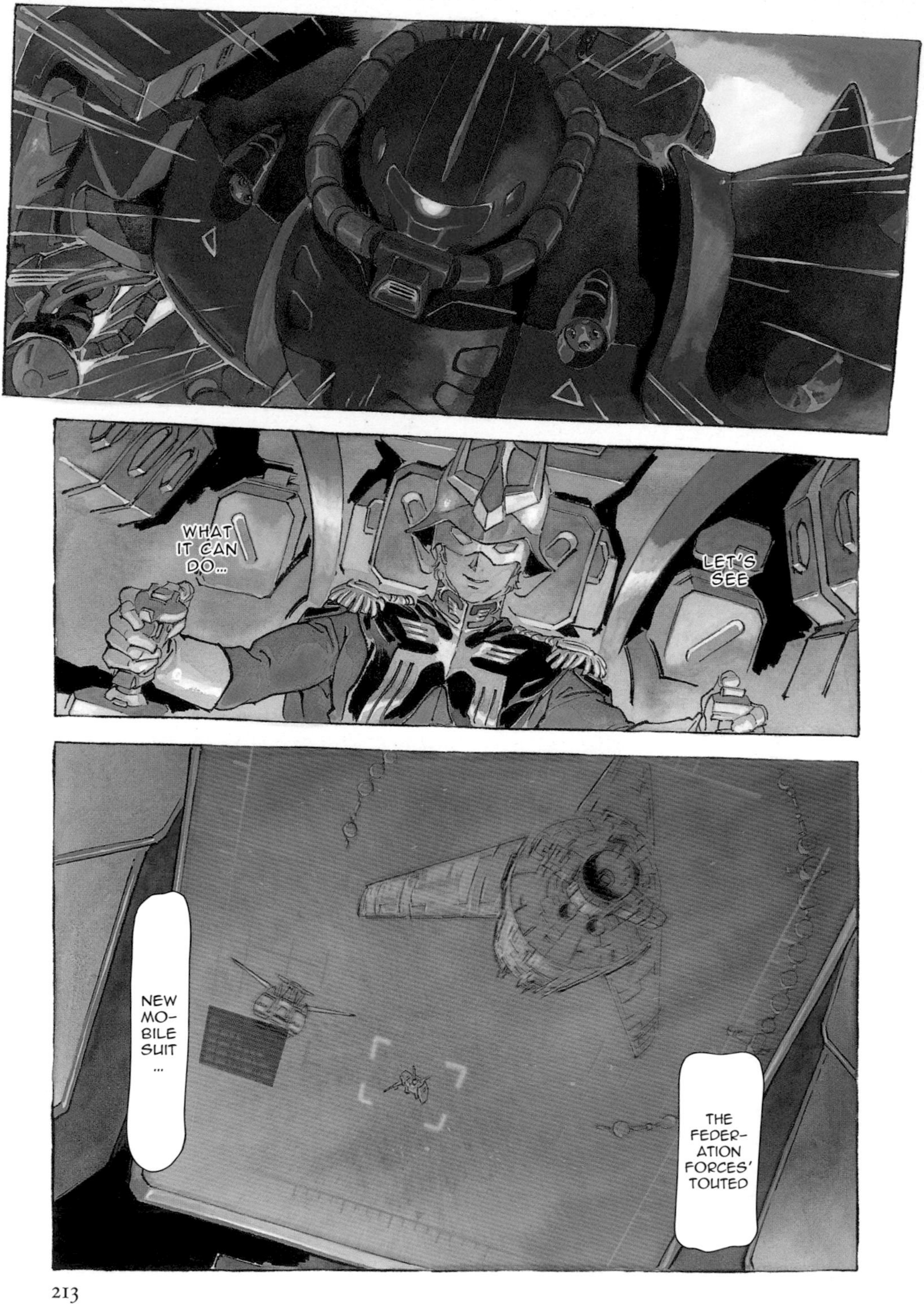
LET'S SEE
WHAT IT CAN DO...
THE FEDER-ATION FORCES' TOUTED
NEW MO-BILE SUIT ...

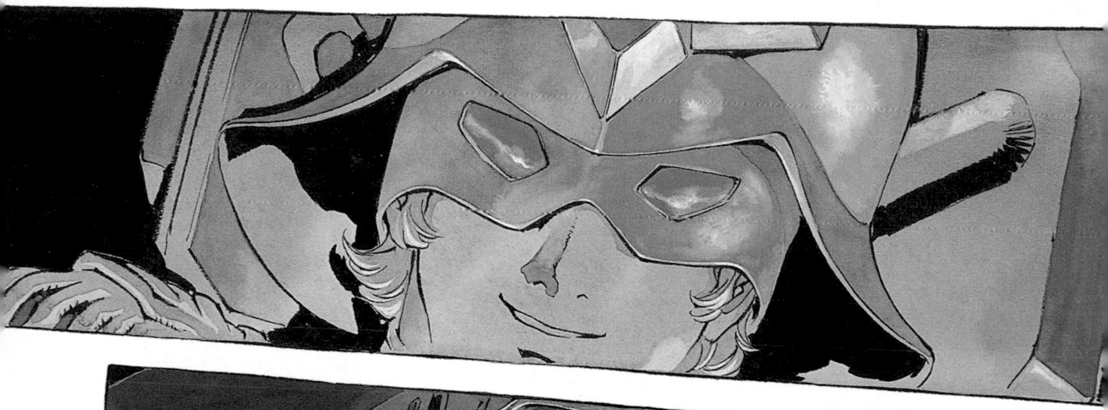
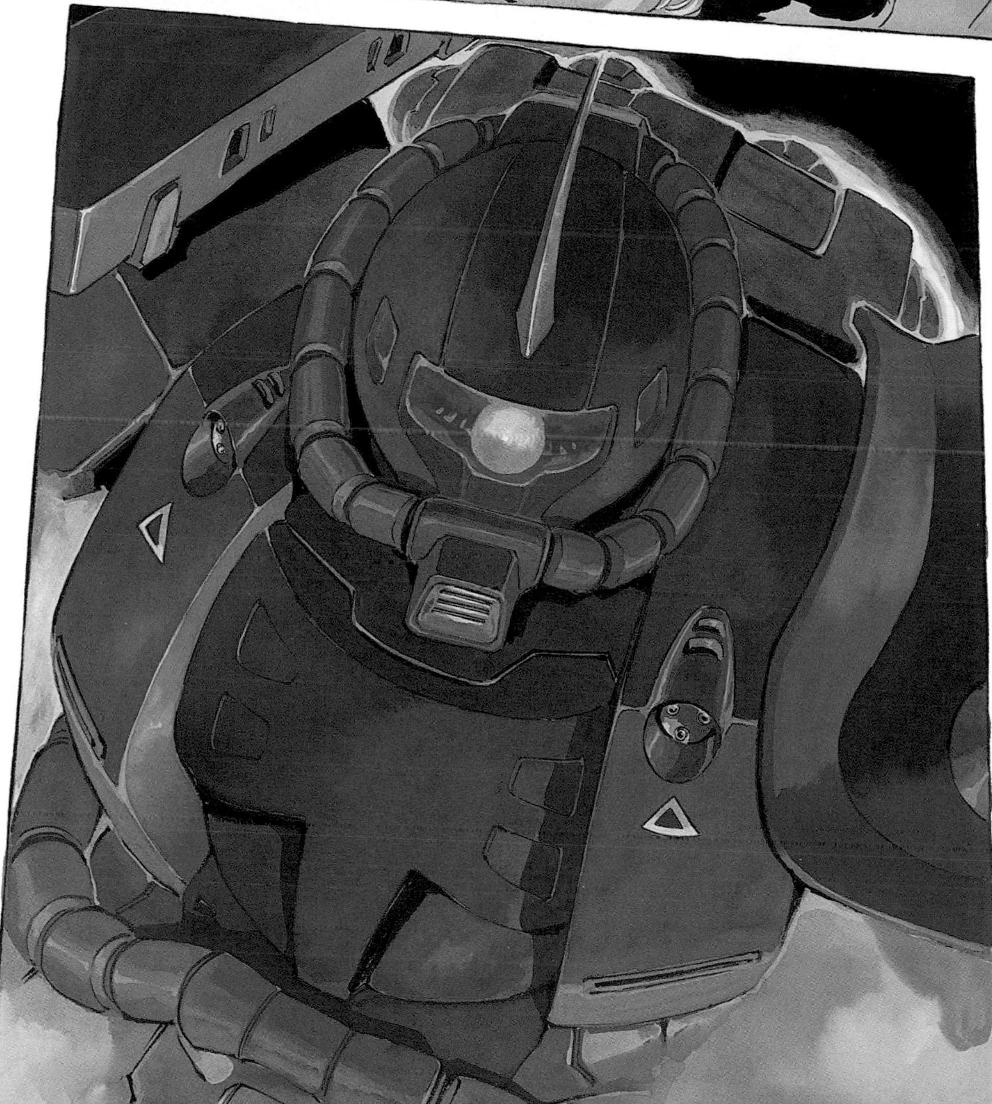

SECTION V

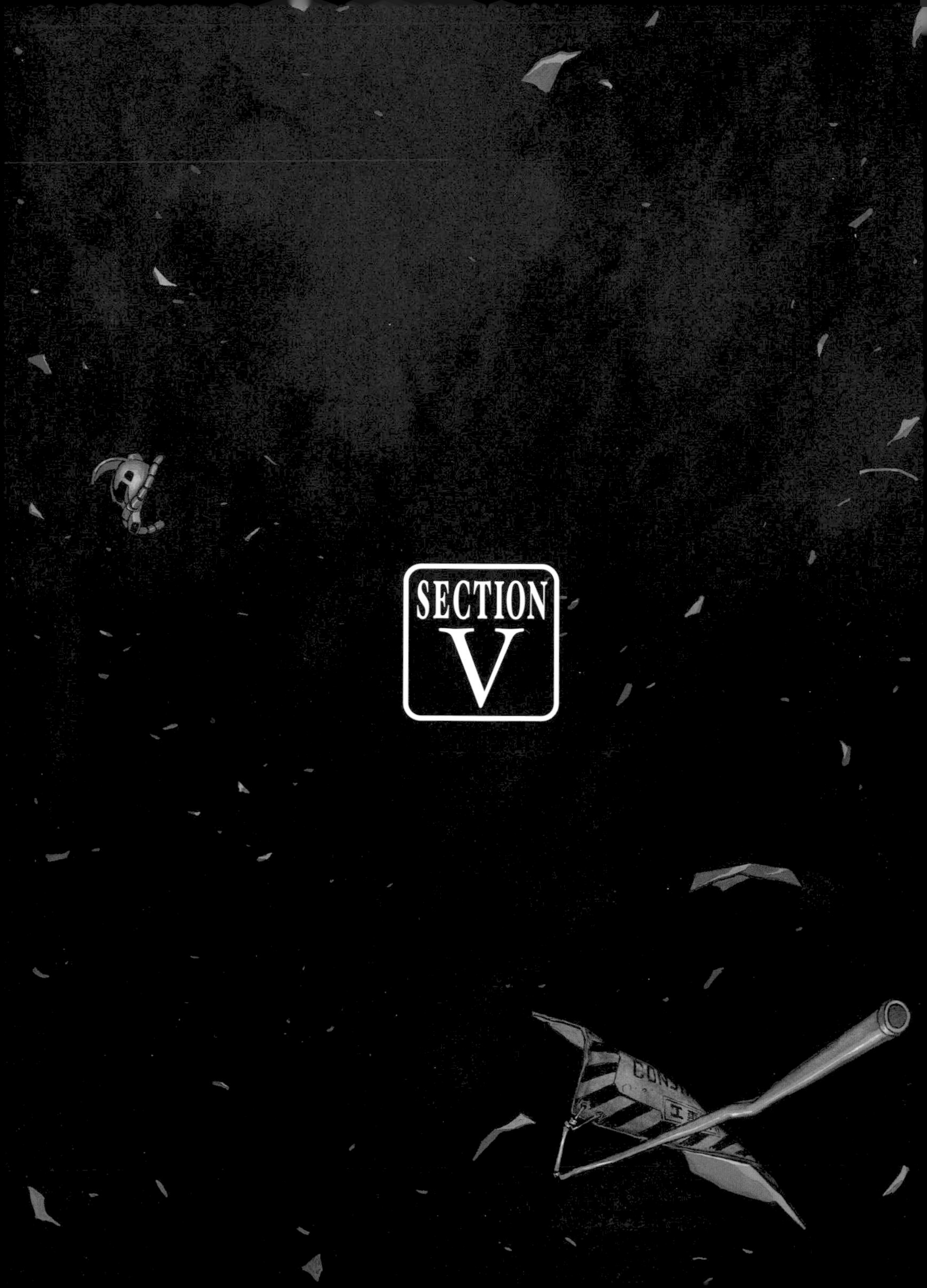

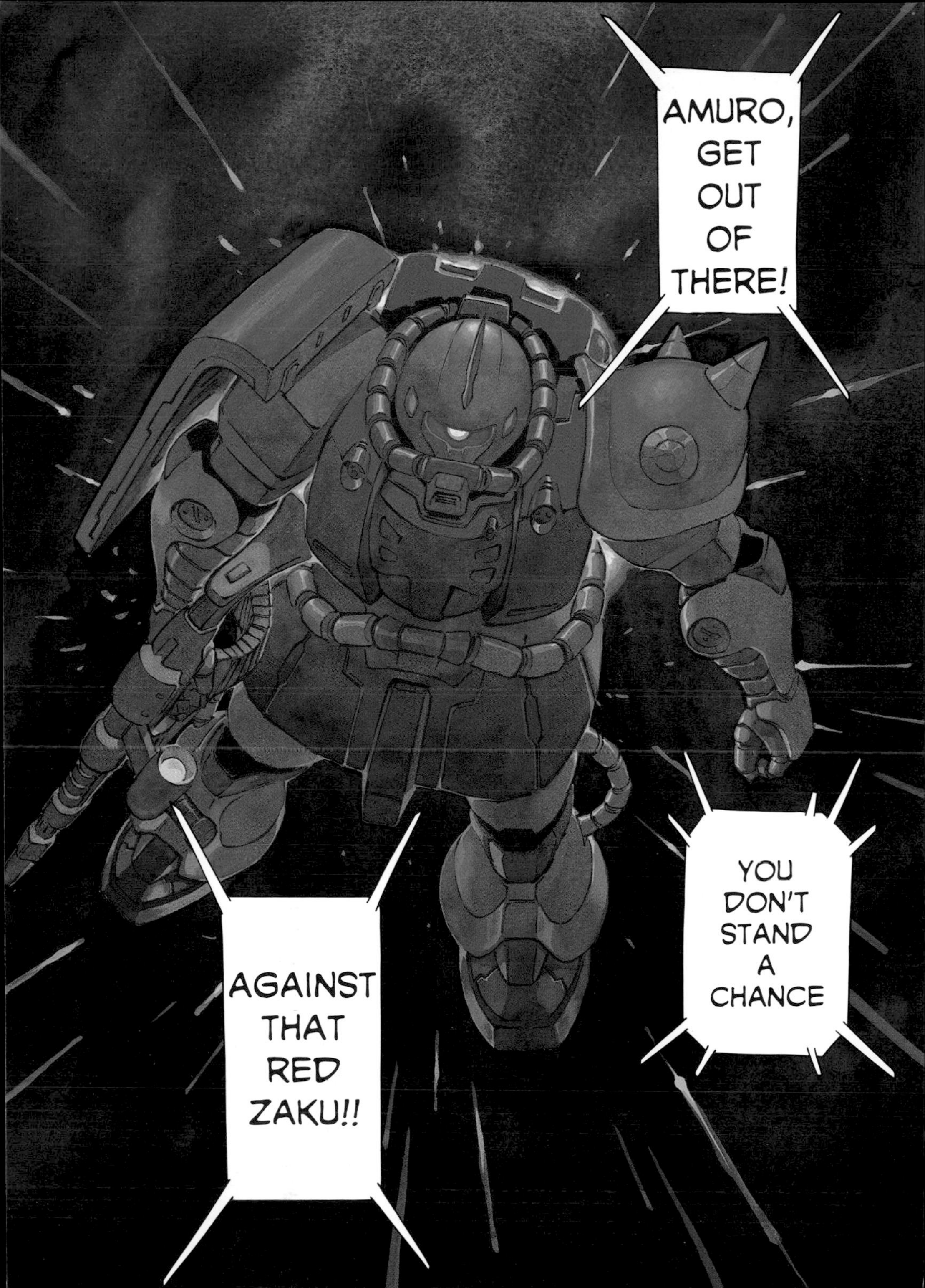
AMURO, GET OUT OF THERE!
YOU DON'T STAND A CHANCE
AGAINST THAT RED ZAKU!!

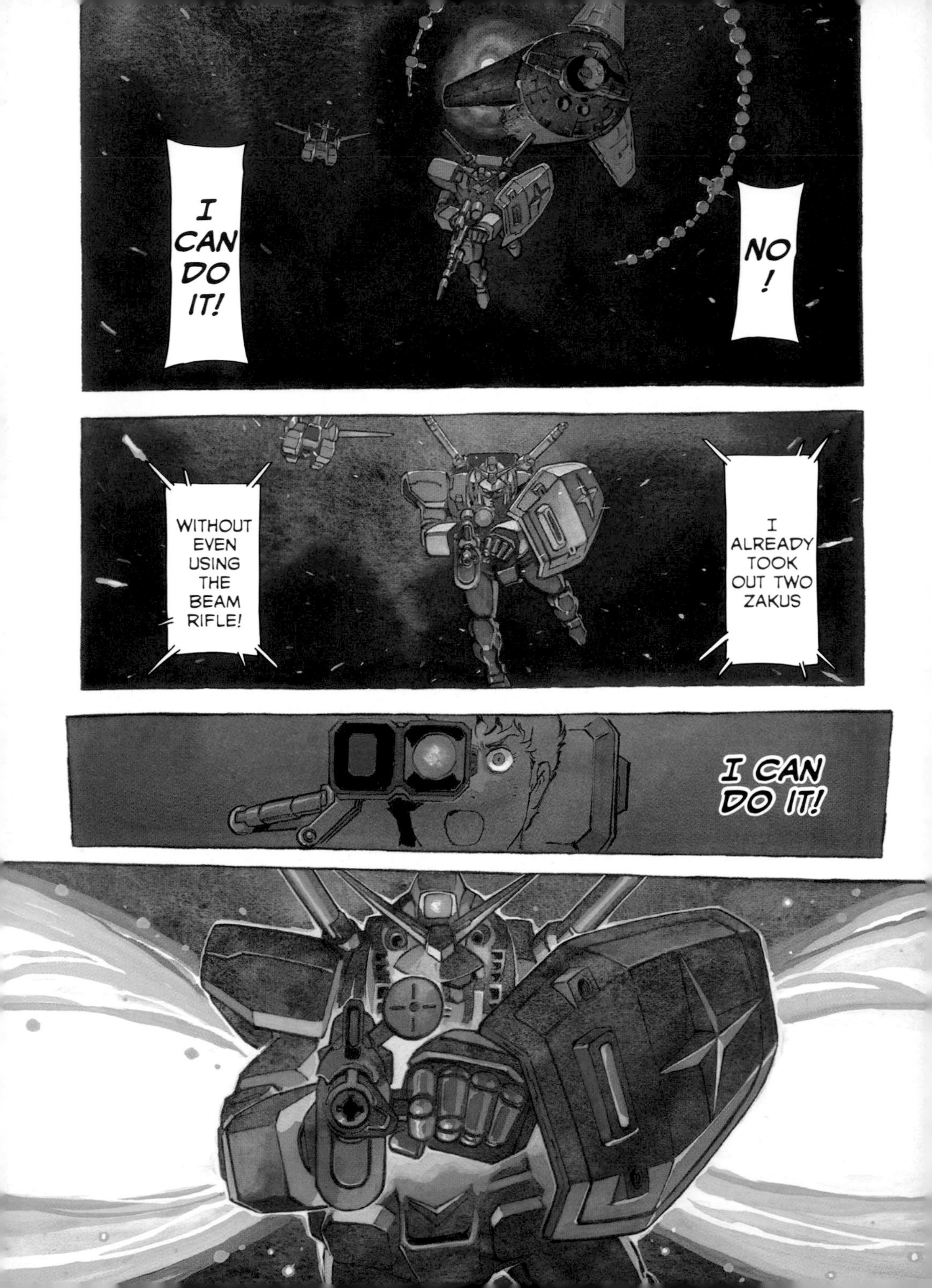
NO!
I CAN DO IT!
I ALREADY TOOK OUT TWO ZAKUS
WITHOUT EVEN USING THE BEAM RIFLE!
I CAN DO IT!

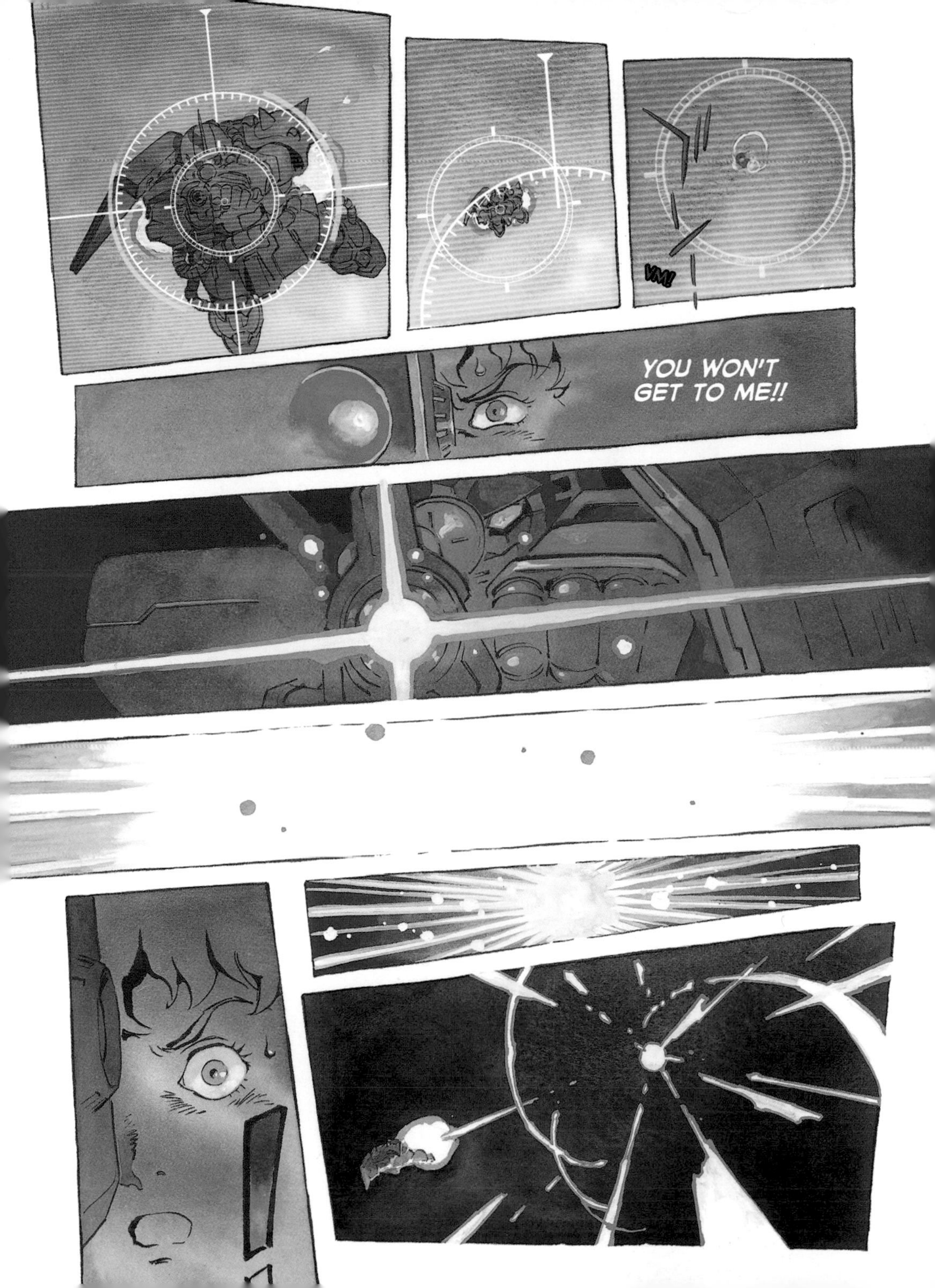
VM!
YOU WON'T GET TO ME!!

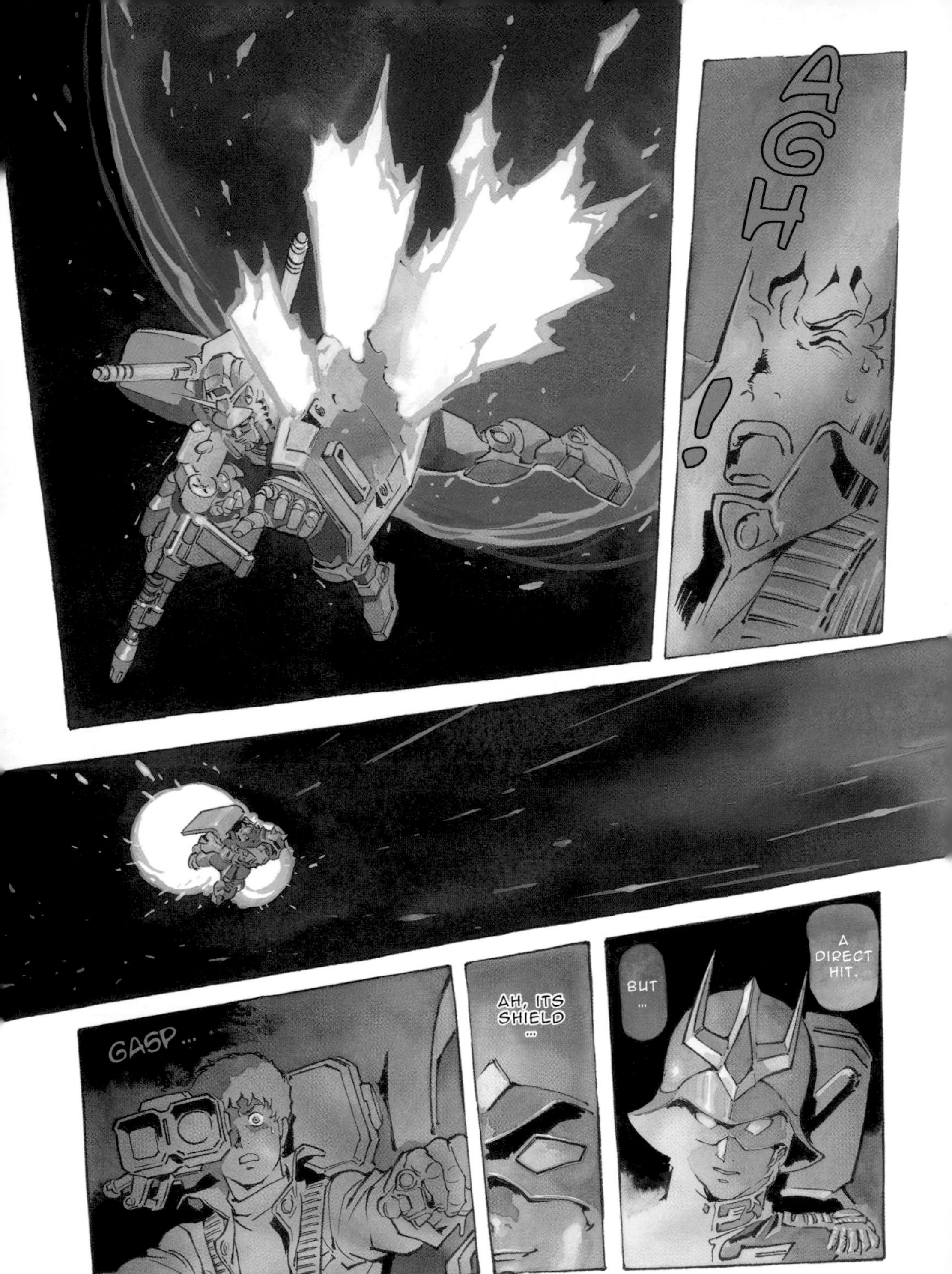
AGH
!
A DIRECT HIT.
BUT ...
AH, ITS SHIELD ...
GASP ...

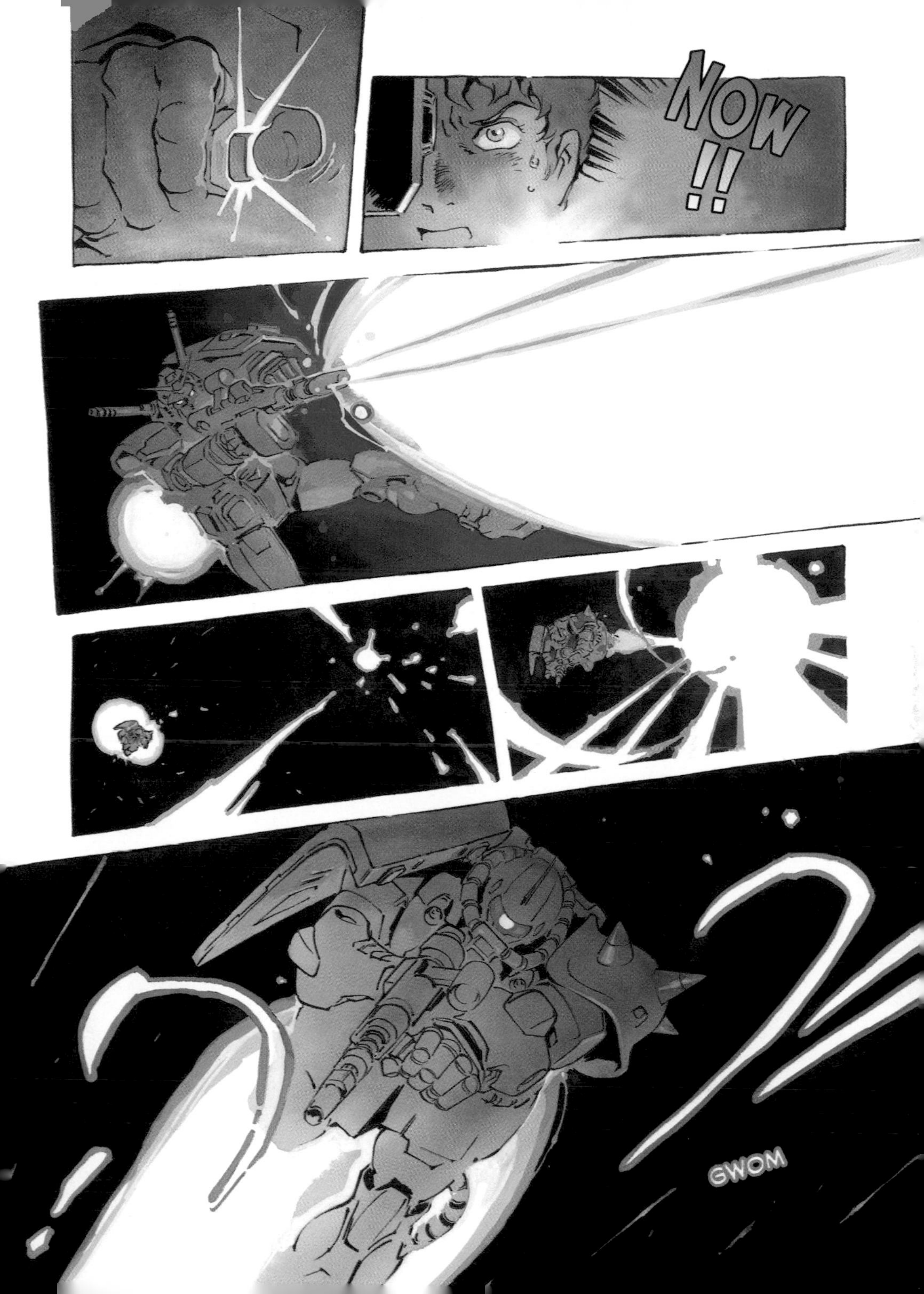
NOW!!
GWOM

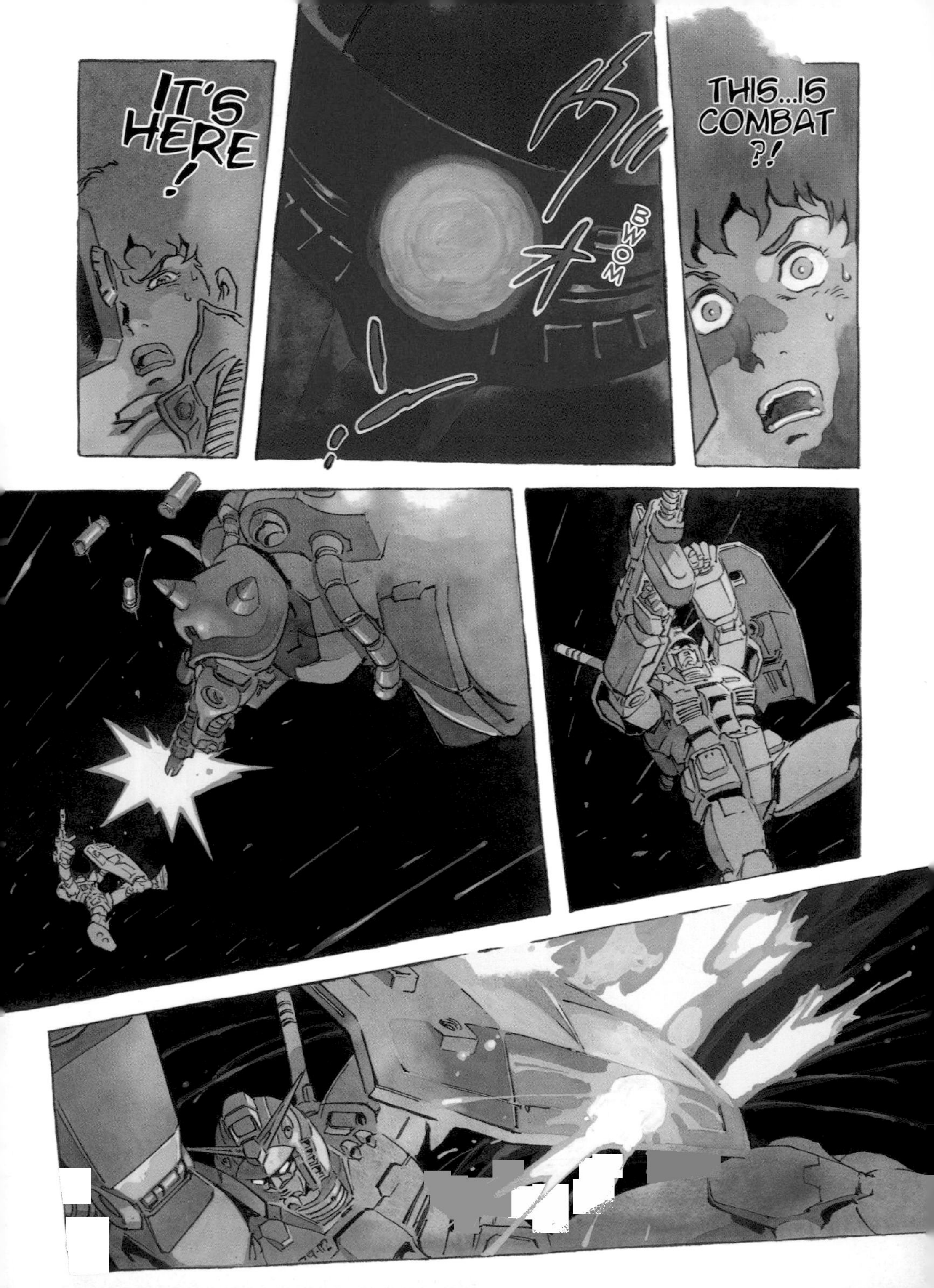
THIS...IS COMBAT ?!
BWOOM
IT'S HERE !

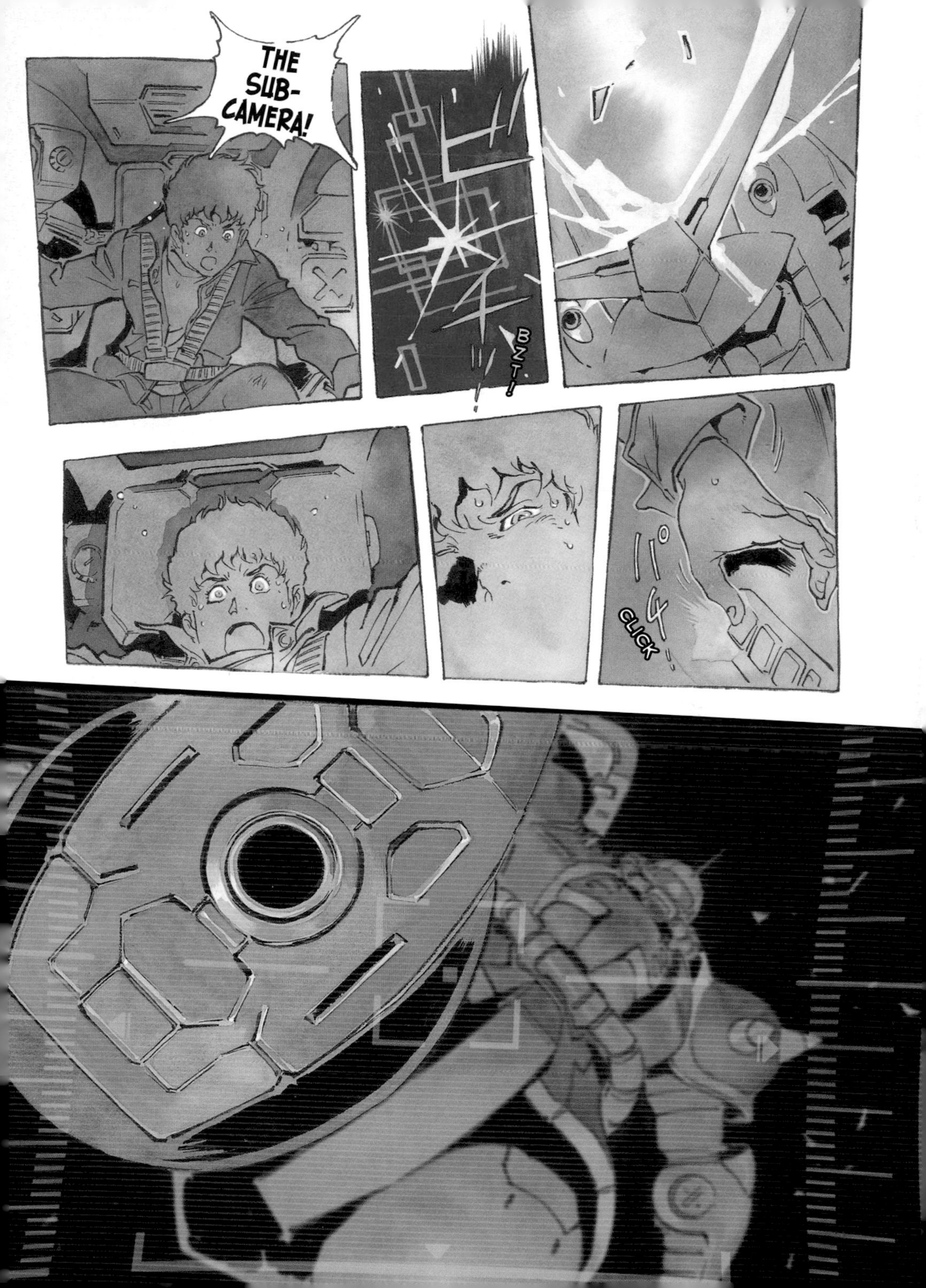
BZT!
THE SUB-CAMERA!
CLICK

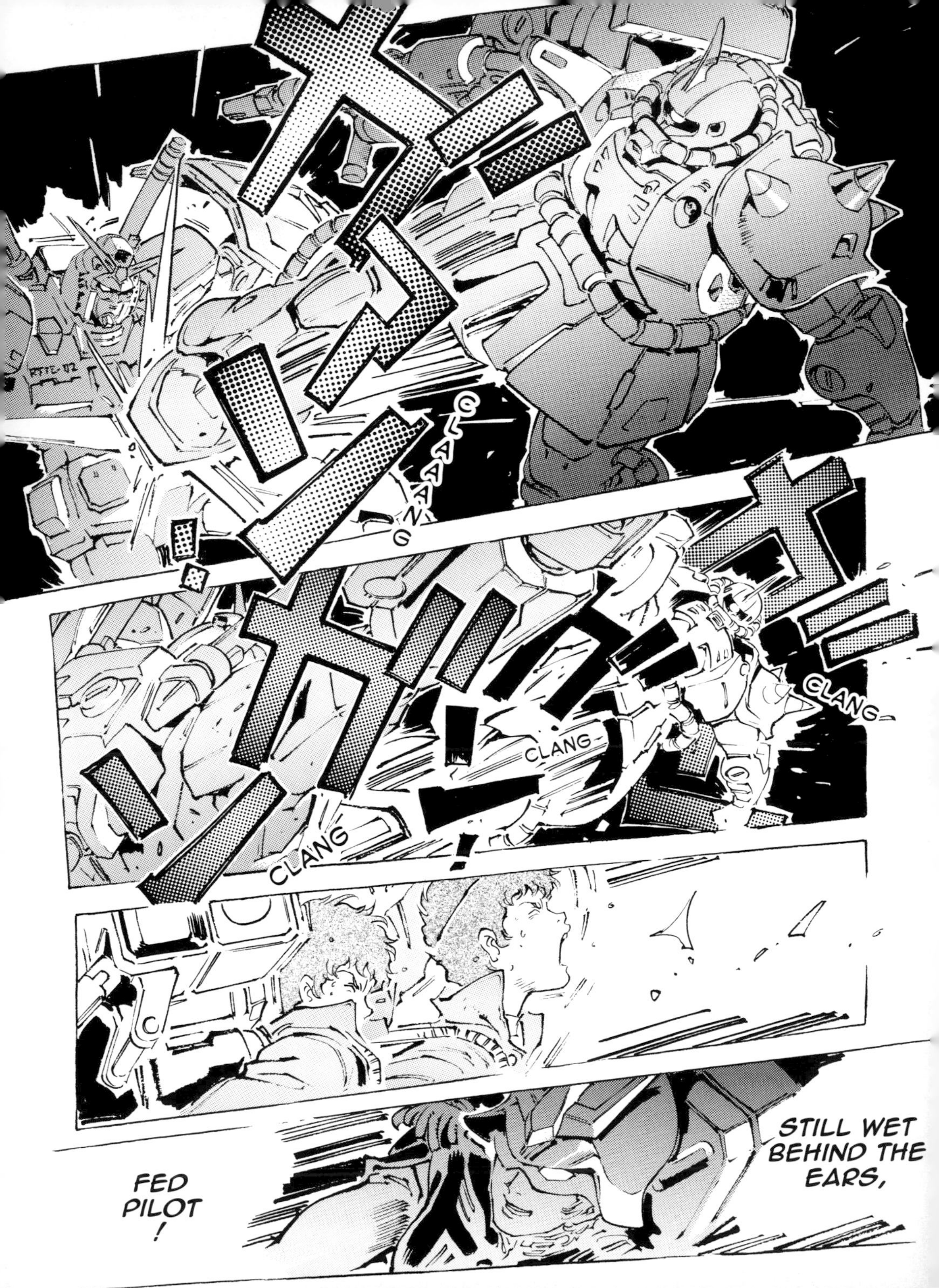
CLAAAANG
CLANG
CLANG
CLANG
STILL WET BEHIND THE EARS,
FED PILOT!

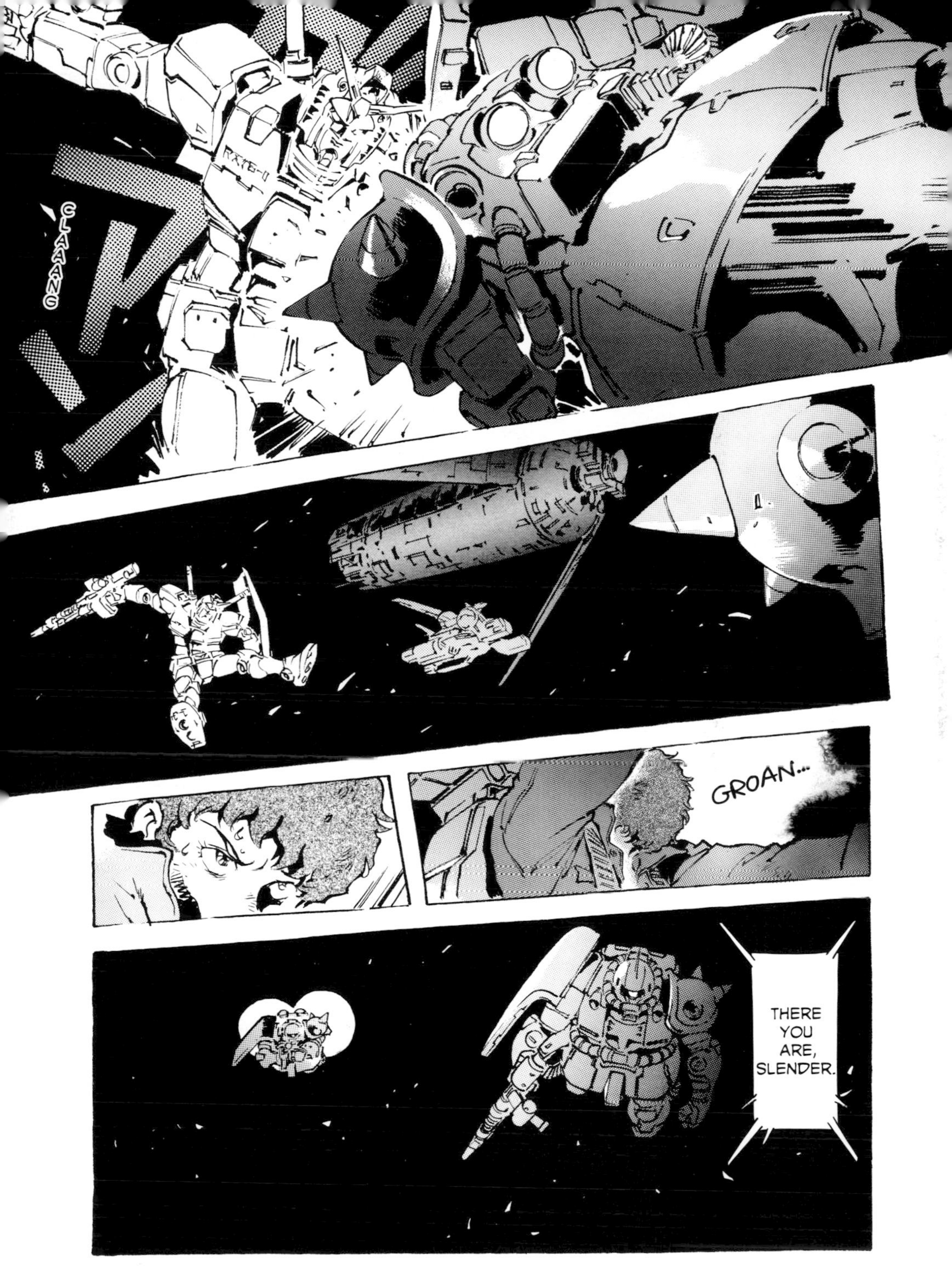
CLAAAANG
GROAN...
THERE YOU ARE, SLENDER.

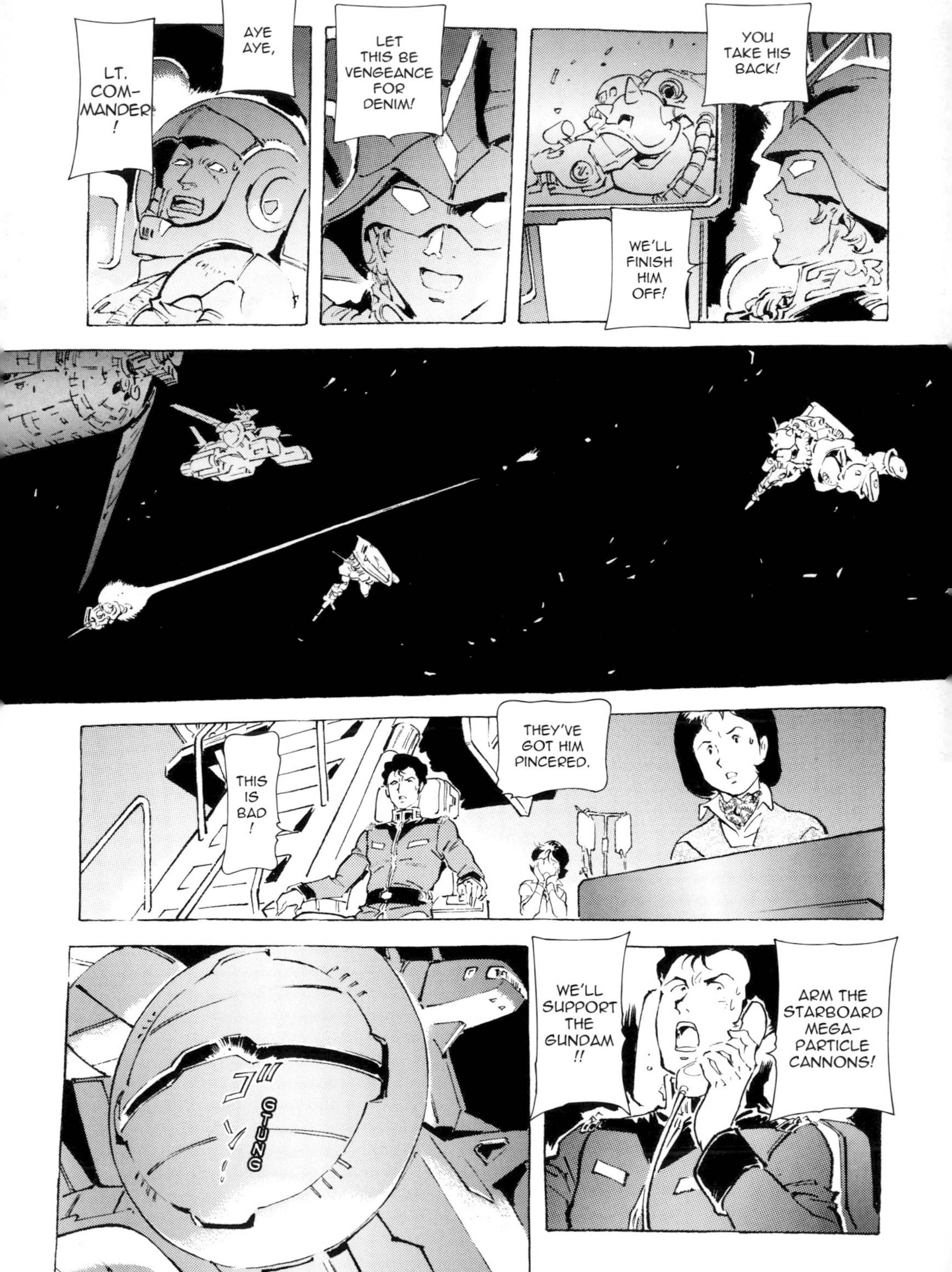
YOU TAKE HIS BACK!
WE'LL FINISH HIM OFF!
LET THIS BE VENGEANCE FOR DENIM!
AYE AYE,
LT. COMMANDER!
THEY'VE GOT HIM PINCERED.
THIS IS BAD!
ARM THE STARBOARD MEGA-PARTICLE CANNONS!
WE'LL SUPPORT THE GUNDAM!!
GTUNG

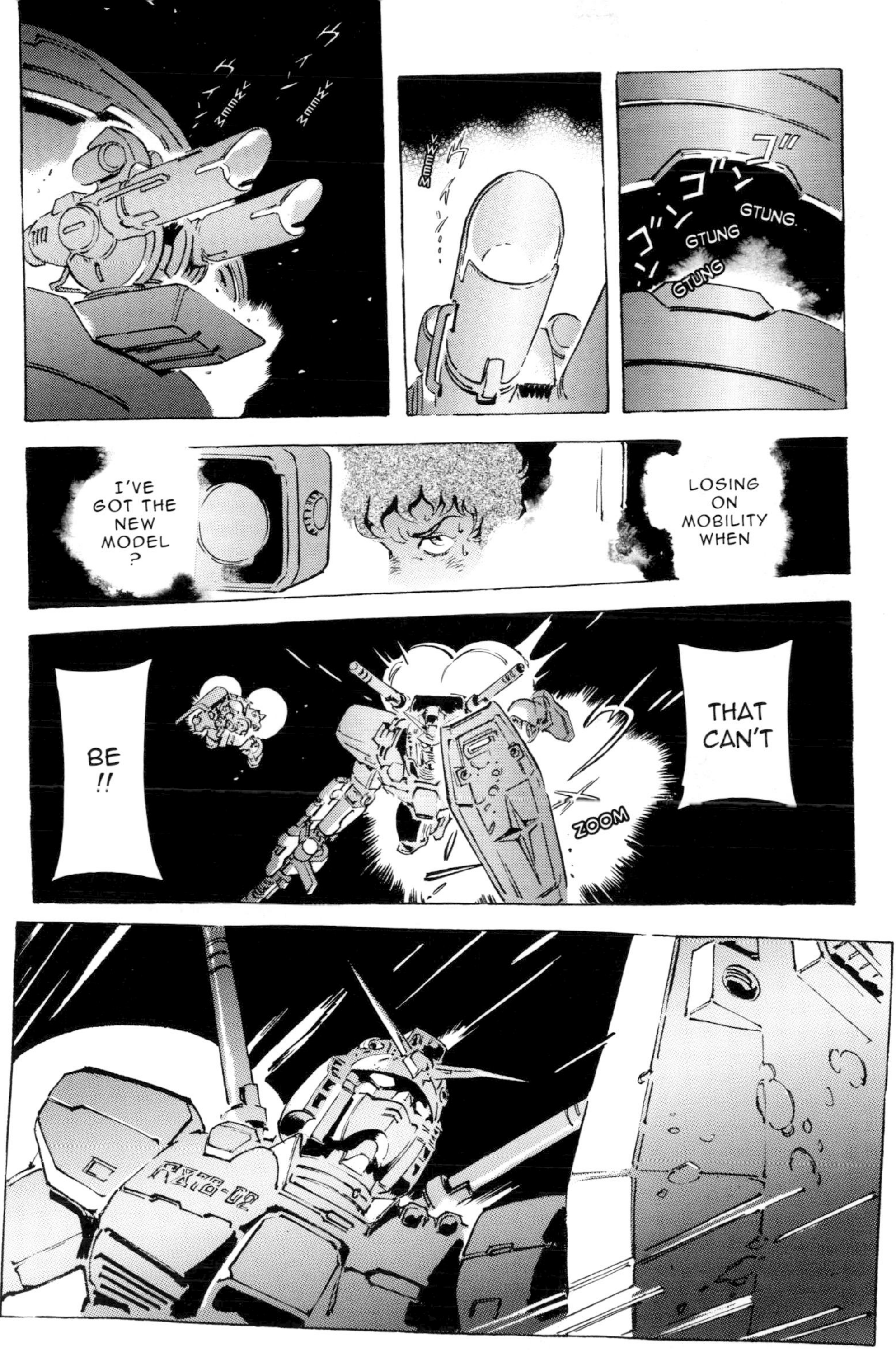
GTUNG
GTUNG
GTUNG
VWEEEM
LOSING ON MOBILITY WHEN
I'VE GOT THE NEW MODEL?
THAT CAN'T
ZOOM
BE!!

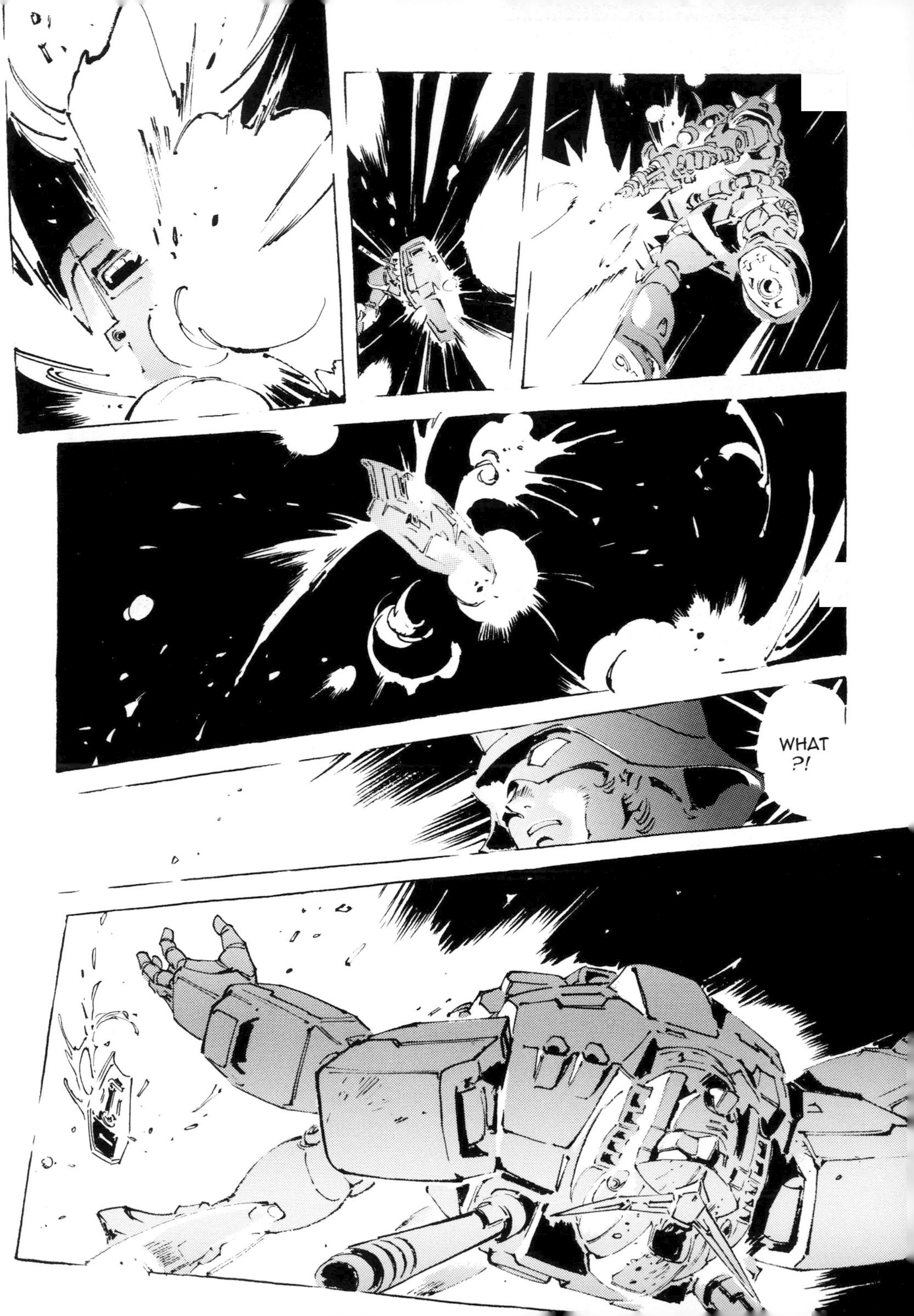
WHAT ?!

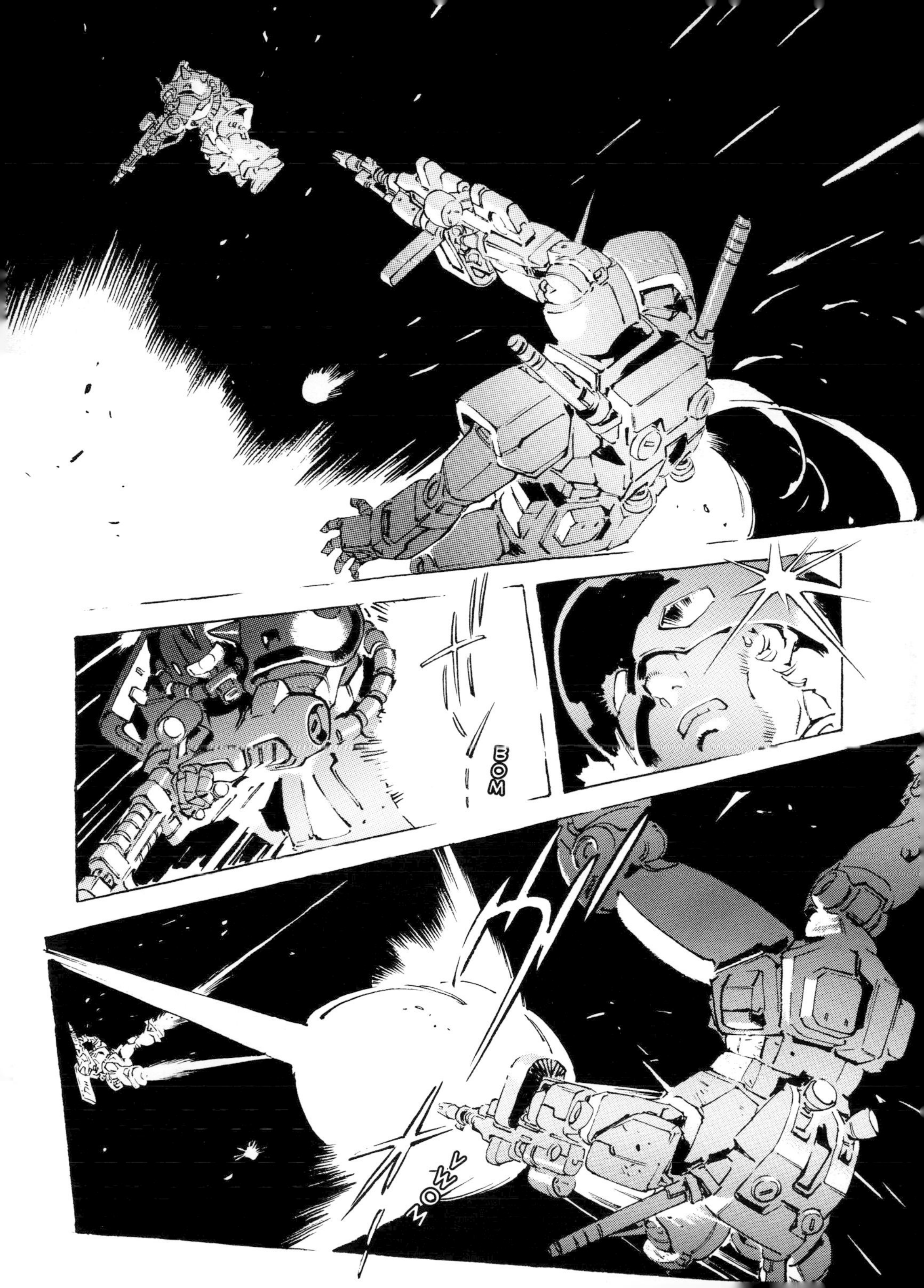
BOM

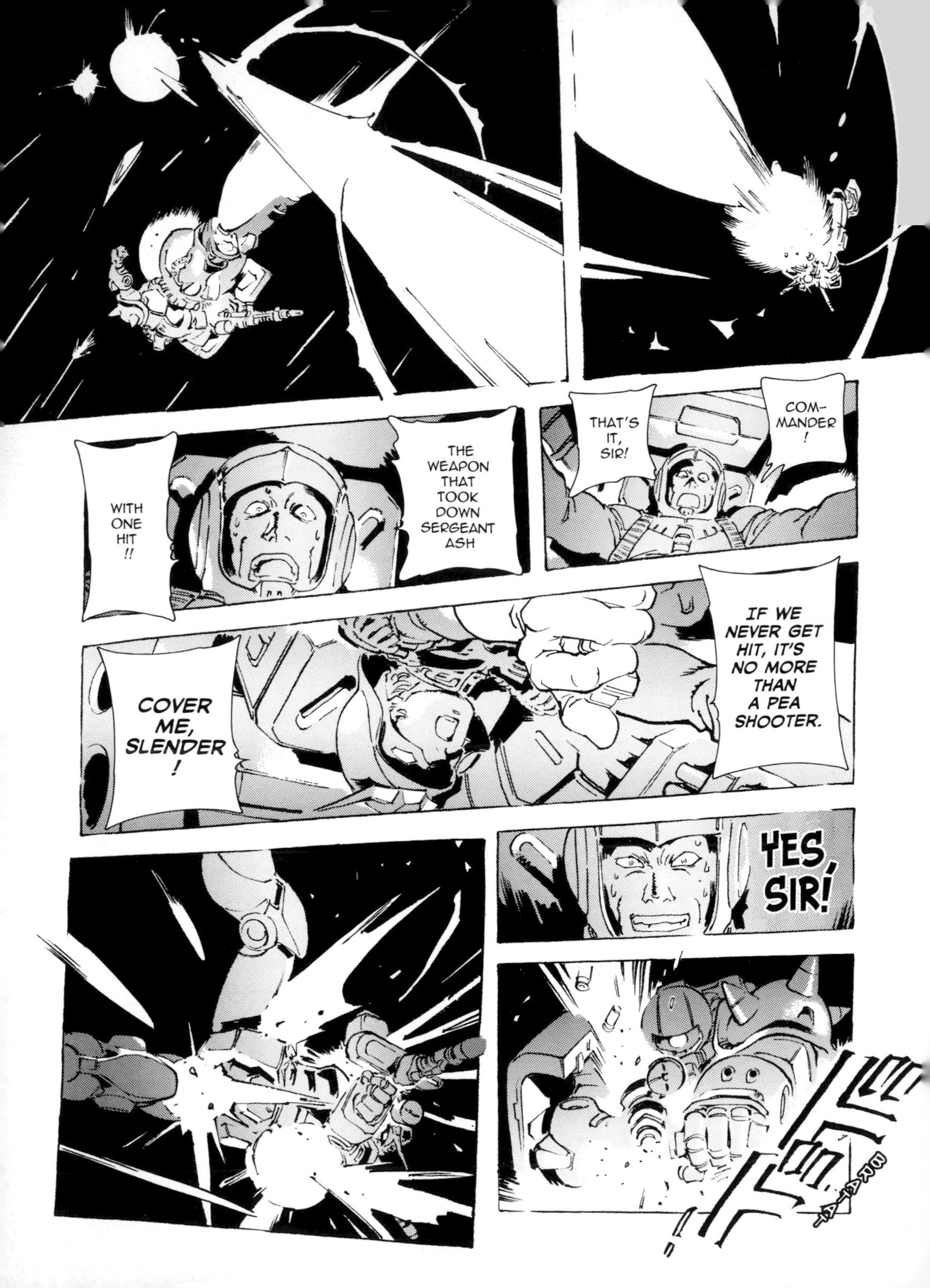
COM-MANDER!
THAT'S IT, SIR!
THE WEAPON THAT TOOK DOWN SERGEANT ASH
WITH ONE HIT!!
IF WE NEVER GET HIT, IT'S NO MORE THAN A PEA SHOOTER.
COVER ME, SLENDER!
YES, SIR!
BRA-TA-T

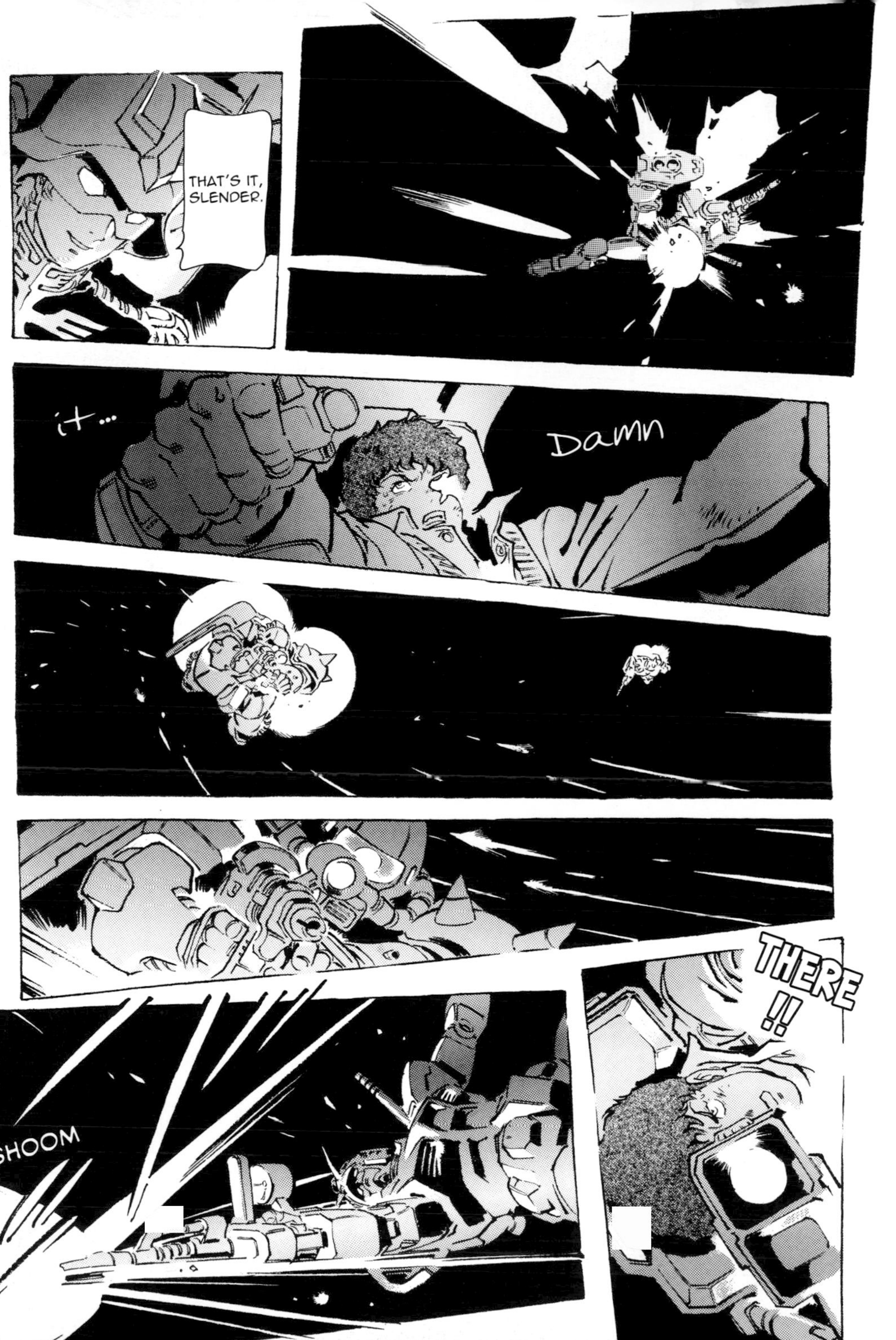
THAT'S IT, SLENDER.
Damn
it...
THERE!!
SHOOM

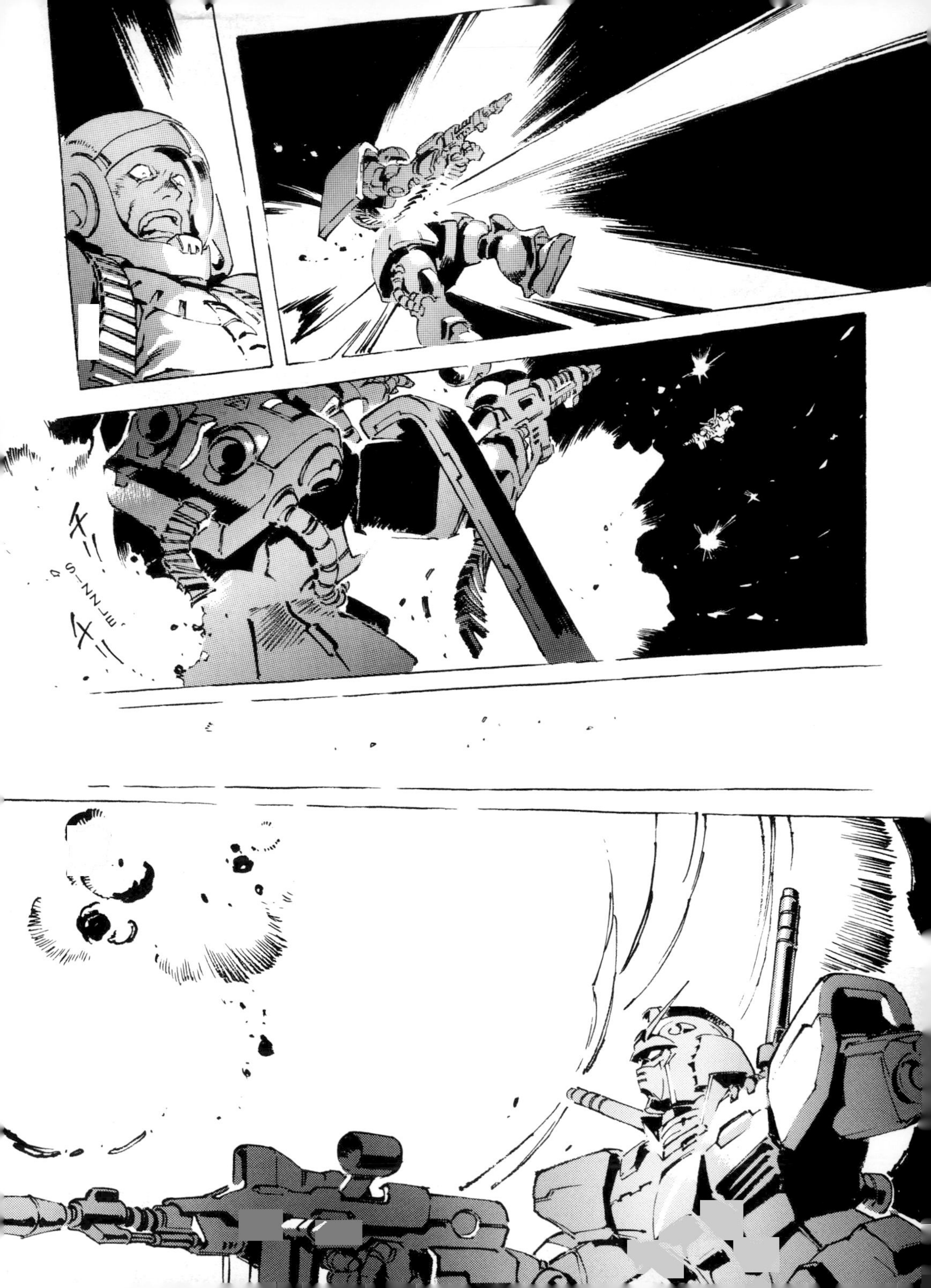

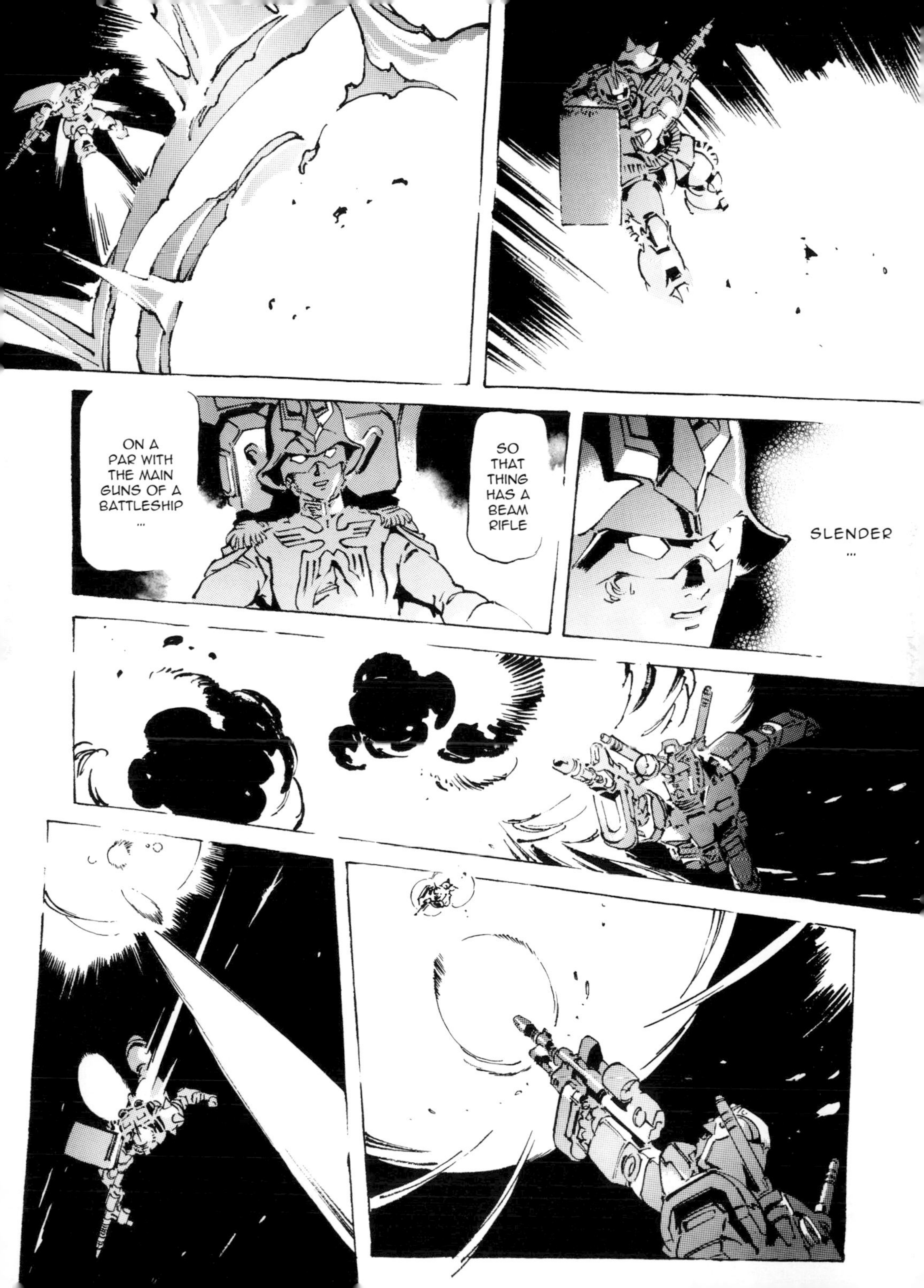
SLENDER ...
SO THAT THING HAS A BEAM RIFLE
ON A PAR WITH THE MAIN GUNS OF A BATTLESHIP ...

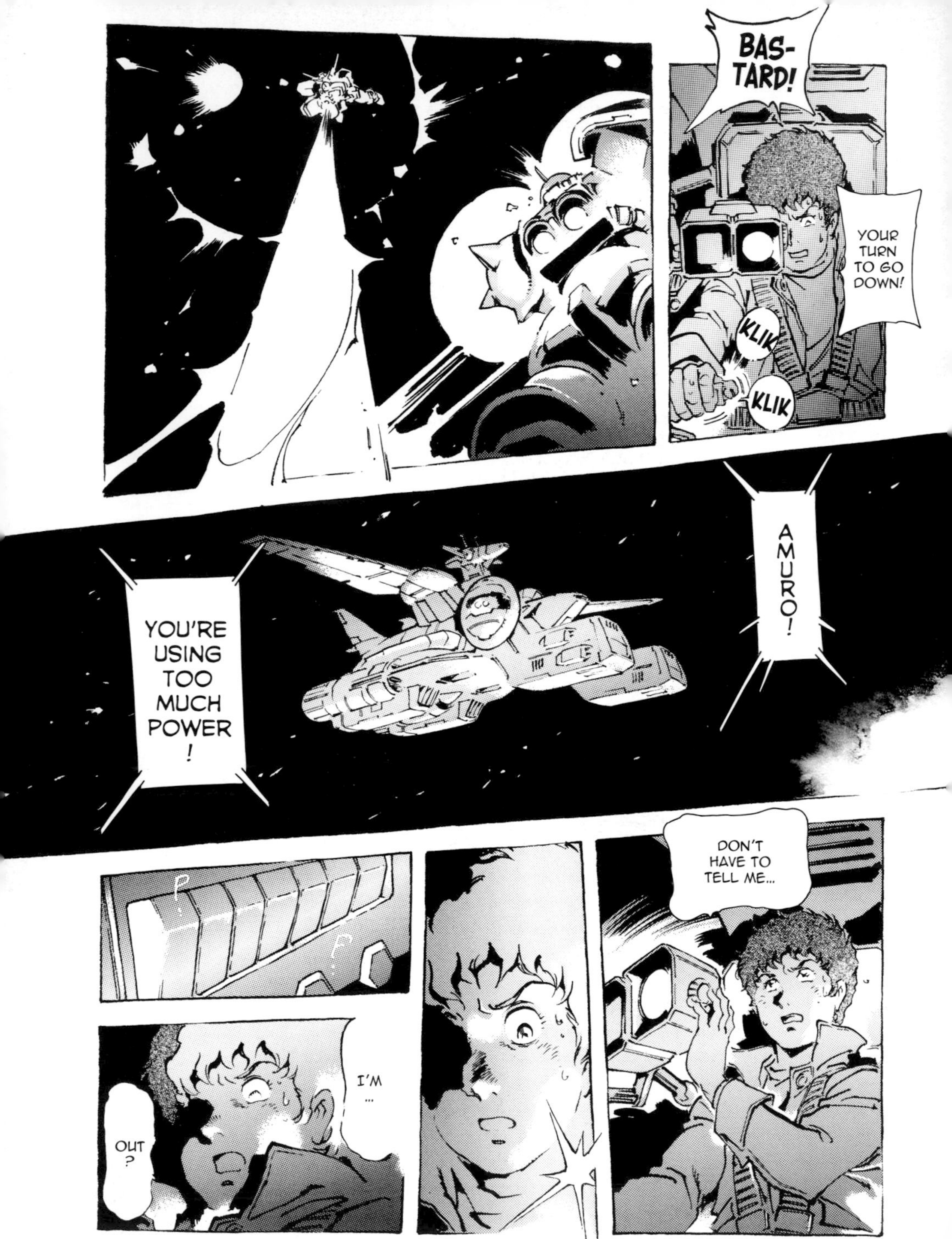
BAS-TARD!
YOUR TURN TO GO DOWN!
KLIK
KLIK
AMURO!
YOU'RE USING TOO MUCH POWER!
DON'T HAVE TO TELL ME...
I'M ...
OUT ?

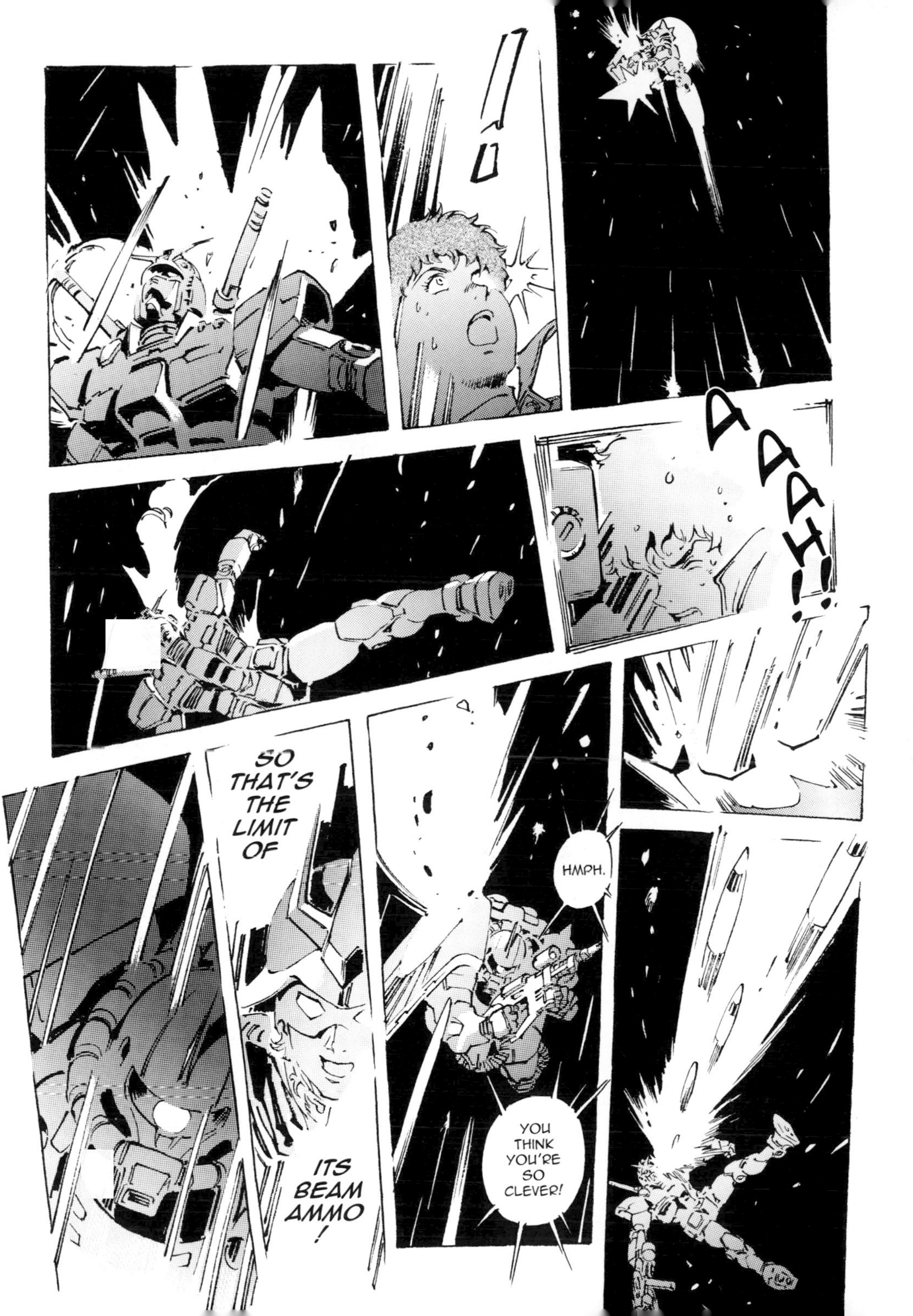
AAAH!!
HMPH.
YOU THINK YOU'RE SO CLEVER!
SO THAT'S THE LIMIT OF
ITS BEAM AMMO!

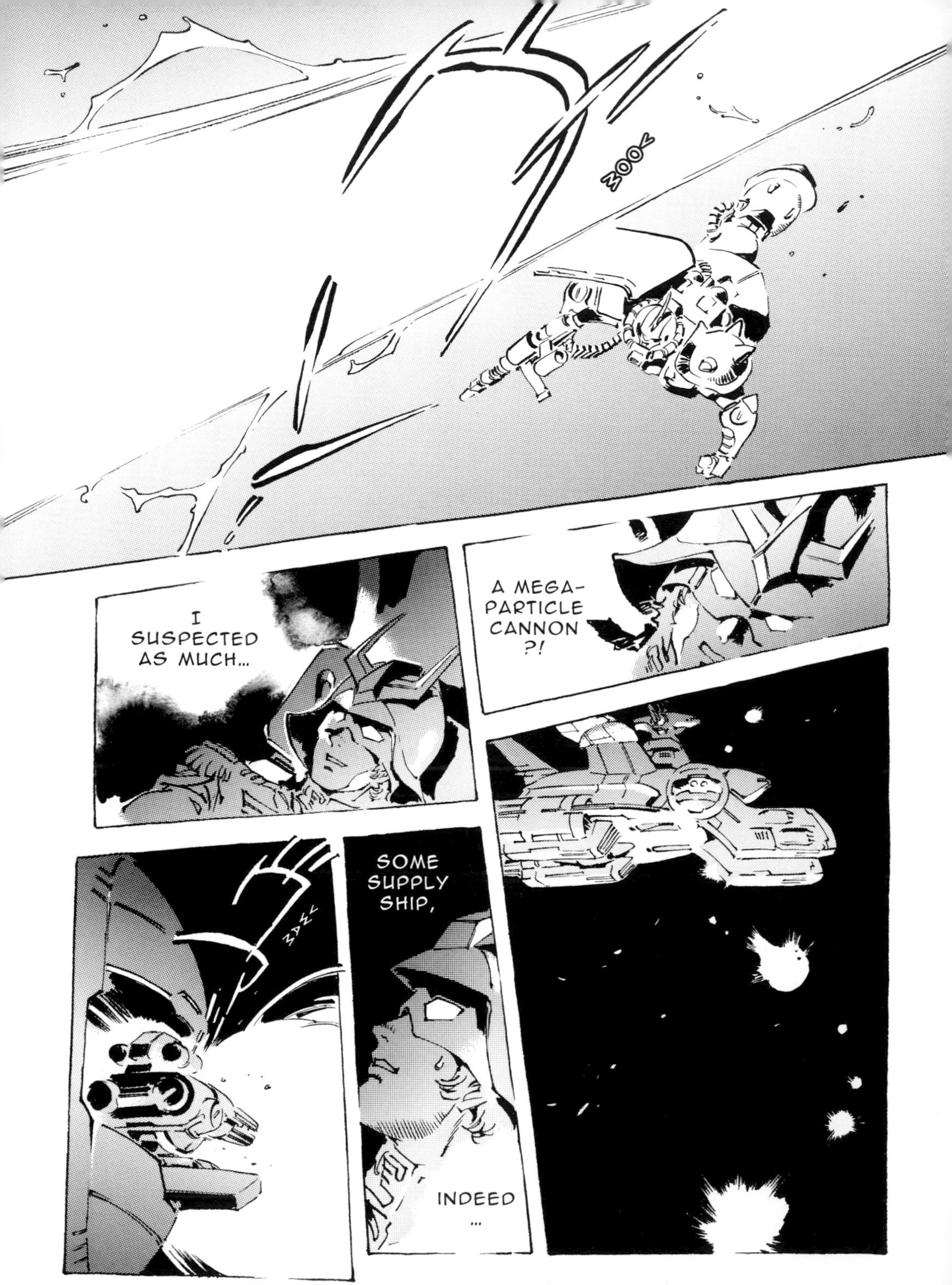
A MEGA-PARTICLE CANNON ?!
I SUSPECTED AS MUCH...
SOME SUPPLY SHIP,
INDEED ...

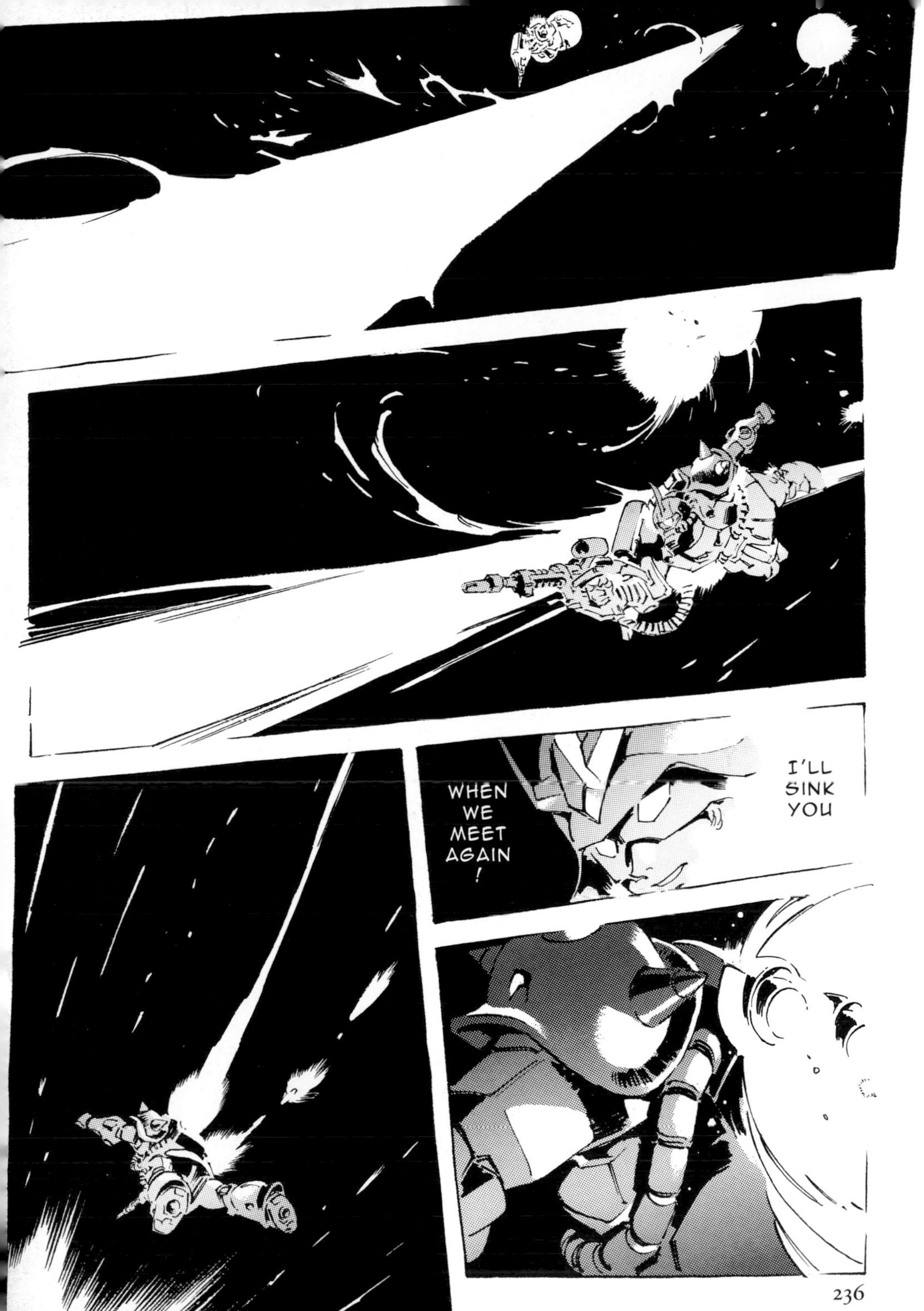
I'LL SINK YOU
WHEN WE MEET AGAIN!

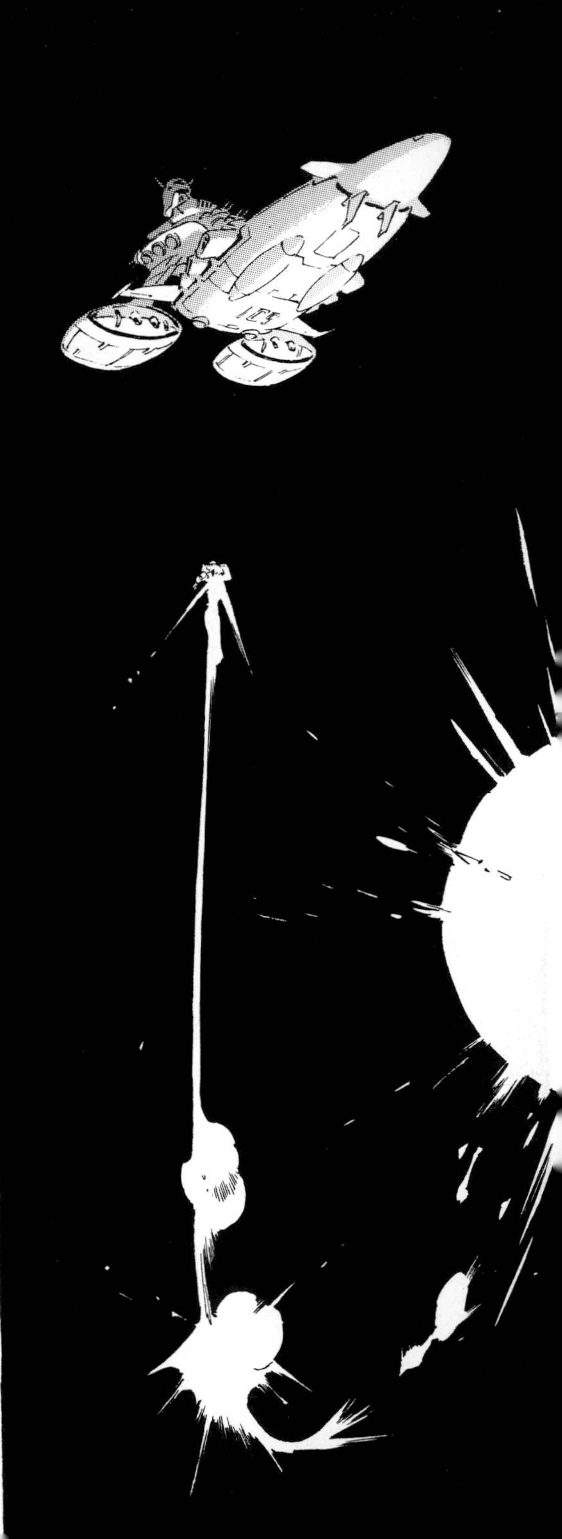
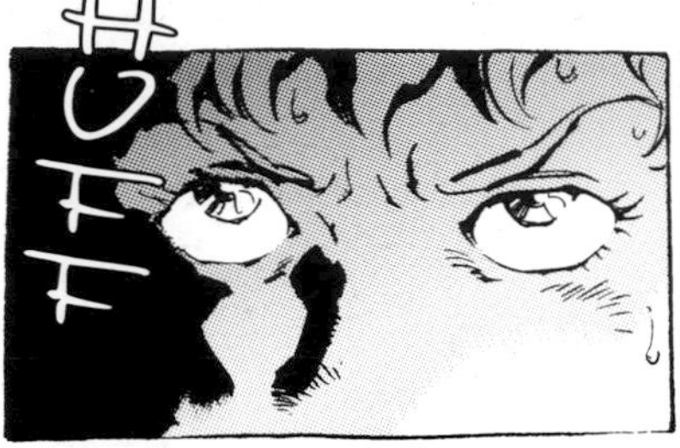
HUFF
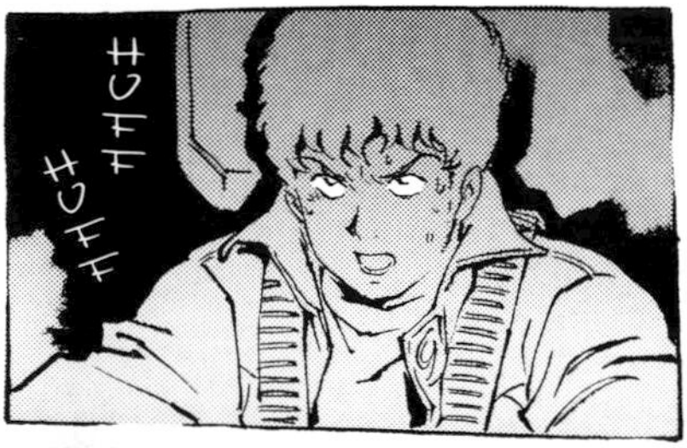
HUFF
HUFF
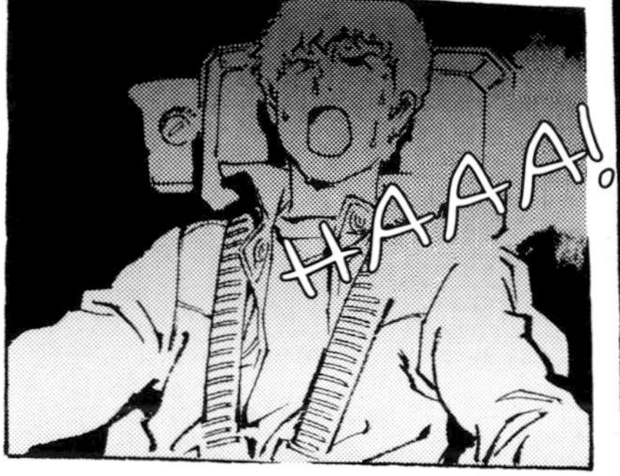
HAAA!
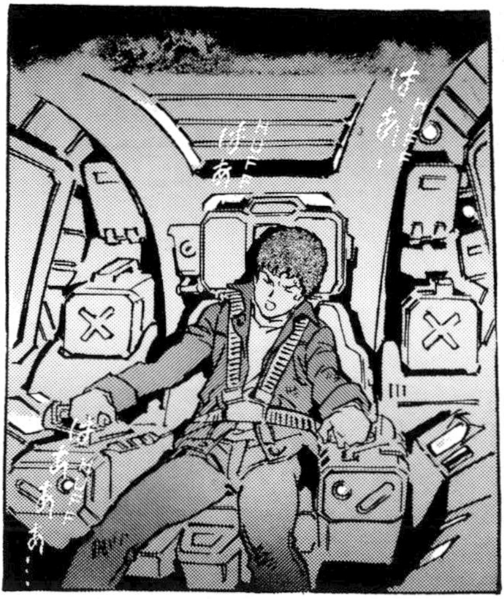
はあ
はあ
はあ あ あ…

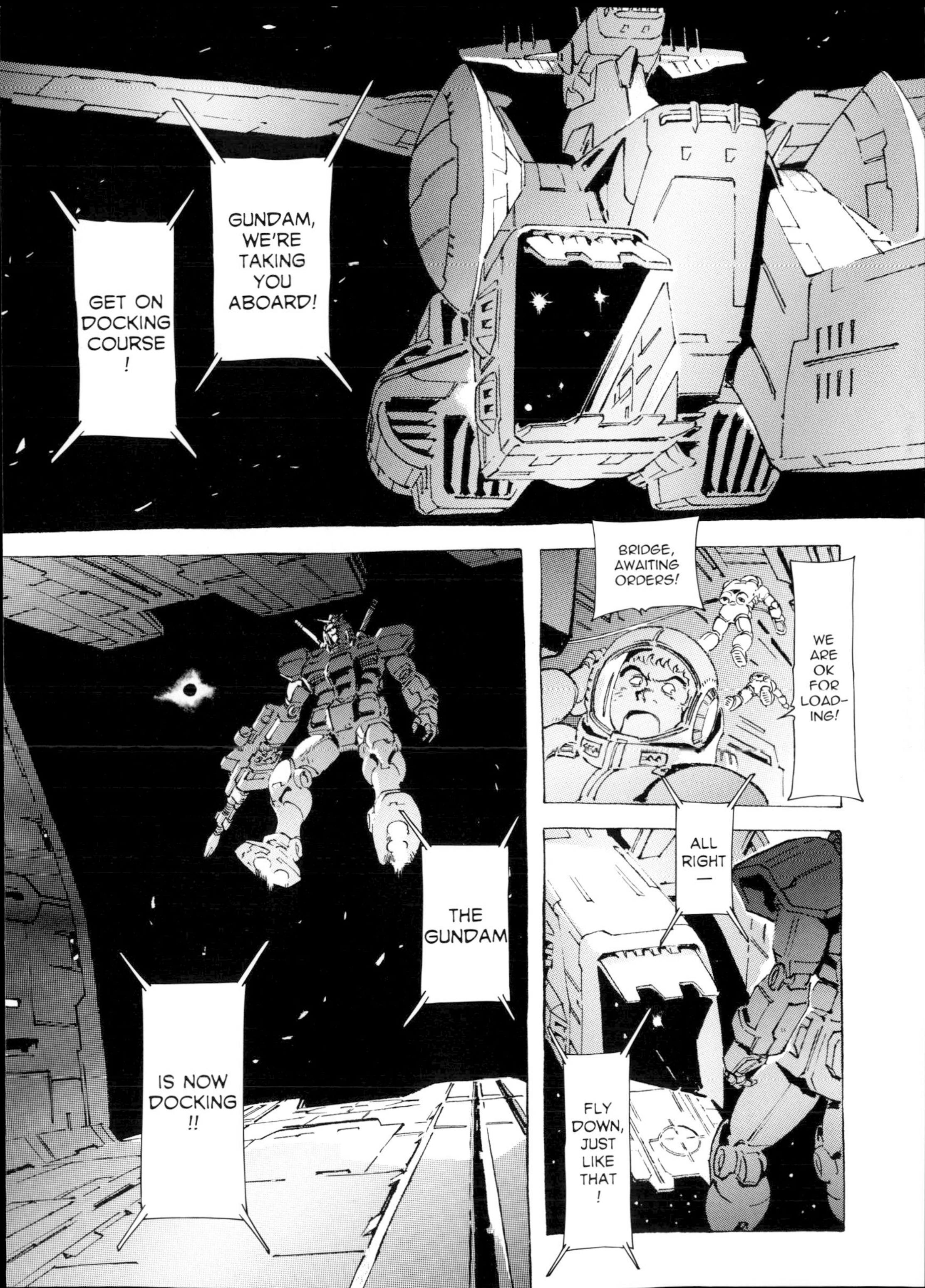
GUNDAM, WE'RE TAKING YOU ABOARD!
GET ON DOCKING COURSE!
BRIDGE, AWAITING ORDERS!
WE ARE OK FOR LOADING!
ALL RIGHT—
FLY DOWN, JUST LIKE THAT!
THE GUNDAM
IS NOW DOCKING!!

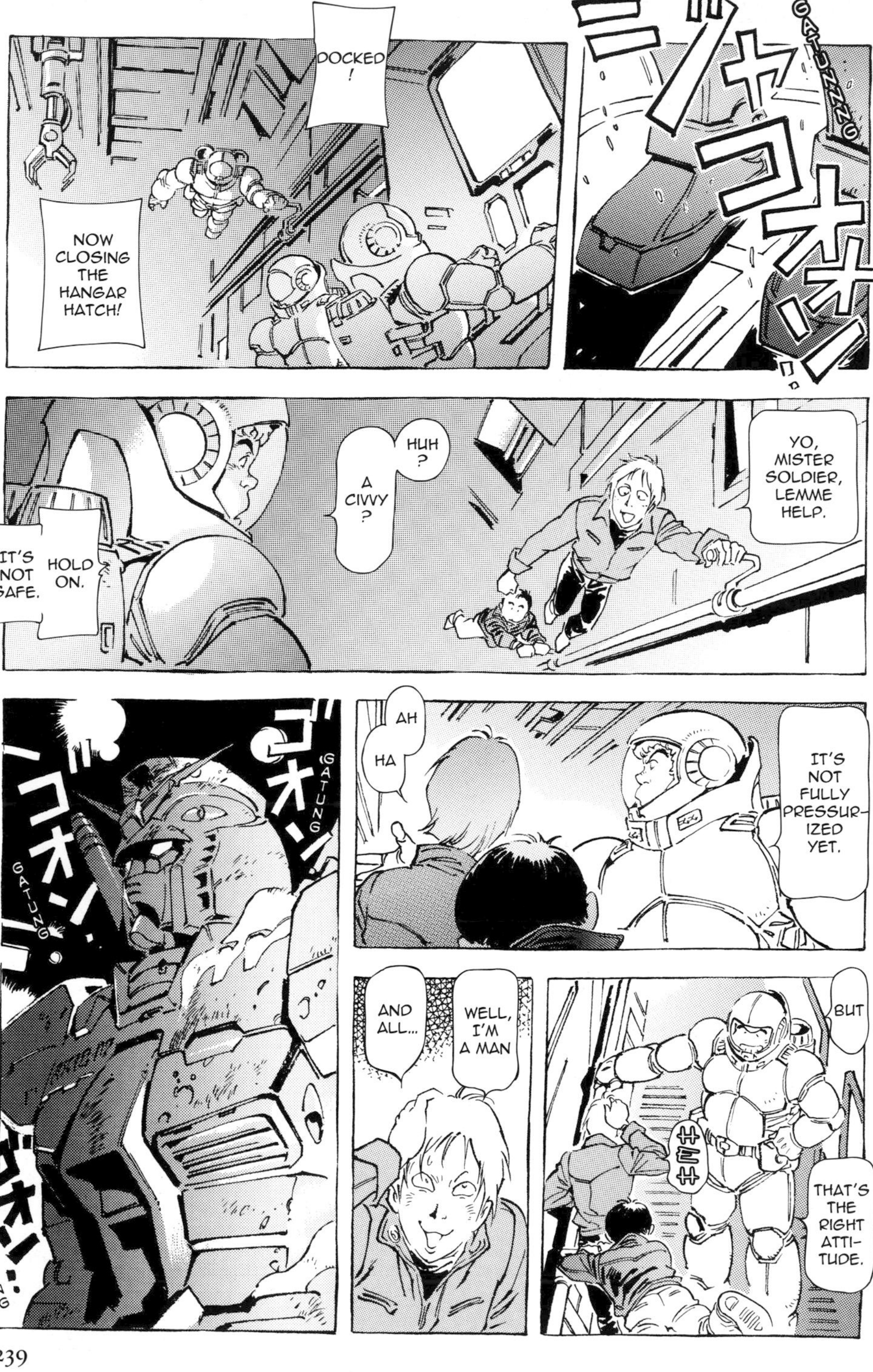
GATUNNNG
DOCKED!
NOW CLOSING THE HANGAR HATCH!
YO, MISTER SOLDIER, LEMME HELP.
HUH?
A CIVVY?
HOLD ON.
IT'S NOT SAFE.
IT'S NOT FULLY PRESSURIZED YET.
AH
HA
BUT
HEH
THAT'S THE RIGHT ATTITUDE.
WELL, I'M A MAN
AND ALL...
GATUNG
GATUNG
GATUNG

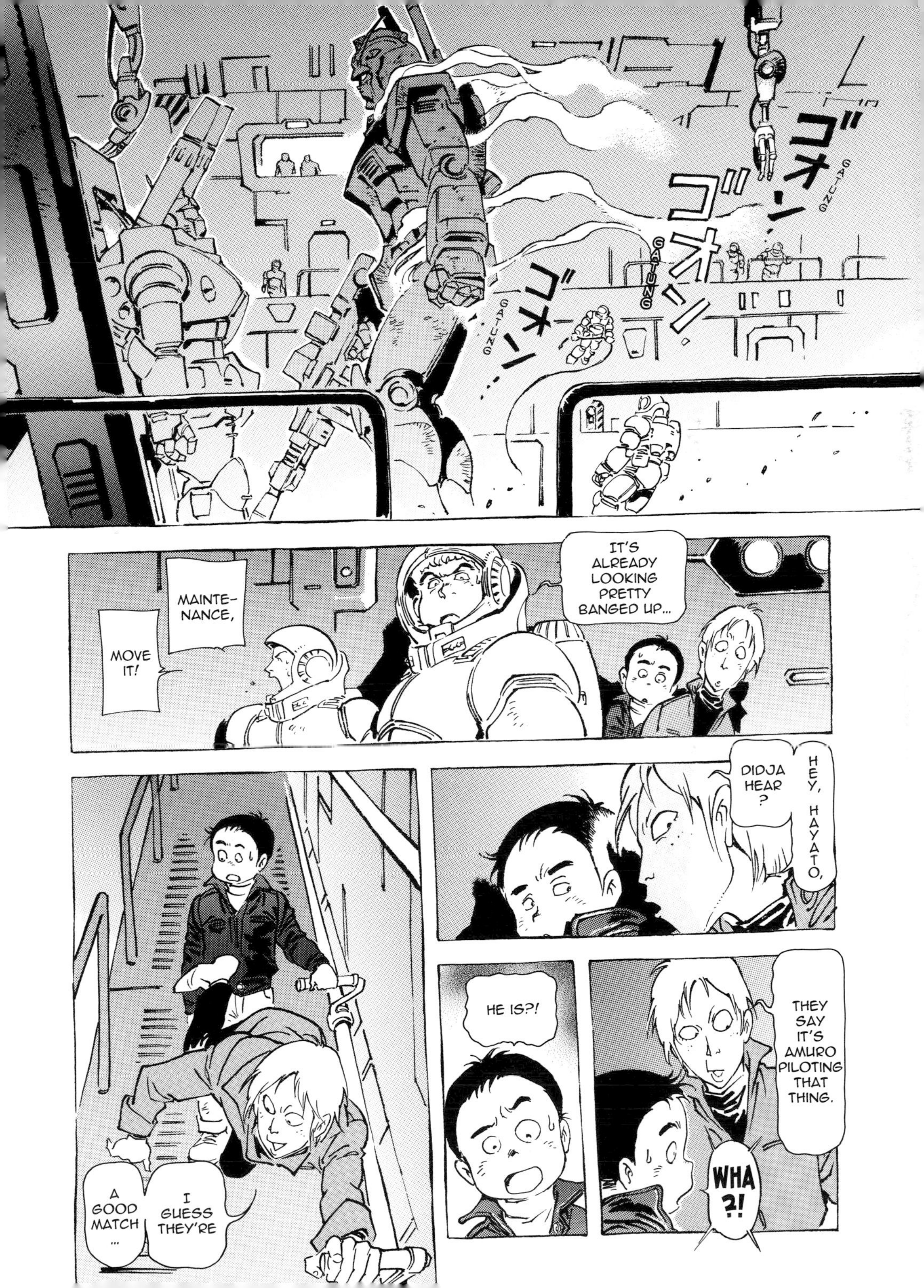
ゴォン!
GATUNG
ゴォン!
GATUNG
ゴォン…
GATUNG
IT'S ALREADY LOOKING PRETTY BANGED UP...
MAINTE-NANCE,
MOVE IT!
HEY, HAYATO,
DIDJA HEAR?
THEY SAY IT'S AMURO PILOTING THAT THING.
WHA?!
HE IS?!
I GUESS THEY'RE
A GOOD MATCH...

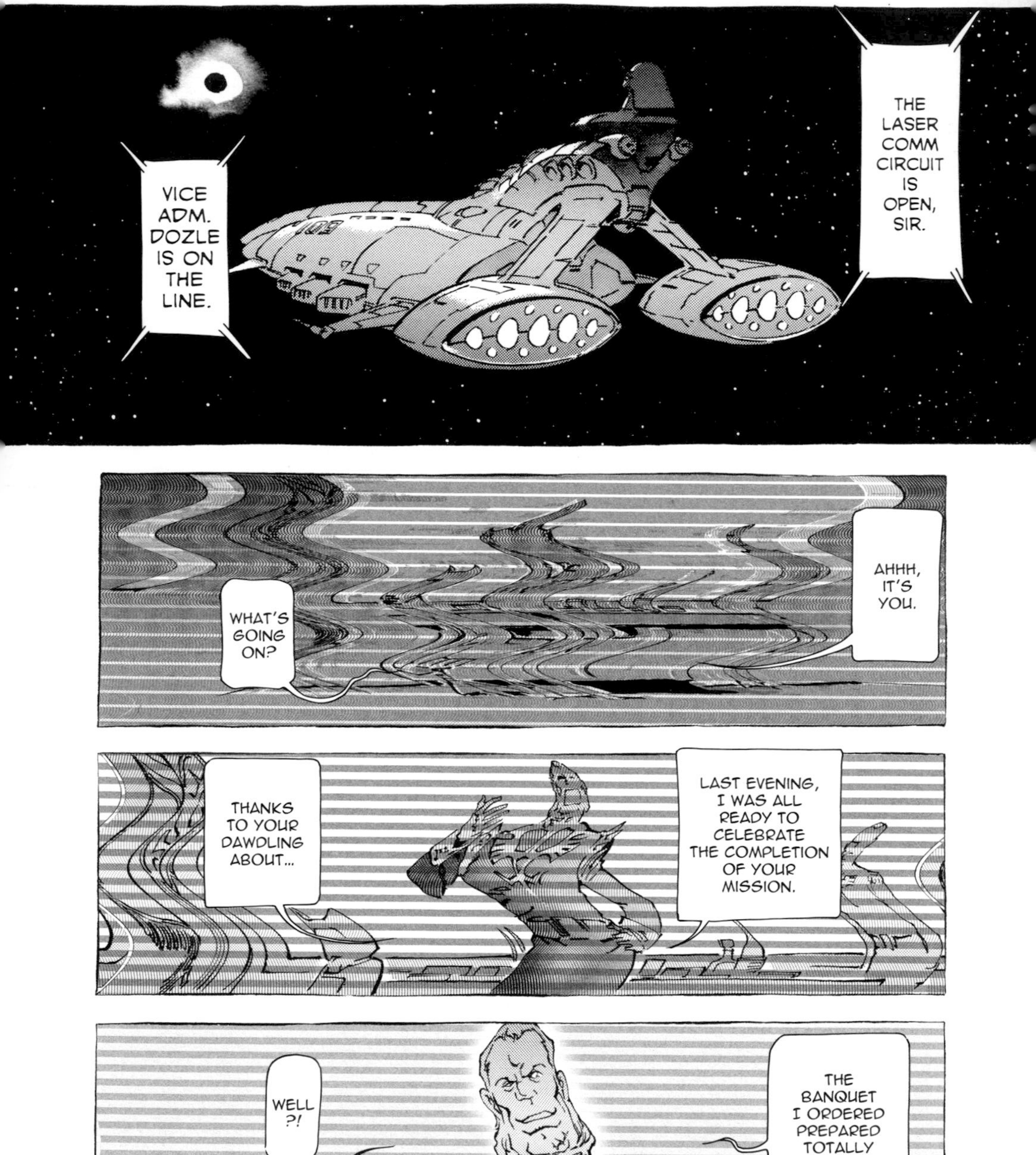
THE LASER COMM CIRCUIT IS OPEN, SIR.
VICE ADM. DOZLE IS ON THE LINE.
AHHH, IT'S YOU.
WHAT'S GOING ON?
LAST EVENING, I WAS ALL READY TO CELEBRATE THE COMPLETION OF YOUR MISSION.
THANKS TO YOUR DAWDLING ABOUT...
THE BANQUET I ORDERED PREPARED TOTALLY WENT TO WASTE.
WELL?!

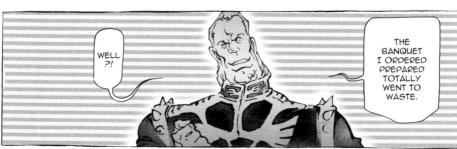

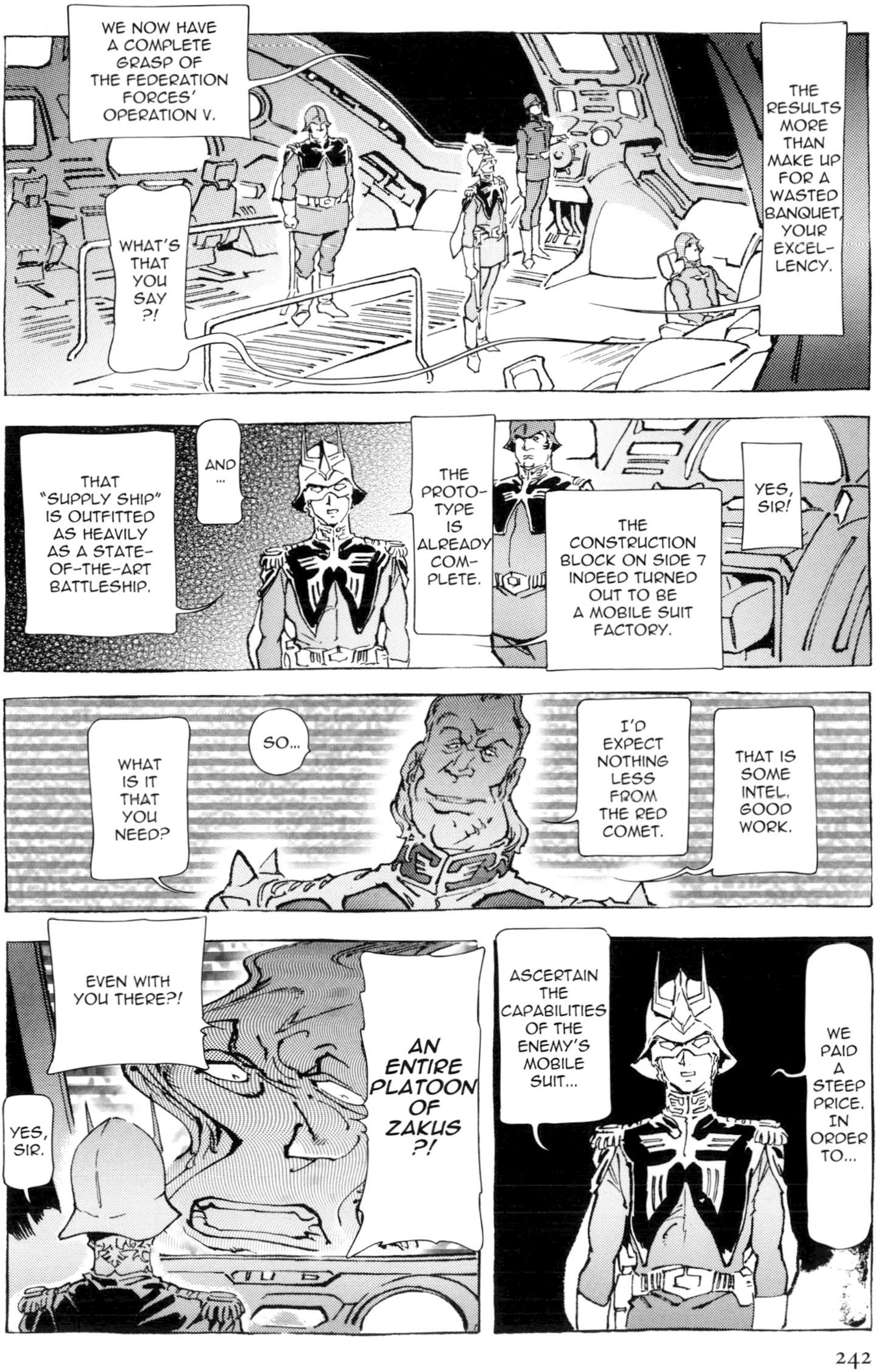
THE RESULTS MORE THAN MAKE UP FOR A WASTED BANQUET, YOUR EXCELLENCY.
WE NOW HAVE A COMPLETE GRASP OF THE FEDERATION FORCES' OPERATION V.
WHAT'S THAT YOU SAY?!
YES, SIR!
THE CONSTRUCTION BLOCK ON SIDE 7 INDEED TURNED OUT TO BE A MOBILE SUIT FACTORY.
THE PROTOTYPE IS ALREADY COMPLETE.
AND ...
THAT "SUPPLY SHIP" IS OUTFITTED AS HEAVILY AS A STATE-OF-THE-ART BATTLESHIP.
THAT IS SOME INTEL. GOOD WORK.
I'D EXPECT NOTHING LESS FROM THE RED COMET.
SO...
WHAT IS IT THAT YOU NEED?
WE PAID A STEEP PRICE. IN ORDER TO...
ASCERTAIN THE CAPABILITIES OF THE ENEMY'S MOBILE SUIT...
AN ENTIRE PLATOON OF ZAKUS?!
EVEN WITH YOU THERE?!
YES, SIR.

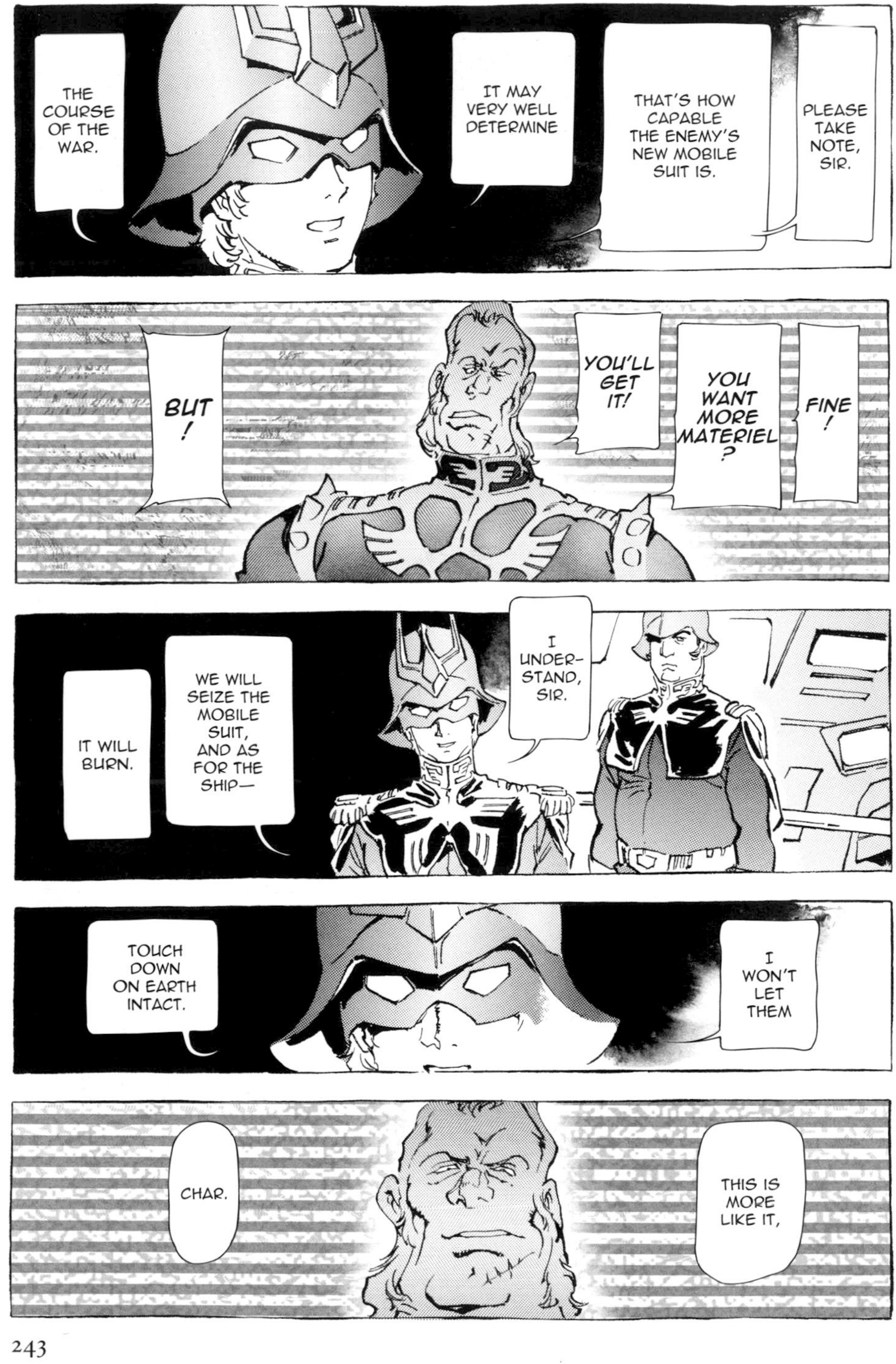
PLEASE TAKE NOTE, SIR.
THAT'S HOW CAPABLE THE ENEMY'S NEW MOBILE SUIT IS.
IT MAY VERY WELL DETERMINE
THE COURSE OF THE WAR.
FINE!
YOU WANT MORE MATERIEL?
YOU'LL GET IT!
BUT!
I UNDER-STAND, SIR.
WE WILL SEIZE THE MOBILE SUIT, AND AS FOR THE SHIP—
IT WILL BURN.
I WON'T LET THEM
TOUCH DOWN ON EARTH INTACT.
THIS IS MORE LIKE IT,
CHAR.

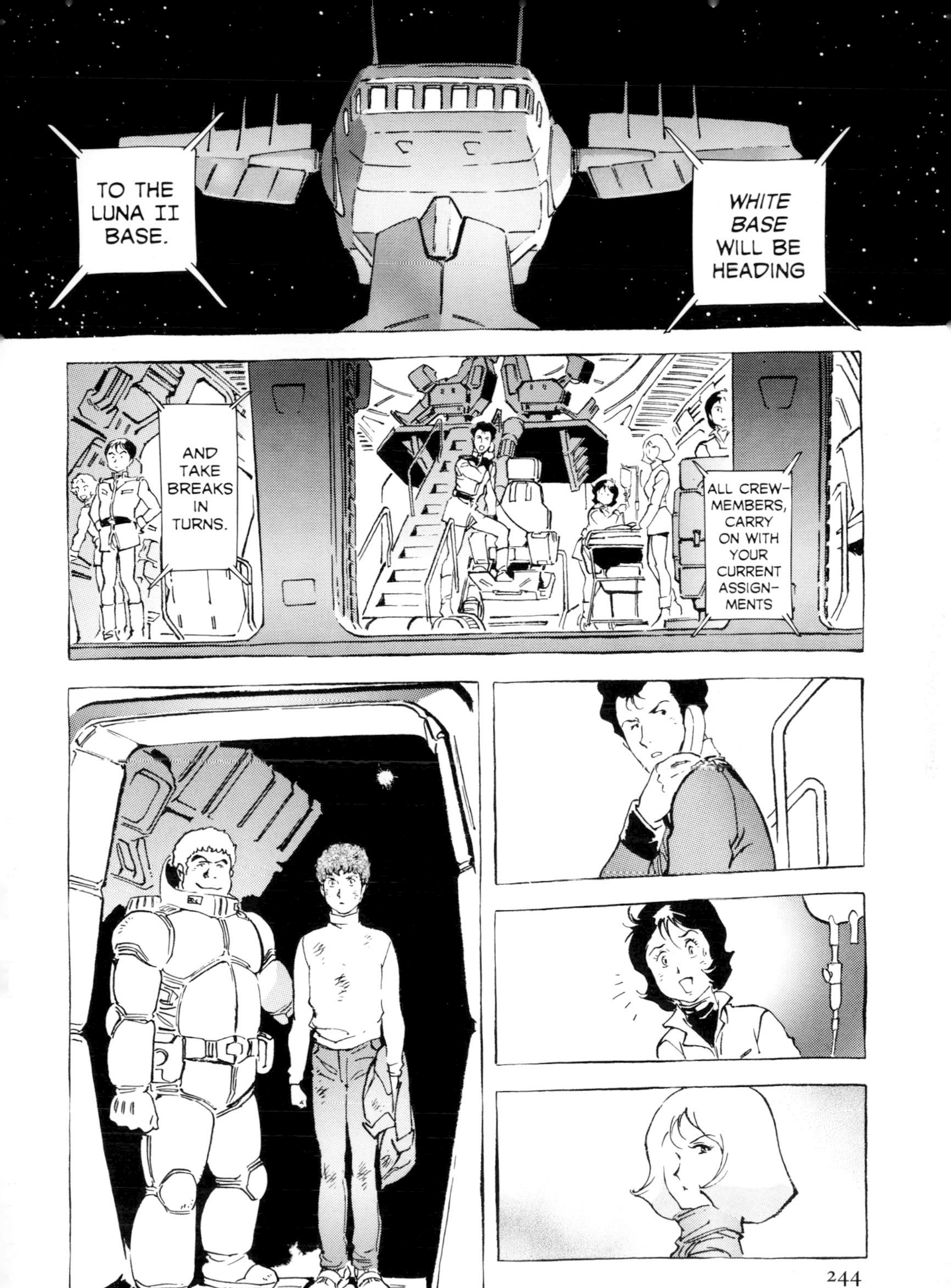
WHITE BASE WILL BE HEADING
TO THE LUNA II BASE.
ALL CREW-MEMBERS, CARRY ON WITH YOUR CURRENT ASSIGNMENTS
AND TAKE BREAKS IN TURNS.

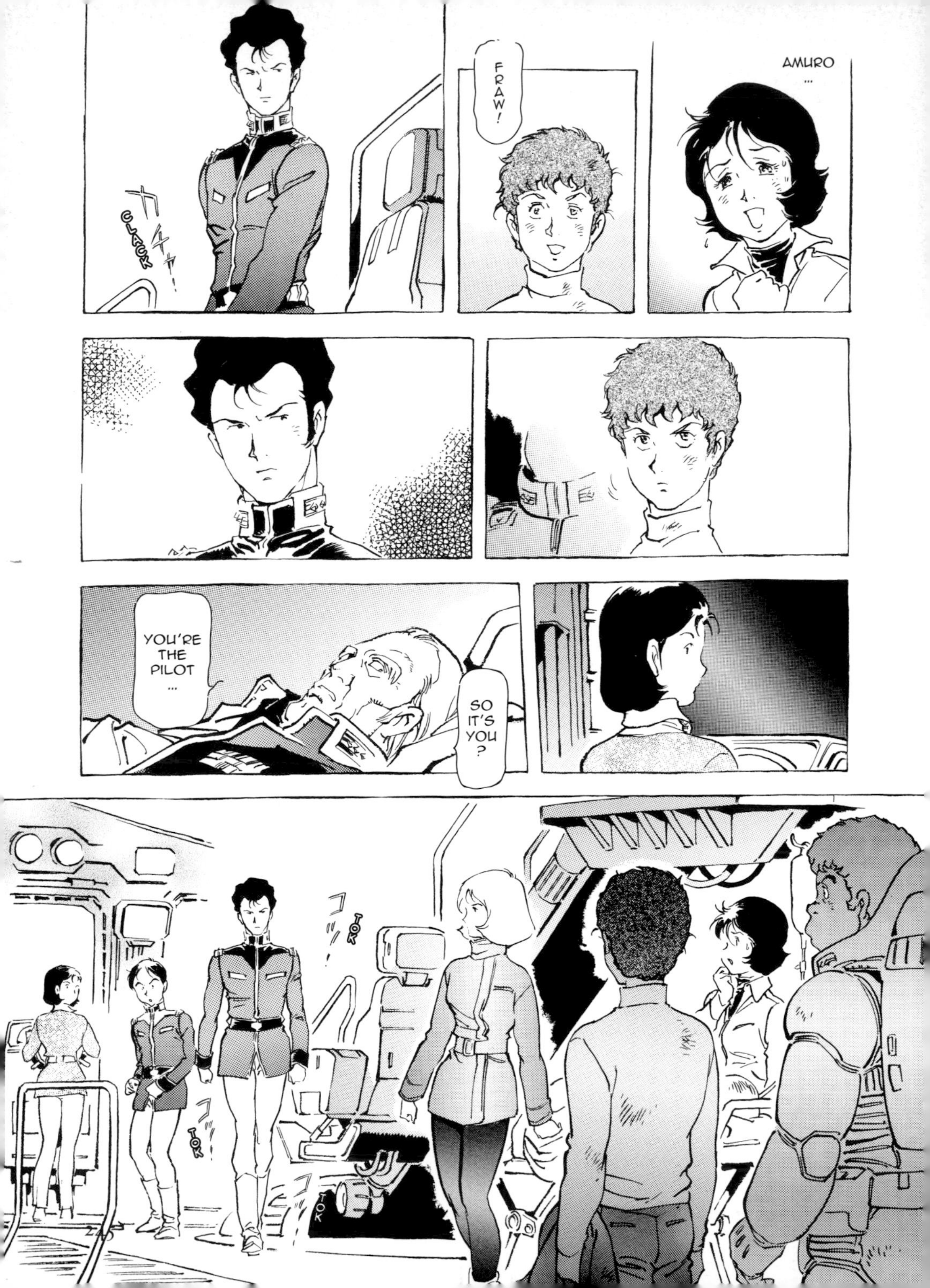

AMURO ...
FRAW!
CLACK
YOU'RE THE PILOT ...
SO IT'S YOU?
TOK
TOK
TOK

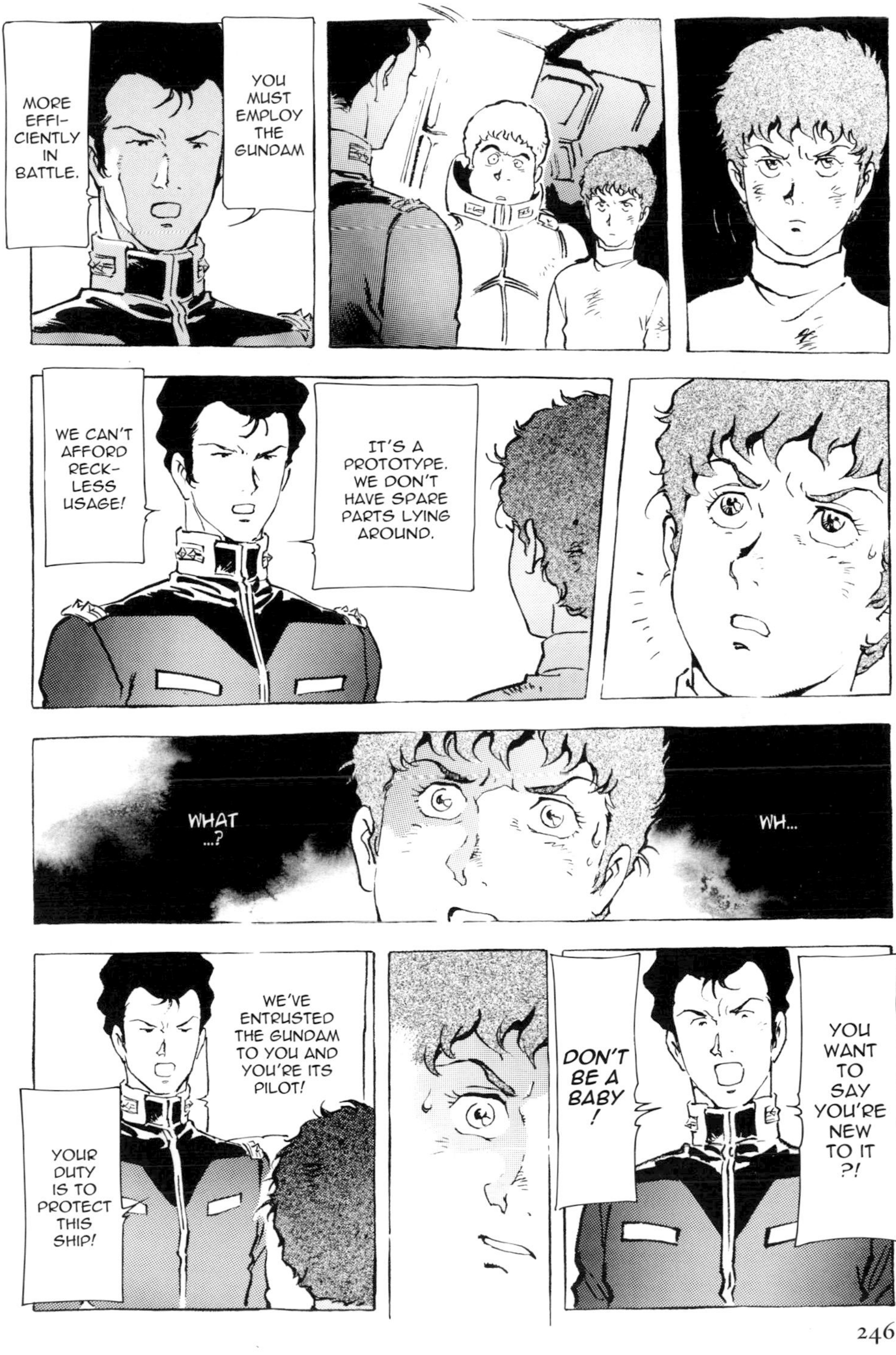
YOU MUST EMPLOY THE GUNDAM
MORE EFFICIENTLY IN BATTLE.
IT'S A PROTOTYPE. WE DON'T HAVE SPARE PARTS LYING AROUND.
WE CAN'T AFFORD RECKLESS USAGE!
WH...
WHAT ...?
YOU WANT TO SAY YOU'RE NEW TO IT ?!
DON'T BE A BABY !
WE'VE ENTRUSTED THE GUNDAM TO YOU AND YOU'RE ITS PILOT!
YOUR DUTY IS TO PROTECT THIS SHIP!

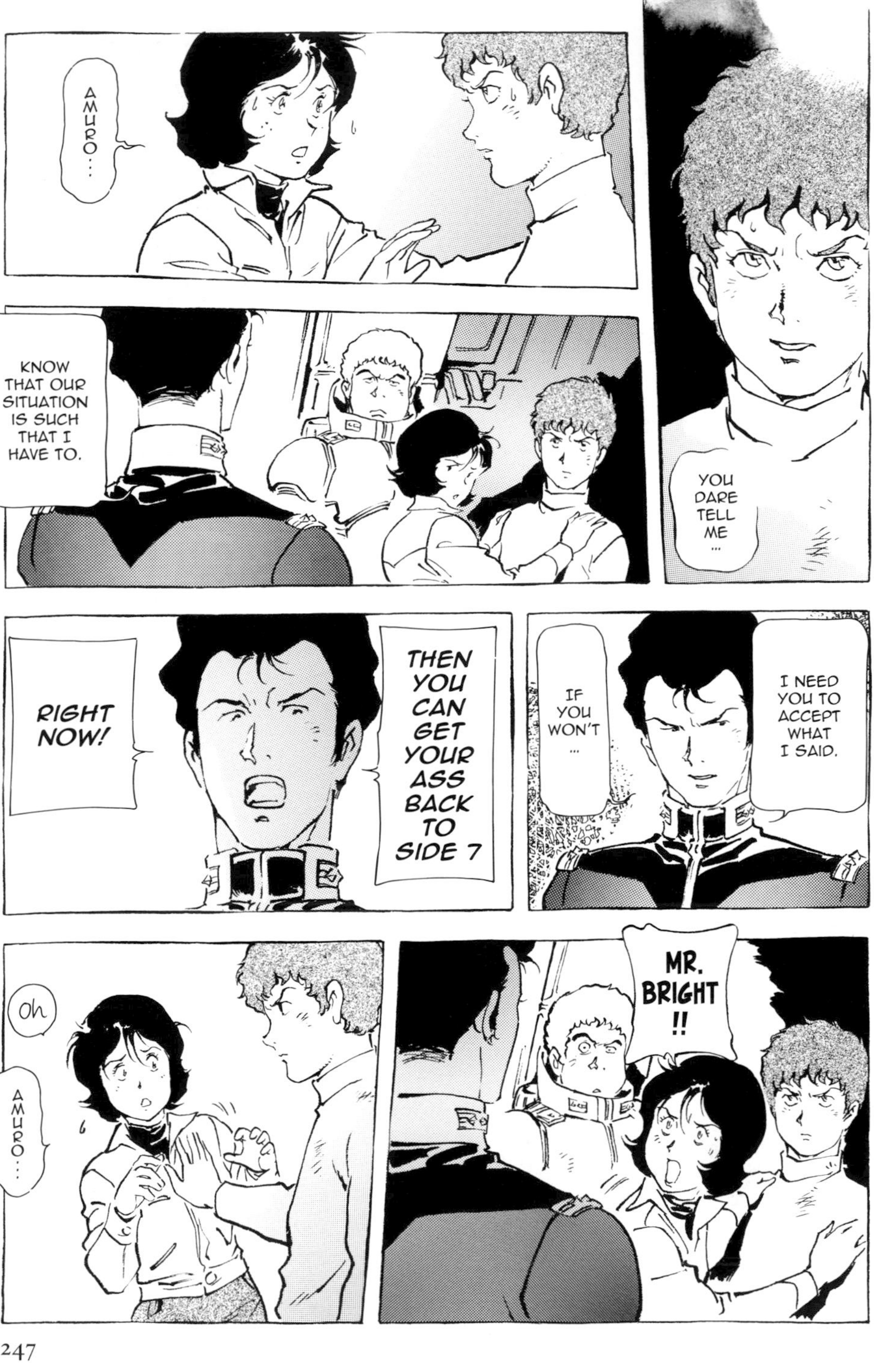
YOU DARE TELL ME ...
AMURO...
KNOW THAT OUR SITUATION IS SUCH THAT I HAVE TO.
I NEED YOU TO ACCEPT WHAT I SAID.
IF YOU WON'T ...
THEN YOU CAN GET YOUR ASS BACK TO SIDE 7
RIGHT NOW!
MR. BRIGHT !!
Oh
AMURO...

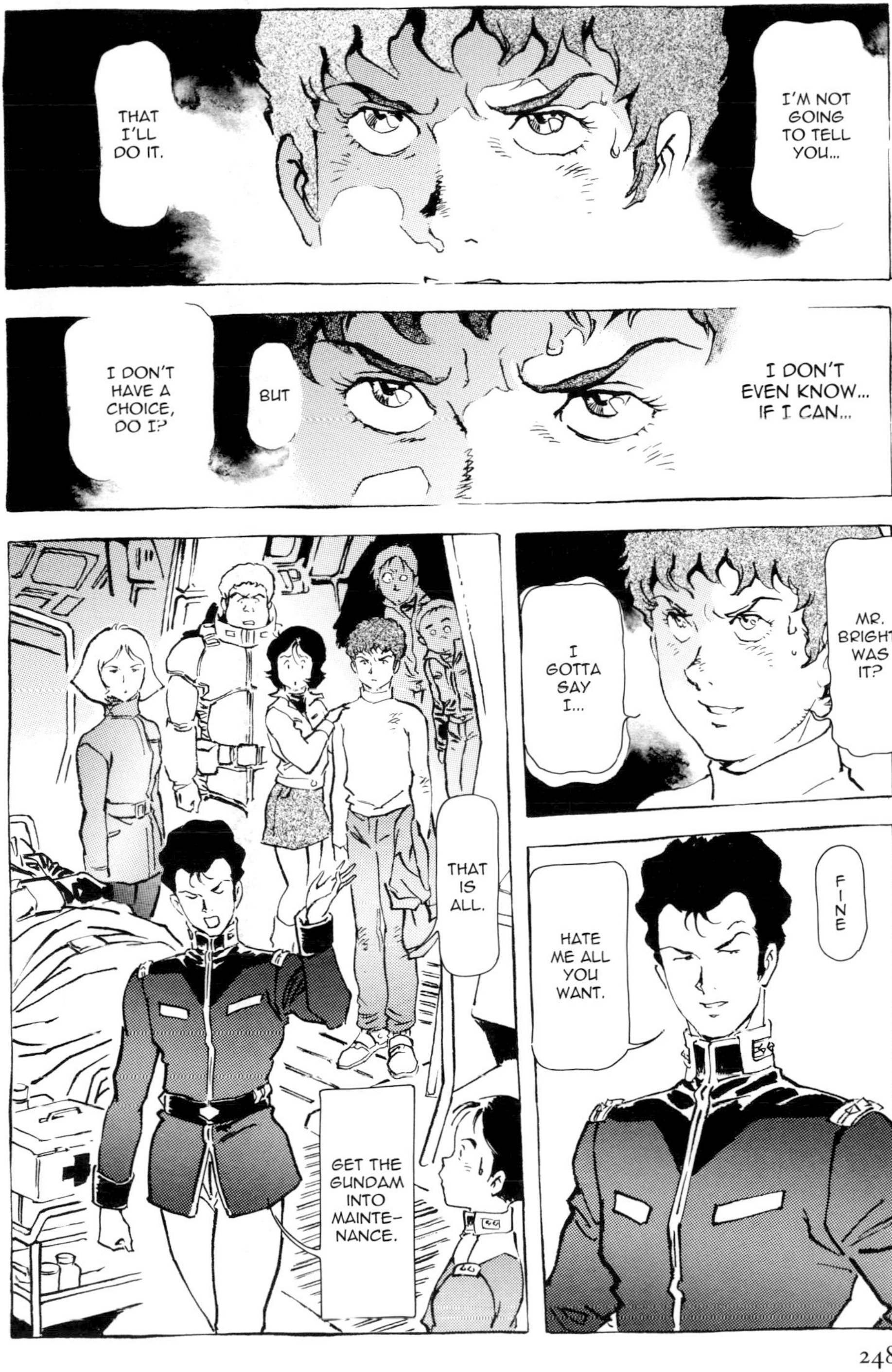
I'M NOT GOING TO TELL YOU...
THAT I'LL DO IT.
I DON'T EVEN KNOW... IF I CAN...
BUT
I DON'T HAVE A CHOICE, DO I?
MR. BRIGHT, WAS IT?
I GOTTA SAY I...
FINE
HATE ME ALL YOU WANT.
THAT IS ALL.
GET THE GUNDAM INTO MAINTE-NANCE.

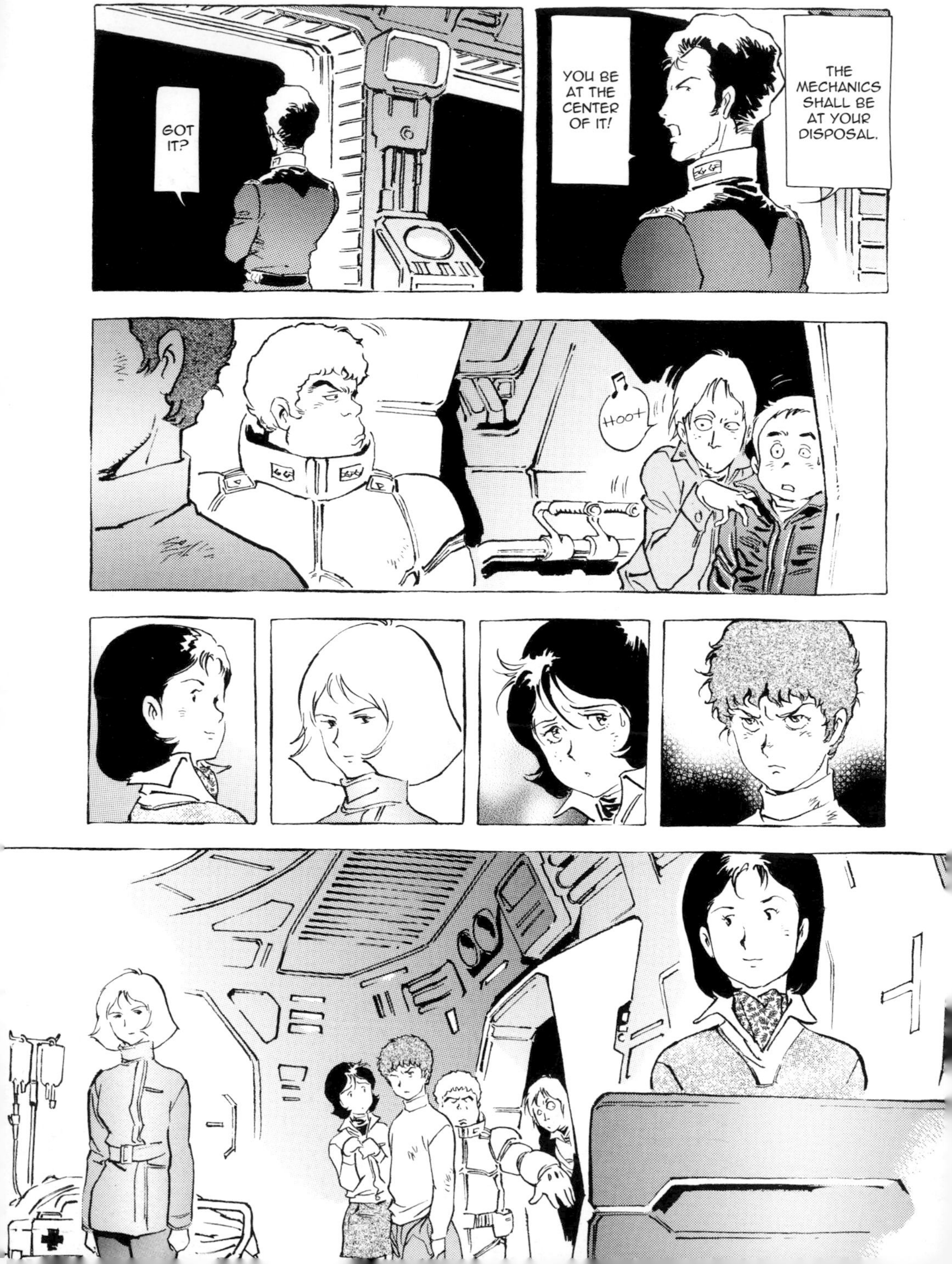
THE MECHANICS SHALL BE AT YOUR DISPOSAL.
YOU BE AT THE CENTER OF IT!
GOT IT?
Hoot

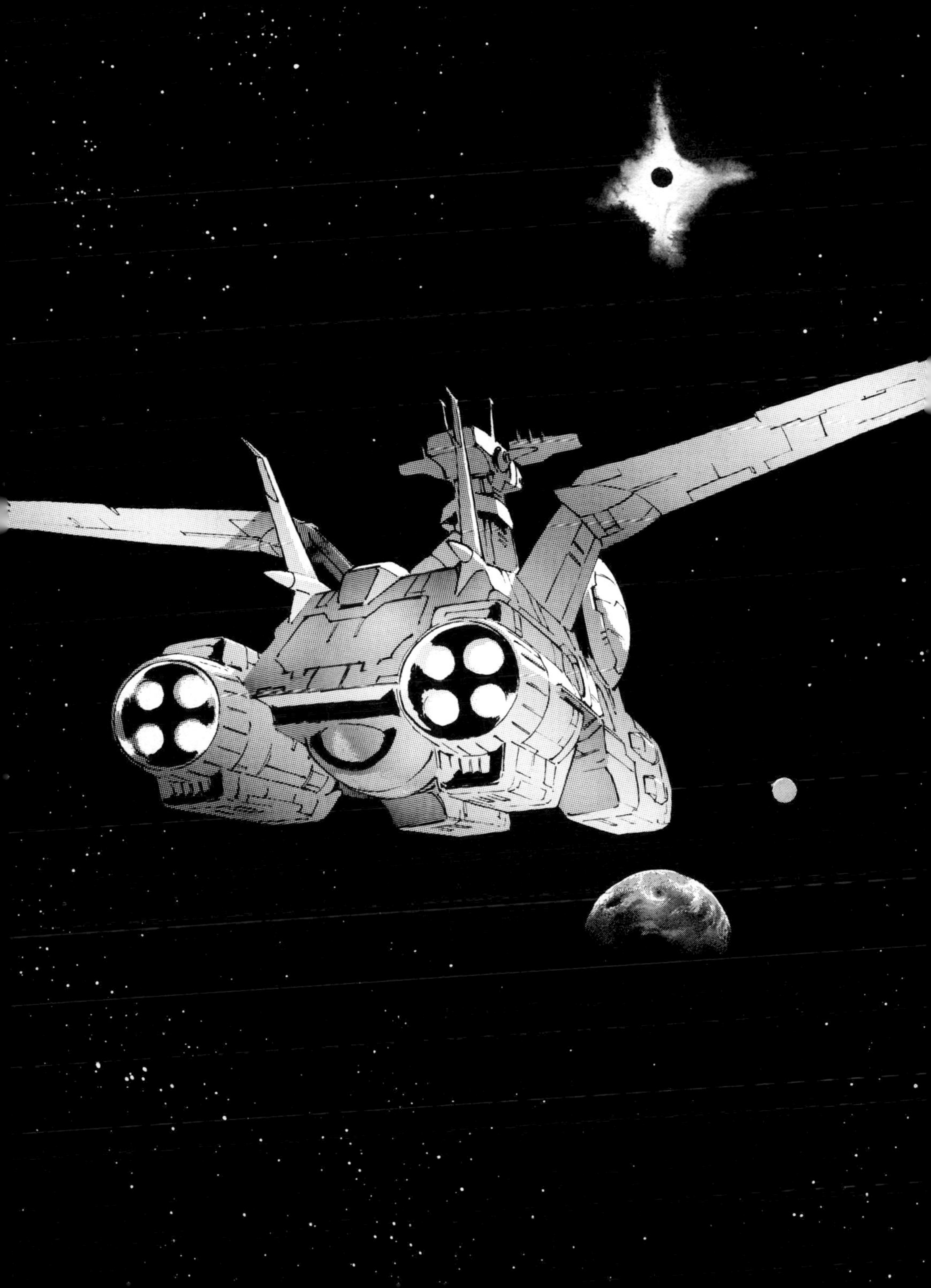

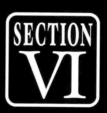

SECTION
VI

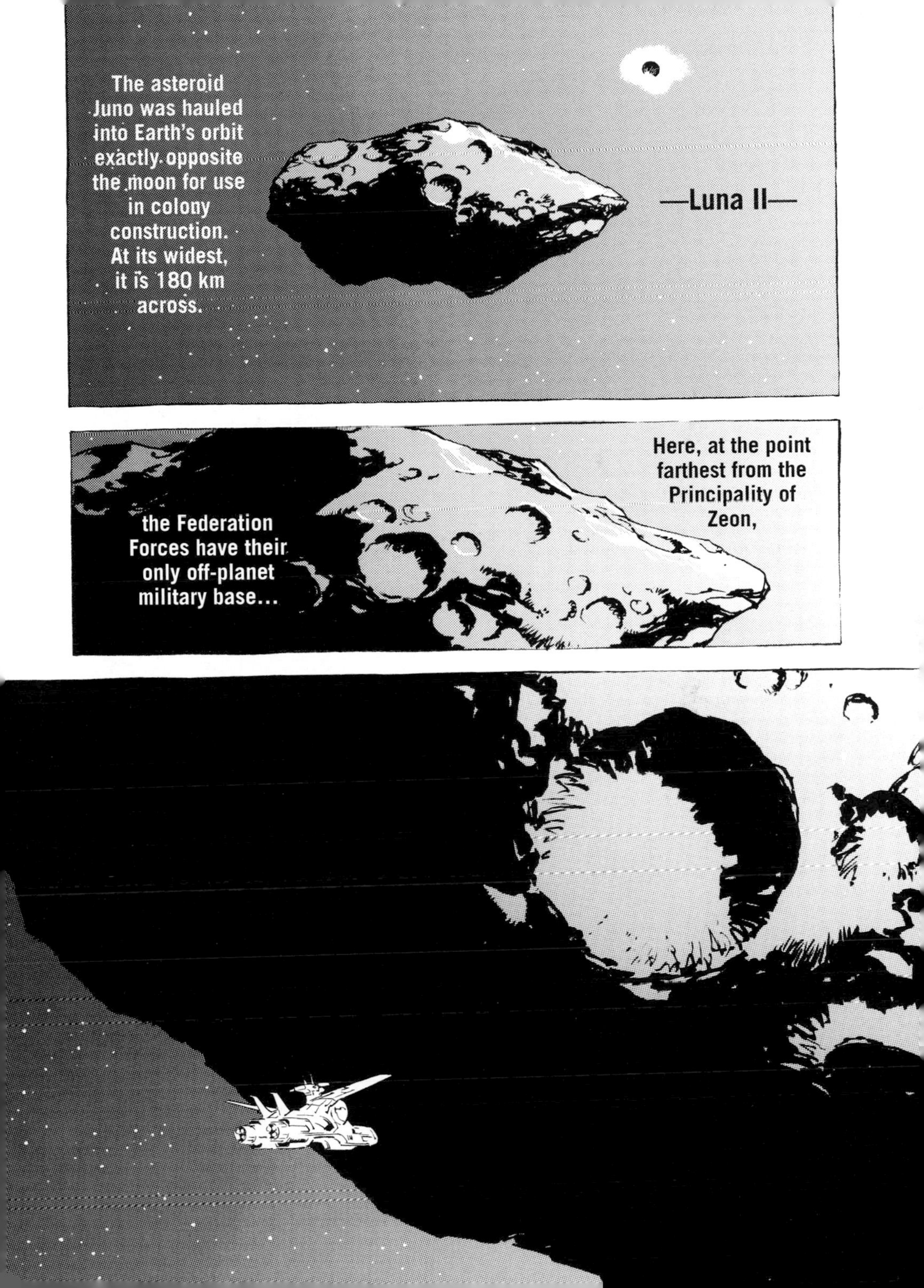
—Luna II—
The asteroid Juno was hauled into Earth's orbit exactly opposite the moon for use in colony construction. At its widest, it is 180 km across.
Here, at the point farthest from the Principality of Zeon,
the Federation Forces have their only off-planet military base...

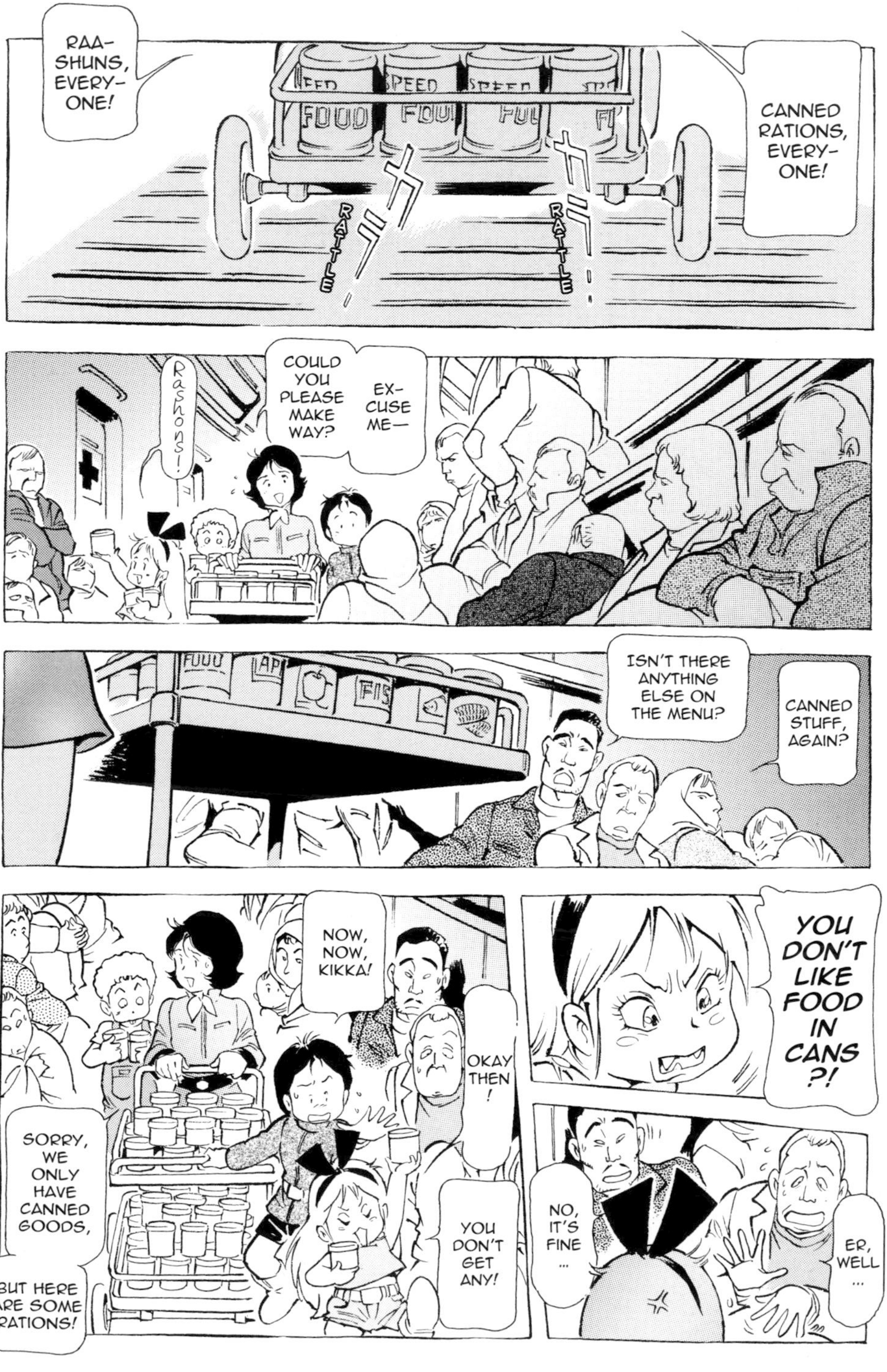
RAA-SHUNS, EVERY-ONE!
CANNED RATIONS, EVERY-ONE!
RATTLE
RATTLE
Rashons!
COULD YOU PLEASE MAKE WAY?
EX-CUSE ME—
ISN'T THERE ANYTHING ELSE ON THE MENU?
CANNED STUFF, AGAIN?
SORRY, WE ONLY HAVE CANNED GOODS,
BUT HERE ARE SOME RATIONS!
NOW, NOW, KIKKA!
OKAY THEN!
YOU DON'T GET ANY!
YOU DON'T LIKE FOOD IN CANS?!
NO, IT'S FINE ...
ER, WELL ...

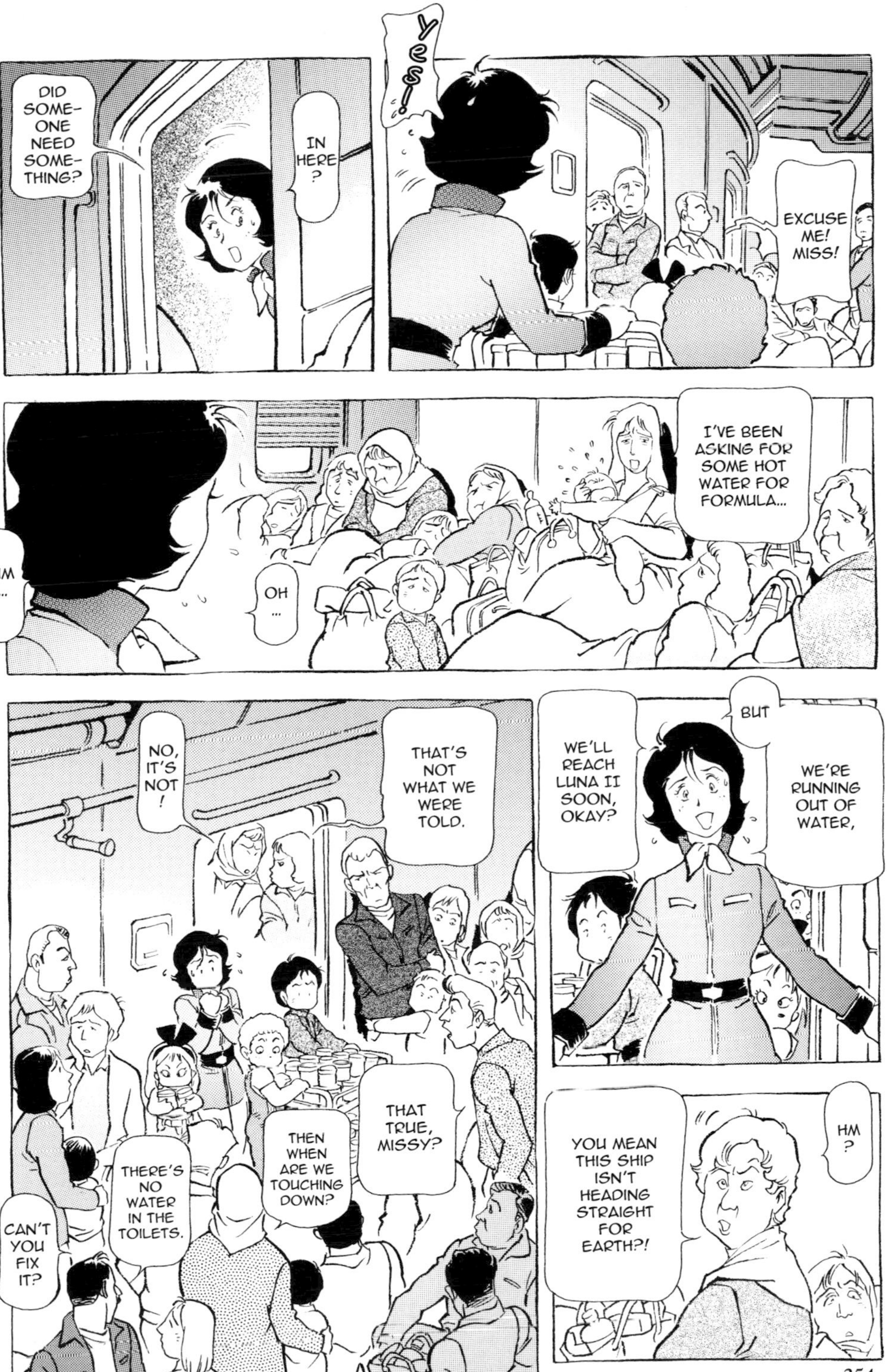
YES!
EXCUSE ME! MISS!
DID SOMEONE NEED SOMETHING?
IN HERE?
I'VE BEEN ASKING FOR SOME HOT WATER FOR FORMULA...
OH ...
UM ...
BUT
WE'RE RUNNING OUT OF WATER,
WE'LL REACH LUNA II SOON, OKAY?
HM ?
YOU MEAN THIS SHIP ISN'T HEADING STRAIGHT FOR EARTH?!
THAT'S NOT WHAT WE WERE TOLD.
NO, IT'S NOT!
THAT TRUE, MISSY?
THEN WHEN ARE WE TOUCHING DOWN?
THERE'S NO WATER IN THE TOILETS.
CAN'T YOU FIX IT?

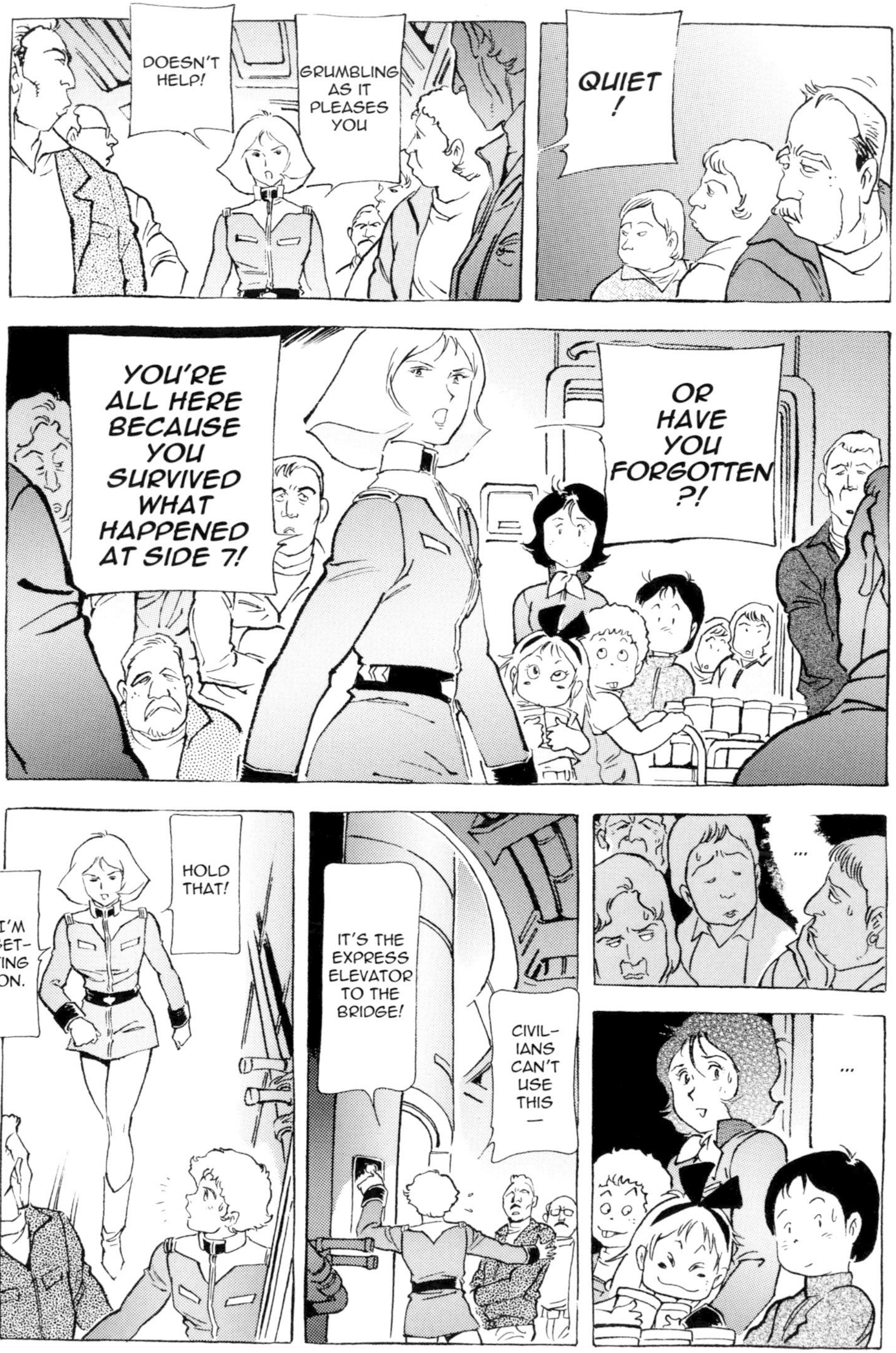
QUIET!
GRUMBLING AS IT PLEASES YOU
DOESN'T HELP!
YOU'RE ALL HERE BECAUSE YOU SURVIVED WHAT HAPPENED AT SIDE 7!
OR HAVE YOU FORGOTTEN?!
...
...
CIVILIANS CAN'T USE THIS—
IT'S THE EXPRESS ELEVATOR TO THE BRIDGE!
HOLD THAT!
I'M GETTING ON.

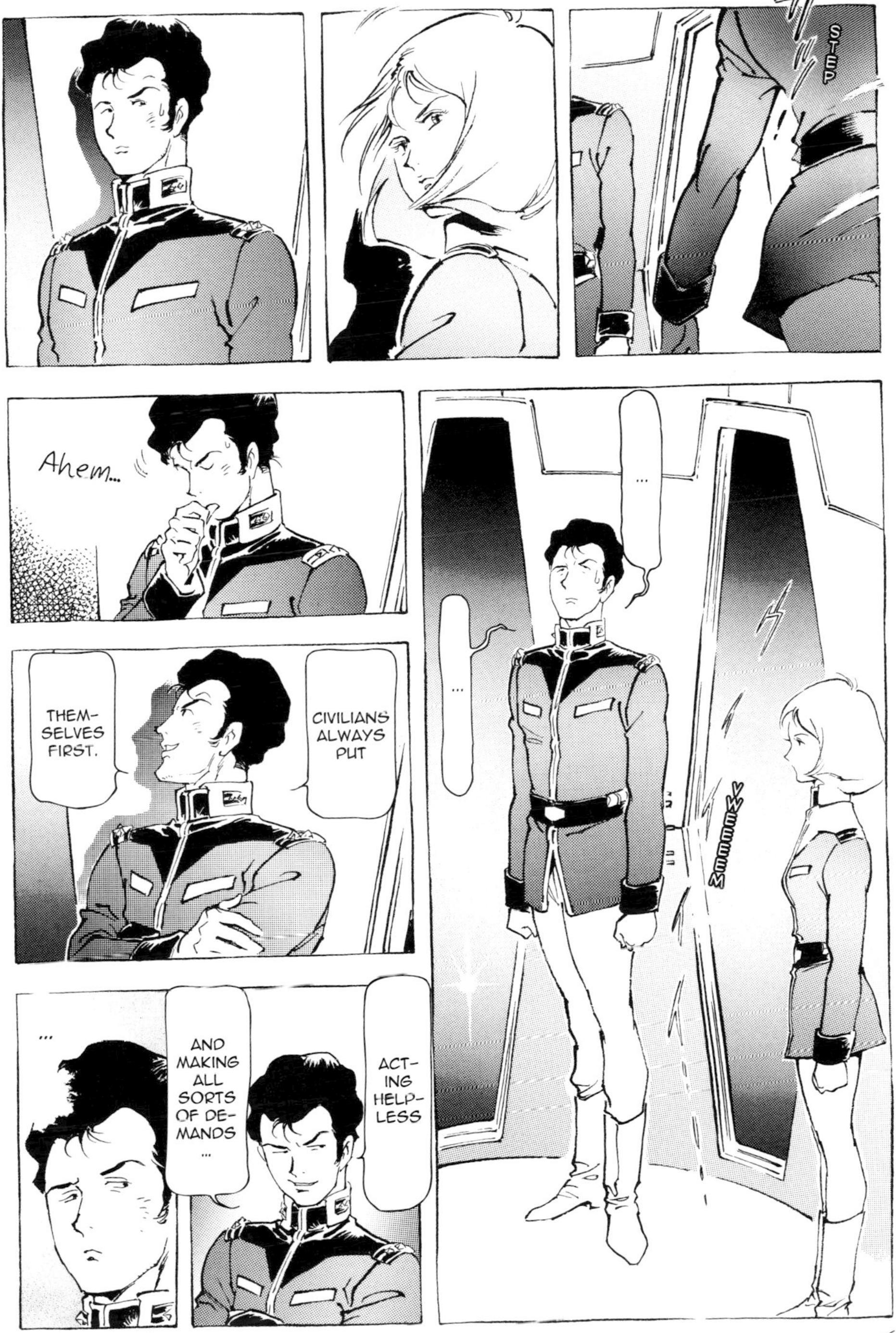
ザッ
STEP
...
...
VWEEEEEM
Ahem...
CIVILIANS ALWAYS PUT
THEMSELVES FIRST.
ACTING HELPLESS
AND MAKING ALL SORTS OF DEMANDS...
...

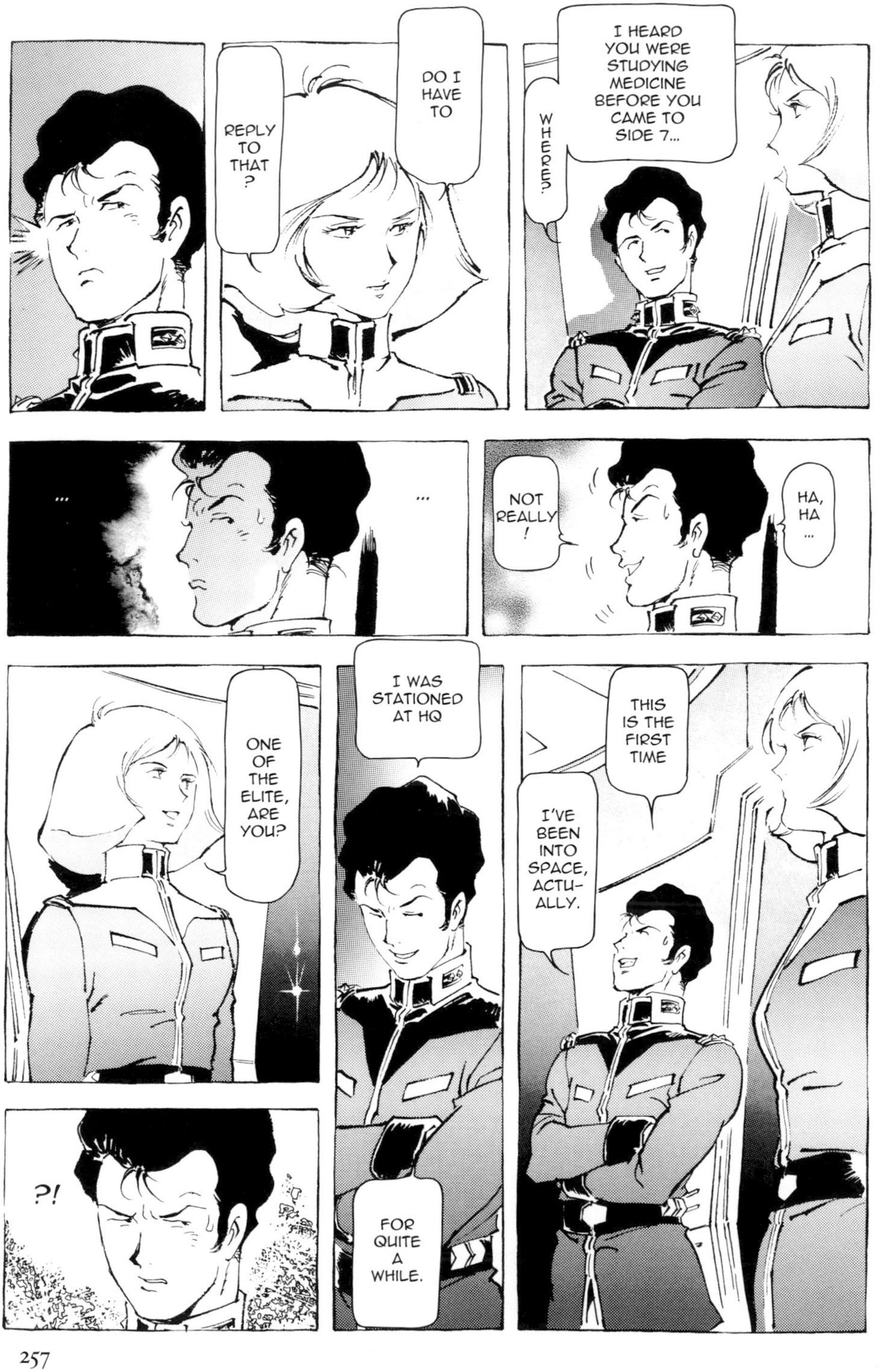
I HEARD YOU WERE STUDYING MEDICINE BEFORE YOU CAME TO SIDE 7...
WHERE?
DO I HAVE TO
REPLY TO THAT ?
HA, HA ...
NOT REALLY !
...
...
THIS IS THE FIRST TIME
I'VE BEEN INTO SPACE, ACTUALLY.
I WAS STATIONED AT HQ
FOR QUITE A WHILE.
ONE OF THE ELITE, ARE YOU?
?!

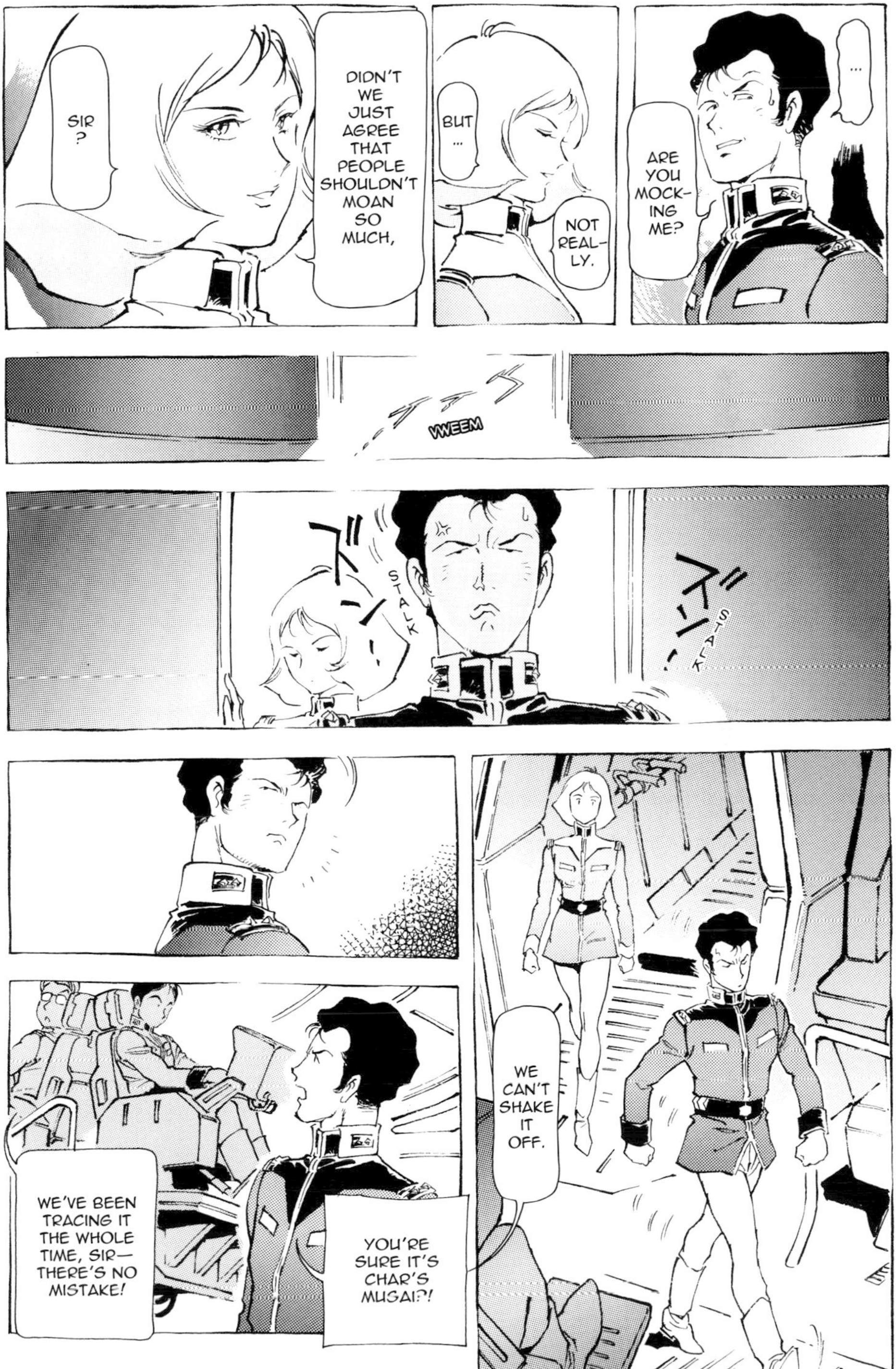
...
ARE YOU MOCKING ME?
NOT REALLY.
BUT ...
DIDN'T WE JUST AGREE THAT PEOPLE SHOULDN'T MOAN SO MUCH,
SIR?
VWEEM
STALK
STALK
WE CAN'T SHAKE IT OFF.
YOU'RE SURE IT'S CHAR'S MUSAI?!
WE'VE BEEN TRACING IT THE WHOLE TIME, SIR— THERE'S NO MISTAKE!

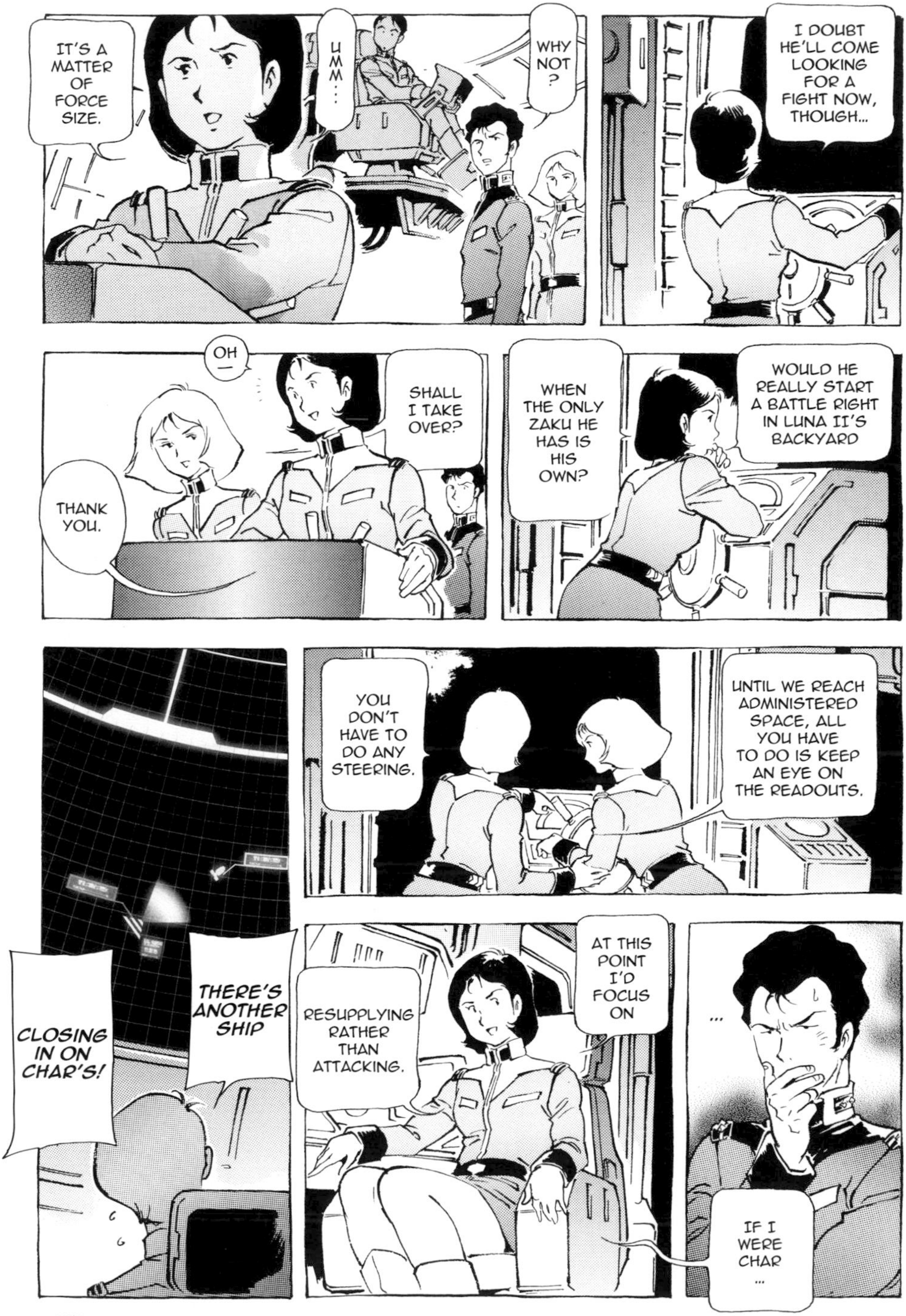
I DOUBT HE'LL COME LOOKING FOR A FIGHT NOW, THOUGH...
WHY NOT?
UMM...
IT'S A MATTER OF FORCE SIZE.
WOULD HE REALLY START A BATTLE RIGHT IN LUNA II'S BACKYARD
WHEN THE ONLY ZAKU HE HAS IS HIS OWN?
SHALL I TAKE OVER?
OH—
THANK YOU.
UNTIL WE REACH ADMINISTERED SPACE, ALL YOU HAVE TO DO IS KEEP AN EYE ON THE READOUTS.
YOU DON'T HAVE TO DO ANY STEERING.
...
IF I WERE CHAR ...
AT THIS POINT I'D FOCUS ON
RESUPPLYING RATHER THAN ATTACKING.
THERE'S ANOTHER SHIP
CLOSING IN ON CHAR'S!

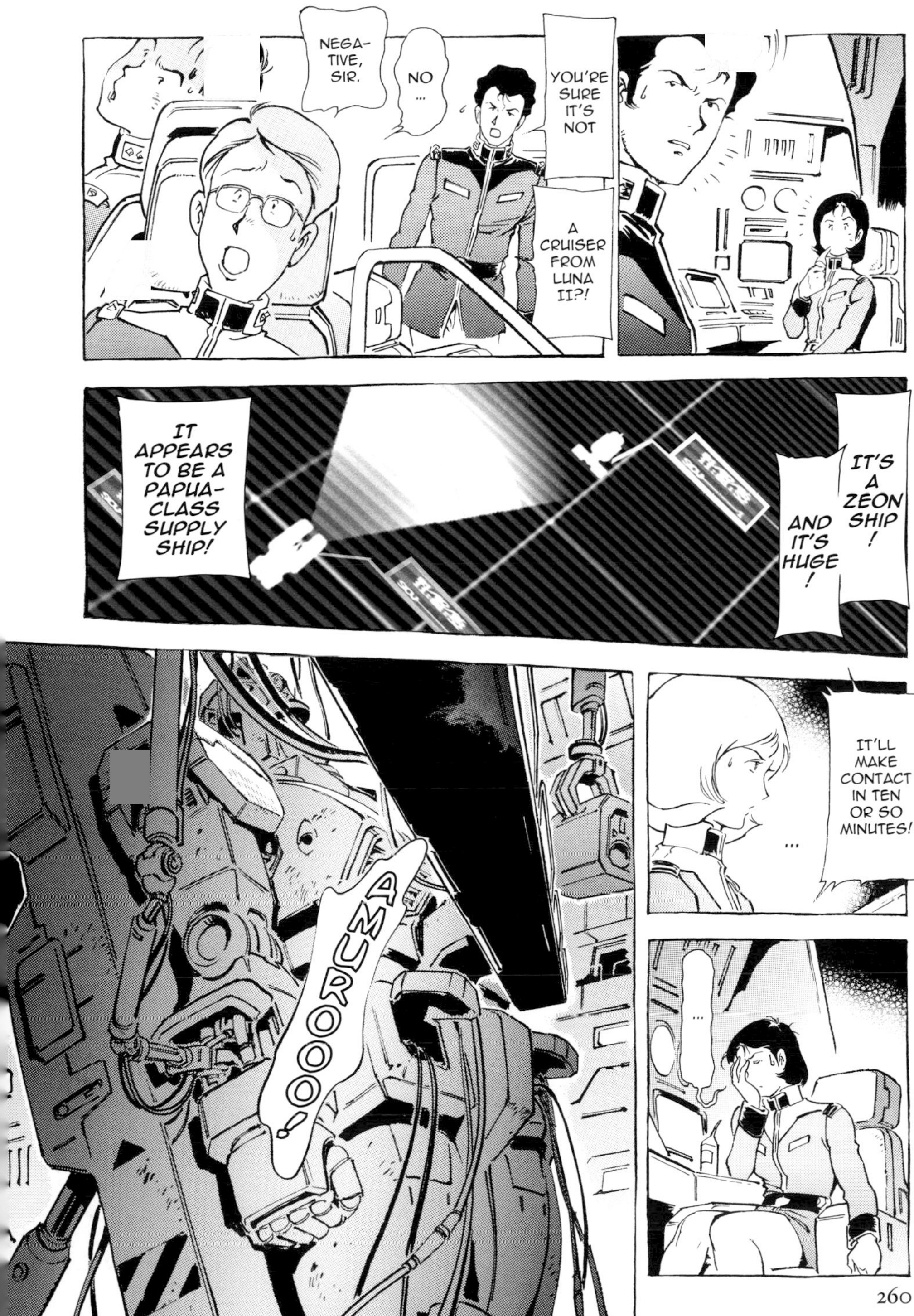

YOU'RE SURE IT'S NOT
A CRUISER FROM LUNA II?!
NO ...
NEGA-TIVE, SIR.
IT'S A ZEON SHIP!
AND IT'S HUGE!
IT APPEARS TO BE A PAPUA-CLASS SUPPLY SHIP!
IT'LL MAKE CONTACT IN TEN OR SO MINUTES!
...
...
AMUROOOOOO!

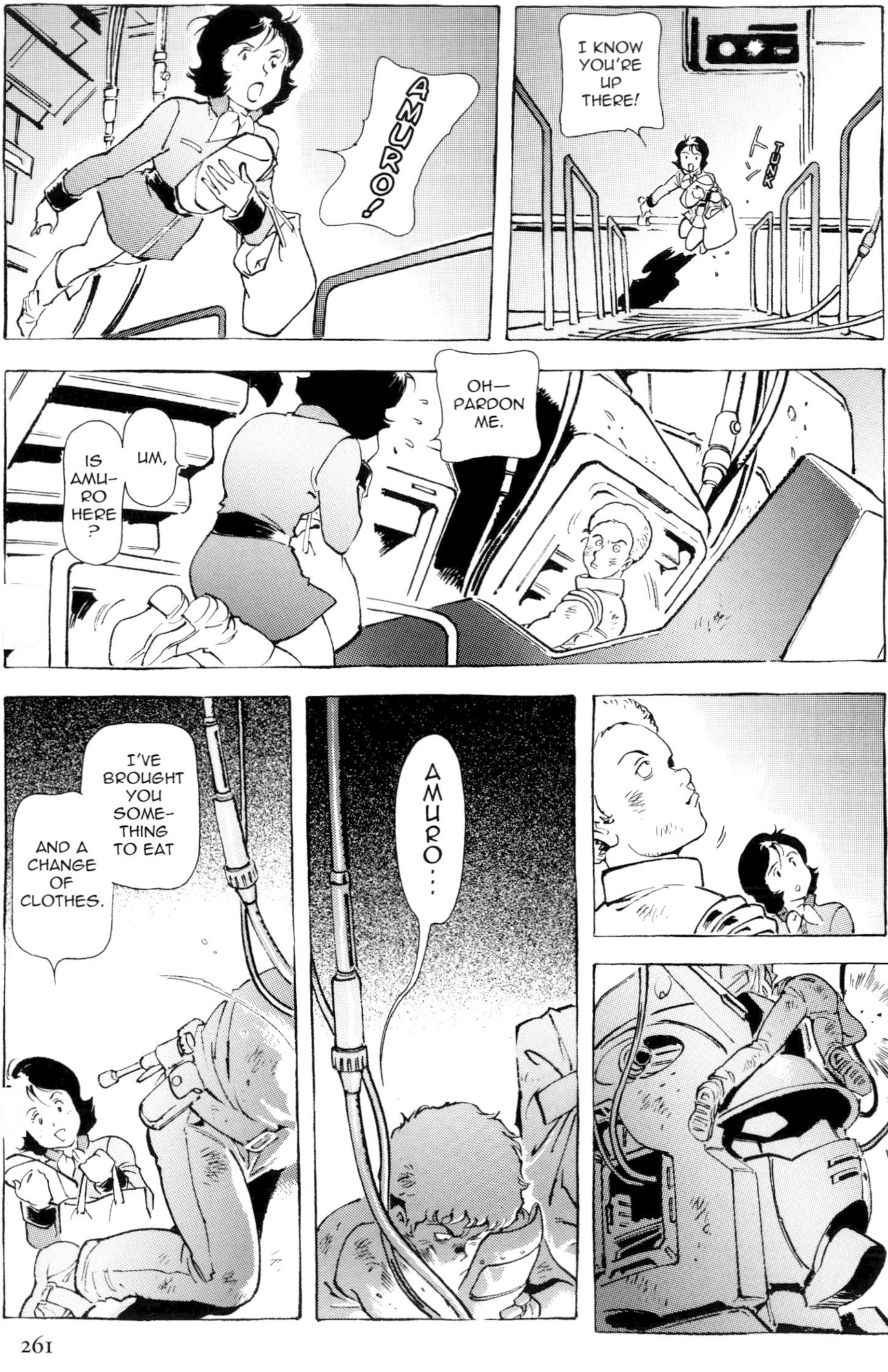
I KNOW YOU'RE UP THERE!
TUNK
トン
AMURO!
OH— PARDON ME.
UM,
IS AMURO HERE?
AMURO...
I'VE BROUGHT YOU SOME-THING TO EAT
AND A CHANGE OF CLOTHES.

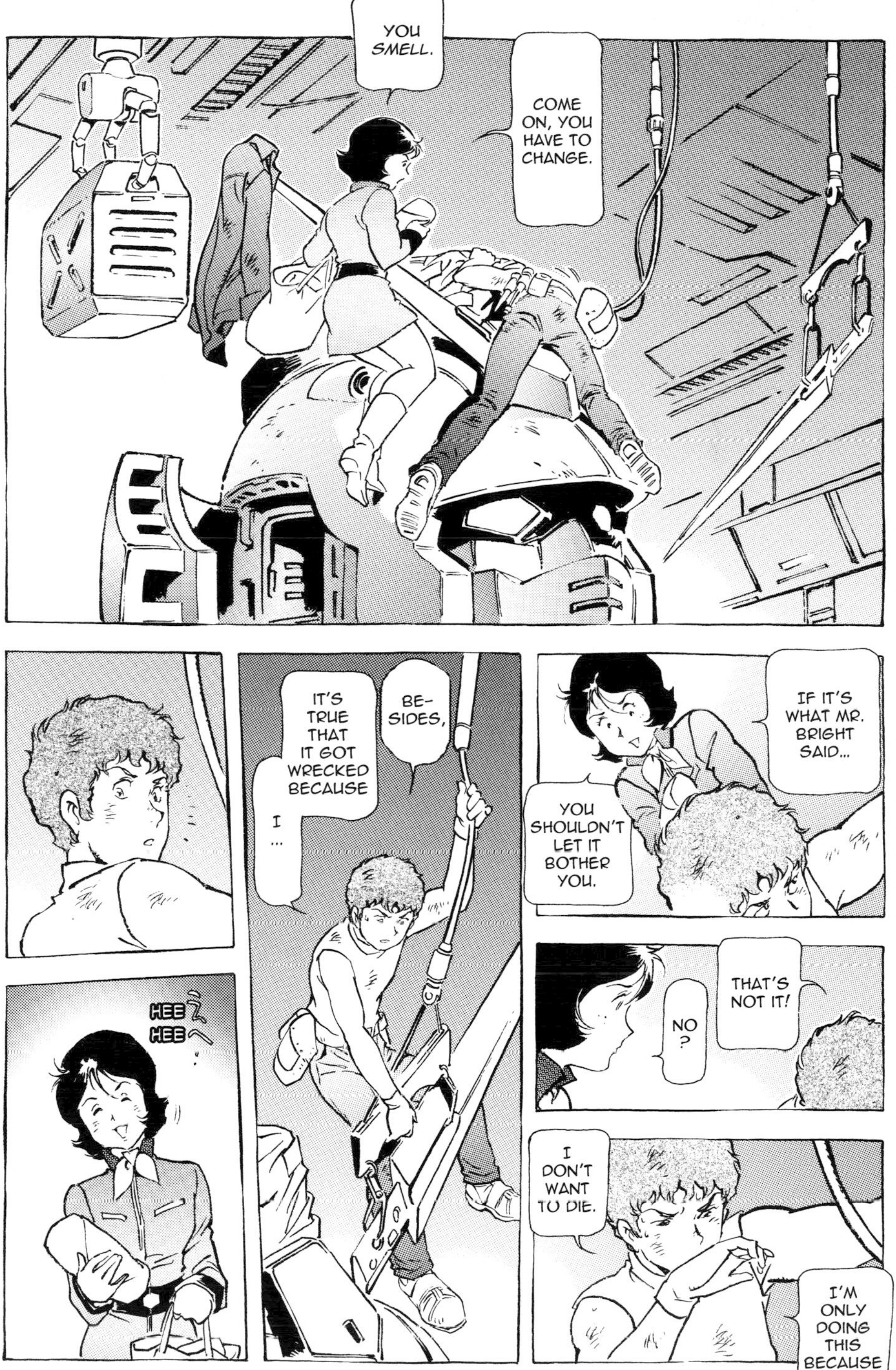
YOU SMELL.
COME ON, YOU HAVE TO CHANGE.
IF IT'S WHAT MR. BRIGHT SAID...
YOU SHOULDN'T LET IT BOTHER YOU.
THAT'S NOT IT!
NO?
I DON'T WANT TO DIE.
I'M ONLY DOING THIS BECAUSE
BE-SIDES,
IT'S TRUE THAT IT GOT WRECKED BECAUSE
I ...
HEE HEE

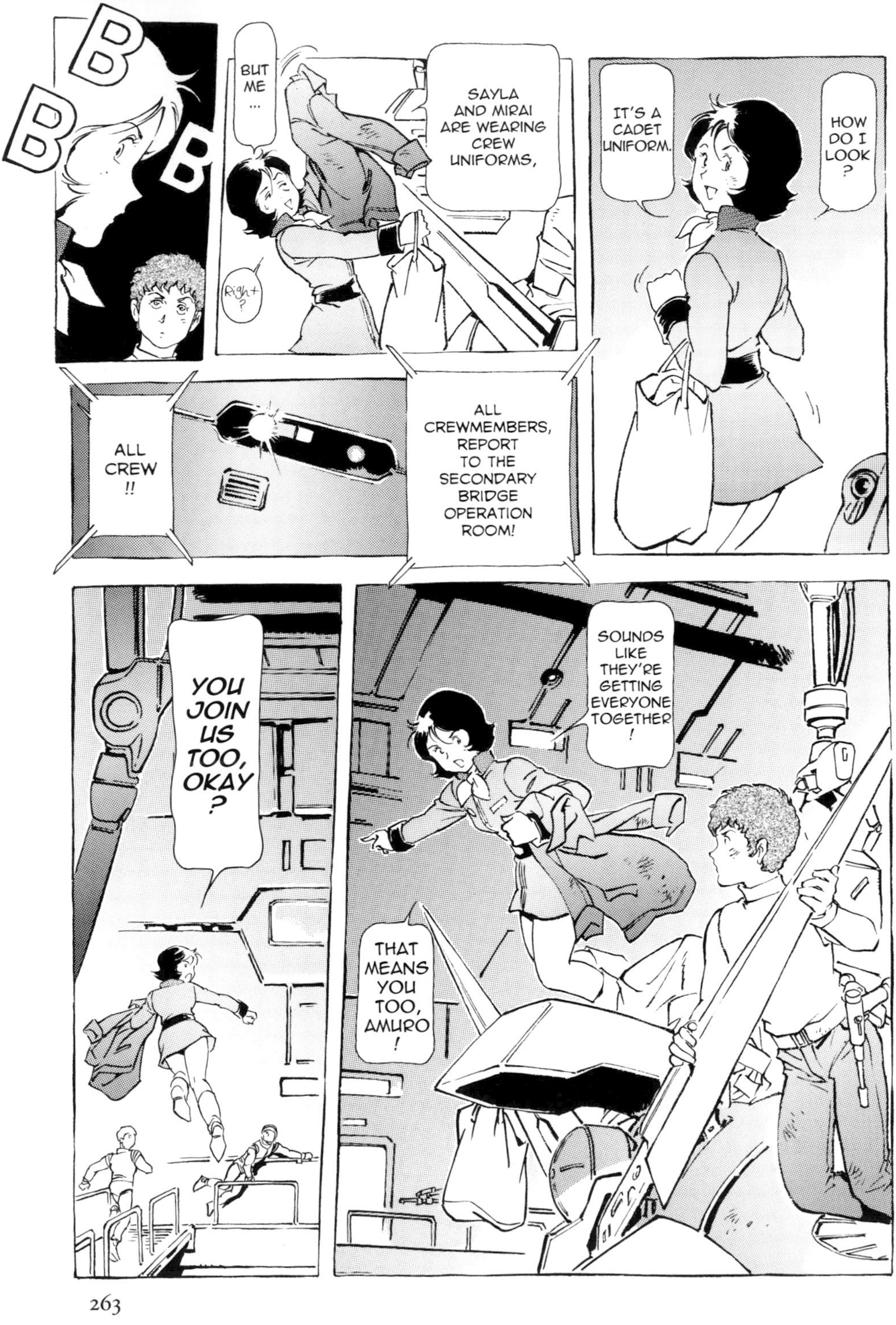

HOW DO I LOOK?
IT'S A CADET UNIFORM.
SAYLA AND MIRAI ARE WEARING CREW UNIFORMS,
BUT ME ...
Right?
B
B
B
ALL CREWMEMBERS, REPORT TO THE SECONDARY BRIDGE OPERATION ROOM!
ALL CREW !!
SOUNDS LIKE THEY'RE GETTING EVERYONE TOGETHER!
THAT MEANS YOU TOO, AMURO!
YOU JOIN US TOO, OKAY?

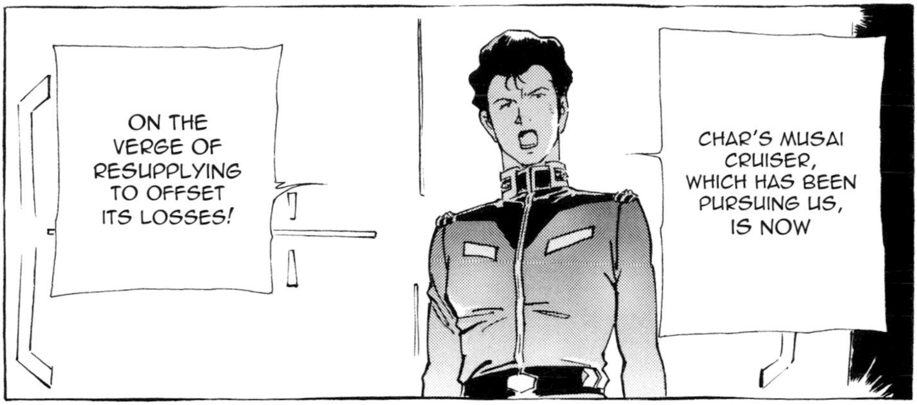
CHAR'S MUSAI CRUISER, WHICH HAS BEEN PURSUING US, IS NOW
ON THE VERGE OF RESUPPLYING TO OFFSET ITS LOSSES!
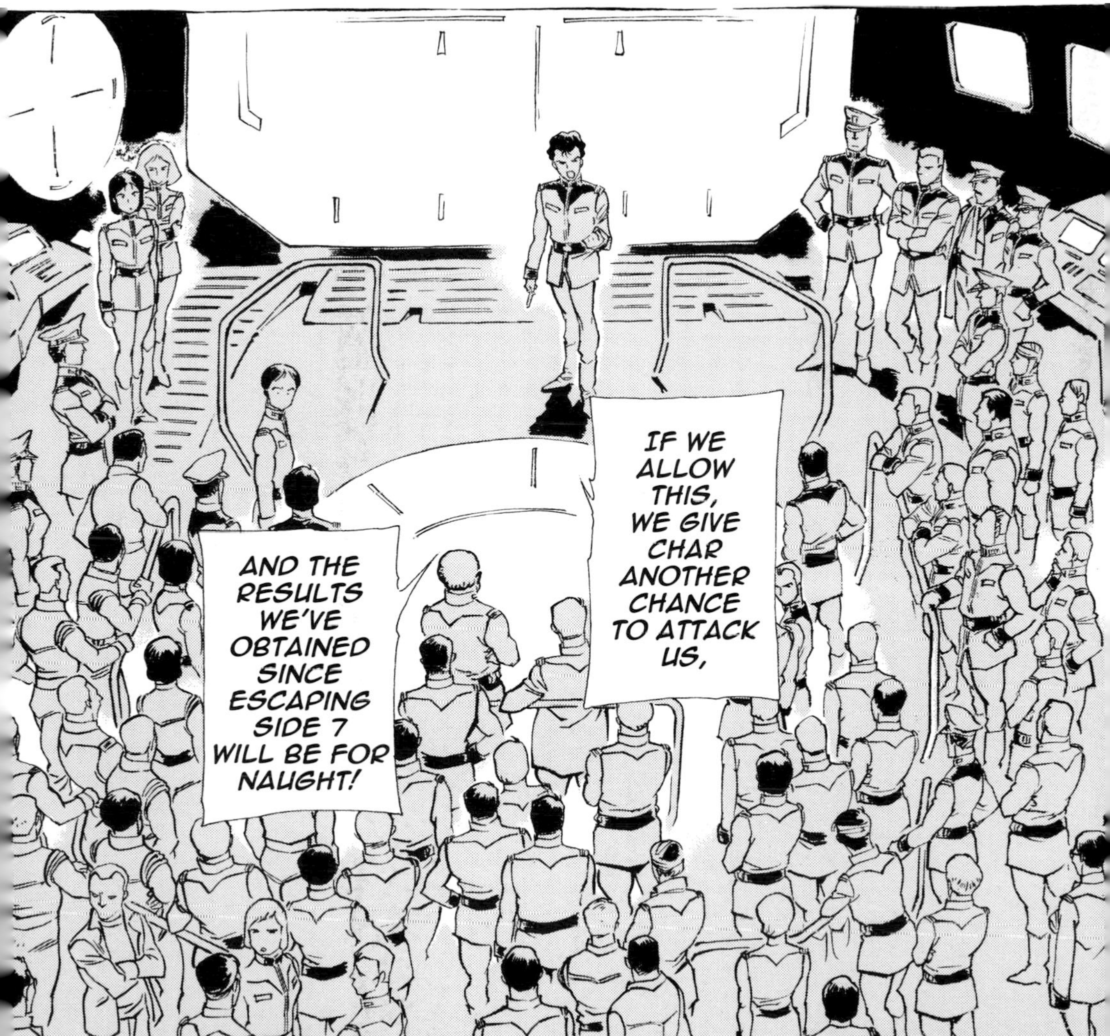
IF WE ALLOW THIS, WE GIVE CHAR ANOTHER CHANCE TO ATTACK US,
AND THE RESULTS WE'VE OBTAINED SINCE ESCAPING SIDE 7 WILL BE FOR NAUGHT!

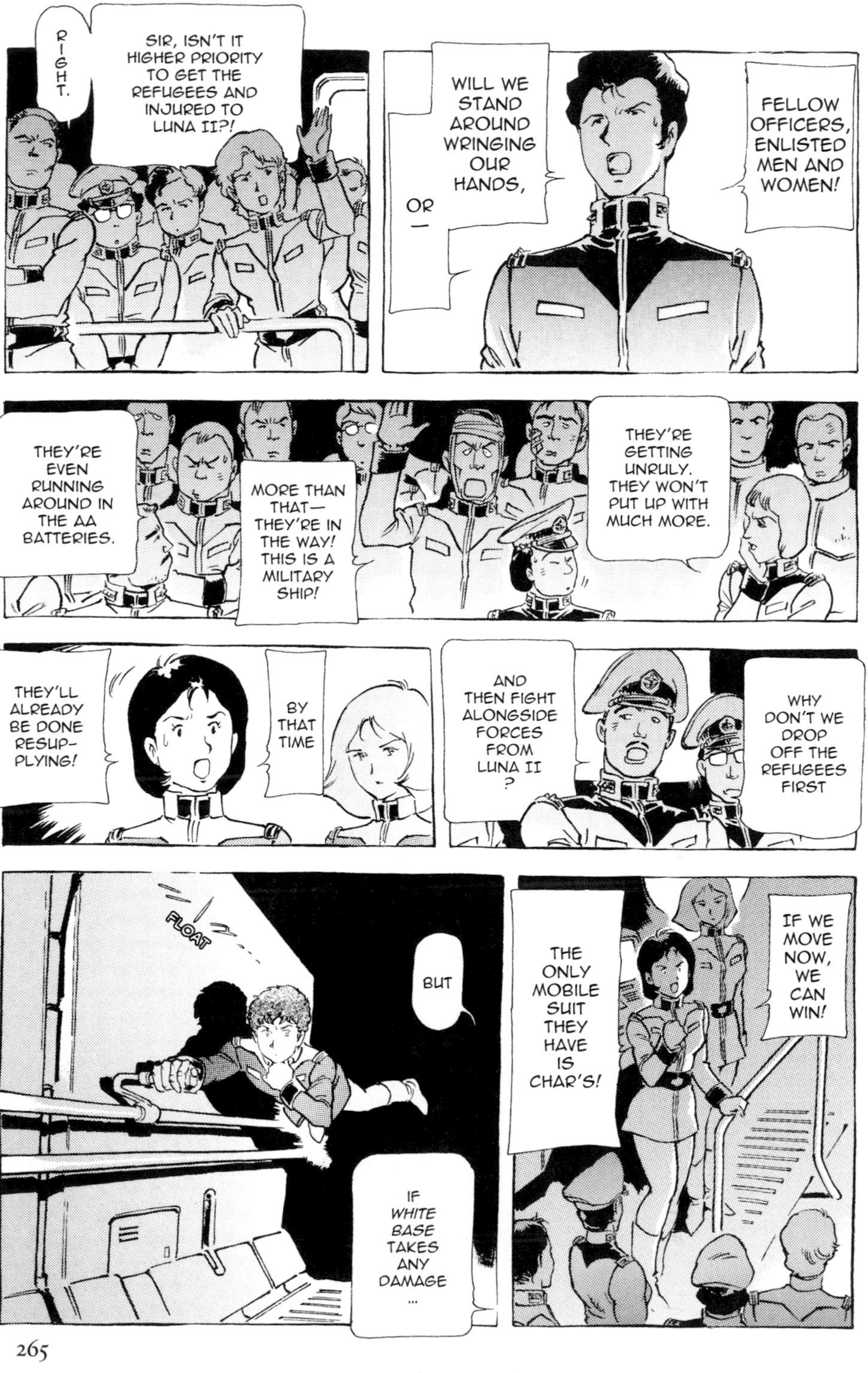
FELLOW OFFICERS, ENLISTED MEN AND WOMEN!
WILL WE STAND AROUND WRINGING OUR HANDS,
OR—
SIR, ISN'T IT HIGHER PRIORITY TO GET THE REFUGEES AND INJURED TO LUNA II?!
RIGHT.
THEY'RE GETTING UNRULY. THEY WON'T PUT UP WITH MUCH MORE.
MORE THAN THAT— THEY'RE IN THE WAY! THIS IS A MILITARY SHIP!
THEY'RE EVEN RUNNING AROUND IN THE AA BATTERIES.
WHY DON'T WE DROP OFF THE REFUGEES FIRST
AND THEN FIGHT ALONGSIDE FORCES FROM LUNA II ?
BY THAT TIME
THEY'LL ALREADY BE DONE RESUP-PLYING!
IF WE MOVE NOW, WE CAN WIN!
THE ONLY MOBILE SUIT THEY HAVE IS CHAR'S!
FLOAT
BUT
IF WHITE BASE TAKES ANY DAMAGE ...

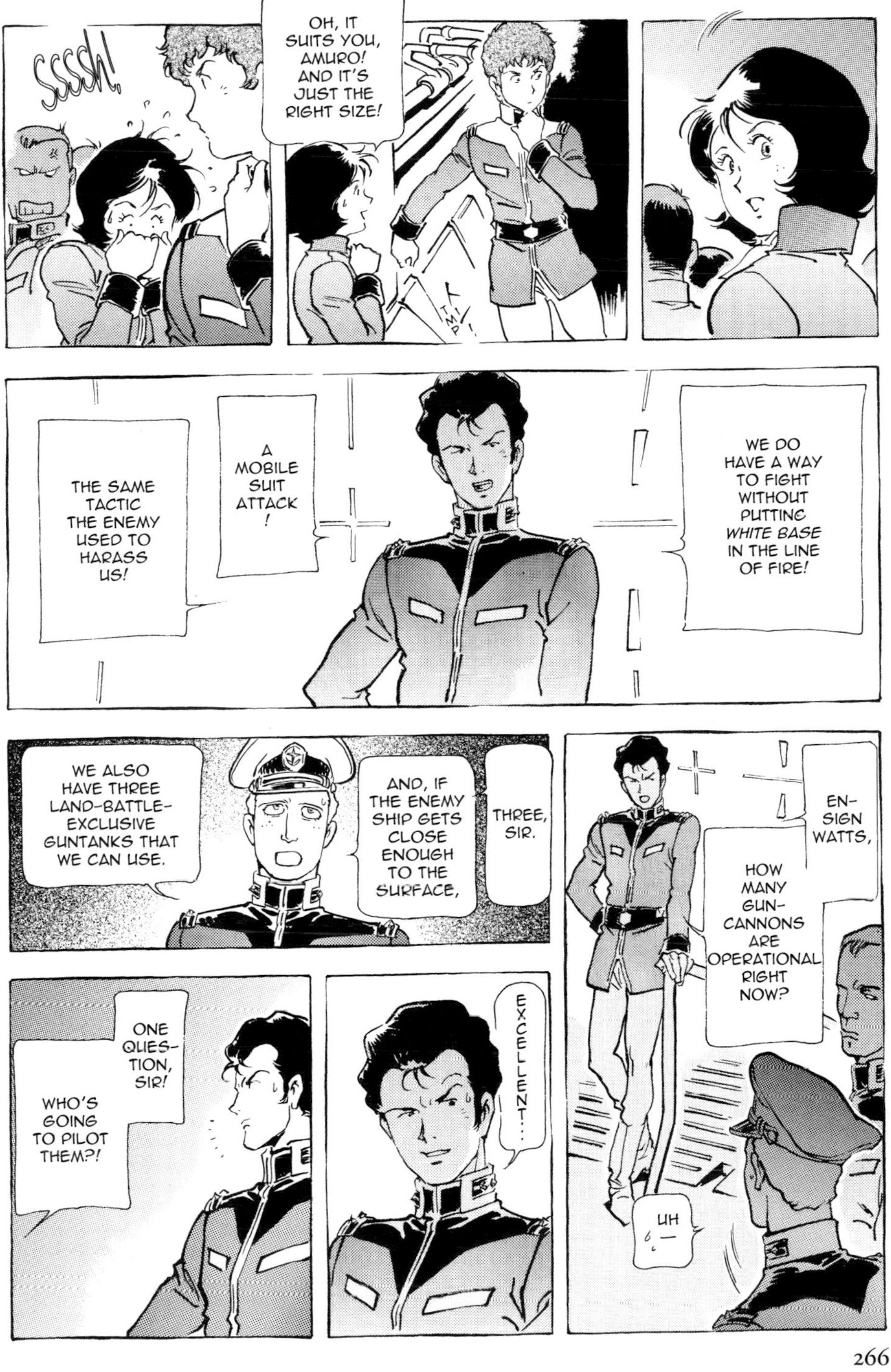
OH, IT SUITS YOU, AMURO! AND IT'S JUST THE RIGHT SIZE!
TMP!
SSSSH!
WE DO HAVE A WAY TO FIGHT WITHOUT PUTTING *WHITE BASE* IN THE LINE OF FIRE!
A MOBILE SUIT ATTACK!
THE SAME TACTIC THE ENEMY USED TO HARASS US!
EN-SIGN WATTS,
HOW MANY GUN-CANNONS ARE OPERATIONAL RIGHT NOW?
UH—
THREE, SIR.
AND, IF THE ENEMY SHIP GETS CLOSE ENOUGH TO THE SURFACE,
WE ALSO HAVE THREE LAND-BATTLE-EXCLUSIVE GUNTANKS THAT WE CAN USE.
EXCELLENT...
ONE QUES-TION, SIR!
WHO'S GOING TO PILOT THEM?!

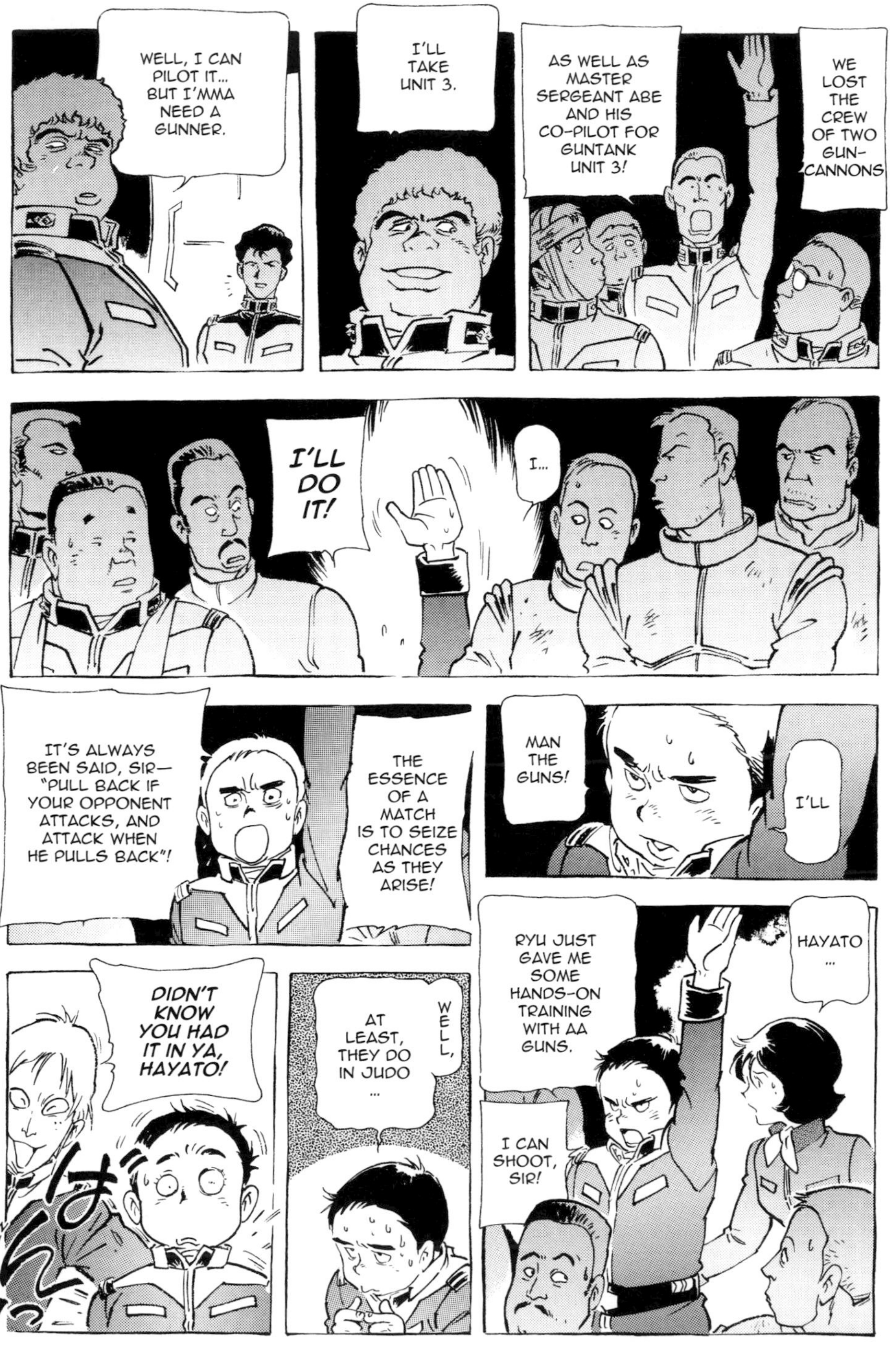

WE LOST THE CREW OF TWO GUN-CANNONS
AS WELL AS MASTER SERGEANT ABE AND HIS CO-PILOT FOR GUNTANK UNIT 3!
I'LL TAKE UNIT 3.
WELL, I CAN PILOT IT... BUT I'MMA NEED A GUNNER.
I...
I'LL DO IT!
I'LL
MAN THE GUNS!
THE ESSENCE OF A MATCH IS TO SEIZE CHANCES AS THEY ARISE!
IT'S ALWAYS BEEN SAID, SIR—"PULL BACK IF YOUR OPPONENT ATTACKS, AND ATTACK WHEN HE PULLS BACK"!
HAYATO...
RYU JUST GAVE ME SOME HANDS-ON TRAINING WITH AA GUNS.
I CAN SHOOT, SIR!
WELL,
AT LEAST, THEY DO IN JUDO...
DIDN'T KNOW YOU HAD IT IN YA, HAYATO!
WHAP!

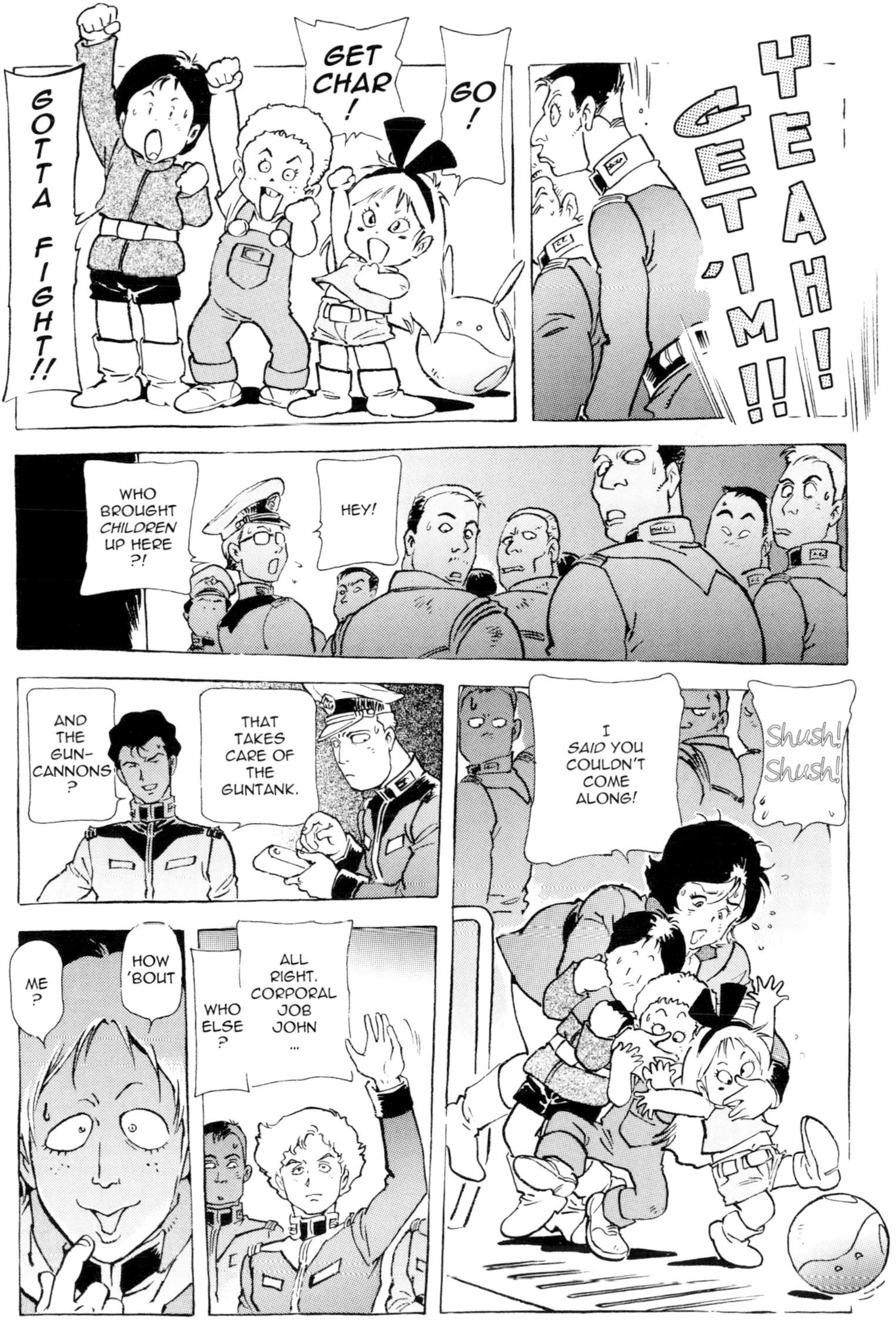
YEAH!
GET 'IM!!
GO!
GET CHAR!
GOTTA FIGHT!!
HEY!
WHO BROUGHT CHILDREN UP HERE?!
Shush! Shush!
I SAID YOU COULDN'T COME ALONG!
THAT TAKES CARE OF THE GUNTANK.
AND THE GUN-CANNONS?
ALL RIGHT. CORPORAL JOB JOHN ...
WHO ELSE?
HOW 'BOUT
ME?

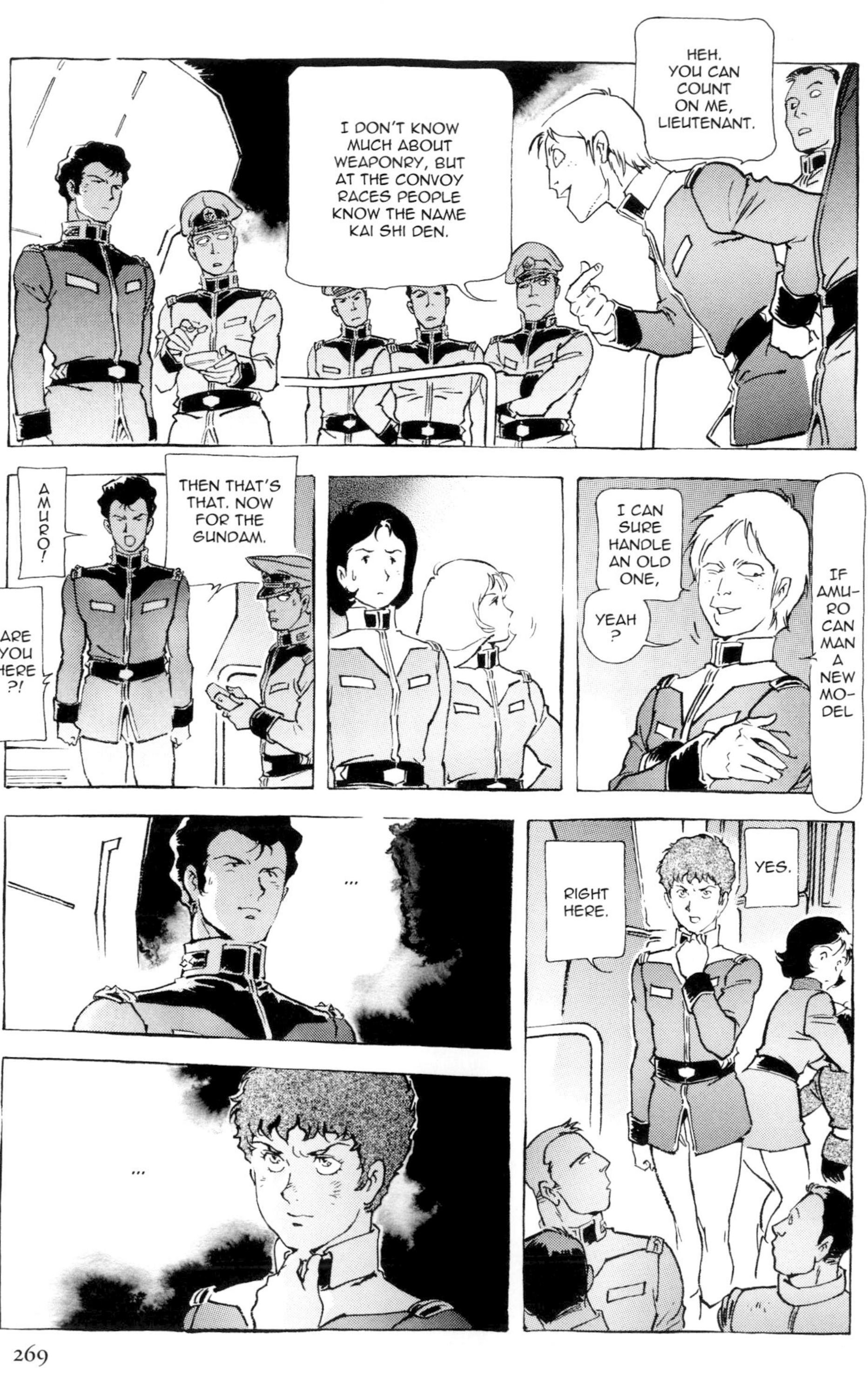
HEH. YOU CAN COUNT ON ME, LIEUTENANT.
I DON'T KNOW MUCH ABOUT WEAPONRY, BUT AT THE CONVOY RACES PEOPLE KNOW THE NAME KAI SHI DEN.
IF AMURO CAN MAN A NEW MODEL
I CAN SURE HANDLE AN OLD ONE,
YEAH?
THEN THAT'S THAT. NOW FOR THE GUNDAM.
AMURO!
ARE YOU HERE?!
YES.
RIGHT HERE.
...
...

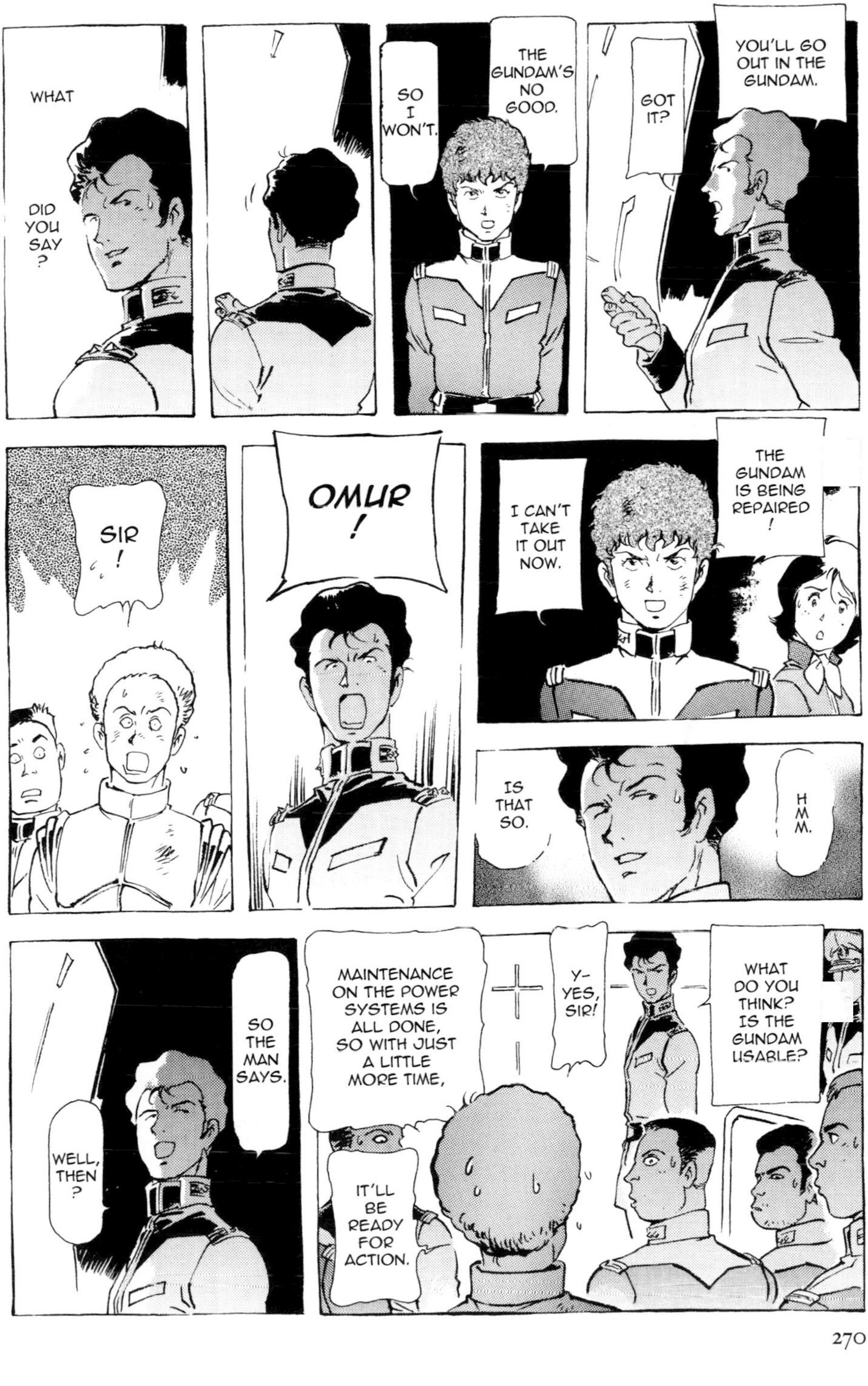
YOU'LL GO OUT IN THE GUNDAM.
GOT IT?
THE GUNDAM'S NO GOOD.
SO I WON'T.
!
WHAT
DID YOU SAY?
THE GUNDAM IS BEING REPAIRED!
I CAN'T TAKE IT OUT NOW.
HMM.
IS THAT SO.
OMUR!
SIR!
WHAT DO YOU THINK? IS THE GUNDAM USABLE?
Y-YES, SIR!
MAINTENANCE ON THE POWER SYSTEMS IS ALL DONE, SO WITH JUST A LITTLE MORE TIME,
IT'LL BE READY FOR ACTION.
SO THE MAN SAYS.
!
WELL, THEN?

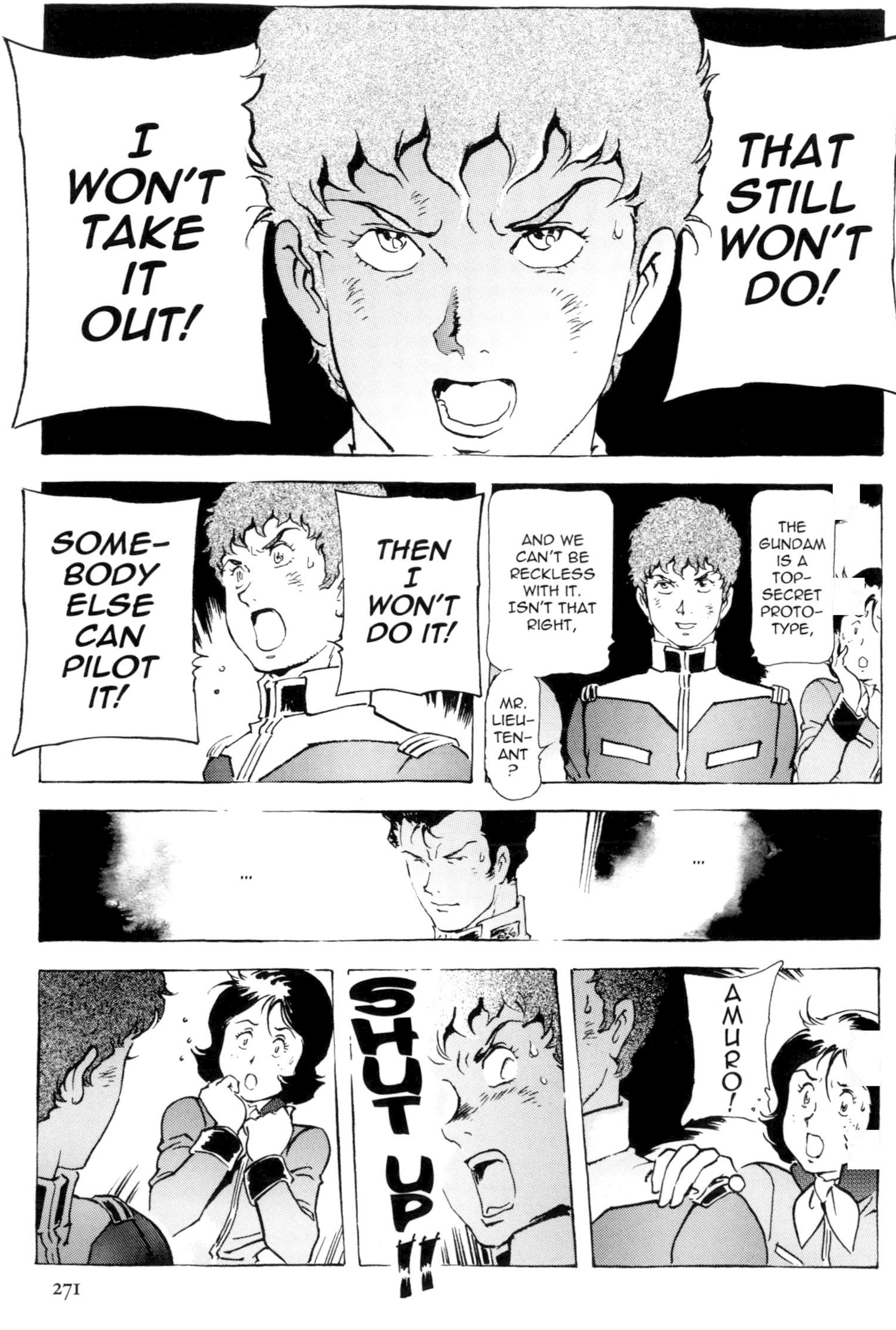
THAT STILL WON'T DO!
I WON'T TAKE IT OUT!
THE GUNDAM IS A TOP-SECRET PROTOTYPE,
AND WE CAN'T BE RECKLESS WITH IT. ISN'T THAT RIGHT,
MR. LIEUTENANT?
THEN I WON'T DO IT!
SOMEBODY ELSE CAN PILOT IT!
...
...
AMURO!
SHUT UP!!

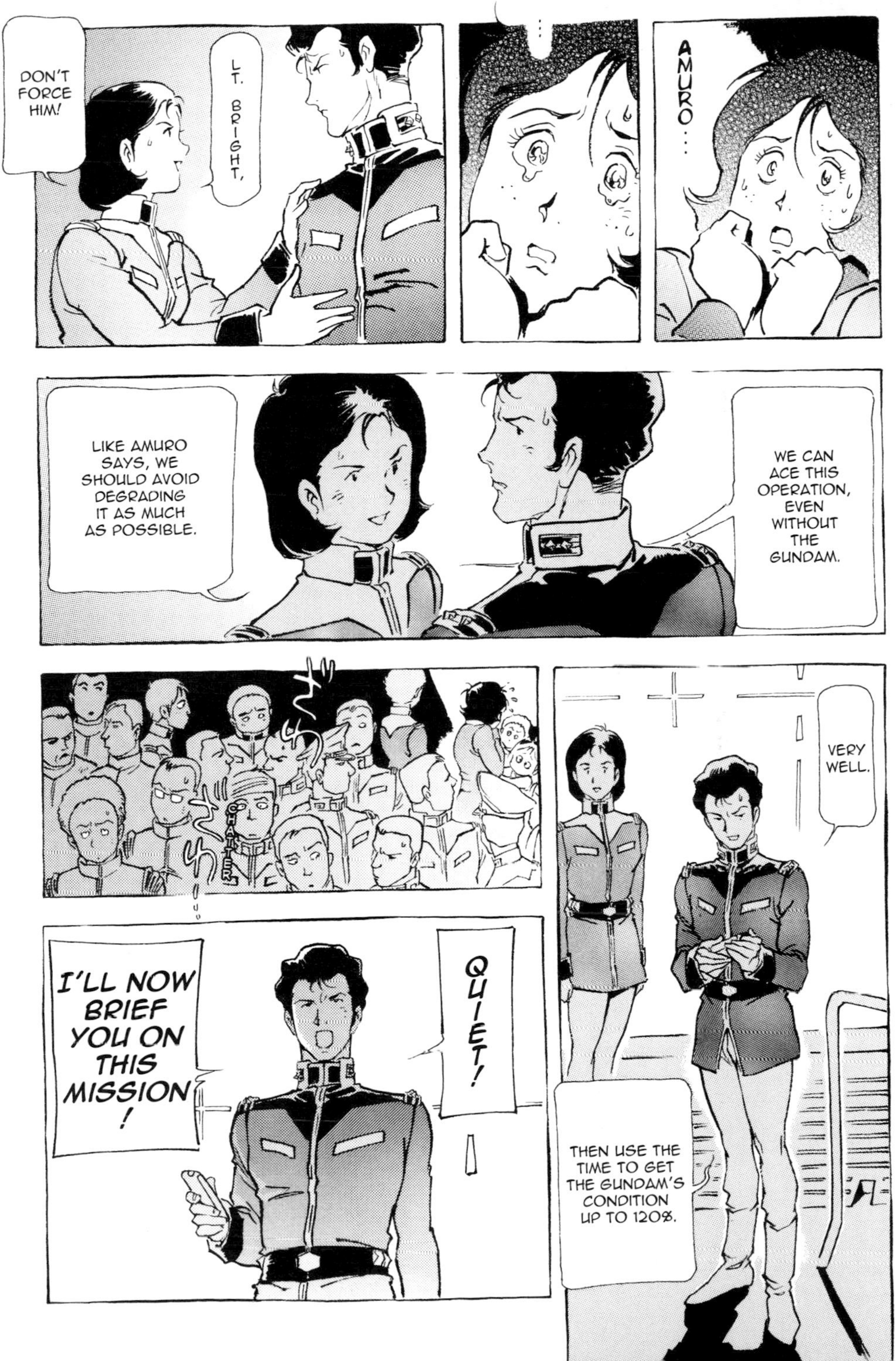
AMURO...
...
LT. BRIGHT,
DON'T FORCE HIM!
WE CAN ACE THIS OPERATION, EVEN WITHOUT THE GUNDAM.
LIKE AMURO SAYS, WE SHOULD AVOID DEGRADING IT AS MUCH AS POSSIBLE.
VERY WELL.
THEN USE THE TIME TO GET THE GUNDAM'S CONDITION UP TO 120%.
CHATTER
QUIET!
I'LL NOW BRIEF YOU ON THIS MISSION!

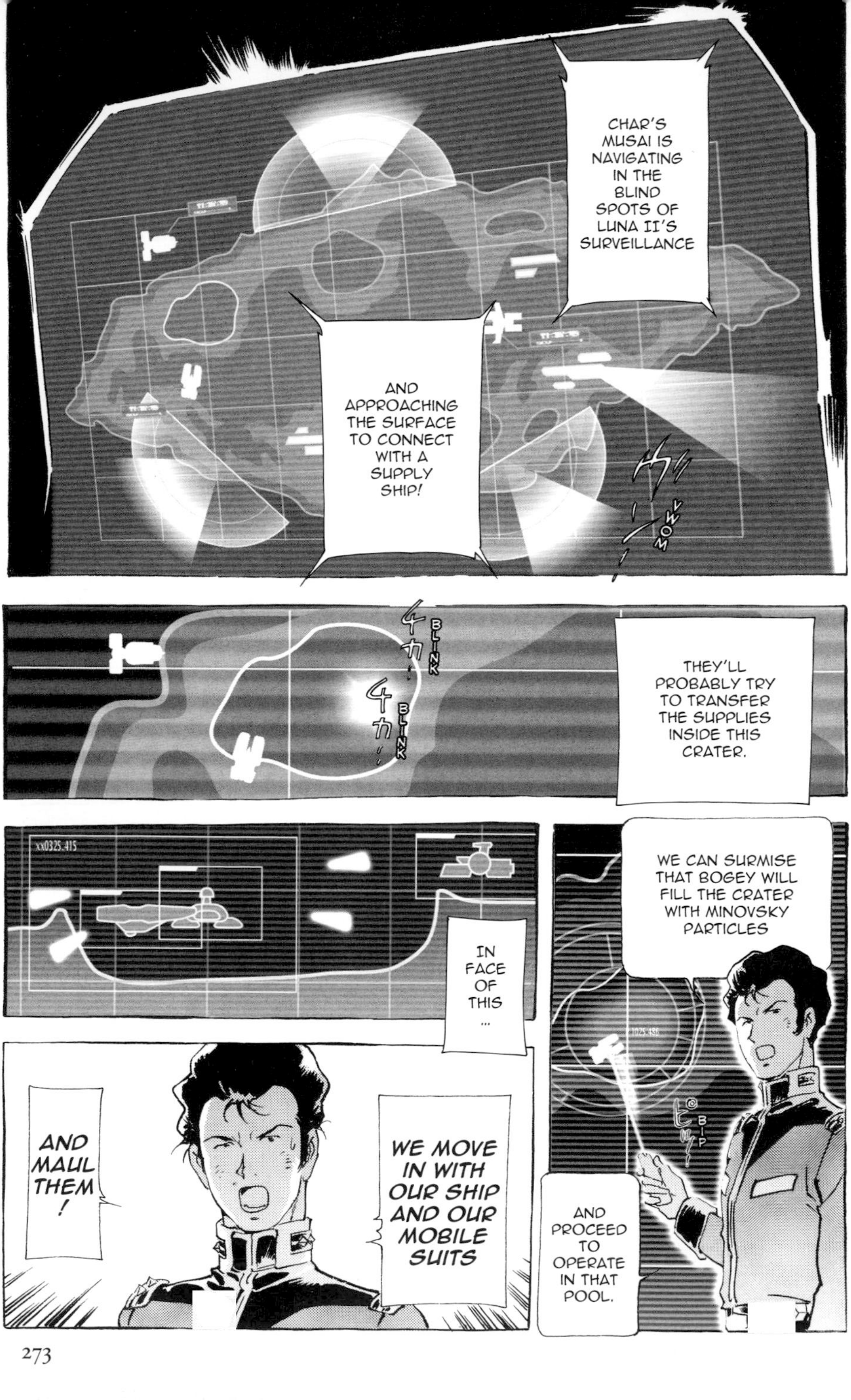
CHAR'S MUSAI IS NAVIGATING IN THE BLIND SPOTS OF LUNA II'S SURVEILLANCE
AND APPROACHING THE SURFACE TO CONNECT WITH A SUPPLY SHIP!
VWOM
BLINK
BLINK
THEY'LL PROBABLY TRY TO TRANSFER THE SUPPLIES INSIDE THIS CRATER.
WE CAN SURMISE THAT BOGEY WILL FILL THE CRATER WITH MINOVSKY PARTICLES
BIP
AND PROCEED TO OPERATE IN THAT POOL.
xx0325.415
IN FACE OF THIS ...
WE MOVE IN WITH OUR SHIP AND OUR MOBILE SUITS
AND MAUL THEM!

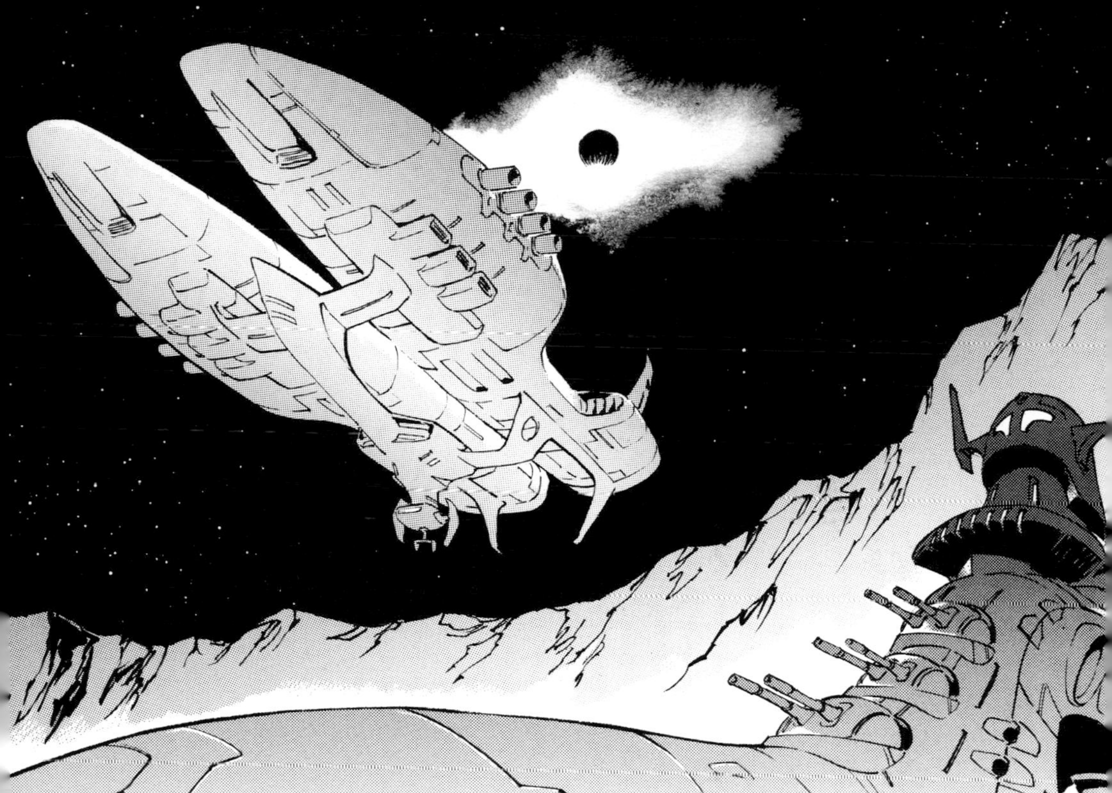

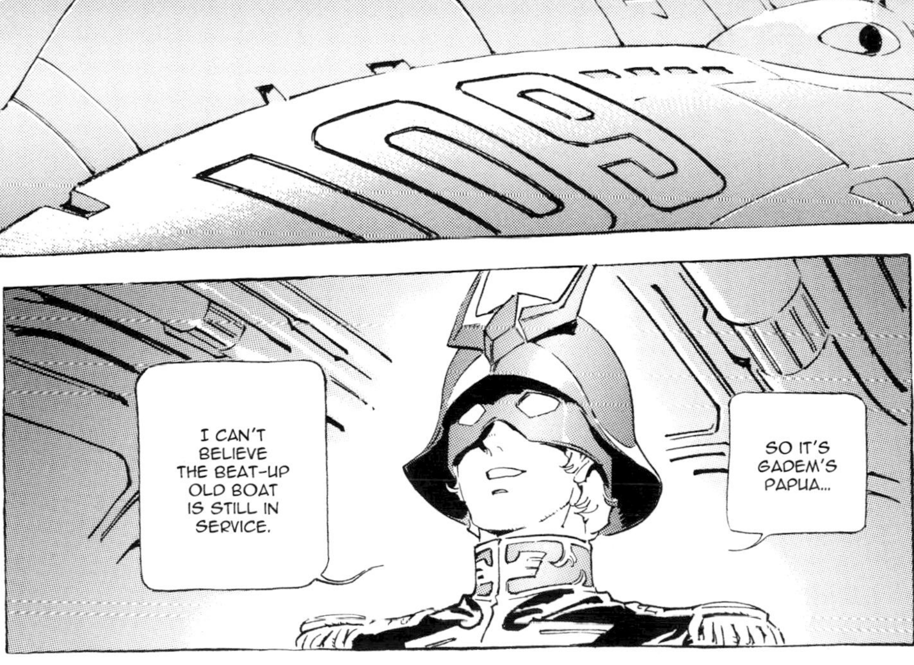
SO IT'S GADEM'S PAPUA...
I CAN'T BELIEVE THE BEAT-UP OLD BOAT IS STILL IN SERVICE.

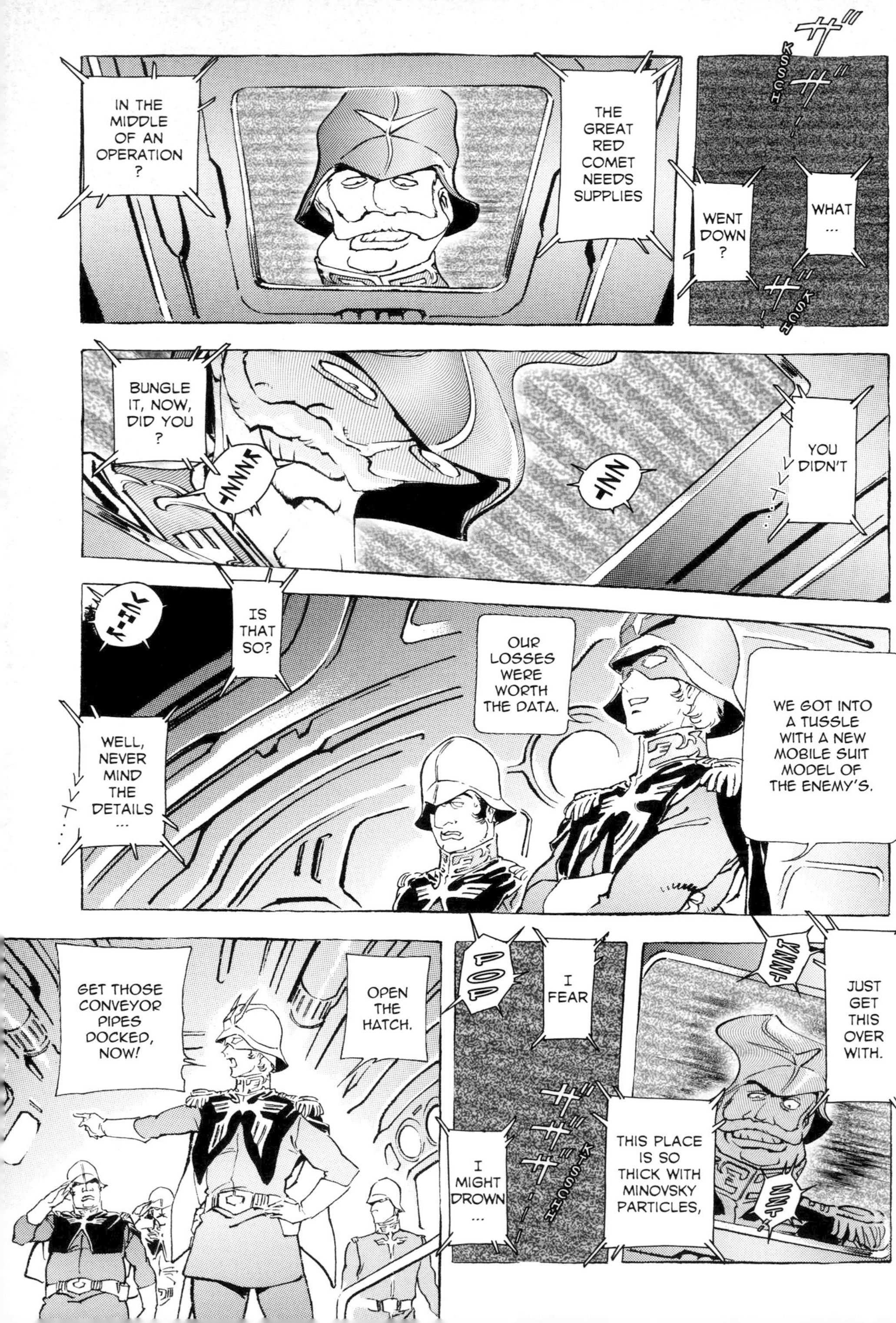
WHAT ...
WENT DOWN ?
KSCH
KSCH
THE GREAT RED COMET NEEDS SUPPLIES
IN THE MIDDLE OF AN OPERATION ?
YOU DIDN'T
NNT
KNNNK
BUNGLE IT, NOW, DID YOU ?
WE GOT INTO A TUSSLE WITH A NEW MOBILE SUIT MODEL OF THE ENEMY'S.
OUR LOSSES WERE WORTH THE DATA.
IS THAT SO?
WELL, NEVER MIND THE DETAILS ...
JUST GET THIS OVER WITH.
KNNK
THIS PLACE IS SO THICK WITH MINOVSKY PARTICLES,
NNT
I FEAR
POP
I MIGHT DROWN ...
KTSCH
OPEN THE HATCH.
GET THOSE CONVEYOR PIPES DOCKED, NOW!

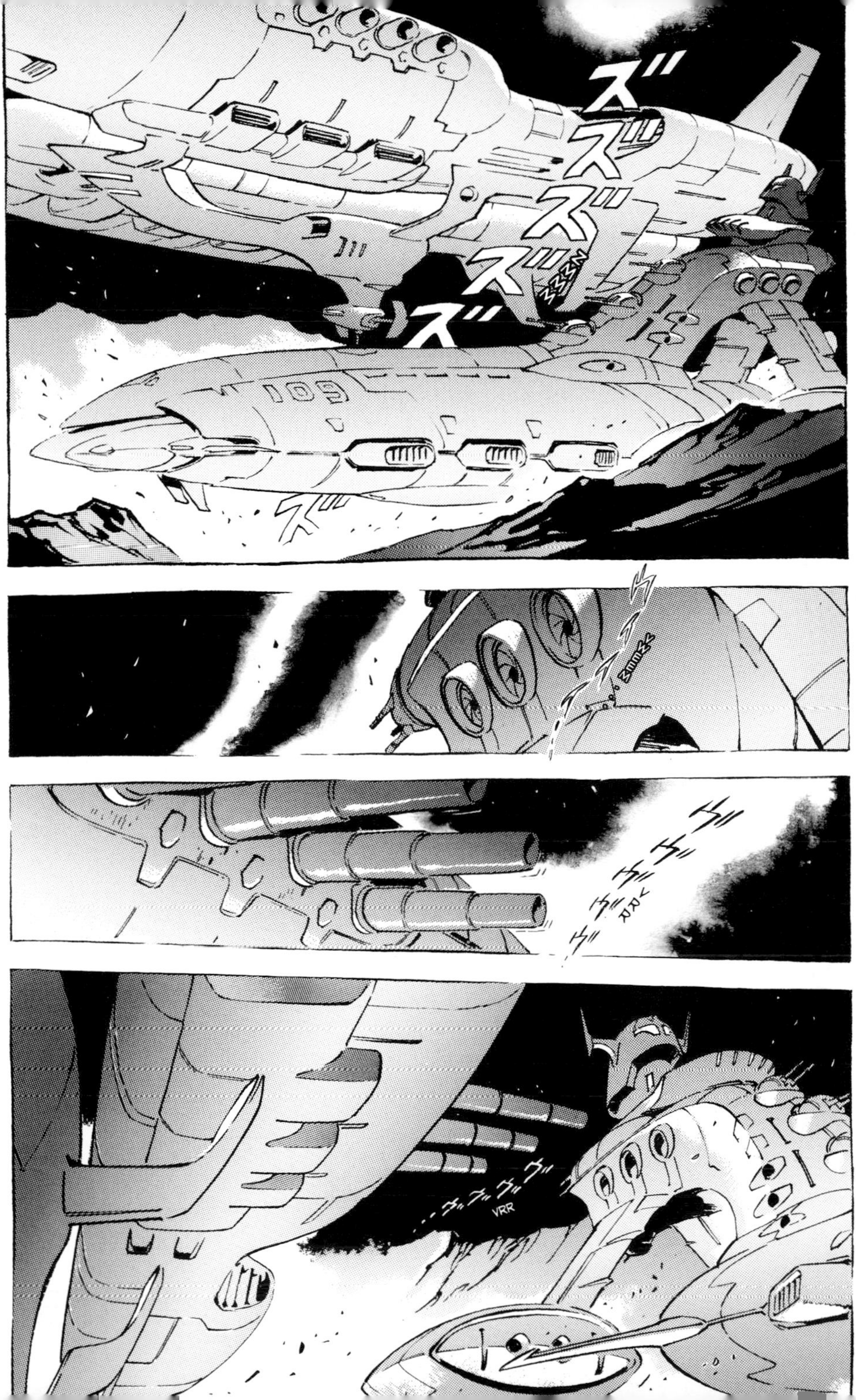
ズ
ズ
ズ
ズ
ズ
ズ
ヴ
ヴ
ヴ
ヴ
ヴ
VRR
ヴ
ヴ
ヴ
ヴ
VRR

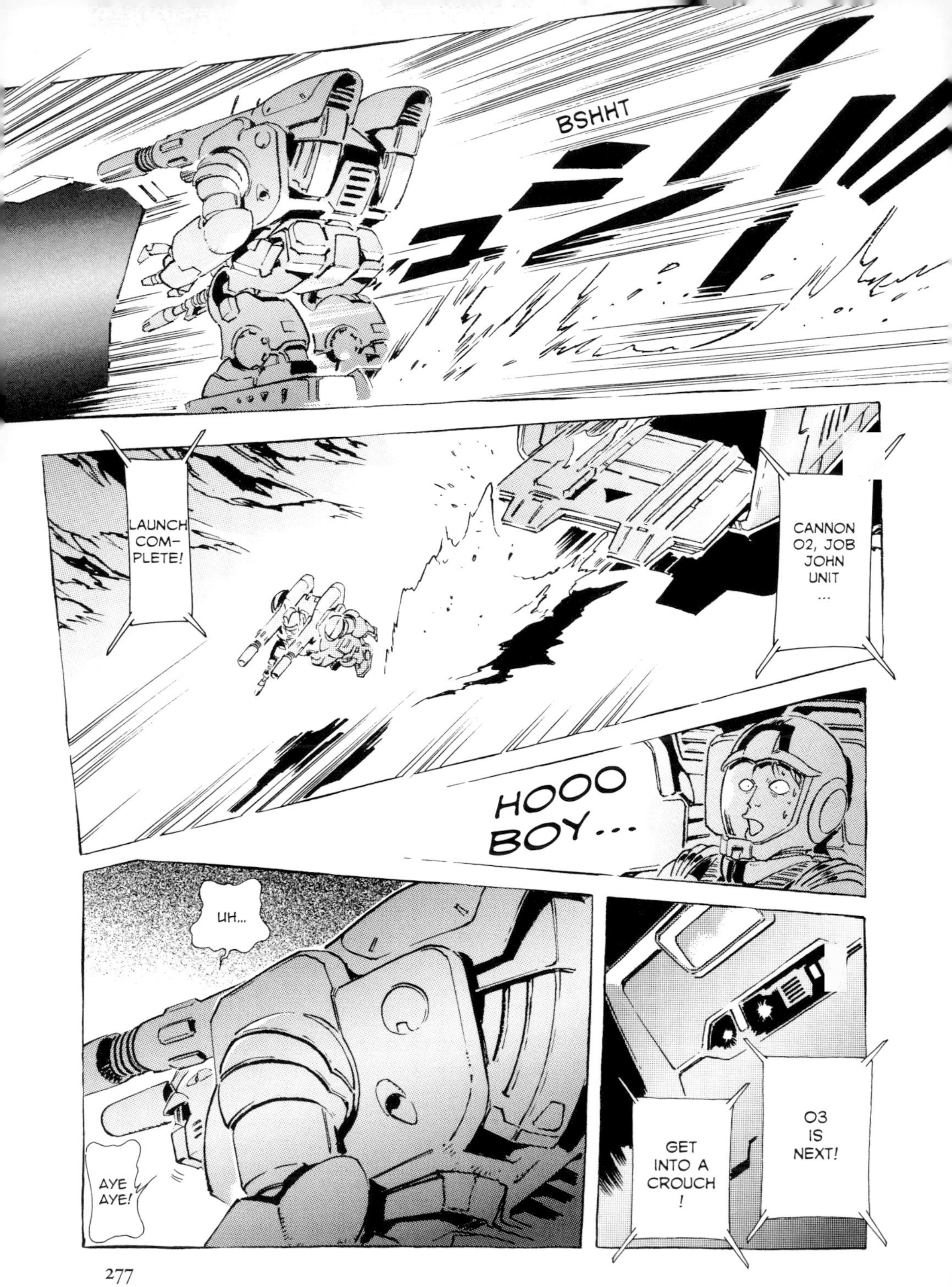
BSHHT
CANNON 02, JOB JOHN UNIT ...
LAUNCH COMPLETE!
HOOO BOY...
03 IS NEXT!
GET INTO A CROUCH!
UH...
AYE AYE!

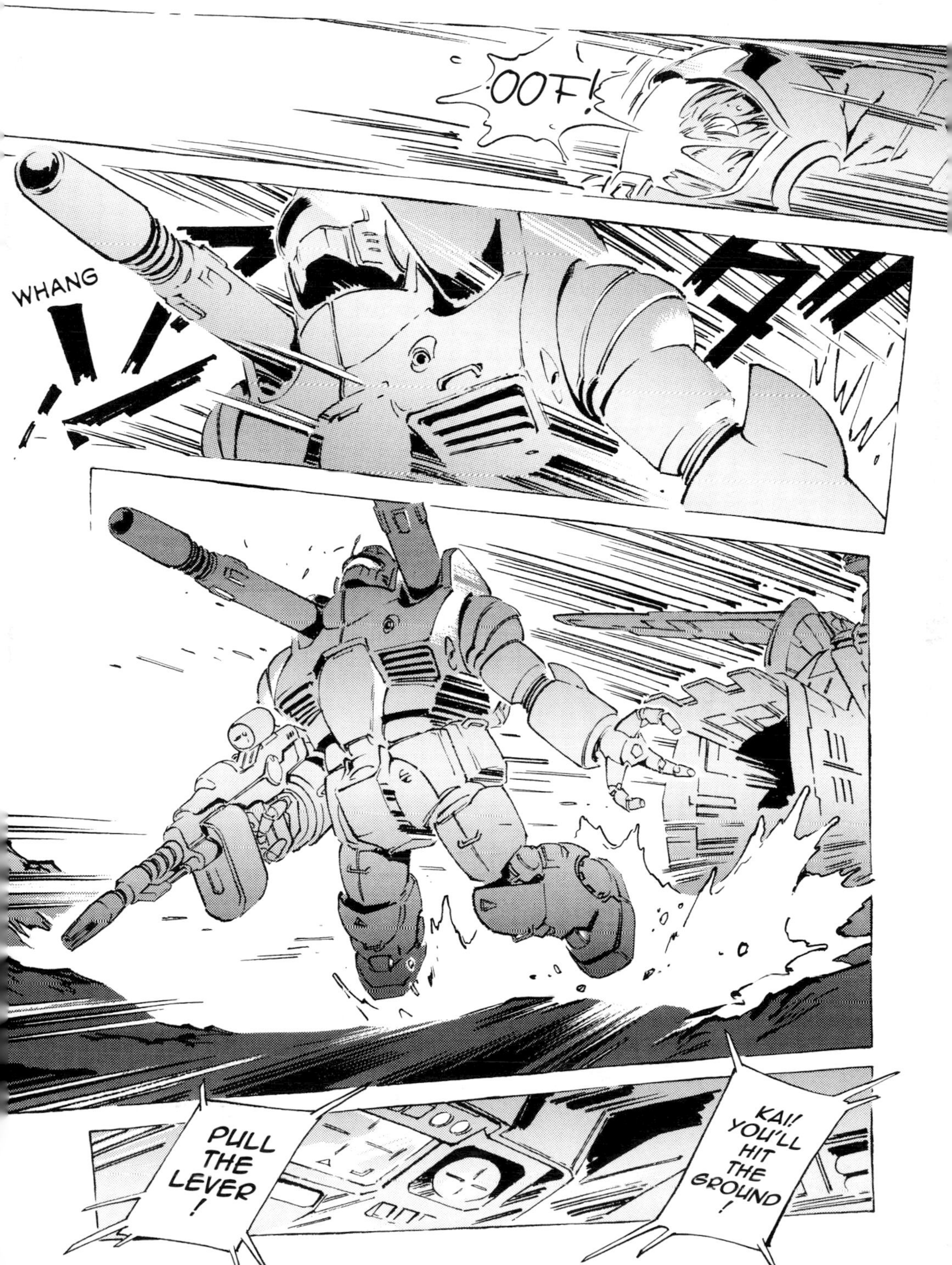
OOF!
WHANG
KAI! YOU'LL HIT THE GROUND!
PULL THE LEVER!

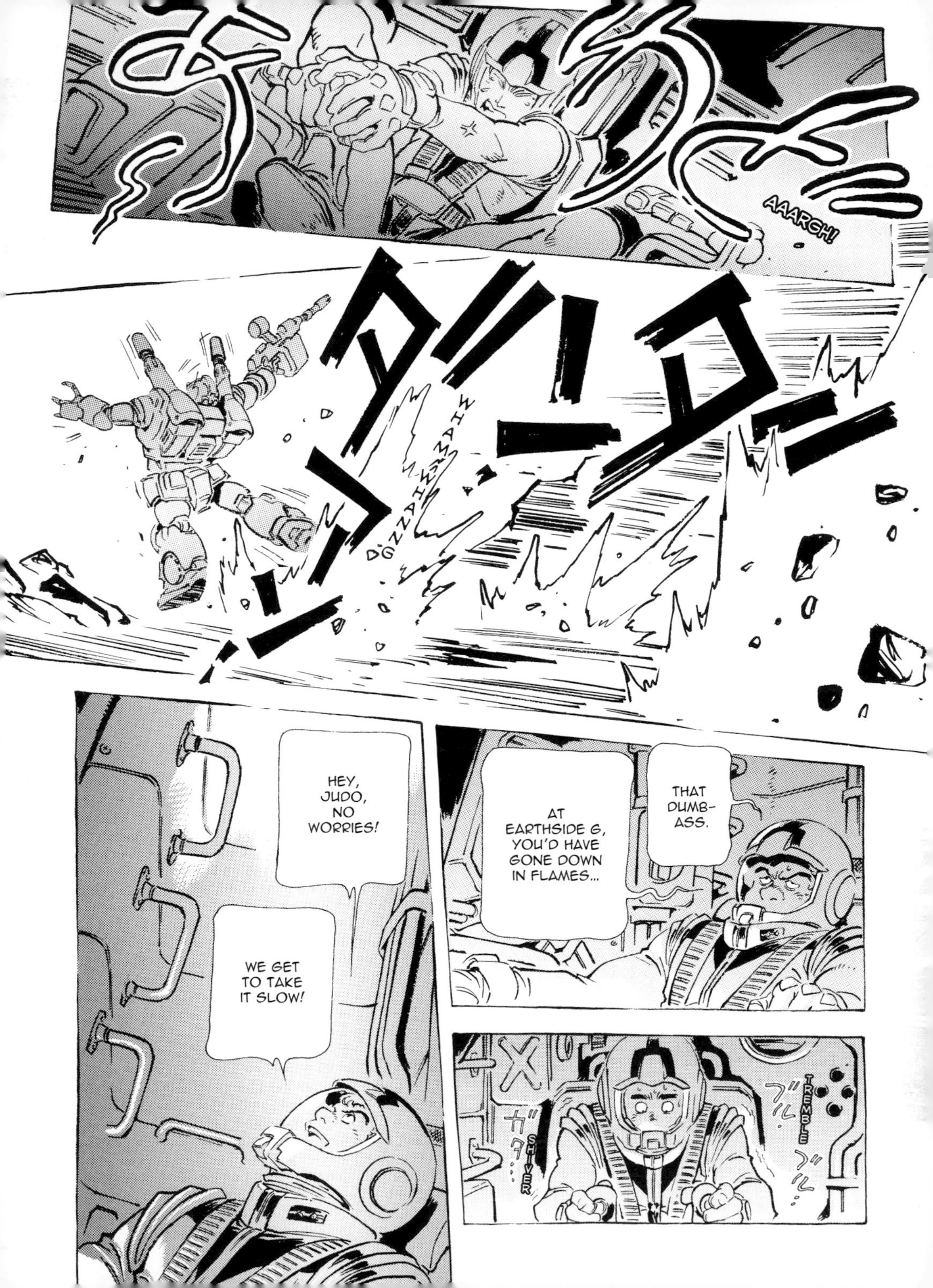
AAARGH!
WHAM
THAT DUMB-ASS.
AT EARTHSIDE 6, YOU'D HAVE GONE DOWN IN FLAMES...
TREMBLE
SHIVER
HEY, JUDO, NO WORRIES!
WE GET TO TAKE IT SLOW!

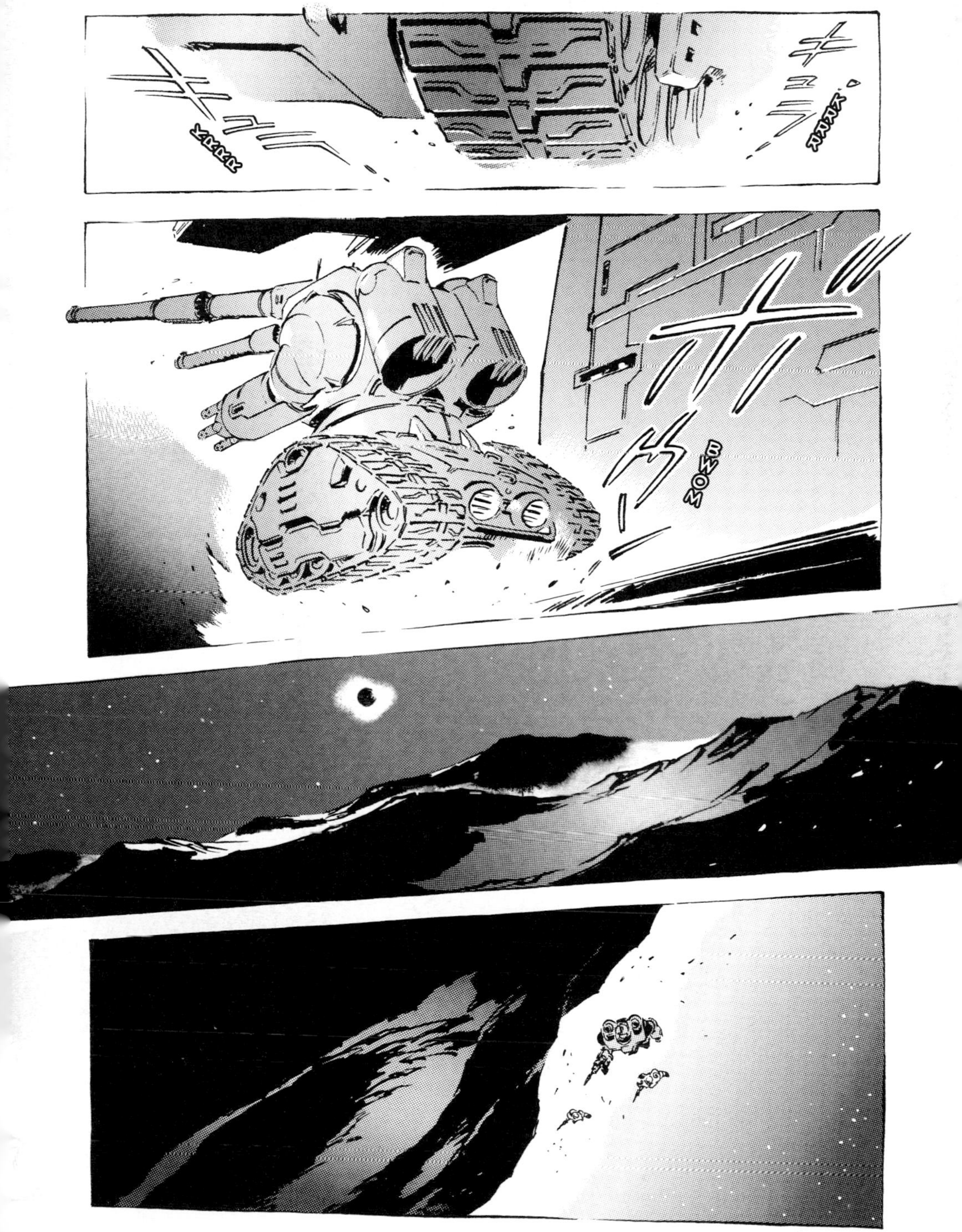
RRRRK
BWOOM

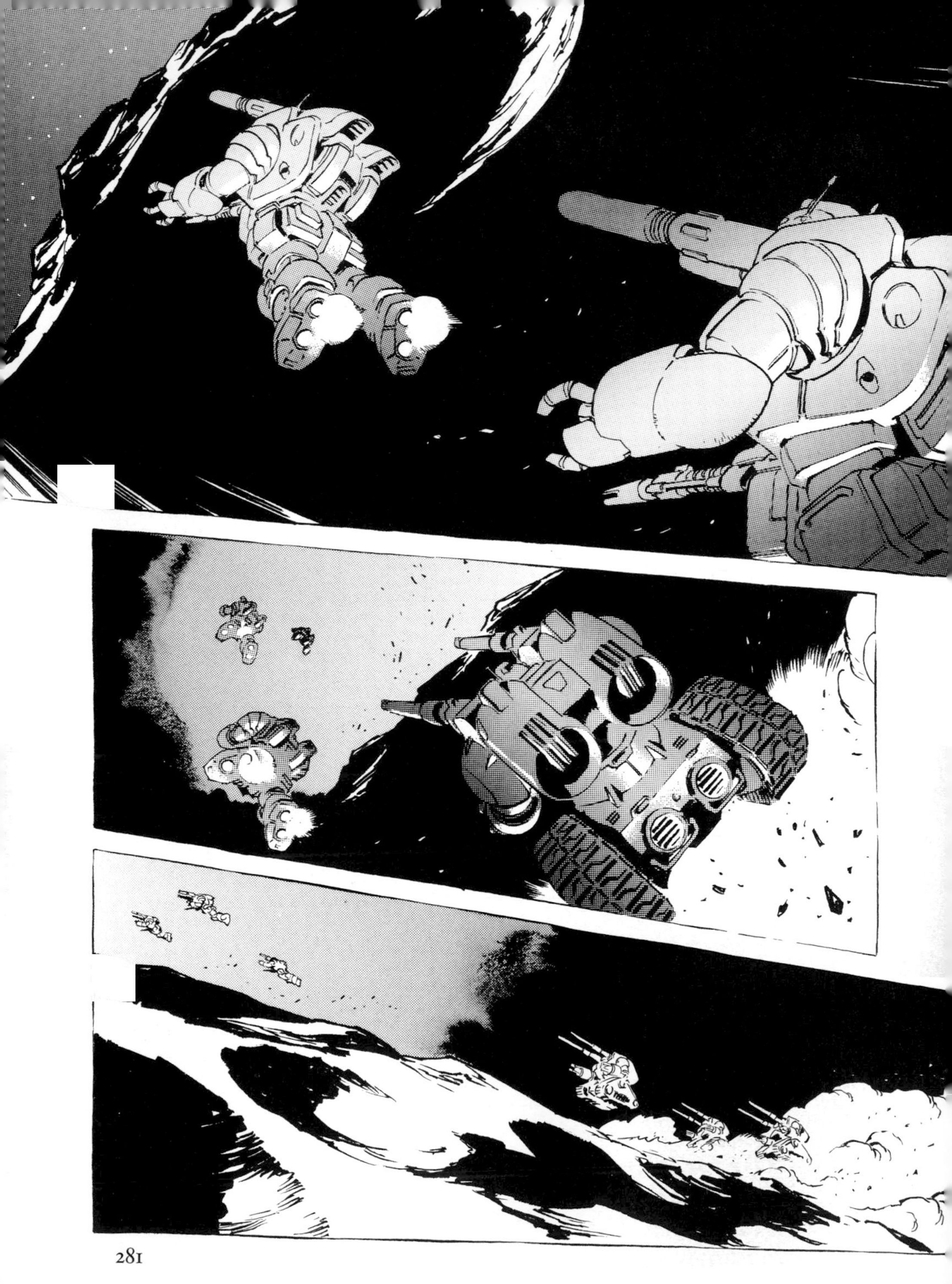

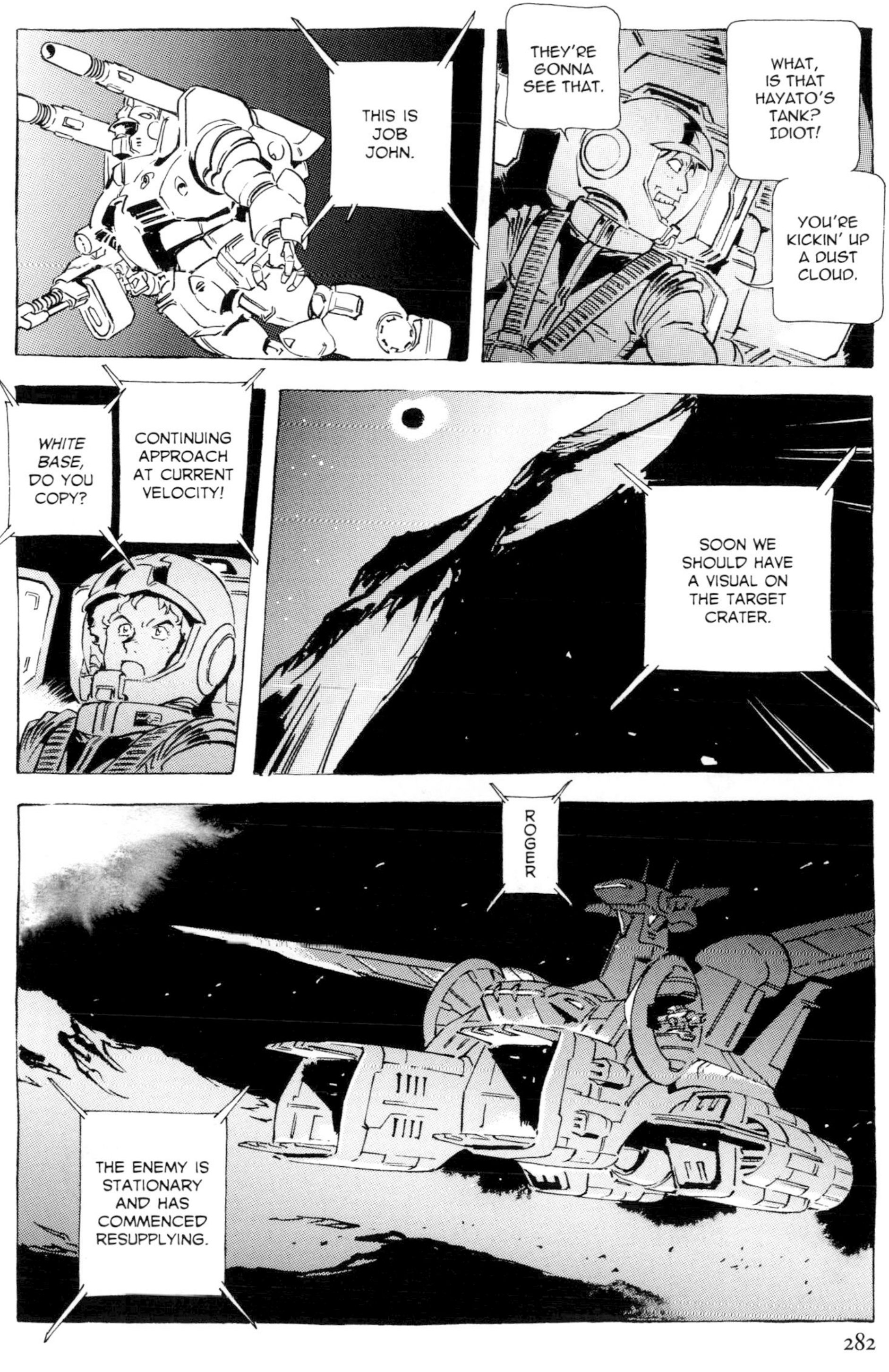
WHAT, IS THAT HAYATO'S TANK? IDIOT!
YOU'RE KICKIN' UP A DUST CLOUD.
THEY'RE GONNA SEE THAT.
THIS IS JOB JOHN.
SOON WE SHOULD HAVE A VISUAL ON THE TARGET CRATER.
CONTINUING APPROACH AT CURRENT VELOCITY!
WHITE BASE, DO YOU COPY?
ROGER
THE ENEMY IS STATIONARY AND HAS COMMENCED RESUPPLYING.

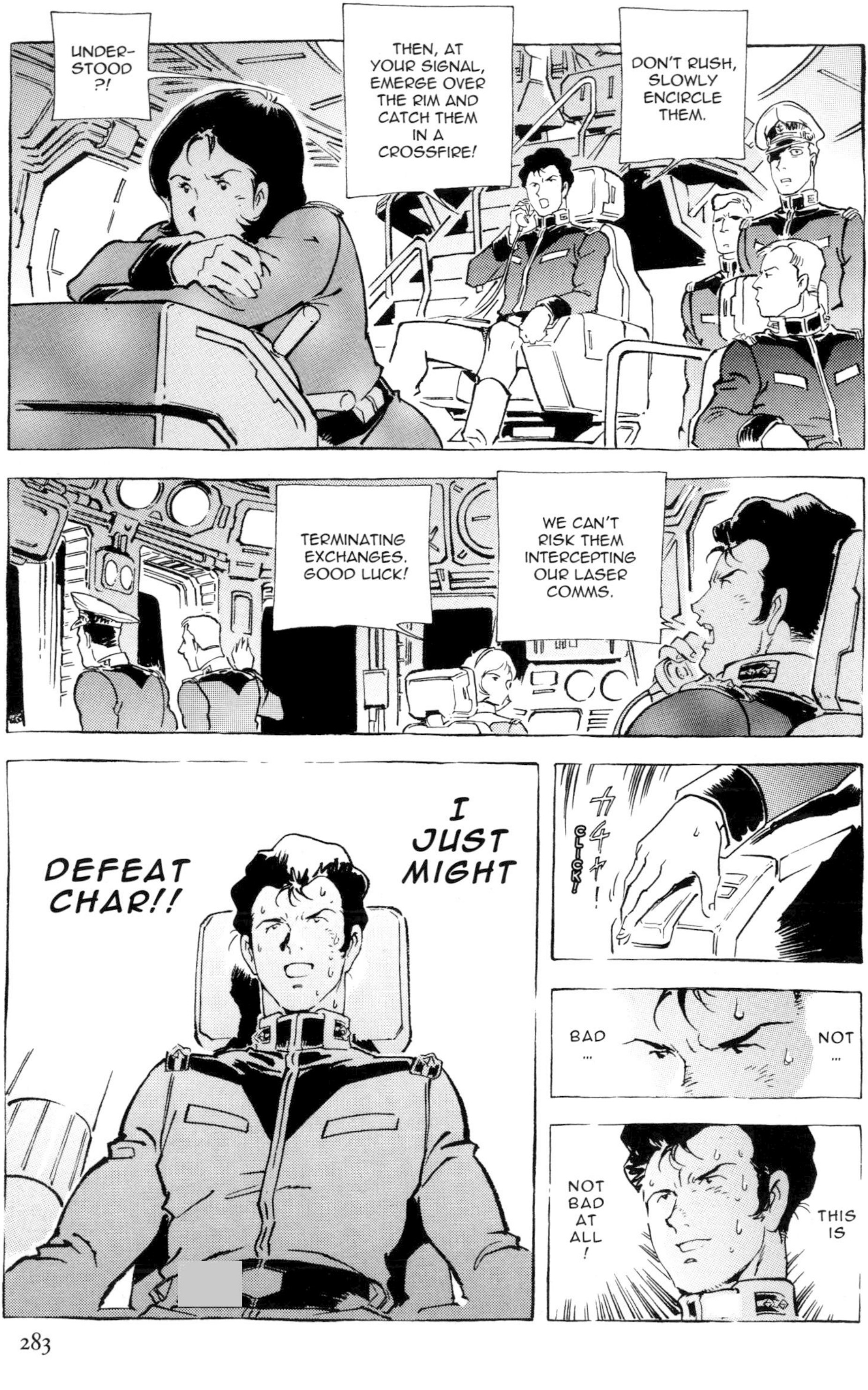
DON'T RUSH, SLOWLY ENCIRCLE THEM.
THEN, AT YOUR SIGNAL, EMERGE OVER THE RIM AND CATCH THEM IN A CROSSFIRE!
UNDER-STOOD?!
WE CAN'T RISK THEM INTERCEPTING OUR LASER COMMS.
TERMINATING EXCHANGES. GOOD LUCK!
カチャ!
CLICK!
NOT ...
BAD ...
THIS IS
NOT BAD AT ALL!
I JUST MIGHT
DEFEAT CHAR!!

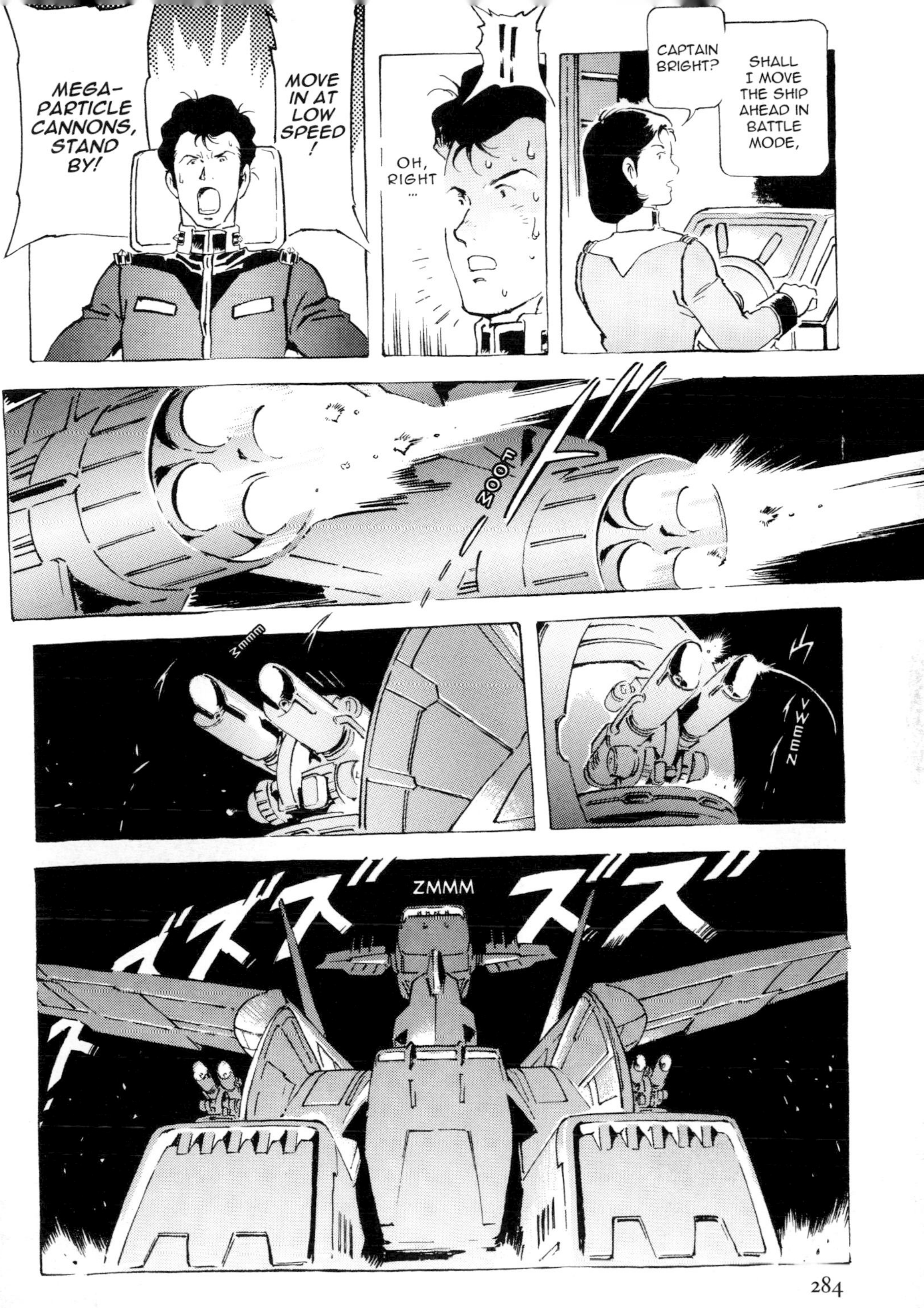

CAPTAIN BRIGHT?
SHALL I MOVE THE SHIP AHEAD IN BATTLE MODE,
OH, RIGHT ...
MOVE IN AT LOW SPEED!
MEGA-PARTICLE CANNONS, STAND BY!
VOOM
VWEEN
ZMMM
ZMMM

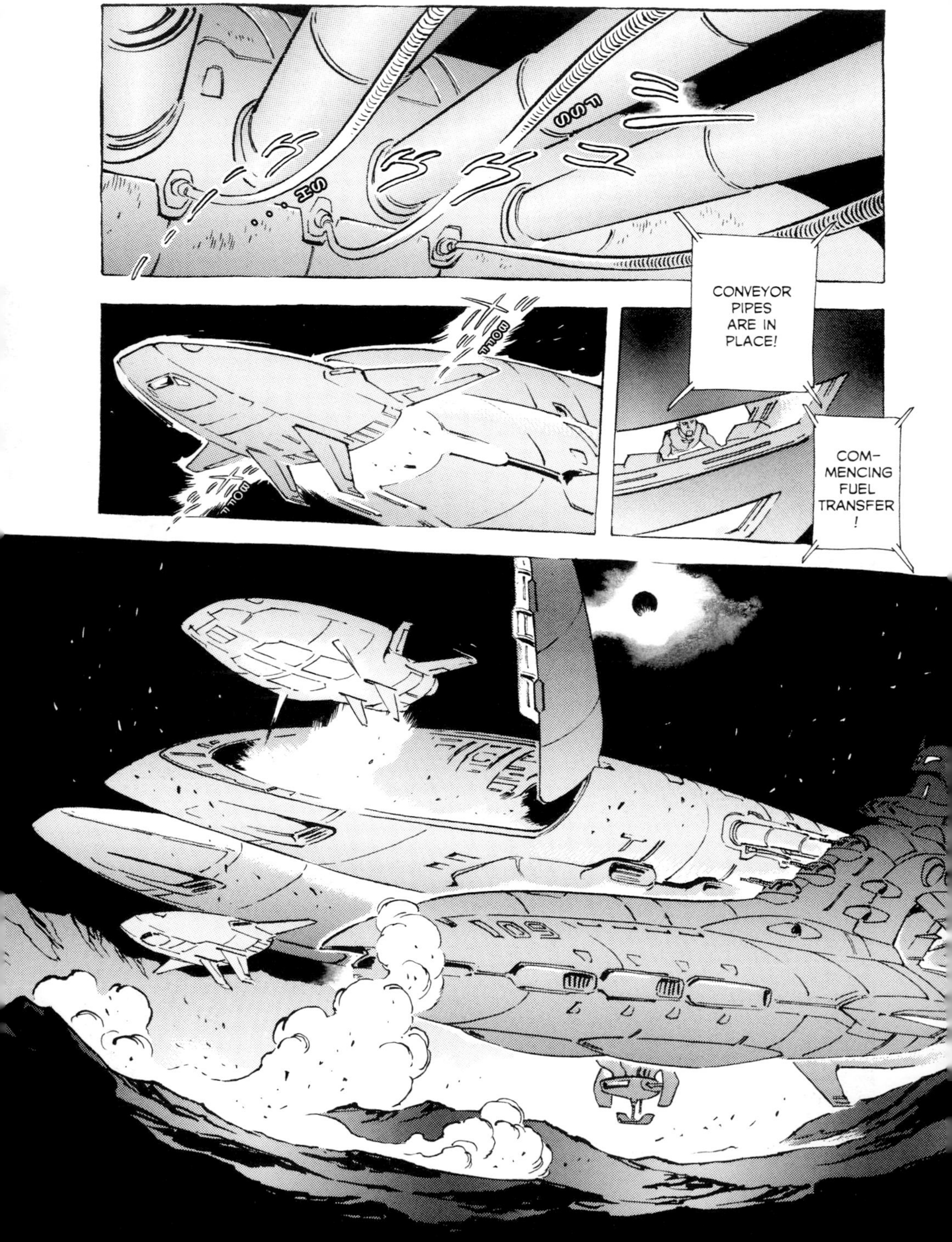
CONVEYOR PIPES ARE IN PLACE!
COM-MENCING FUEL TRANSFER !

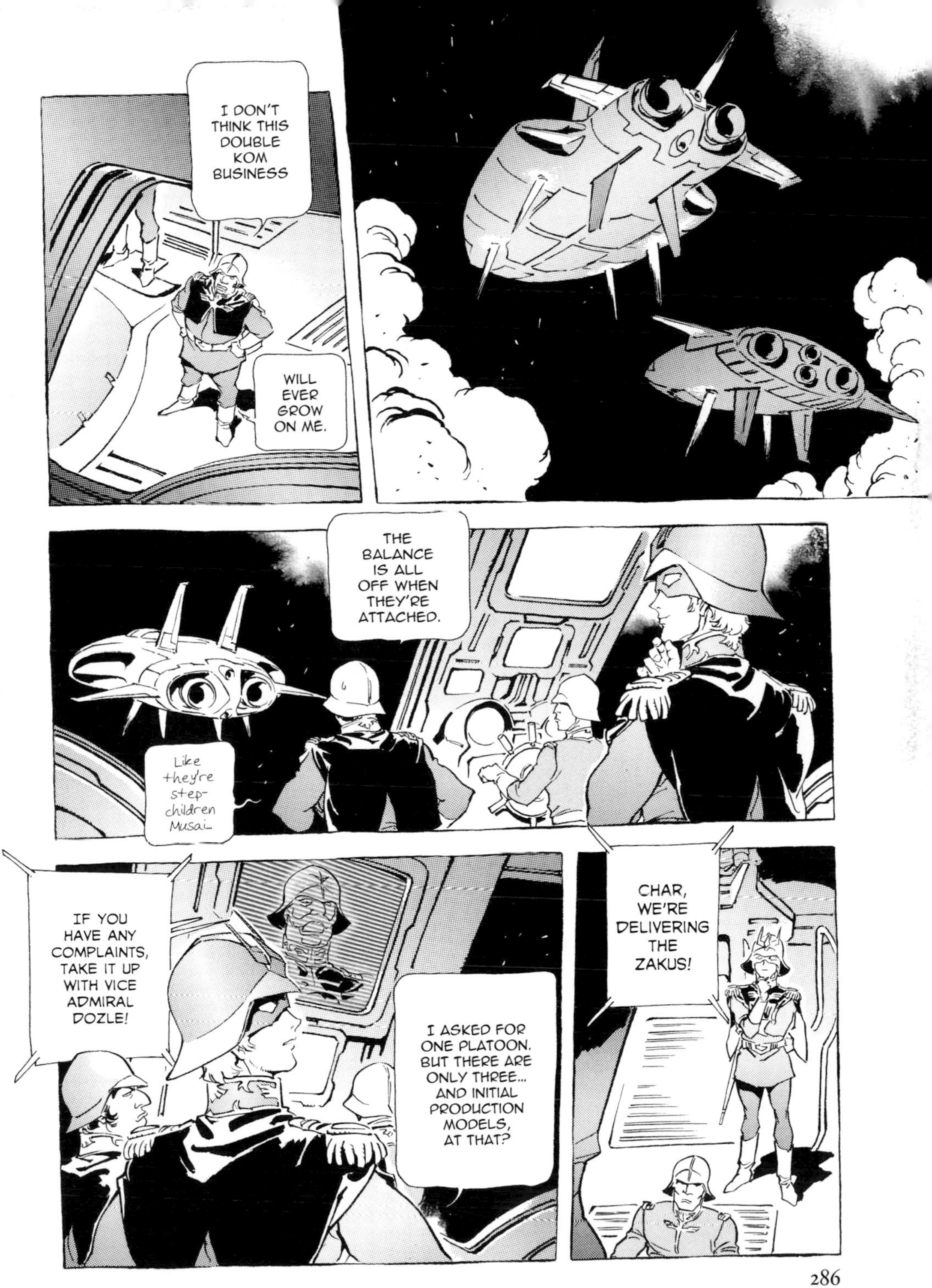
I DON'T THINK THIS DOUBLE KOM BUSINESS
WILL EVER GROW ON ME.
THE BALANCE IS ALL OFF WHEN THEY'RE ATTACHED.
Like they're step-children Musai...
CHAR, WE'RE DELIVERING THE ZAKUS!
I ASKED FOR ONE PLATOON. BUT THERE ARE ONLY THREE... AND INITIAL PRODUCTION MODELS, AT THAT?
IF YOU HAVE ANY COMPLAINTS, TAKE IT UP WITH VICE ADMIRAL DOZLE!

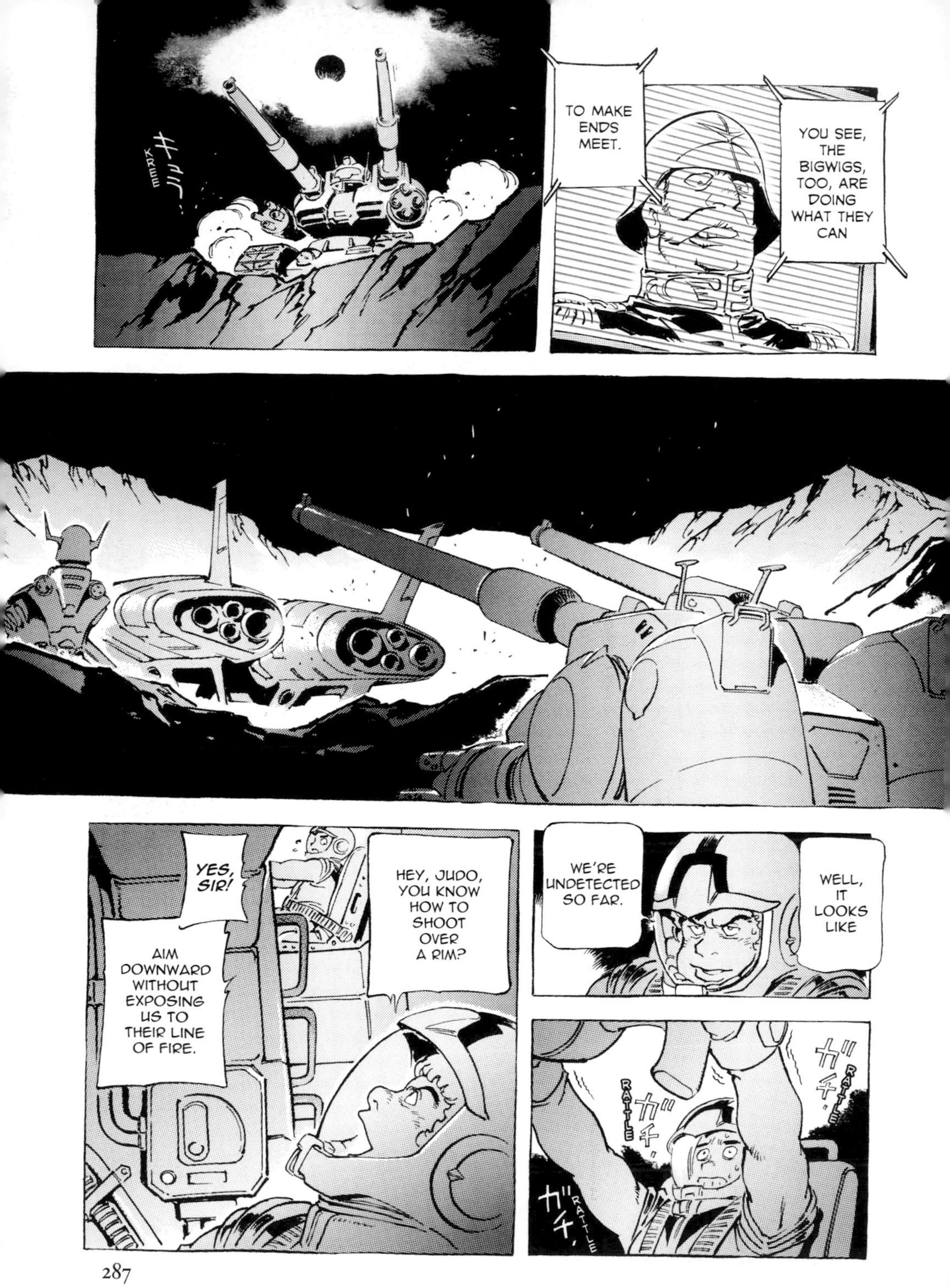

YOU SEE, THE BIGWIGS, TOO, ARE DOING WHAT THEY CAN
TO MAKE ENDS MEET.
KREE
WELL, IT LOOKS LIKE
WE'RE UNDETECTED SO FAR.
RATTLE
RATTLE
RATTLE
HEY, JUDO, YOU KNOW HOW TO SHOOT OVER A RIM?
YES, SIR!
AIM DOWNWARD WITHOUT EXPOSING US TO THEIR LINE OF FIRE.

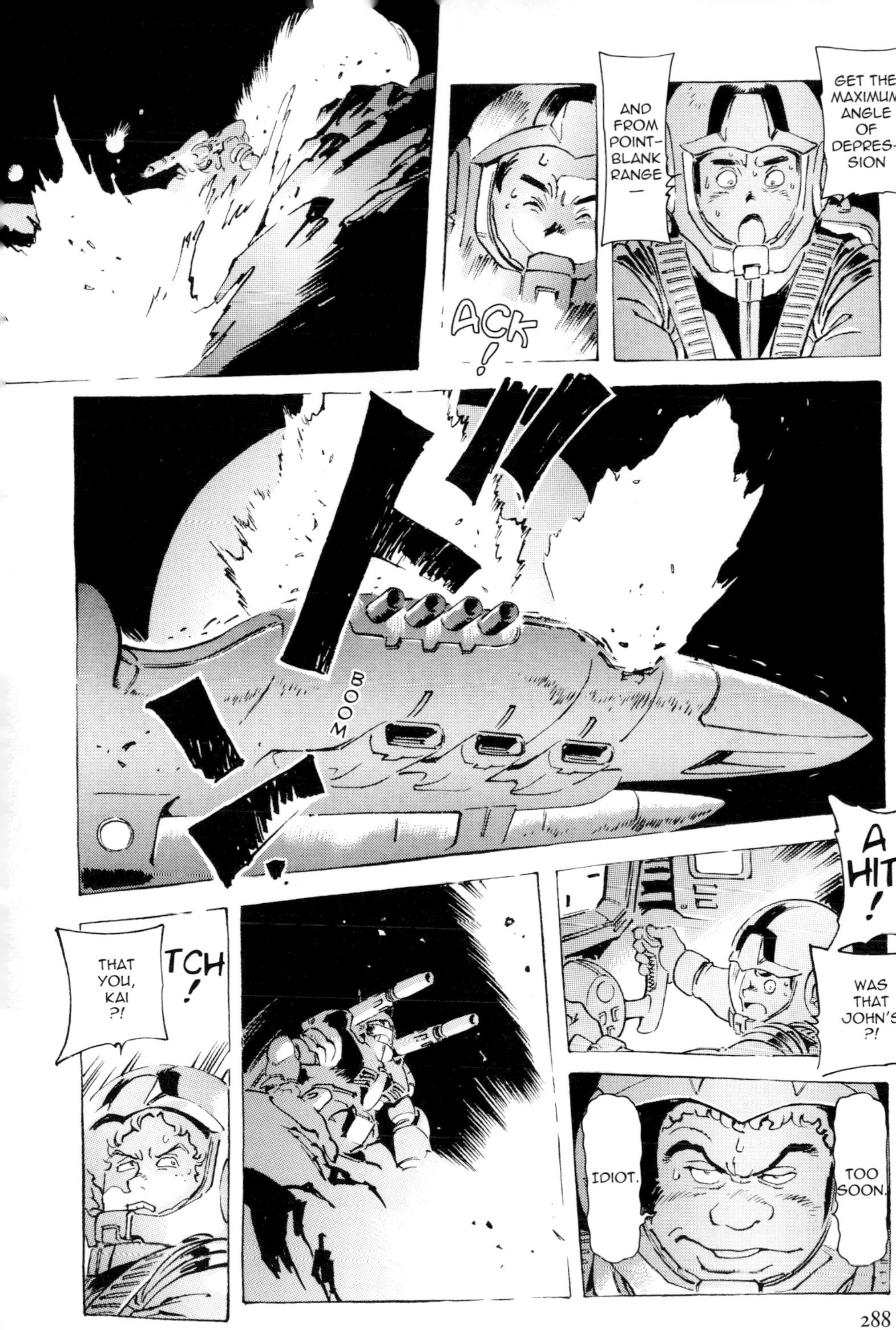
GET THE MAXIMUM ANGLE OF DEPRESSION
AND FROM POINT-BLANK RANGE —
ACK!
BOOM
A HIT!
WAS THAT JOHN'S ?!
TOO SOON.
IDIOT.
TCH!
THAT YOU, KAI ?!

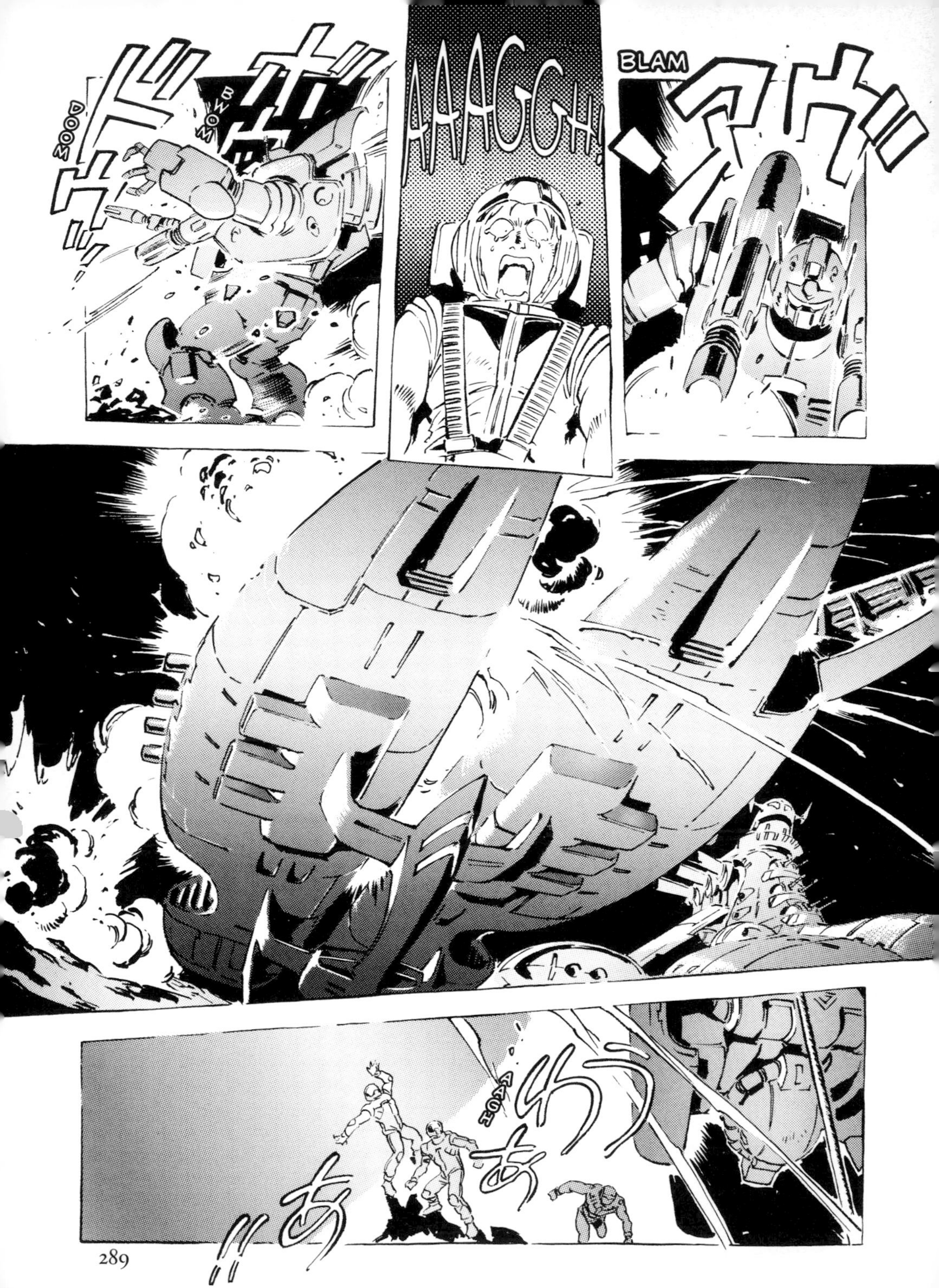
BLAM
AAAGGH!
BWOM
DOOOM
AAGH

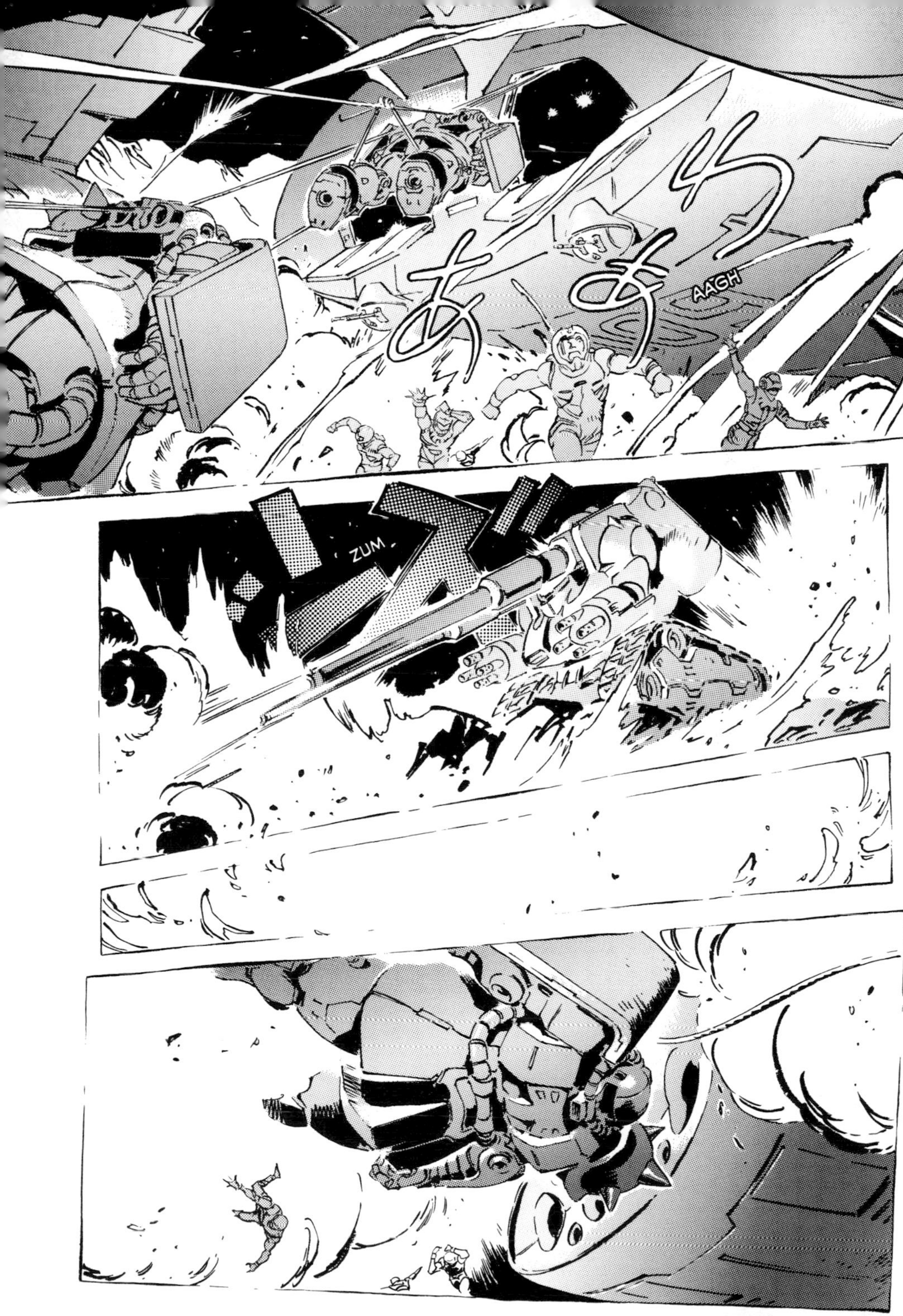
AAGH
ZUM

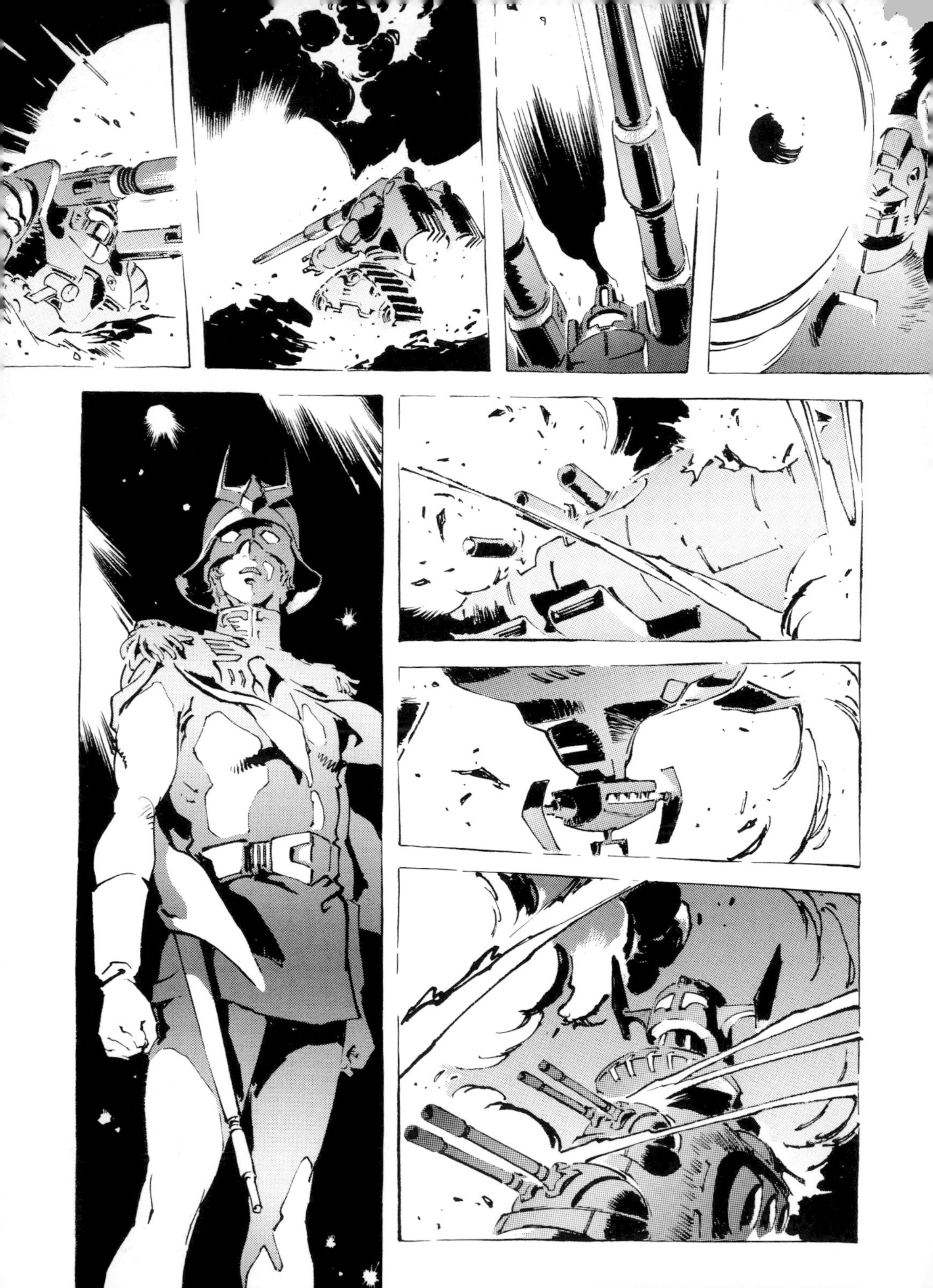

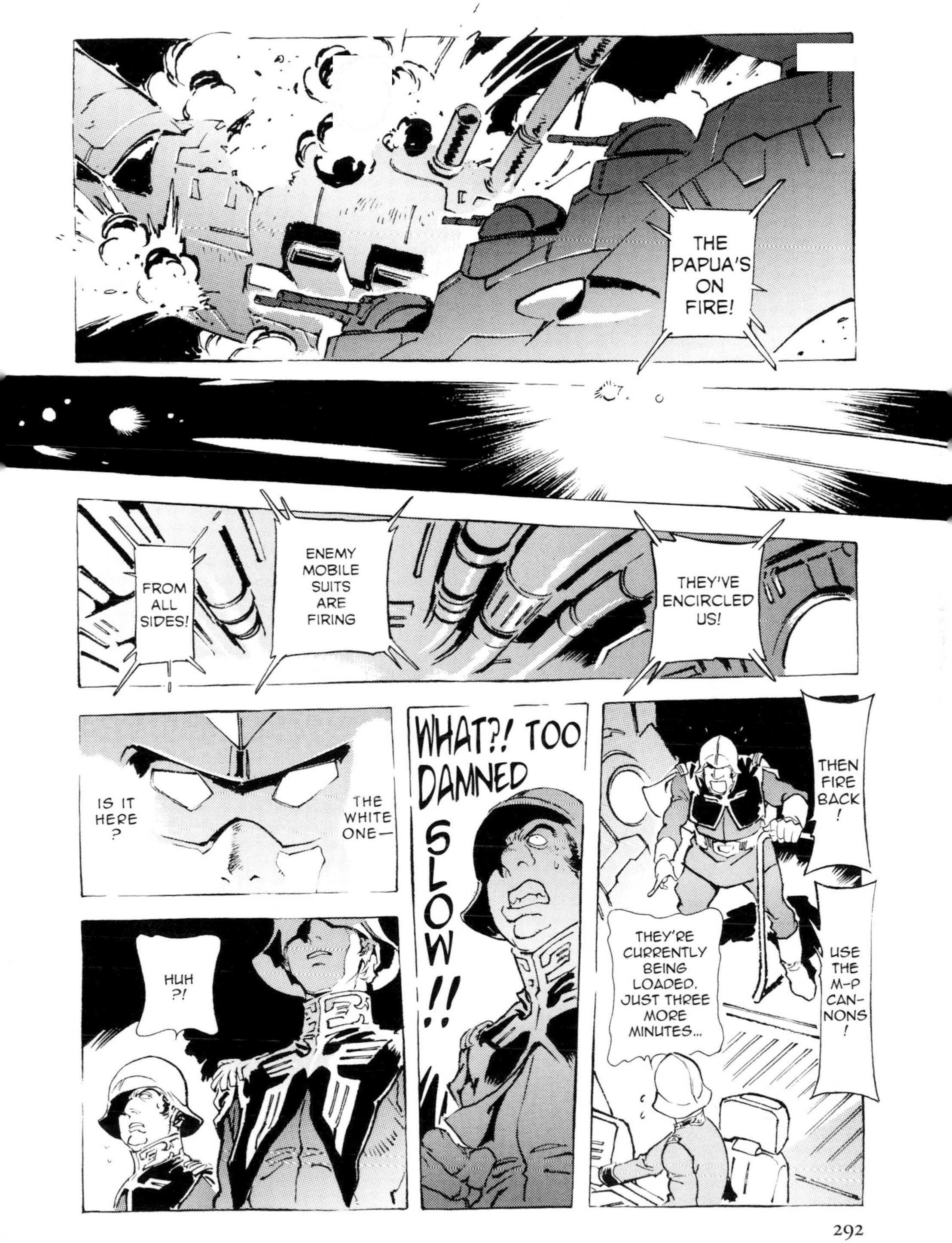
THE PAPUA'S ON FIRE!
THEY'VE ENCIRCLED US!
ENEMY MOBILE SUITS ARE FIRING
FROM ALL SIDES!
THEN FIRE BACK!
USE THE M-P CAN-NONS!
THEY'RE CURRENTLY BEING LOADED. JUST THREE MORE MINUTES...
WHAT?! TOO DAMNED SLOW!!
THE WHITE ONE—
IS IT HERE?
HUH?!

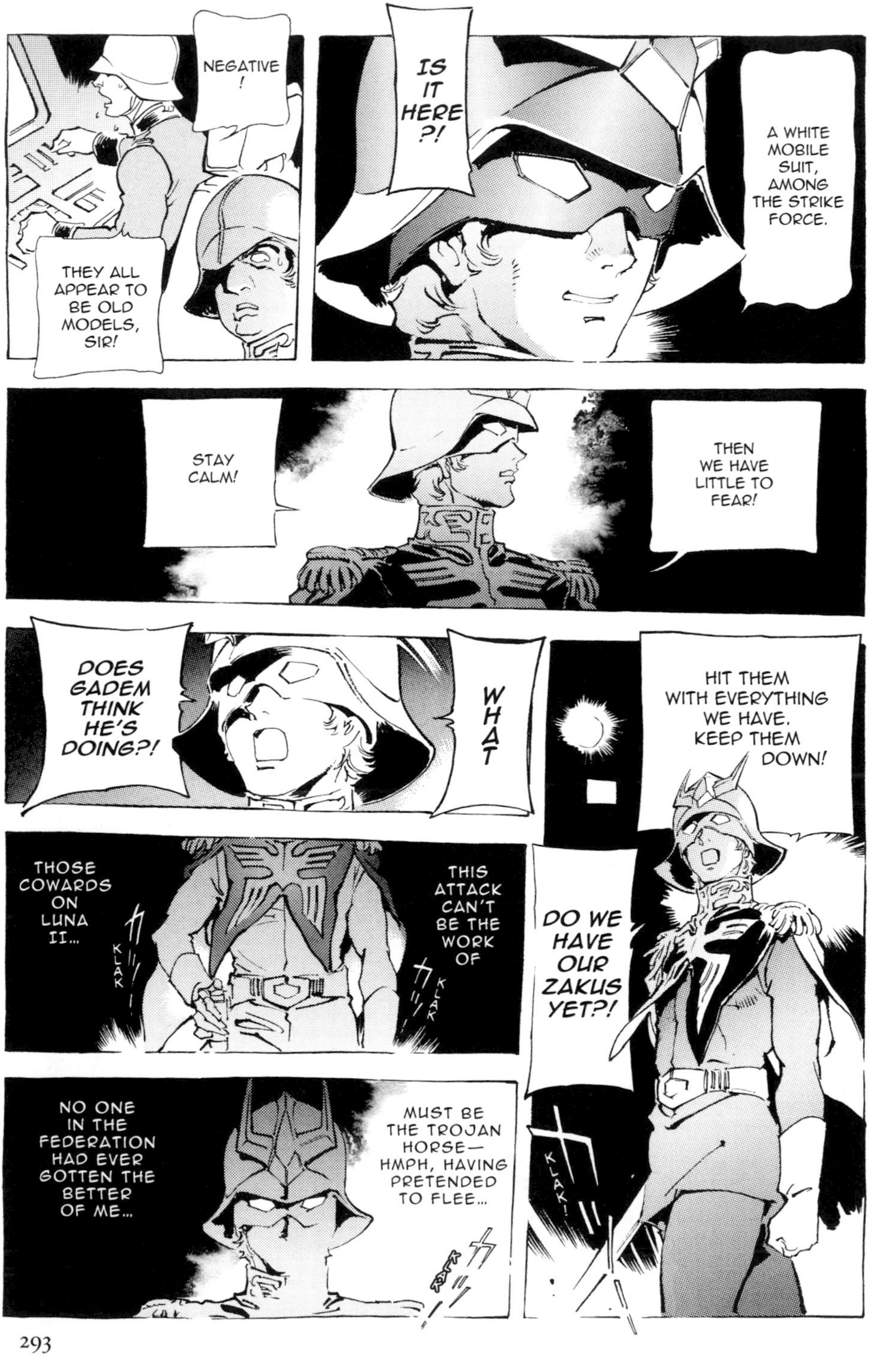
IS IT HERE?!
A WHITE MOBILE SUIT, AMONG THE STRIKE FORCE.
NEGATIVE!
THEY ALL APPEAR TO BE OLD MODELS, SIR!
THEN WE HAVE LITTLE TO FEAR!
STAY CALM!
HIT THEM WITH EVERYTHING WE HAVE. KEEP THEM DOWN!
DO WE HAVE OUR ZAKUS YET?!
KLAK!
WHAT
DOES GADEM THINK HE'S DOING?!
THIS ATTACK CAN'T BE THE WORK OF
KLAK
THOSE COWARDS ON LUNA II...
KLAK
MUST BE THE TROJAN HORSE— HMPH, HAVING PRETENDED TO FLEE...
NO ONE IN THE FEDERATION HAD EVER GOTTEN THE BETTER OF ME...

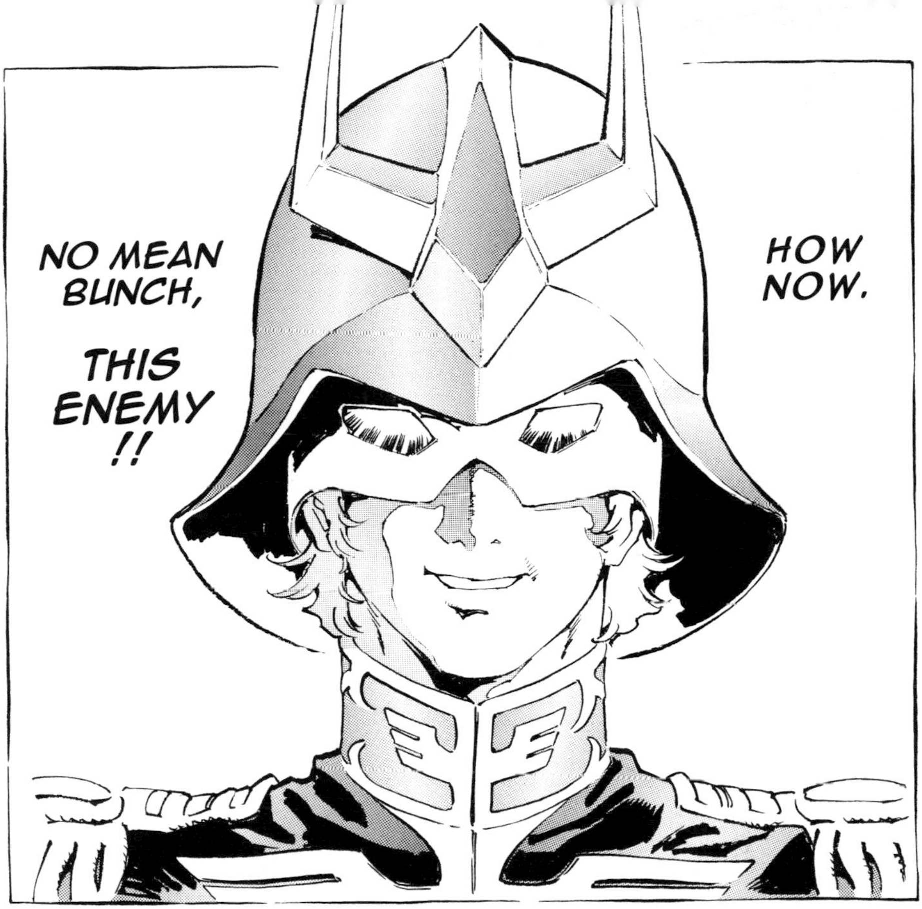
HOW NOW.
NO MEAN BUNCH,
THIS ENEMY!!

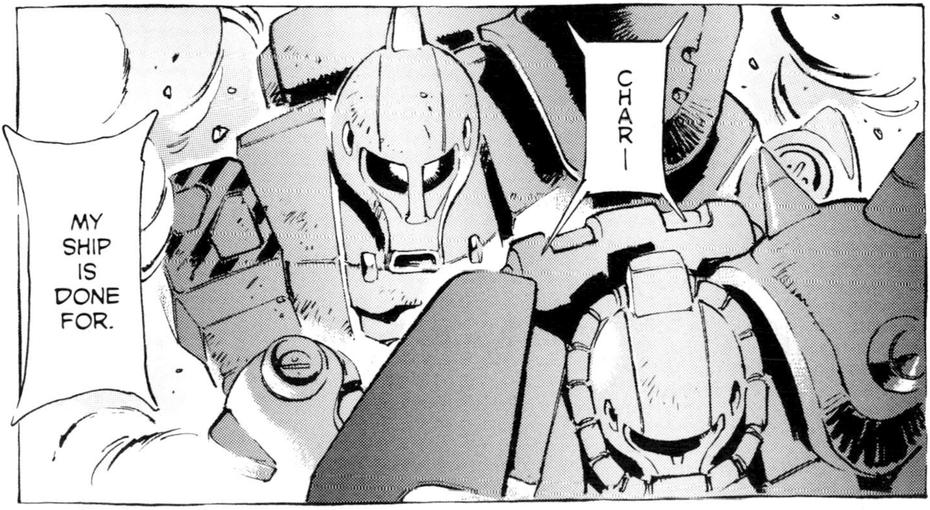
CHARI
MY SHIP IS DONE FOR.

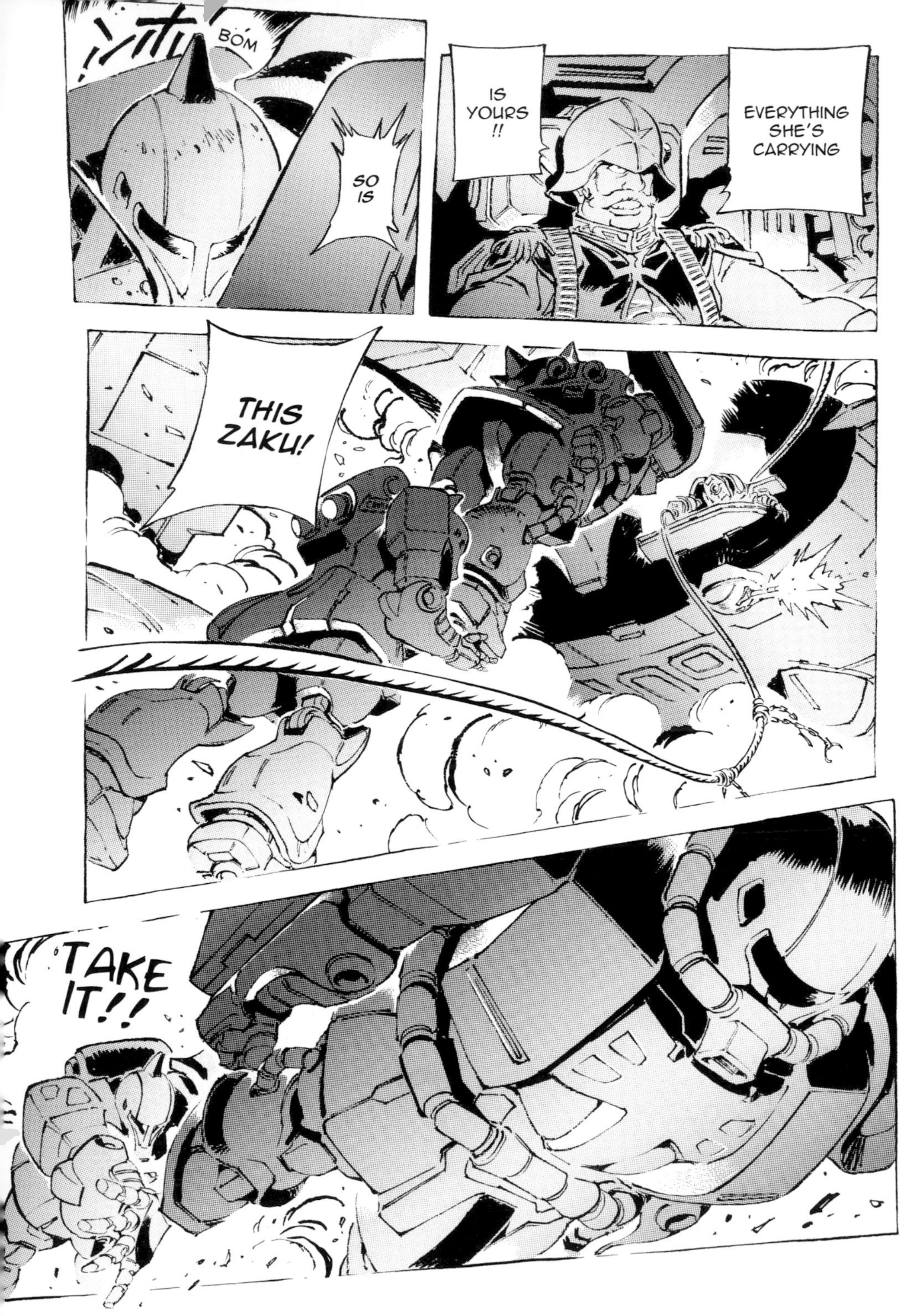
EVERYTHING SHE'S CARRYING
IS YOURS !!
BOM
SO IS
THIS ZAKU!
TAKE IT!!

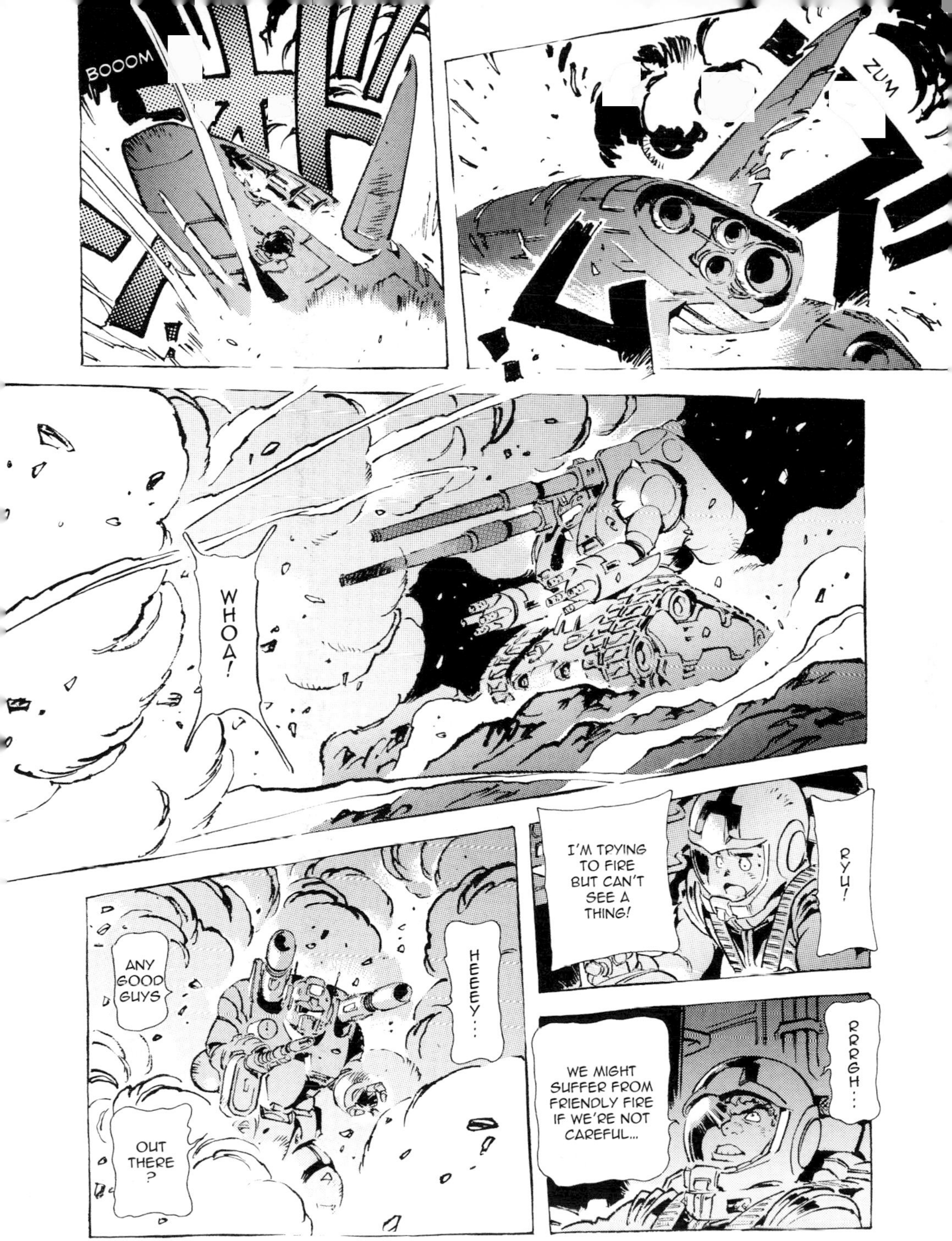
ZUM
BOOOM
WHOA!
RYU!
I'M TRYING TO FIRE BUT CAN'T SEE A THING!
RRRGH...
WE MIGHT SUFFER FROM FRIENDLY FIRE IF WE'RE NOT CAREFUL...
HEEEY...
ANY GOOD GUYS
OUT THERE?

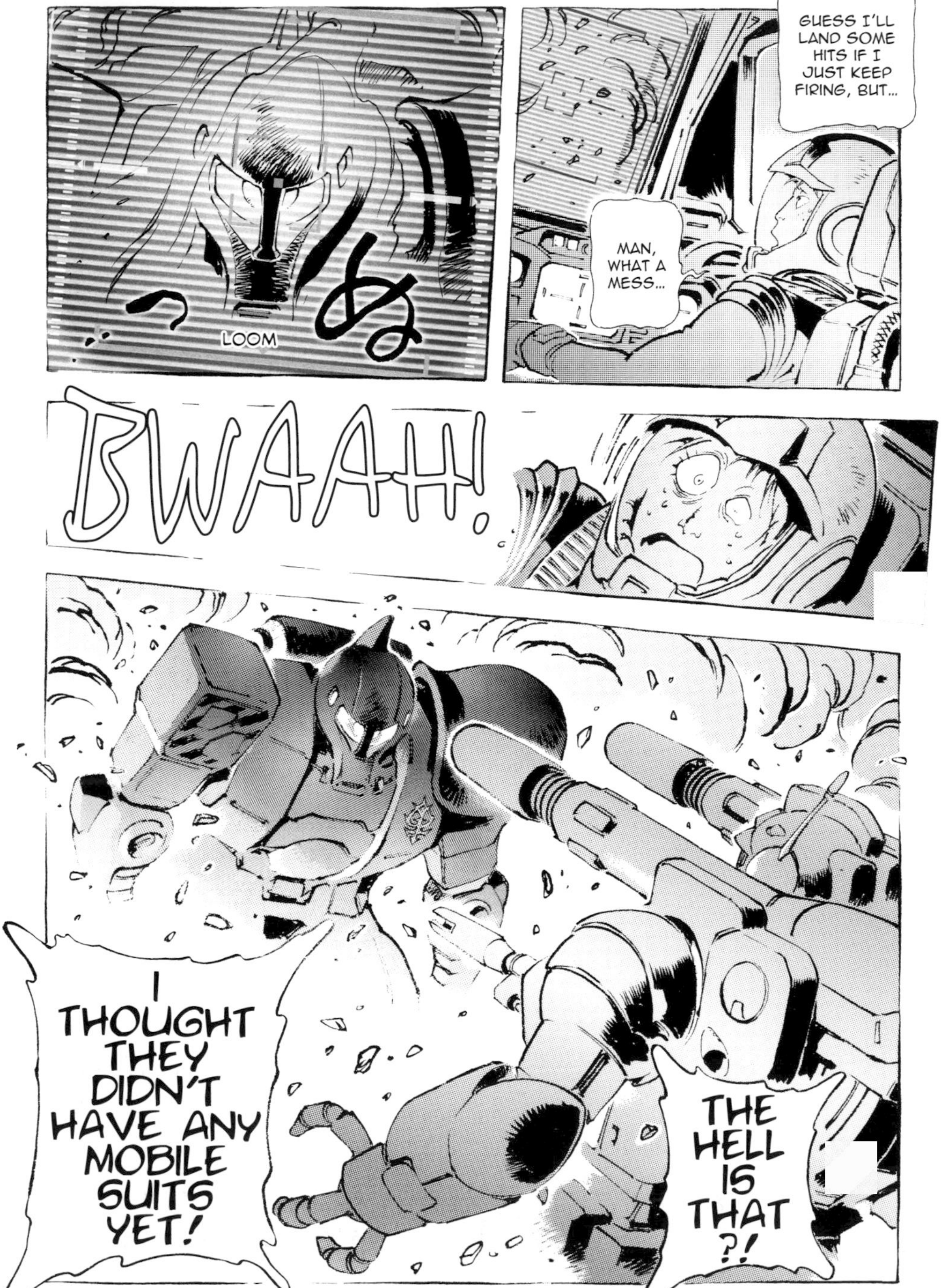
GUESS I'LL LAND SOME HITS IF I JUST KEEP FIRING, BUT...
MAN, WHAT A MESS...
ぬっ
LOOM
BWAAH!
THE HELL IS THAT?!
I THOUGHT THEY DIDN'T HAVE ANY MOBILE SUITS YET!

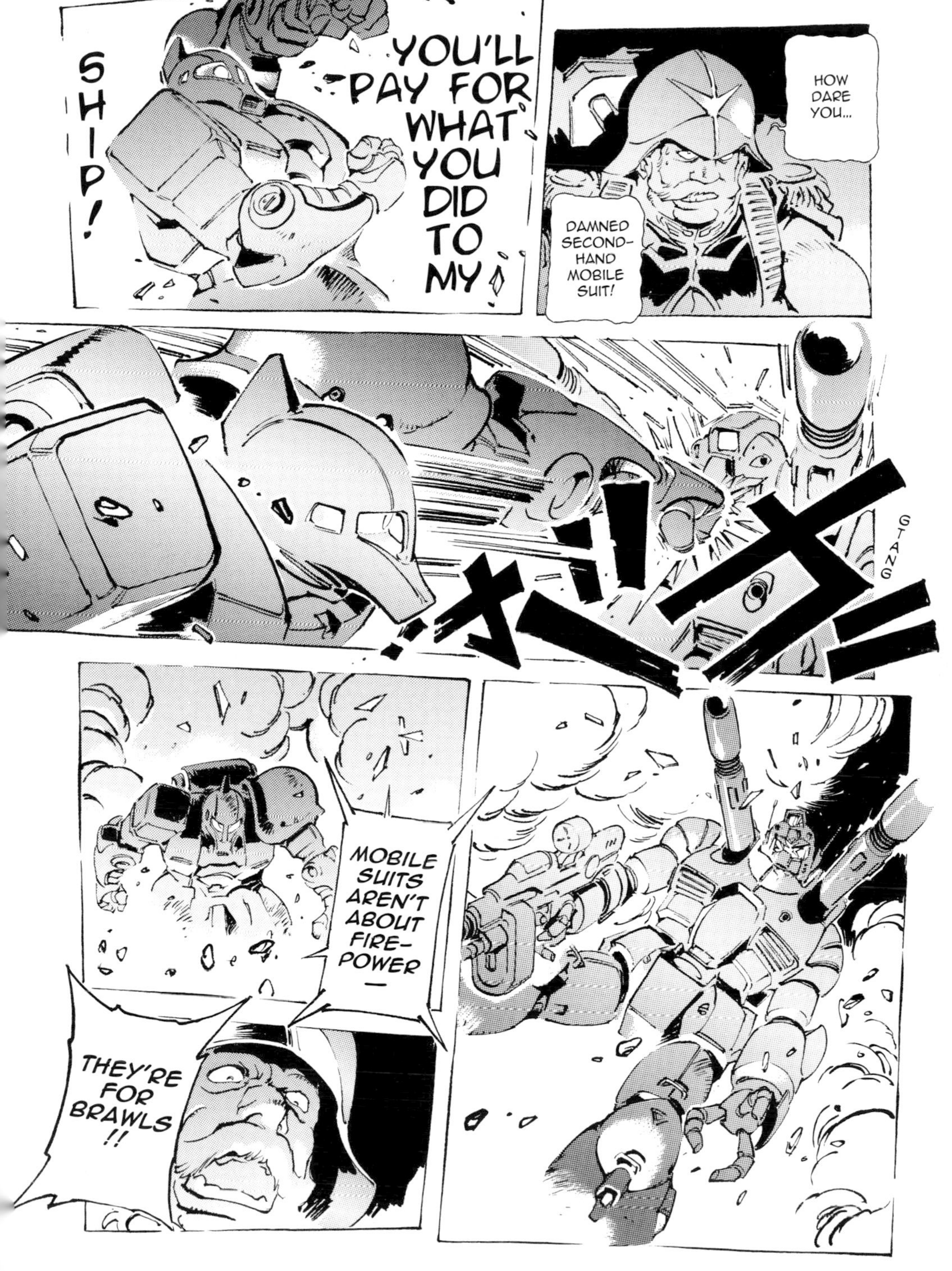
HOW DARE YOU...
DAMNED SECOND-HAND MOBILE SUIT!
YOU'LL PAY FOR WHAT YOU DID TO MY
SHIP!
GIANG
MOBILE SUITS AREN'T ABOUT FIRE-POWER—
THEY'RE FOR BRAWLS!!

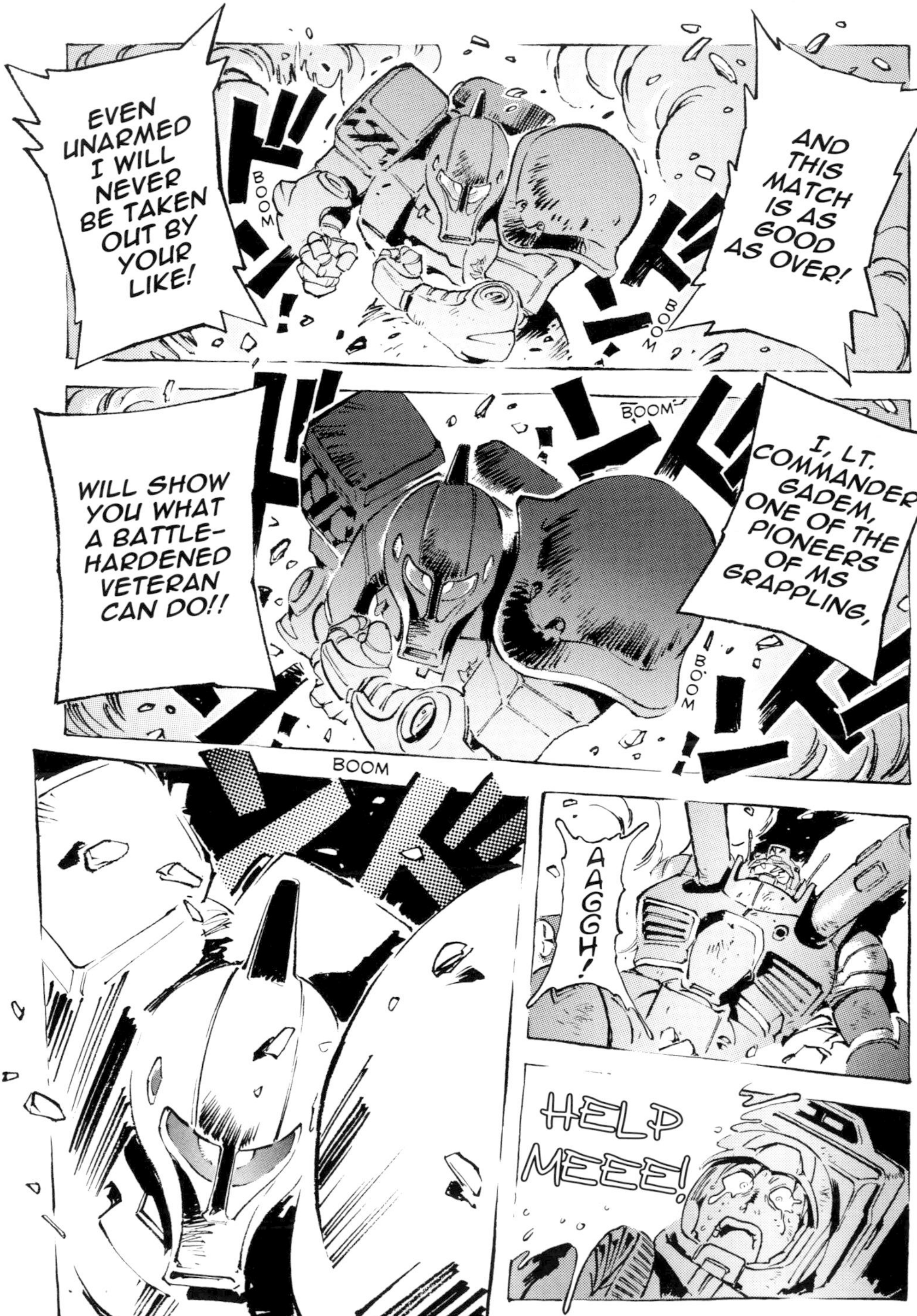
AND THIS MATCH IS AS GOOD AS OVER!
BOOM
EVEN UNARMED I WILL NEVER BE TAKEN OUT BY YOUR LIKE!
BOOM
BOOM
I, LT. COMMANDER GADEM, ONE OF THE PIONEERS OF MS GRAPPLING,
BOOM
WILL SHOW YOU WHAT A BATTLE-HARDENED VETERAN CAN DO!!
AAGGH!
HELP MEEEE!
BOOM

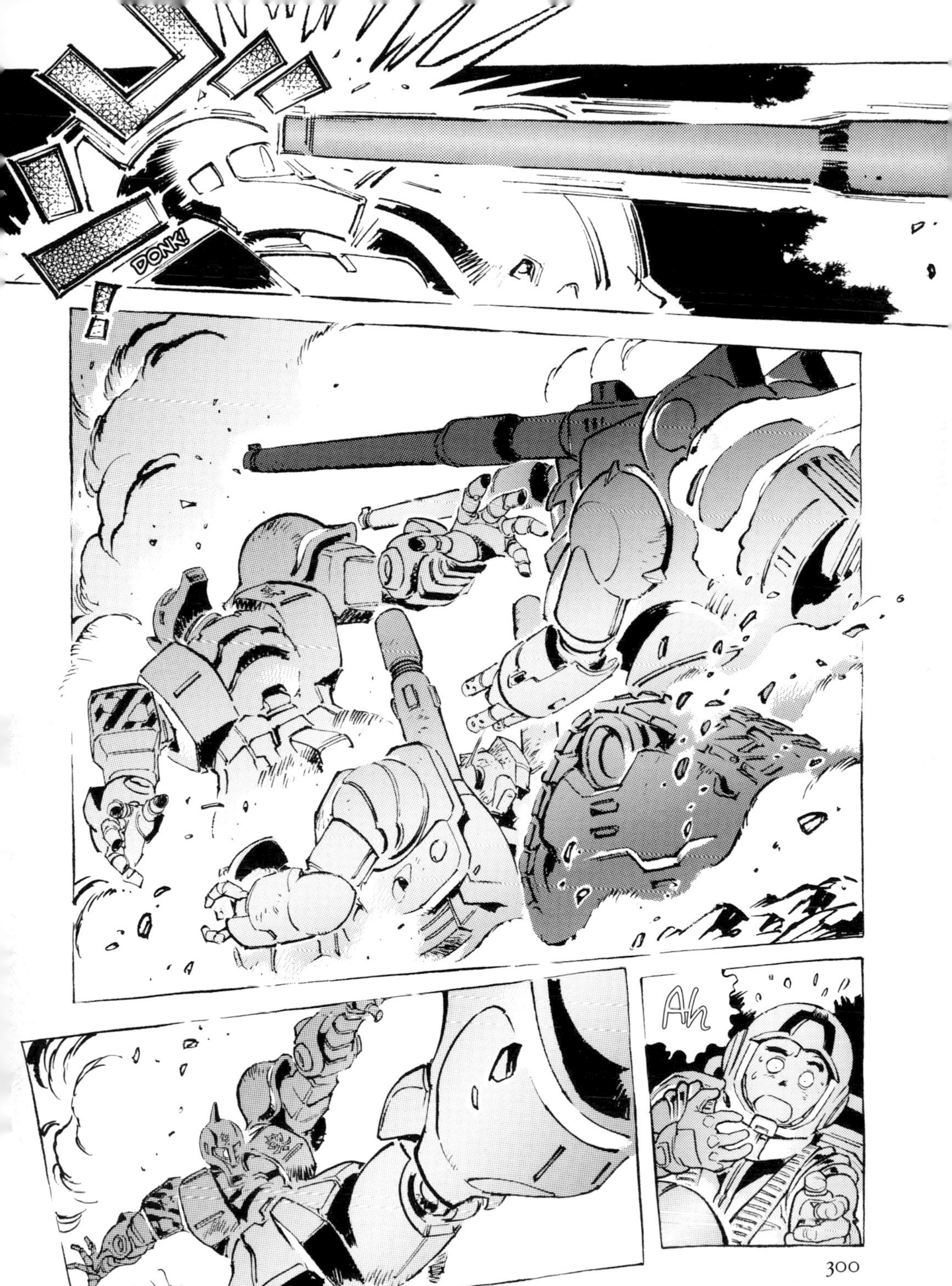
DONK!
!
Ah

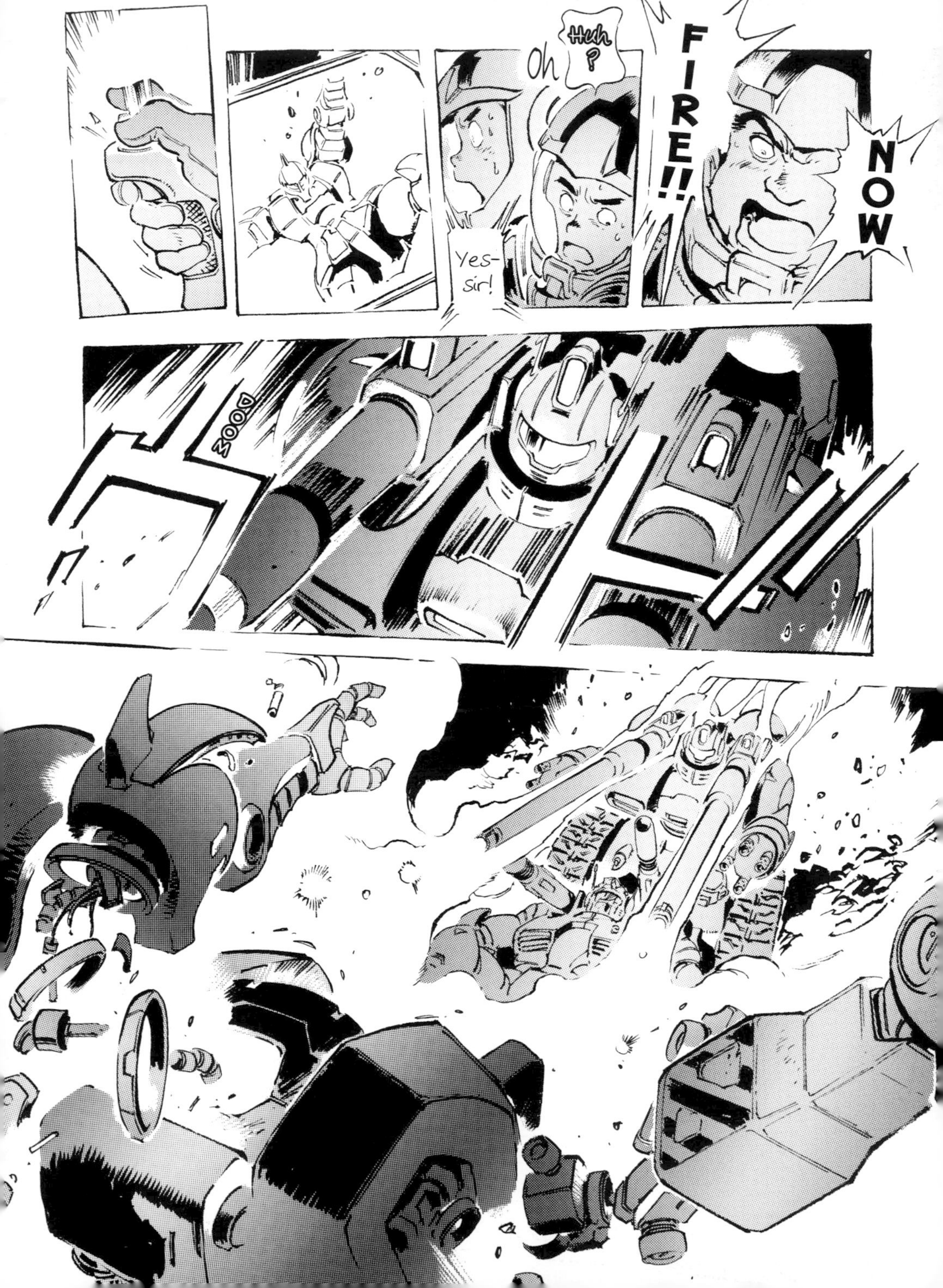
FIRE!!
NOW
Huh?
Oh
Yes-sir!
DOOM

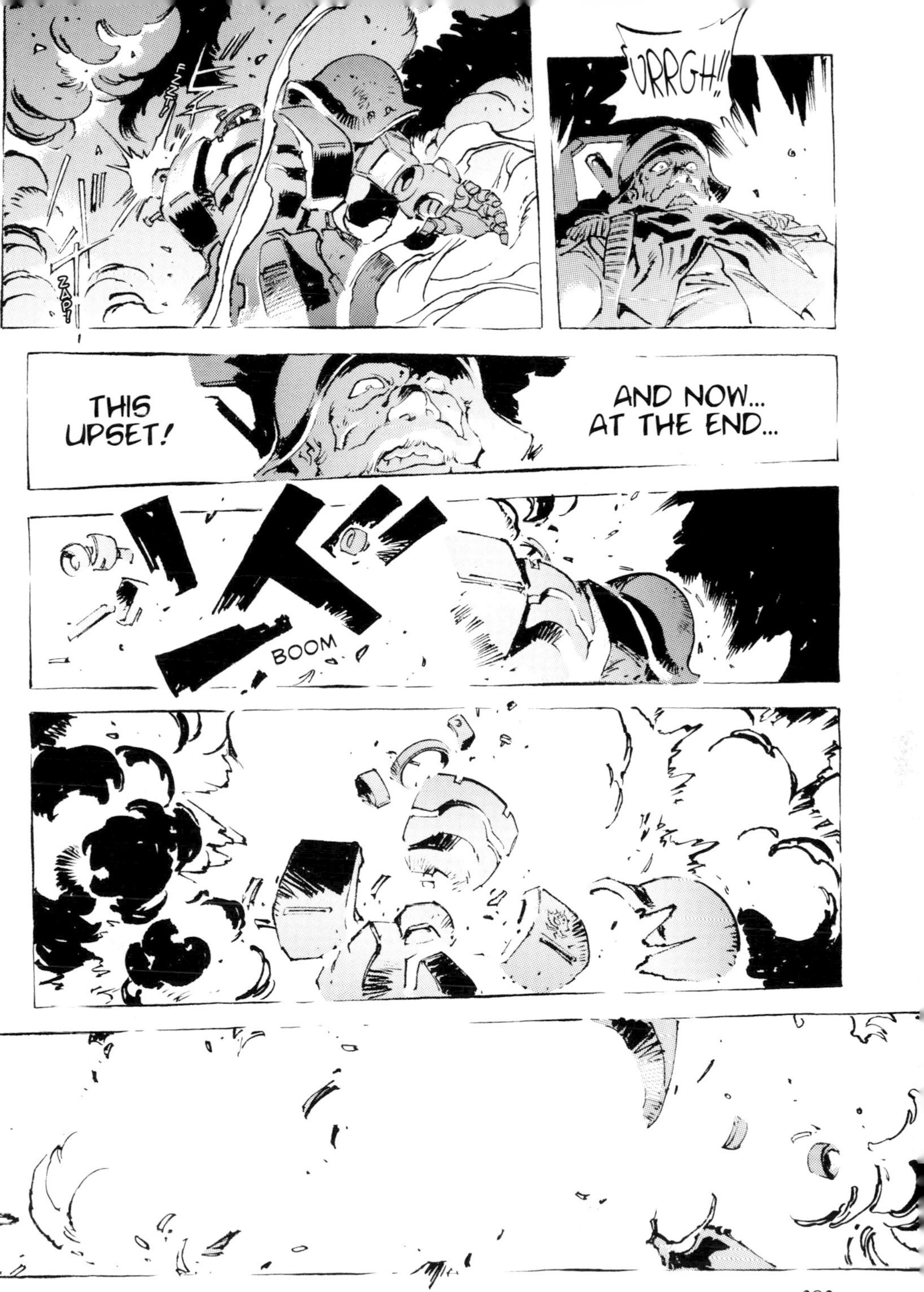
URRGH!!
FZZT!
ZAP!
AND NOW... AT THE END...
THIS UPSET!
BOOM

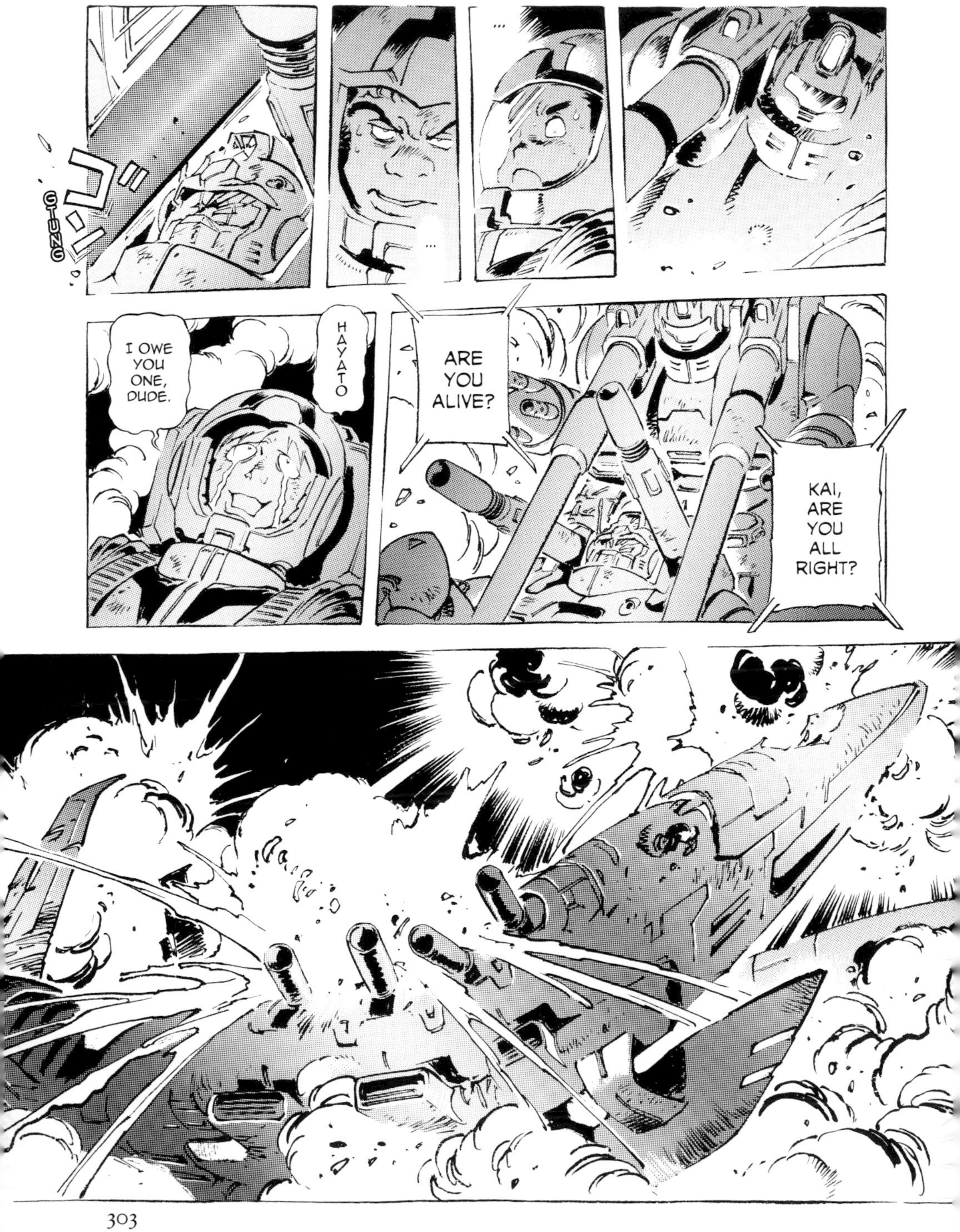
...
...
GTUNG
KAI, ARE YOU ALL RIGHT?
ARE YOU ALIVE?
HAYATO
I OWE YOU ONE, DUDE.

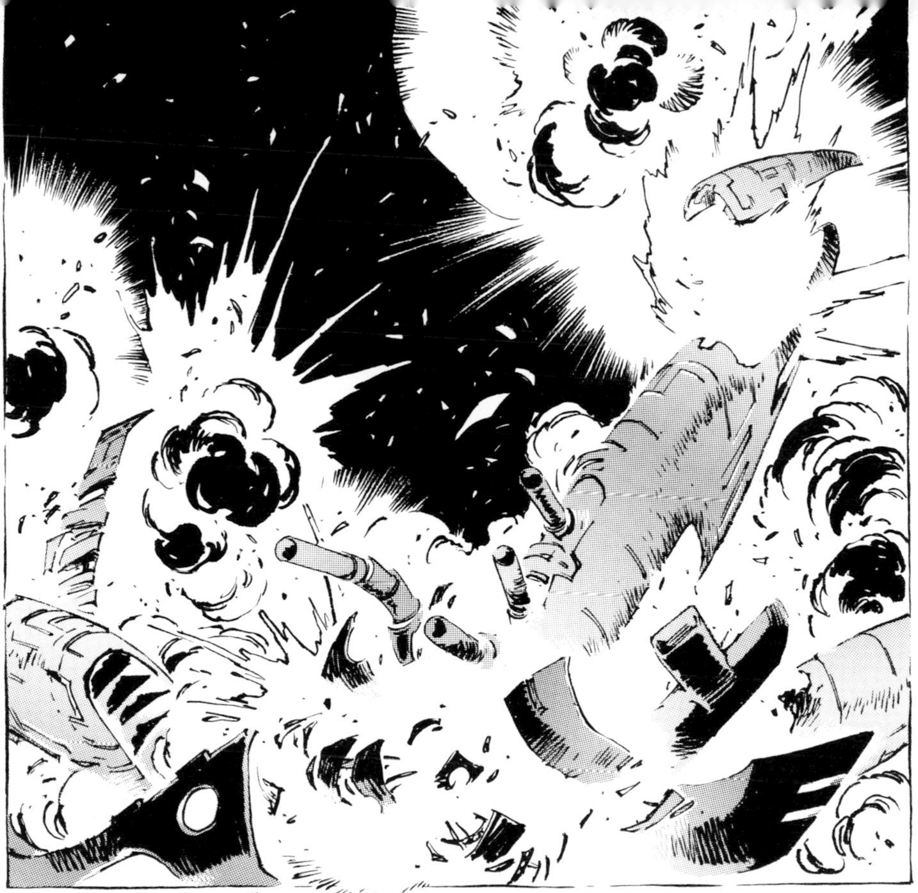
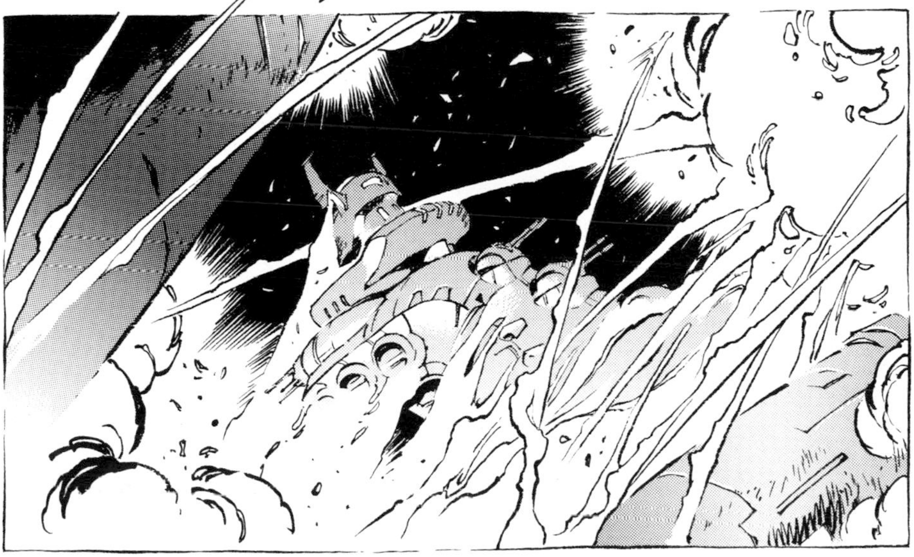

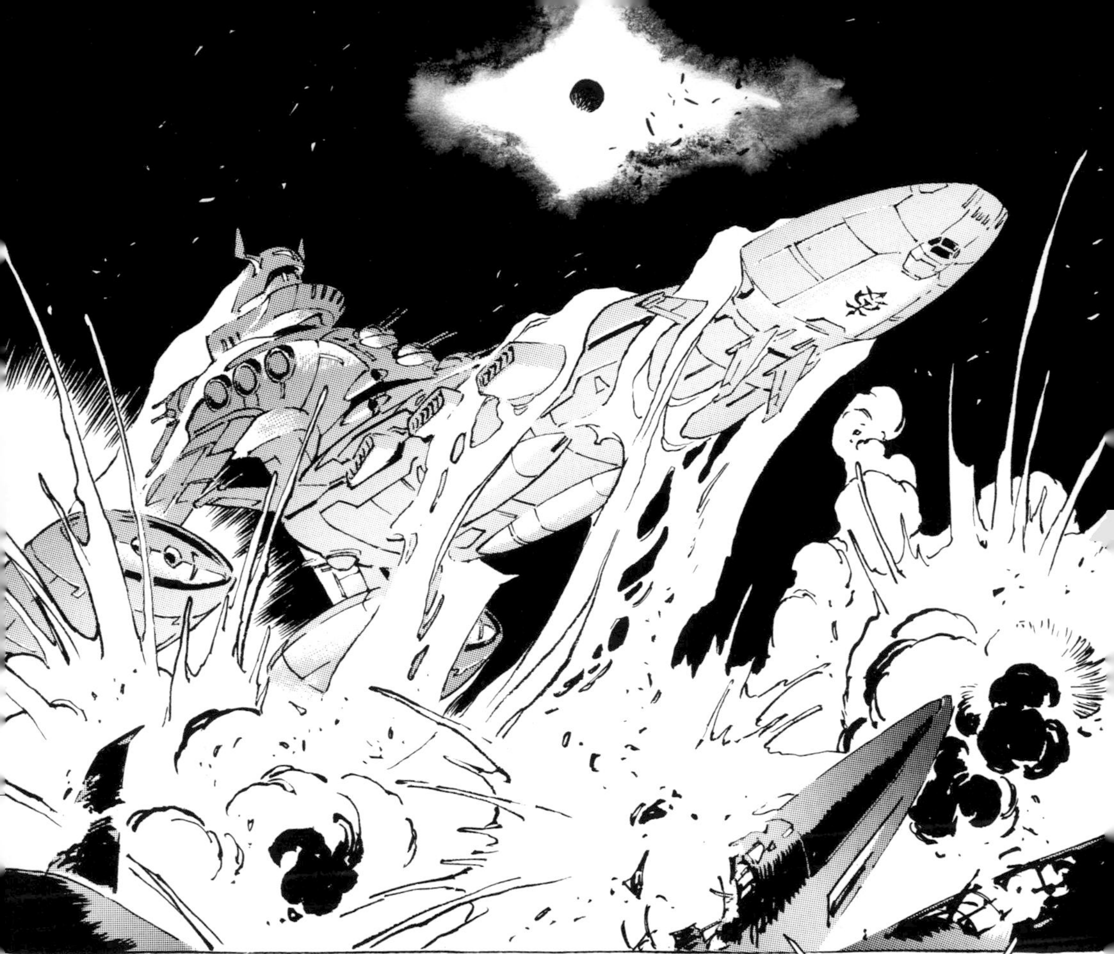

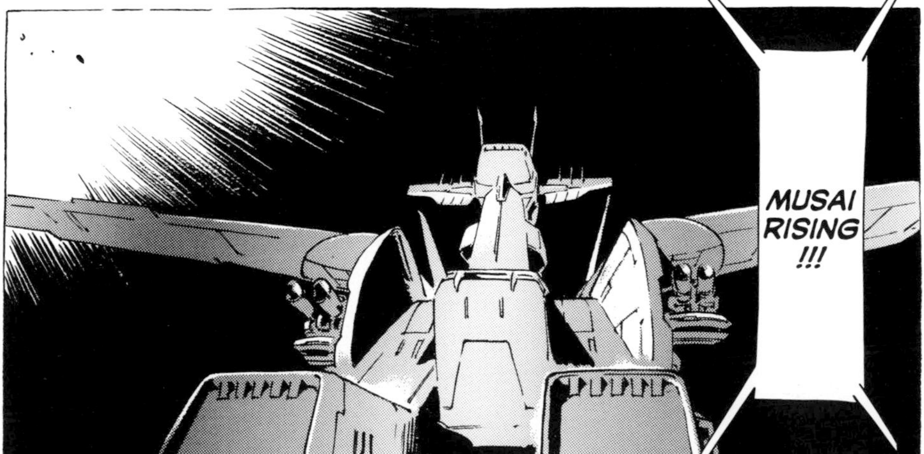
MUSAI
RISING
!!!

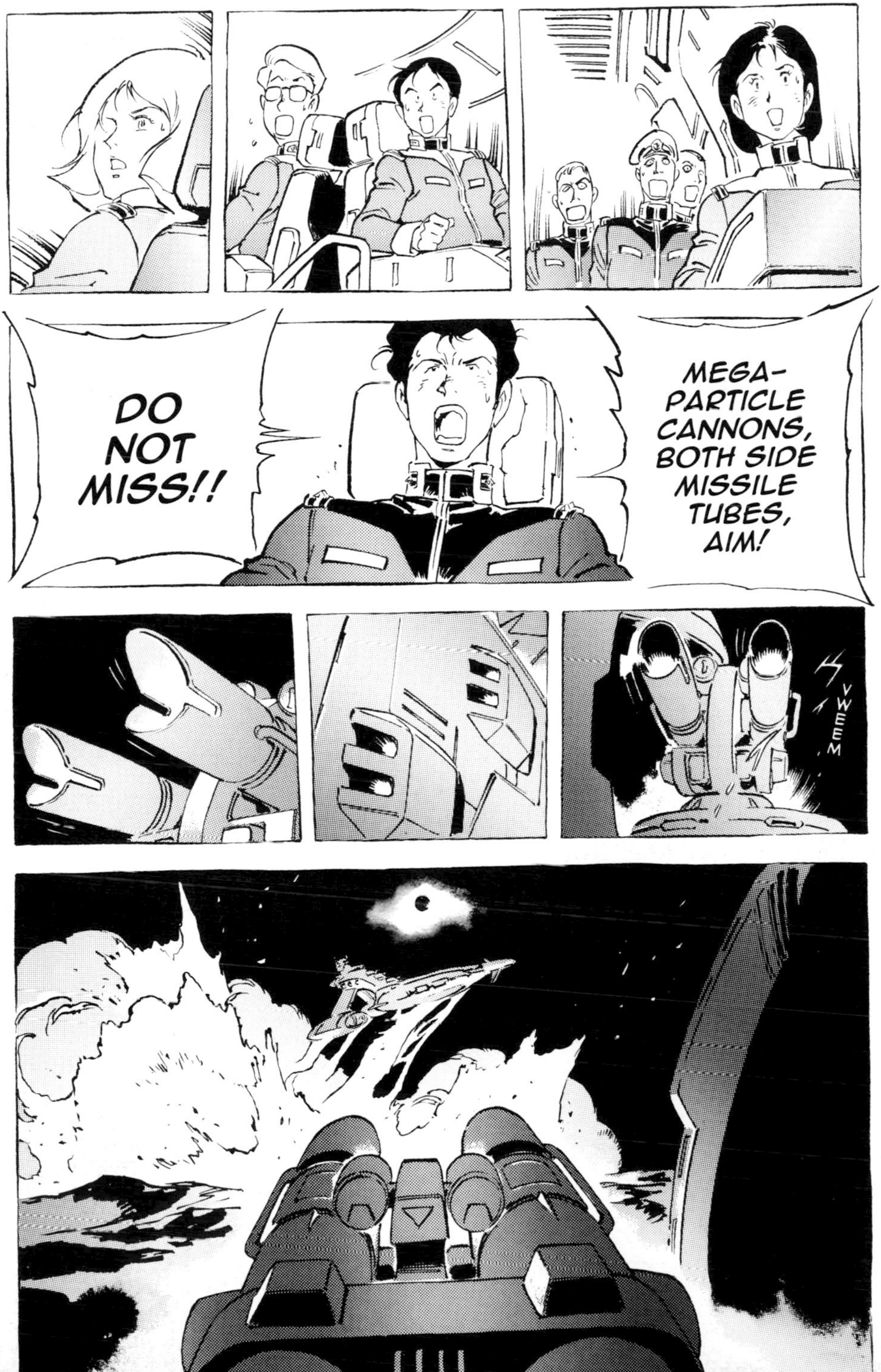
MEGA-PARTICLE CANNONS, BOTH SIDE MISSILE TUBES, AIM!
DO NOT MISS!!
VWEEM

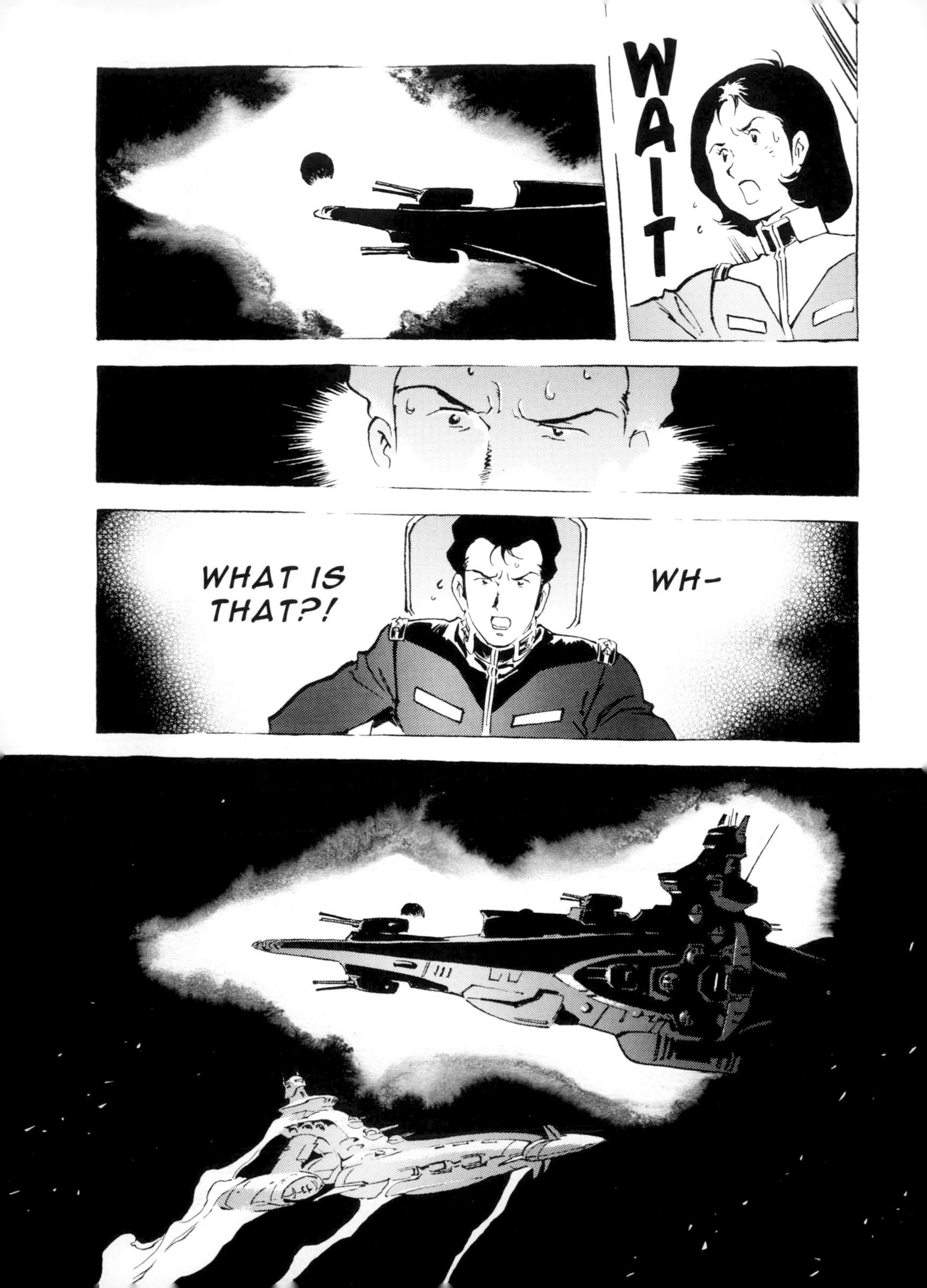
WAIT
WH-
WHAT IS THAT?!

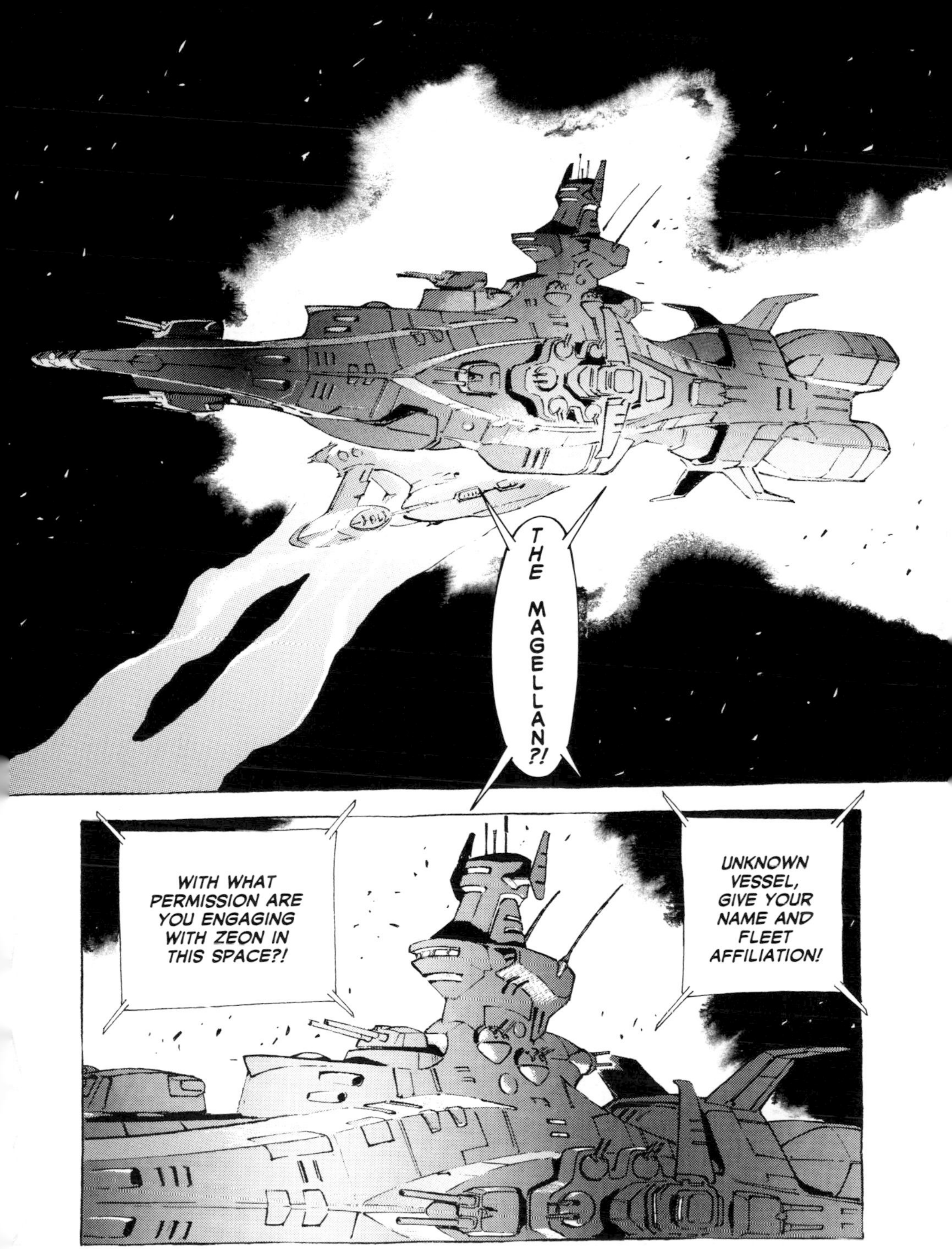
THE MAGELLAN?!
UNKNOWN VESSEL, GIVE YOUR NAME AND FLEET AFFILIATION!
WITH WHAT PERMISSION ARE YOU ENGAGING WITH ZEON IN THIS SPACE?!

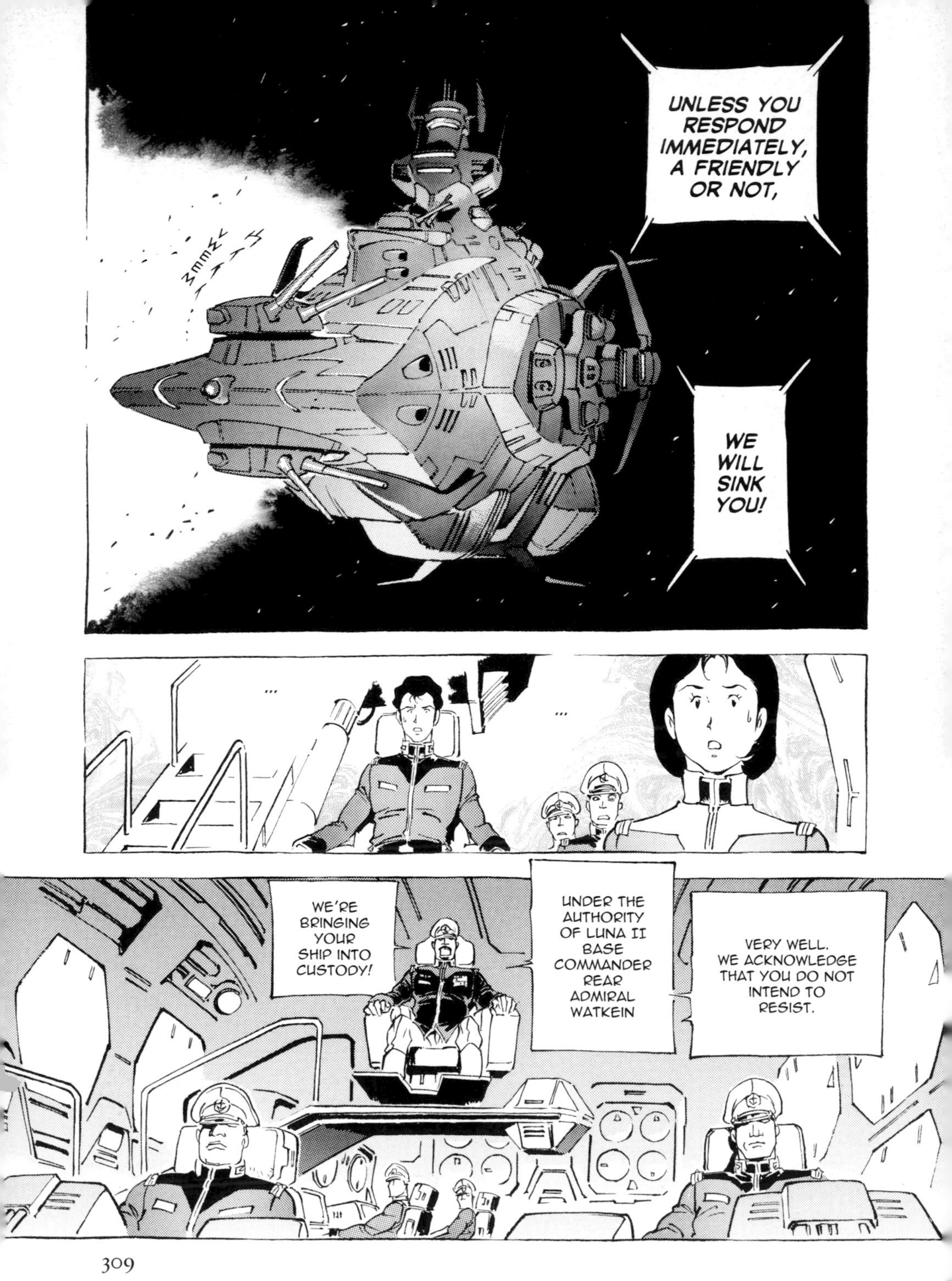
UNLESS YOU RESPOND IMMEDIATELY, A FRIENDLY OR NOT,
WE WILL SINK YOU!
...
...
VERY WELL. WE ACKNOWLEDGE THAT YOU DO NOT INTEND TO RESIST.
UNDER THE AUTHORITY OF LUNA II BASE COMMANDER REAR ADMIRAL WATKEIN
WE'RE BRINGING YOUR SHIP INTO CUSTODY!

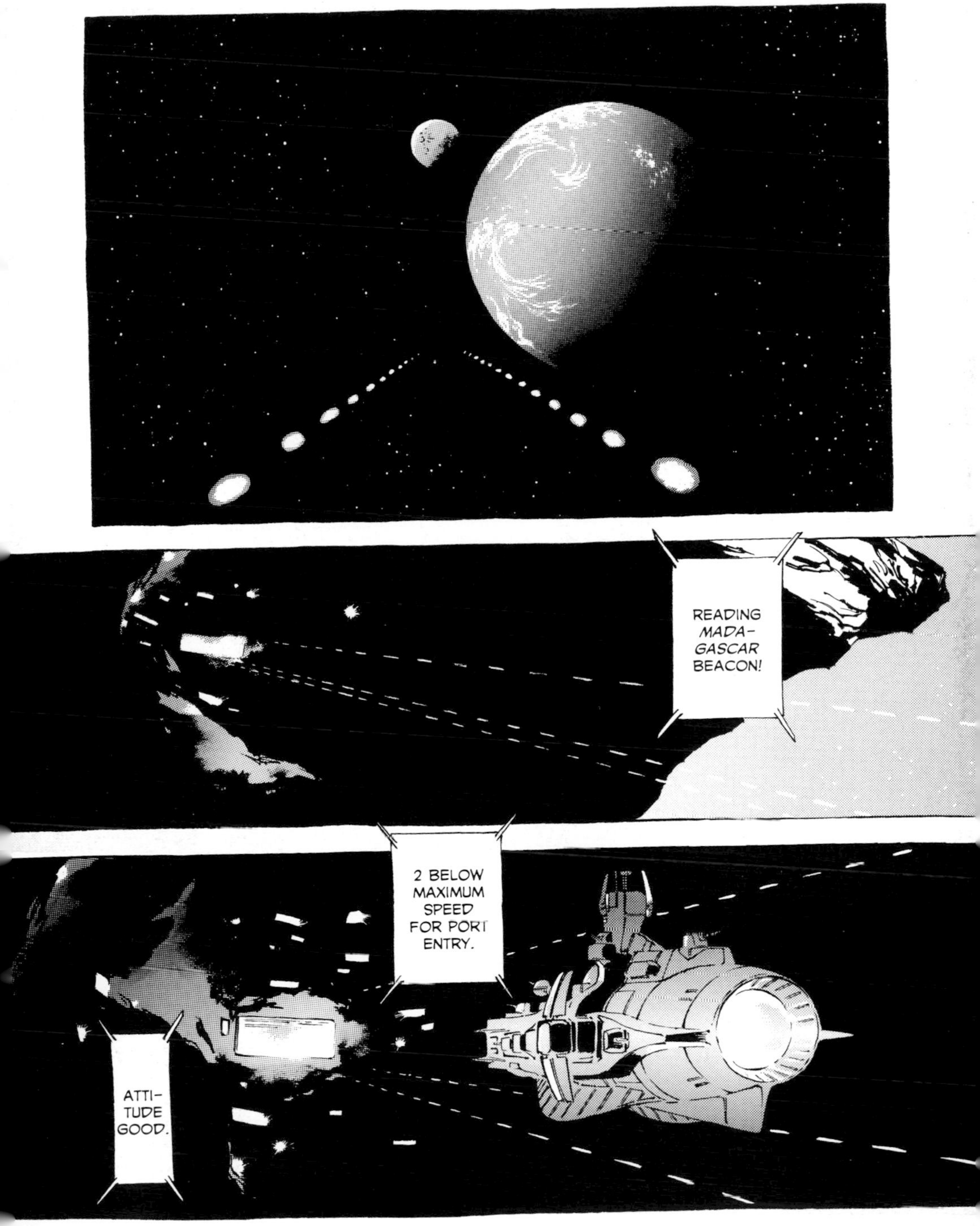
READING *MADA-GASCAR* BEACON!
2 BELOW MAXIMUM SPEED FOR PORT ENTRY.
ATTI-TUDE GOOD.

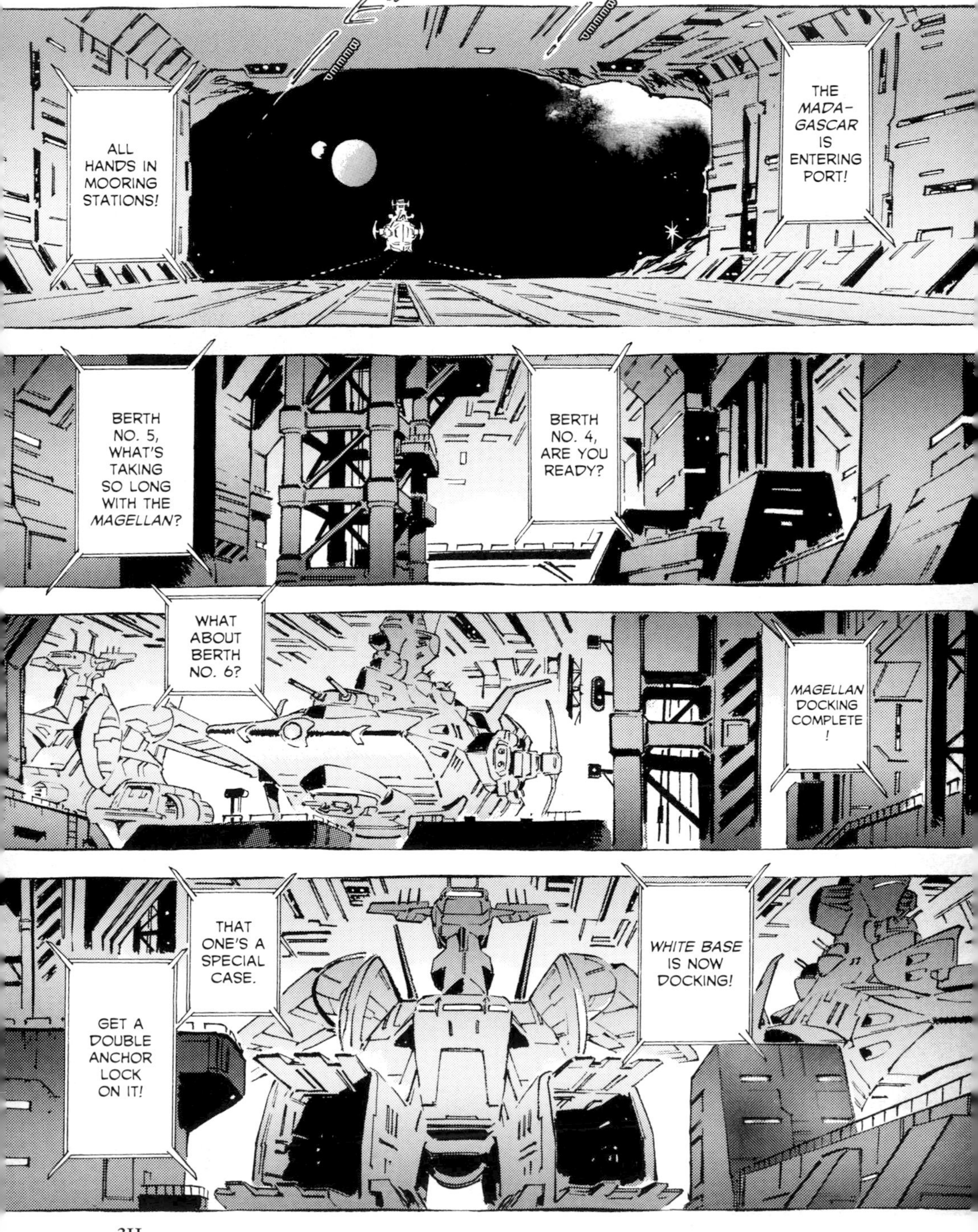
THE MADA-GASCAR IS ENTERING PORT!
ALL HANDS IN MOORING STATIONS!
BERTH NO. 4, ARE YOU READY?
BERTH NO. 5, WHAT'S TAKING SO LONG WITH THE MAGELLAN?
MAGELLAN DOCKING COMPLETE!
WHAT ABOUT BERTH NO. 6?
WHITE BASE IS NOW DOCKING!
THAT ONE'S A SPECIAL CASE.
GET A DOUBLE ANCHOR LOCK ON IT!

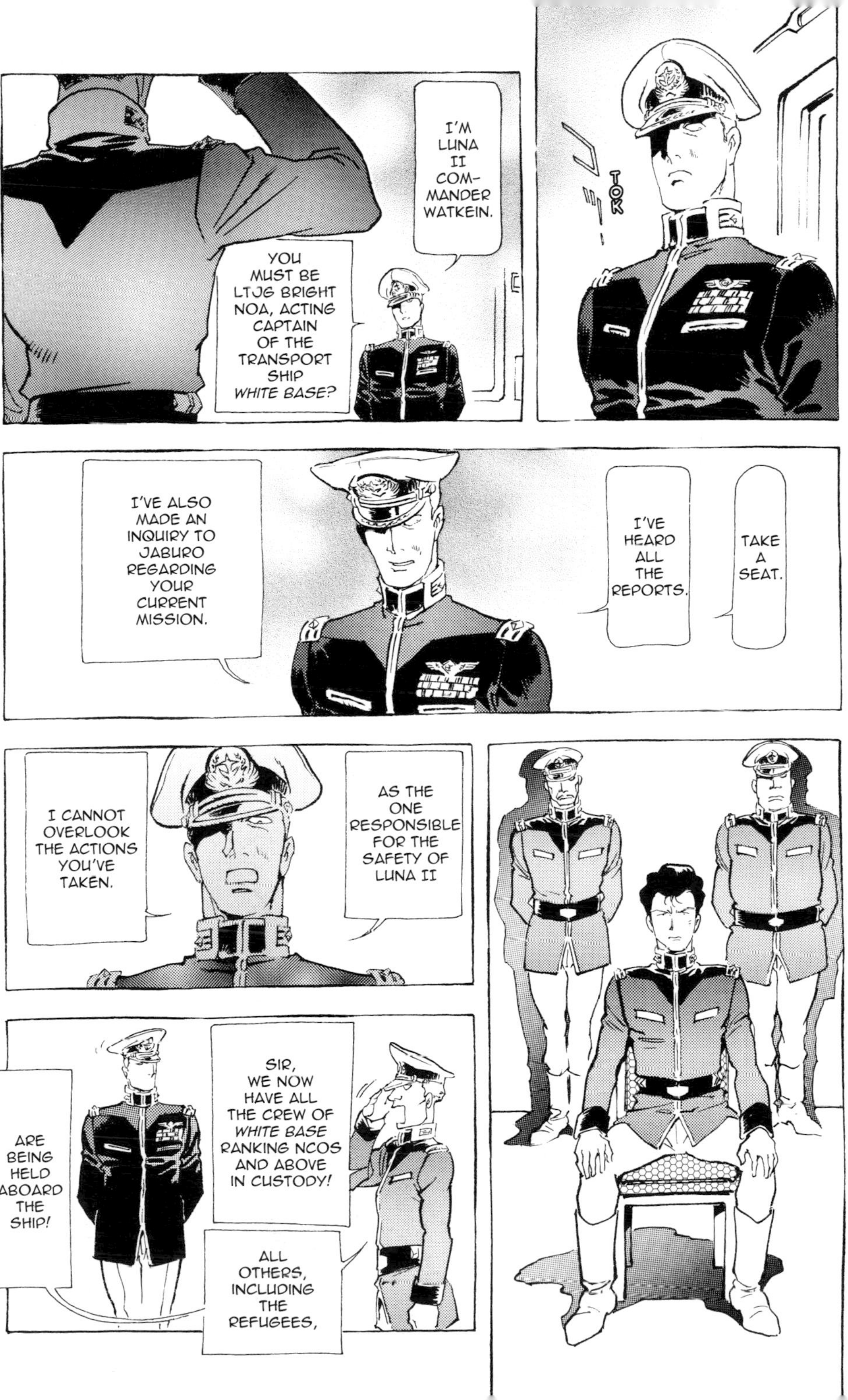
TOK
I'M LUNA II COM-MANDER WATKEIN.
YOU MUST BE LTJG BRIGHT NOA, ACTING CAPTAIN OF THE TRANSPORT SHIP *WHITE BASE*?
TAKE A SEAT.
I'VE HEARD ALL THE REPORTS.
I'VE ALSO MADE AN INQUIRY TO JABURO REGARDING YOUR CURRENT MISSION.
AS THE ONE RESPONSIBLE FOR THE SAFETY OF LUNA II
I CANNOT OVERLOOK THE ACTIONS YOU'VE TAKEN.
SIR, WE NOW HAVE ALL THE CREW OF *WHITE BASE* RANKING NCOS AND ABOVE IN CUSTODY!
ALL OTHERS, INCLUDING THE REFUGEES,
ARE BEING HELD ABOARD THE SHIP!

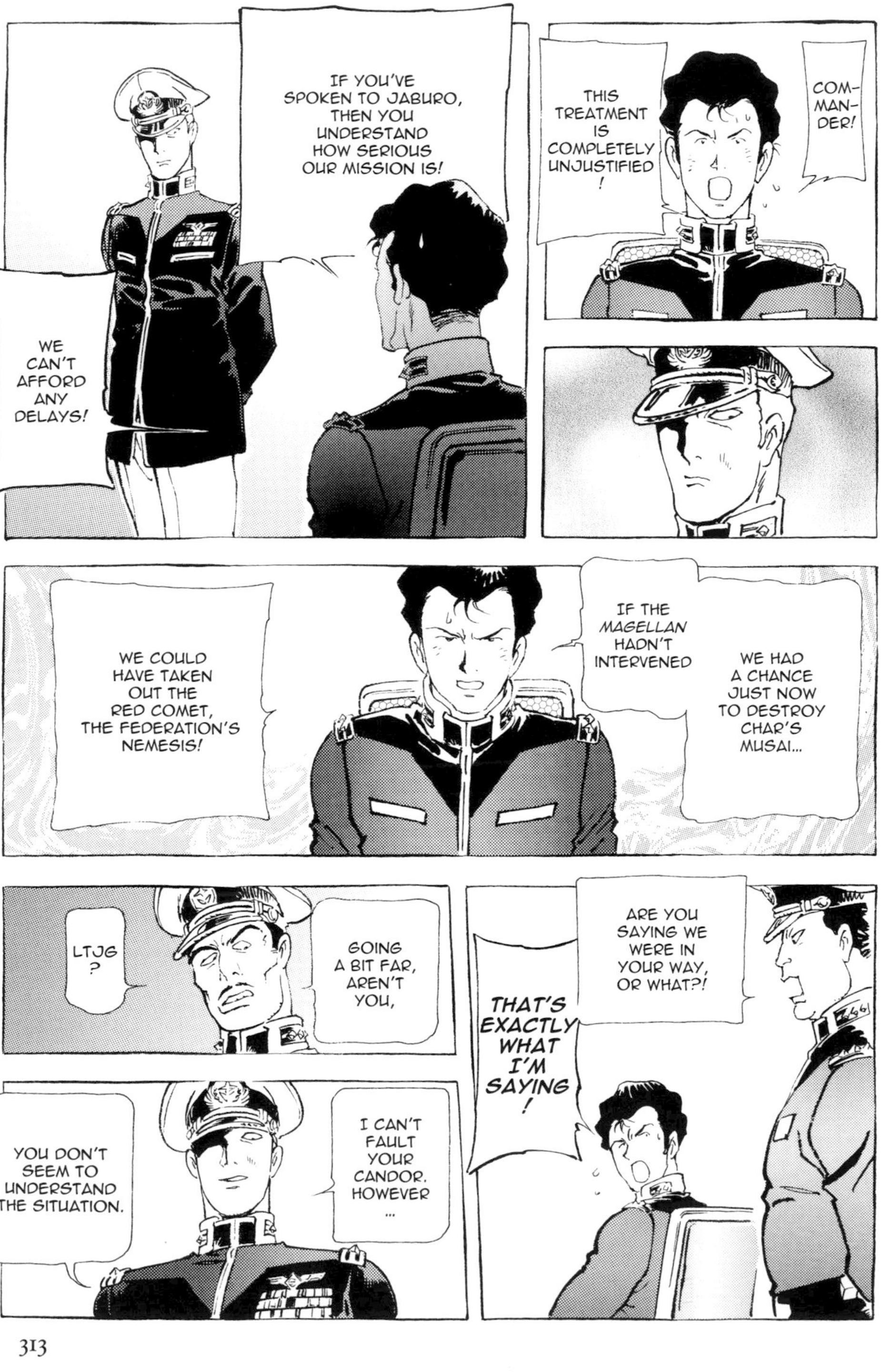
COM-MAN-DER!
THIS TREATMENT IS COMPLETELY UNJUSTIFIED!
IF YOU'VE SPOKEN TO JABURO, THEN YOU UNDERSTAND HOW SERIOUS OUR MISSION IS!
WE CAN'T AFFORD ANY DELAYS!
WE HAD A CHANCE JUST NOW TO DESTROY CHAR'S MUSAI...
IF THE MAGELLAN HADN'T INTERVENED
WE COULD HAVE TAKEN OUT THE RED COMET, THE FEDERATION'S NEMESIS!
ARE YOU SAYING WE WERE IN YOUR WAY, OR WHAT?!
THAT'S EXACTLY WHAT I'M SAYING!
GOING A BIT FAR, AREN'T YOU,
LTJG?
I CAN'T FAULT YOUR CANDOR. HOWEVER...
YOU DON'T SEEM TO UNDERSTAND THE SITUATION.

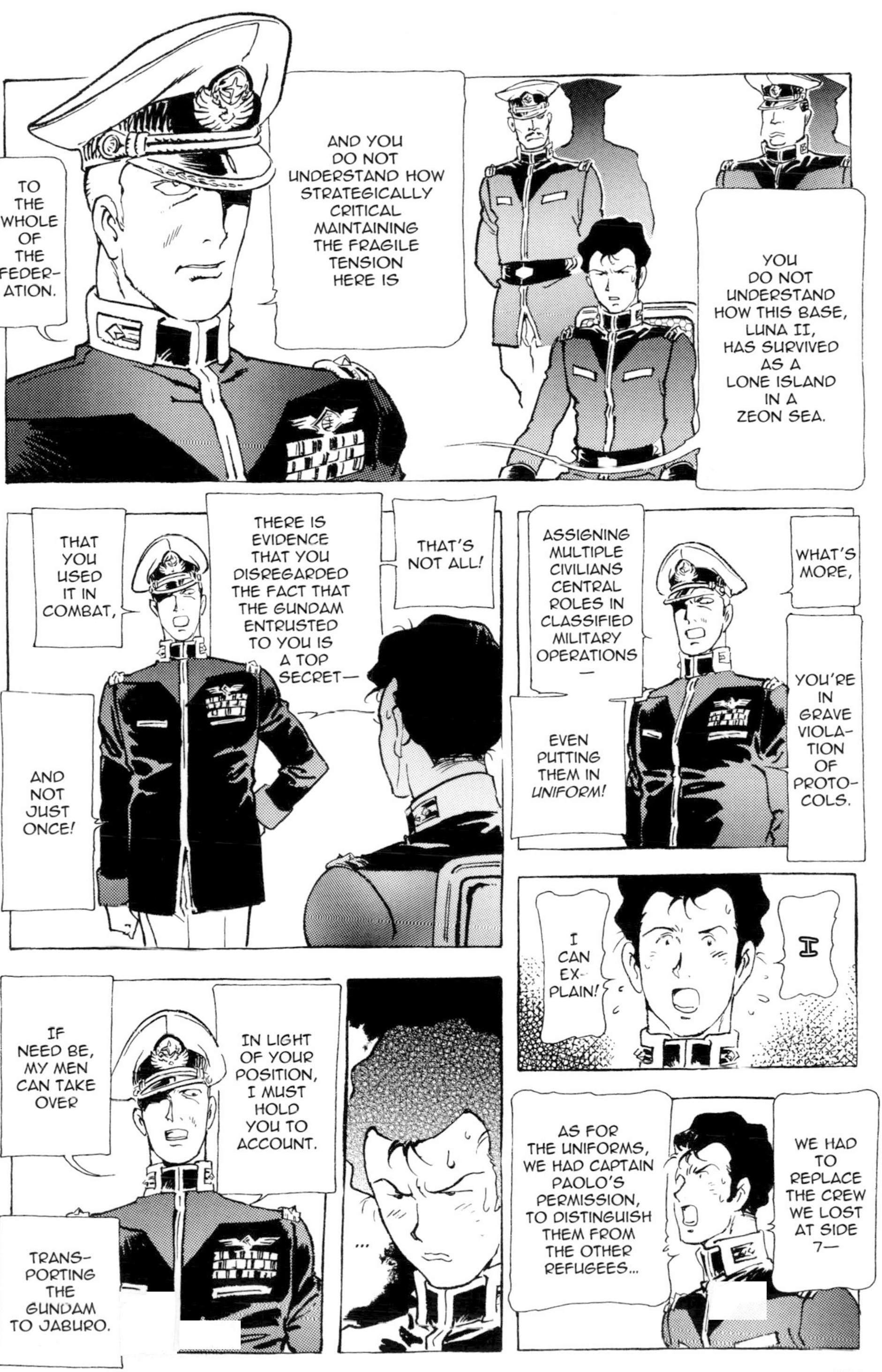
YOU DO NOT UNDERSTAND HOW THIS BASE, LUNA II, HAS SURVIVED AS A LONE ISLAND IN A ZEON SEA.
AND YOU DO NOT UNDERSTAND HOW STRATEGICALLY CRITICAL MAINTAINING THE FRAGILE TENSION HERE IS
TO THE WHOLE OF THE FEDERATION.
WHAT'S MORE,
YOU'RE IN GRAVE VIOLATION OF PROTOCOLS.
ASSIGNING MULTIPLE CIVILIANS CENTRAL ROLES IN CLASSIFIED MILITARY OPERATIONS—
EVEN PUTTING THEM IN *UNIFORM!*
I
I CAN EXPLAIN!
THAT'S NOT ALL!
THERE IS EVIDENCE THAT YOU DISREGARDED THE FACT THAT THE GUNDAM ENTRUSTED TO YOU IS A TOP SECRET—
THAT YOU USED IT IN COMBAT,
AND NOT JUST ONCE!
WE HAD TO REPLACE THE CREW WE LOST AT SIDE 7—
AS FOR THE UNIFORMS, WE HAD CAPTAIN PAOLO'S PERMISSION, TO DISTINGUISH THEM FROM THE OTHER REFUGEES...
...
IN LIGHT OF YOUR POSITION, I MUST HOLD YOU TO ACCOUNT.
IF NEED BE, MY MEN CAN TAKE OVER
TRANSPORTING THE GUNDAM TO JABURO.

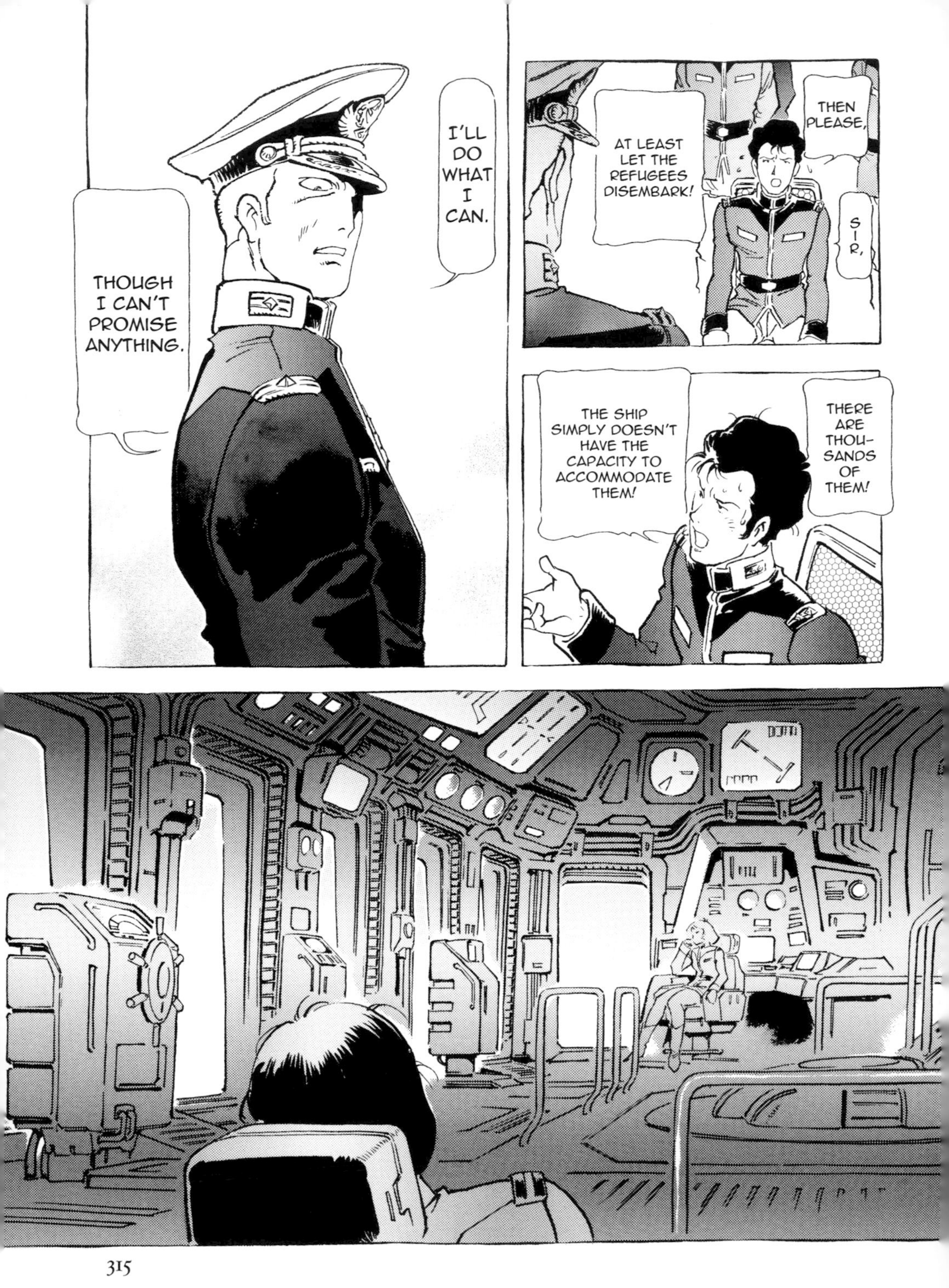
THEN PLEASE,
SIR,
AT LEAST LET THE REFUGEES DISEMBARK!
THERE ARE THOU-SANDS OF THEM!
THE SHIP SIMPLY DOESN'T HAVE THE CAPACITY TO ACCOMMODATE THEM!
I'LL DO WHAT I CAN.
THOUGH I CAN'T PROMISE ANYTHING.

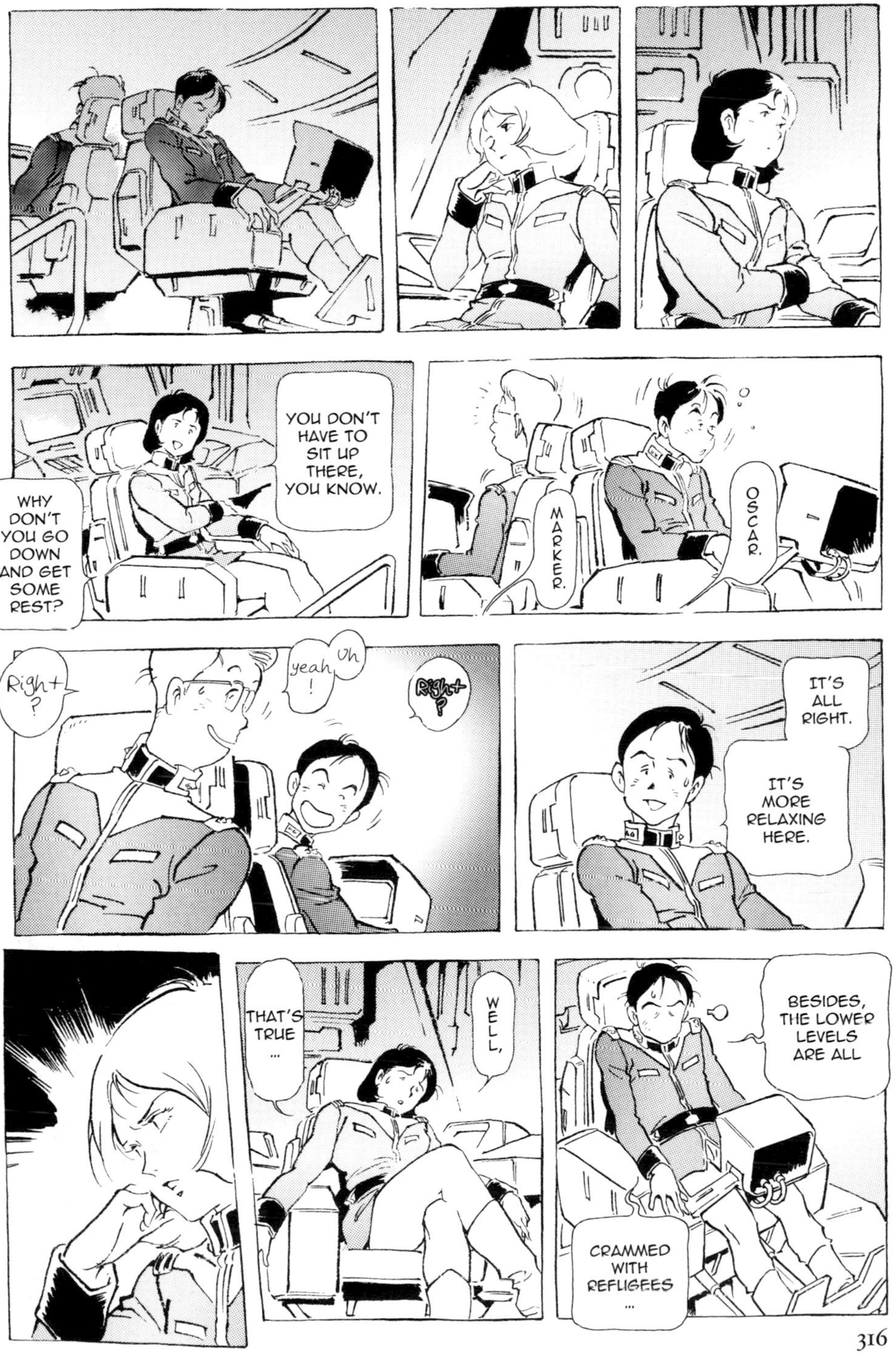
OSCAR.
MARKER.
YOU DON'T HAVE TO SIT UP THERE, YOU KNOW.
WHY DON'T YOU GO DOWN AND GET SOME REST?
IT'S ALL RIGHT.
IT'S MORE RELAXING HERE.
Right?
Uh yeah!
Right?
BESIDES, THE LOWER LEVELS ARE ALL
CRAMMED WITH REFUGEES ...
WELL,
THAT'S TRUE ...

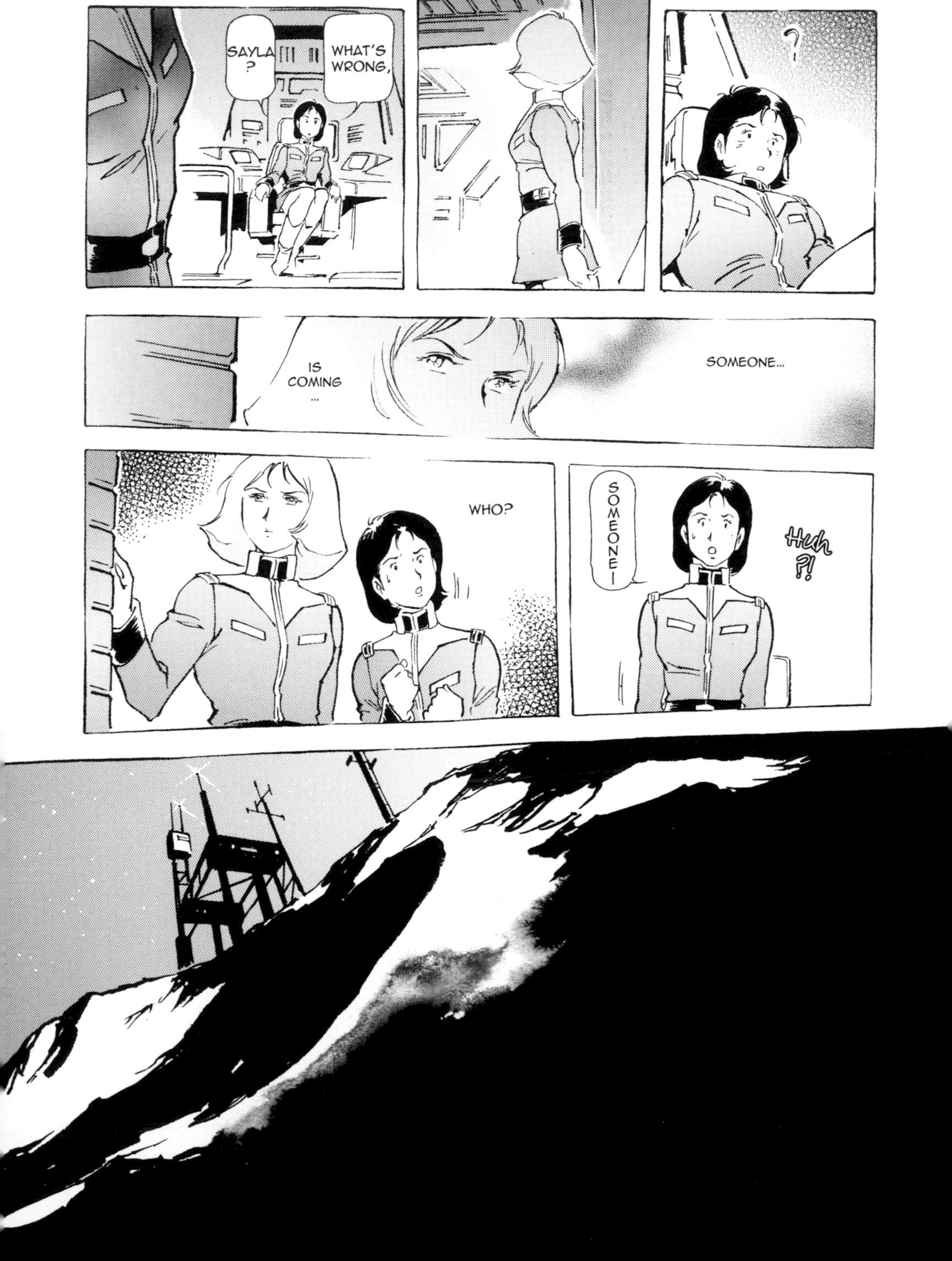
?
WHAT'S WRONG,
SAYLA?
SOMEONE...
IS COMING...
Huh?!
SOMEONE!
WHO?

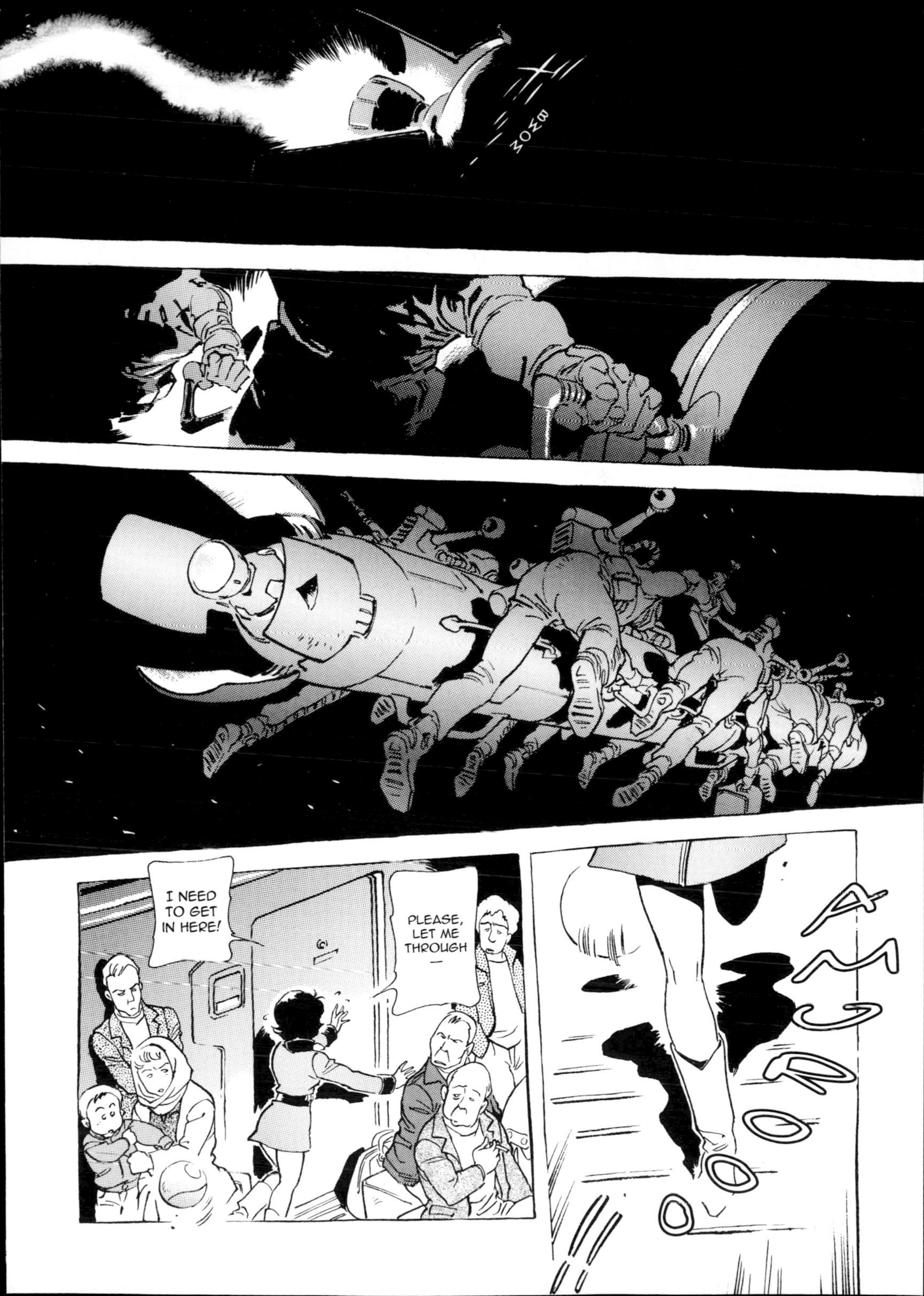
AMUROOOO
PLEASE, LET ME THROUGH —
I NEED TO GET IN HERE!

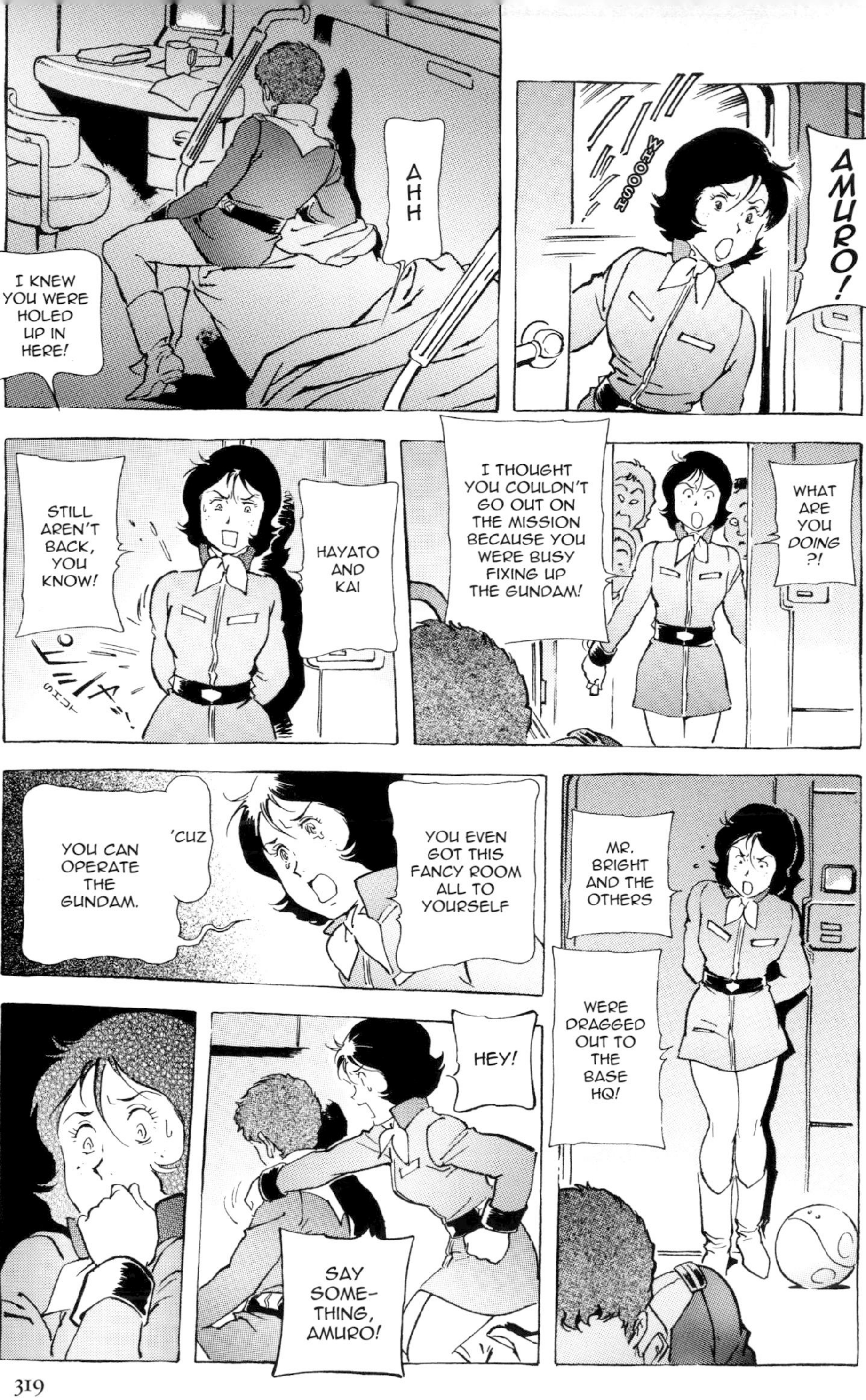
AMURO!
WHOOSH
AHH
I KNEW YOU WERE HOLED UP IN HERE!
WHAT ARE YOU DOING?!
I THOUGHT YOU COULDN'T GO OUT ON THE MISSION BECAUSE YOU WERE BUSY FIXING UP THE GUNDAM!
HAYATO AND KAI
STILL AREN'T BACK, YOU KNOW!
MR. BRIGHT AND THE OTHERS
WERE DRAGGED OUT TO THE BASE HQ!
YOU EVEN GOT THIS FANCY ROOM ALL TO YOURSELF
'CUZ
YOU CAN OPERATE THE GUNDAM.
HEY!
SAY SOME-THING, AMURO!

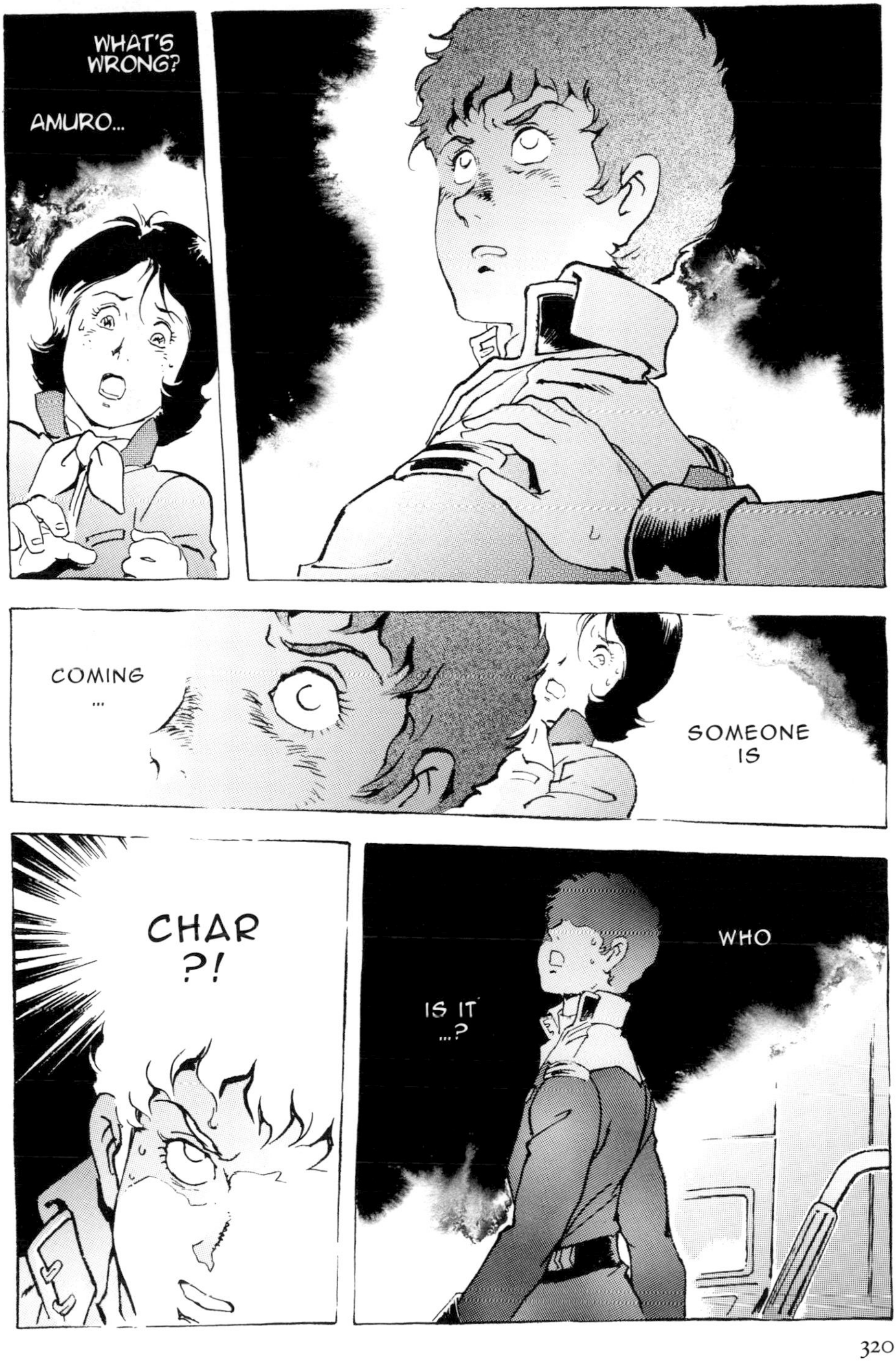
WHAT'S WRONG?
AMURO...
SOMEONE IS
COMING ...
WHO
IS IT ...?
CHAR ?!

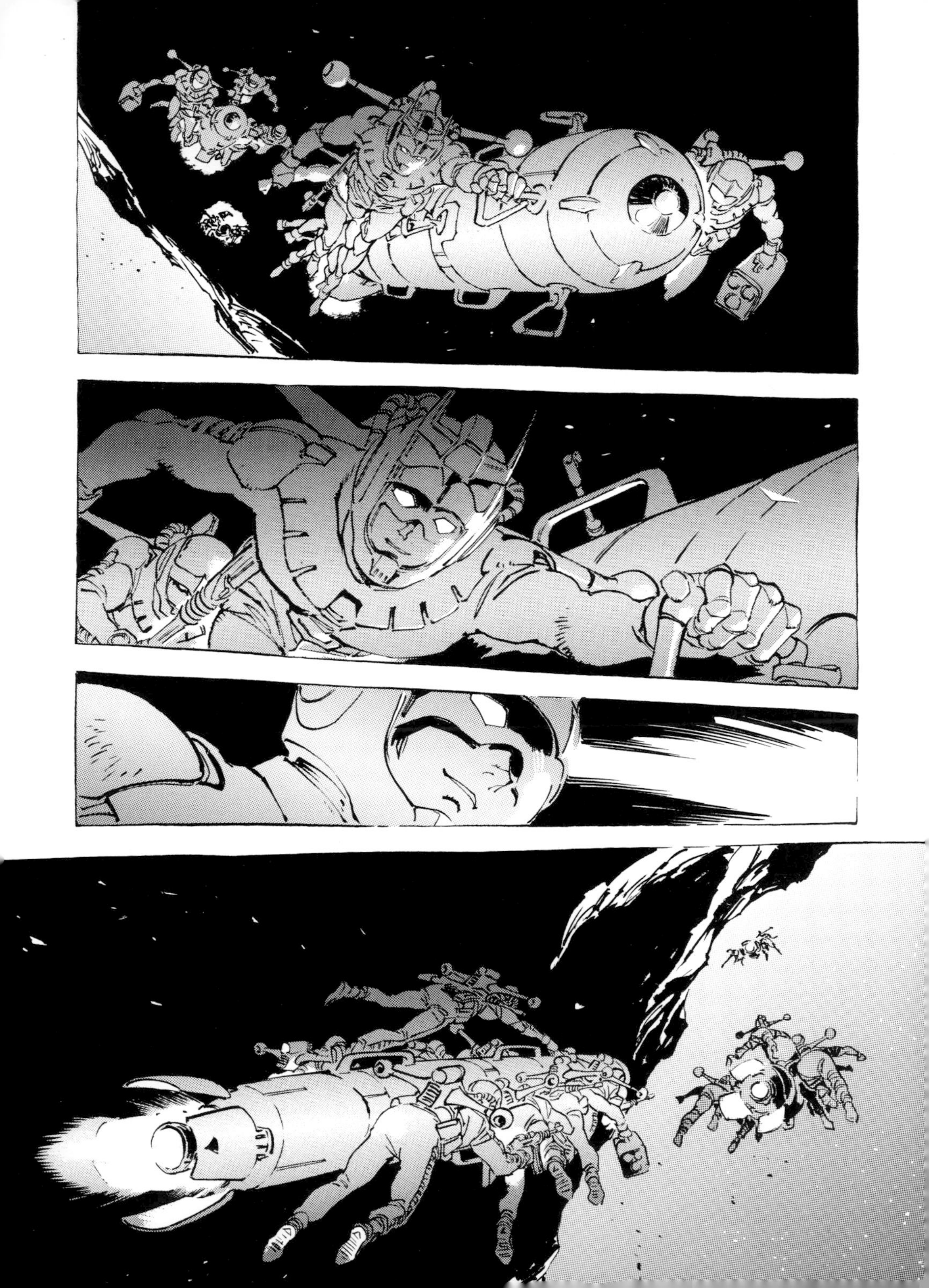

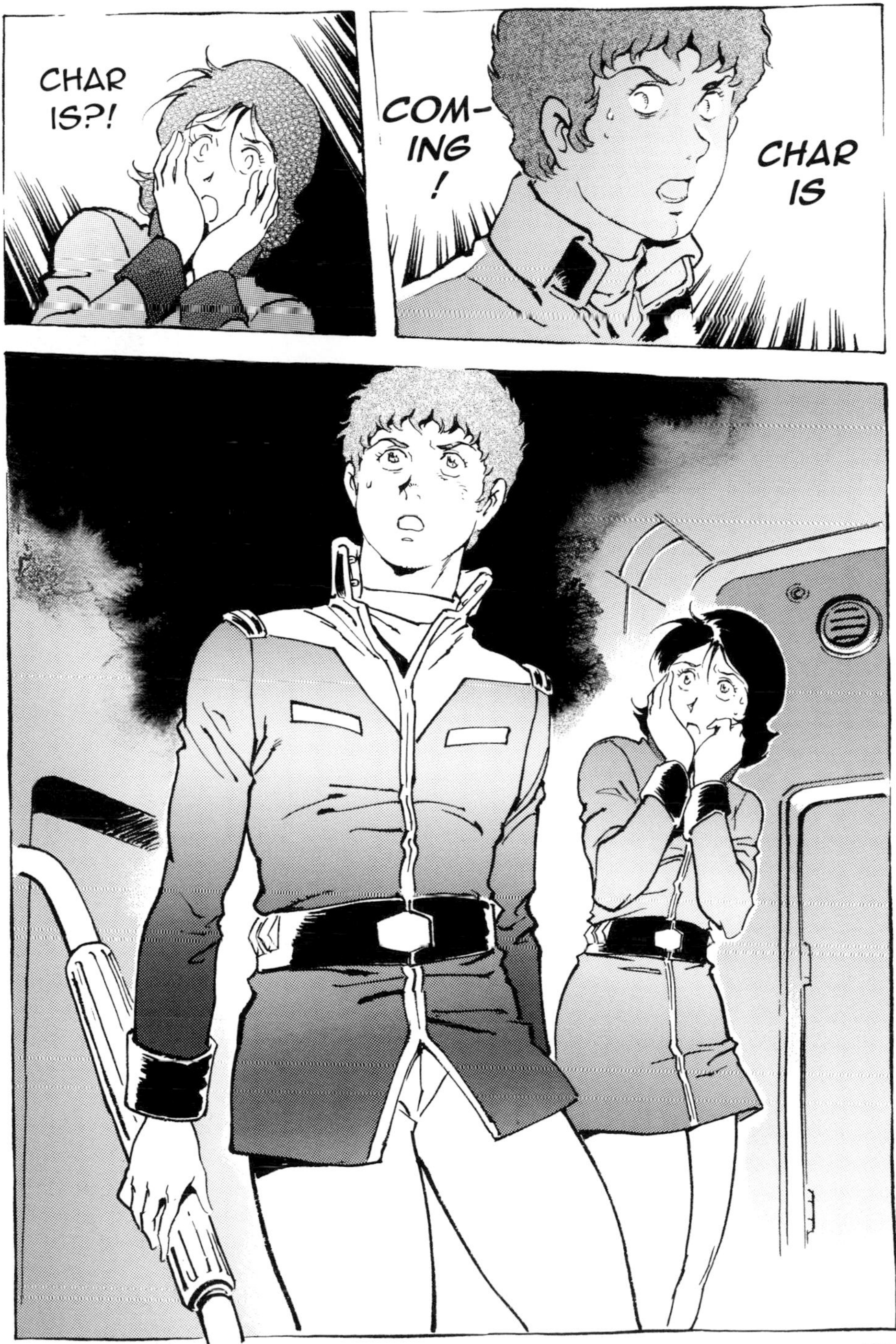
CHAR IS
COM-ING!
CHAR IS?!

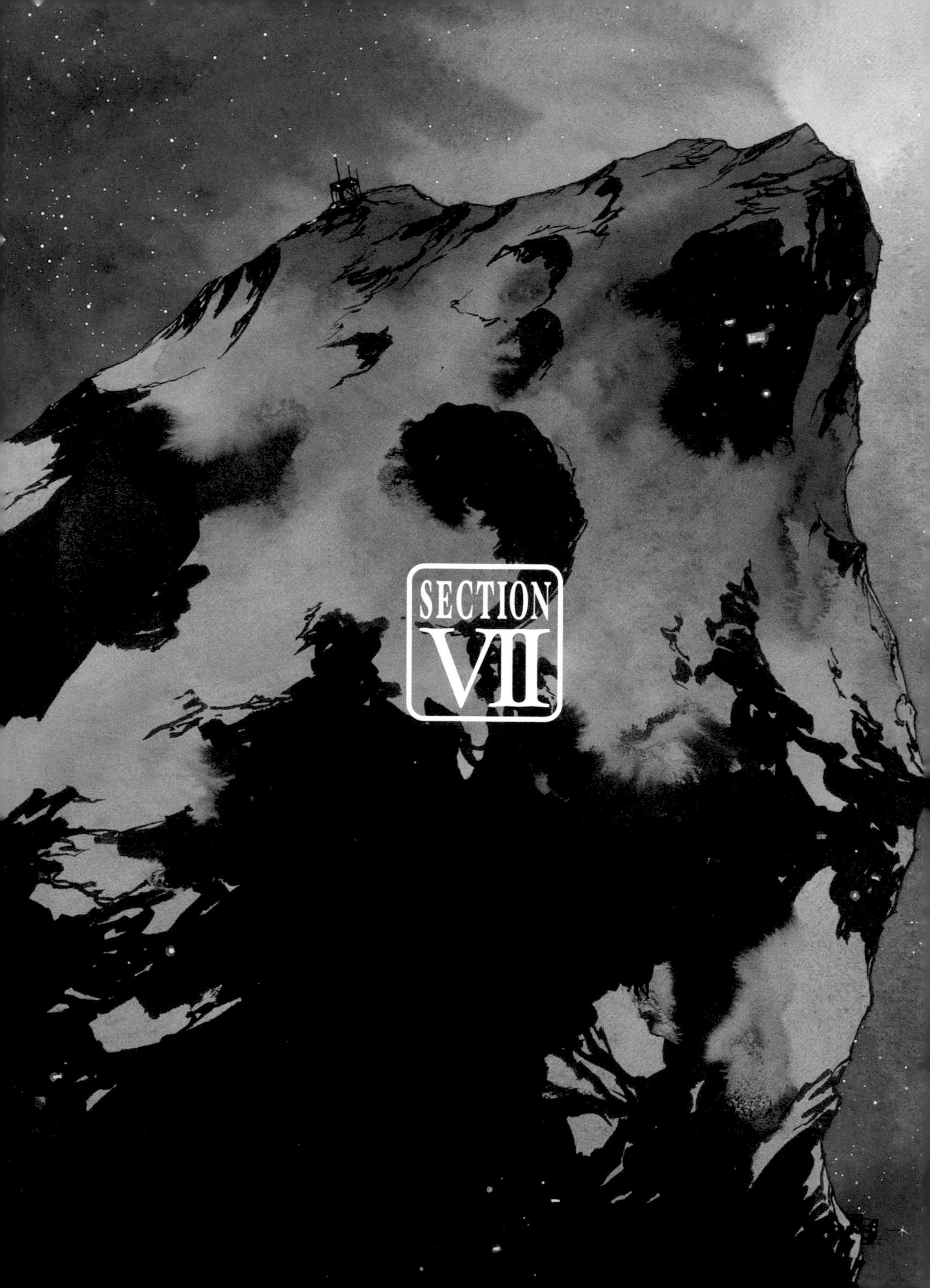
SECTION
VII

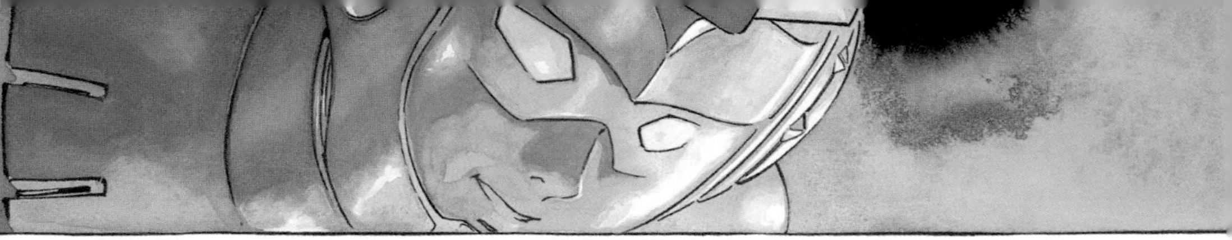

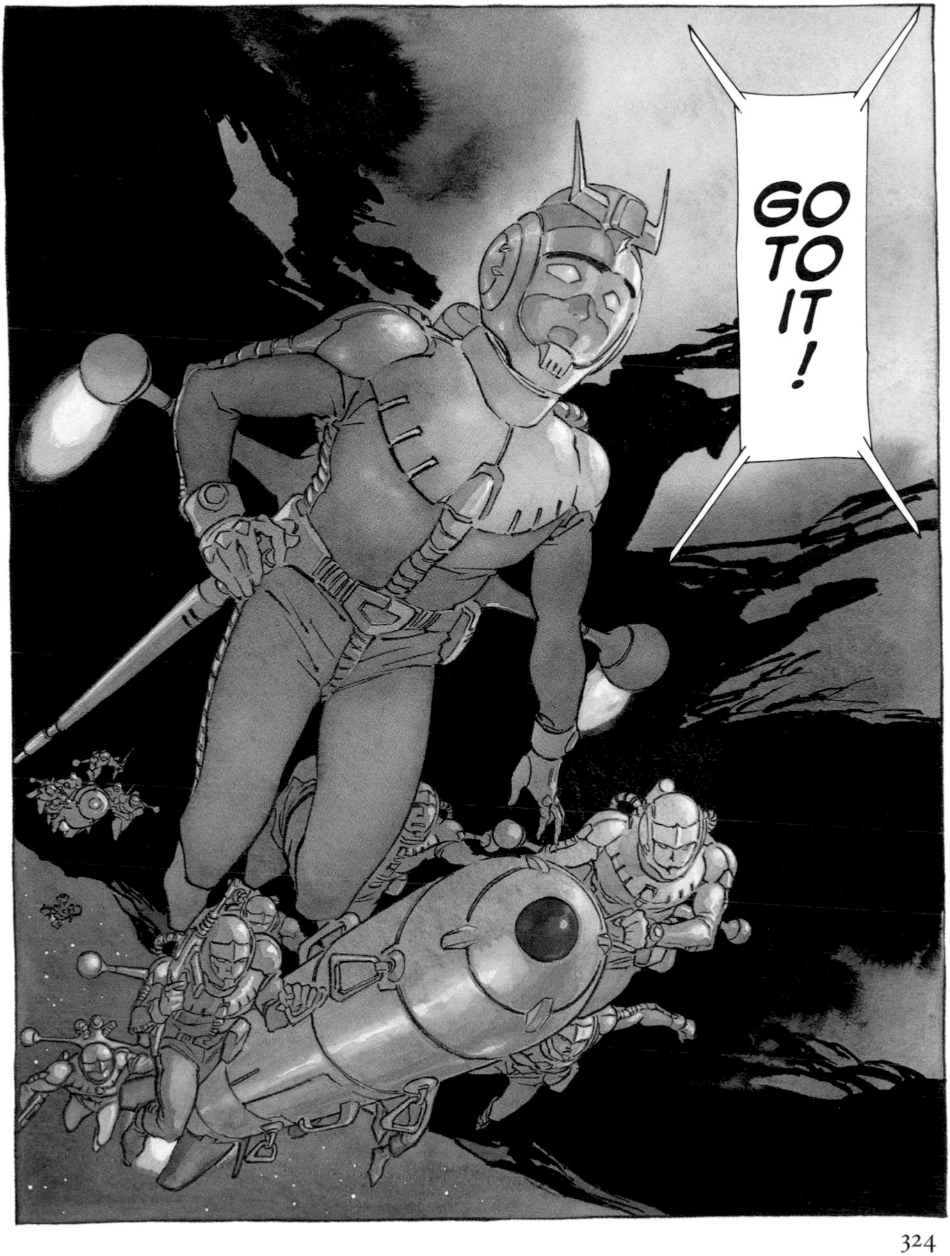
GO TO IT!

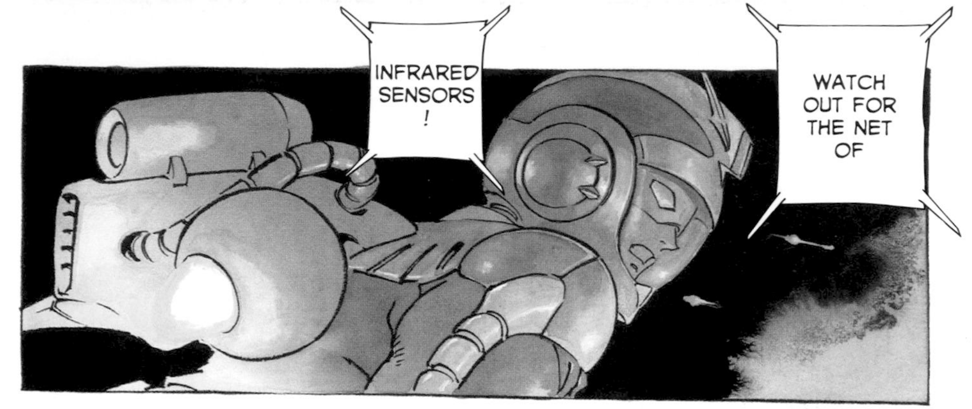
WATCH OUT FOR THE NET OF
INFRARED SENSORS!
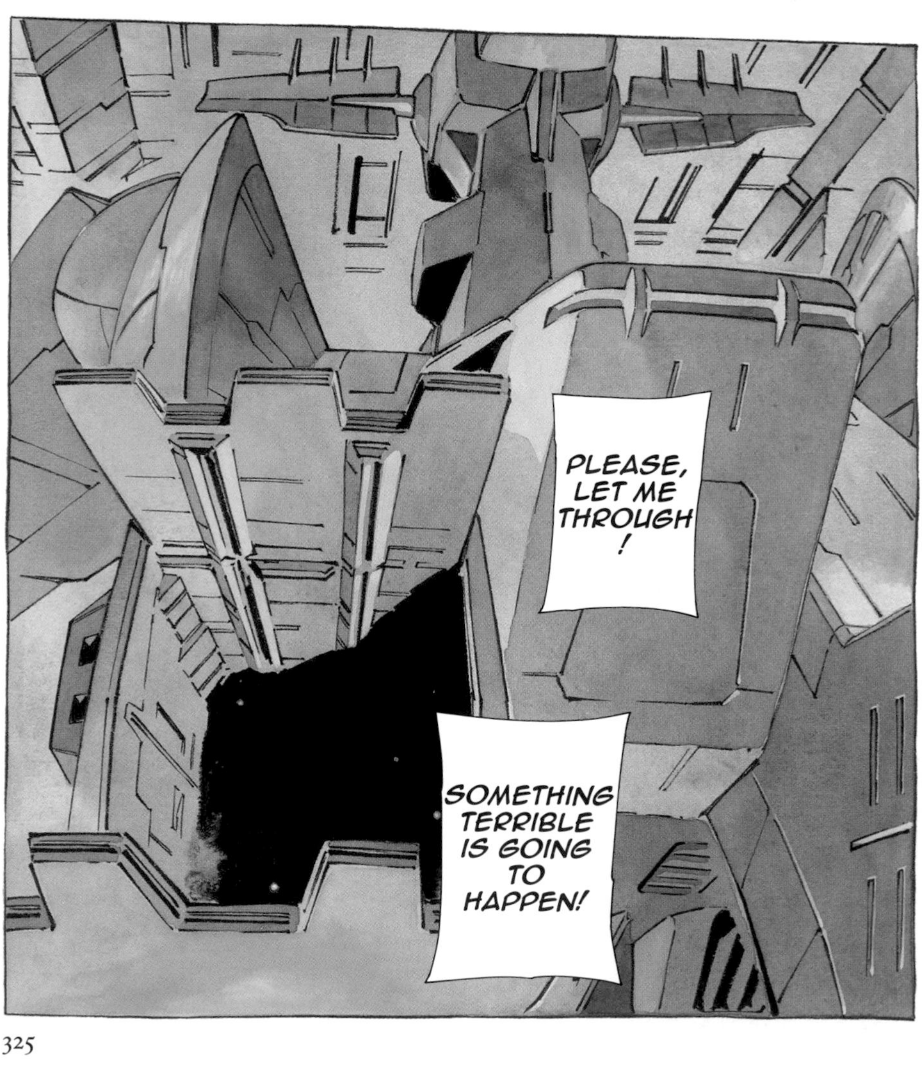
PLEASE, LET ME THROUGH!
SOMETHING TERRIBLE IS GOING TO HAPPEN!

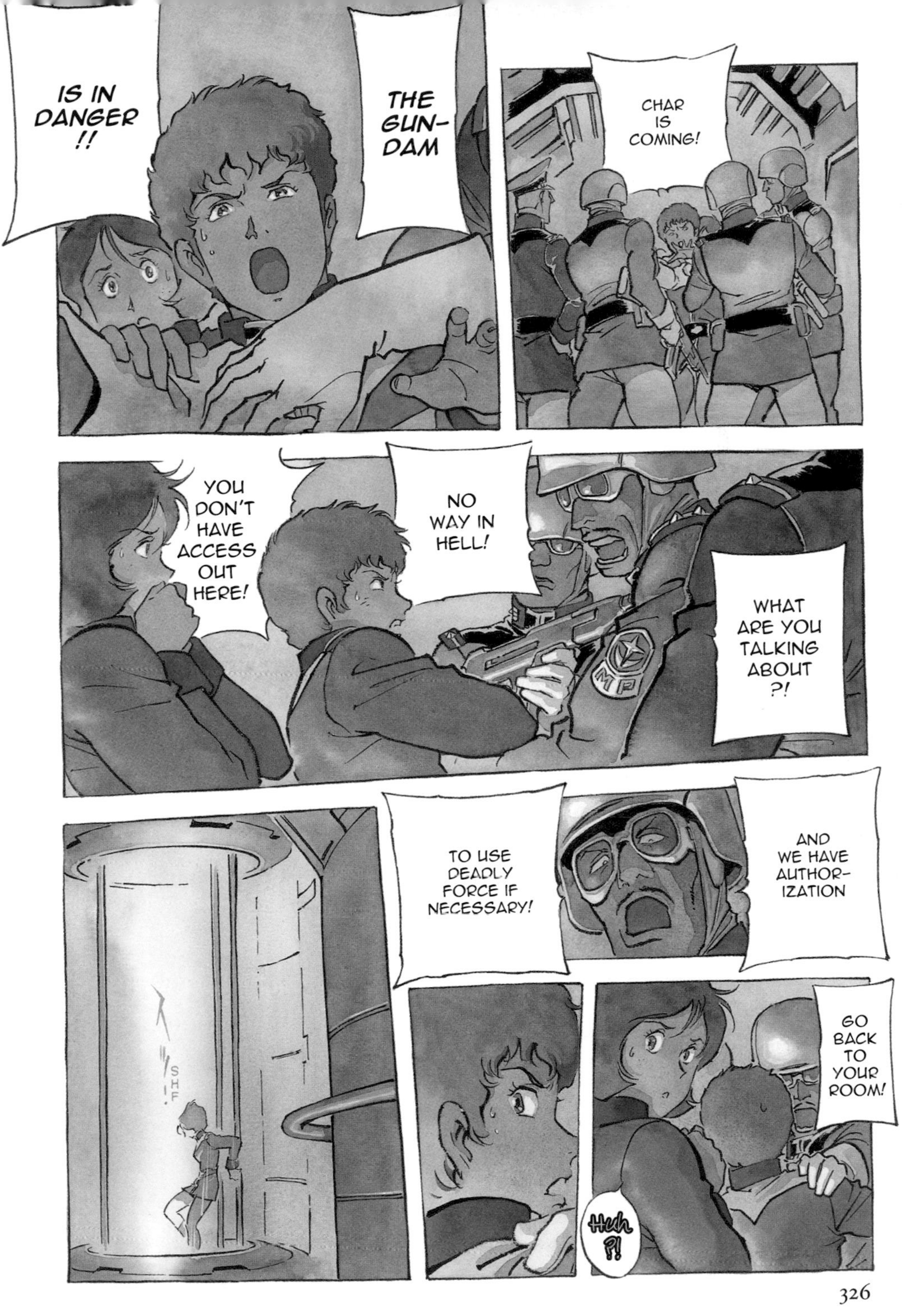
CHAR IS COMING!
THE GUN-DAM
IS IN DANGER!!
WHAT ARE YOU TALKING ABOUT?!
NO WAY IN HELL!
YOU DON'T HAVE ACCESS OUT HERE!
AND WE HAVE AUTHOR-IZATION
TO USE DEADLY FORCE IF NECESSARY!
GO BACK TO YOUR ROOM!
Huh?!
SHF

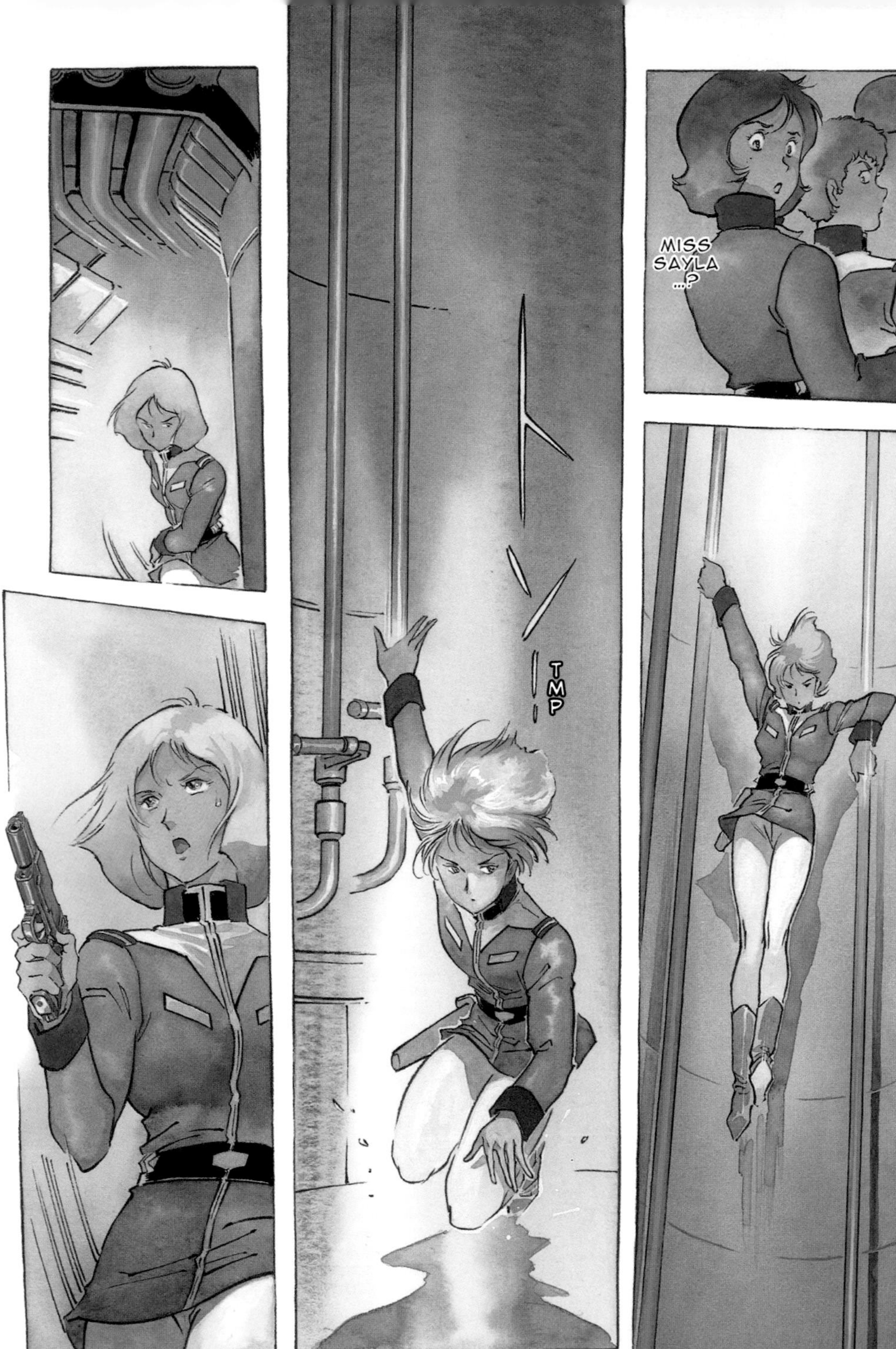
MISS SAYLA ...?
TMP

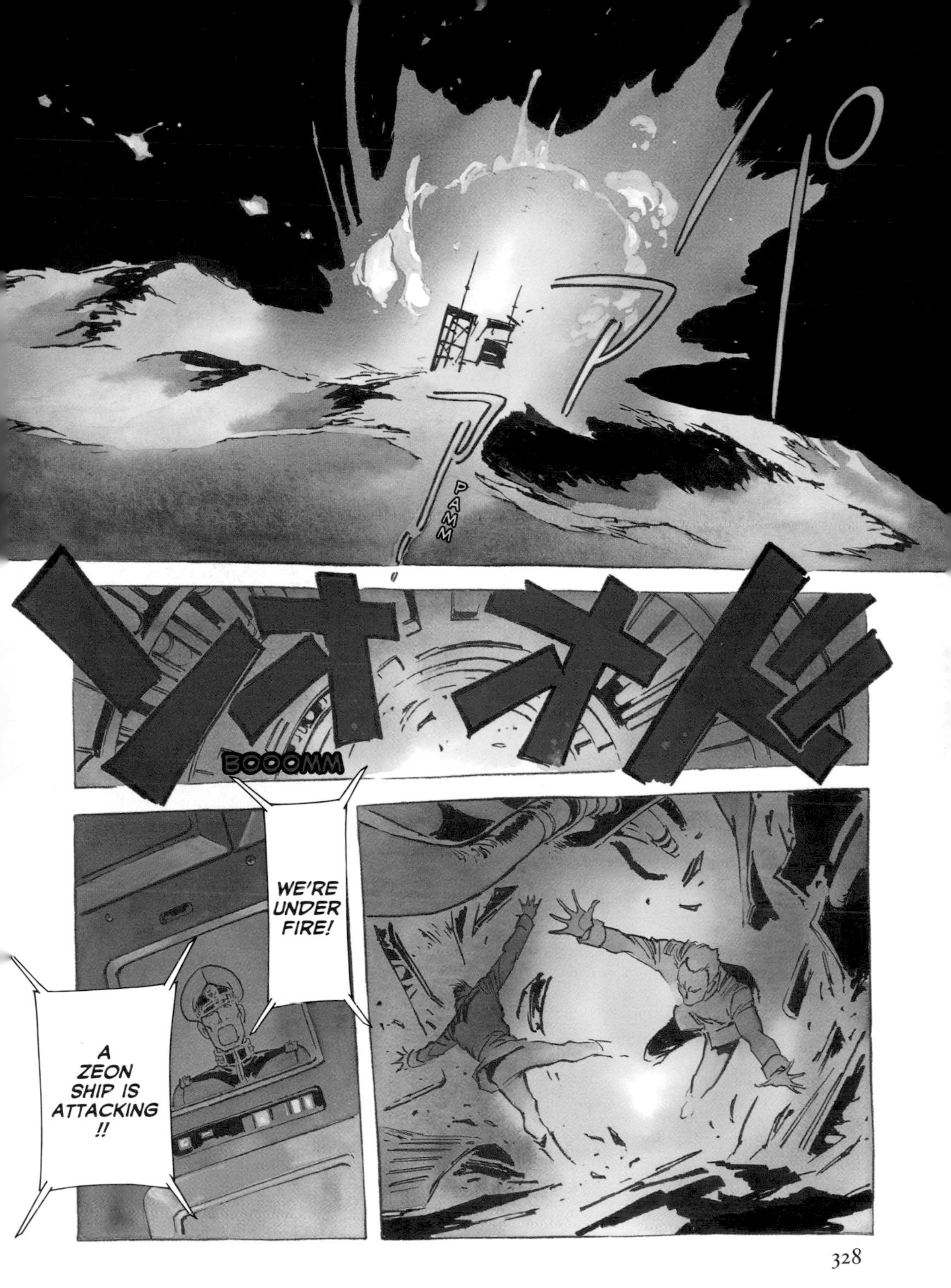
PAMM
BOOOMM
WE'RE UNDER FIRE!
A ZEON SHIP IS ATTACKING!!

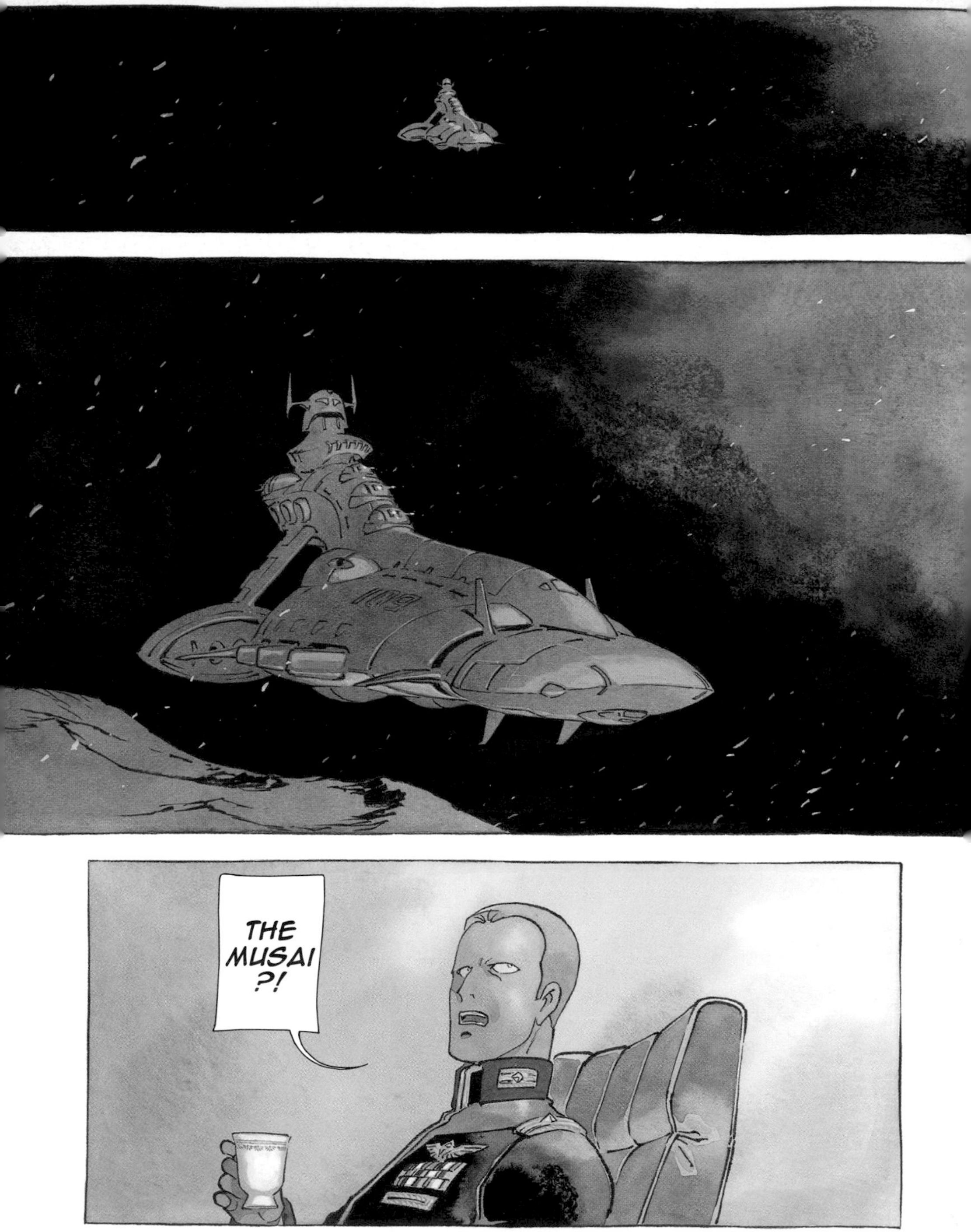
THE MUSAI ?!

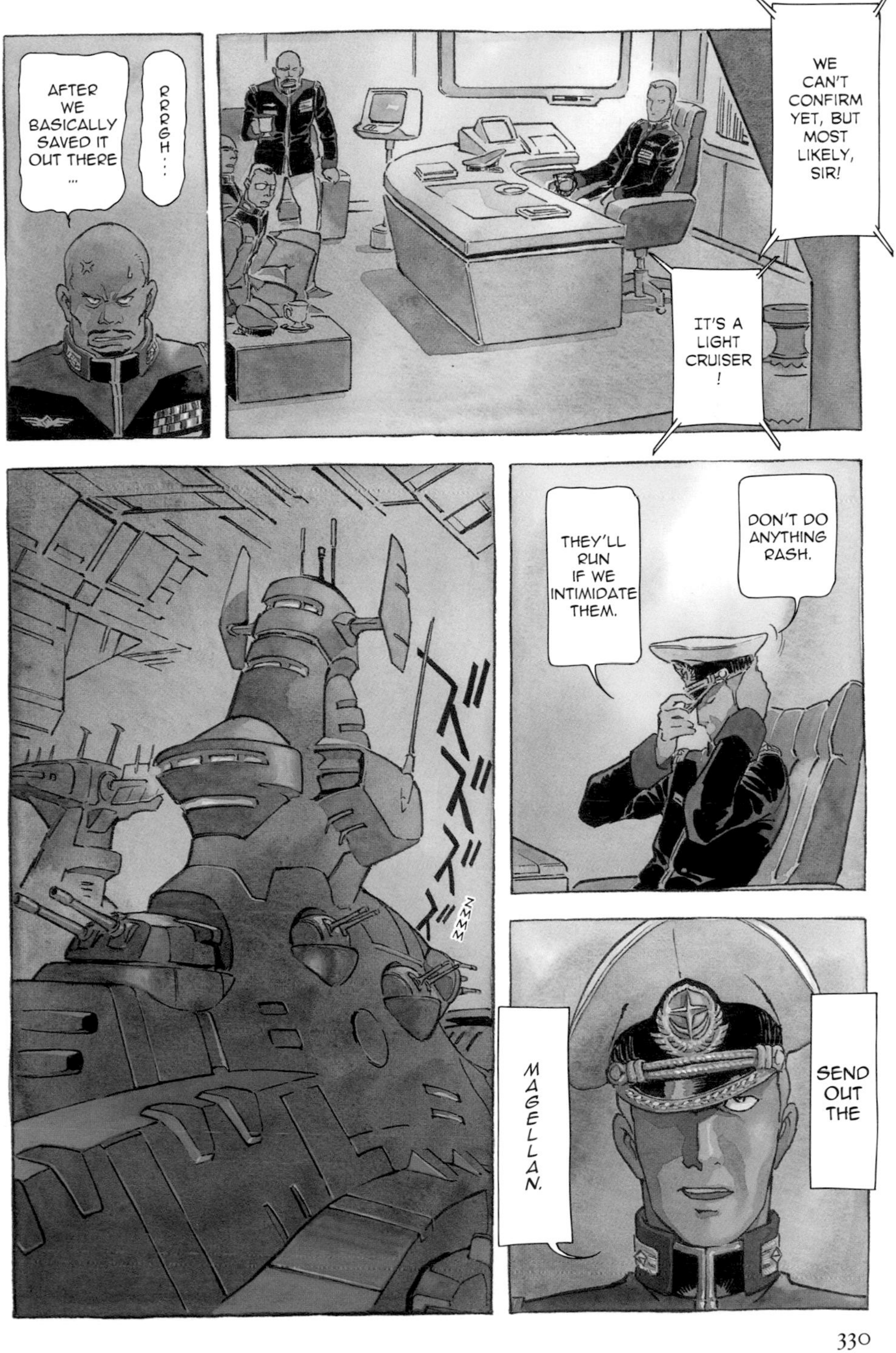
WE CAN'T CONFIRM YET, BUT MOST LIKELY, SIR!
IT'S A LIGHT CRUISER!
RRRGH...
AFTER WE BASICALLY SAVED IT OUT THERE...
DON'T DO ANYTHING RASH.
THEY'LL RUN IF WE INTIMIDATE THEM.
SEND OUT THE
MAGELLAN.
ZMMM

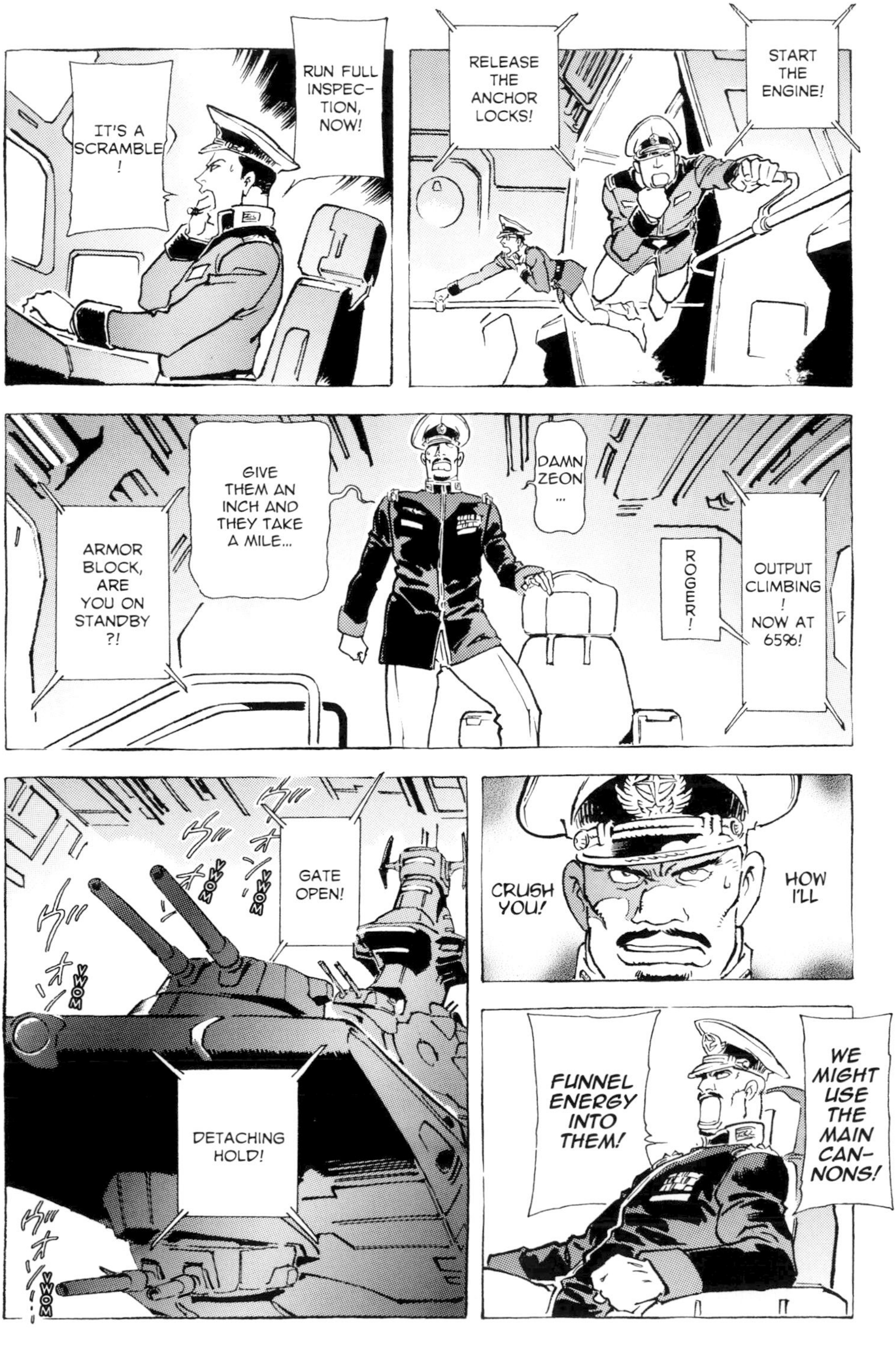
START THE ENGINE!
RELEASE THE ANCHOR LOCKS!
RUN FULL INSPECTION, NOW!
IT'S A SCRAMBLE!
OUTPUT CLIMBING! NOW AT 65%!
ROGER!
DAMN ZEON...
GIVE THEM AN INCH AND THEY TAKE A MILE...
ARMOR BLOCK, ARE YOU ON STANDBY?!
HOW I'LL
CRUSH YOU!
WE MIGHT USE THE MAIN CANNONS!
FUNNEL ENERGY INTO THEM!
VWOM
GATE OPEN!
VWOM
VWOM
DETACHING HOLD!
VWOM

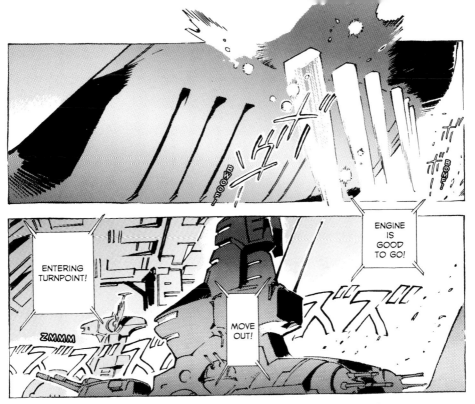

ENGINE
IS
GOOD
TO GO!

ENTERING
TURNPOINT!

MOVE
OUT!

ZMMM

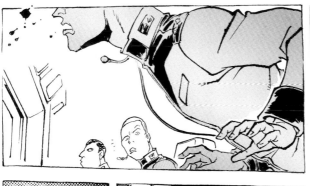

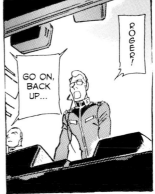

GO ON,
BACK
UP...

ROGER!

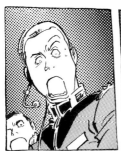

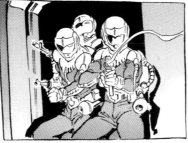

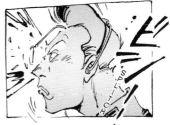

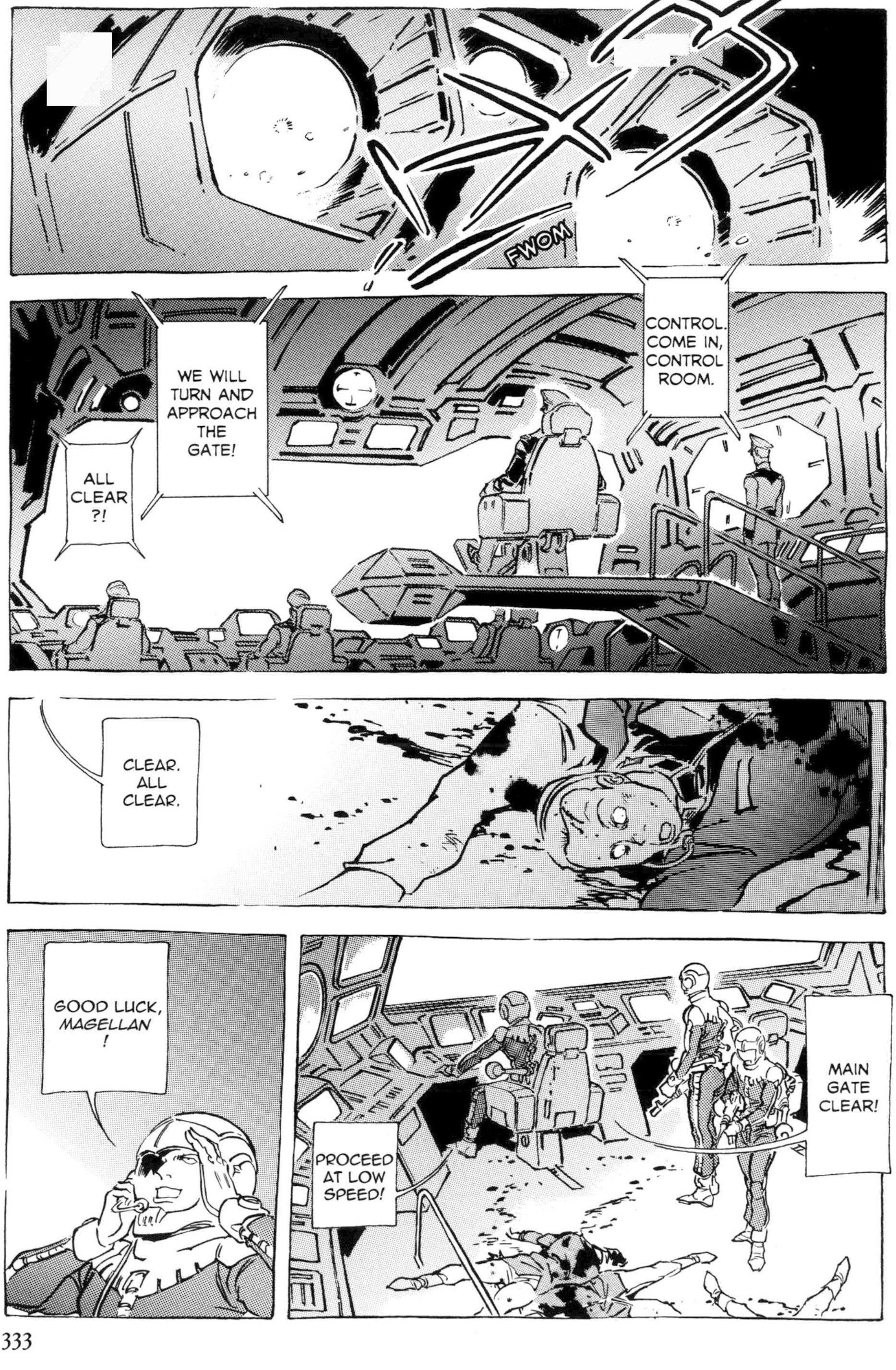
FWOM
CONTROL. COME IN, CONTROL ROOM.
WE WILL TURN AND APPROACH THE GATE!
ALL CLEAR ?!
CLEAR. ALL CLEAR.
MAIN GATE CLEAR!
PROCEED AT LOW SPEED!
GOOD LUCK, MAGELLAN !

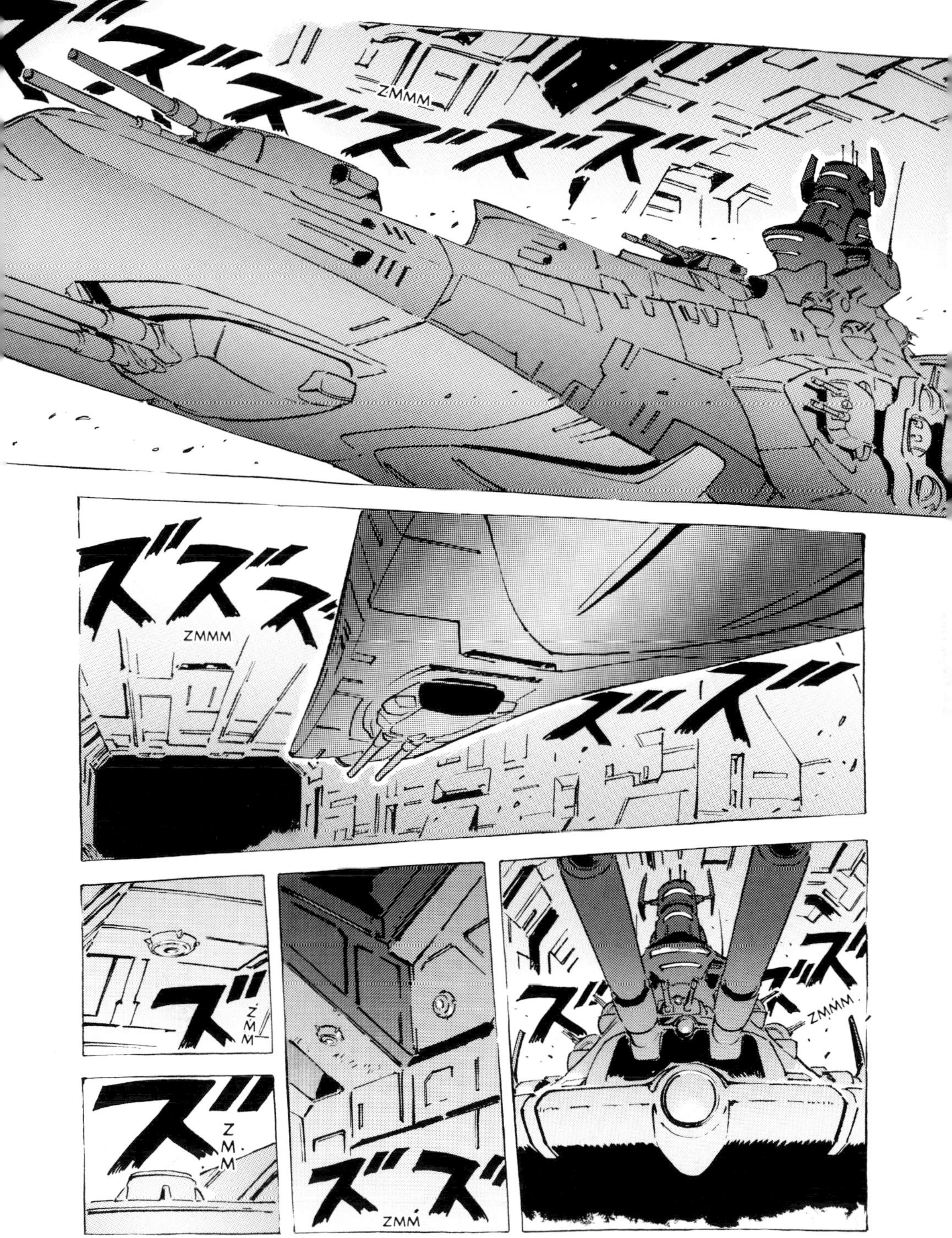
ズズズズズズズ
ZMMM
ズズズ
ZMMM
ズズ
ズズズ
ZMMM
ズズ
ZMM
ズ
ZMM
ズ
ZMM

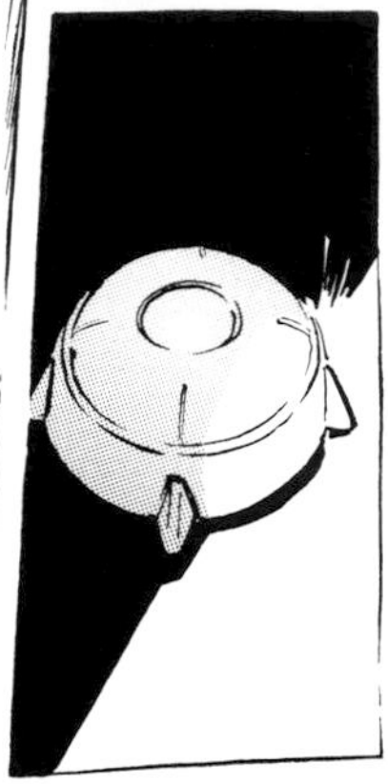

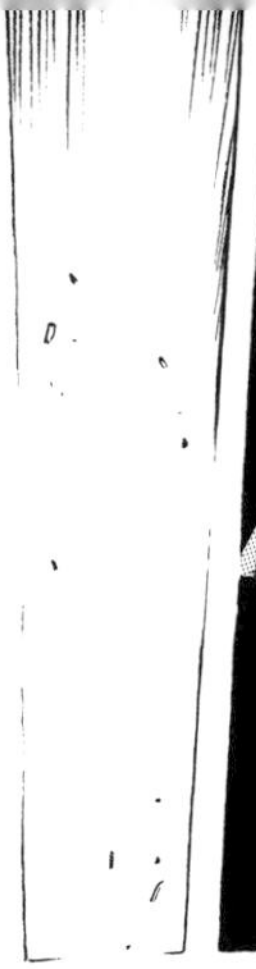

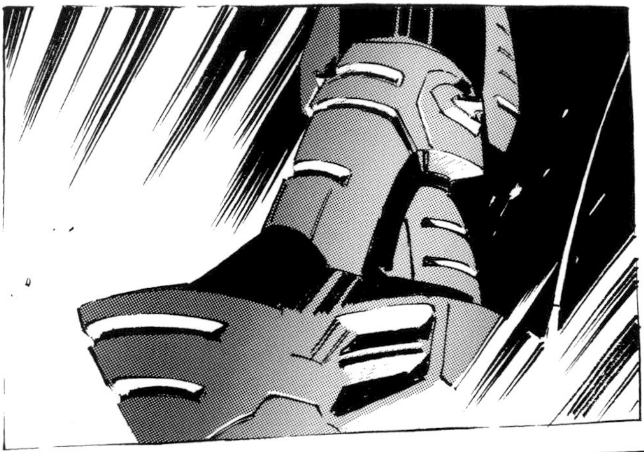

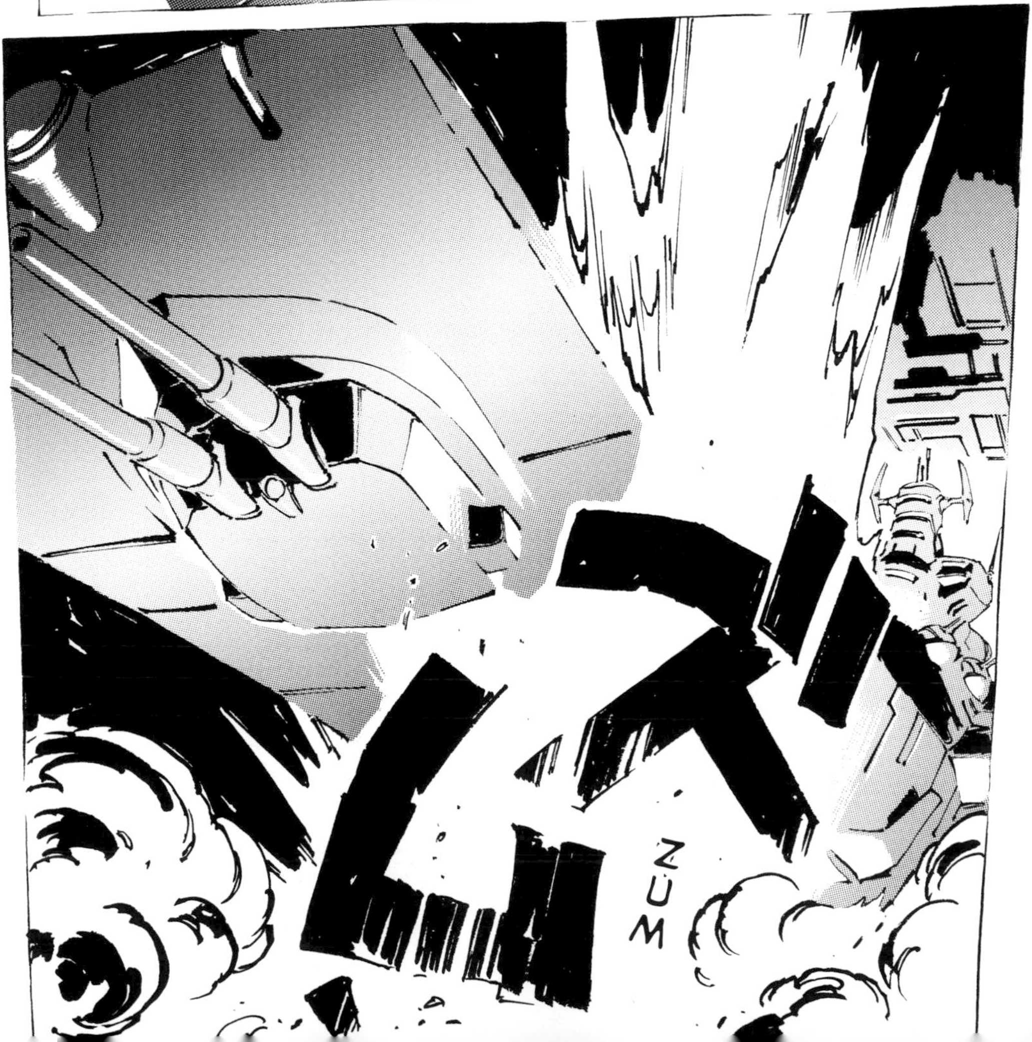
ZUM

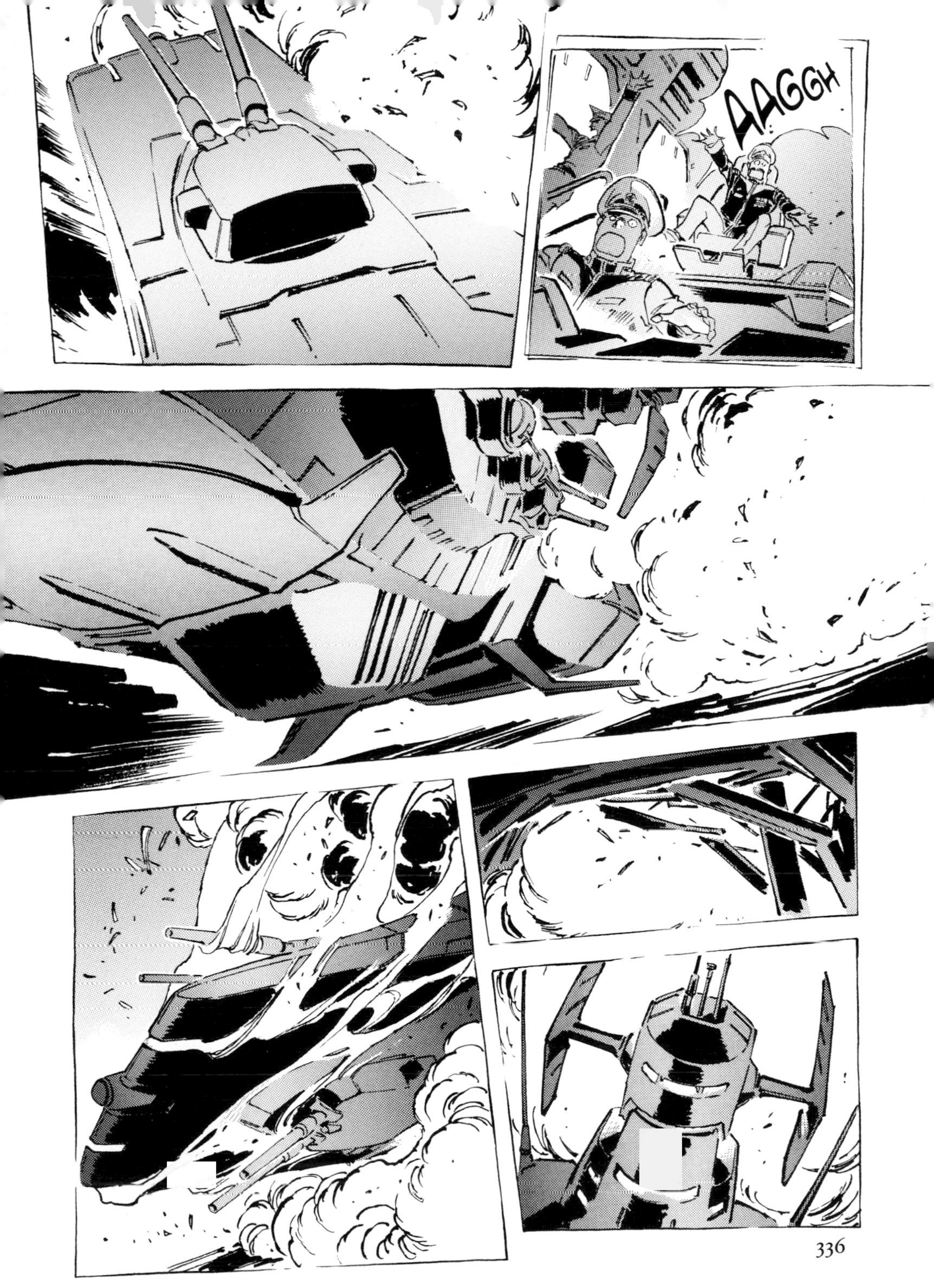
AAGGH

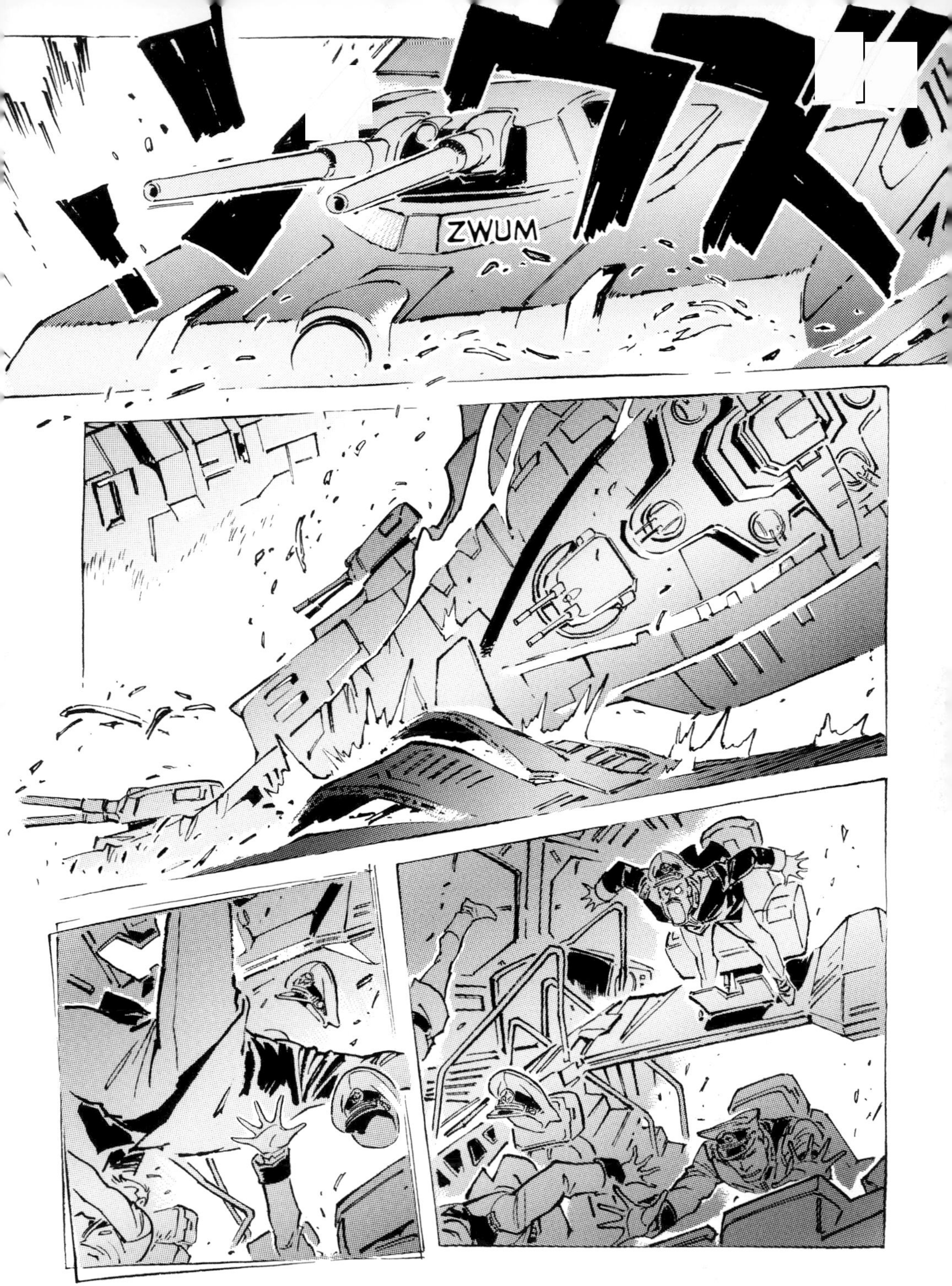
ZWUM

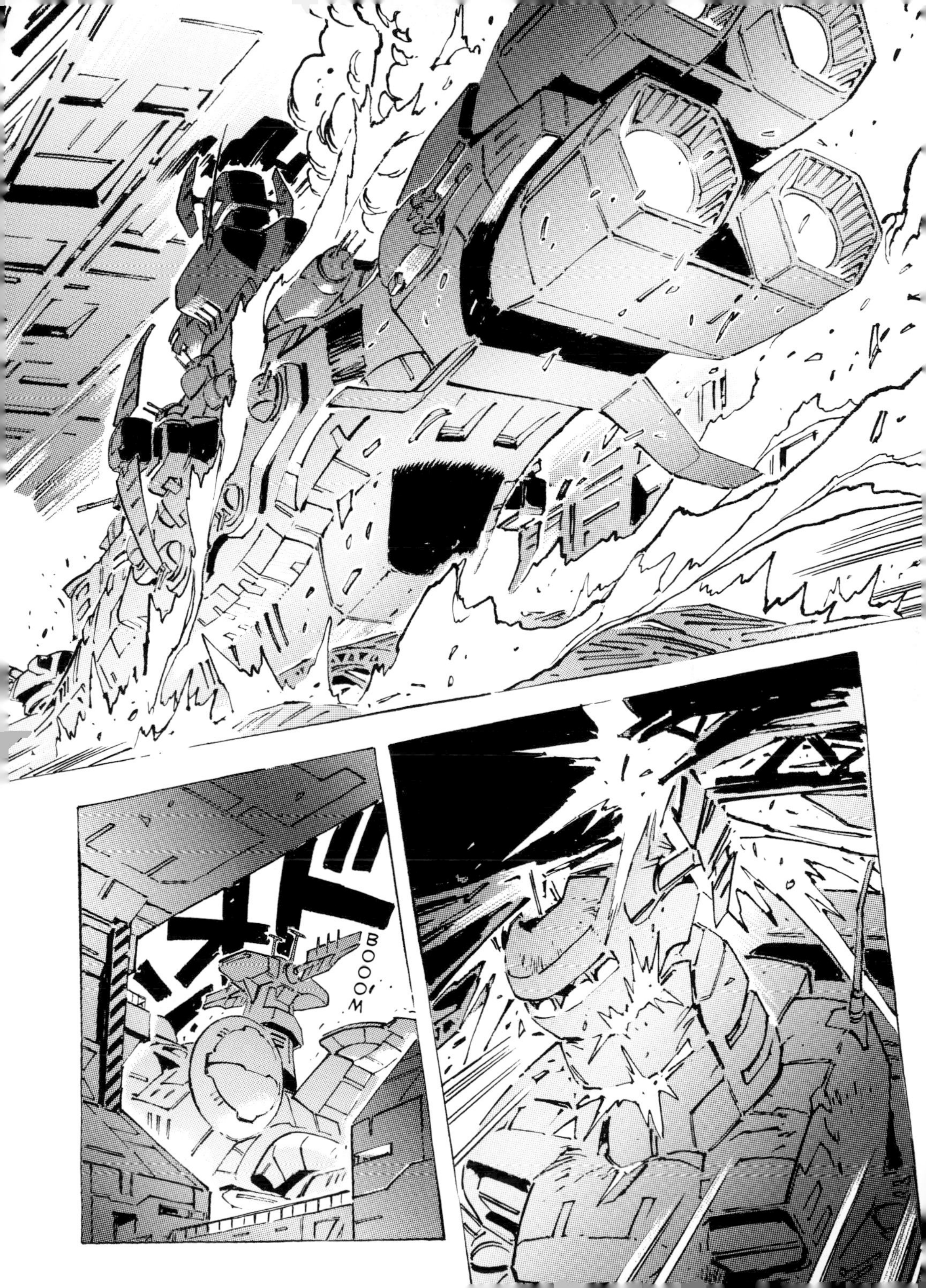
BOOOM

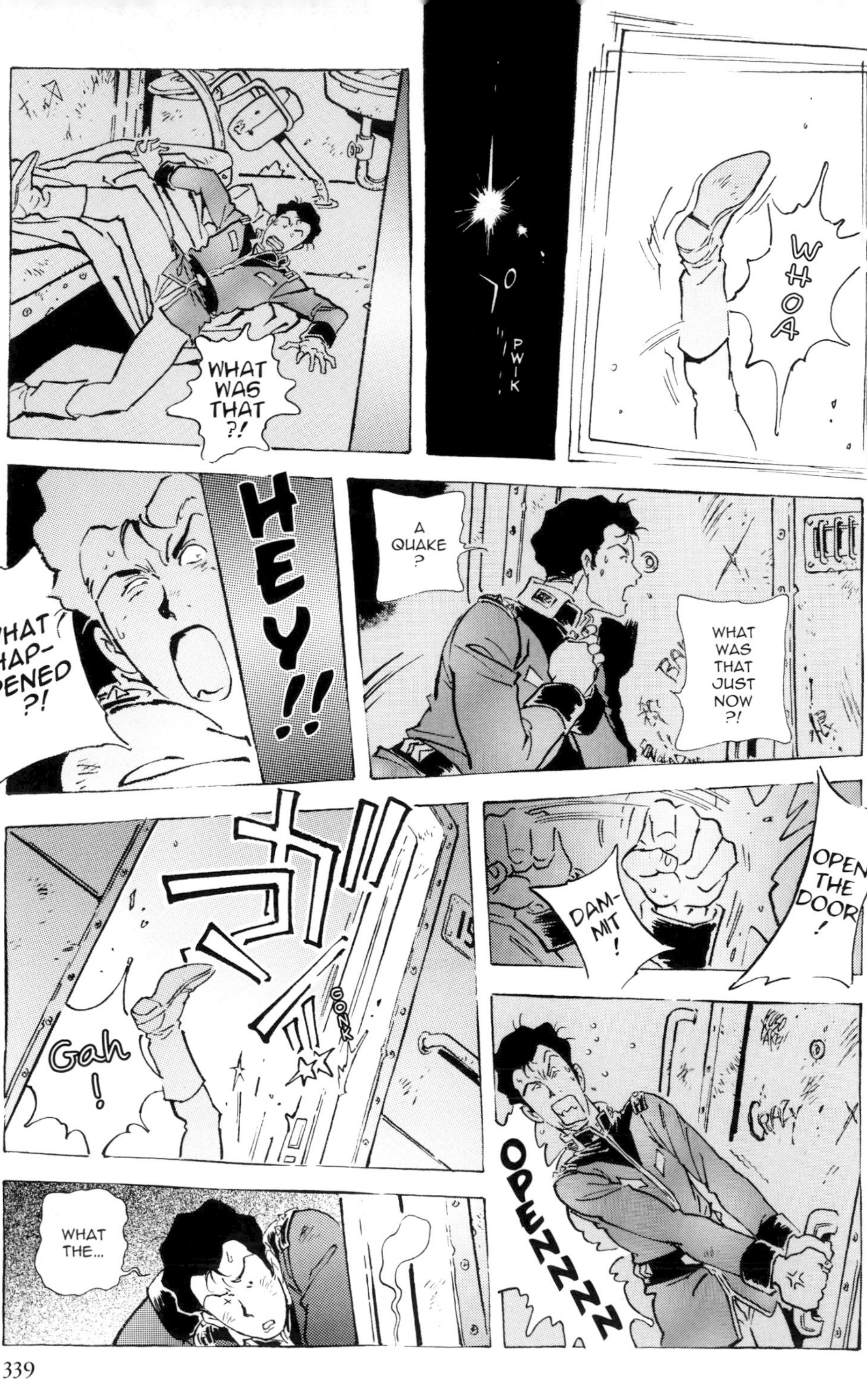
WHOA
PWIK
WHAT WAS THAT ?!
A QUAKE ?
WHAT WAS THAT JUST NOW ?!
HEY!!
WHAT HAP-PENED ?!
OPEN THE DOOR !
DAM-MIT !
OPENNNN
GONK
Gah !
WHAT THE...

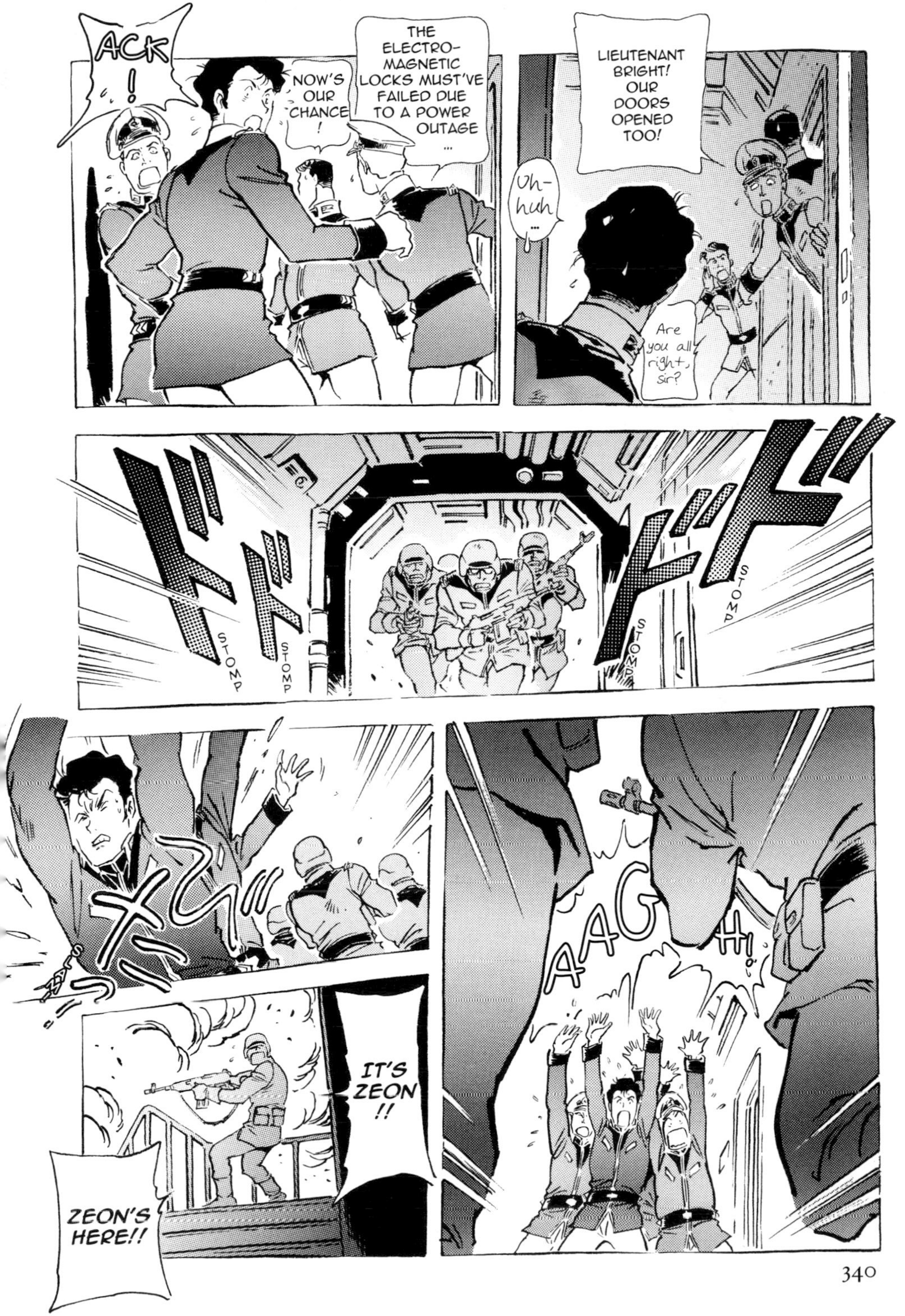
LIEUTENANT BRIGHT! OUR DOORS OPENED TOO!
Uh-huh...
Are you all right, sir?
THE ELECTRO-MAGNETIC LOCKS MUST'VE FAILED DUE TO A POWER OUTAGE...
NOW'S OUR CHANCE!
ACK!
STOMP
STOMP
STOMP
STOMP
AAGH!
IT'S ZEON!!
ZEON'S HERE!!

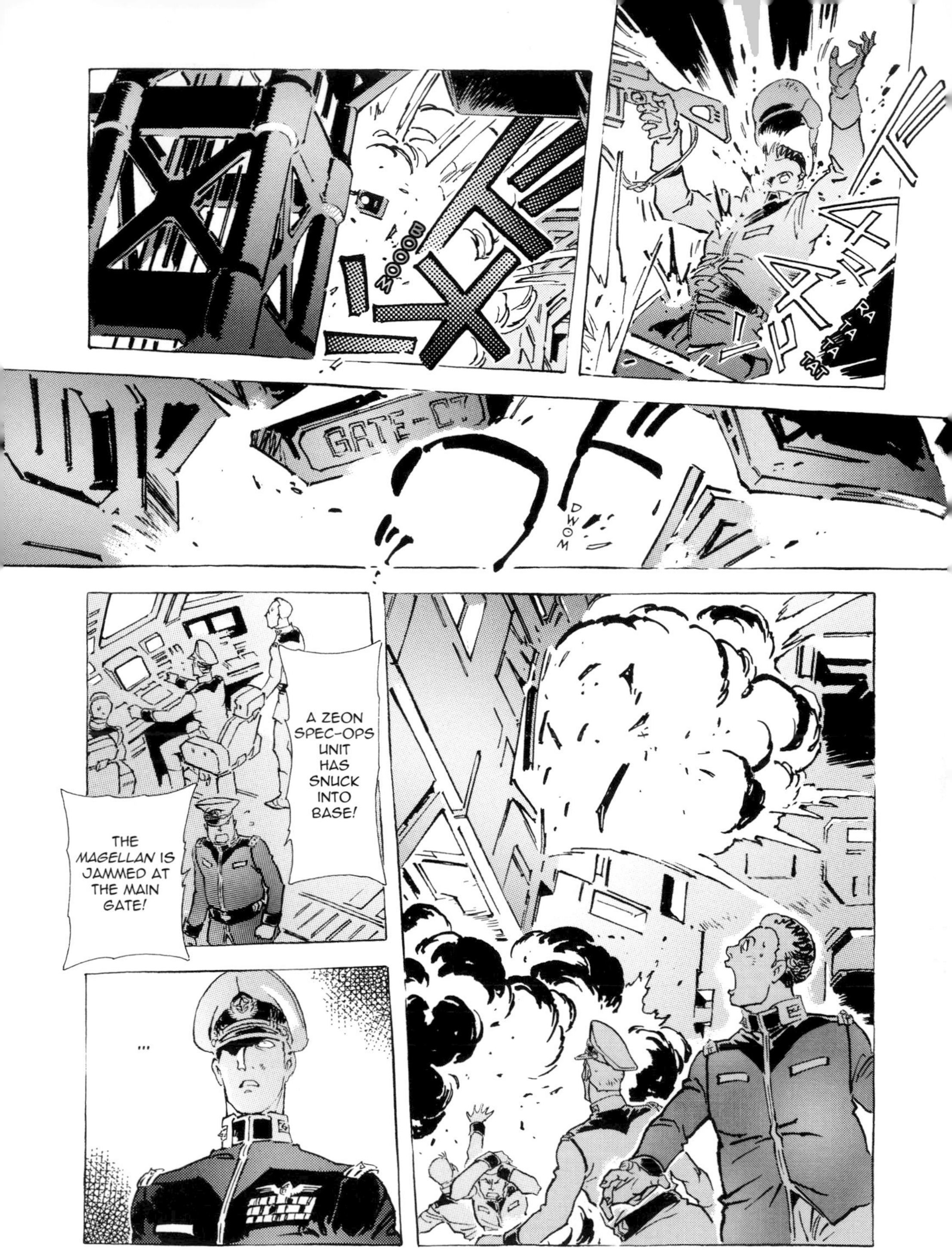
RA TA TA TAT
WOOOM
GATE-C7
DWOM
A ZEON SPEC-OPS UNIT HAS SNUCK INTO BASE!
THE MAGELLAN IS JAMMED AT THE MAIN GATE!
...

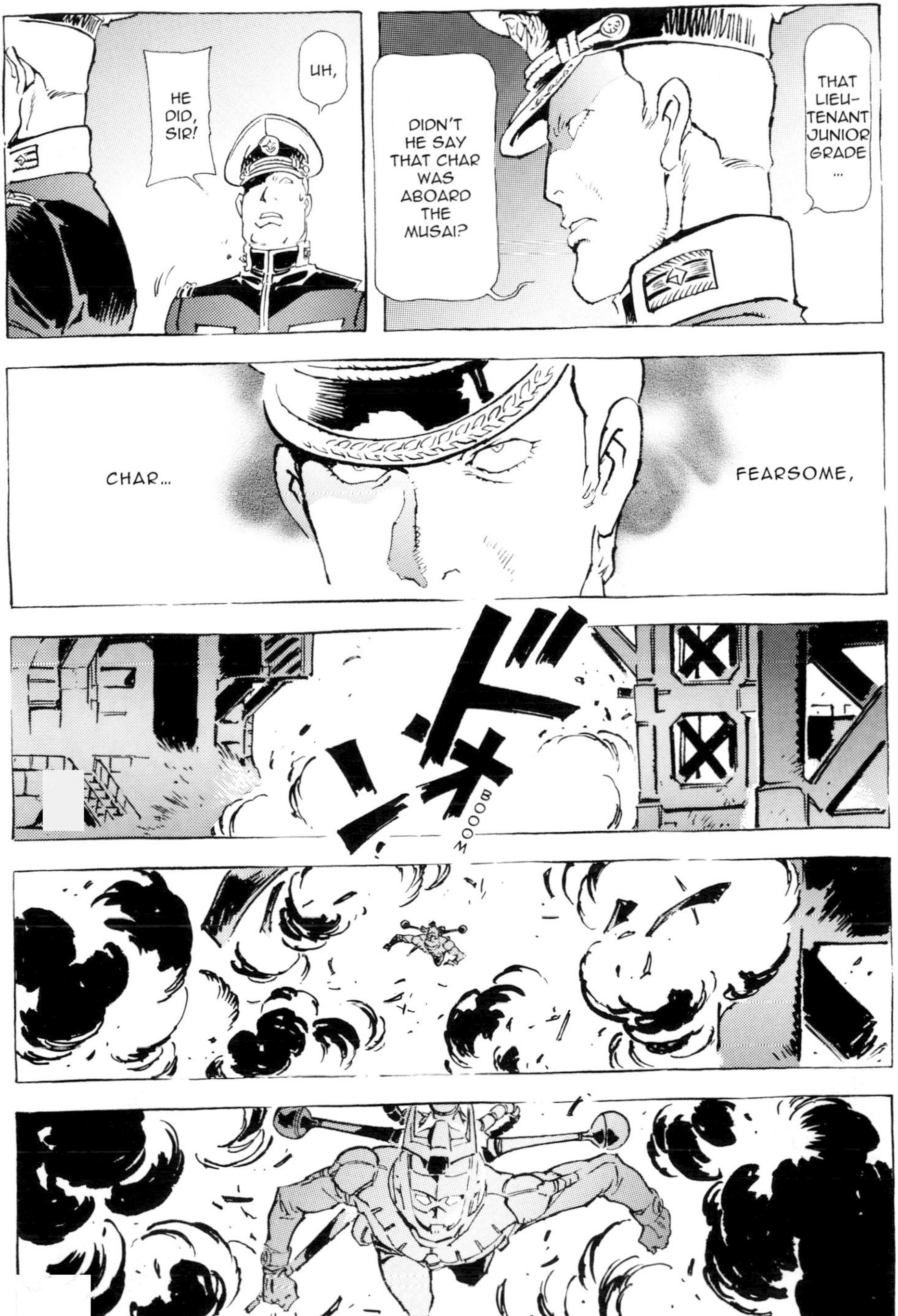

THAT LIEU-TENANT JUNIOR GRADE ...
DIDN'T HE SAY THAT CHAR WAS ABOARD THE MUSAI?
UH,
HE DID, SIR!
CHAR...
FEARSOME,
ドォン
BOOOM

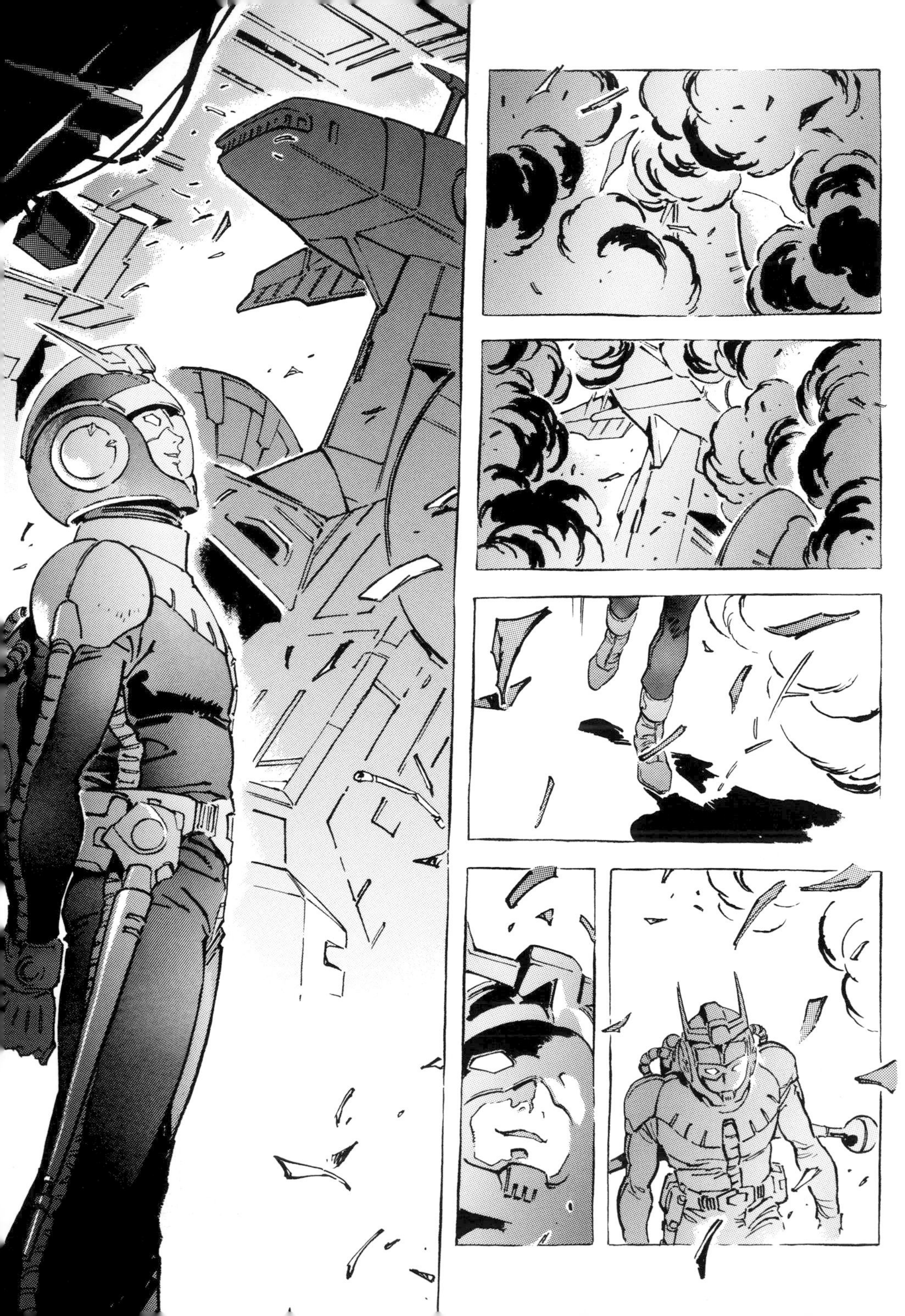

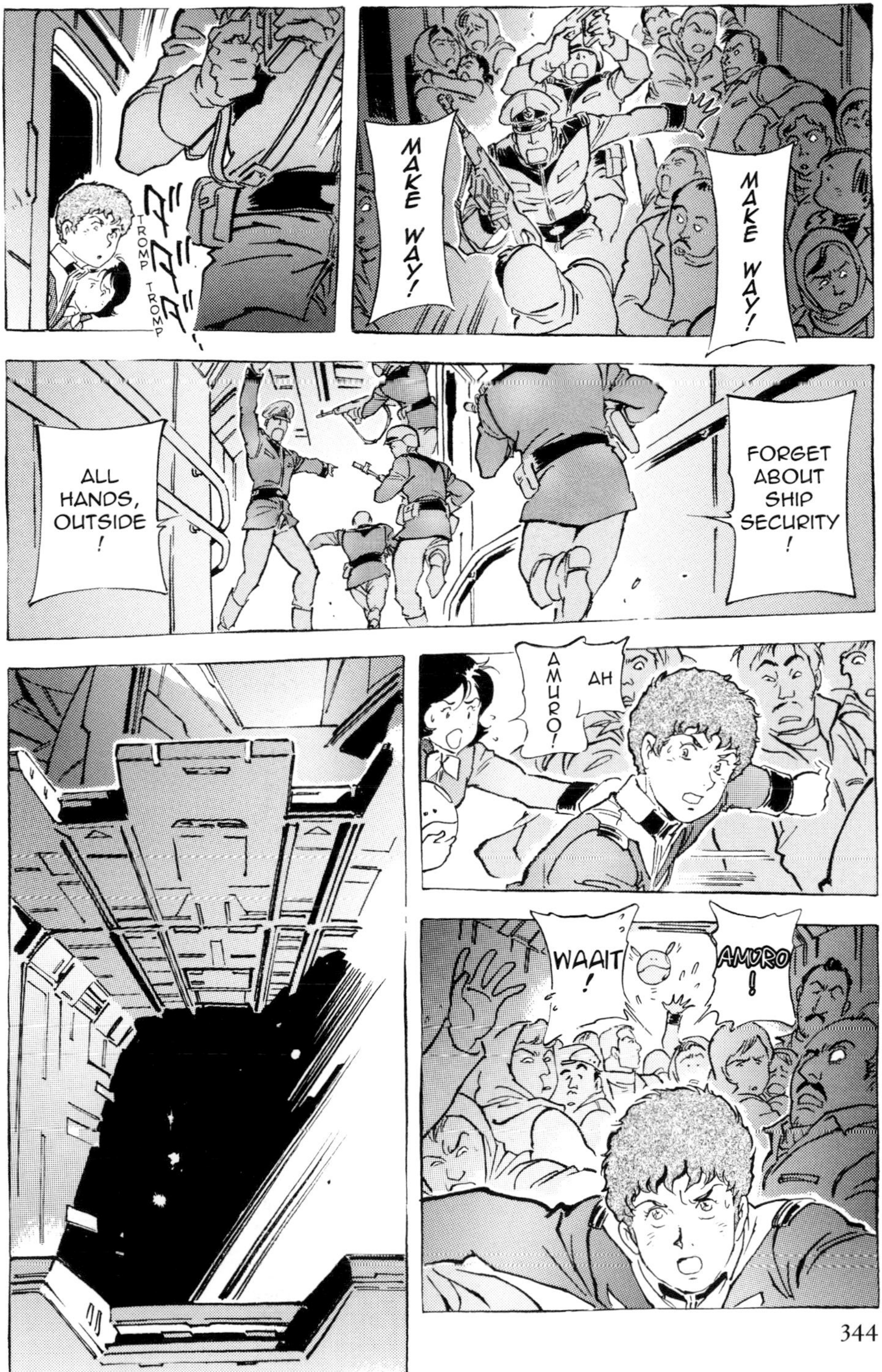
MAKE WAY!
MAKE WAY!
TROMP TROMP
FORGET ABOUT SHIP SECURITY!
ALL HANDS, OUTSIDE!
AH
AMURO!
AMURO!
WAAIT!

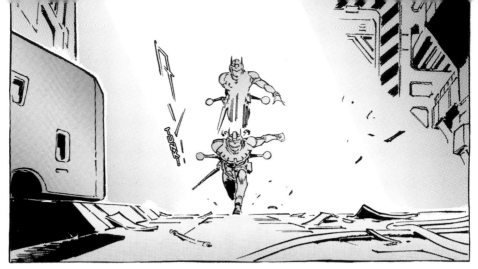

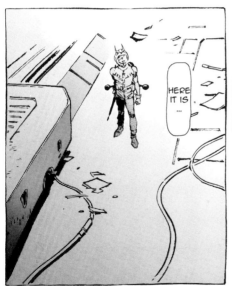

HERE IT IS ...

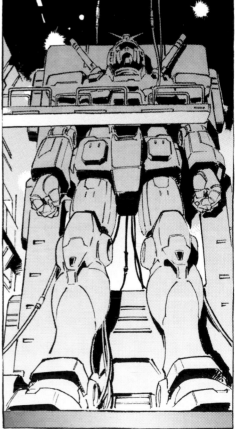

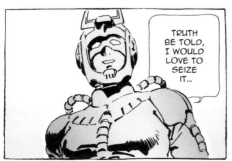

TRUTH BE TOLD, I WOULD LOVE TO SEIZE IT...

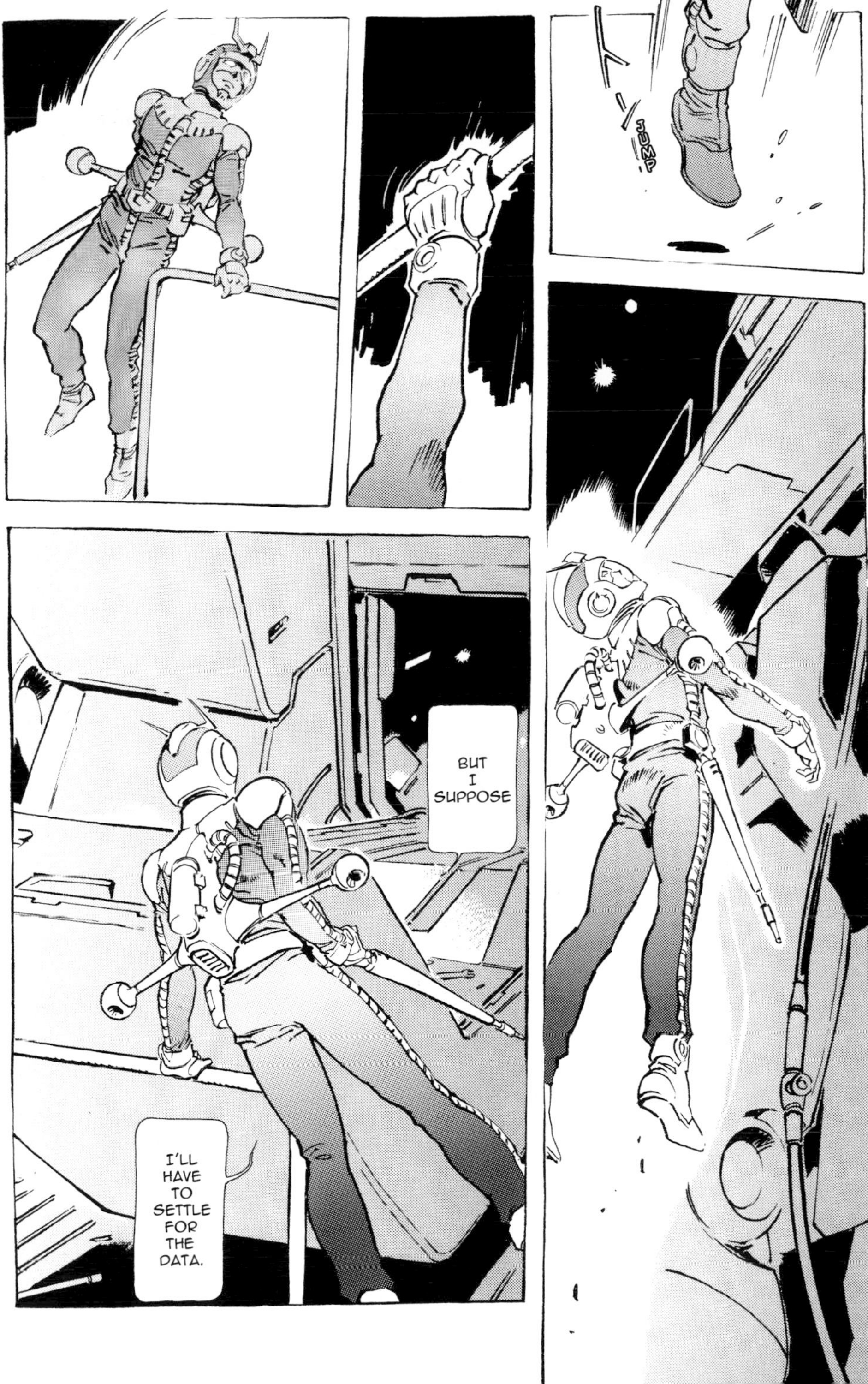
JUMP
BUT I SUPPOSE
I'LL HAVE TO SETTLE FOR THE DATA.

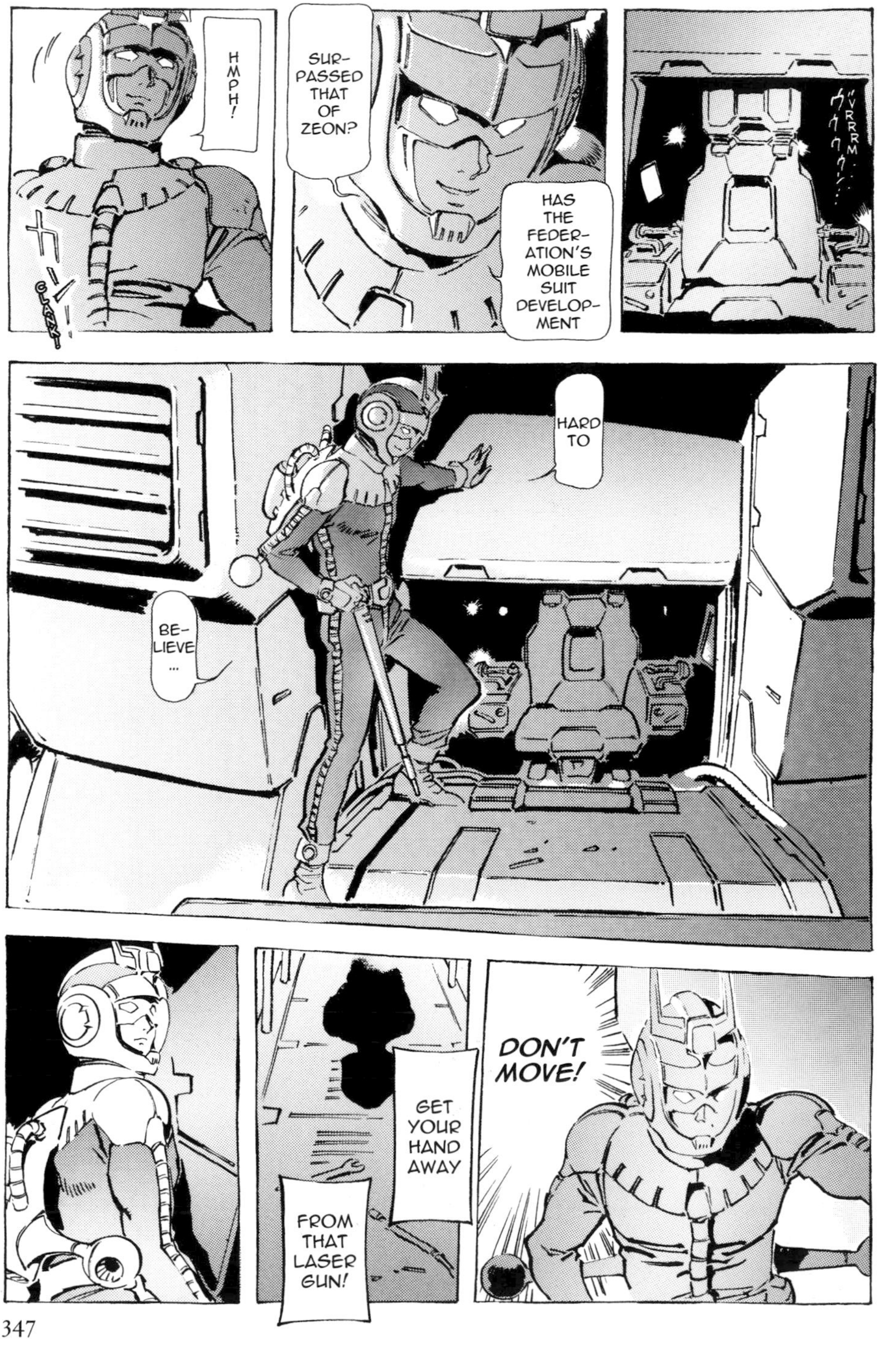
VRRM...
HAS THE FEDERATION'S MOBILE SUIT DEVELOPMENT
SURPASSED THAT OF ZEON?
HMPH!
CLANK!
HARD TO
BELIEVE...
DON'T MOVE!
GET YOUR HAND AWAY
FROM THAT LASER GUN!

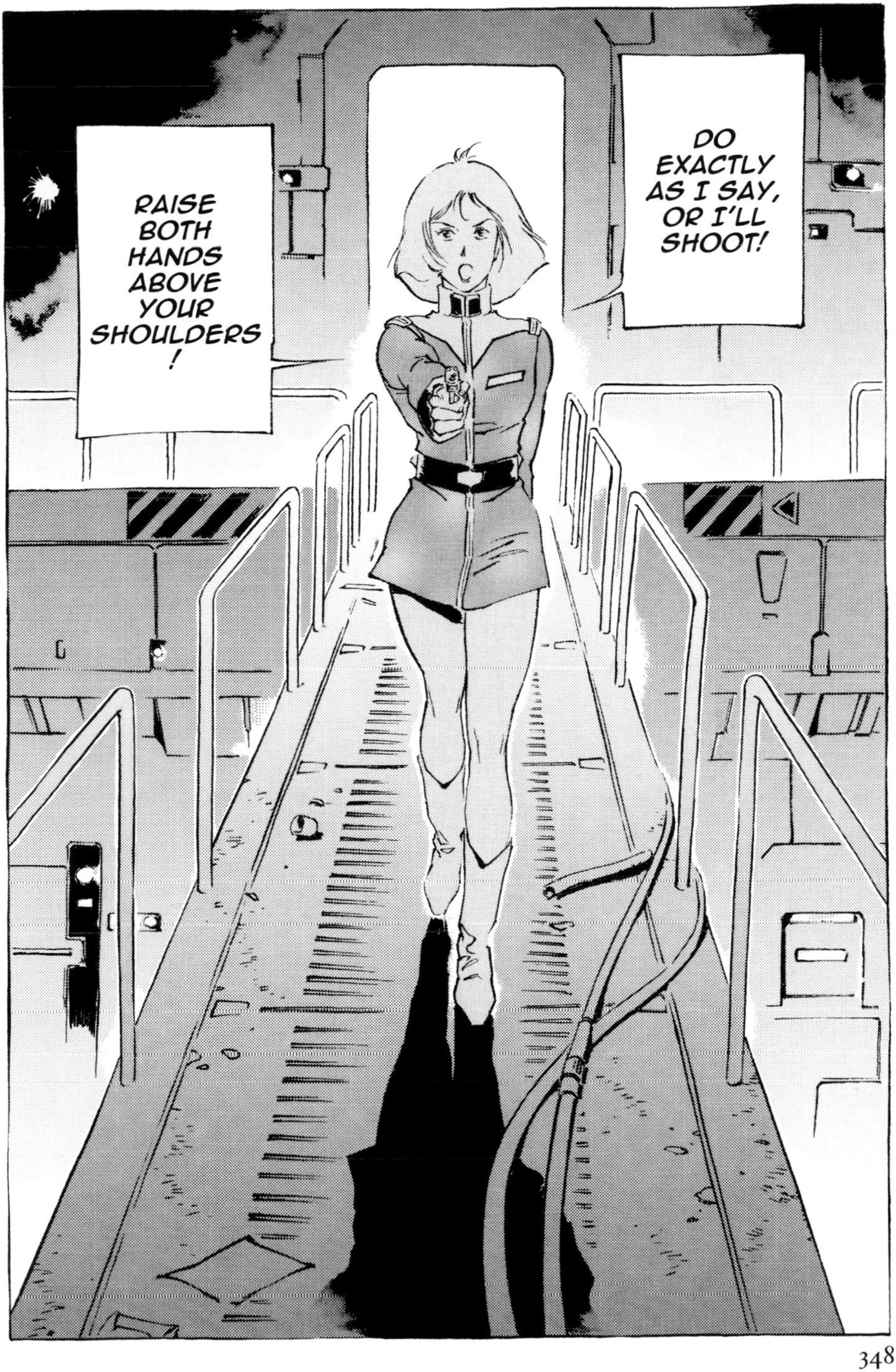
DO EXACTLY AS I SAY, OR I'LL SHOOT!
RAISE BOTH HANDS ABOVE YOUR SHOULDERS!

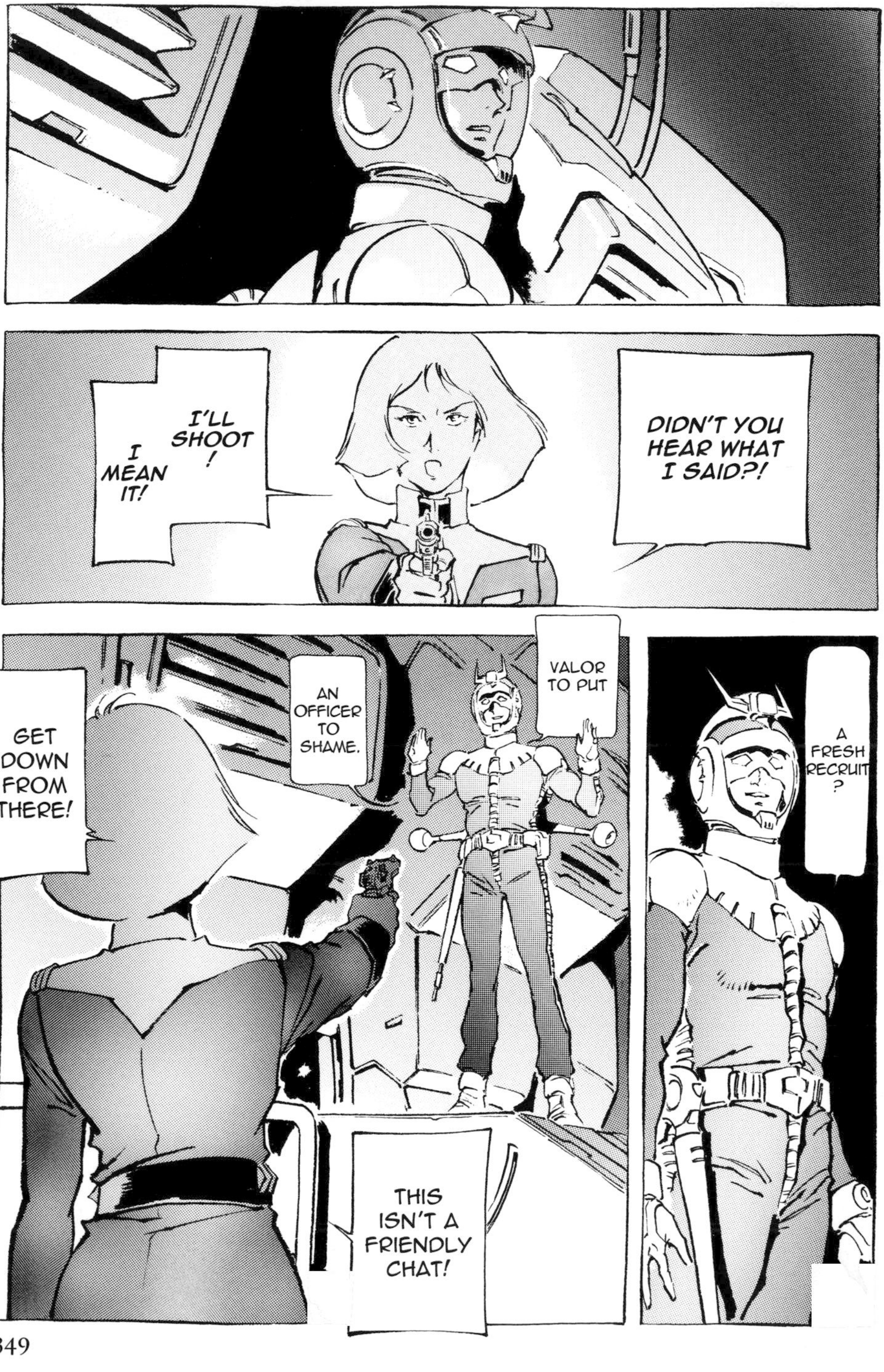
DIDN'T YOU HEAR WHAT I SAID?!
I'LL SHOOT!
I MEAN IT!
A FRESH RECRUIT?
VALOR TO PUT
AN OFFICER TO SHAME.
GET DOWN FROM THERE!
THIS ISN'T A FRIENDLY CHAT!

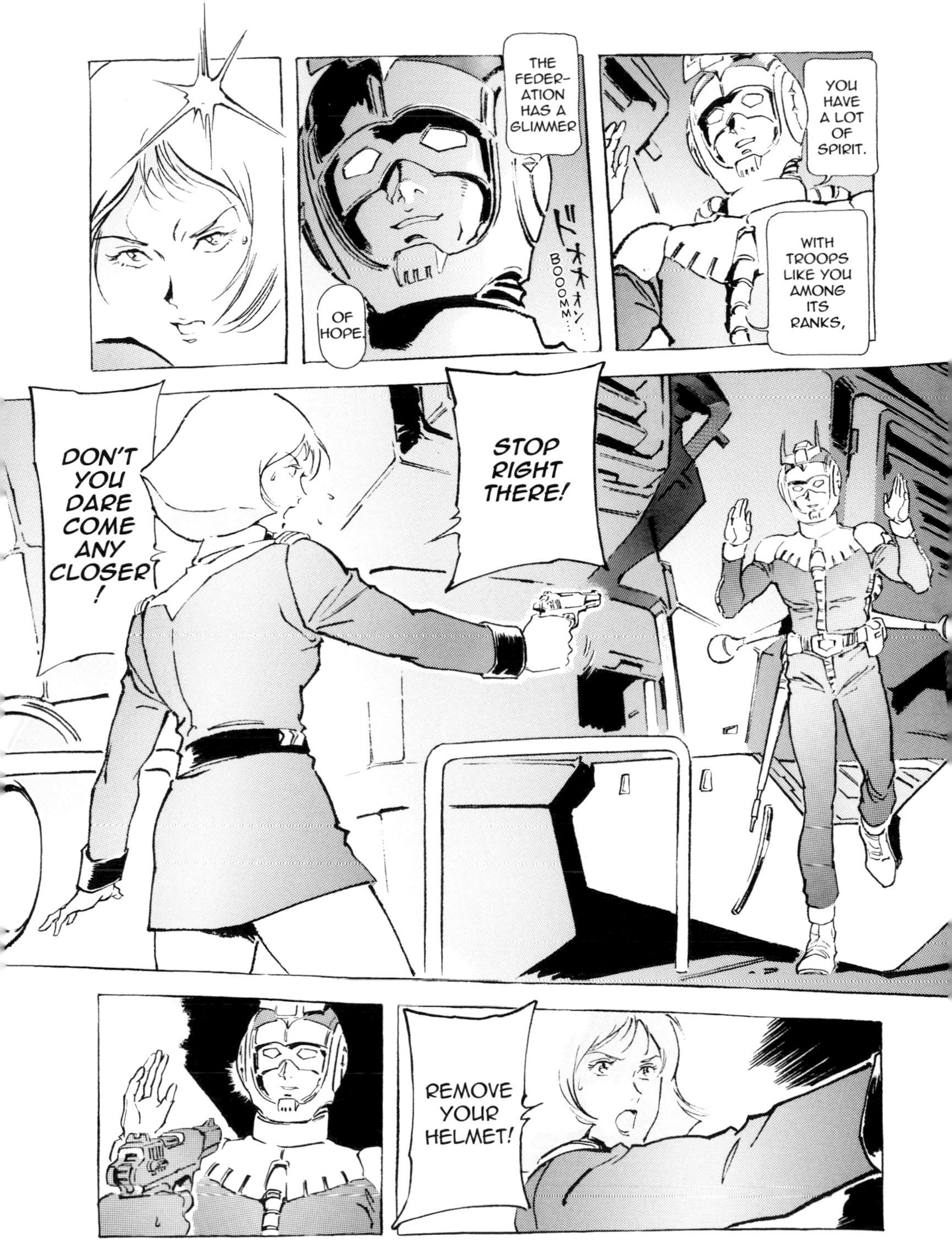
YOU HAVE A LOT OF SPIRIT.
WITH TROOPS LIKE YOU AMONG ITS RANKS,
THE FEDERATION HAS A GLIMMER
OF HOPE.
BOOOOMM...
STOP RIGHT THERE!
DON'T YOU DARE COME ANY CLOSER!
REMOVE YOUR HELMET!

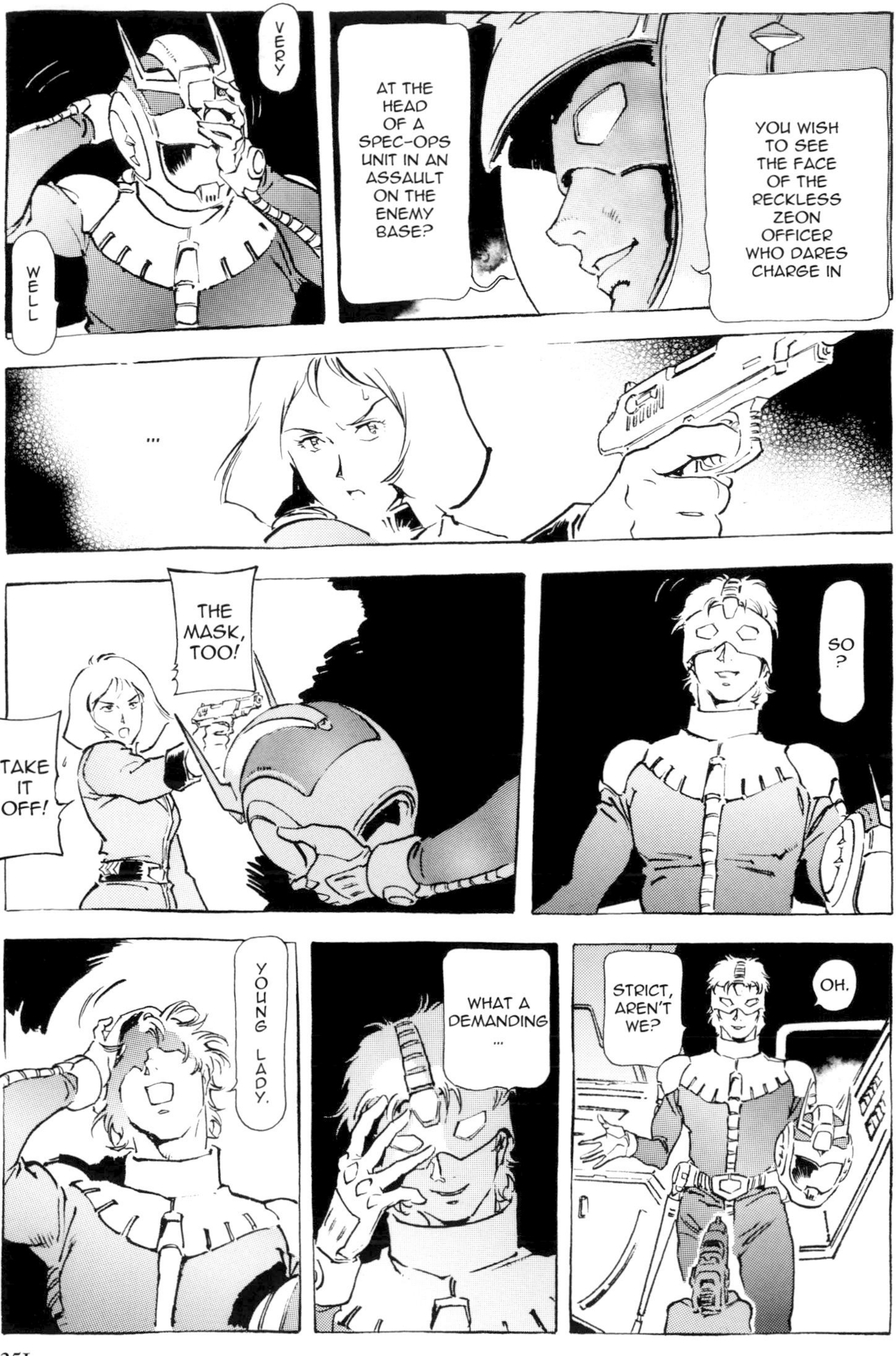
YOU WISH TO SEE THE FACE OF THE RECKLESS ZEON OFFICER WHO DARES CHARGE IN
AT THE HEAD OF A SPEC-OPS UNIT IN AN ASSAULT ON THE ENEMY BASE?
VERY
WELL
...
SO?
THE MASK, TOO!
TAKE IT OFF!
OH.
STRICT, AREN'T WE?
WHAT A DEMANDING ...
YOUNG LADY.

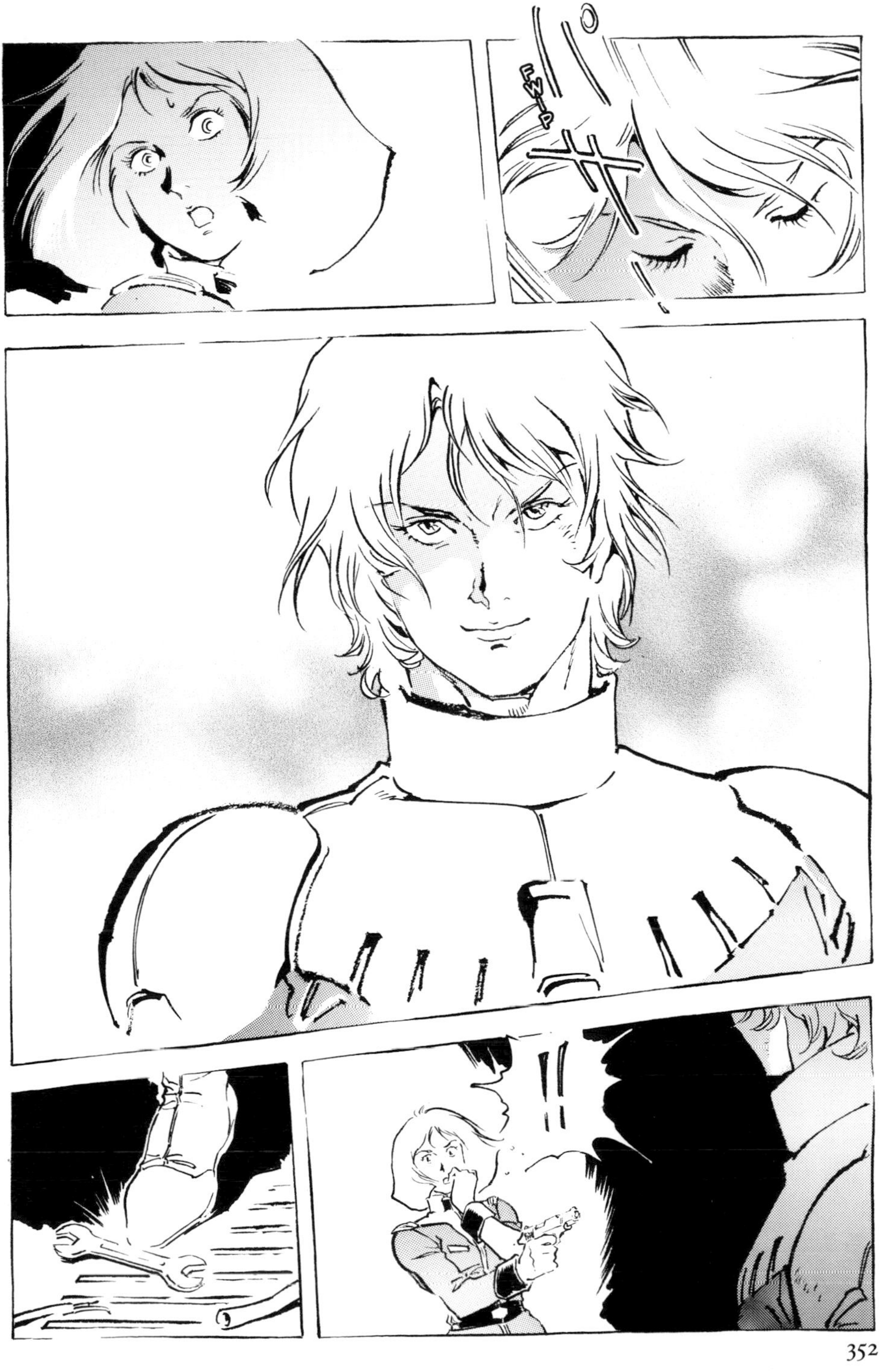
FWIP

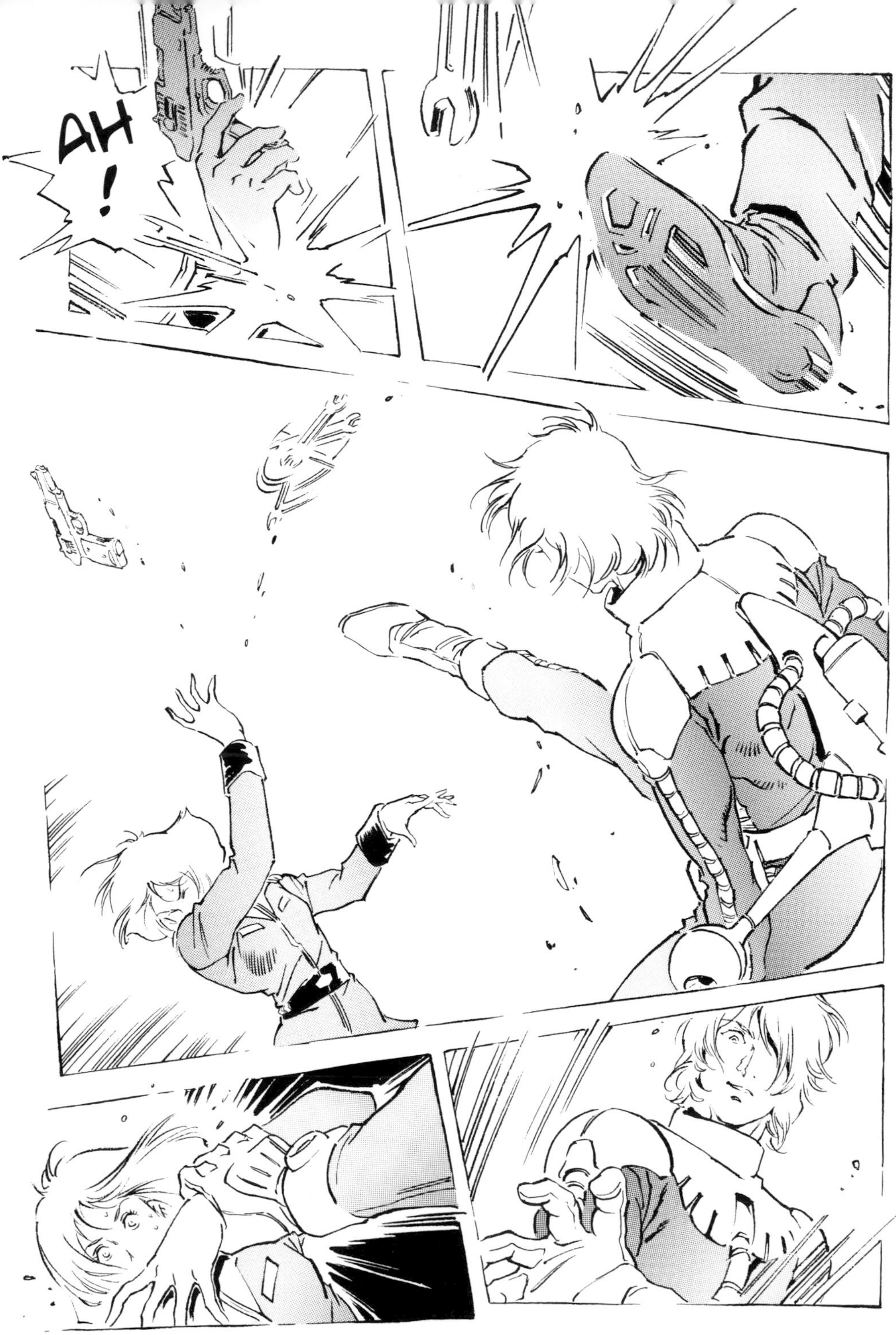
AH!

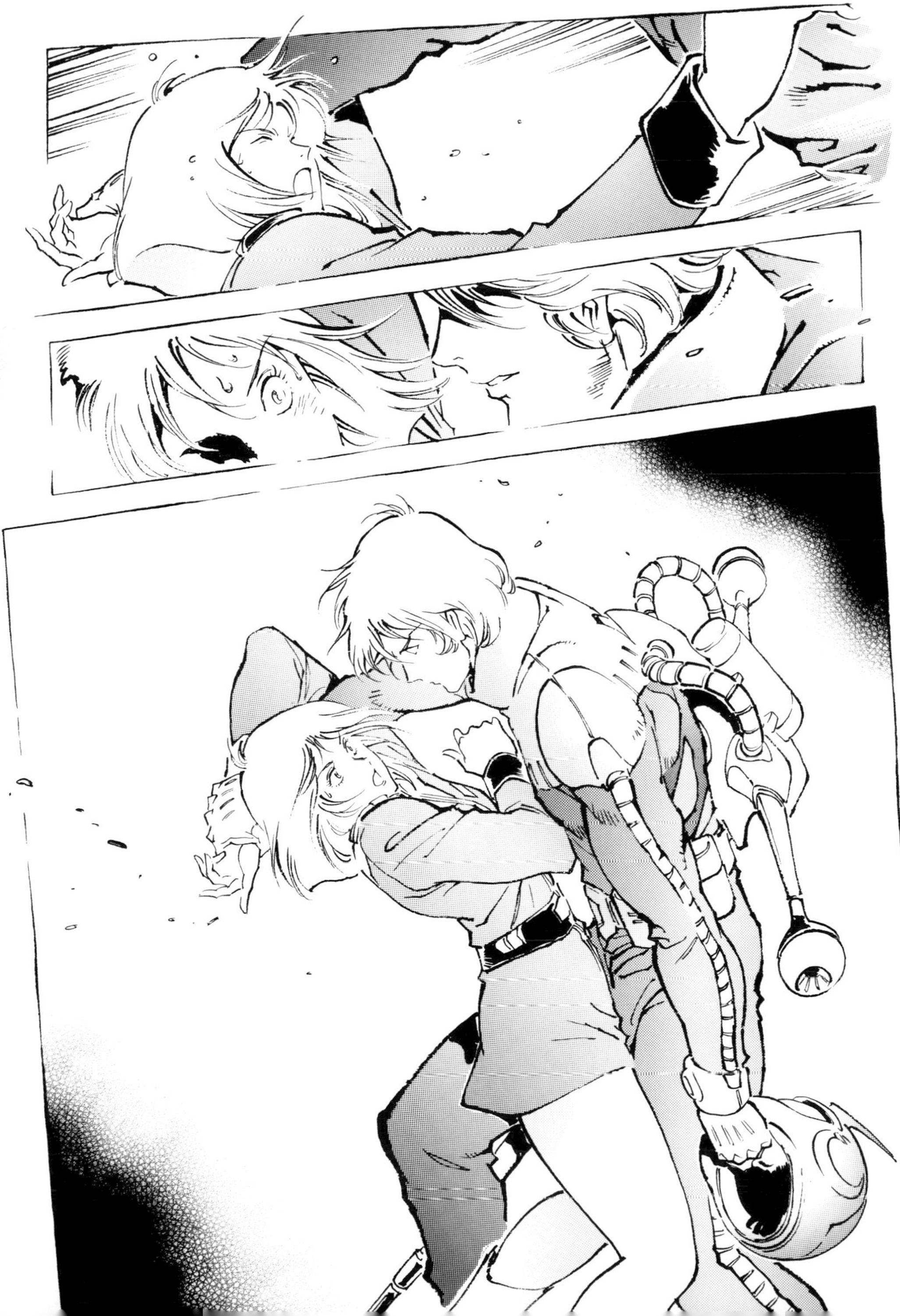

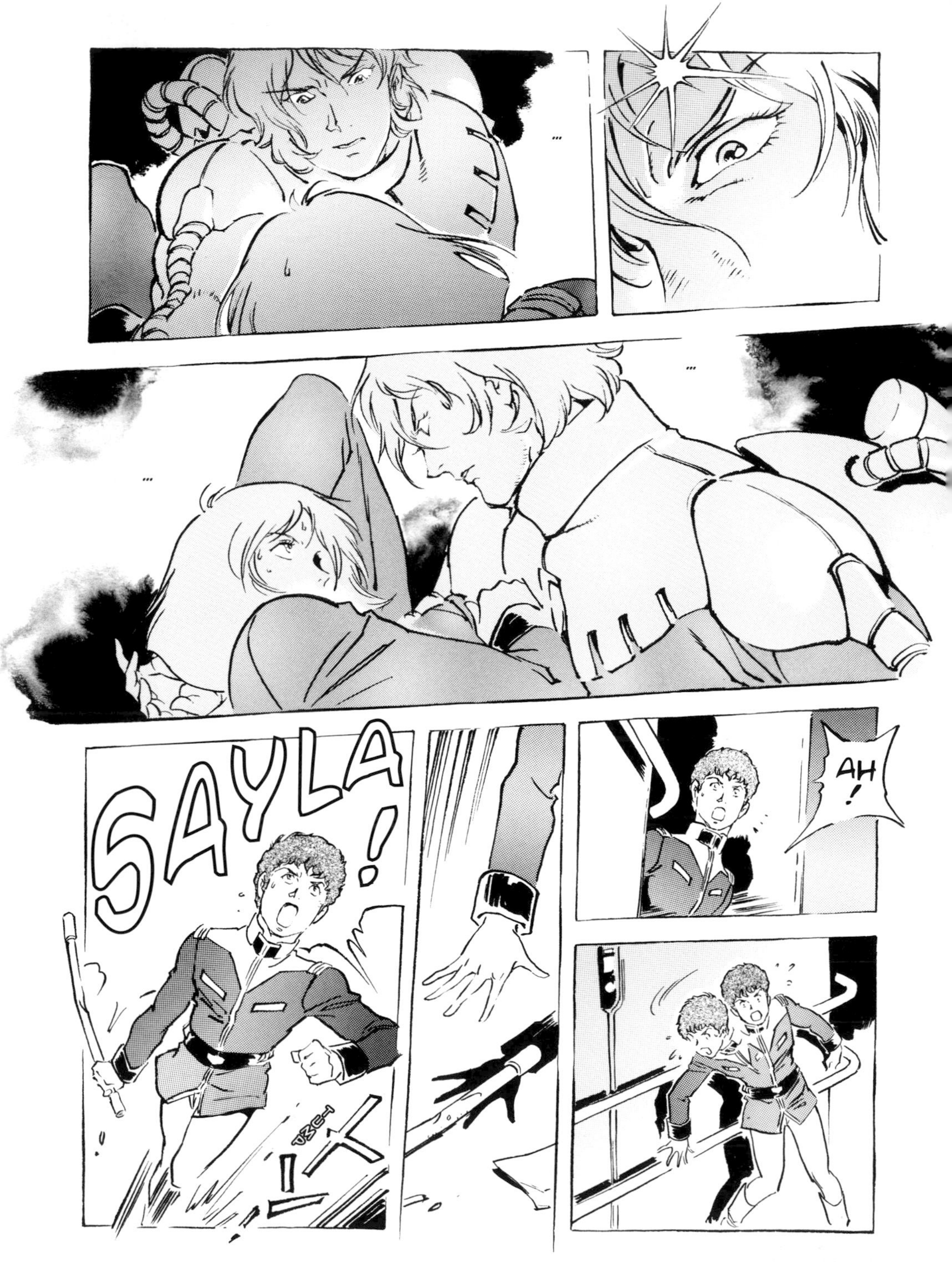
...
...
...
AH!
SAYLA!

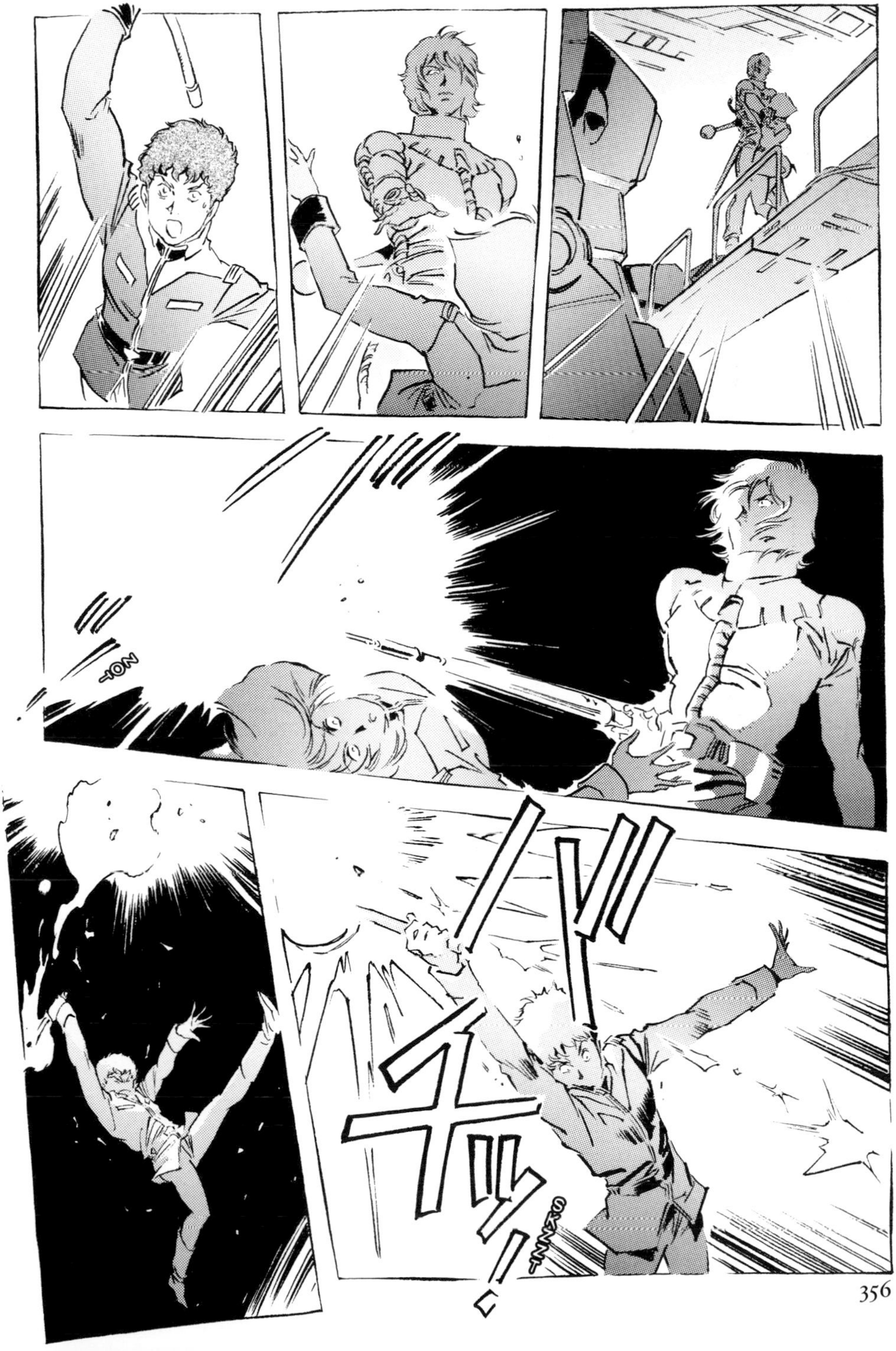
NO—!
SKWNT—

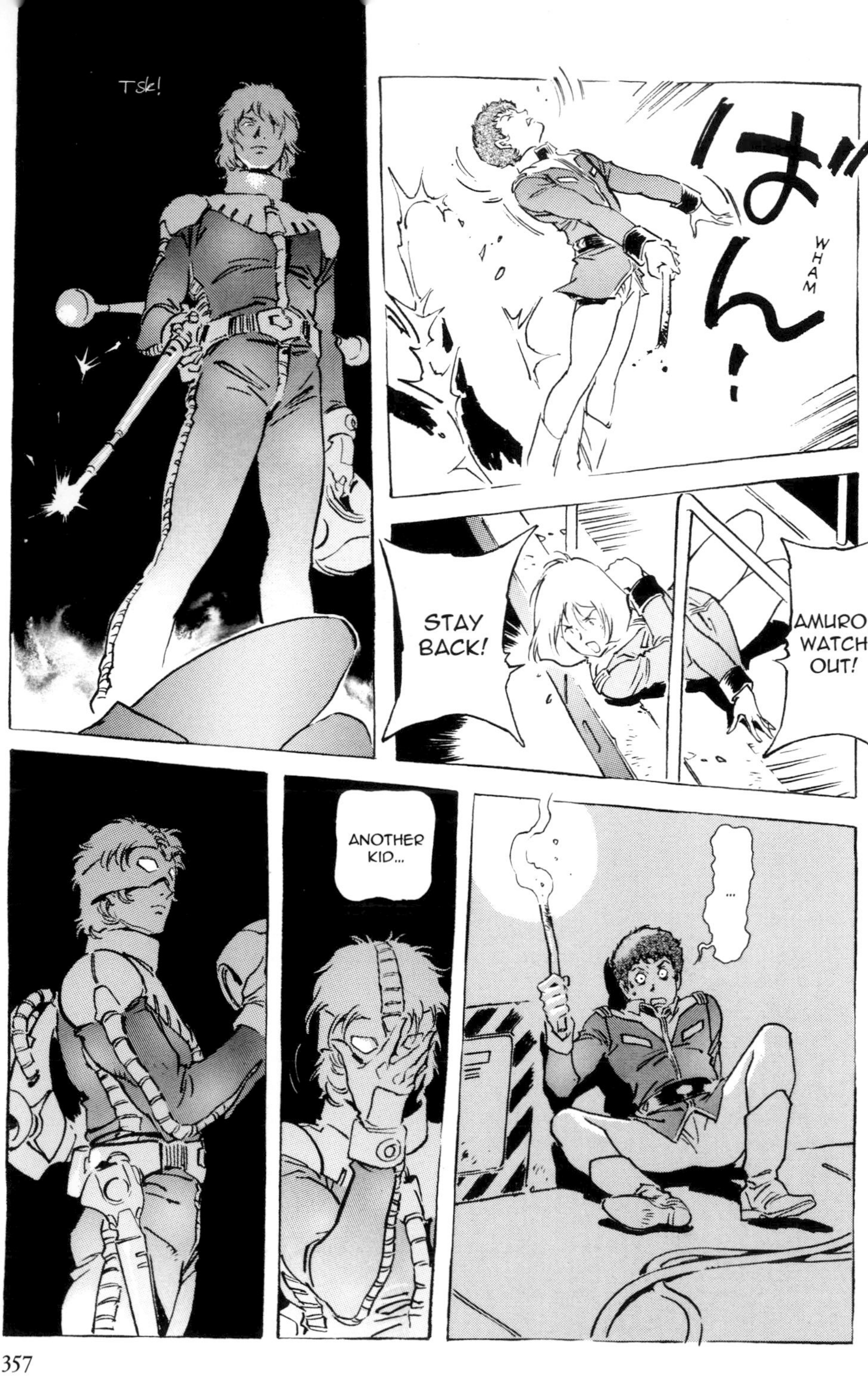
ばん～！
WHAM
AMURO, WATCH OUT!
STAY BACK!
TSK!
...
ANOTHER KID...

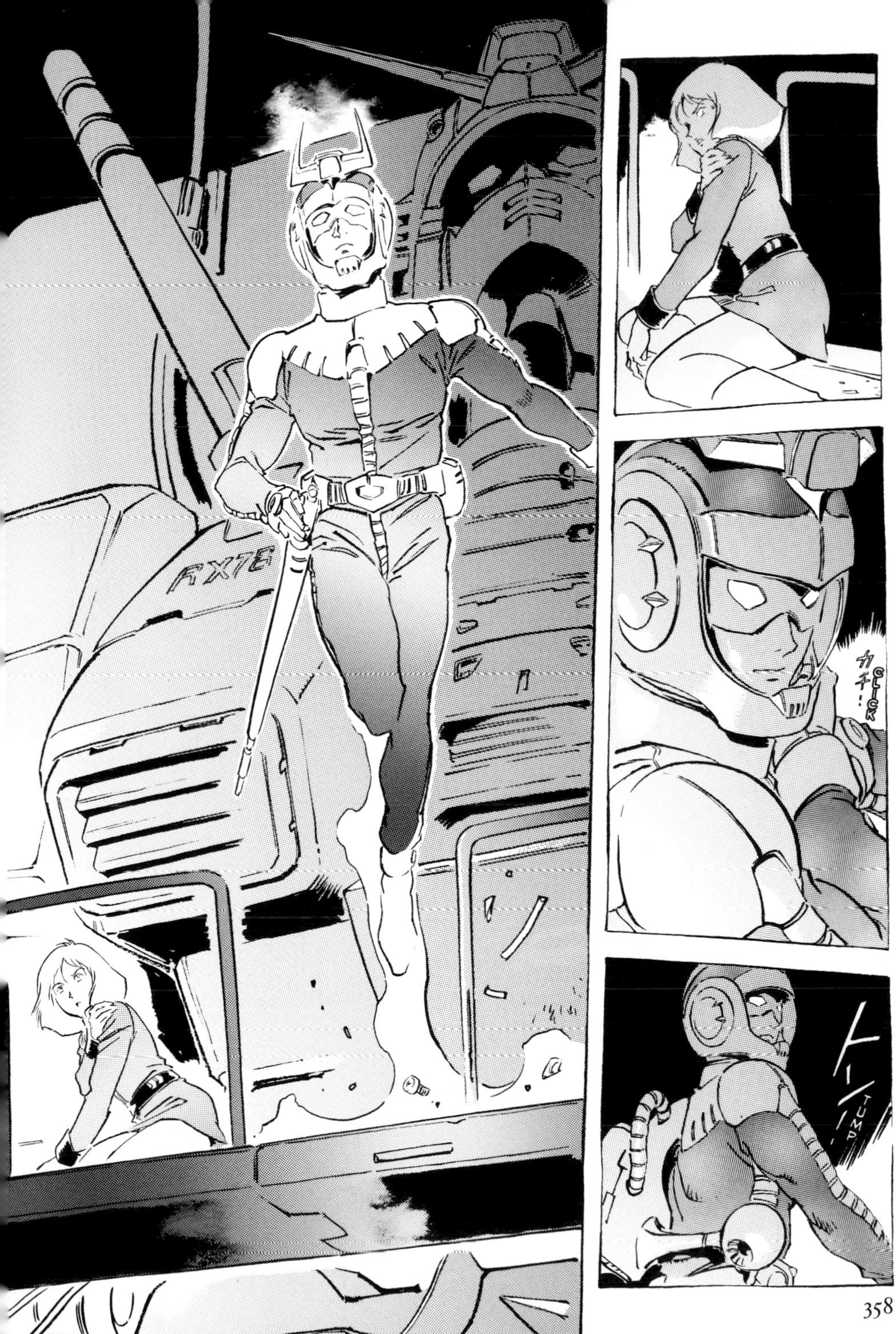
カチ!
CLICK
トン!
TUMP

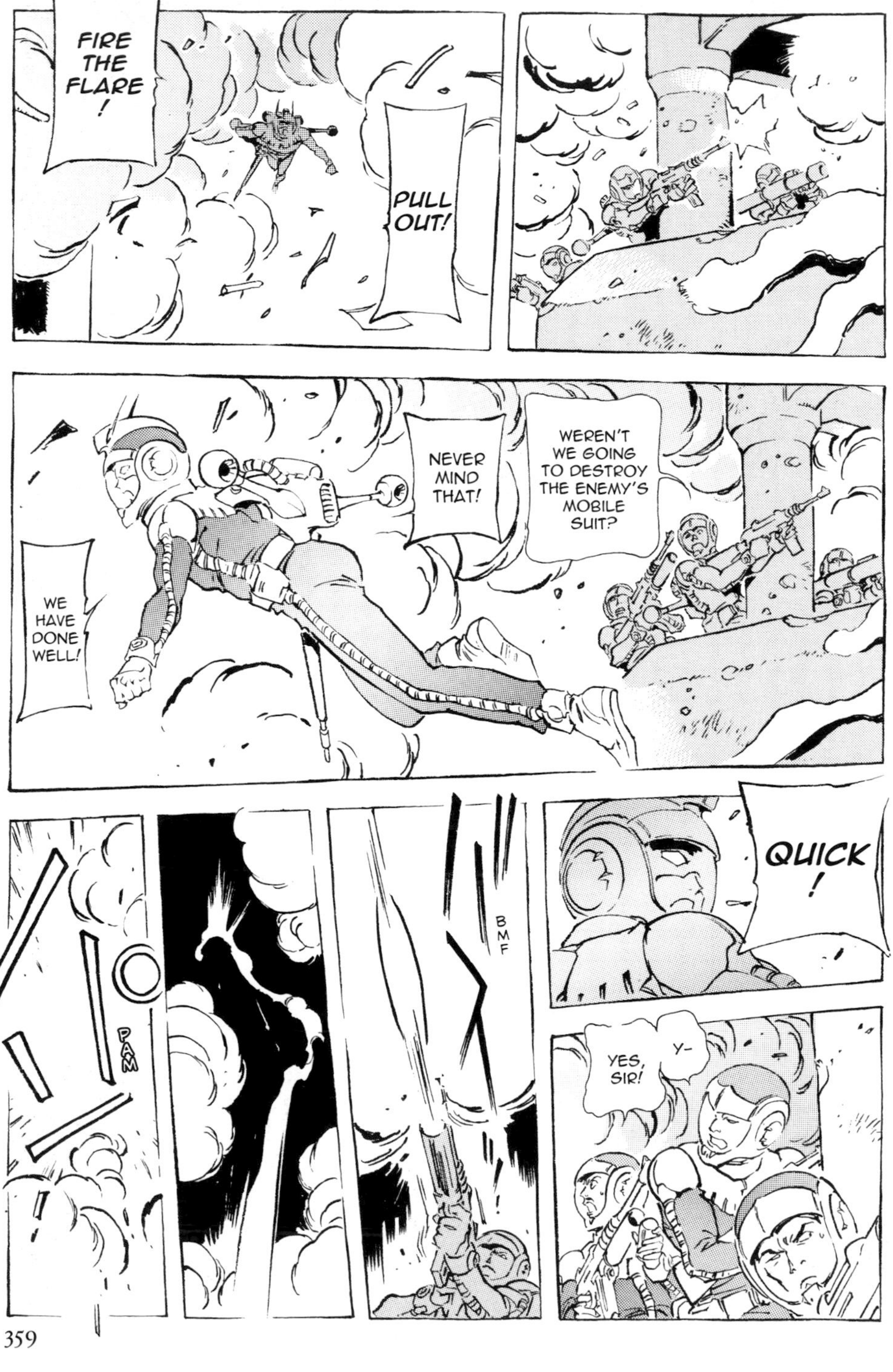
FIRE THE FLARE!
PULL OUT!
WEREN'T WE GOING TO DESTROY THE ENEMY'S MOBILE SUIT?
NEVER MIND THAT!
WE HAVE DONE WELL!
QUICK!
Y-
YES, SIR!
BMF
PAM

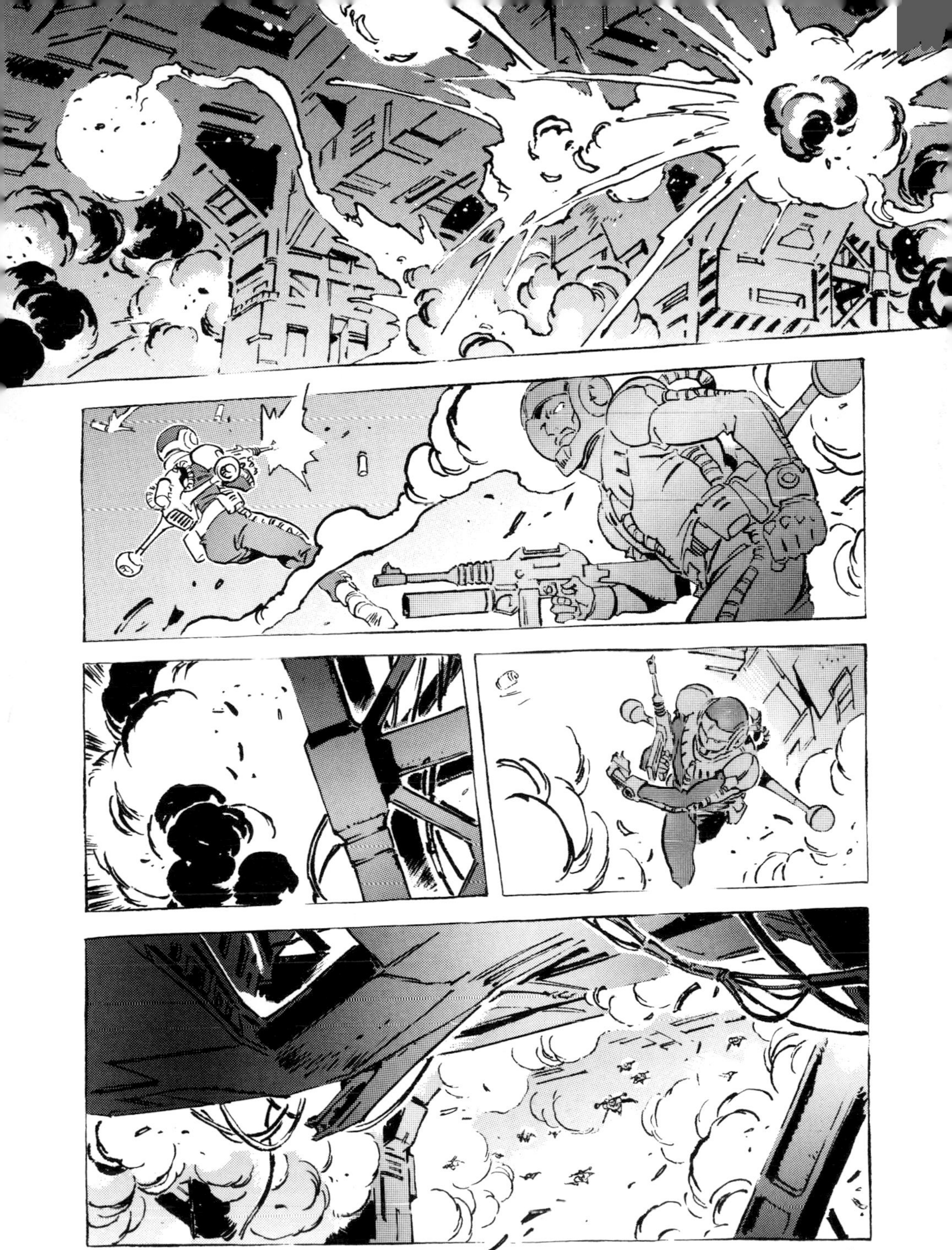

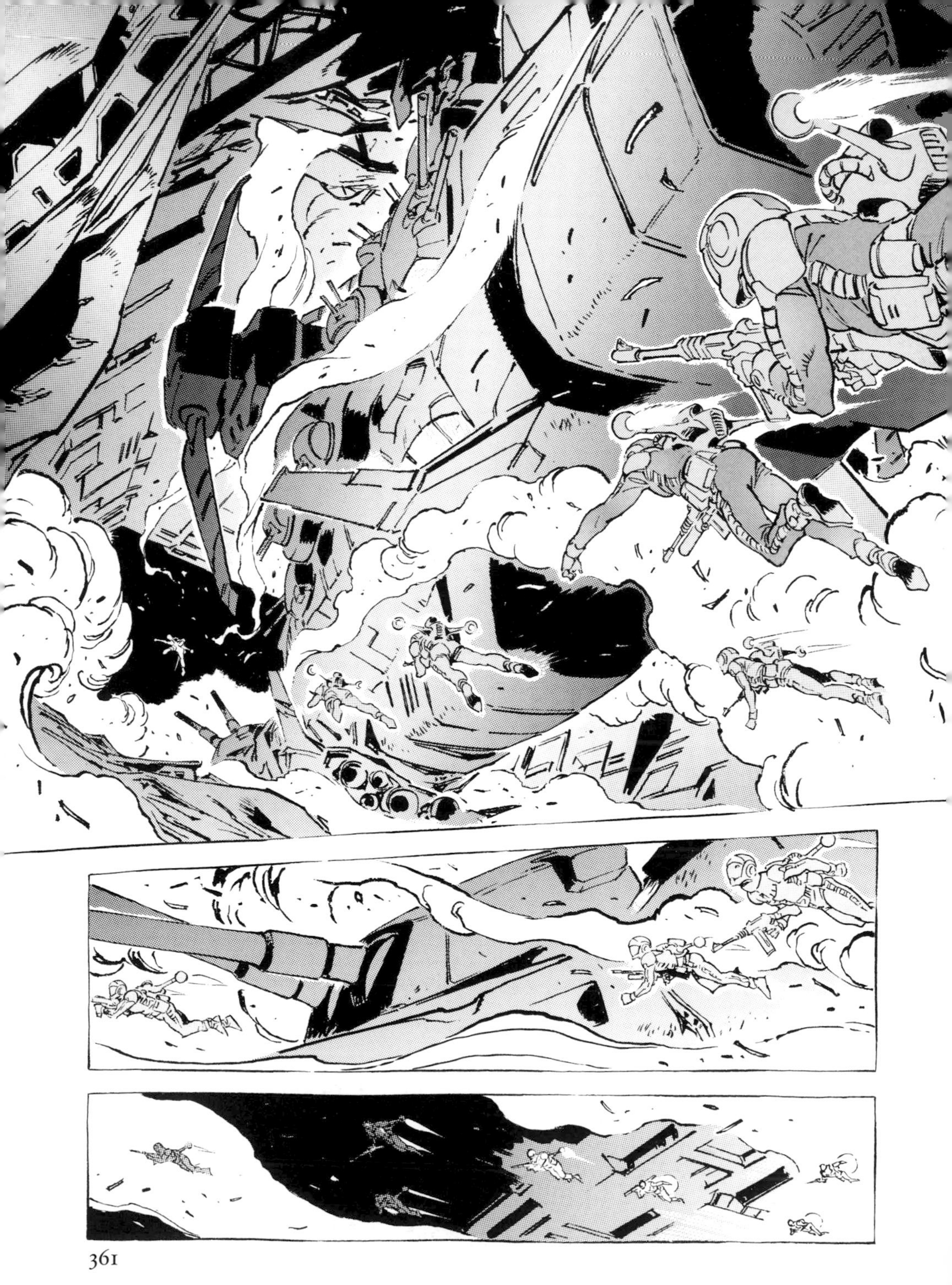

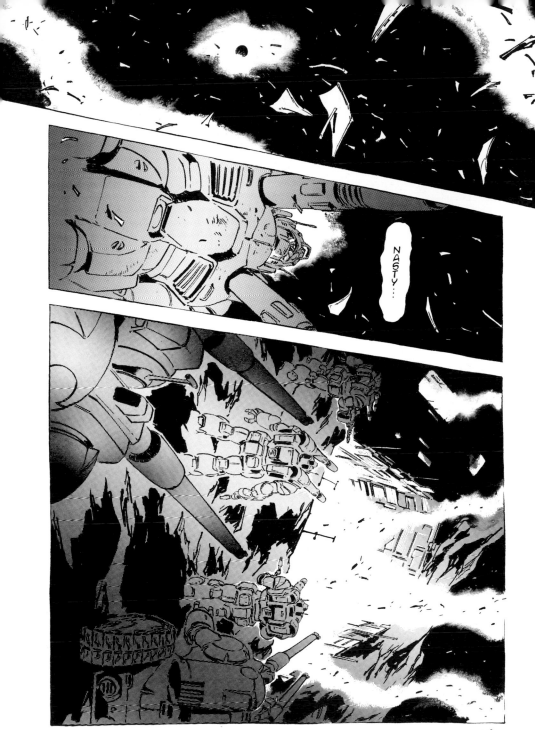

NASTY...

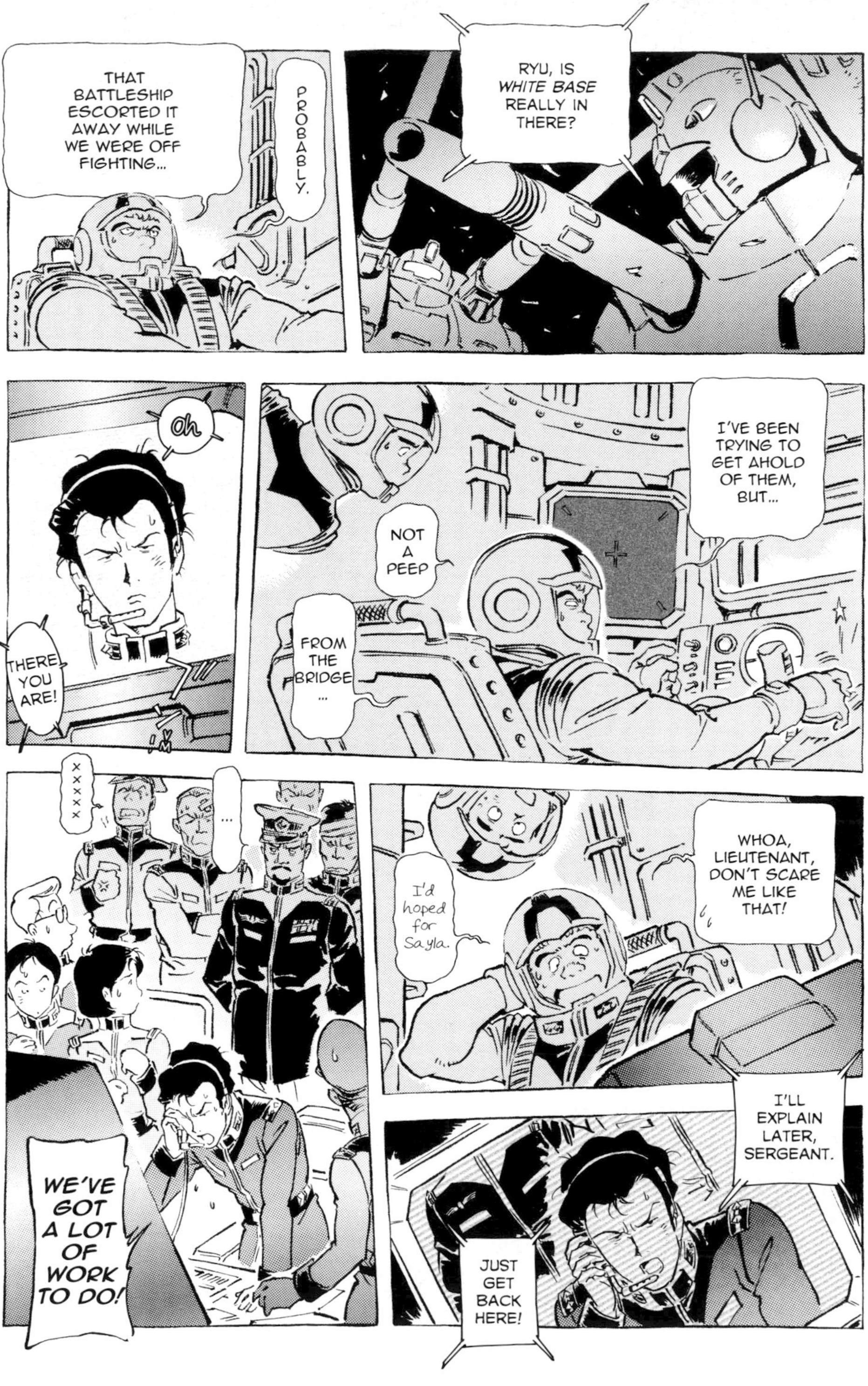
RYU, IS *WHITE BASE* REALLY IN THERE?
PROBABLY.
THAT BATTLESHIP ESCORTED IT AWAY WHILE WE WERE OFF FIGHTING...
I'VE BEEN TRYING TO GET AHOLD OF THEM, BUT...
NOT A PEEP
FROM THE BRIDGE ...
Oh
THERE YOU ARE!
WHOA, LIEUTENANT, DON'T SCARE ME LIKE THAT!
I'd hoped for Sayla.
I'LL EXPLAIN LATER, SERGEANT.
JUST GET BACK HERE!
xxxxx
...
WE'VE GOT A LOT OF WORK TO DO!

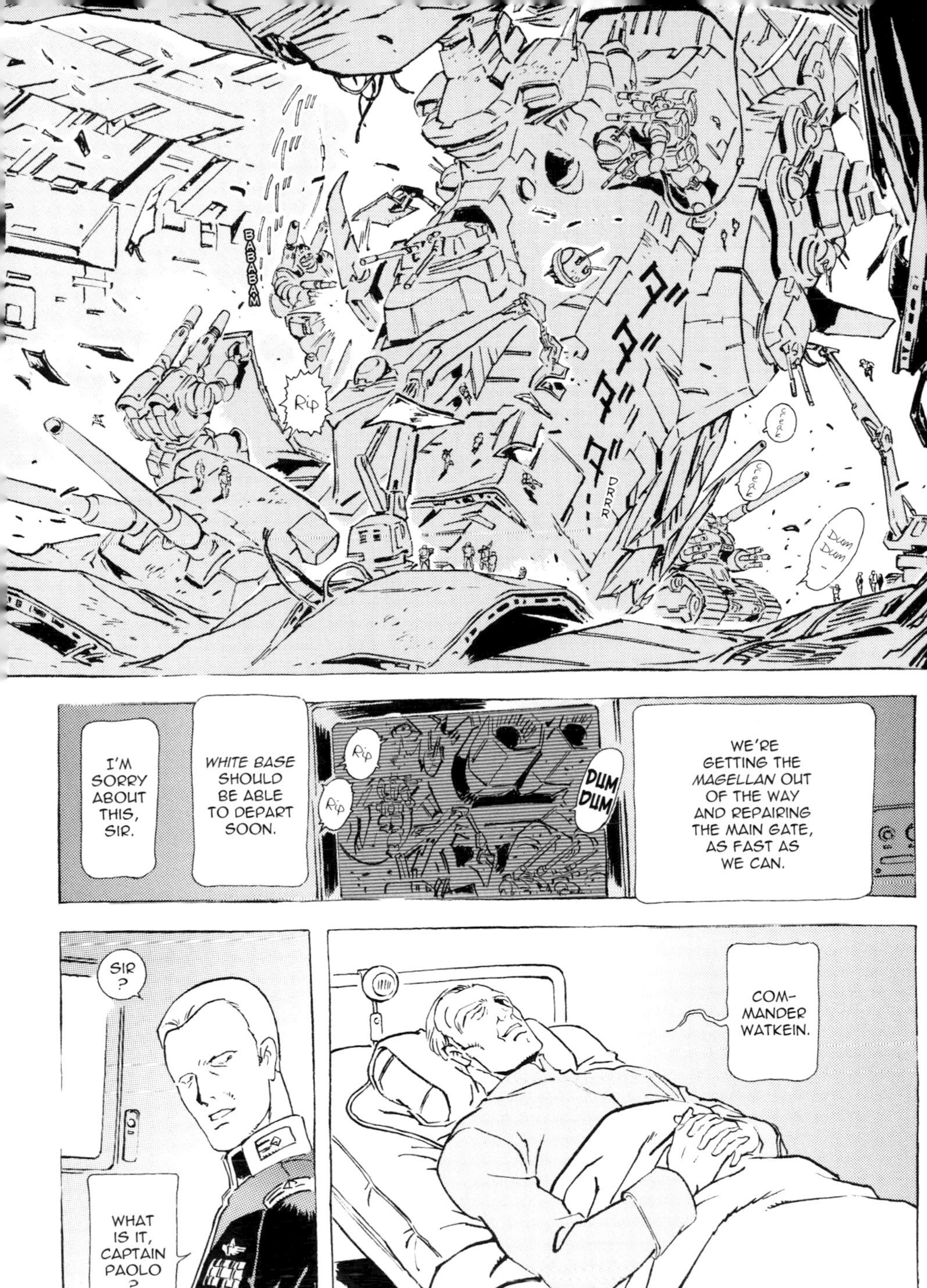
Creak
Creak
Dum Dum …
ダダダダ
DRRR
Rip
BABABAM
WE'RE GETTING THE *MAGELLAN* OUT OF THE WAY AND REPAIRING THE MAIN GATE, AS FAST AS WE CAN.
DUM DUM
Rip
Rip
WHITE BASE SHOULD BE ABLE TO DEPART SOON.
I'M SORRY ABOUT THIS, SIR.
COM-MANDER WATKEIN.
SIR?
WHAT IS IT, CAPTAIN PAOLO?

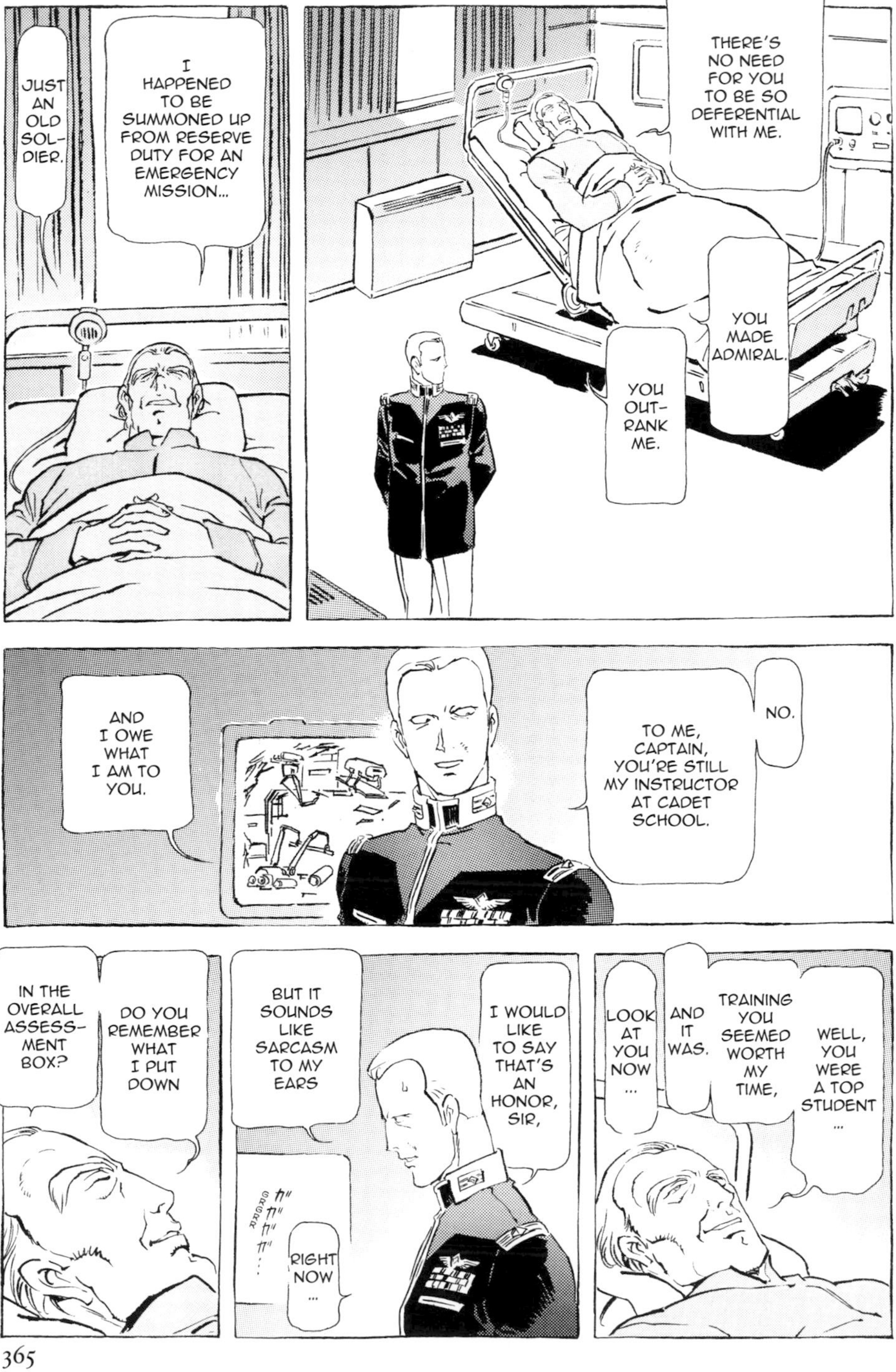
THERE'S NO NEED FOR YOU TO BE SO DEFERENTIAL WITH ME.
YOU MADE ADMIRAL.
YOU OUT-RANK ME.
I HAPPENED TO BE SUMMONED UP FROM RESERVE DUTY FOR AN EMERGENCY MISSION...
JUST AN OLD SOL-DIER.
NO.
TO ME, CAPTAIN, YOU'RE STILL MY INSTRUCTOR AT CADET SCHOOL.
AND I OWE WHAT I AM TO YOU.
WELL, YOU WERE A TOP STUDENT...
TRAINING YOU SEEMED WORTH MY TIME,
AND IT WAS.
LOOK AT YOU NOW...
I WOULD LIKE TO SAY THAT'S AN HONOR, SIR,
BUT IT SOUNDS LIKE SARCASM TO MY EARS
RIGHT NOW...
ガガガ…
DO YOU REMEMBER WHAT I PUT DOWN
IN THE OVERALL ASSESS-MENT BOX?

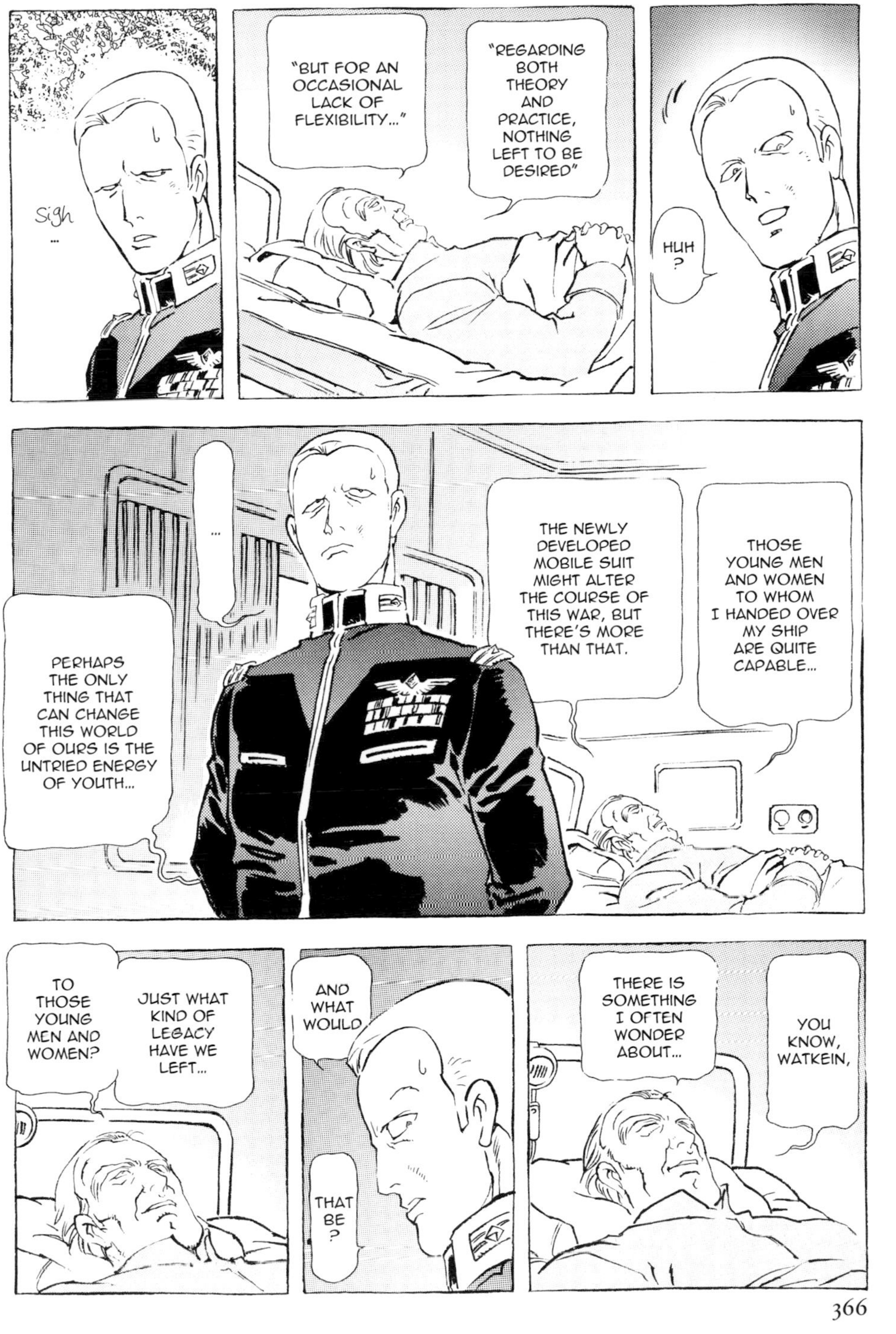
HUH ?
"REGARDING BOTH THEORY AND PRACTICE, NOTHING LEFT TO BE DESIRED"
"BUT FOR AN OCCASIONAL LACK OF FLEXIBILITY..."
Sigh ...
THOSE YOUNG MEN AND WOMEN TO WHOM I HANDED OVER MY SHIP ARE QUITE CAPABLE...
THE NEWLY DEVELOPED MOBILE SUIT MIGHT ALTER THE COURSE OF THIS WAR, BUT THERE'S MORE THAN THAT.
...
PERHAPS THE ONLY THING THAT CAN CHANGE THIS WORLD OF OURS IS THE UNTRIED ENERGY OF YOUTH...
YOU KNOW, WATKEIN,
THERE IS SOMETHING I OFTEN WONDER ABOUT...
AND WHAT WOULD
THAT BE ?
JUST WHAT KIND OF LEGACY HAVE WE LEFT...
TO THOSE YOUNG MEN AND WOMEN?

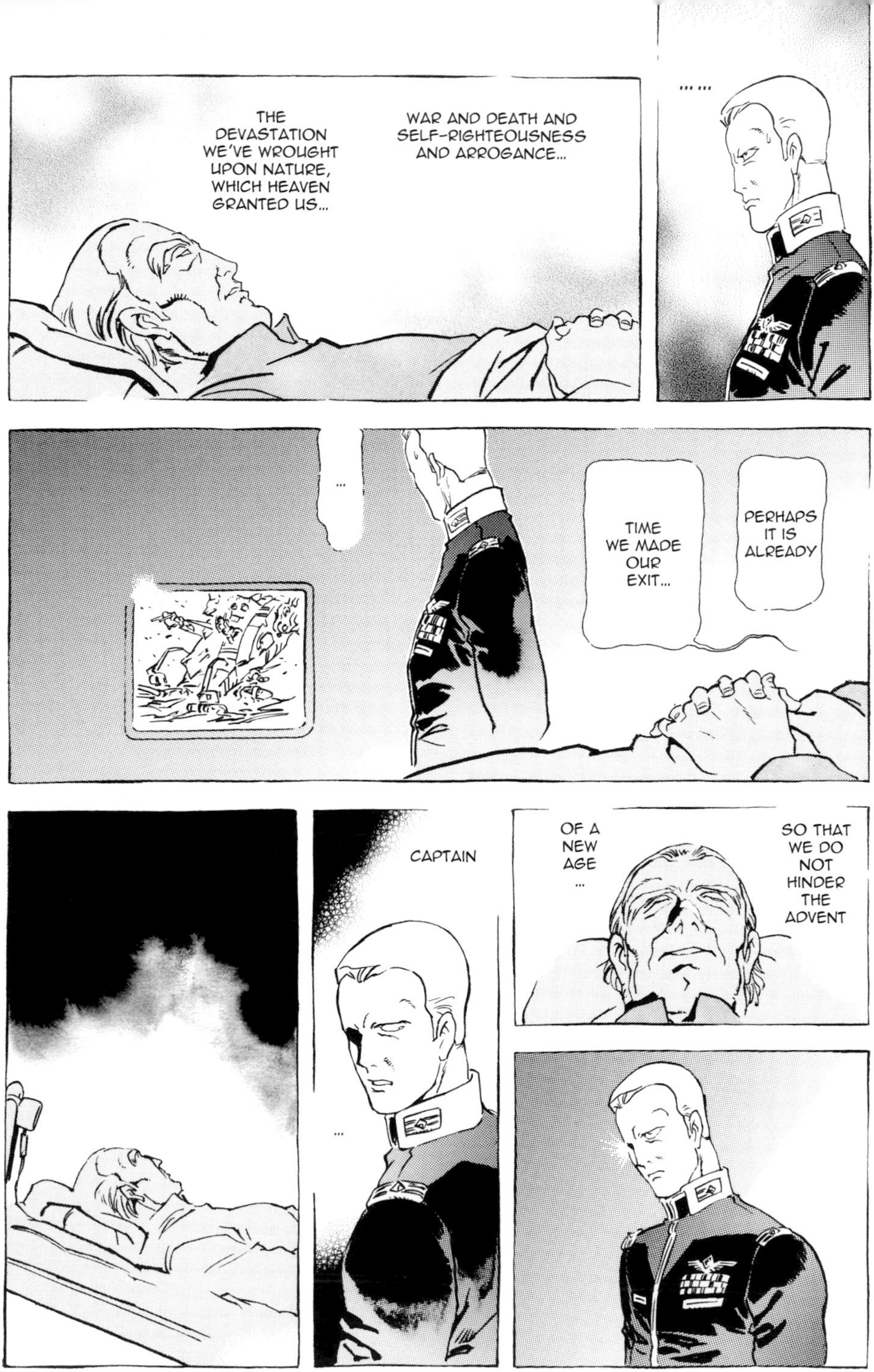
……
WAR AND DEATH AND SELF-RIGHTEOUSNESS AND ARROGANCE...
THE DEVASTATION WE'VE WROUGHT UPON NATURE, WHICH HEAVEN GRANTED US...
PERHAPS IT IS ALREADY
TIME WE MADE OUR EXIT...
...
SO THAT WE DO NOT HINDER THE ADVENT
OF A NEW AGE ...
CAPTAIN
...

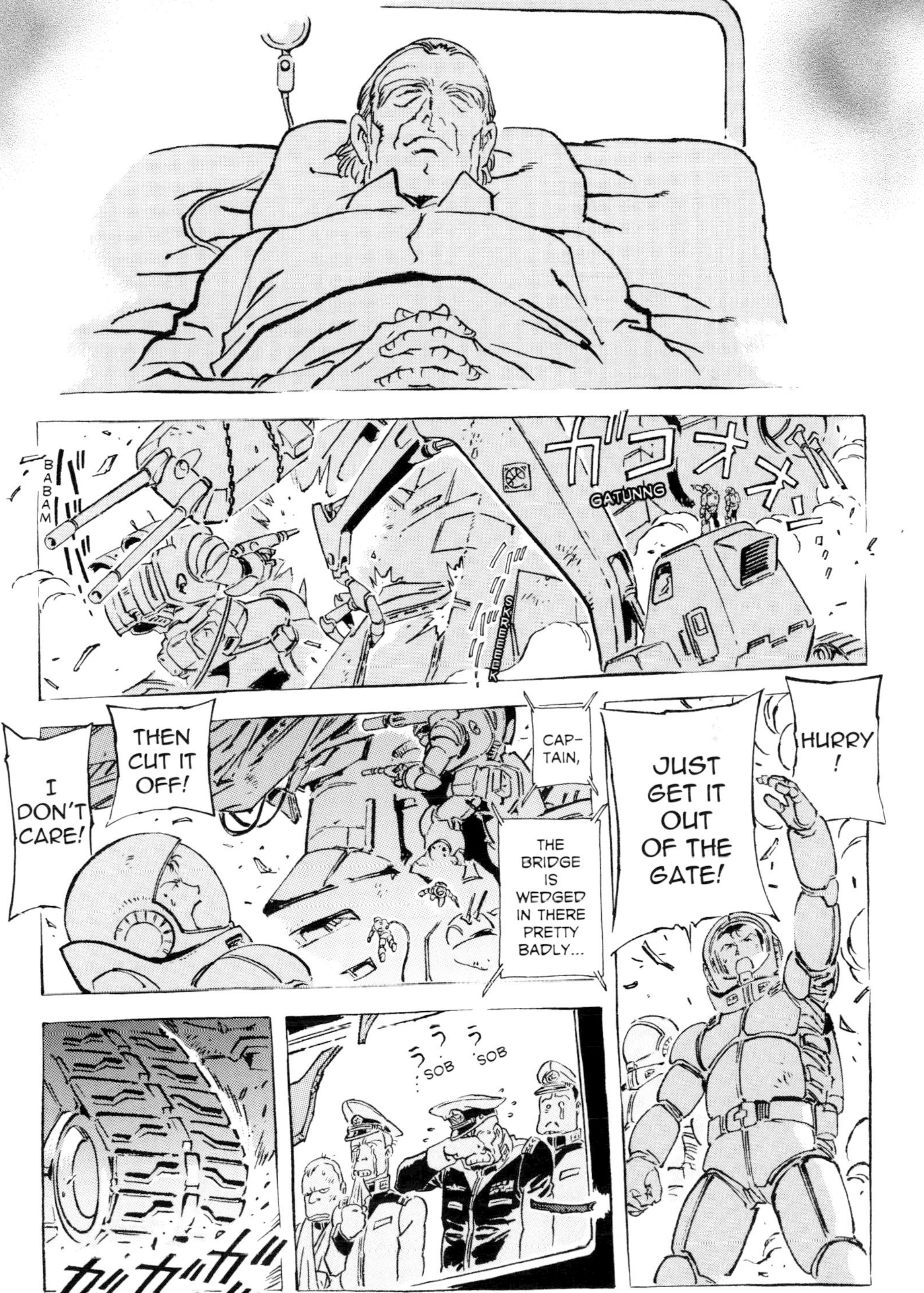
GATUNNG
SKREEEEK
BABAM
HURRY!
JUST GET IT OUT OF THE GATE!
CAPTAIN,
THE BRIDGE IS WEDGED IN THERE PRETTY BADLY...
THEN CUT IT OFF!
I DON'T CARE!
SOB SOB
GR GR GR

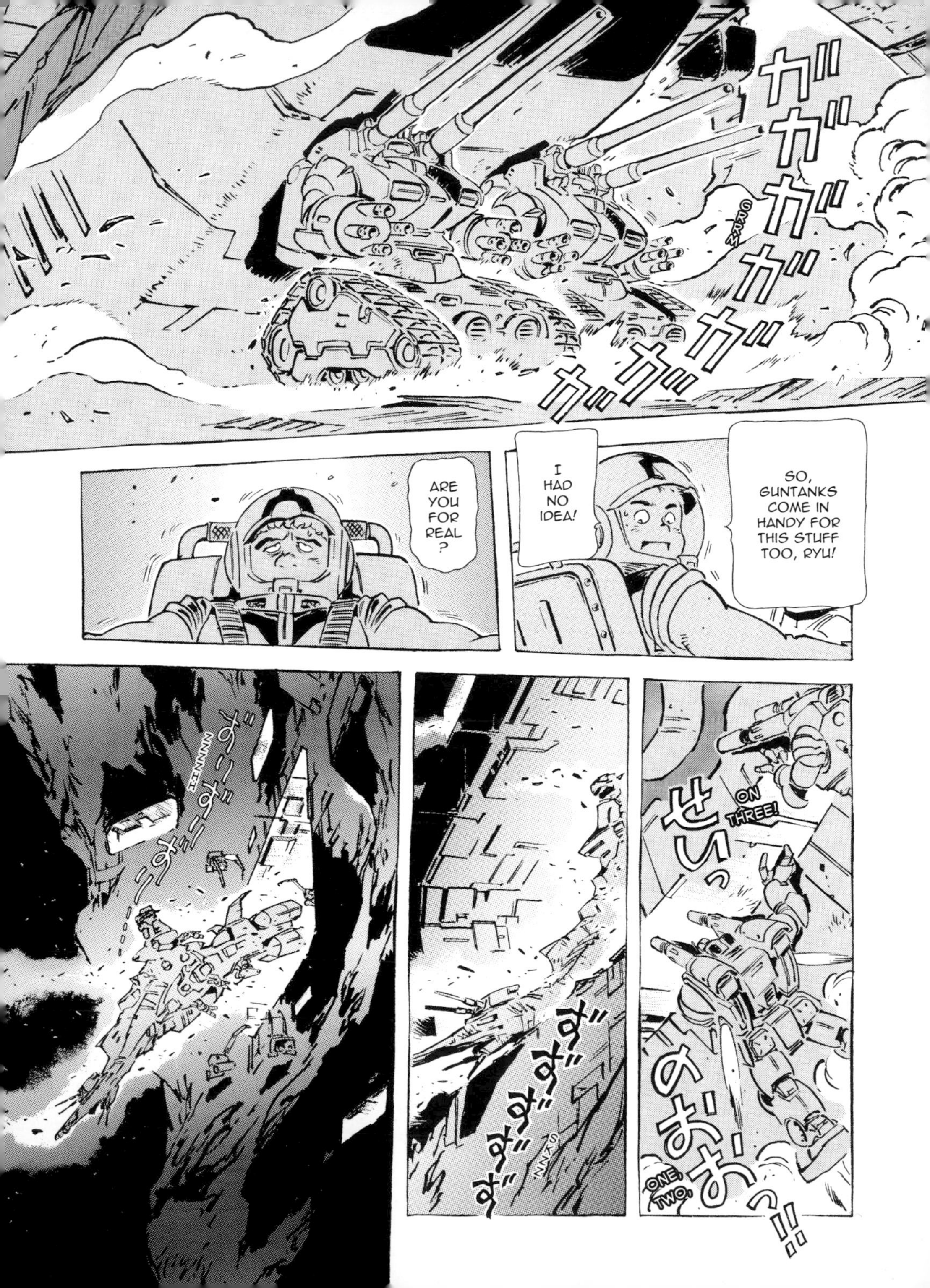

GRRM
SO, GUNTANKS COME IN HANDY FOR THIS STUFF TOO, RYU!
I HAD NO IDEA!
ARE YOU FOR REAL?
ON THREE!
ONE, TWO,
SKNNN
HNNNN

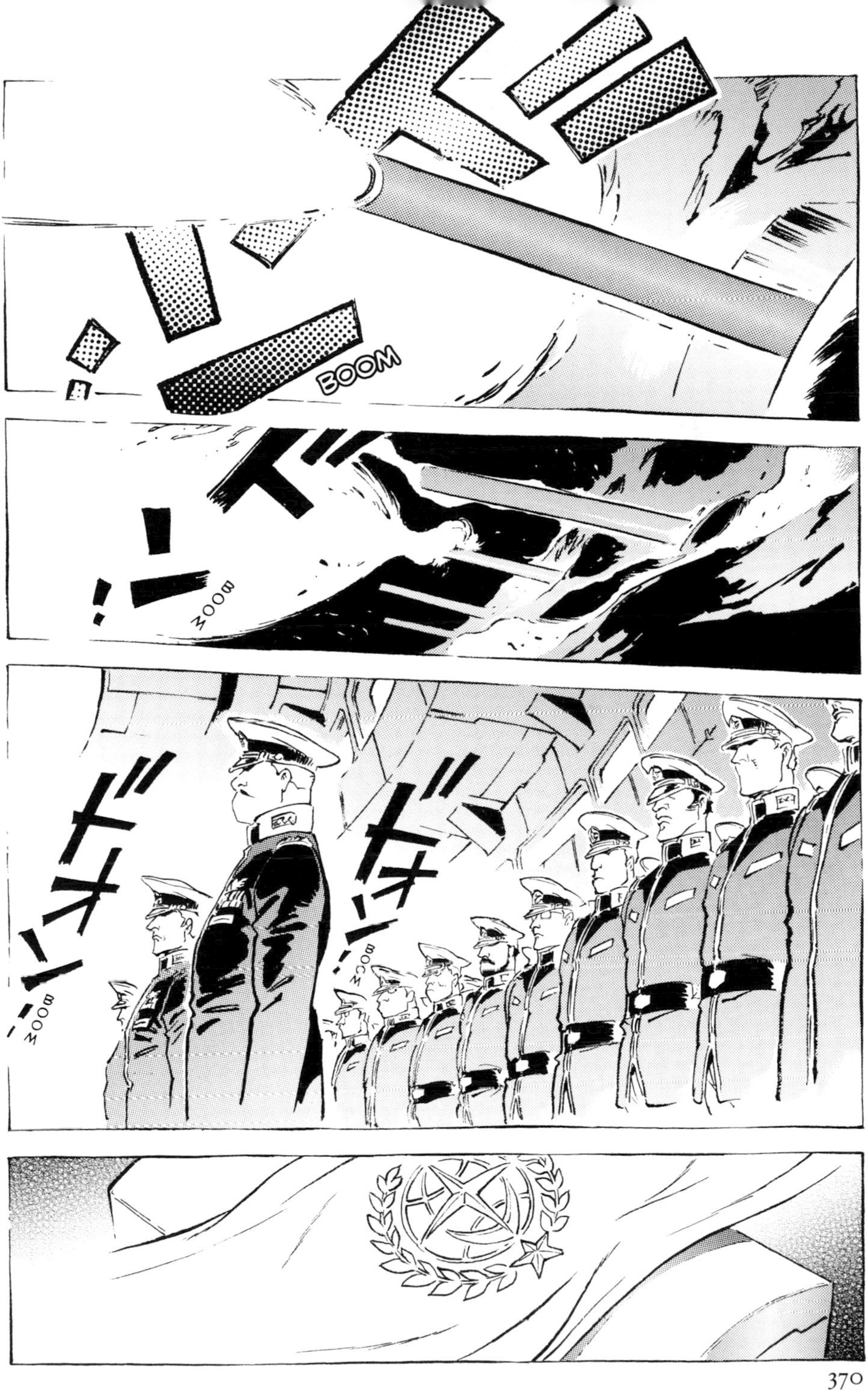
BOOM
BOOM
BOOM
BOOM

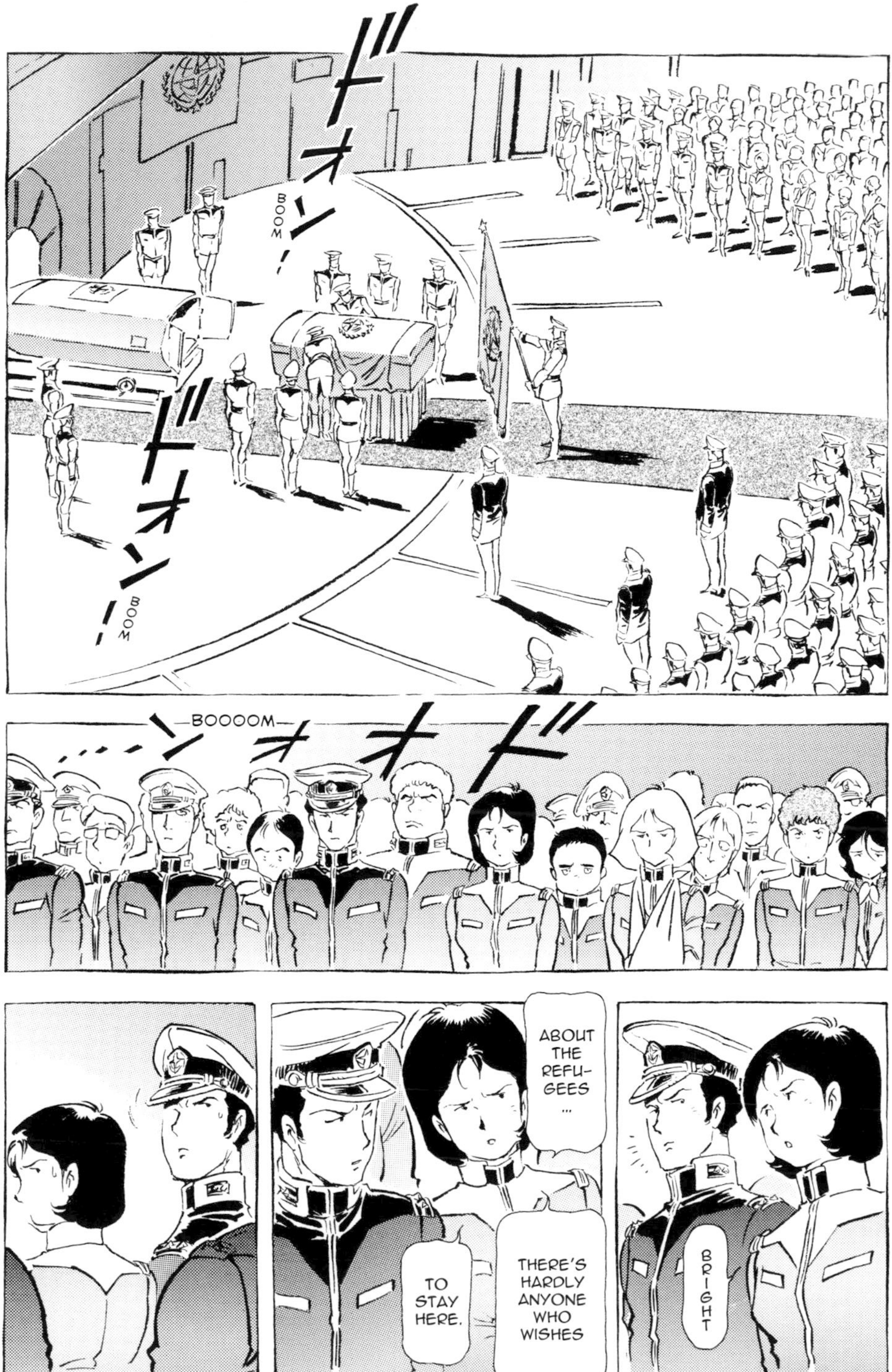
ドオーン
BOOM
ドオーン
BOOM
ドオオーン
BOOOOM
BRIGHT
ABOUT THE REFUGEES ...
THERE'S HARDLY ANYONE WHO WISHES
TO STAY HERE.

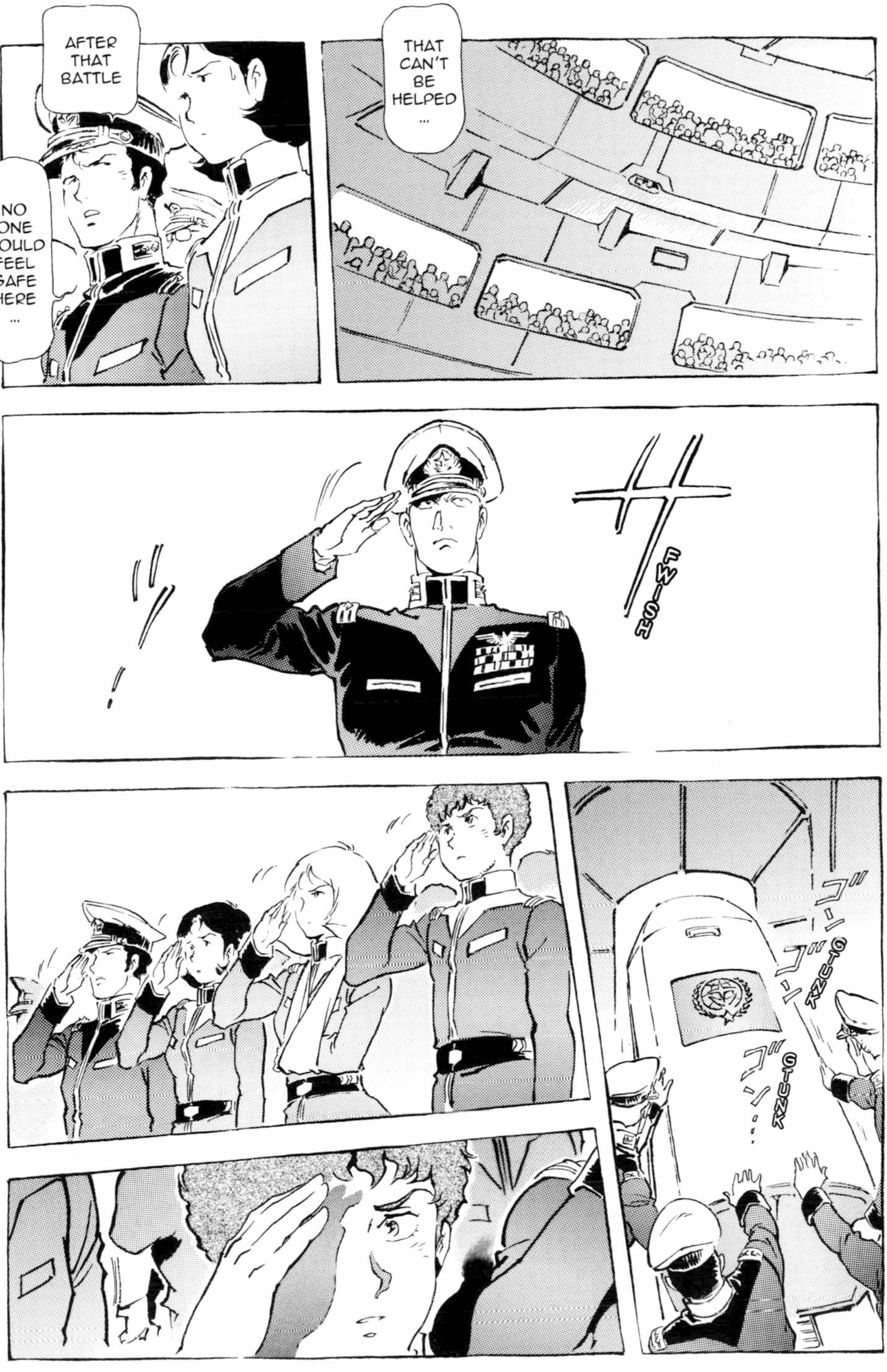

THAT CAN'T BE HELPED ...
AFTER THAT BATTLE
NO ONE WOULD FEEL SAFE HERE ...
TWISH
G-LUNK
G-UNK

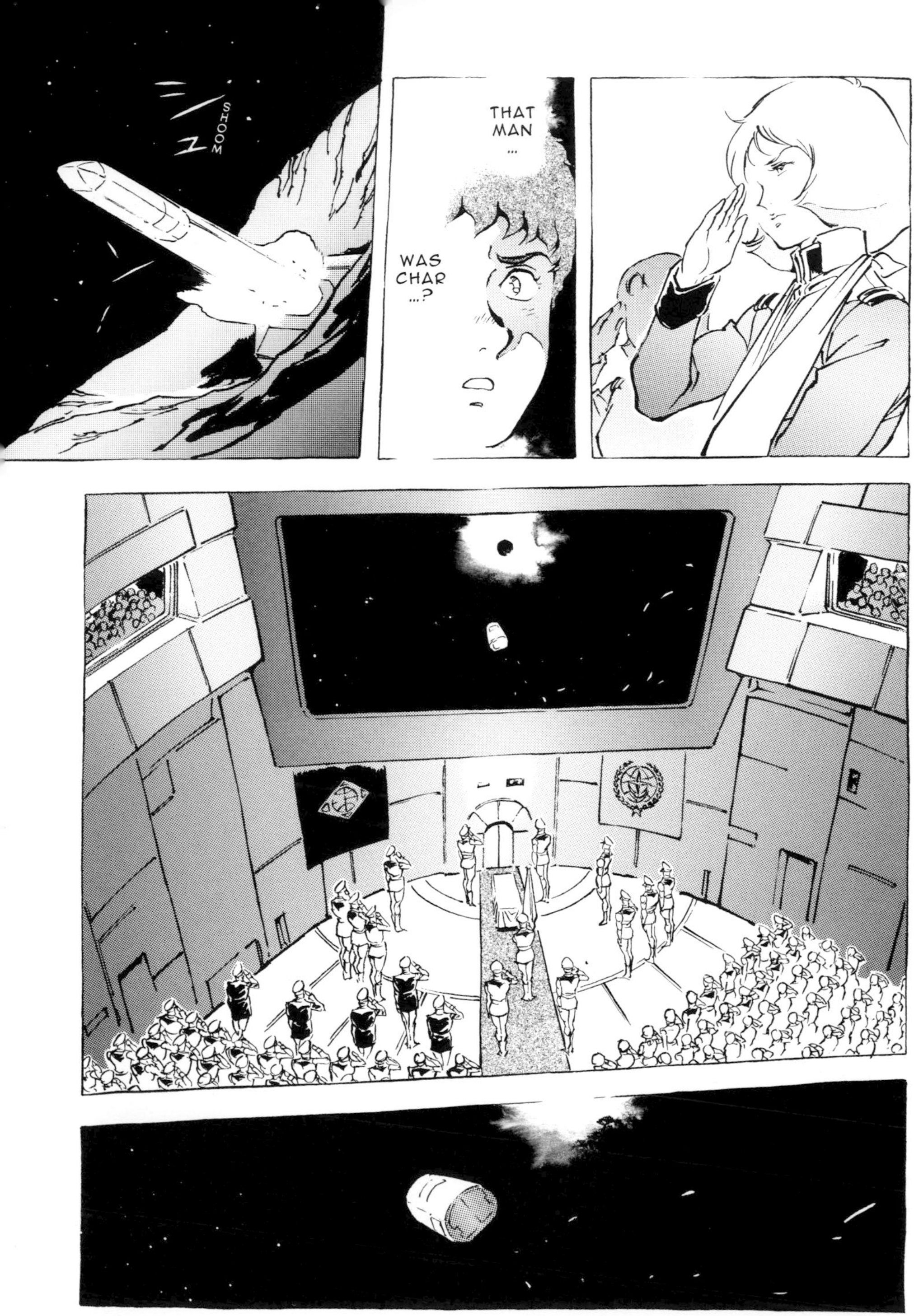
THAT MAN ...
WAS CHAR ...?
SHOOM

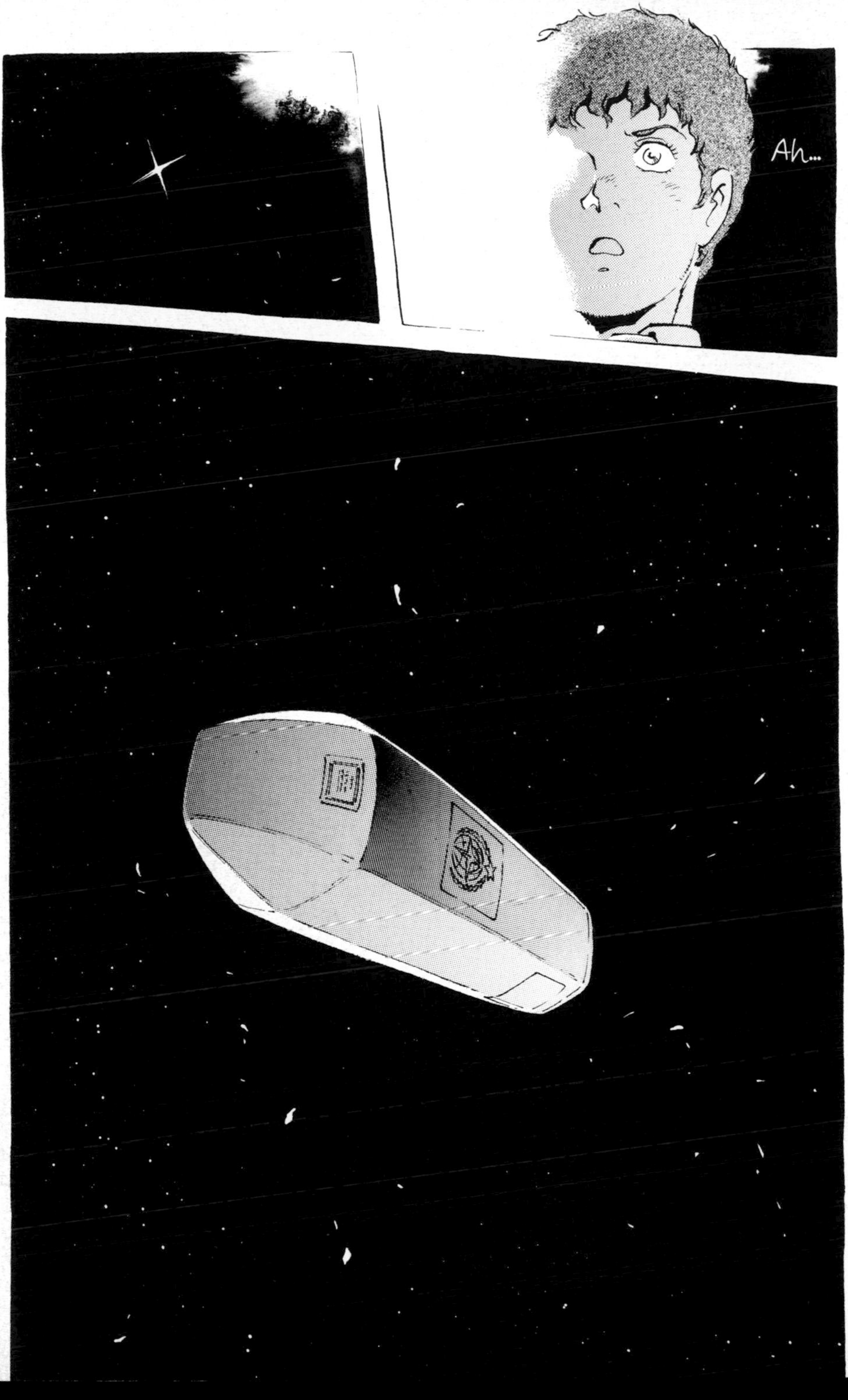
Ah...

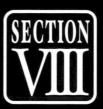

SECTION
VIII

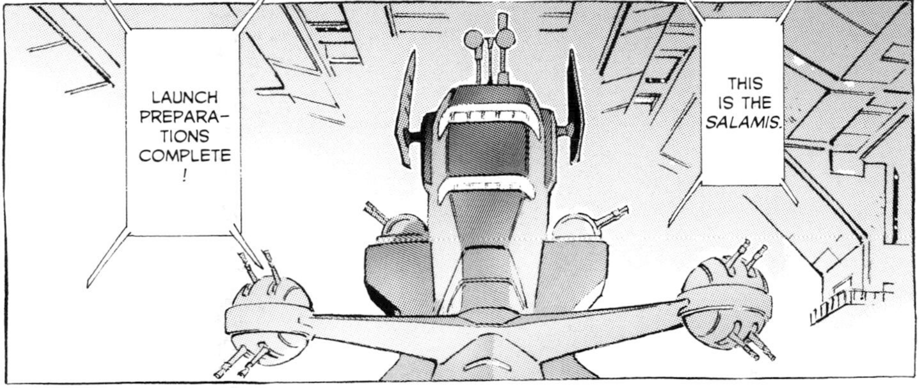
THIS IS THE *SALAMIS*.
LAUNCH PREPARA-TIONS COMPLETE!

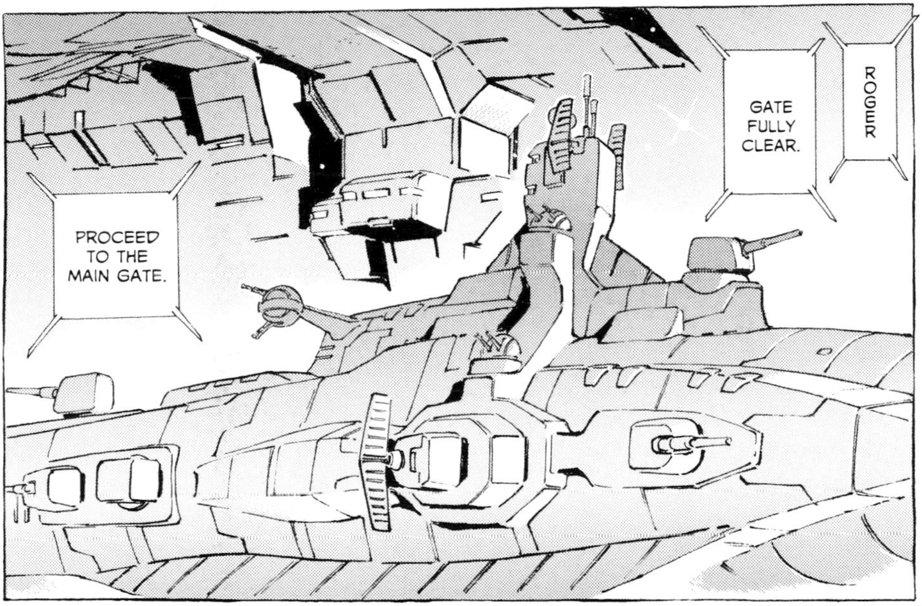
ROGER
GATE FULLY CLEAR.
PROCEED TO THE MAIN GATE.

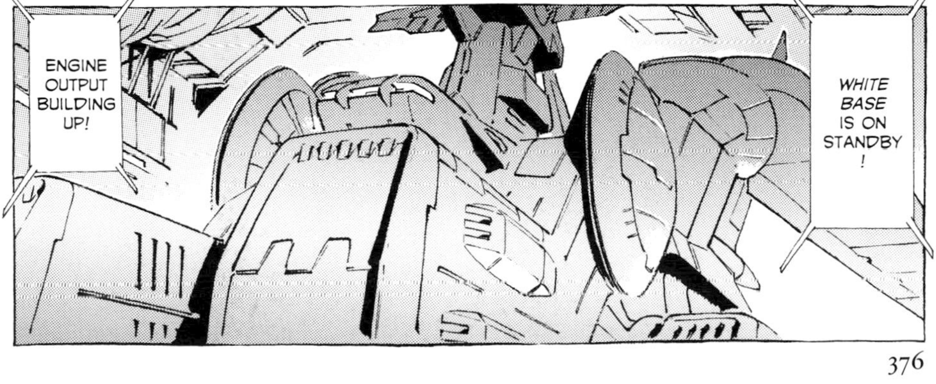
WHITE BASE IS ON STANDBY!
ENGINE OUTPUT BUILDING UP!

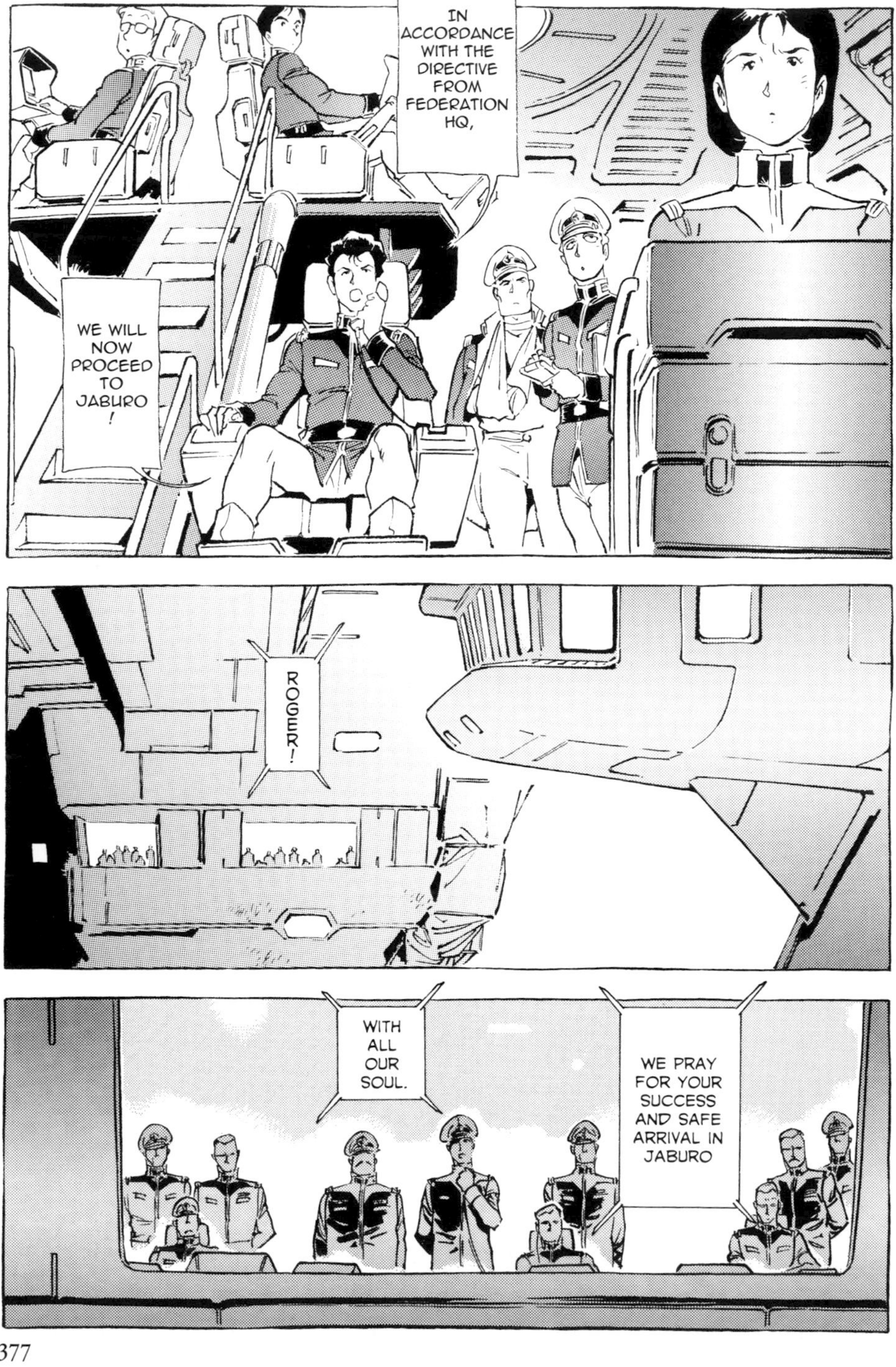
IN ACCORDANCE WITH THE DIRECTIVE FROM FEDERATION HQ,
WE WILL NOW PROCEED TO JABURO!
ROGER!
WE PRAY FOR YOUR SUCCESS AND SAFE ARRIVAL IN JABURO
WITH ALL OUR SOUL.

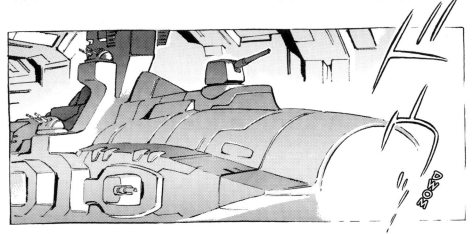

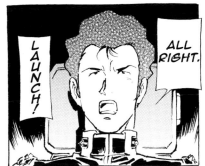

LAUNCH!

ALL RIGHT.

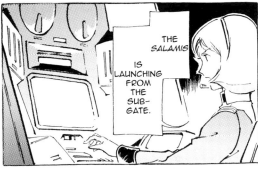

THE SALAMIS IS LAUNCHING FROM THE SUB-GATE.

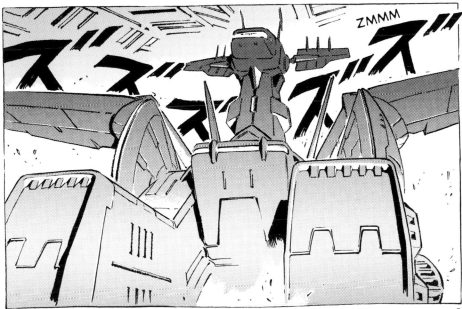

ZMMM

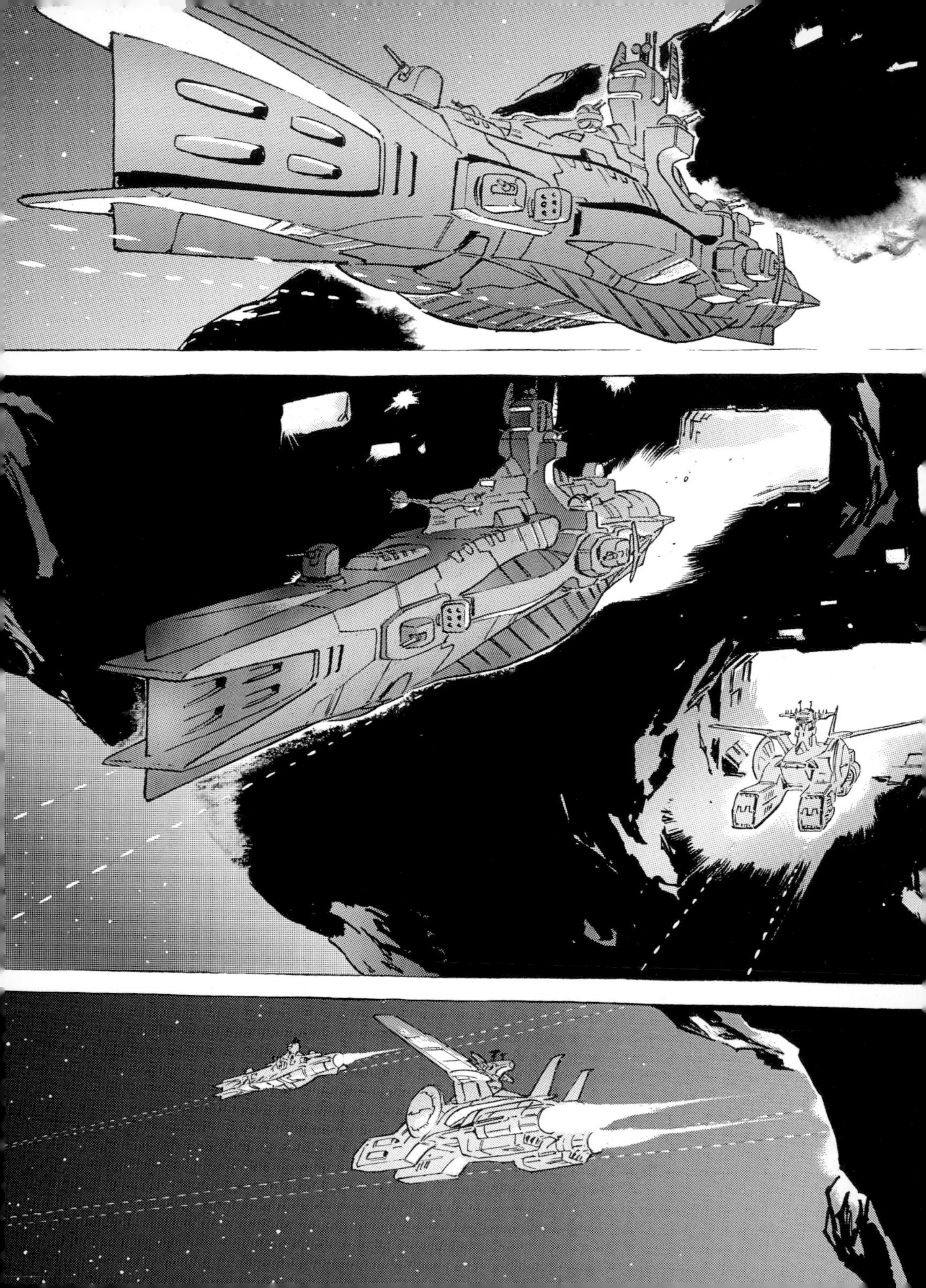

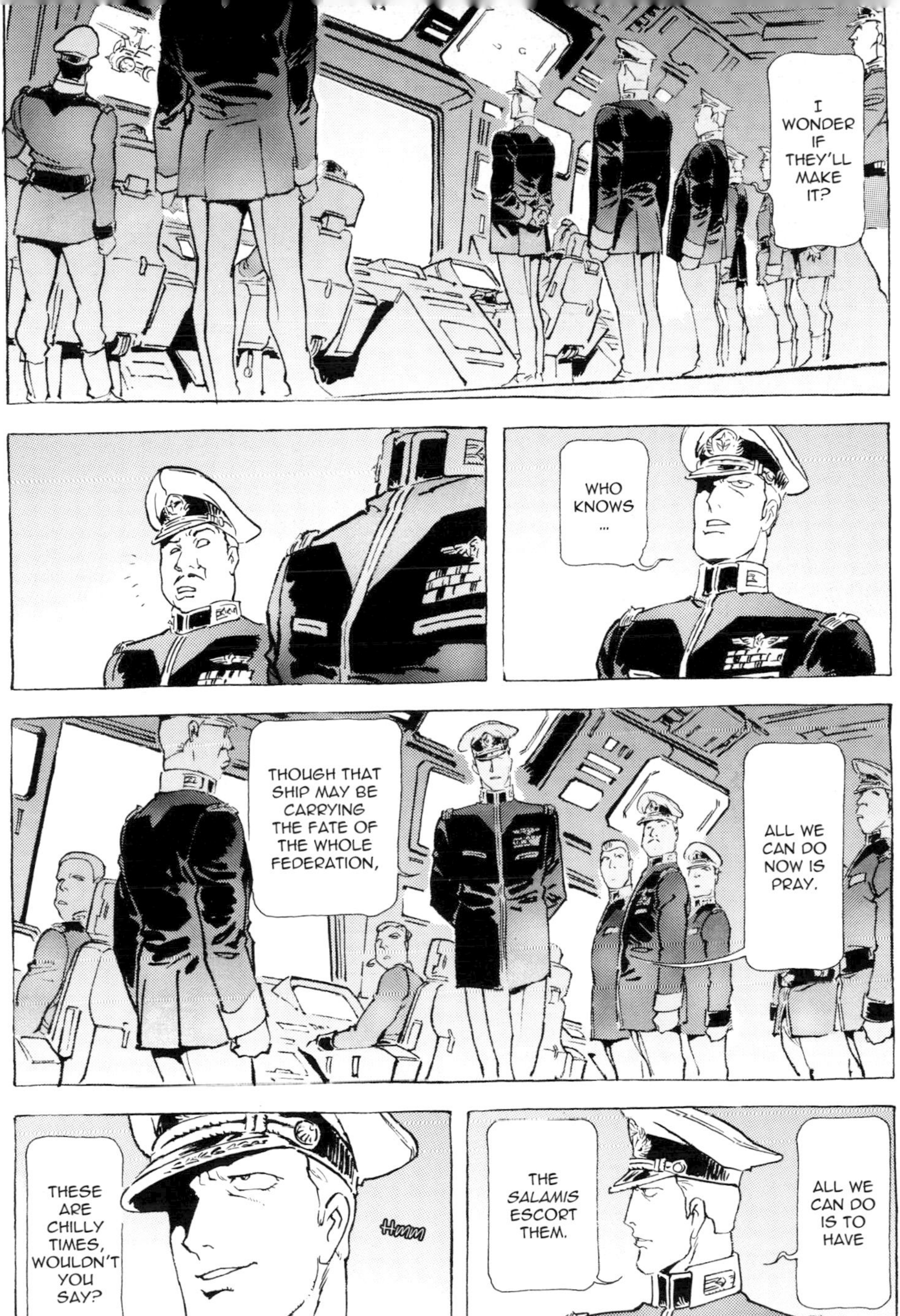
I WONDER IF THEY'LL MAKE IT?
WHO KNOWS ...
THOUGH THAT SHIP MAY BE CARRYING THE FATE OF THE WHOLE FEDERATION,
ALL WE CAN DO NOW IS PRAY.
THESE ARE CHILLY TIMES, WOULDN'T YOU SAY?
Hmm
ALL WE CAN DO IS TO HAVE
THE SALAMIS ESCORT THEM.

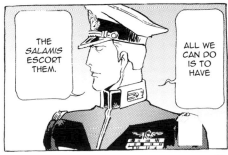

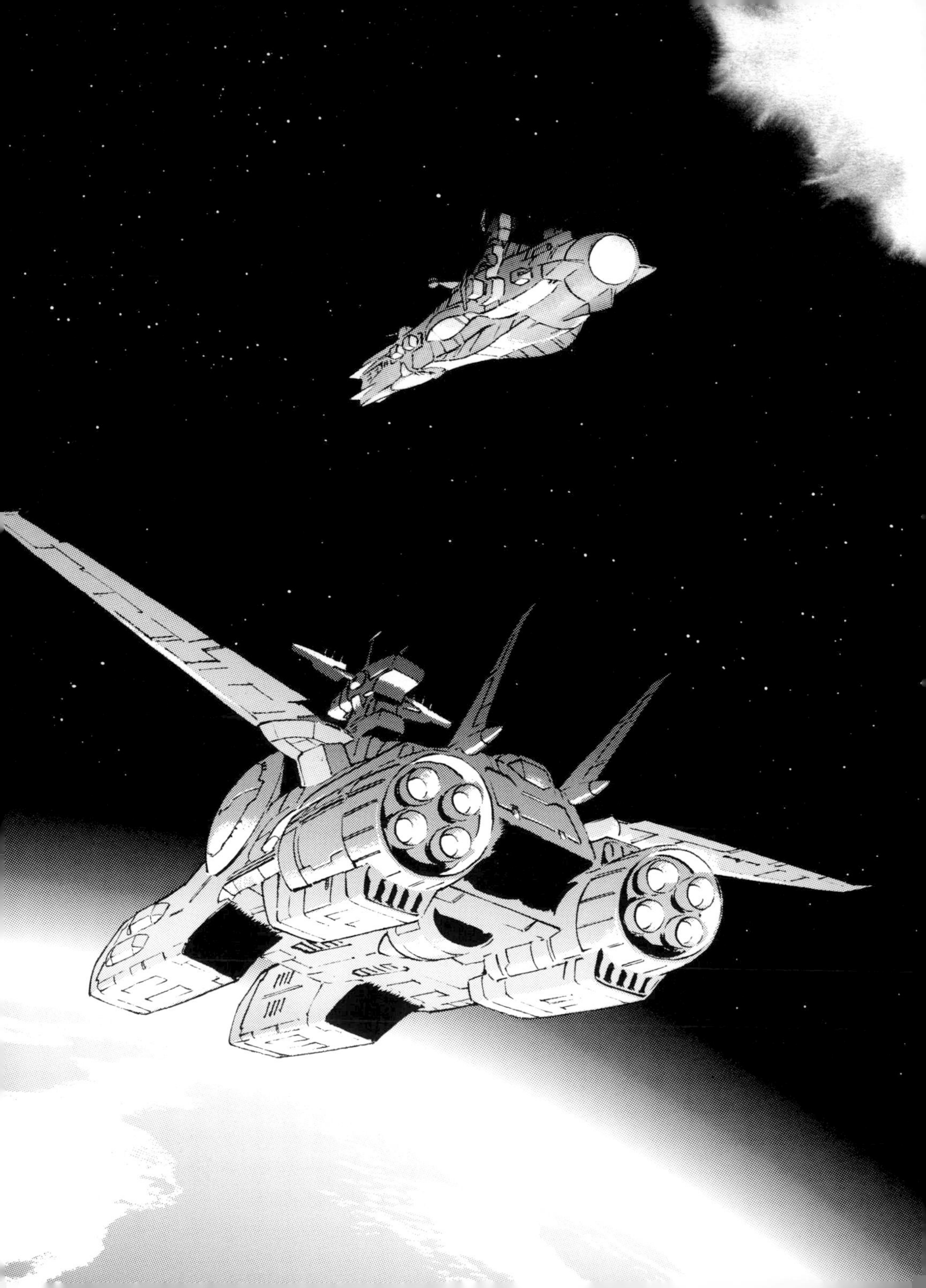

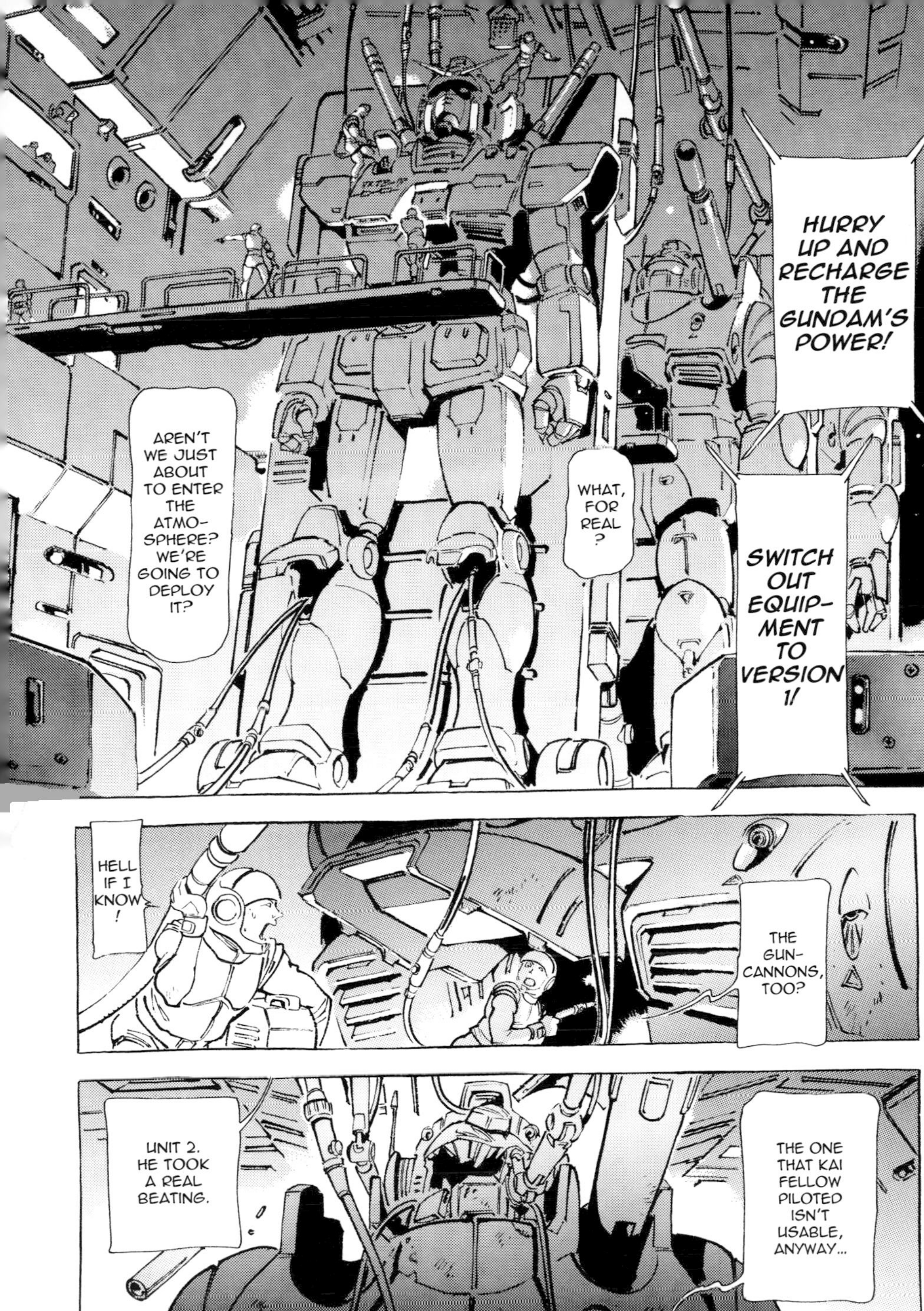
HURRY UP AND RECHARGE THE GUNDAM'S POWER!
SWITCH OUT EQUIPMENT TO VERSION 1!
WHAT, FOR REAL?
AREN'T WE JUST ABOUT TO ENTER THE ATMOSPHERE? WE'RE GOING TO DEPLOY IT?
THE GUN-CANNONS, TOO?
HELL IF I KNOW!
THE ONE THAT KAI FELLOW PILOTED ISN'T USABLE, ANYWAY...
UNIT 2. HE TOOK A REAL BEATING.

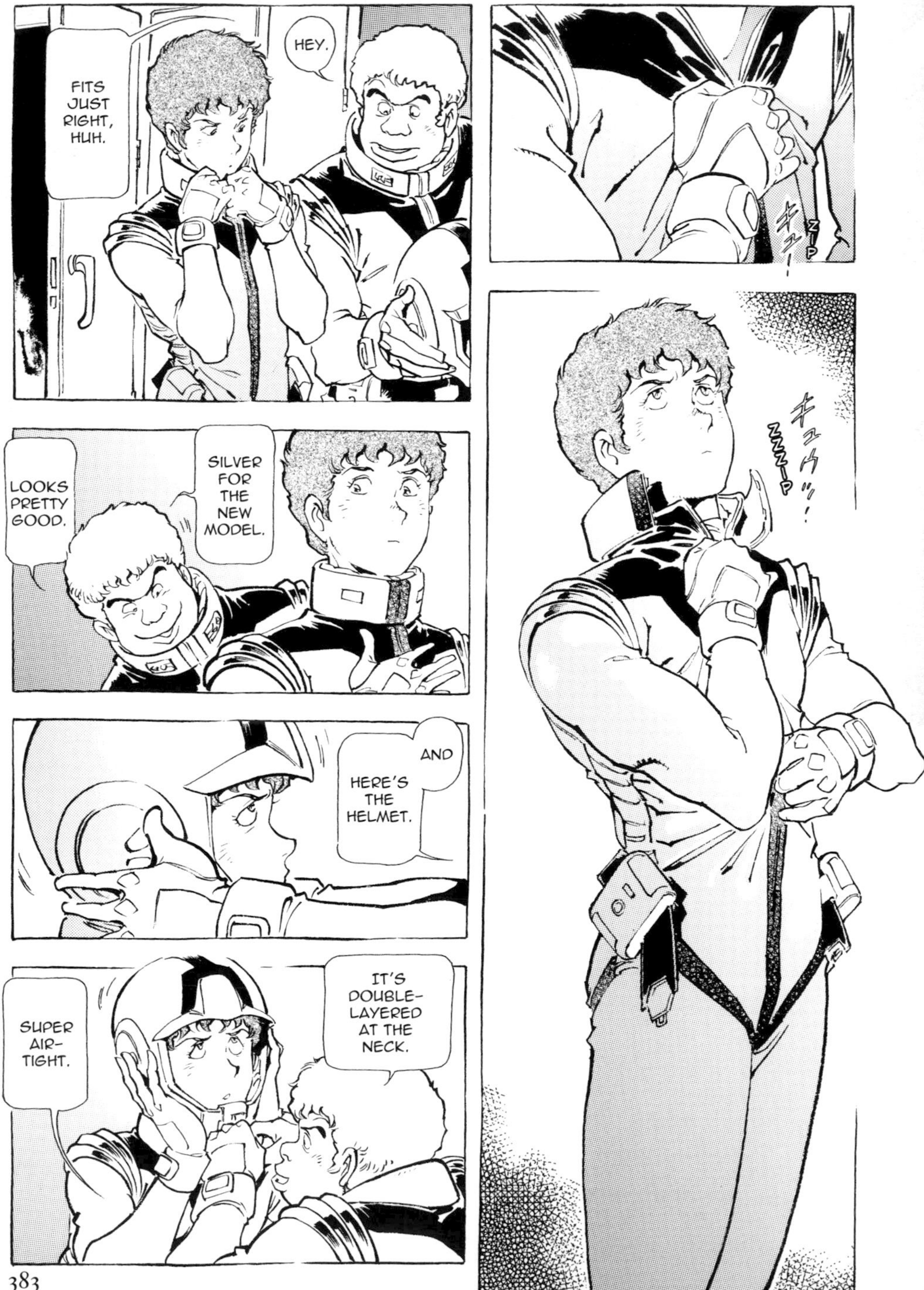
キュ
ZIP
キュウッ!
ZZZIP
HEY.
FITS JUST RIGHT, HUH.
SILVER FOR THE NEW MODEL.
LOOKS PRETTY GOOD.
AND HERE'S THE HELMET.
IT'S DOUBLE-LAYERED AT THE NECK.
SUPER AIR-TIGHT.

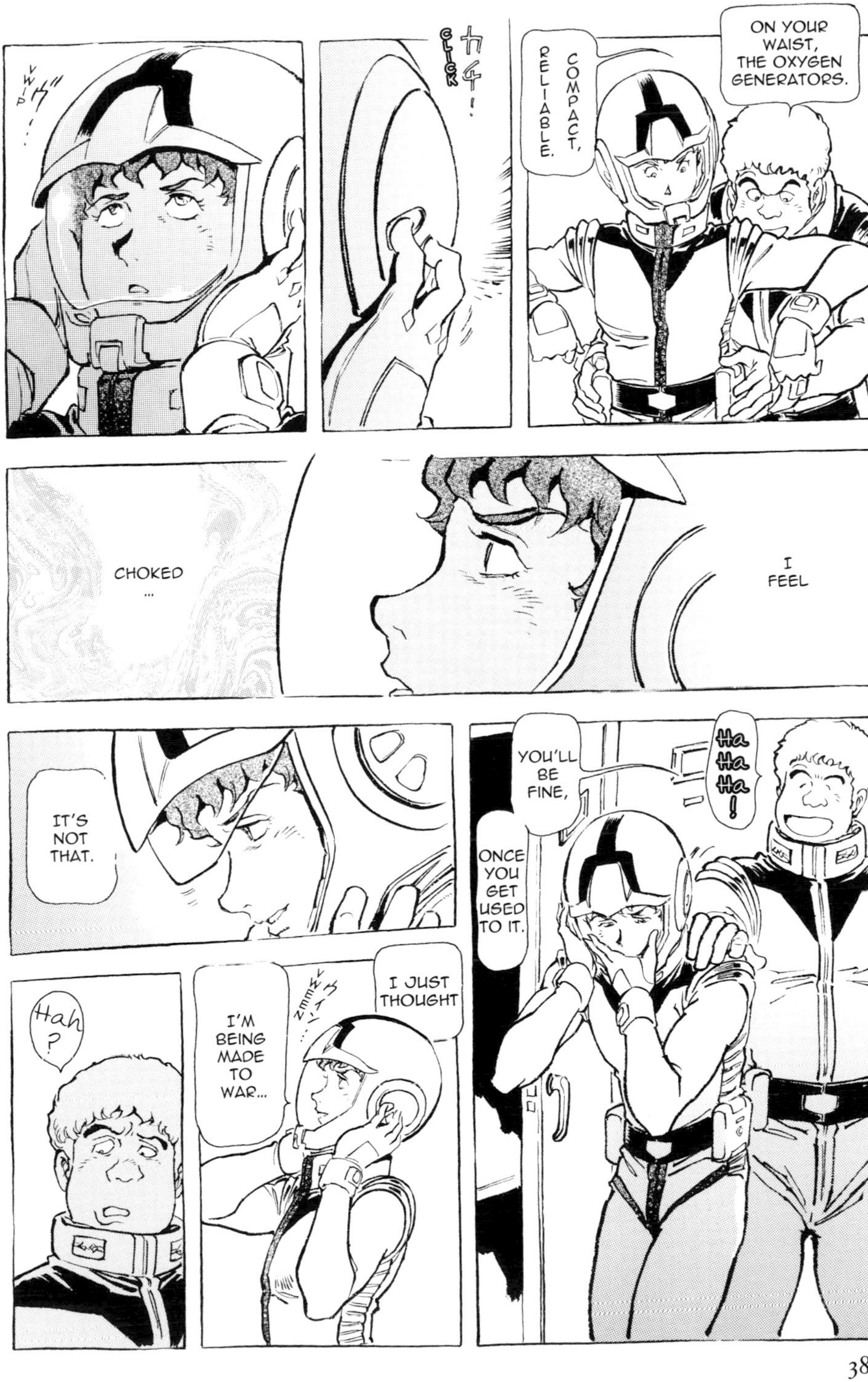
ON YOUR WAIST, THE OXYGEN GENERATORS.
COMPACT, RELIABLE.
CLICK
VWIP
I FEEL
CHOKED ...
Ha Ha Ha!
YOU'LL BE FINE,
ONCE YOU GET USED TO IT.
IT'S NOT THAT.
I JUST THOUGHT
VWEEN
I'M BEING MADE TO WAR...
Hah?

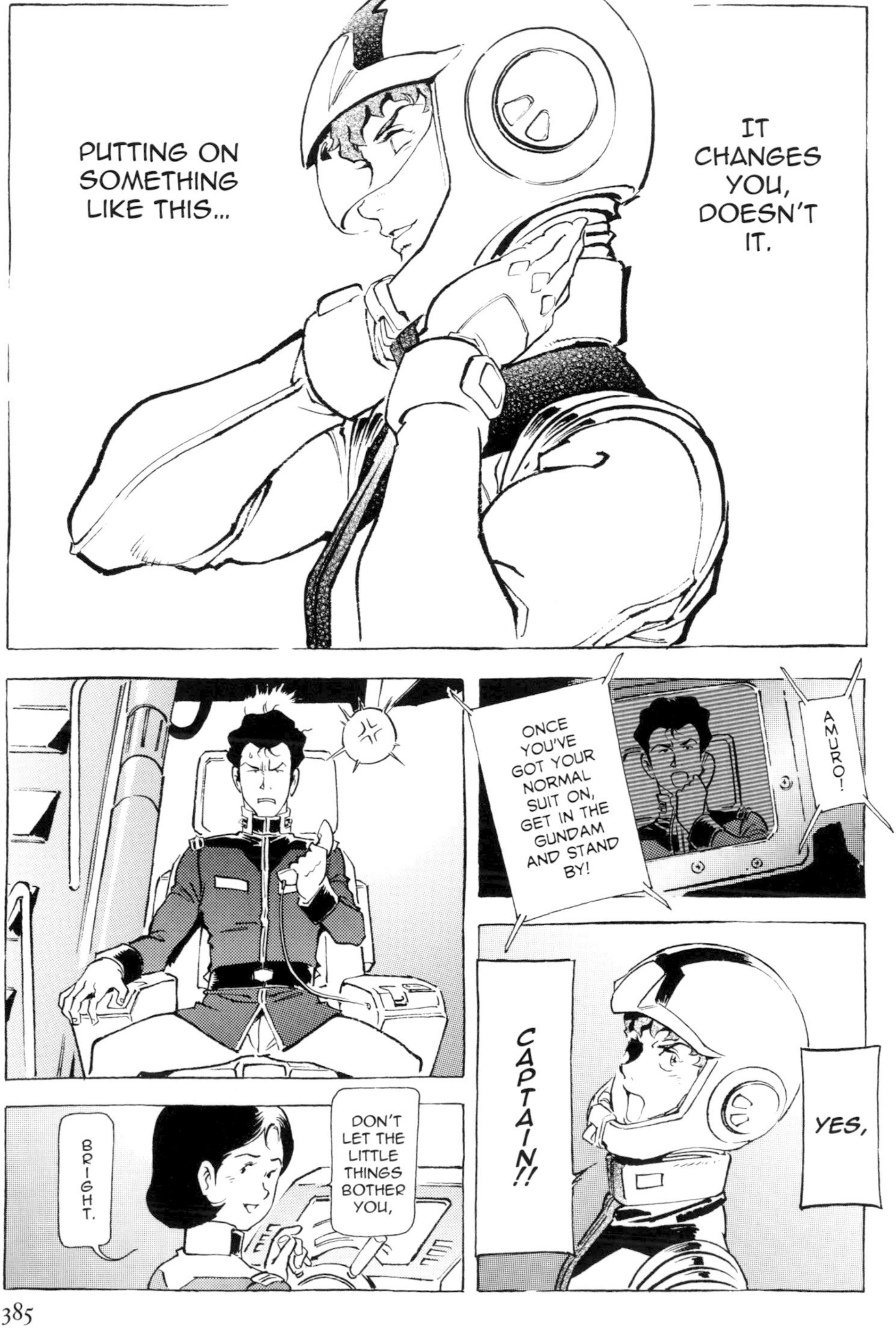
IT CHANGES YOU, DOESN'T IT.
PUTTING ON SOMETHING LIKE THIS...
AMURO!
ONCE YOU'VE GOT YOUR NORMAL SUIT ON, GET IN THE GUNDAM AND STAND BY!
YES,
CAPTAIN!!
DON'T LET THE LITTLE THINGS BOTHER YOU,
BRIGHT.

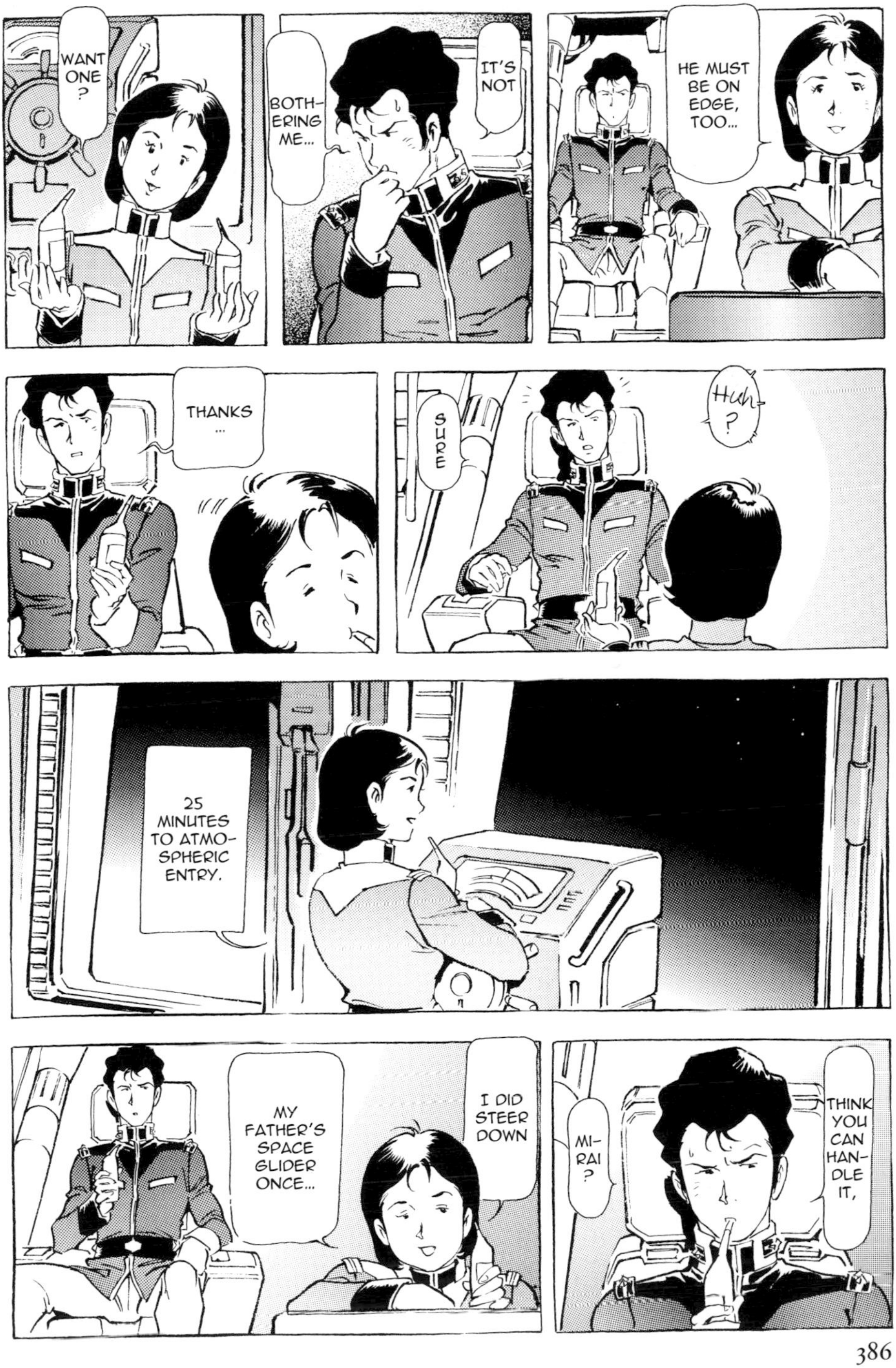
HE MUST BE ON EDGE, TOO...
IT'S NOT BOTHERING ME...
WANT ONE?
Huh-?
SURE
THANKS ...
25 MINUTES TO ATMOSPHERIC ENTRY.
THINK YOU CAN HANDLE IT,
MIRAI?
I DID STEER DOWN
MY FATHER'S SPACE GLIDER ONCE...

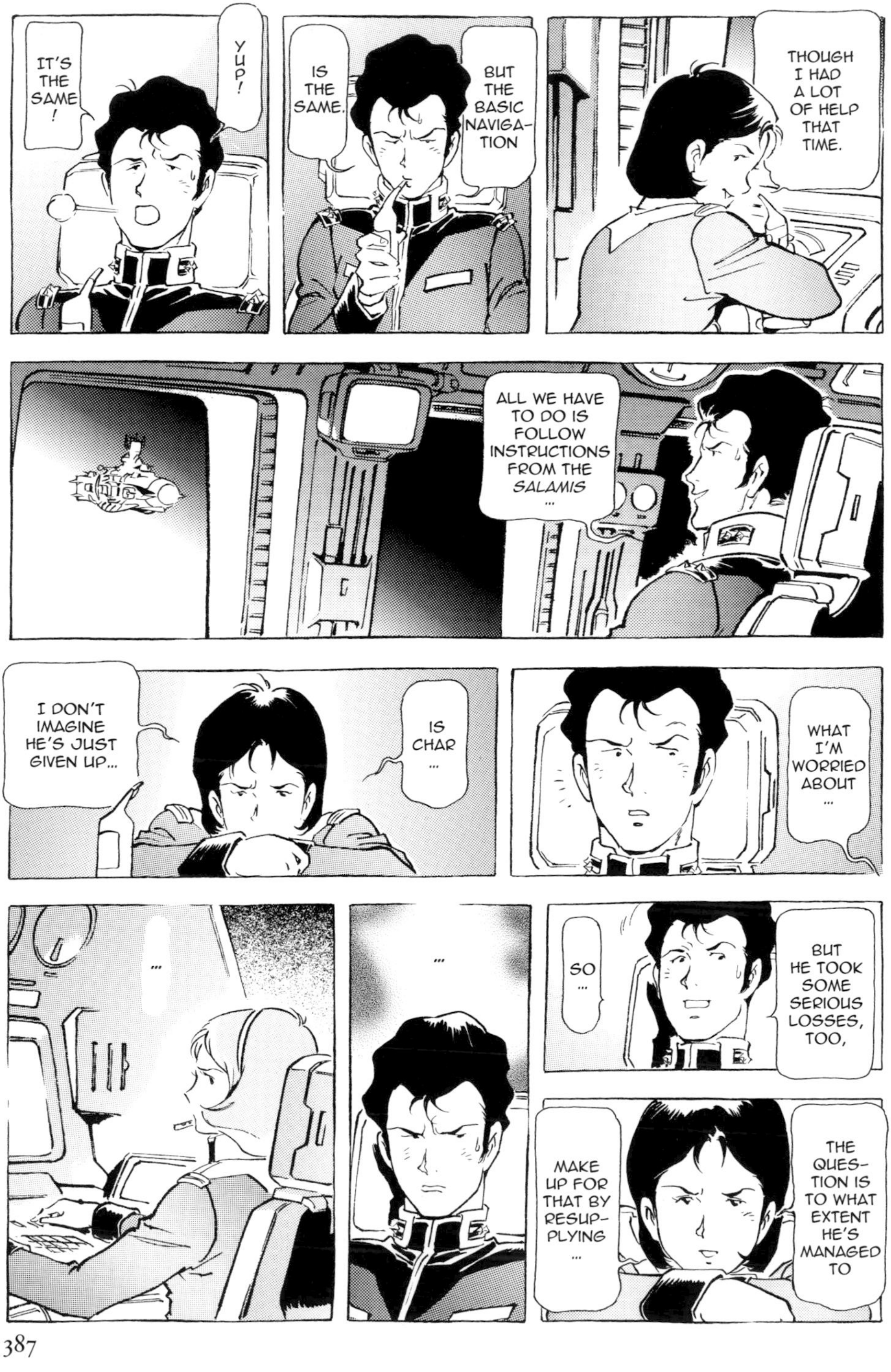
THOUGH I HAD A LOT OF HELP THAT TIME.
BUT THE BASIC NAVIGA-TION
IS THE SAME.
YUP!
IT'S THE SAME!
ALL WE HAVE TO DO IS FOLLOW INSTRUCTIONS FROM THE *SALAMIS* ...
WHAT I'M WORRIED ABOUT ...
IS CHAR ...
I DON'T IMAGINE HE'S JUST GIVEN UP...
BUT HE TOOK SOME SERIOUS LOSSES, TOO,
SO ...
THE QUES-TION IS TO WHAT EXTENT HE'S MANAGED TO
MAKE UP FOR THAT BY RESUP-PLYING ...
...
...

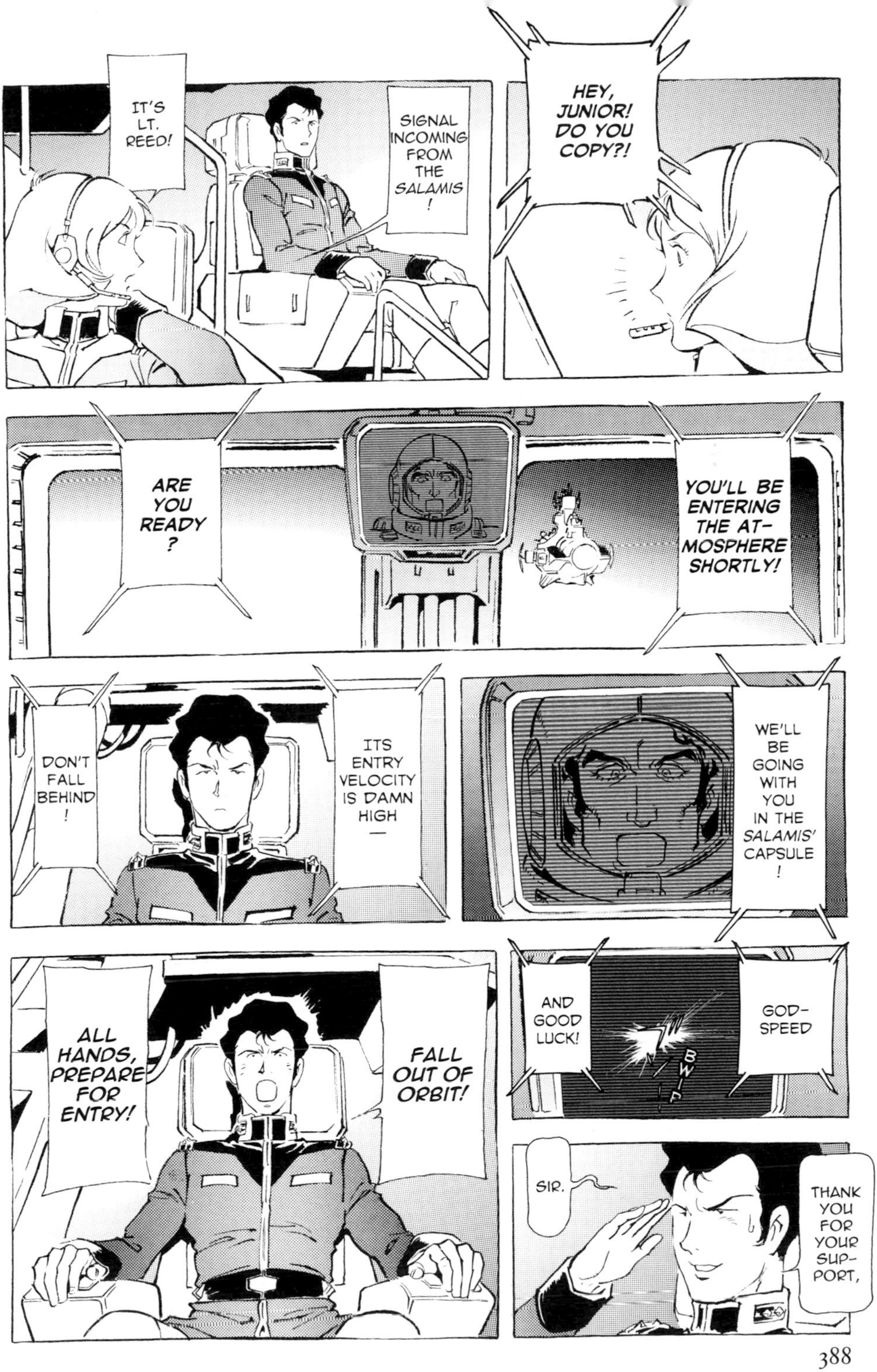
HEY, JUNIOR! DO YOU COPY?!
SIGNAL INCOMING FROM THE *SALAMIS*!
IT'S LT. REED!
YOU'LL BE ENTERING THE AT-MOSPHERE SHORTLY!
ARE YOU READY?
WE'LL BE GOING WITH YOU IN THE *SALAMIS'* CAPSULE!
ITS ENTRY VELOCITY IS DAMN HIGH—
DON'T FALL BEHIND!
GOD-SPEED
AND GOOD LUCK!
BWIP
THANK YOU FOR YOUR SUP-PORT,
SIR.
FALL OUT OF ORBIT!
ALL HANDS, PREPARE FOR ENTRY!

ズ"
ZMM
ズ"ズ"
ZMMM
ズ"ズ"ズ"ズ"ズ"
ウィ…
イ…
WMMM
ゴ"ゴ"ゴ"
GRMM

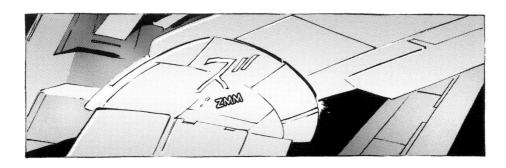

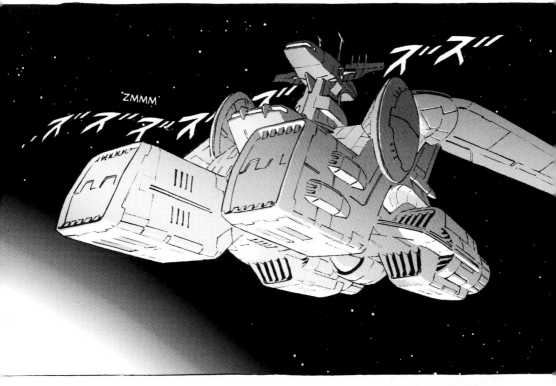

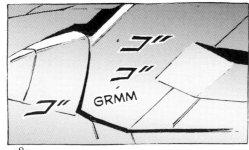

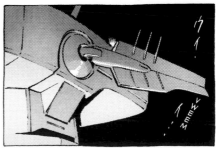

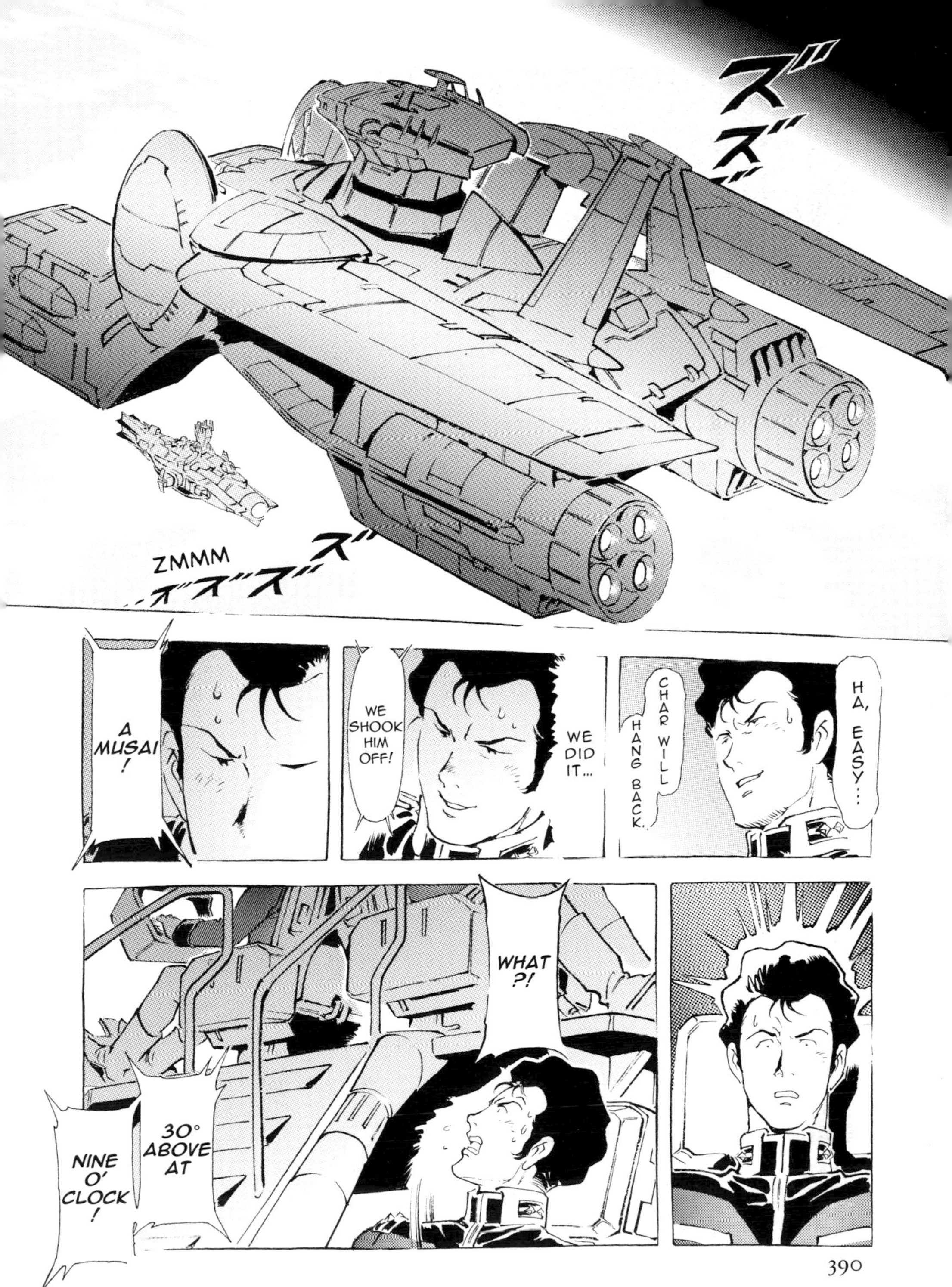
ズズ
ZMMM
ズズズズ
HA, EASY...
CHAR WILL HANG BACK.
WE DID IT...
WE SHOOK HIM OFF!
A MUSAI!
WHAT?!
30° ABOVE AT
NINE O' CLOCK!

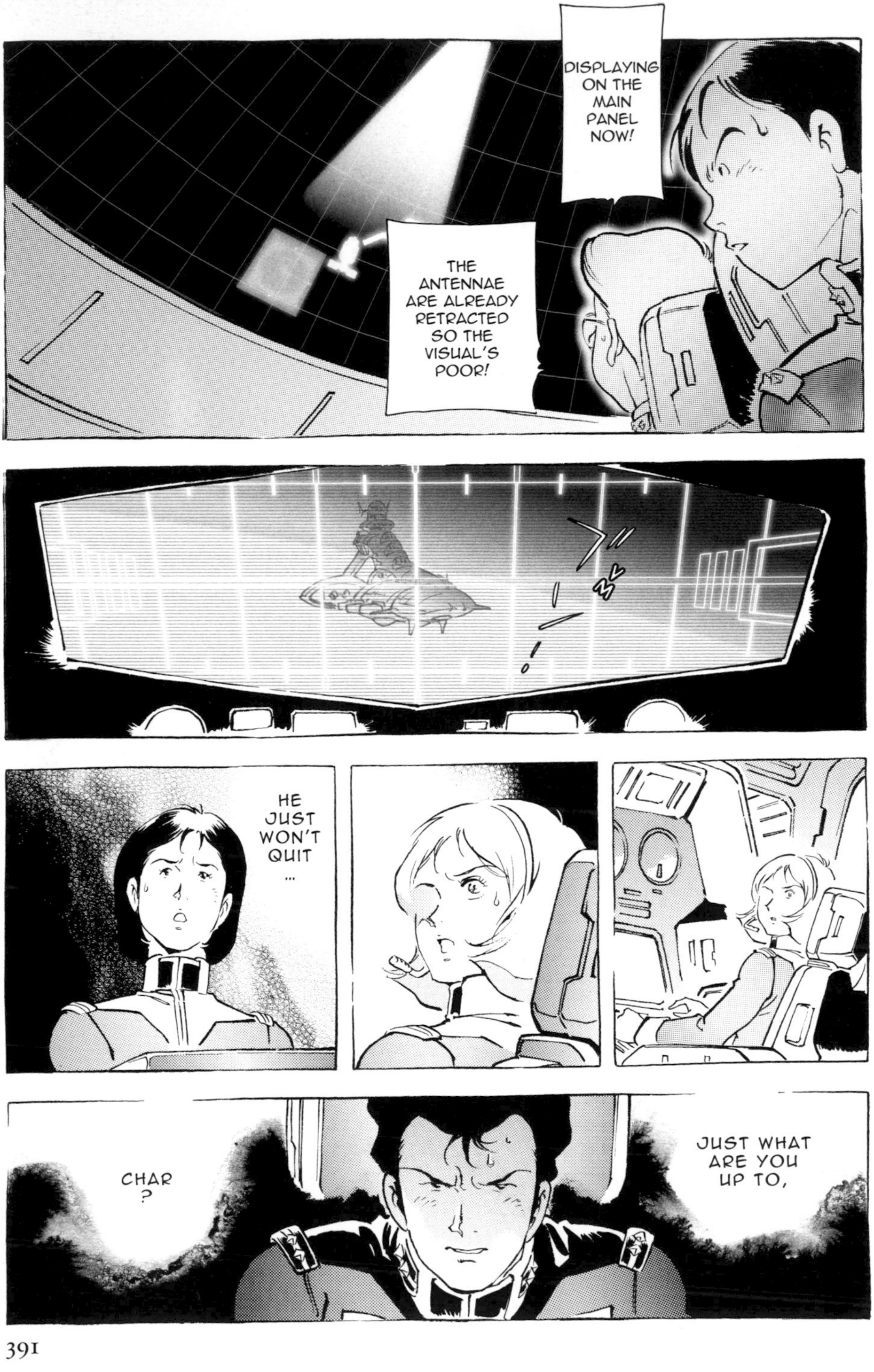
DISPLAYING ON THE MAIN PANEL NOW!
THE ANTENNAE ARE ALREADY RETRACTED SO THE VISUAL'S POOR!
HE JUST WON'T QUIT ...
JUST WHAT ARE YOU UP TO,
CHAR ?

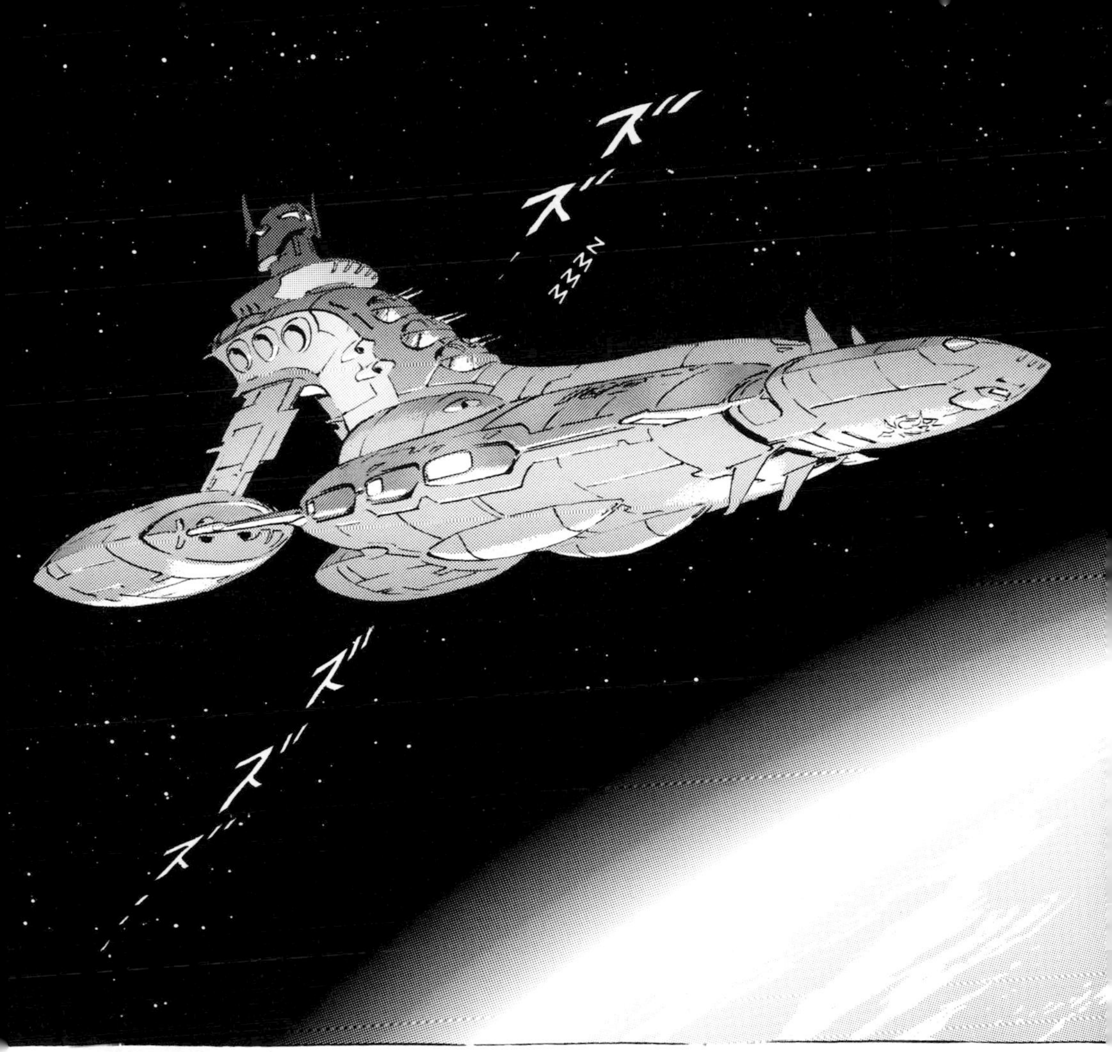

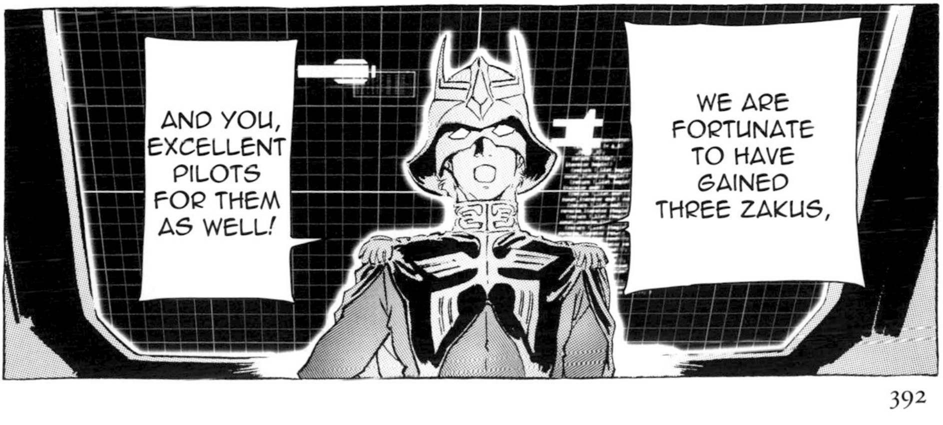
WE ARE FORTUNATE TO HAVE GAINED THREE ZAKUS,
AND YOU, EXCELLENT PILOTS FOR THEM AS WELL!

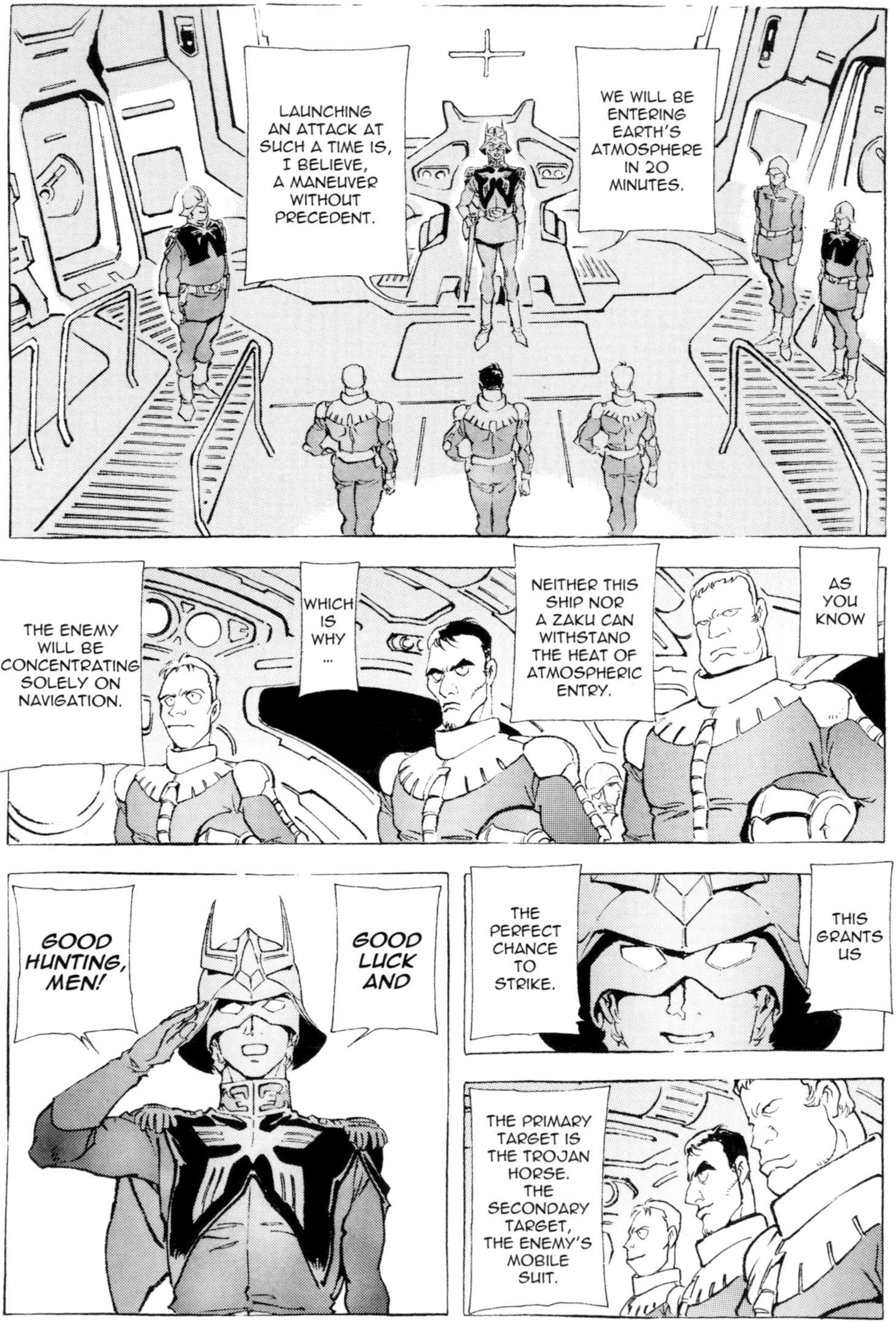
WE WILL BE ENTERING EARTH'S ATMOSPHERE IN 20 MINUTES.
LAUNCHING AN ATTACK AT SUCH A TIME IS, I BELIEVE, A MANEUVER WITHOUT PRECEDENT.
AS YOU KNOW
NEITHER THIS SHIP NOR A ZAKU CAN WITHSTAND THE HEAT OF ATMOSPHERIC ENTRY.
WHICH IS WHY ...
THE ENEMY WILL BE CONCENTRATING SOLELY ON NAVIGATION.
THIS GRANTS US
THE PERFECT CHANCE TO STRIKE.
THE PRIMARY TARGET IS THE TROJAN HORSE. THE SECONDARY TARGET, THE ENEMY'S MOBILE SUIT.
GOOD LUCK AND
GOOD HUNTING, MEN!

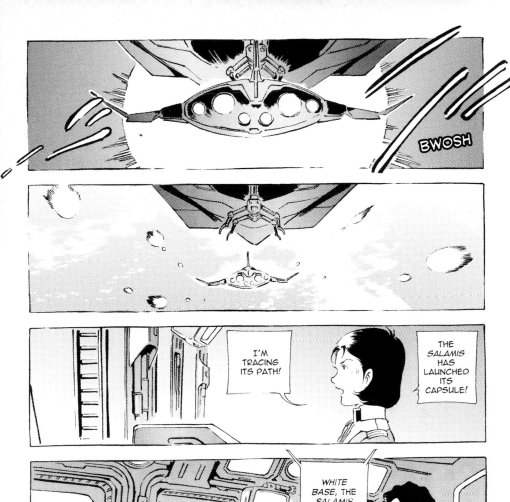

BWOSH

I'M TRACING ITS PATH!

THE SALAMIS HAS LAUNCHED ITS CAPSULE!

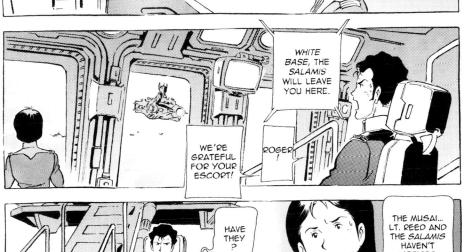

WHITE BASE, THE SALAMIS WILL LEAVE YOU HERE.

WE'RE GRATEFUL FOR YOUR ESCORT!

ROGER!

HAVE THEY?

THE MUSAI... LT. REED AND THE SALAMIS HAVEN'T NOTICED...

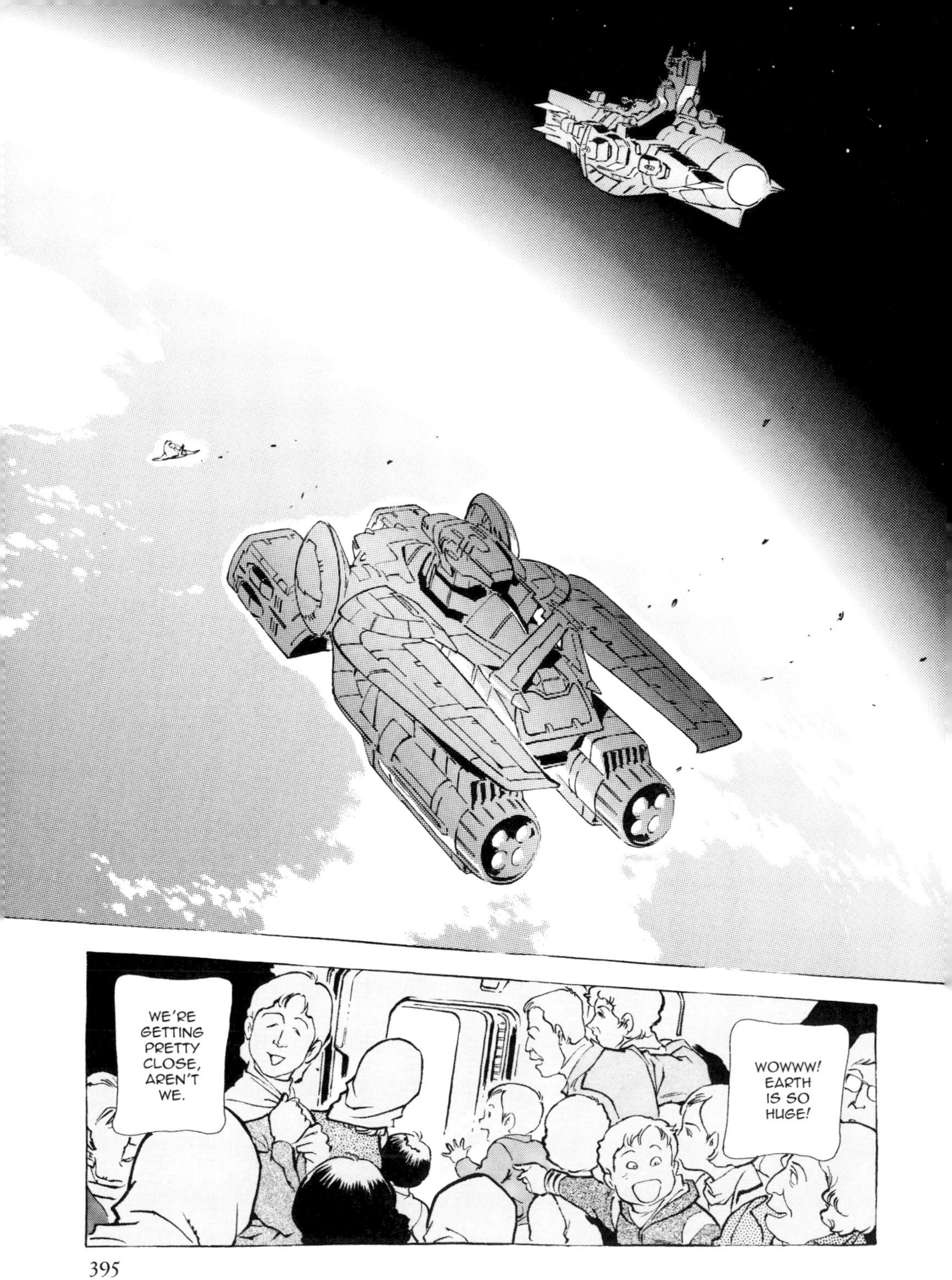
WOWWW! EARTH IS SO HUGE!
WE'RE GETTING PRETTY CLOSE, AREN'T WE.

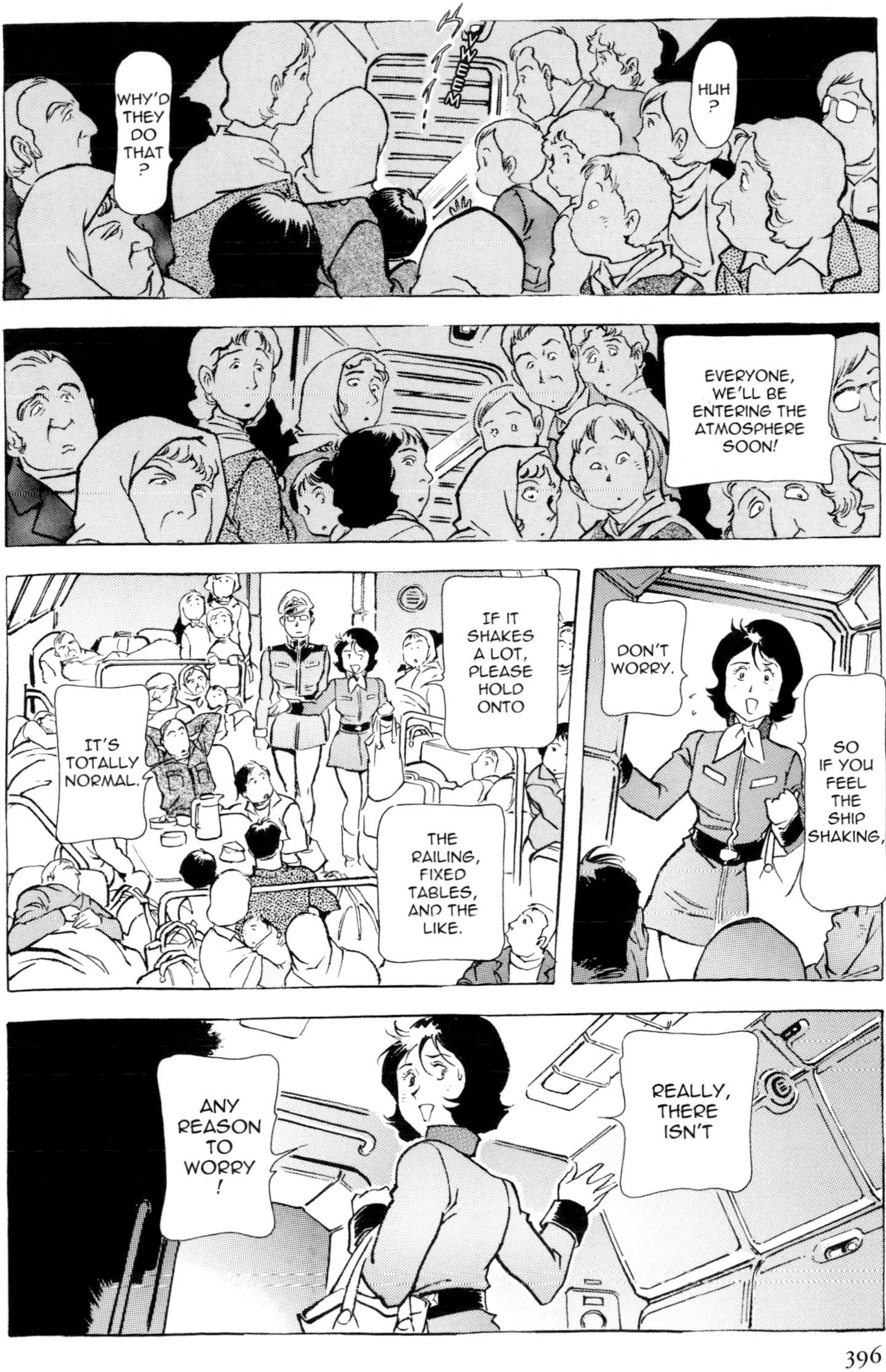
HUH ?
VWEEM
WHY'D THEY DO THAT ?
EVERYONE, WE'LL BE ENTERING THE ATMOSPHERE SOON!
SO IF YOU FEEL THE SHIP SHAKING,
DON'T WORRY.
IF IT SHAKES A LOT, PLEASE HOLD ONTO
THE RAILING, FIXED TABLES, AND THE LIKE.
IT'S TOTALLY NORMAL.
REALLY, THERE ISN'T
ANY REASON TO WORRY !

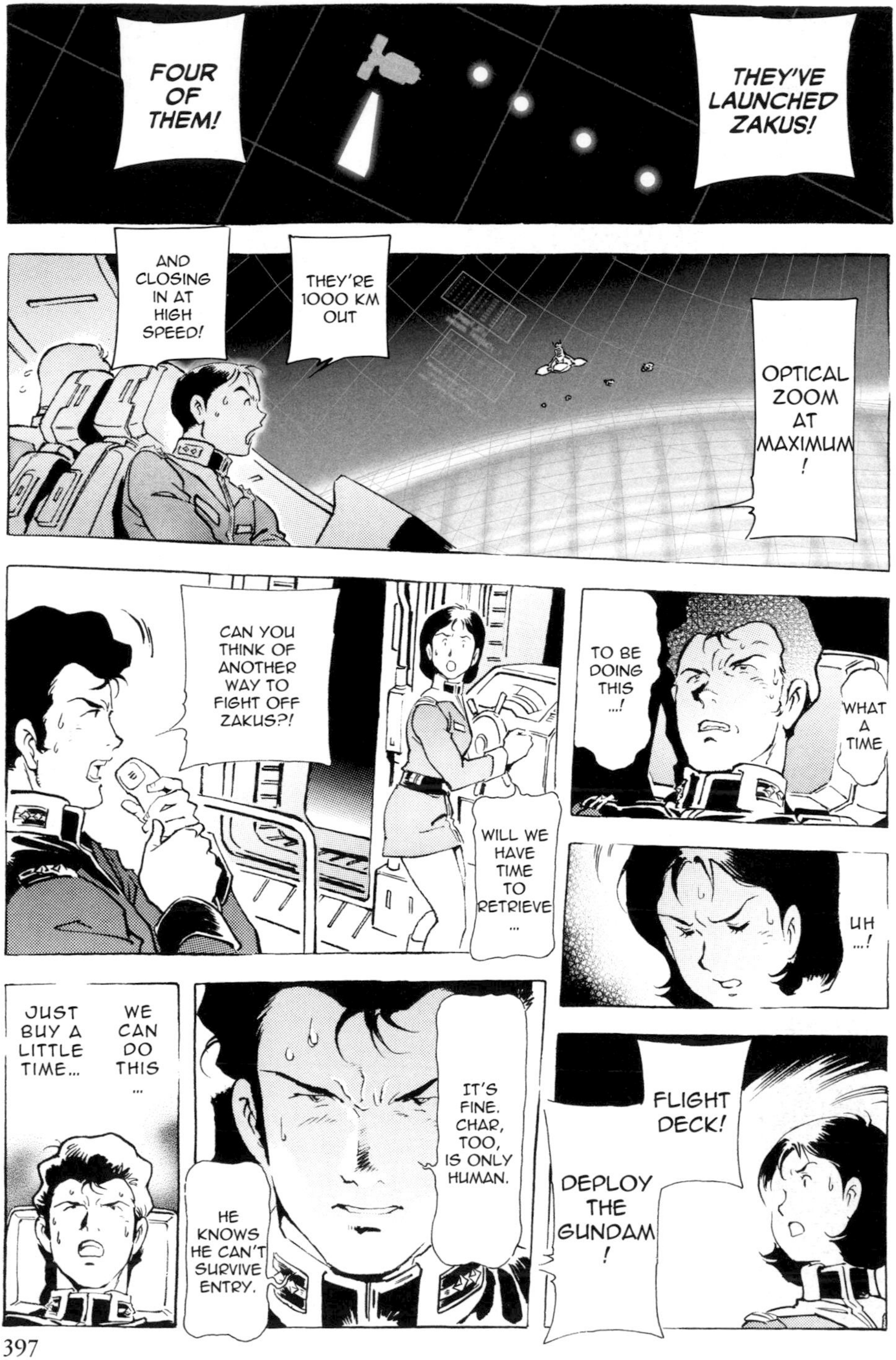

THEY'VE LAUNCHED ZAKUS!
FOUR OF THEM!
OPTICAL ZOOM AT MAXIMUM!
THEY'RE 1000 KM OUT
AND CLOSING IN AT HIGH SPEED!
WHAT A TIME
TO BE DOING THIS ...!
UH ...!
WILL WE HAVE TIME TO RETRIEVE ...
CAN YOU THINK OF ANOTHER WAY TO FIGHT OFF ZAKUS?!
FLIGHT DECK!
DEPLOY THE GUNDAM!
IT'S FINE. CHAR, TOO, IS ONLY HUMAN.
HE KNOWS HE CAN'T SURVIVE ENTRY.
WE CAN DO THIS ...
JUST BUY A LITTLE TIME...

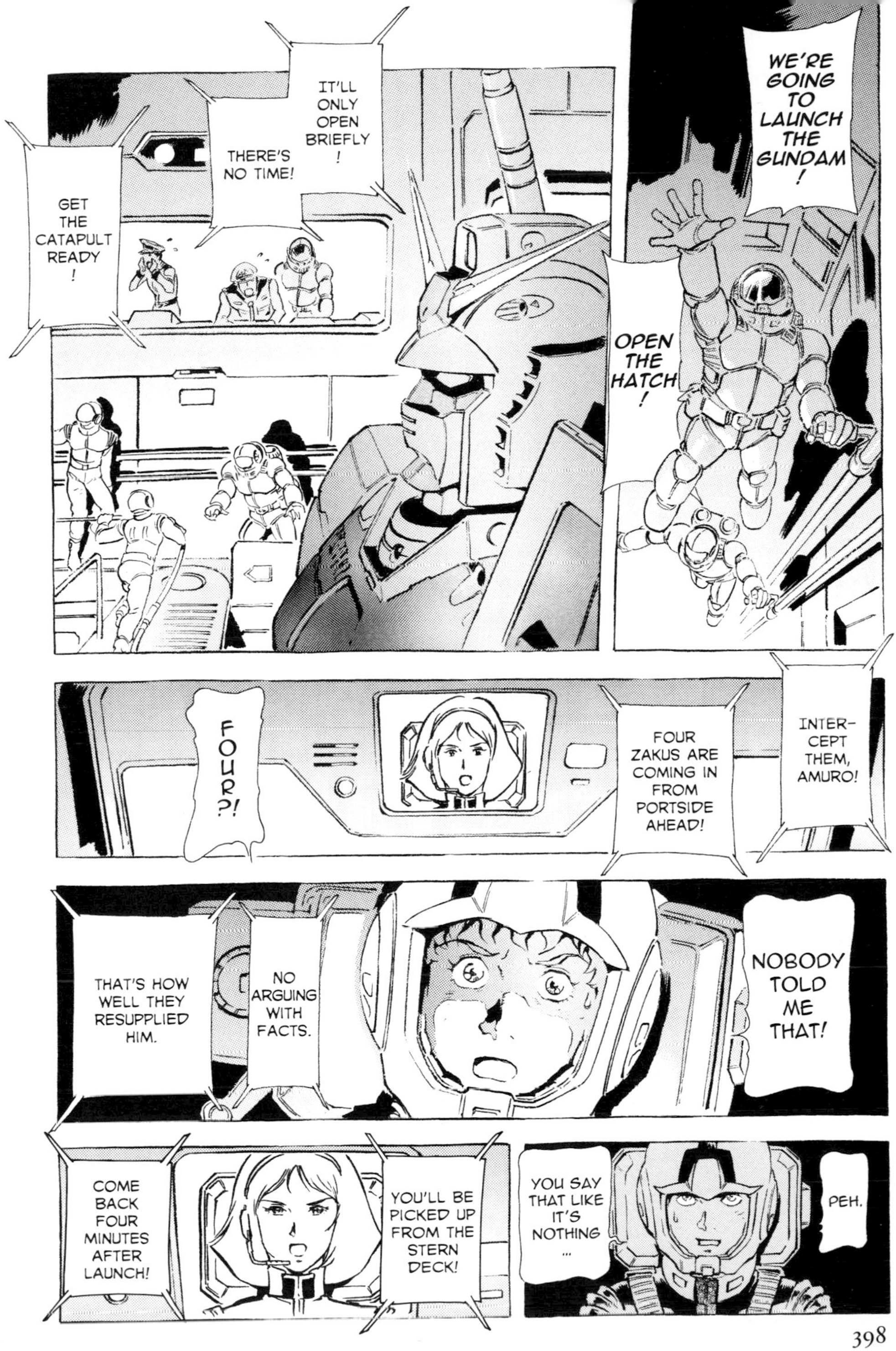
WE'RE GOING TO LAUNCH THE GUNDAM!
OPEN THE HATCH!
IT'LL ONLY OPEN BRIEFLY!
THERE'S NO TIME!
GET THE CATAPULT READY!
INTER-CEPT THEM, AMURO!
FOUR ZAKUS ARE COMING IN FROM PORTSIDE AHEAD!
FOUR?!
NOBODY TOLD ME THAT!
NO ARGUING WITH FACTS.
THAT'S HOW WELL THEY RESUPPLIED HIM.
PEH.
YOU SAY THAT LIKE IT'S NOTHING ...
YOU'LL BE PICKED UP FROM THE STERN DECK!
COME BACK FOUR MINUTES AFTER LAUNCH!

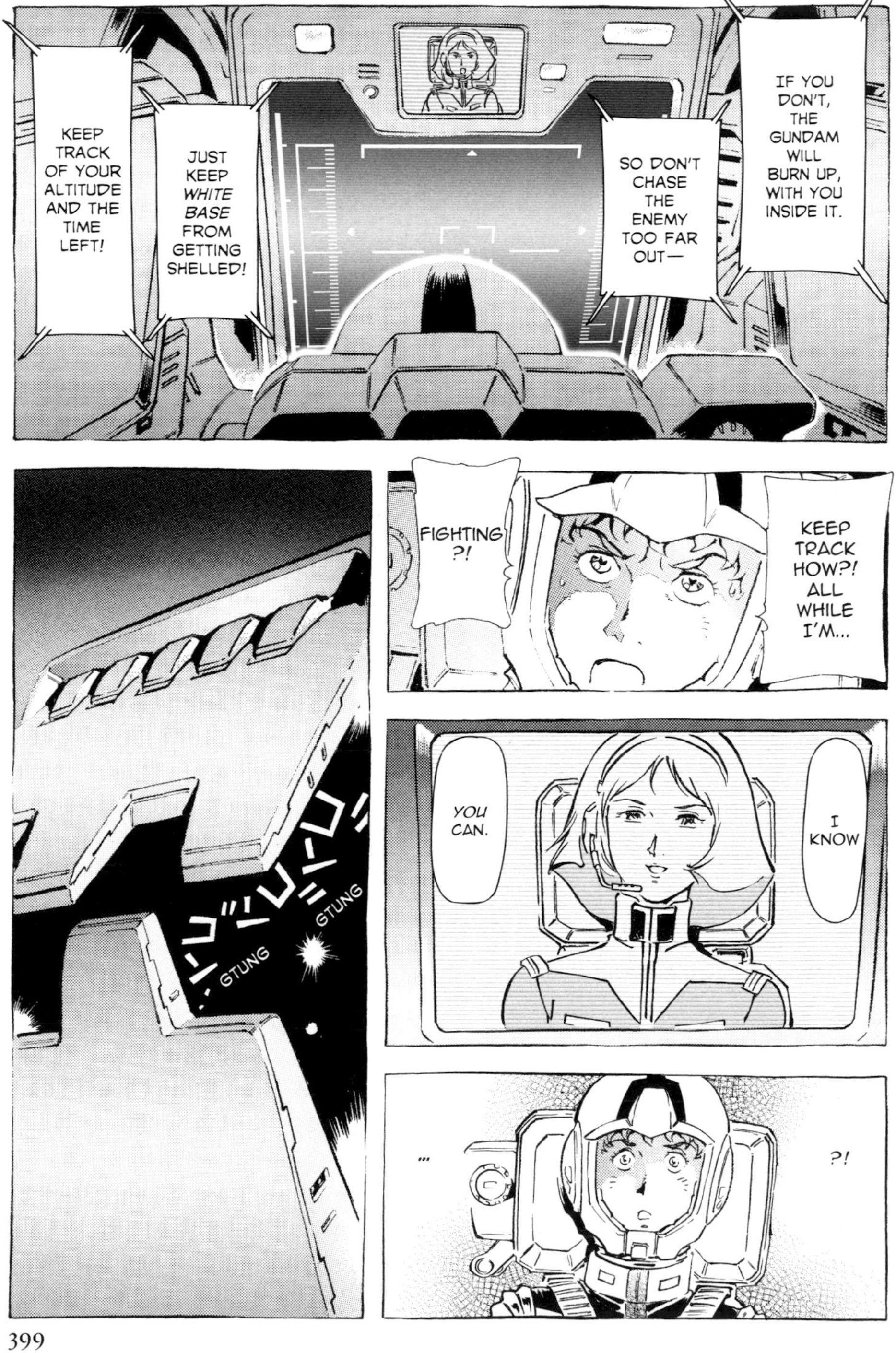
IF YOU DON'T, THE GUNDAM WILL BURN UP, WITH YOU INSIDE IT.
SO DON'T CHASE THE ENEMY TOO FAR OUT—
JUST KEEP *WHITE BASE* FROM GETTING SHELLED!
KEEP TRACK OF YOUR ALTITUDE AND THE TIME LEFT!
KEEP TRACK HOW?! ALL WHILE I'M...
FIGHTING?!
I KNOW
YOU CAN.
?!
...
GTUNG
GTUNG

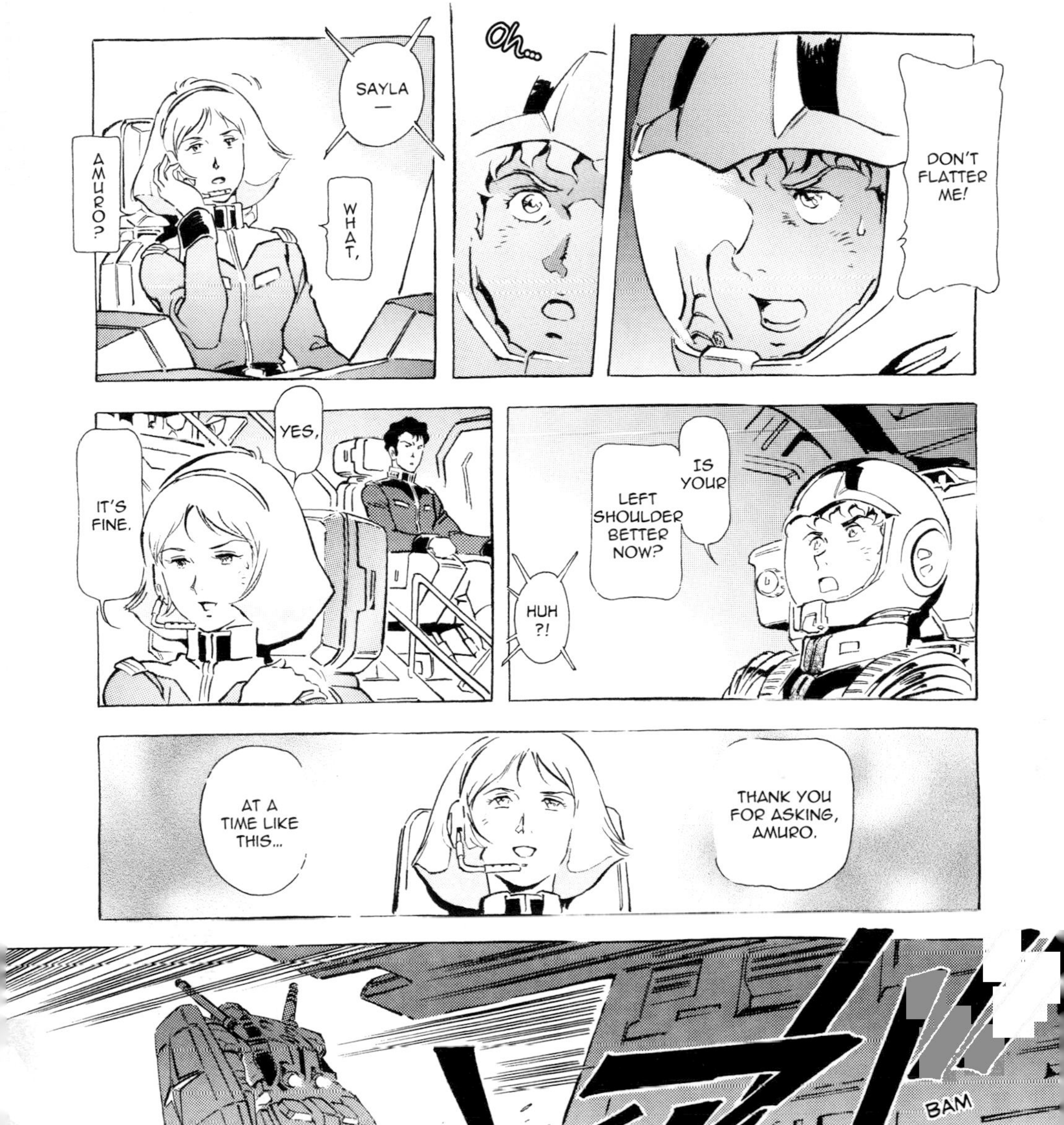
DON'T FLATTER ME!
Oh...
SAYLA —
WHAT,
AMURO?
IS YOUR LEFT SHOULDER BETTER NOW?
HUH?!
YES,
IT'S FINE.
THANK YOU FOR ASKING, AMURO.
AT A TIME LIKE THIS...
BAM

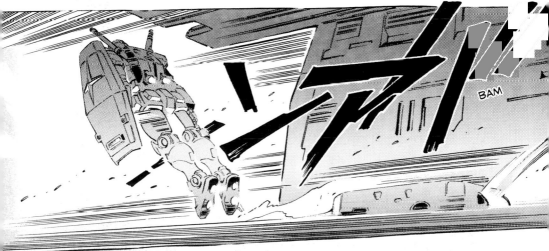

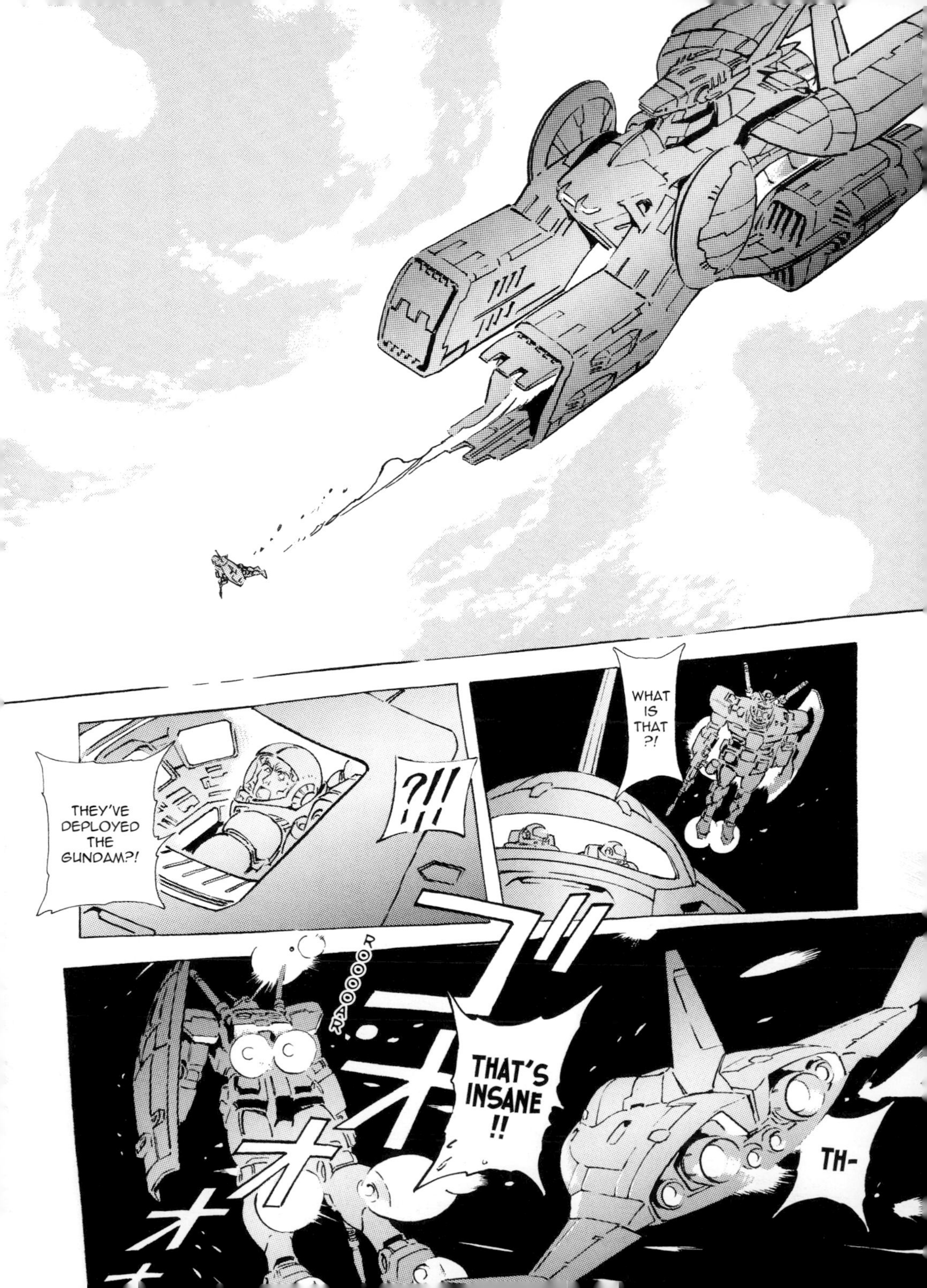
WHAT IS THAT?!
?!!
THEY'VE DEPLOYED THE GUNDAM?!
TH-
ブオオ
ROOOOAR
THAT'S INSANE!!

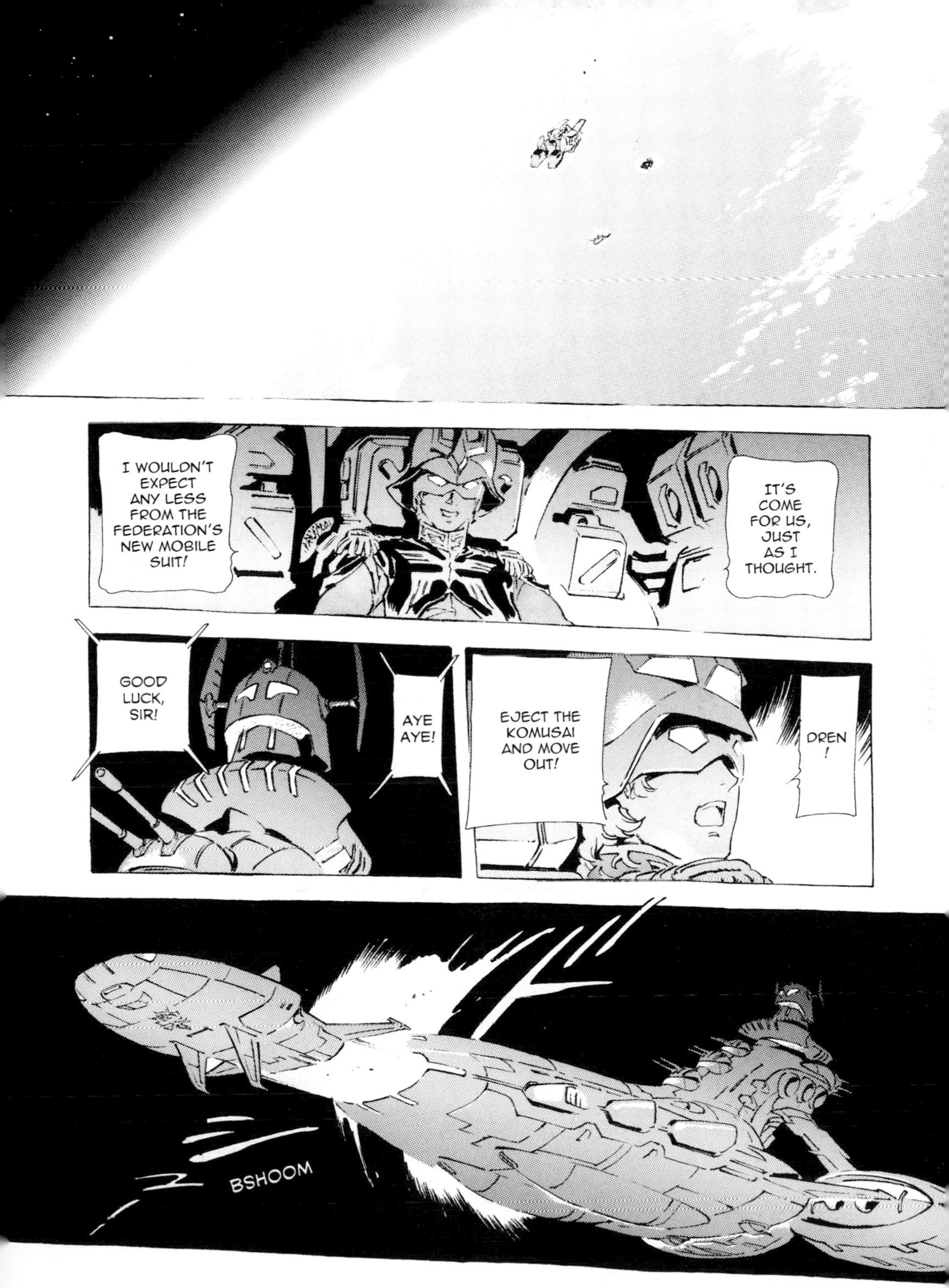
IT'S COME FOR US, JUST AS I THOUGHT.
I WOULDN'T EXPECT ANY LESS FROM THE FEDERATION'S NEW MOBILE SUIT!
DREN!
EJECT THE KOMUSAI AND MOVE OUT!
AYE AYE!
GOOD LUCK, SIR!
BSHOOM

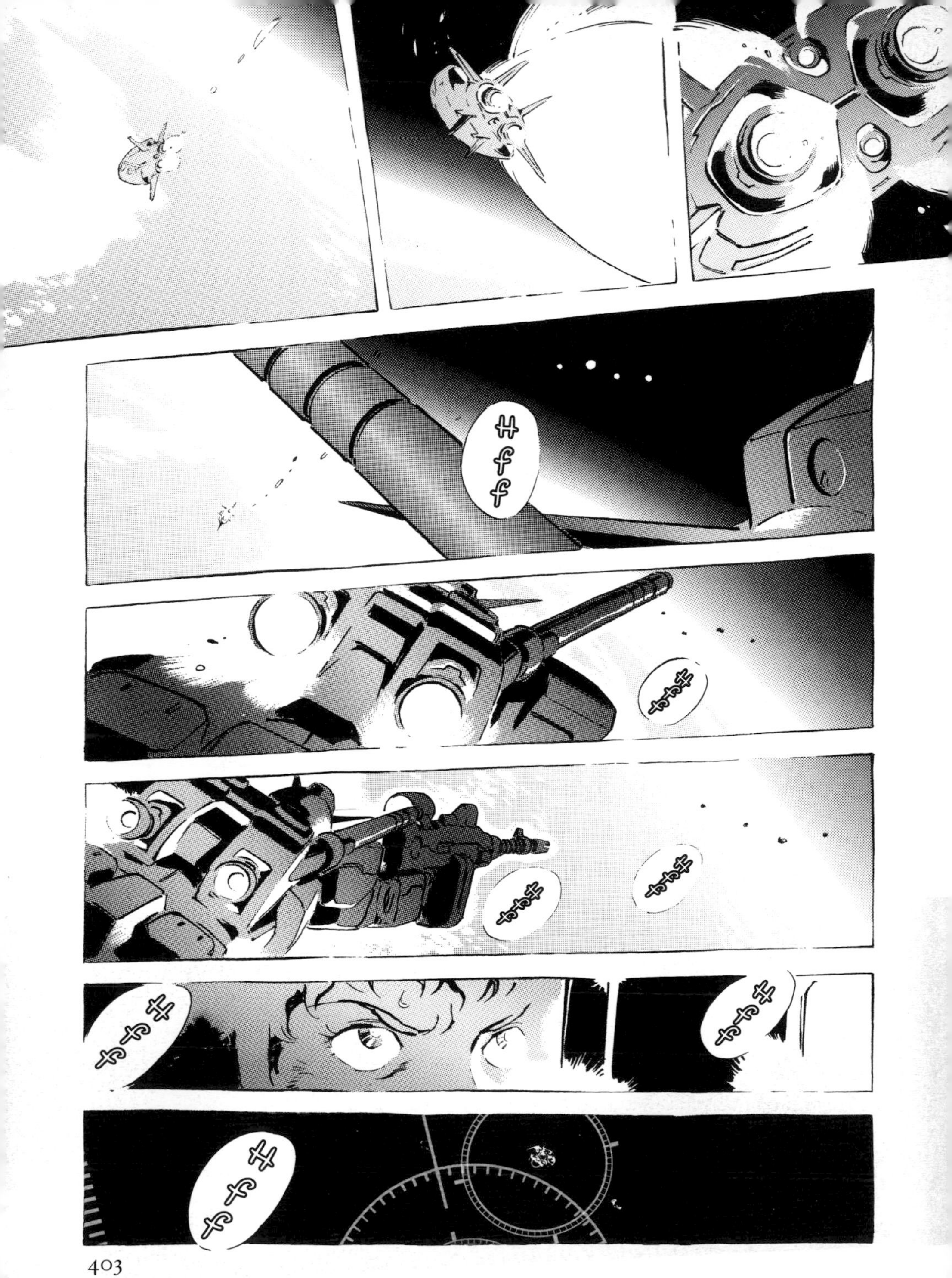
キチチ
キチチ
キチチ
キチチ
キチチ
キチチ
キチチ

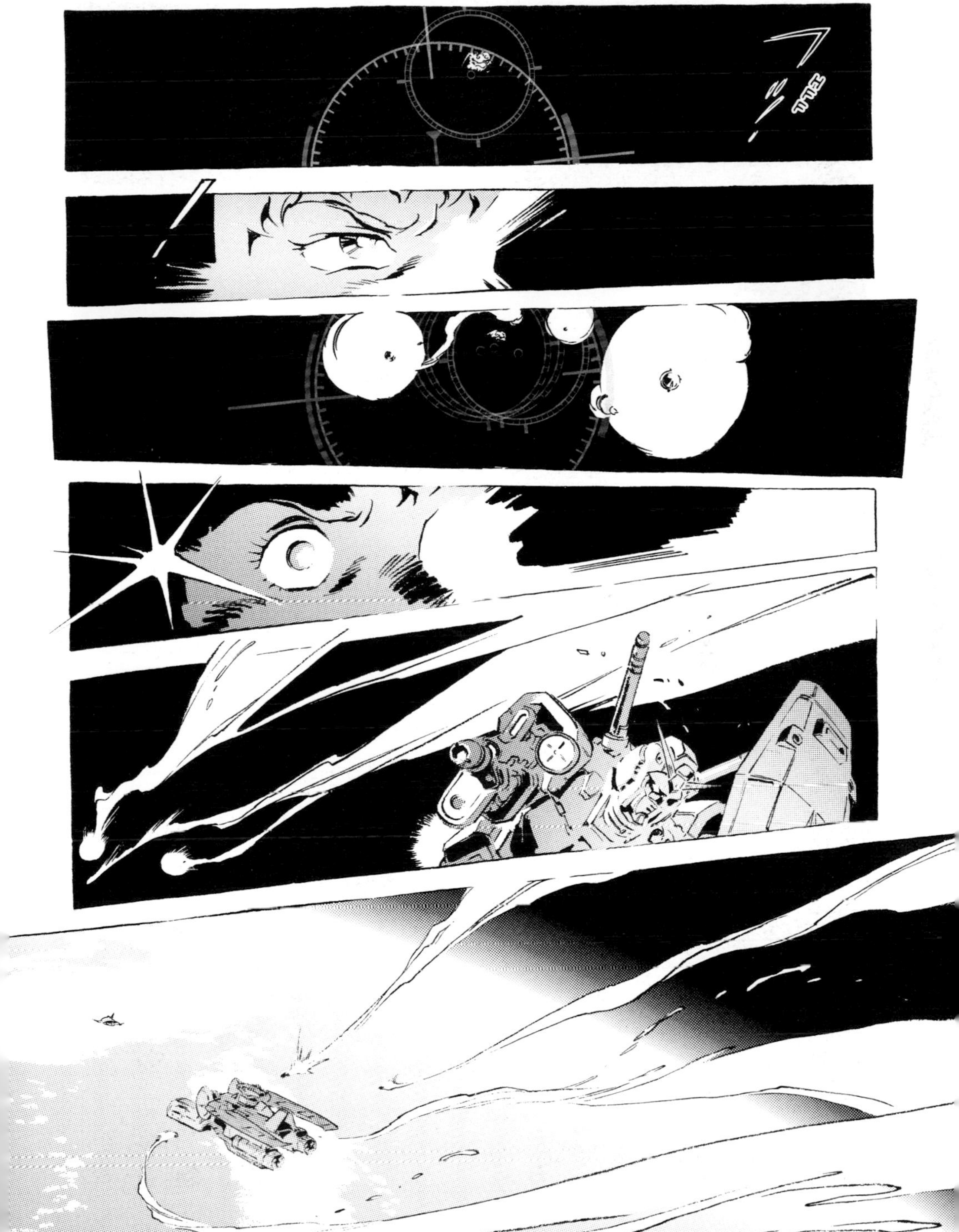
フッ!

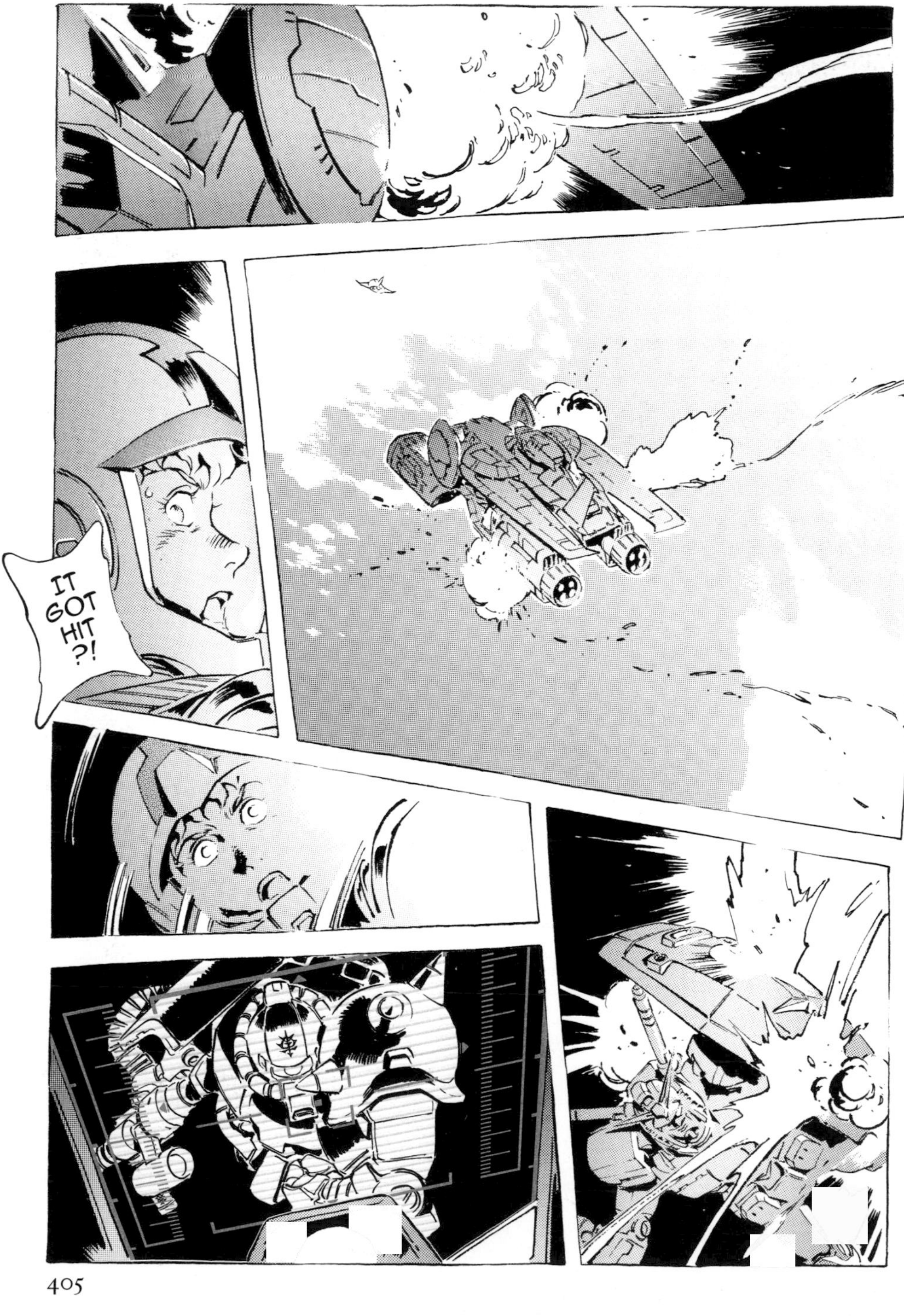
IT GOT HIT?!

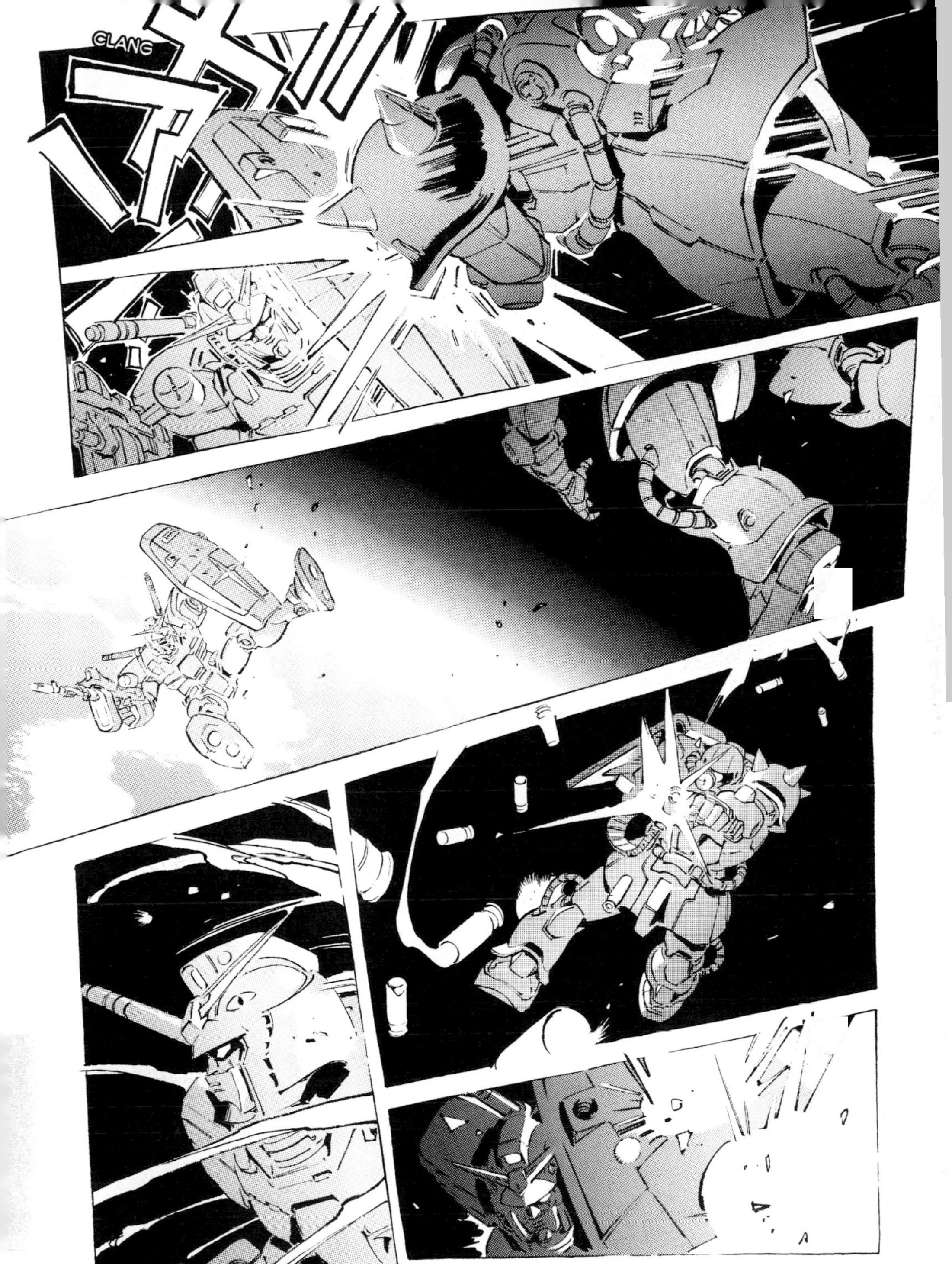
CLANG

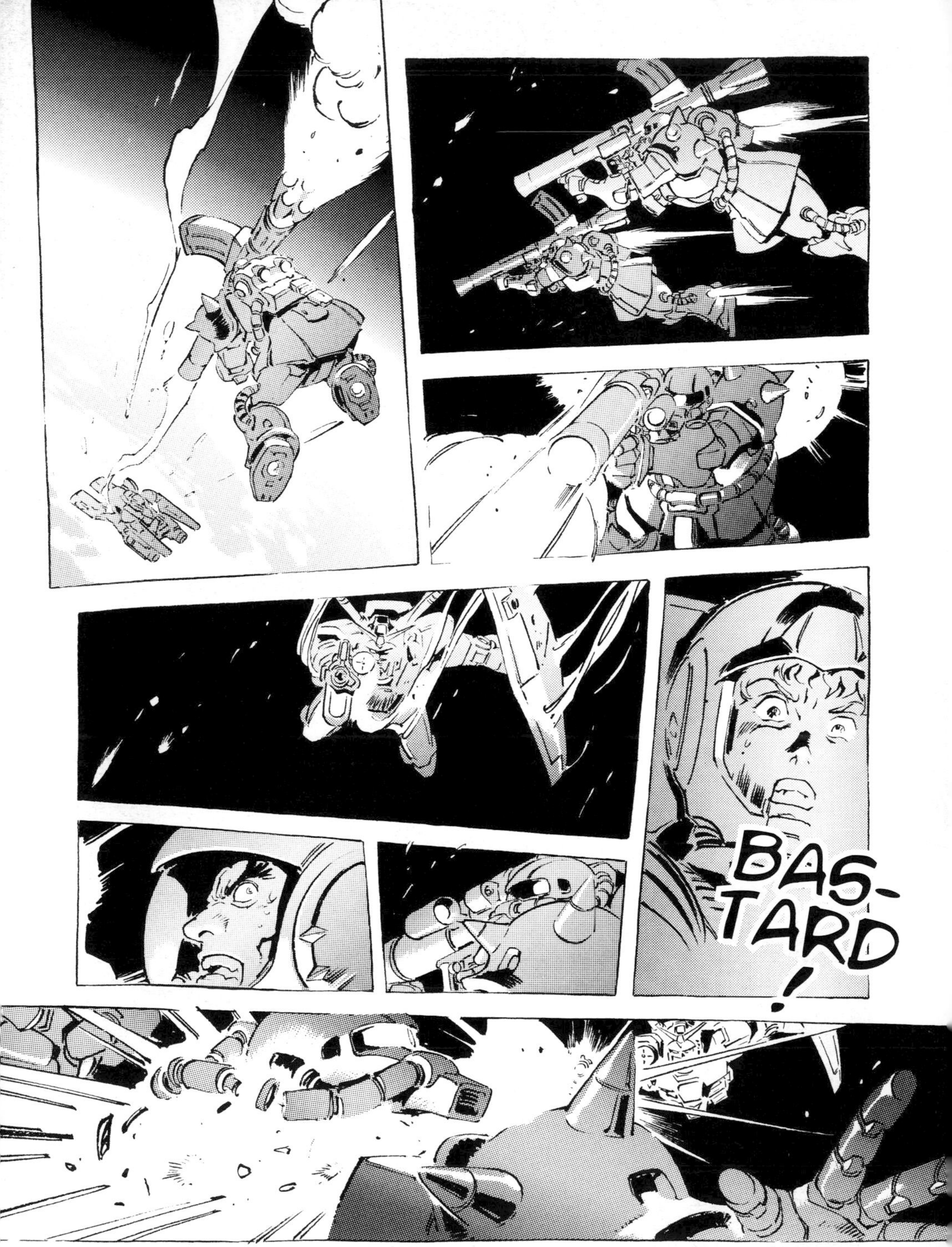
BAS-
TARD
!

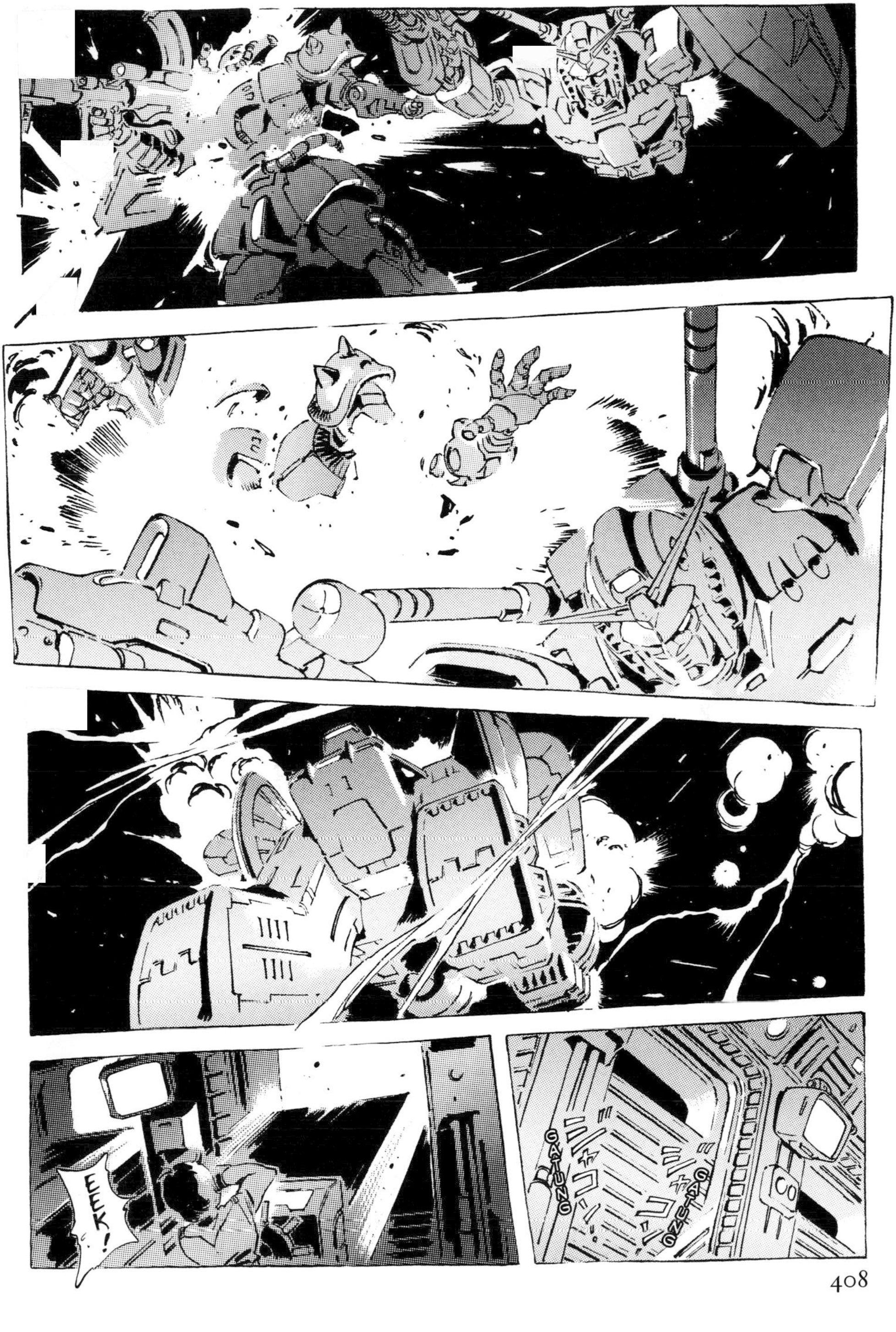
GATUNG
GATUNG
EEK!

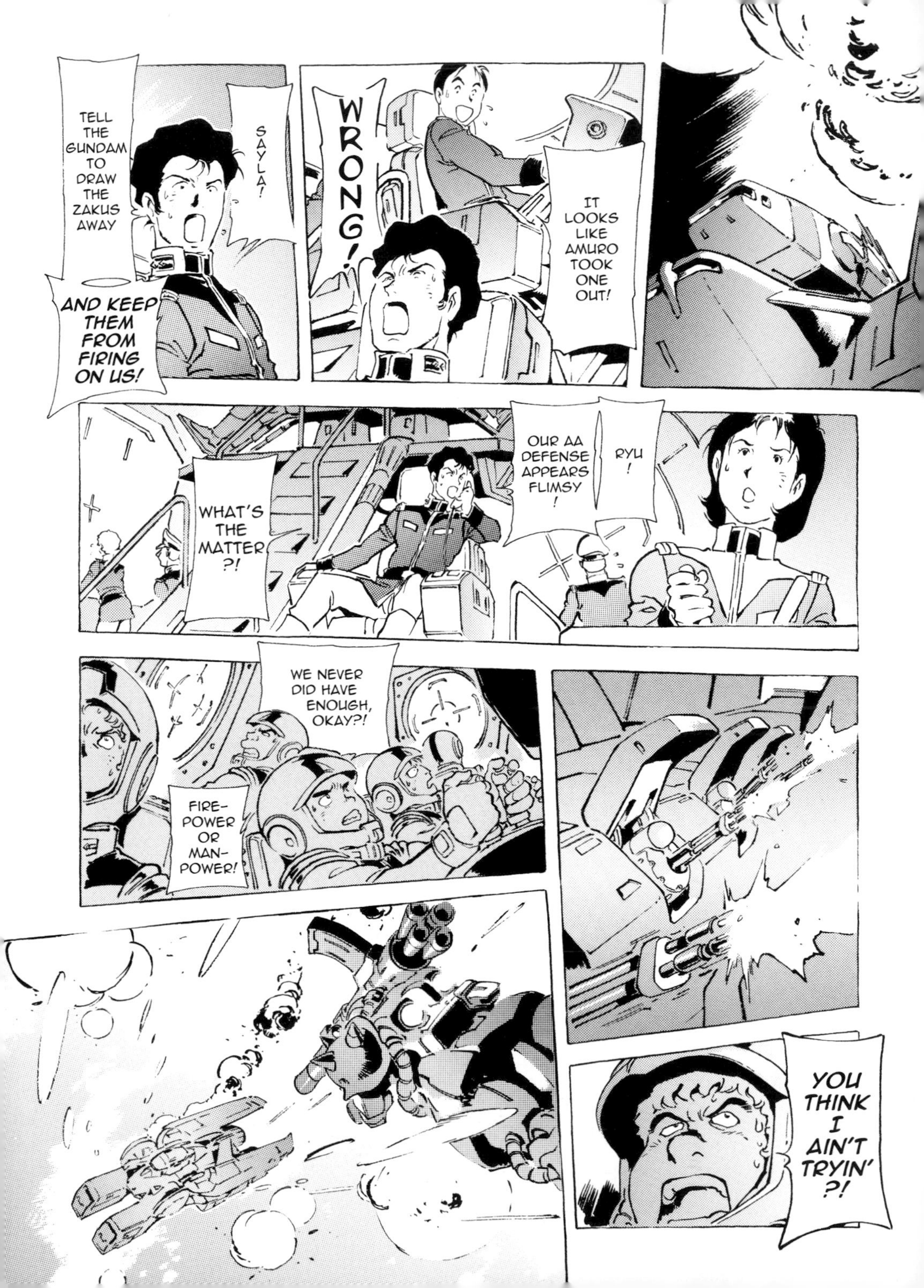
IT LOOKS LIKE AMURO TOOK ONE OUT!
WRONG!
SAYLA!
TELL THE GUNDAM TO DRAW THE ZAKUS AWAY
AND KEEP THEM FROM FIRING ON US!
RYU!
OUR AA DEFENSE APPEARS FLIMSY!
WHAT'S THE MATTER?!
WE NEVER DID HAVE ENOUGH, OKAY?!
FIRE-POWER OR MAN-POWER!
YOU THINK I AIN'T TRYIN'?!

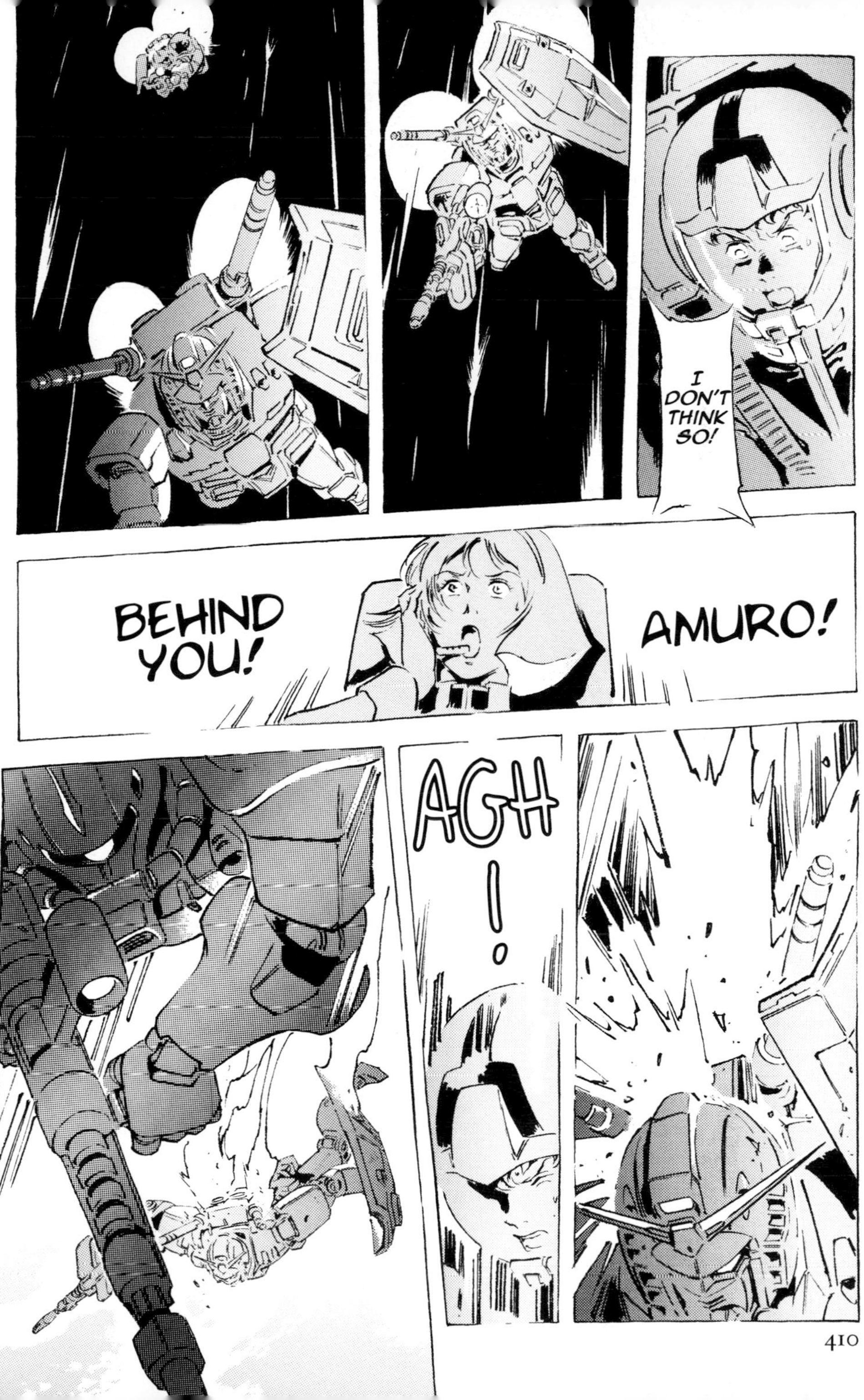
I DON'T THINK SO!
AMURO!
BEHIND YOU!
AGH!

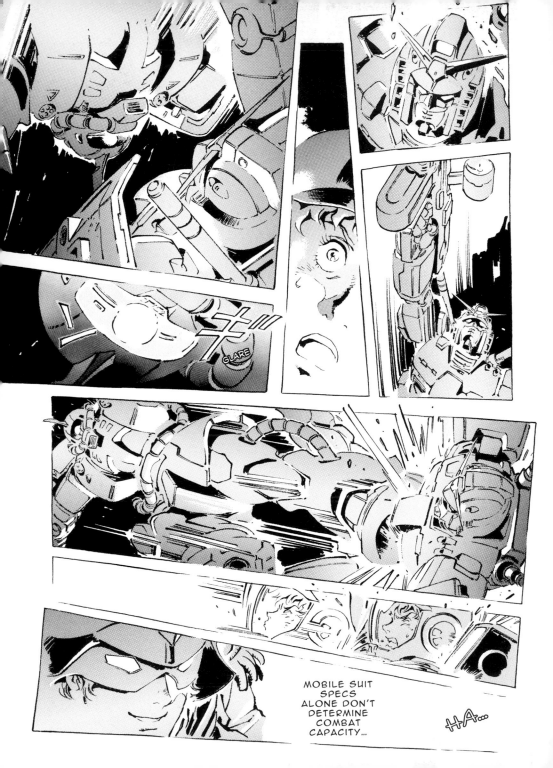

MOBILE SUIT
SPECS
ALONE DON'T
DETERMINE
COMBAT
CAPACITY...

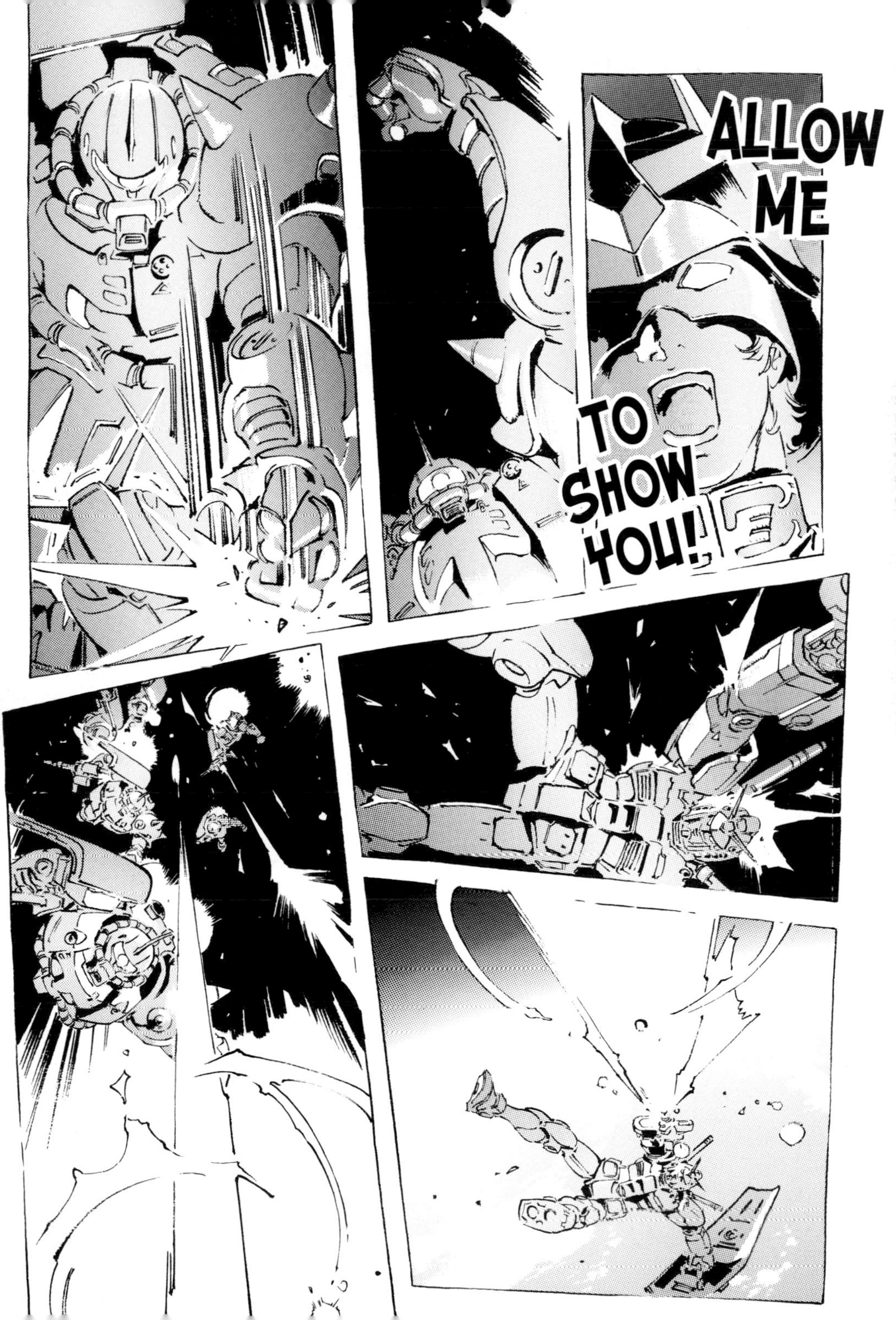

ALLOW ME
TO SHOW YOU!

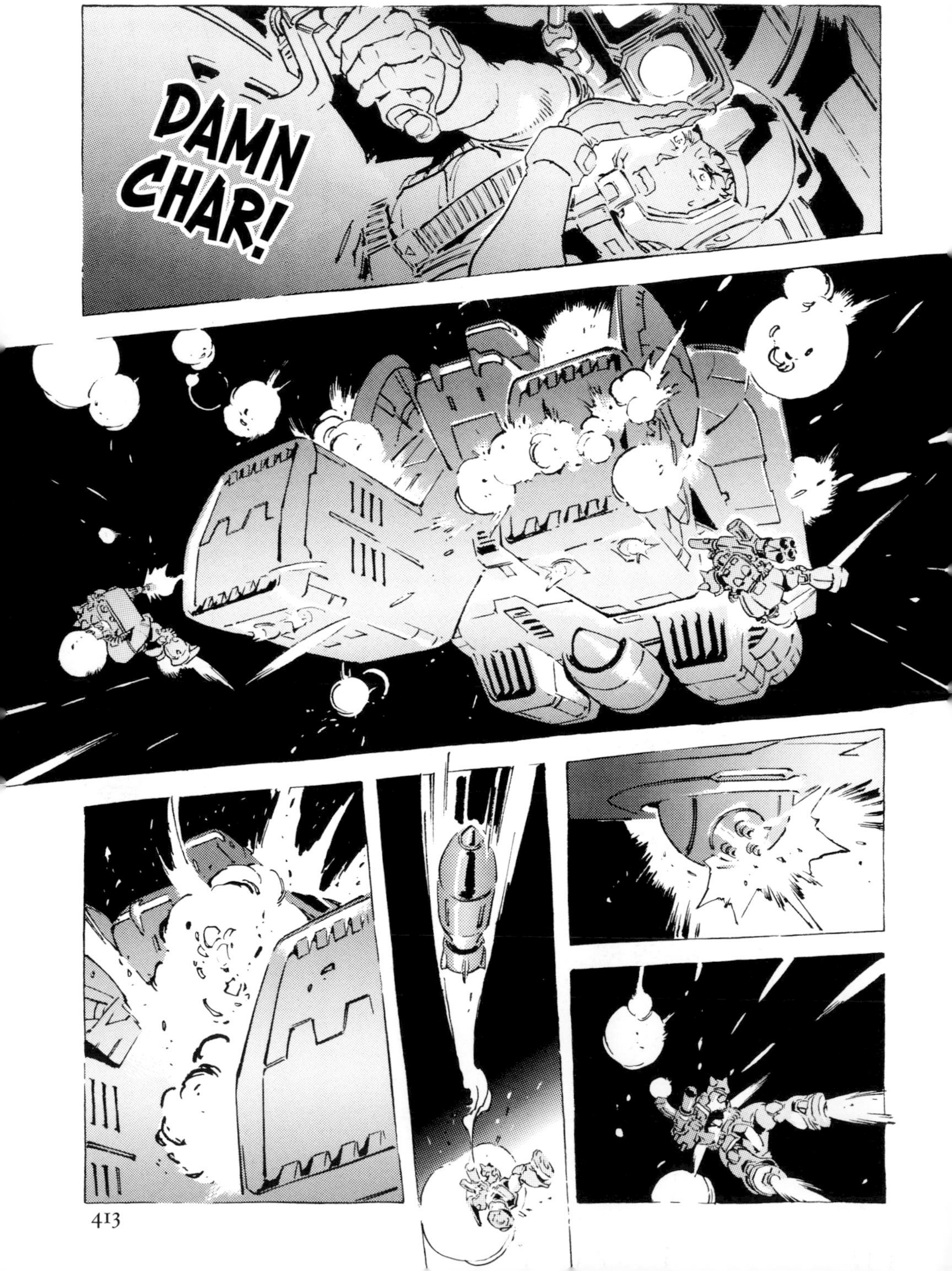
DAMN CHAR!

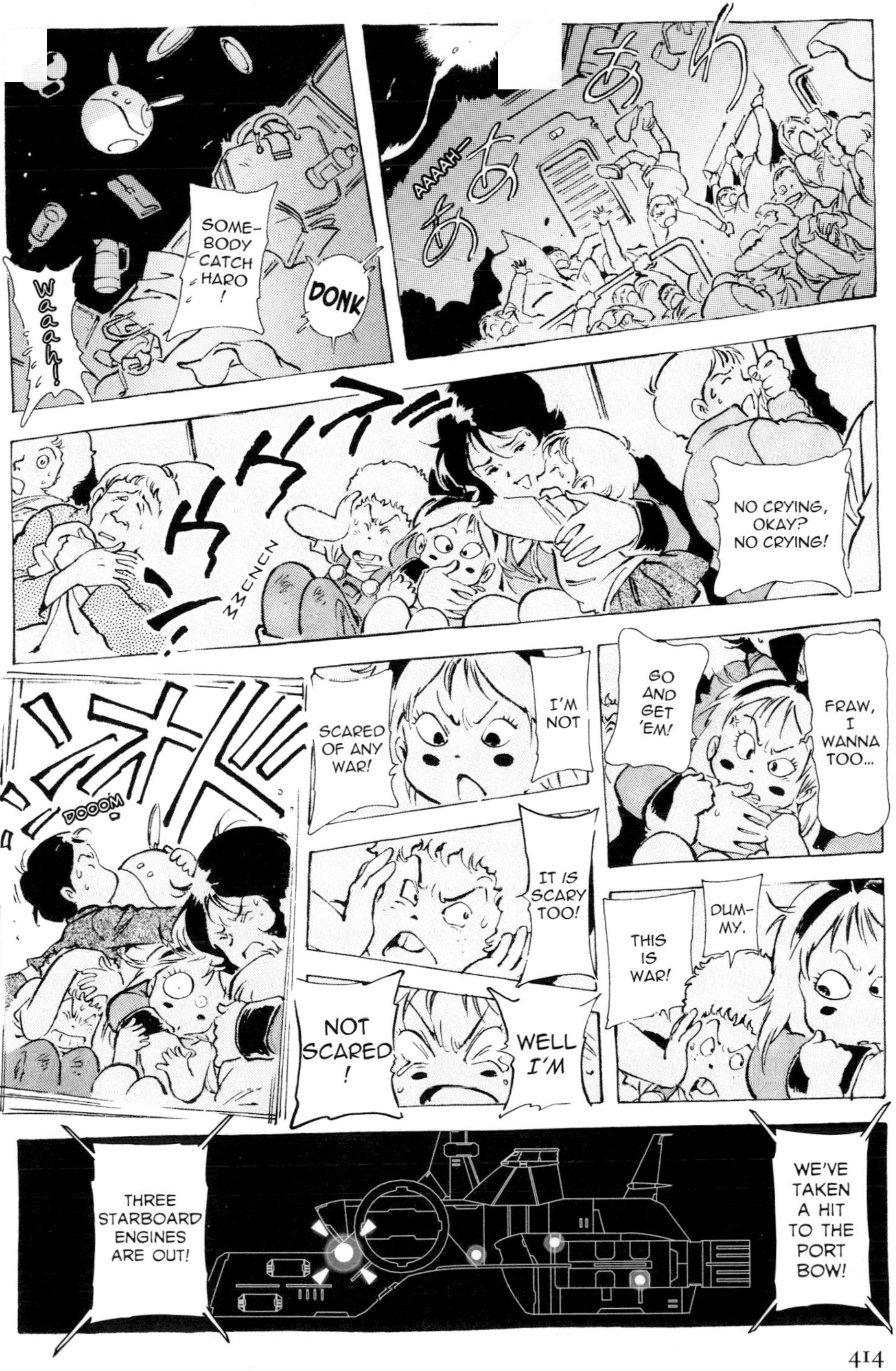
AAAAH—
SOMEBODY CATCH HARO!
DONK
Waaah!
NO CRYING, OKAY? NO CRYING!
GO AND GET 'EM!
FRAW, I WANNA TOO...
I'M NOT
SCARED OF ANY WAR!
DUM-MY.
THIS IS WAR!
IT IS SCARY TOO!
WELL I'M
NOT SCARED!
DOOOM
WE'VE TAKEN A HIT TO THE PORT BOW!
THREE STARBOARD ENGINES ARE OUT!

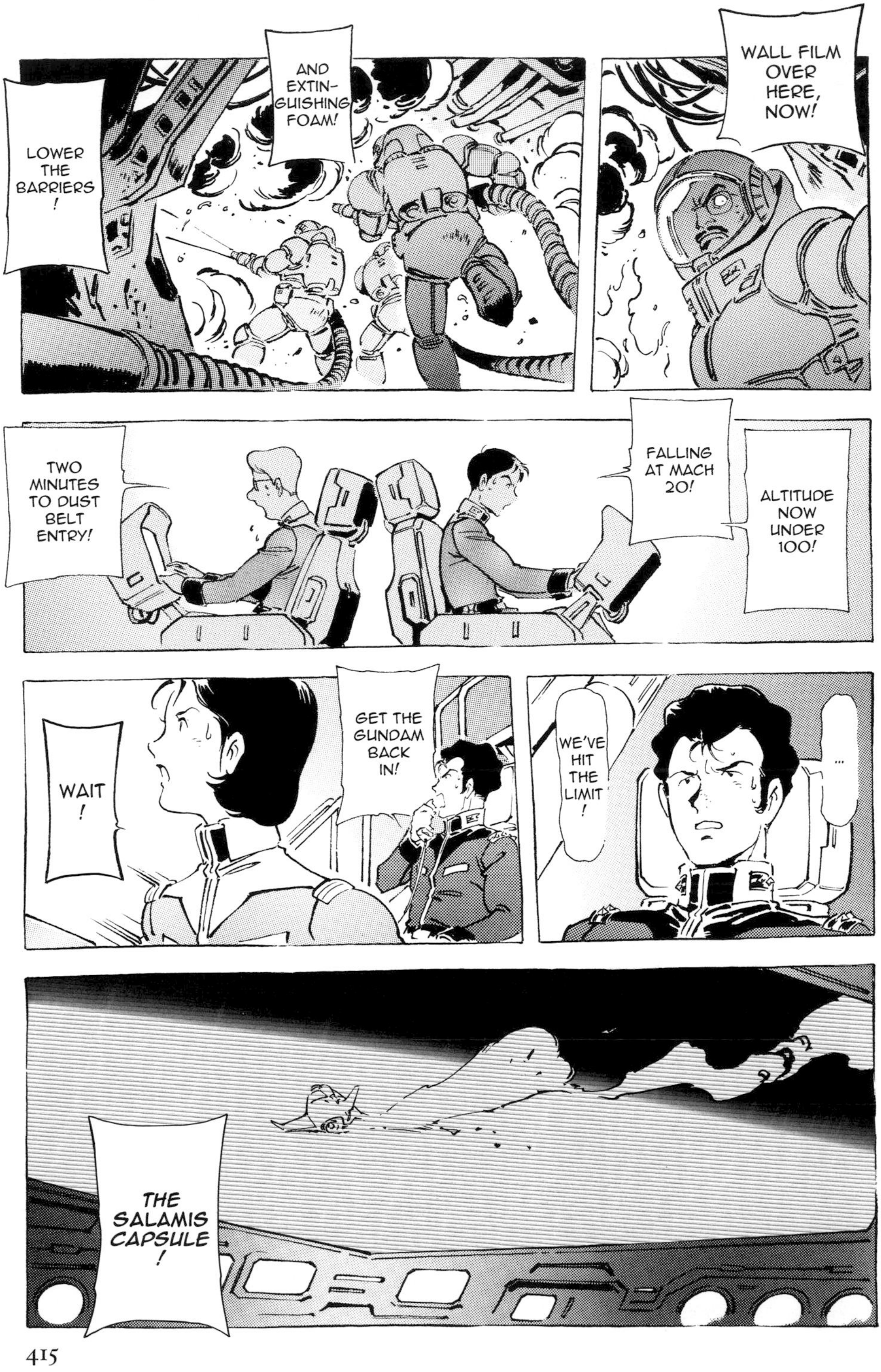
WALL FILM OVER HERE, NOW!
AND EXTIN-GUISHING FOAM!
LOWER THE BARRIERS!
ALTITUDE NOW UNDER 100!
FALLING AT MACH 20!
TWO MINUTES TO DUST BELT ENTRY!
...
WE'VE HIT THE LIMIT!
GET THE GUNDAM BACK IN!
WAIT!
THE SALAMIS CAPSULE!

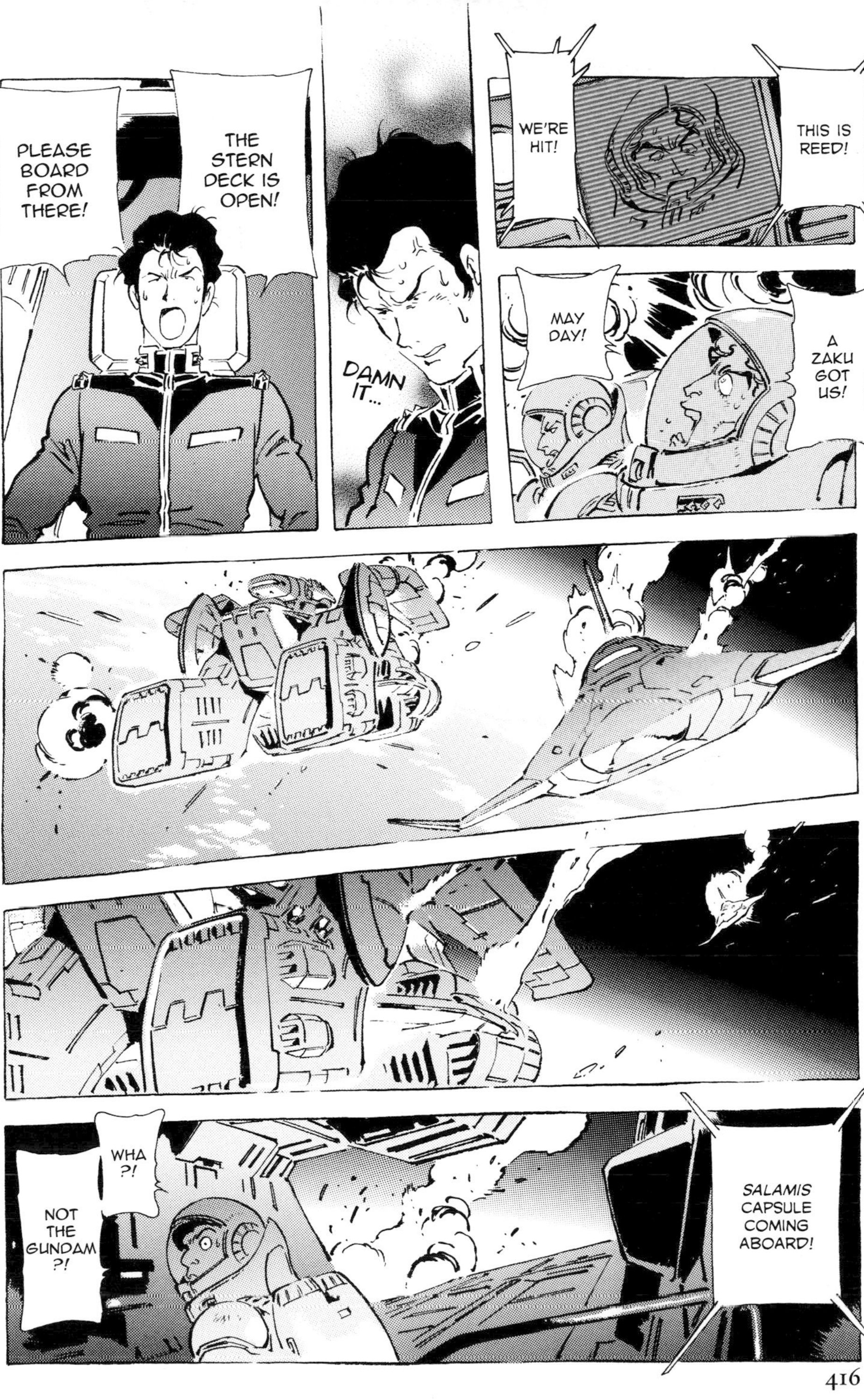
THIS IS REED!
WE'RE HIT!
A ZAKU GOT US!
MAY DAY!
DAMN IT...
THE STERN DECK IS OPEN!
PLEASE BOARD FROM THERE!
SALAMIS CAPSULE COMING ABOARD!
WHA?!
NOT THE GUNDAM?!

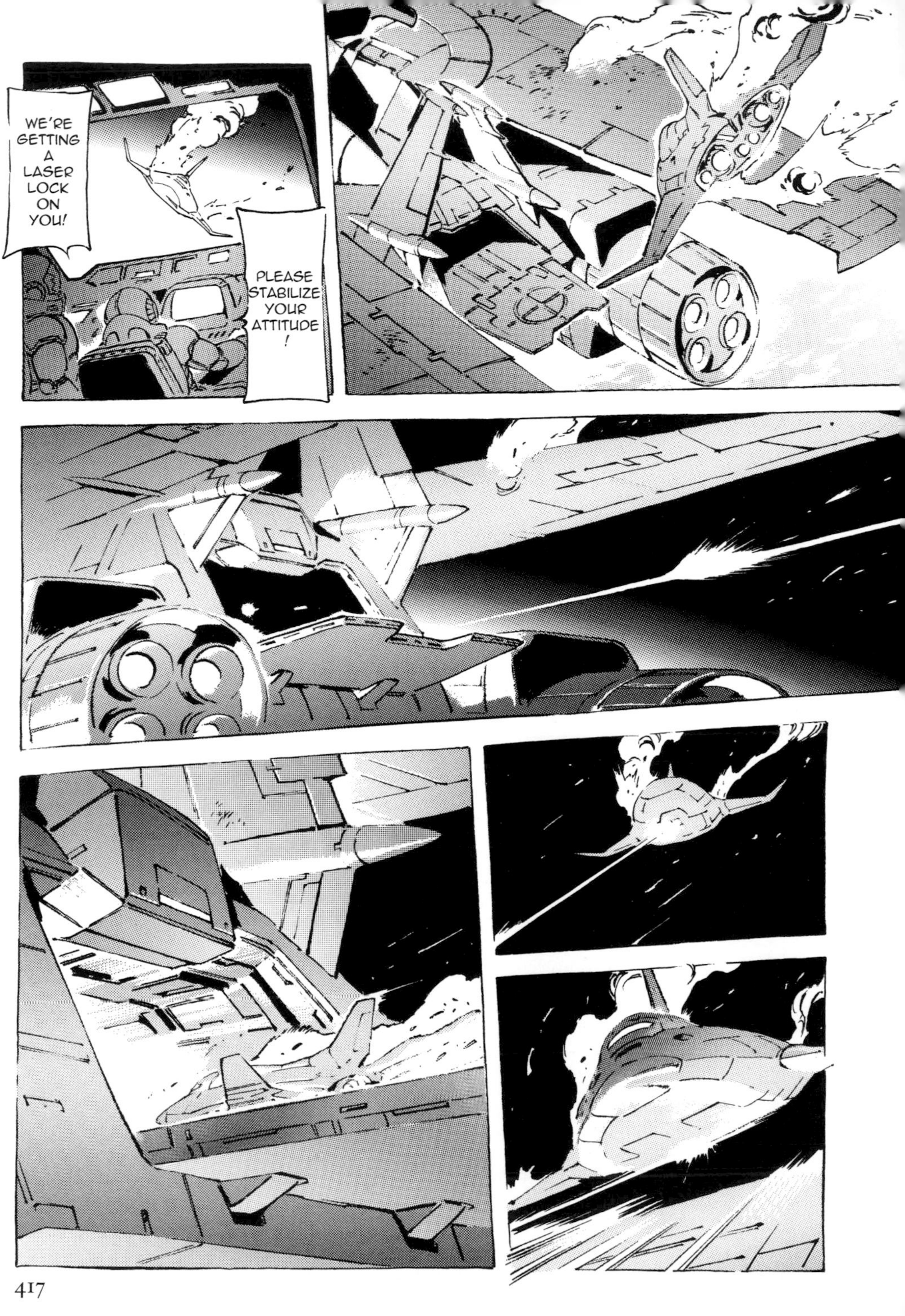
WE'RE GETTING A LASER LOCK ON YOU!
PLEASE STABILIZE YOUR ATTITUDE!

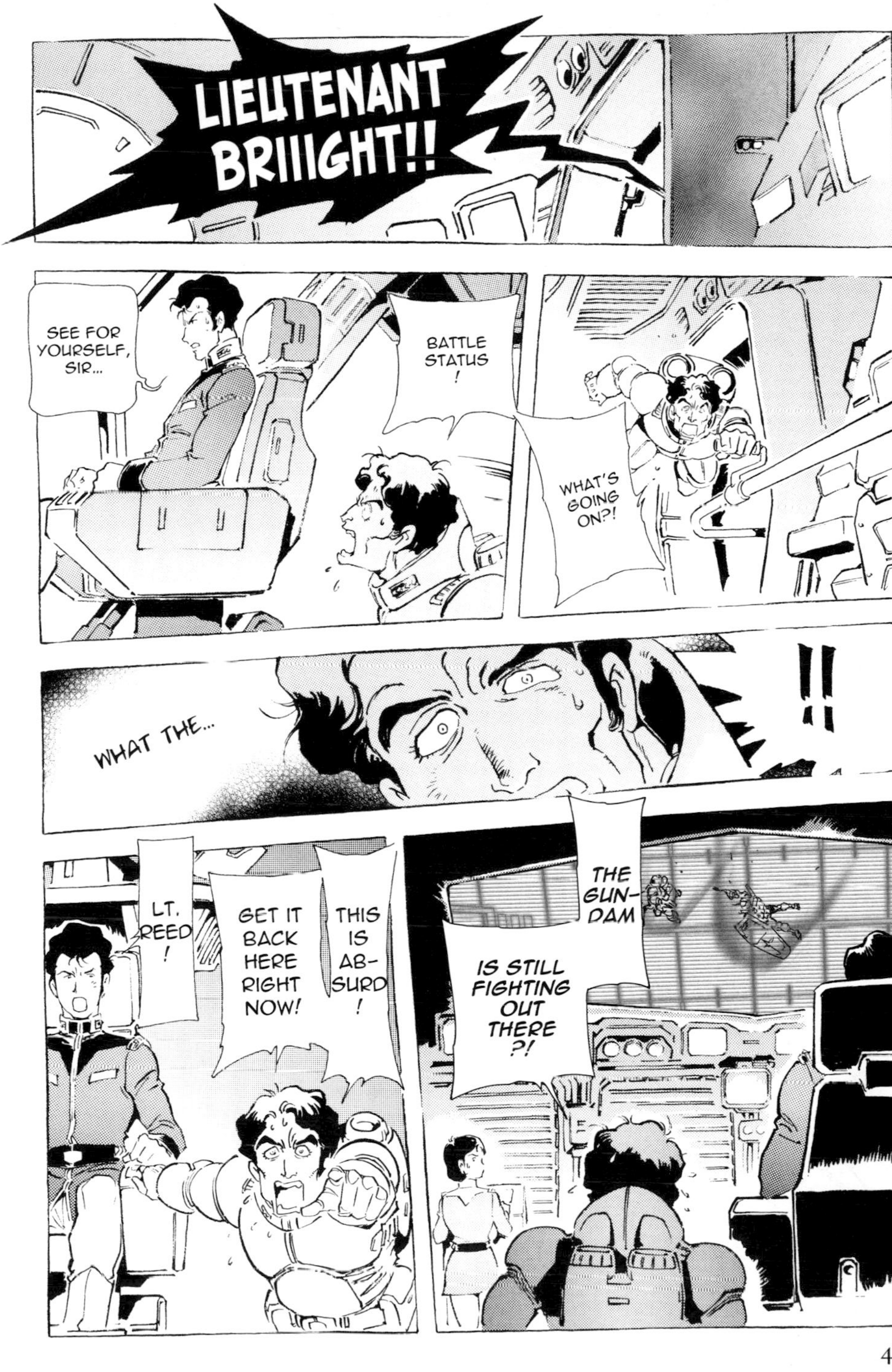
LIEUTENANT BRIIIGHT!!
WHAT'S GOING ON?!
BATTLE STATUS !
SEE FOR YOURSELF, SIR...
WHAT THE...
!!
THE GUNDAM
IS STILL FIGHTING OUT THERE ?!
THIS IS ABSURD !
GET IT BACK HERE RIGHT NOW!
LT. REED !

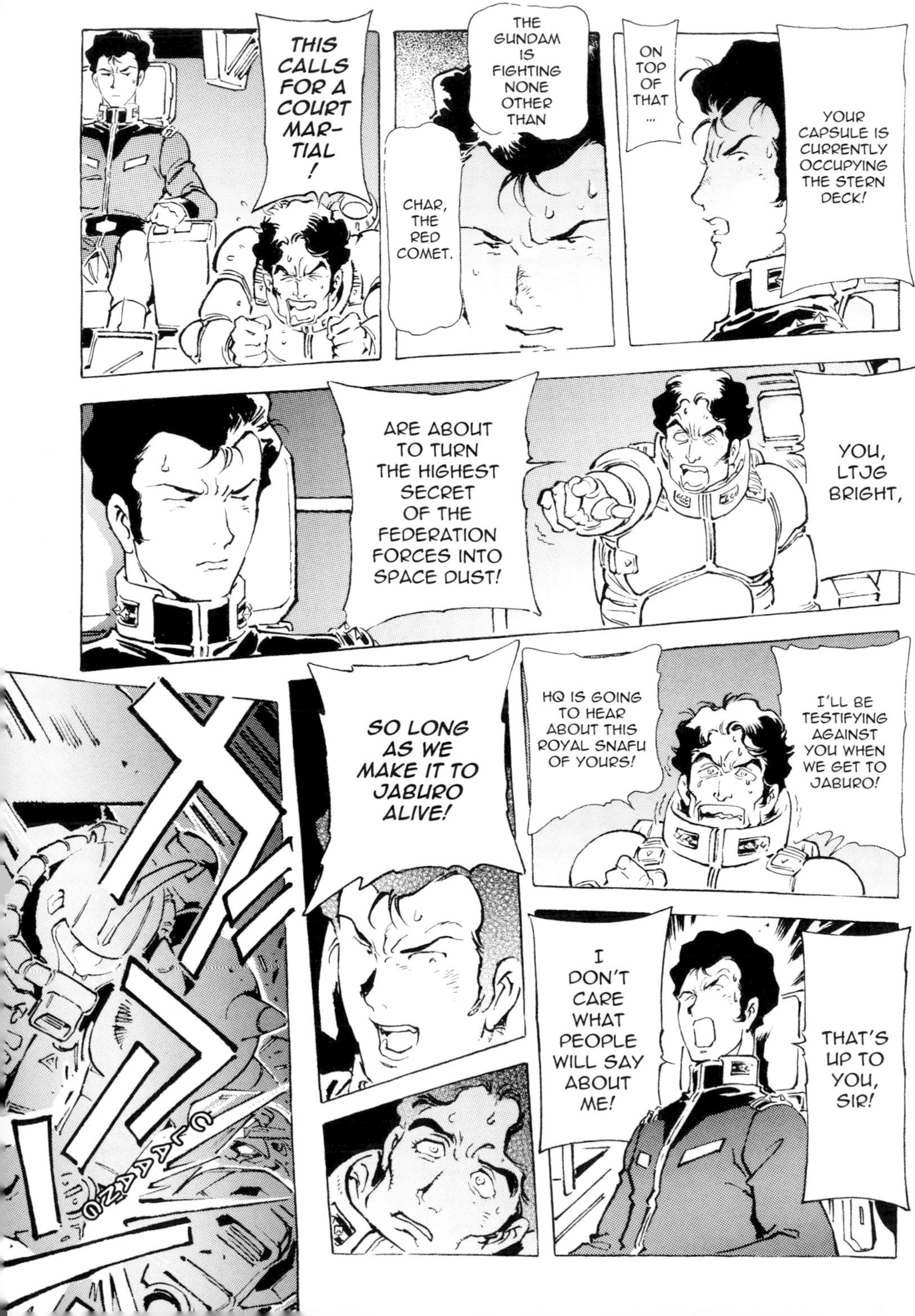
YOUR CAPSULE IS CURRENTLY OCCUPYING THE STERN DECK!
ON TOP OF THAT ...
THE GUNDAM IS FIGHTING NONE OTHER THAN
CHAR, THE RED COMET.
THIS CALLS FOR A COURT MAR-TIAL!
YOU, LTJG BRIGHT,
ARE ABOUT TO TURN THE HIGHEST SECRET OF THE FEDERATION FORCES INTO SPACE DUST!
I'LL BE TESTIFYING AGAINST YOU WHEN WE GET TO JABURO!
HQ IS GOING TO HEAR ABOUT THIS ROYAL SNAFU OF YOURS!
THAT'S UP TO YOU, SIR!
I DON'T CARE WHAT PEOPLE WILL SAY ABOUT ME!
SO LONG AS WE MAKE IT TO JABURO ALIVE!
CLAAANG

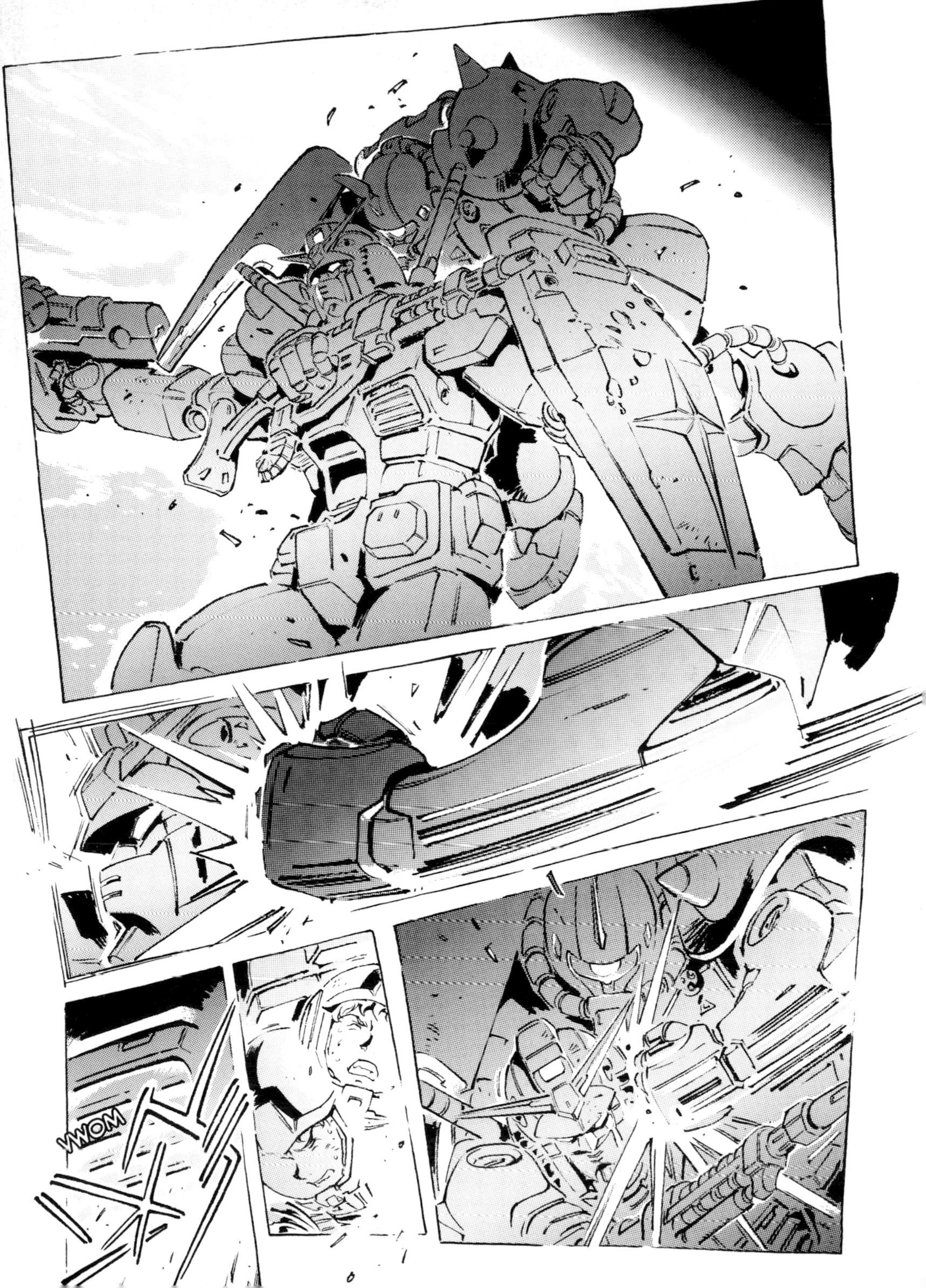
VWOM

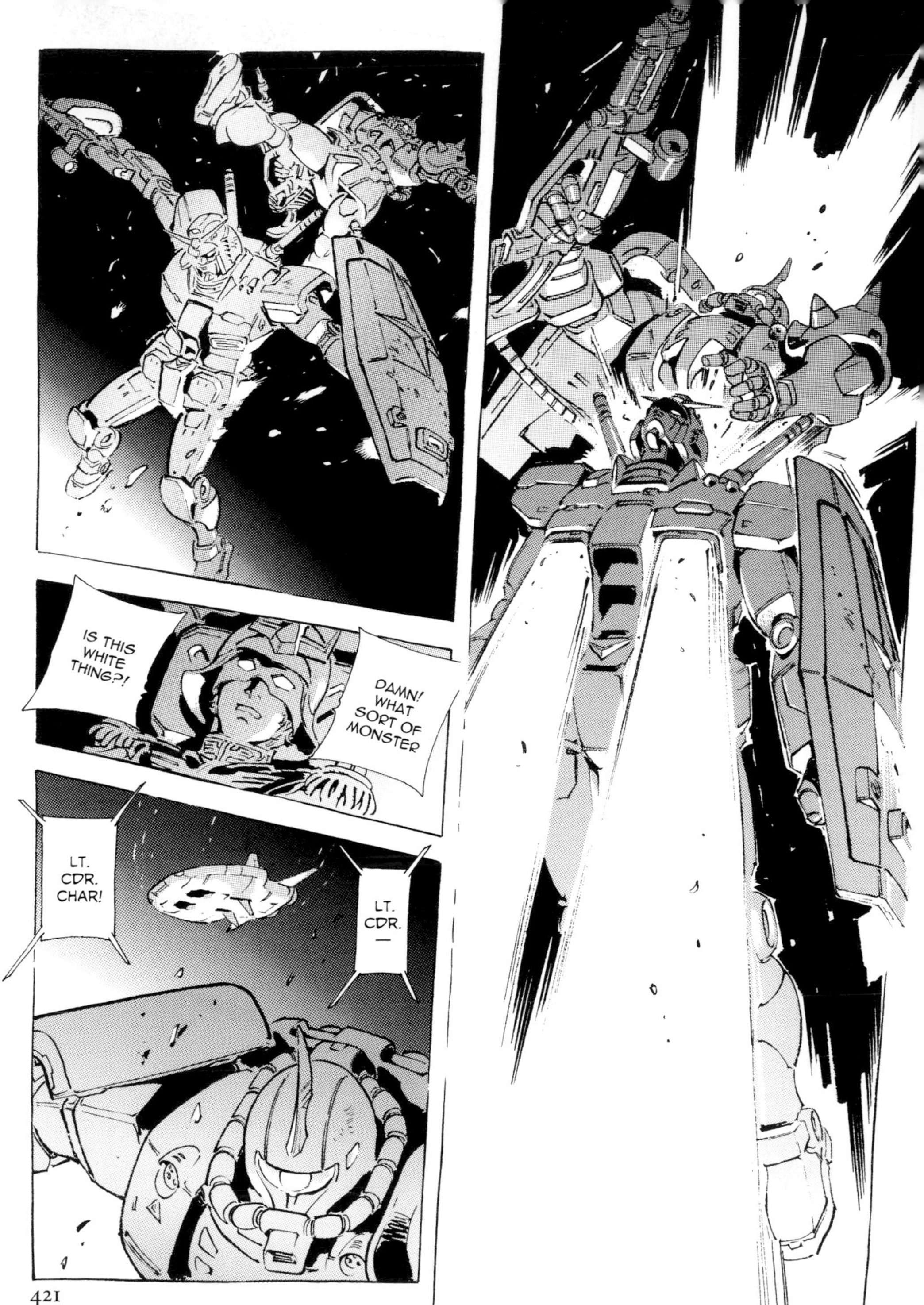
DAMN! WHAT SORT OF MONSTER
IS THIS WHITE THING?!
LT. CDR. —
LT. CDR. CHAR!

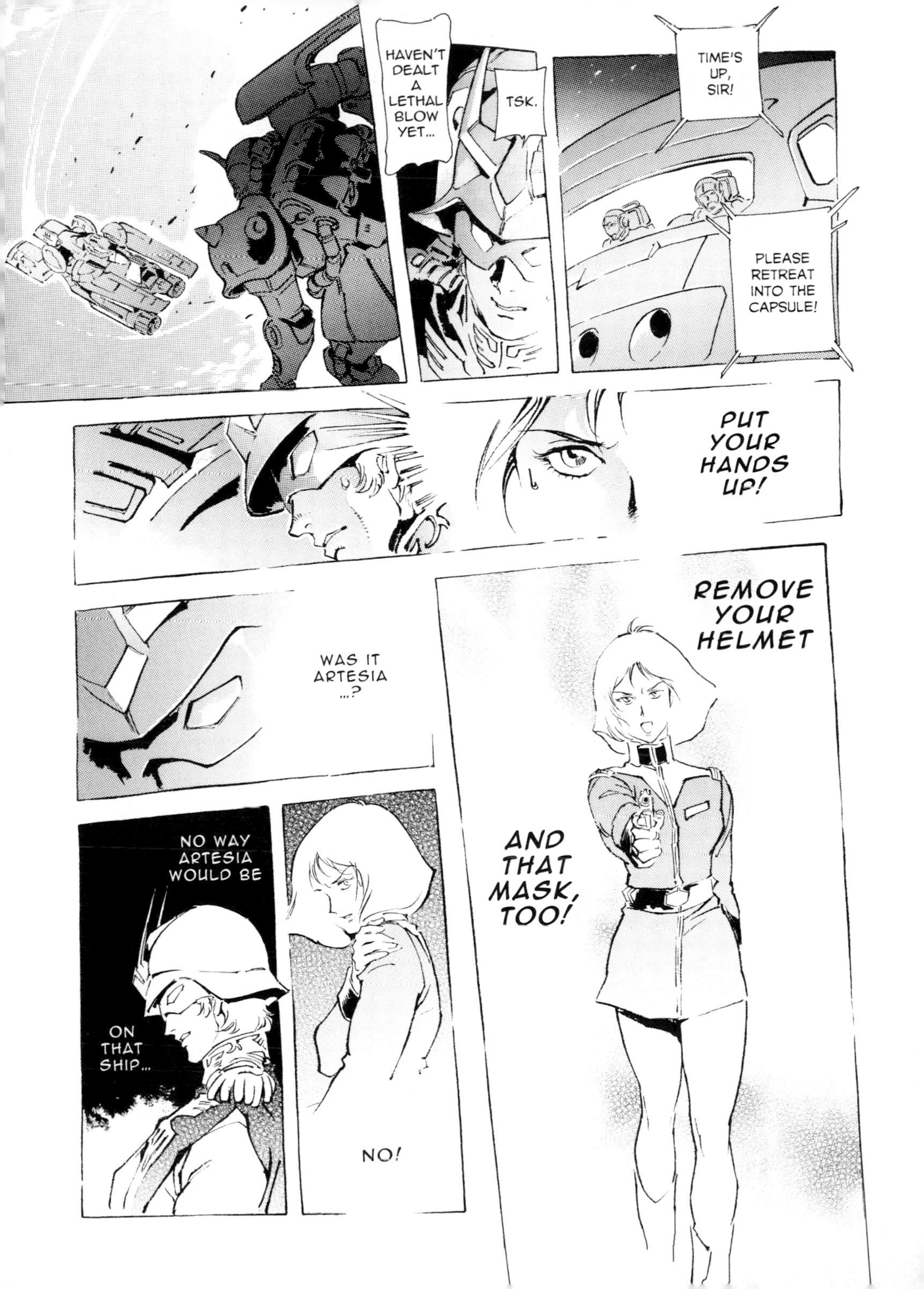
TIME'S UP, SIR!
PLEASE RETREAT INTO THE CAPSULE!
TSK.
HAVEN'T DEALT A LETHAL BLOW YET...
PUT YOUR HANDS UP!
REMOVE YOUR HELMET
AND THAT MASK, TOO!
WAS IT ARTESIA ...?
NO!
NO WAY ARTESIA WOULD BE
ON THAT SHIP...

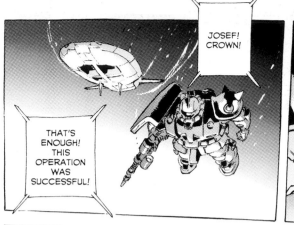

JOSEF! CROWN!

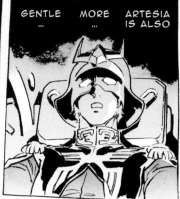

GENTLE ... MORE ... ARTESIA IS ALSO

THAT'S ENOUGH! THIS OPERATION WAS SUCCESSFUL!

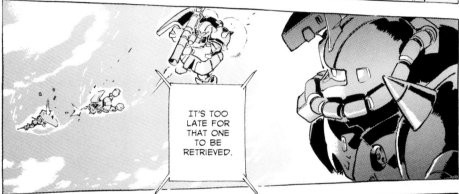

IT'S TOO LATE FOR THAT ONE TO BE RETRIEVED.

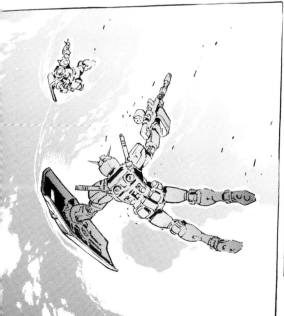

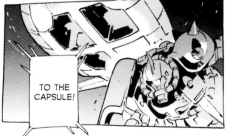

TO THE CAPSULE!

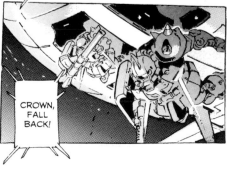

CROWN, FALL BACK!

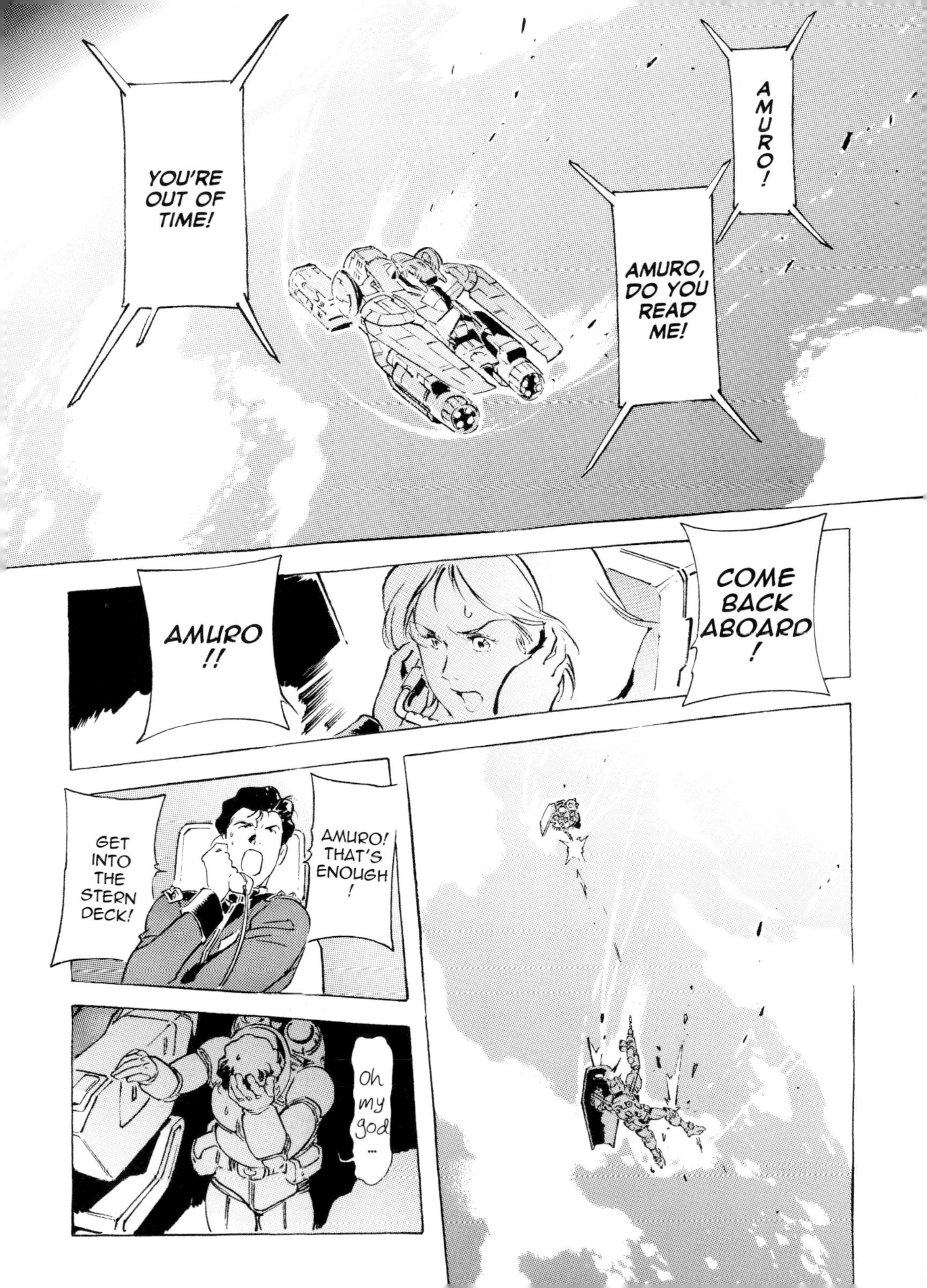
AMURO!
AMURO, DO YOU READ ME!
YOU'RE OUT OF TIME!
COME BACK ABOARD!
AMURO!!
AMURO! THAT'S ENOUGH!
GET INTO THE STERN DECK!
Oh my god ...

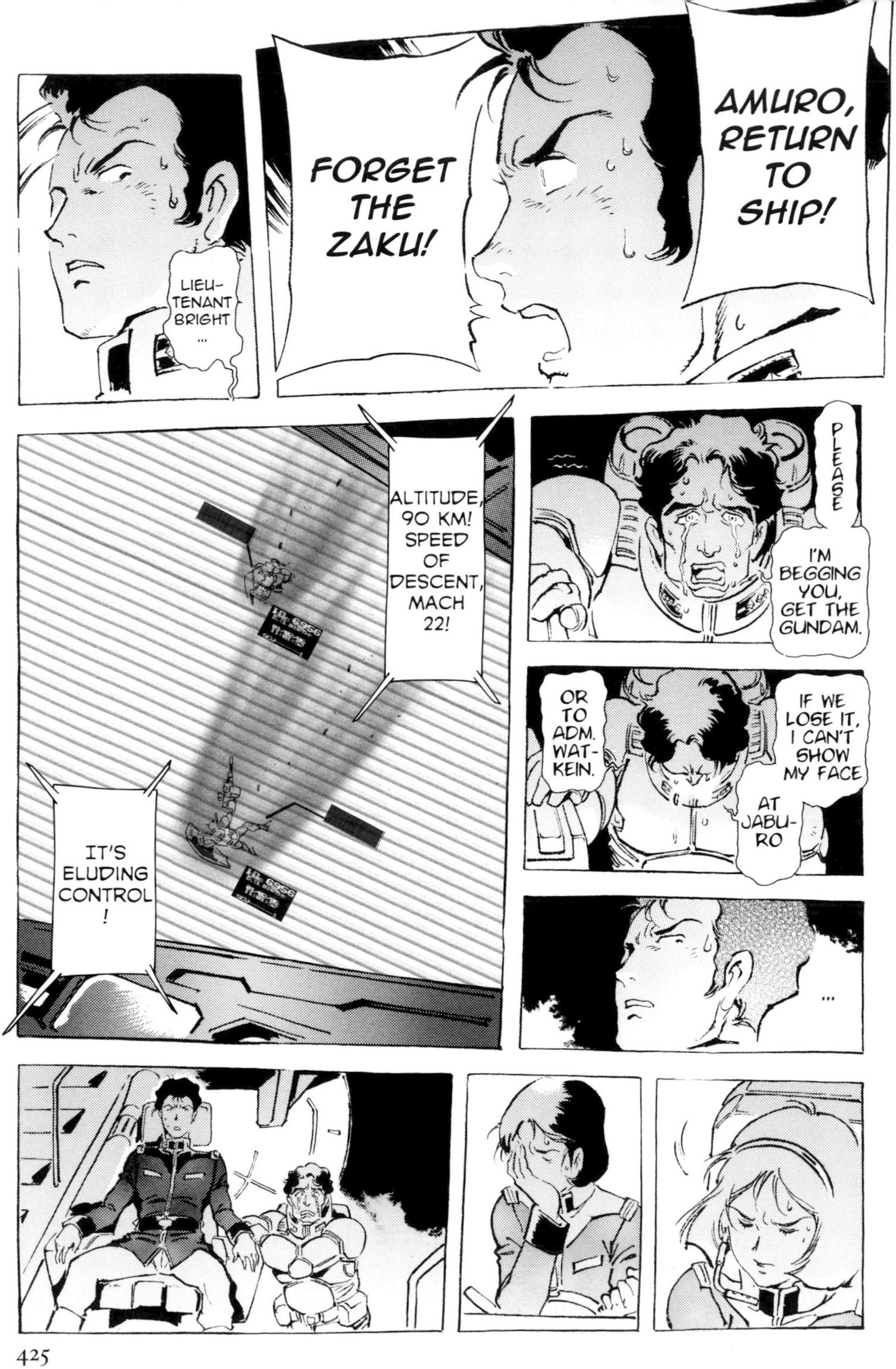
AMURO, RETURN TO SHIP!
FORGET THE ZAKU!
LIEU-TENANT BRIGHT ...
PLEASE
I'M BEGGING YOU, GET THE GUNDAM.
IF WE LOSE IT, I CAN'T SHOW MY FACE
AT JABU-RO
OR TO ADM. WAT-KEIN.
...
ALTITUDE, 90 KM! SPEED OF DESCENT, MACH 22!
IT'S ELUDING CONTROL!

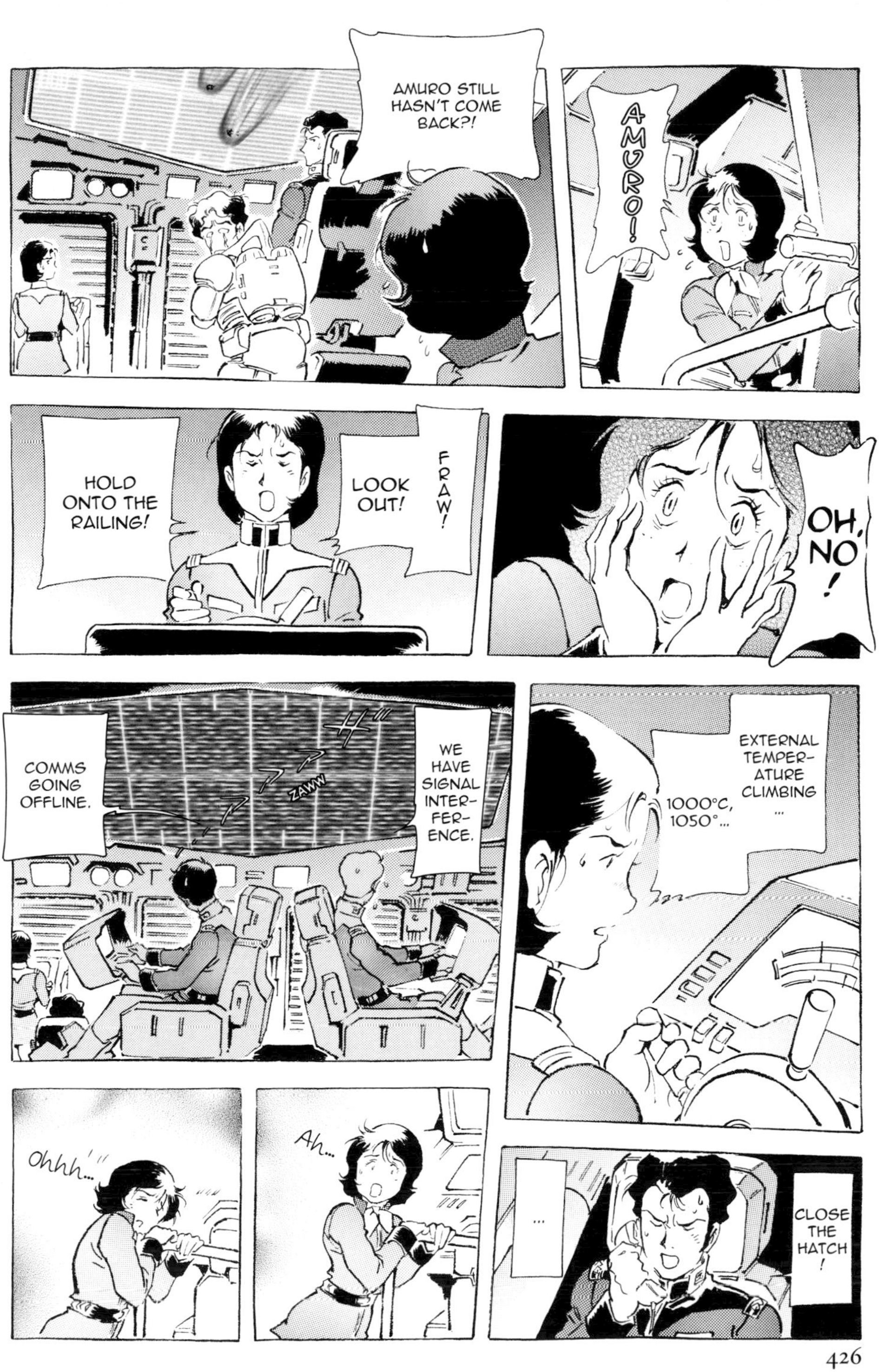
AMURO!
AMURO STILL HASN'T COME BACK?!
OH, NO!
FRAW!
LOOK OUT!
HOLD ONTO THE RAILING!
EXTERNAL TEMPERATURE CLIMBING...
1000°C, 1050°...
WE HAVE SIGNAL INTERFERENCE.
ZAWW
COMMS GOING OFFLINE.
CLOSE THE HATCH!
...
Ah...
Ohhh...

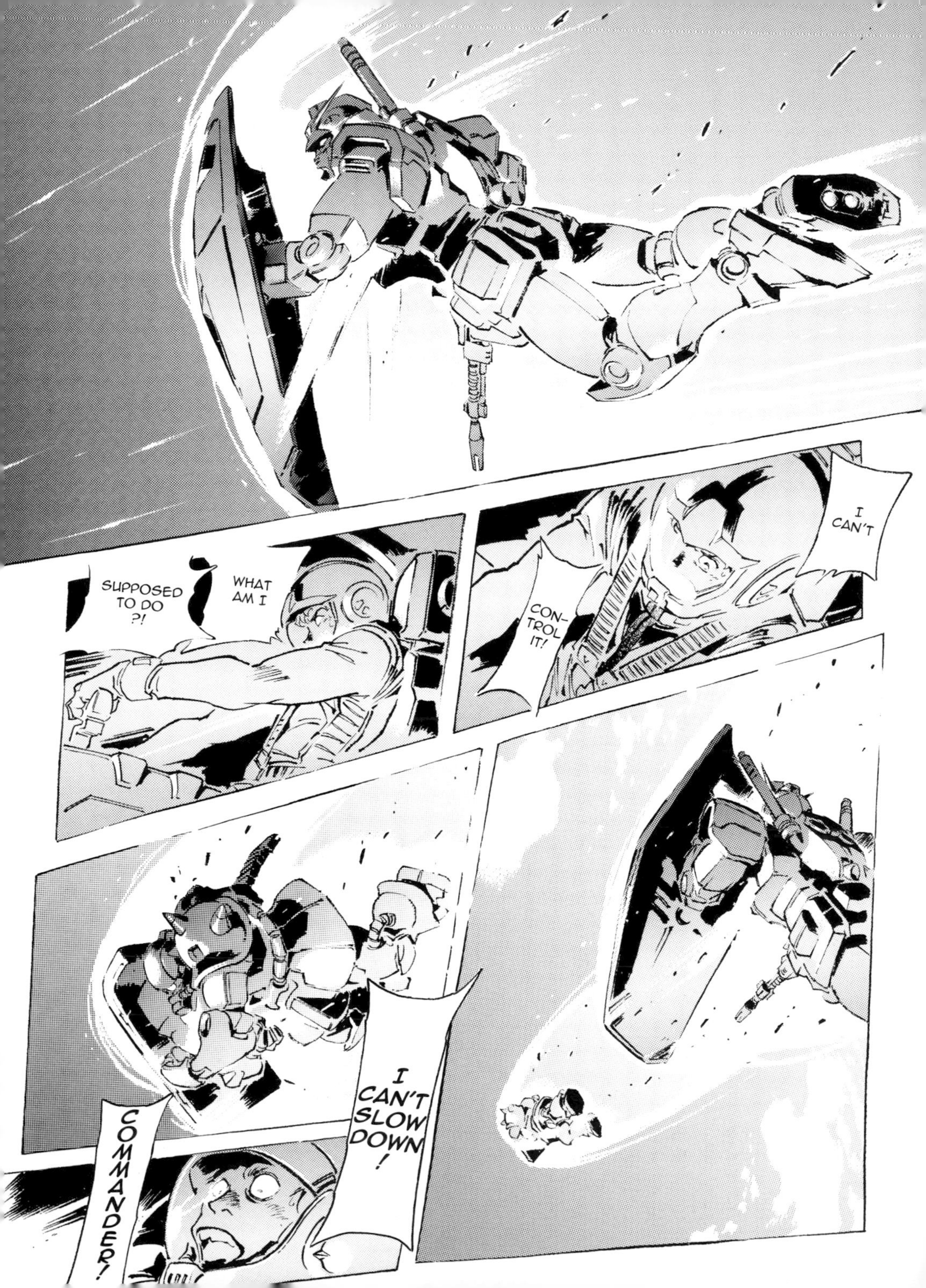
I CAN'T CONTROL IT!
WHAT AM I SUPPOSED TO DO ?!
I CAN'T SLOW DOWN!
COMMANDER!

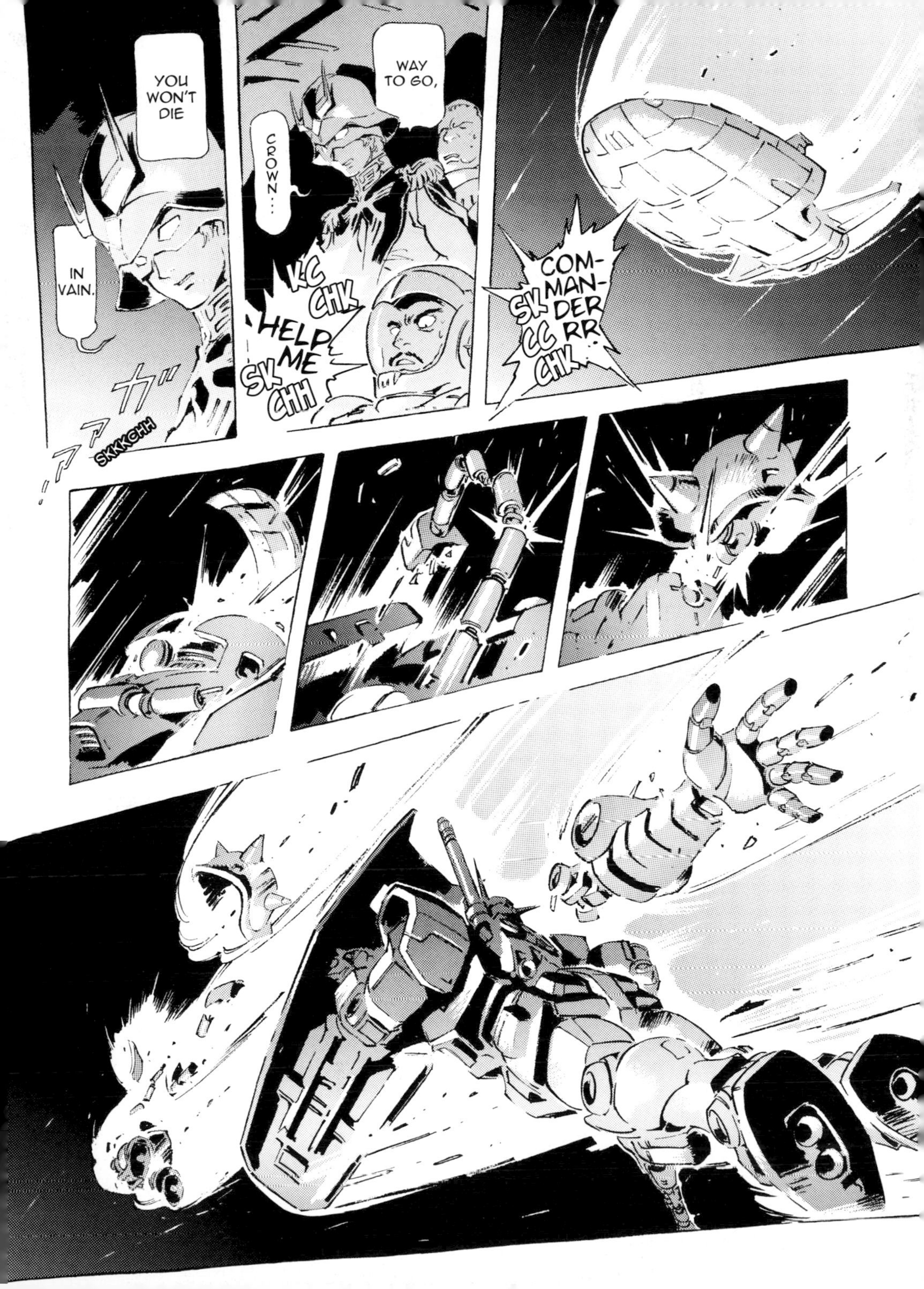
COM-MAN-DER RR CHK
SK CC
WAY TO GO,
CROWN...
KC CHK
HELP ME
SK CHH
YOU WON'T DIE
IN VAIN.
SKKKCHH

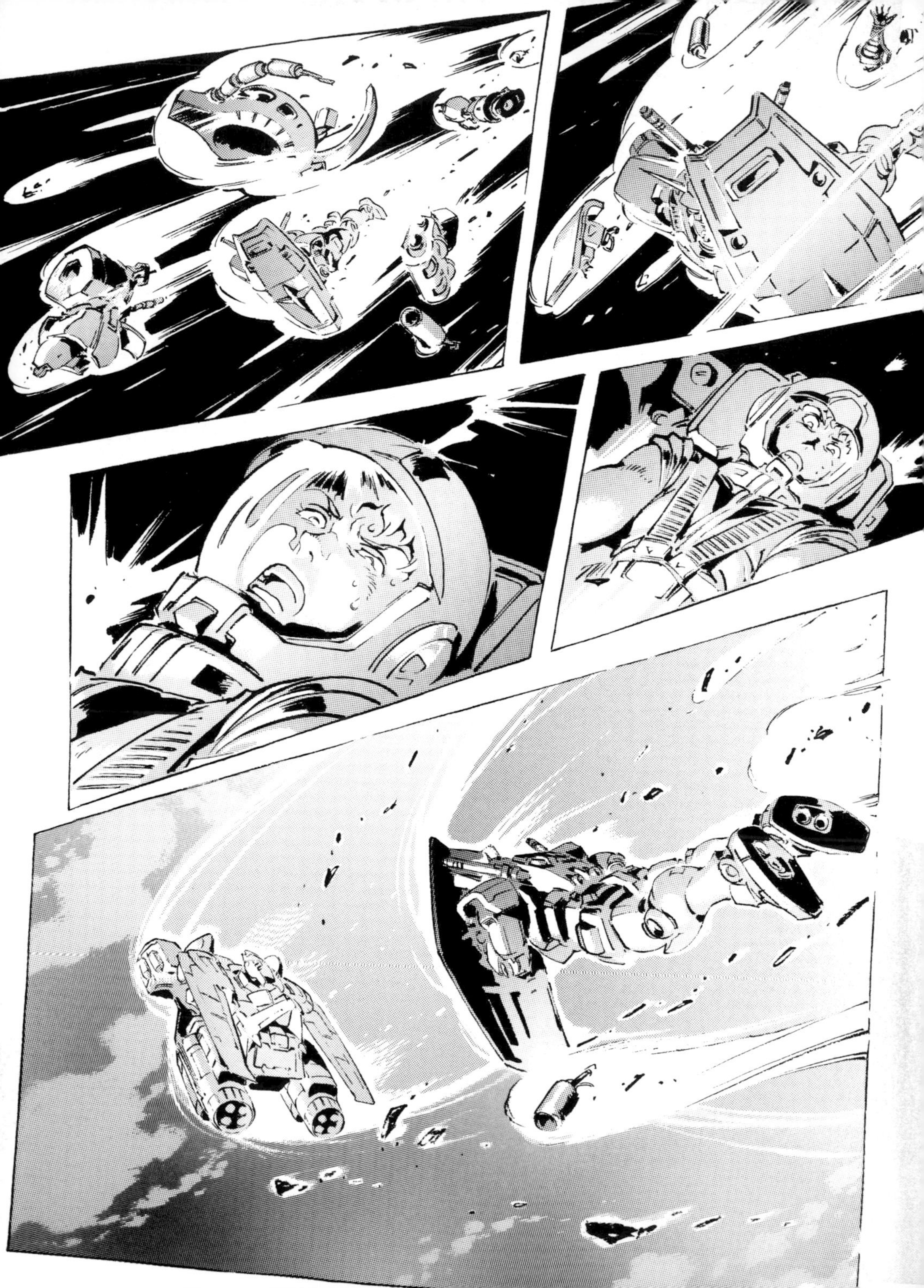

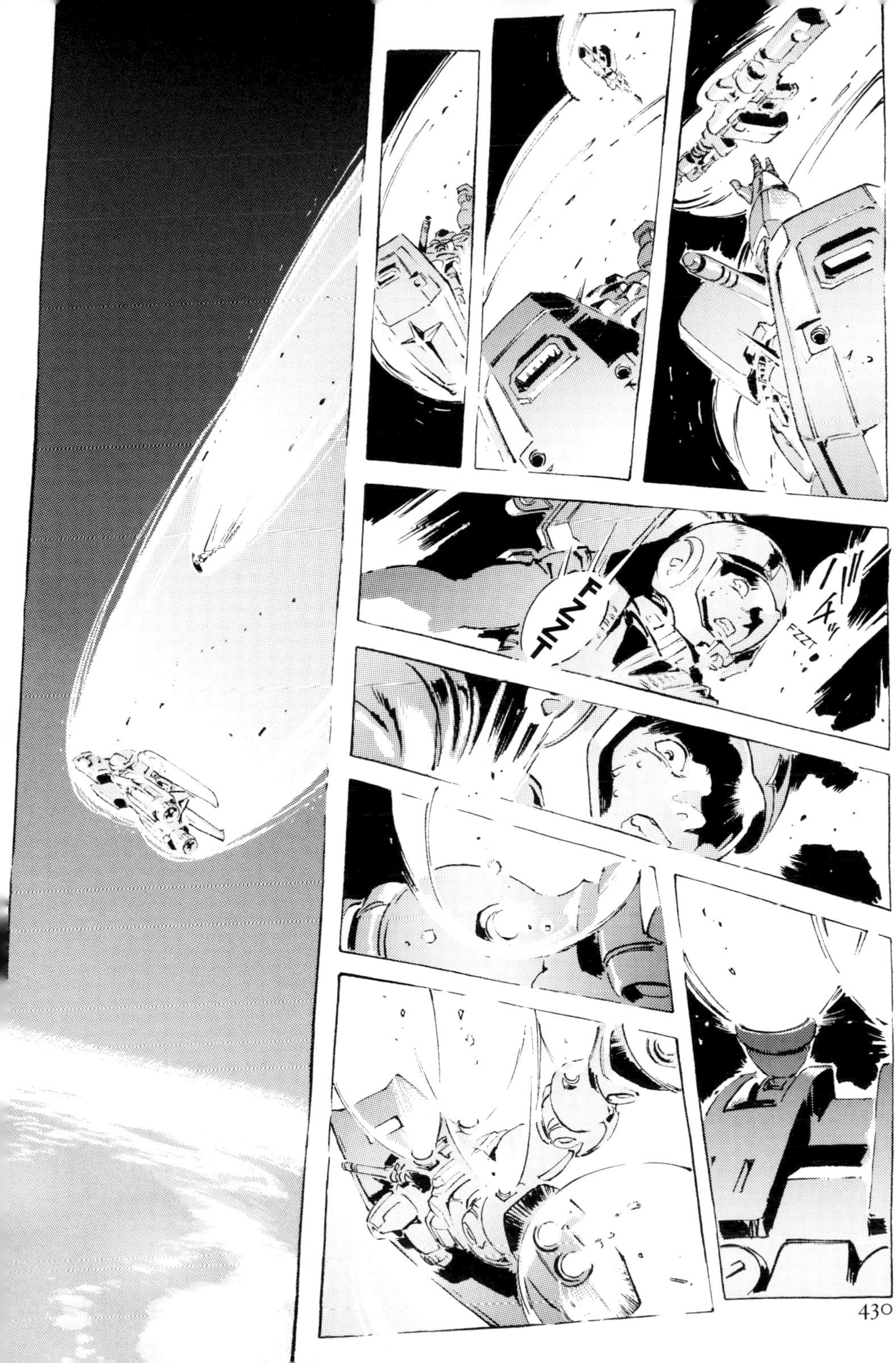
ズッ
FZZT
FNNT

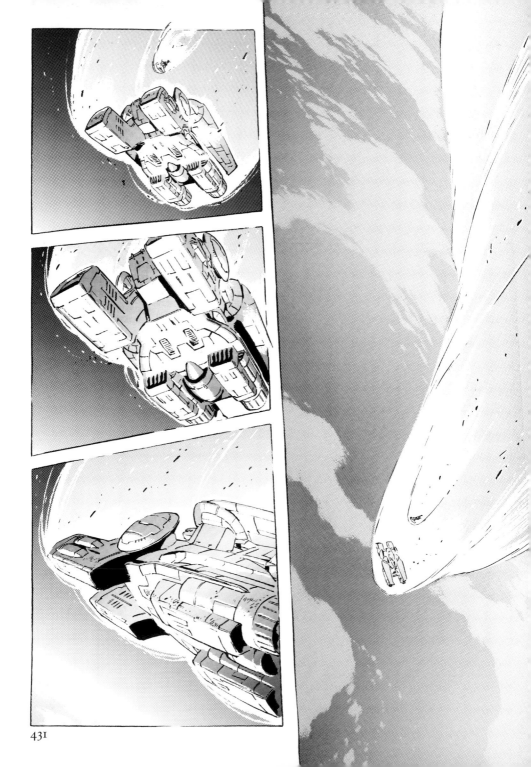

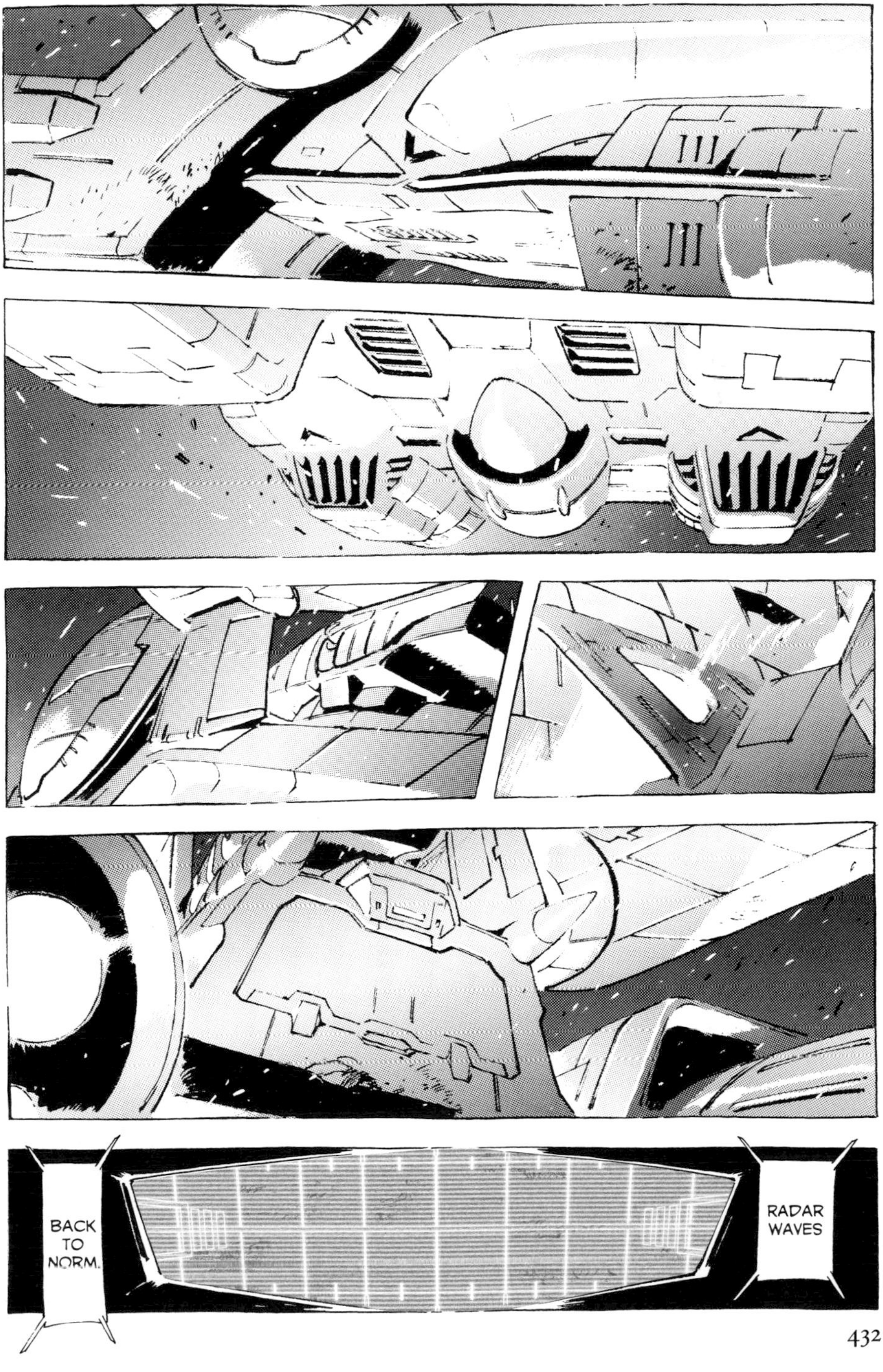
RADAR WAVES
BACK TO NORM.

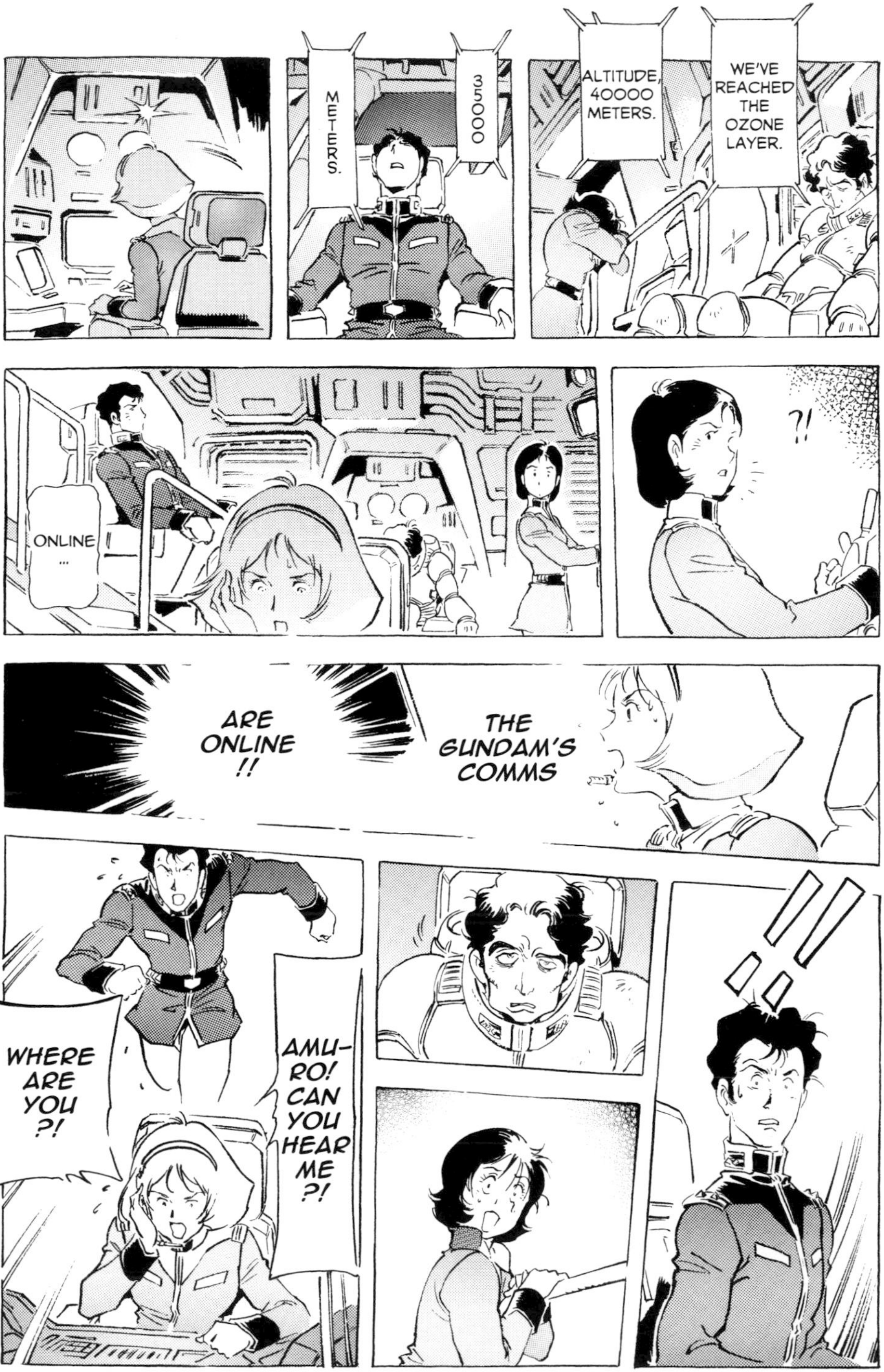
WE'VE REACHED THE OZONE LAYER.
ALTITUDE, 40000 METERS.
35000 METERS.
?!
ONLINE ...
THE GUNDAM'S COMMS
ARE ONLINE !!
AMURO! CAN YOU HEAR ME?!
WHERE ARE YOU ?!

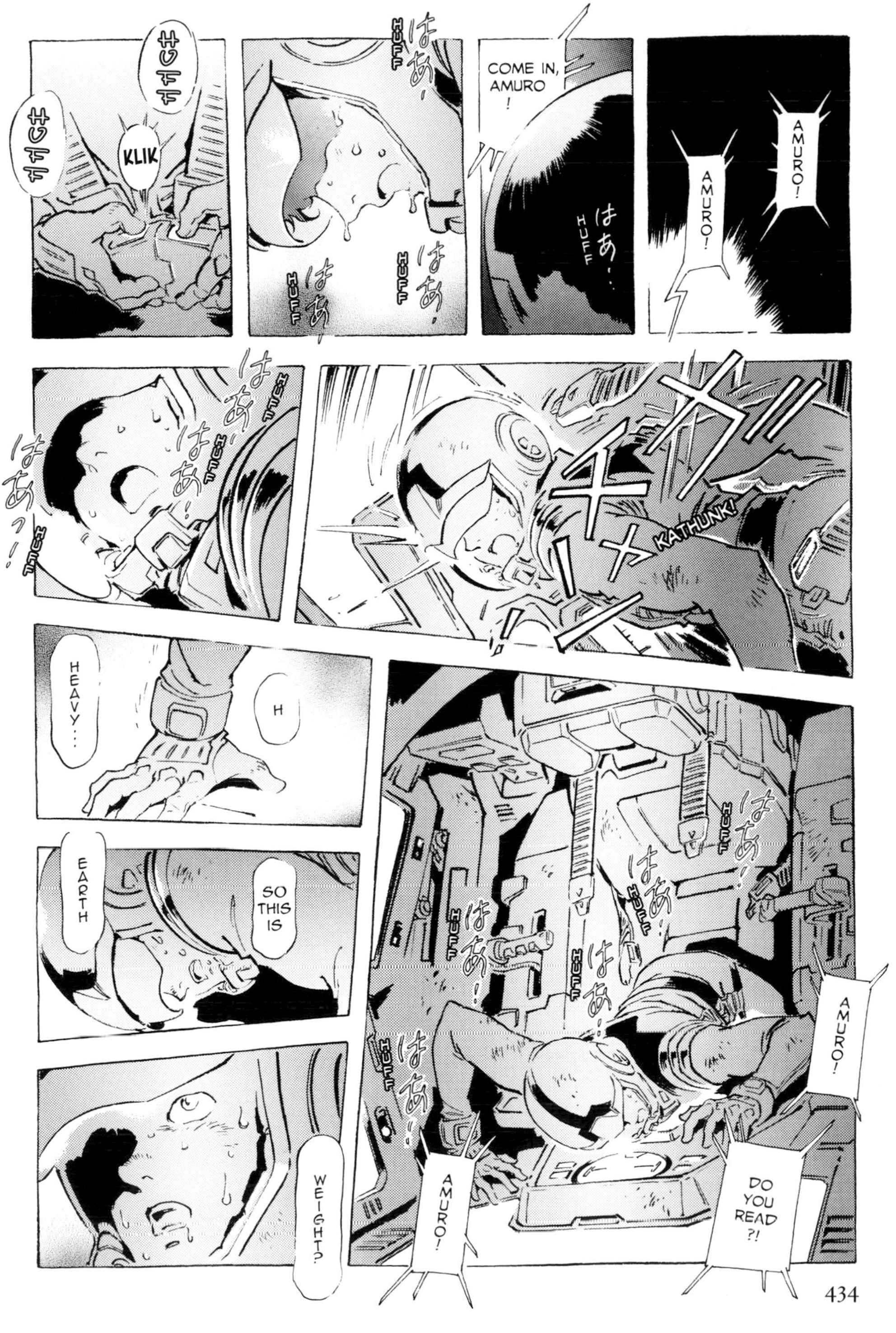
AMURO!
AMURO!
COME IN, AMURO!
はあ…
HUFF
はあ、
HUFF
はあ、
HUFF
はあ
HUFF
KLIK
HUFF
HUFF
ガキャ
KATHUNK!
はあ
TCH
はあ!
TCH
はあっ!
TCH
はあ!
HUFF
はあ…
HUFF
はあ!
HUFF
はあ!
HUFF
はあ!
HUFF
AMURO!
DO YOU READ?!
AMURO!
H
HEAVY…
SO THIS IS
EARTH
WEIGHT?

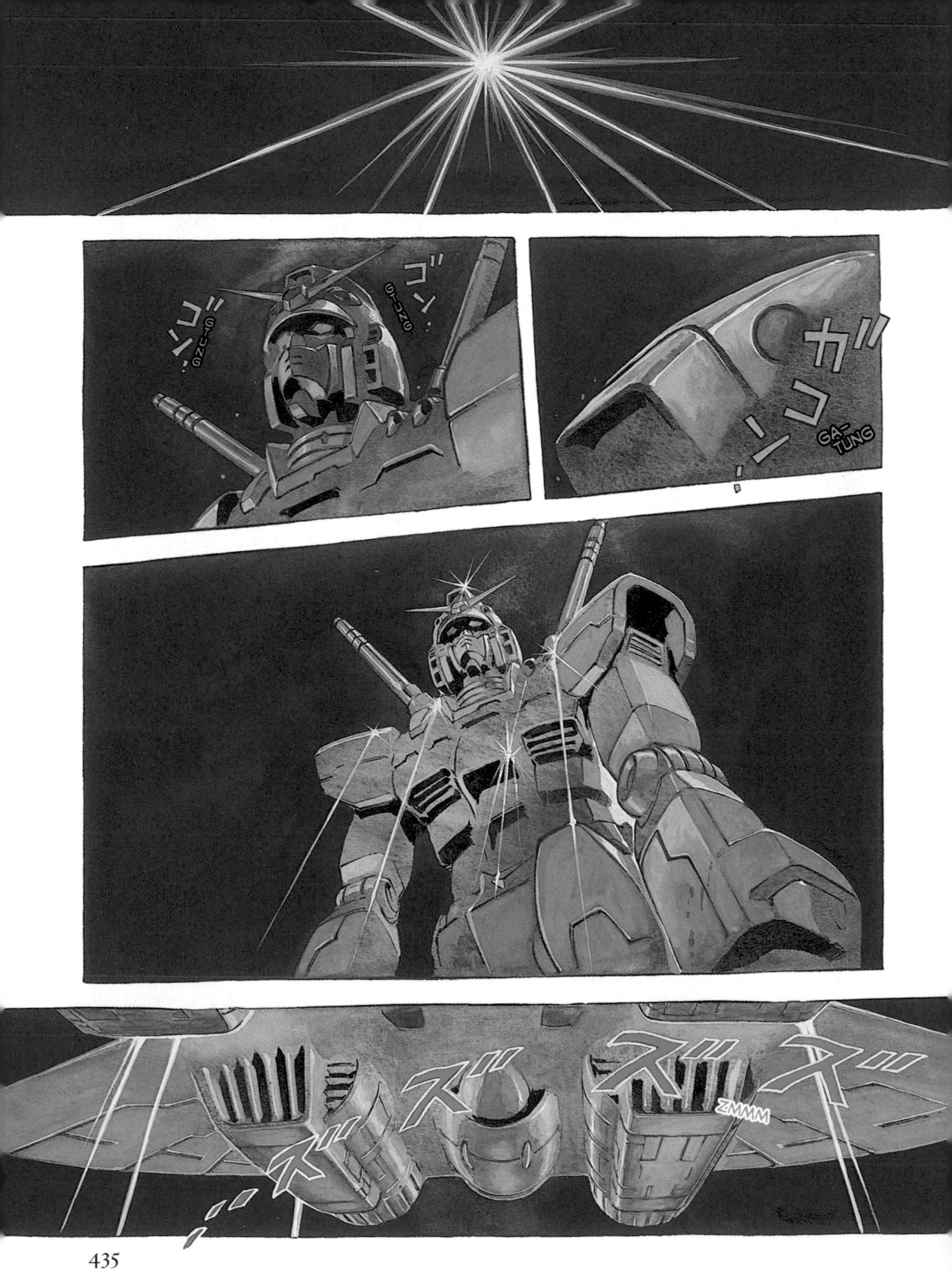
ガコン
GA-TUNG
ゴン
G-TUNG
ゴン
G-TUNG
ズズズズ
ZMMM

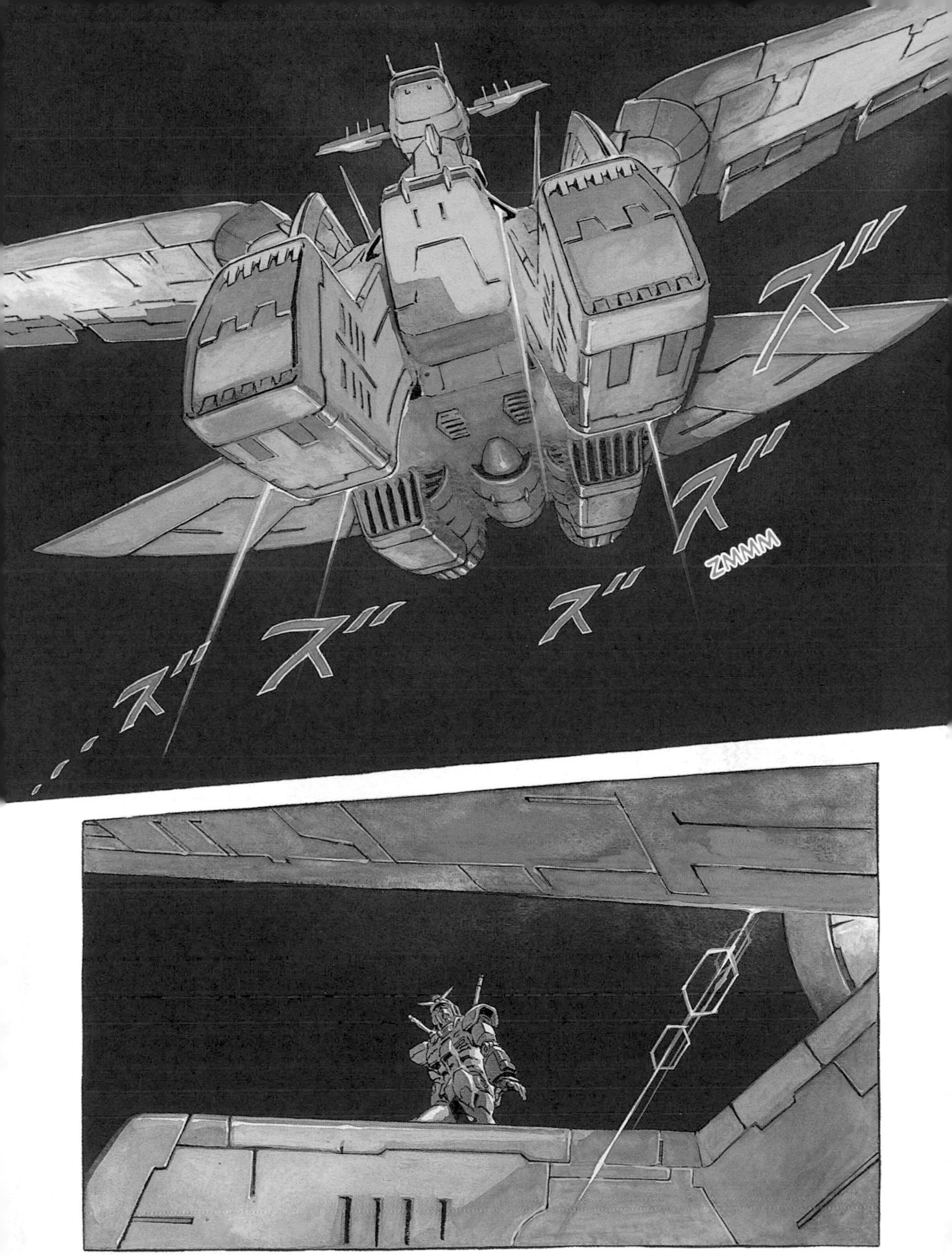
ズズズズズ…
ZMMMM

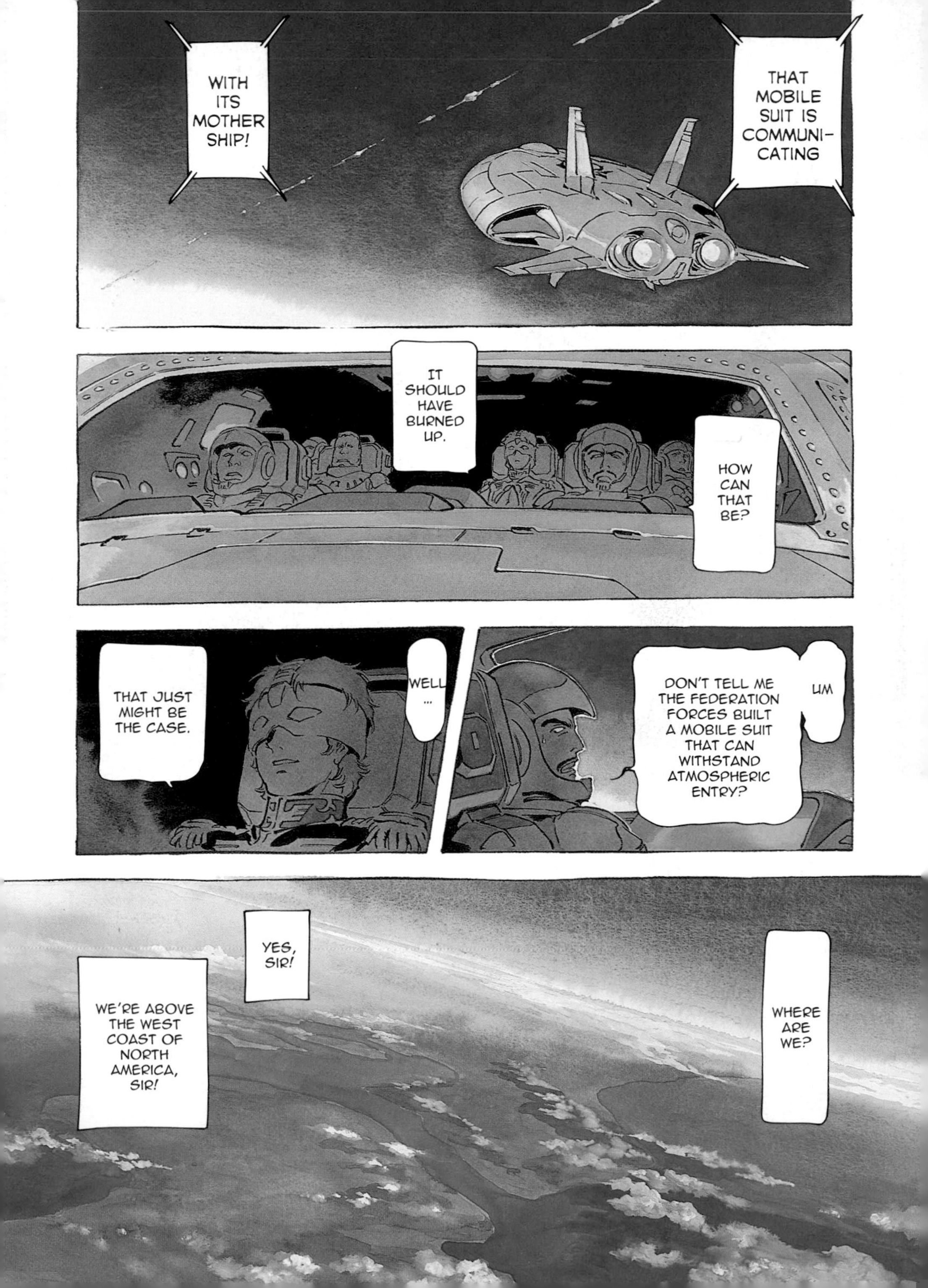
THAT MOBILE SUIT IS COMMUNICATING
WITH ITS MOTHER SHIP!
HOW CAN THAT BE?
IT SHOULD HAVE BURNED UP.
UM
DON'T TELL ME THE FEDERATION FORCES BUILT A MOBILE SUIT THAT CAN WITHSTAND ATMOSPHERIC ENTRY?
WELL ...
THAT JUST MIGHT BE THE CASE.
WHERE ARE WE?
YES, SIR!
WE'RE ABOVE THE WEST COAST OF NORTH AMERICA, SIR!

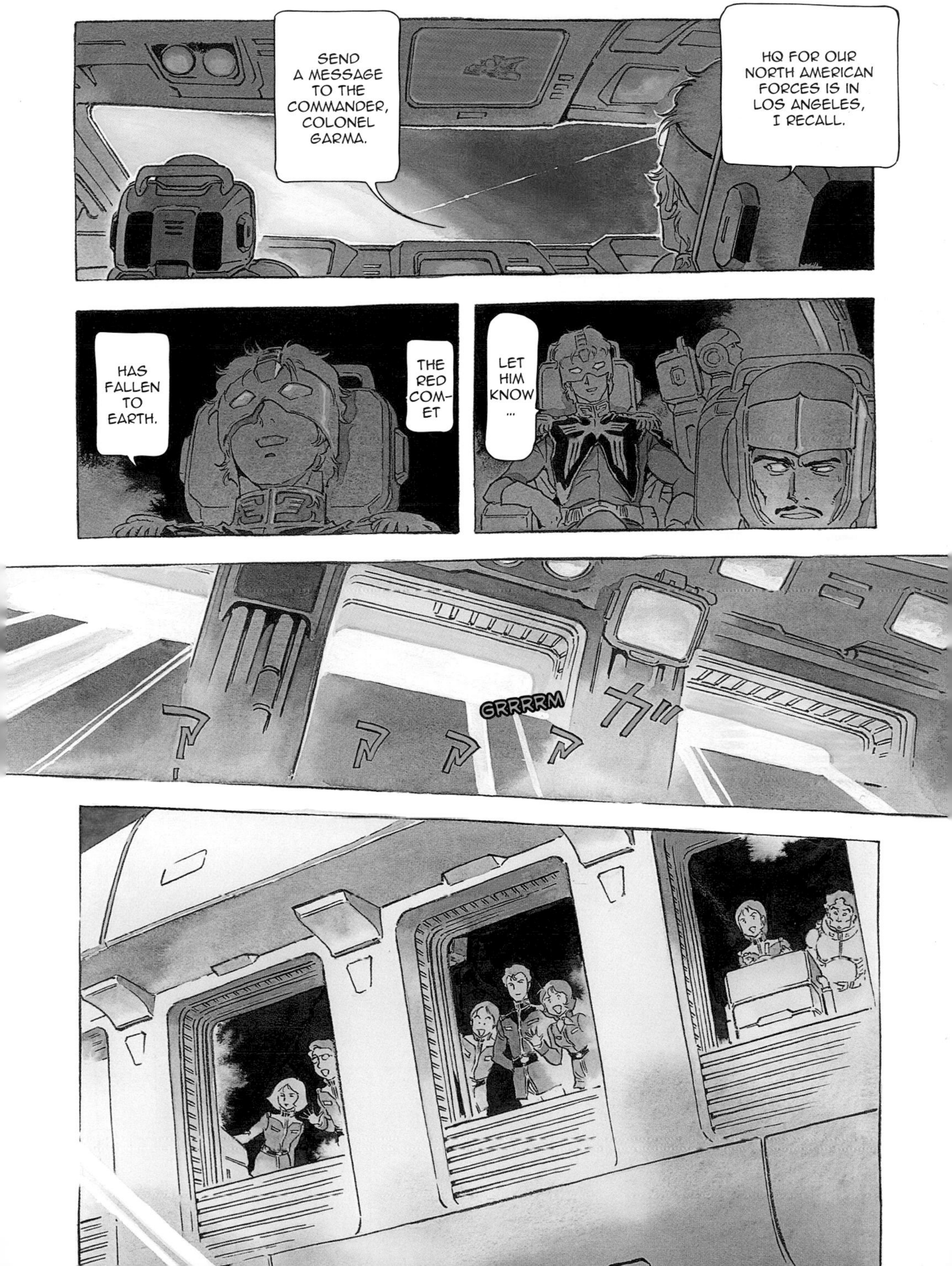
HQ FOR OUR NORTH AMERICAN FORCES IS IN LOS ANGELES, I RECALL.
SEND A MESSAGE TO THE COMMANDER, COLONEL GARMA.
LET HIM KNOW ...
THE RED COM-ET
HAS FALLEN TO EARTH.
GRRRRM

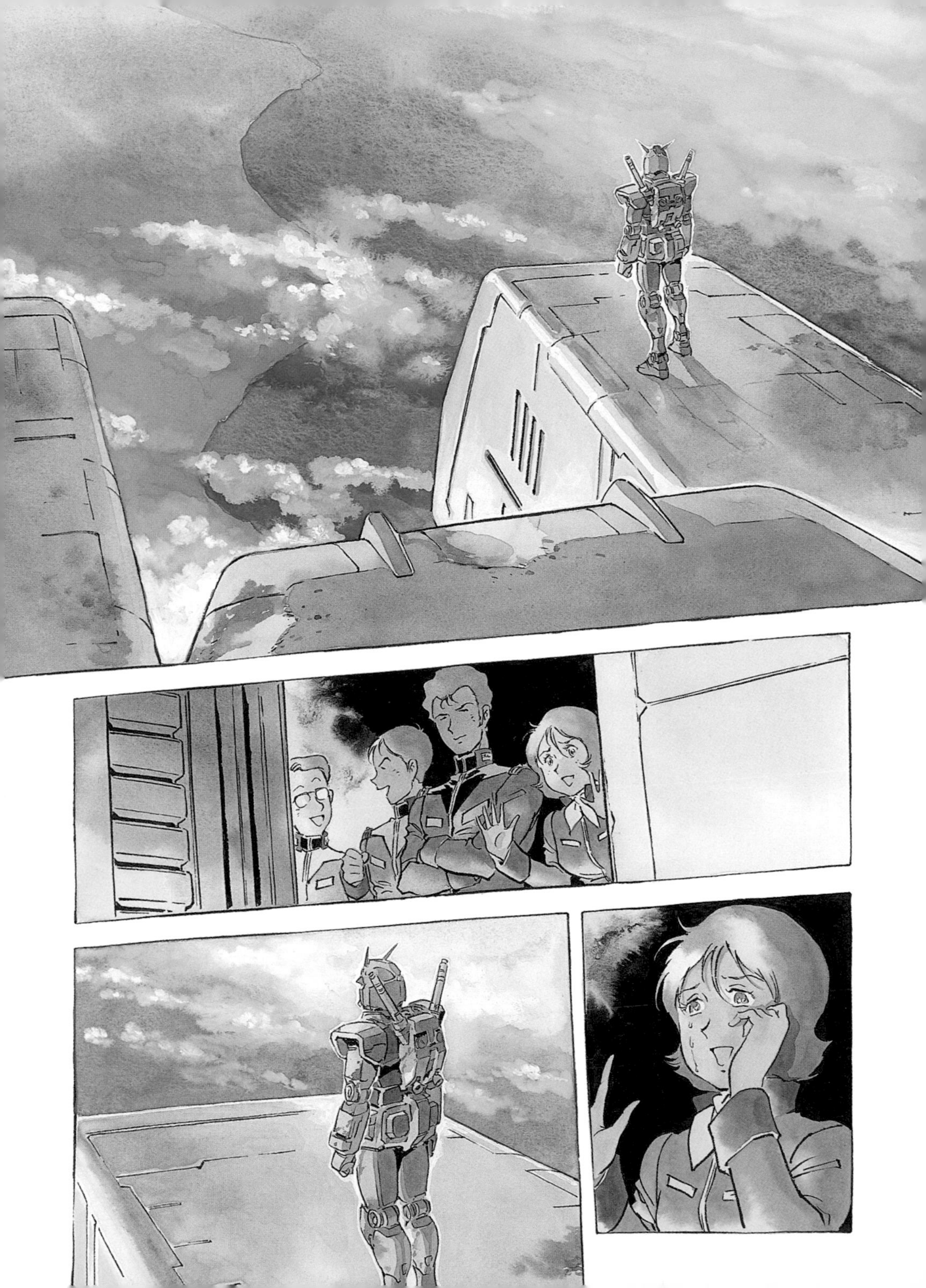

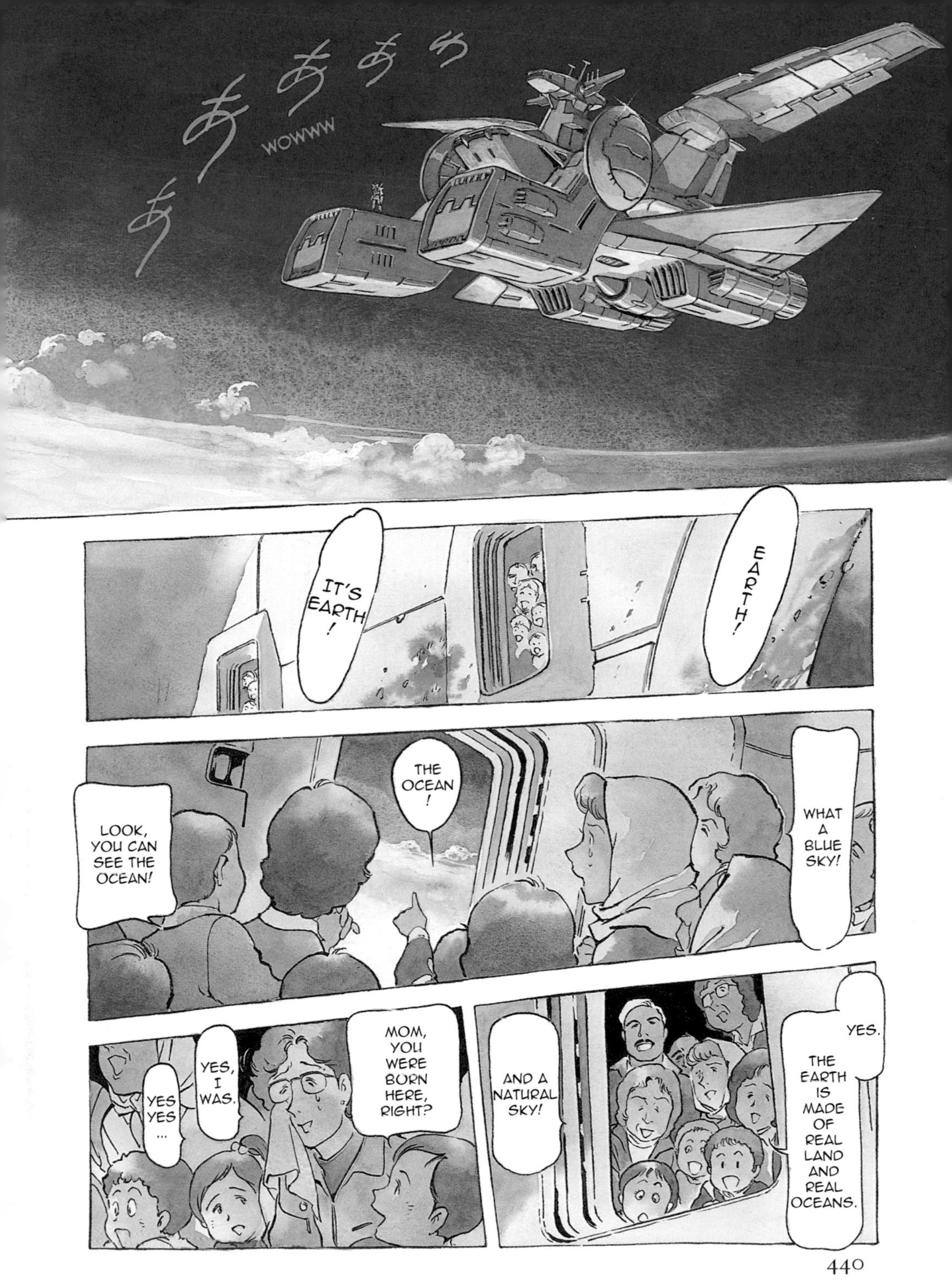
WOWWW
EARTH!
IT'S EARTH!
WHAT A BLUE SKY!
THE OCEAN!
LOOK, YOU CAN SEE THE OCEAN!
YES.
THE EARTH IS MADE OF REAL LAND AND REAL OCEANS.
AND A NATURAL SKY!
MOM, YOU WERE BORN HERE, RIGHT?
YES, I WAS.
YES YES ...

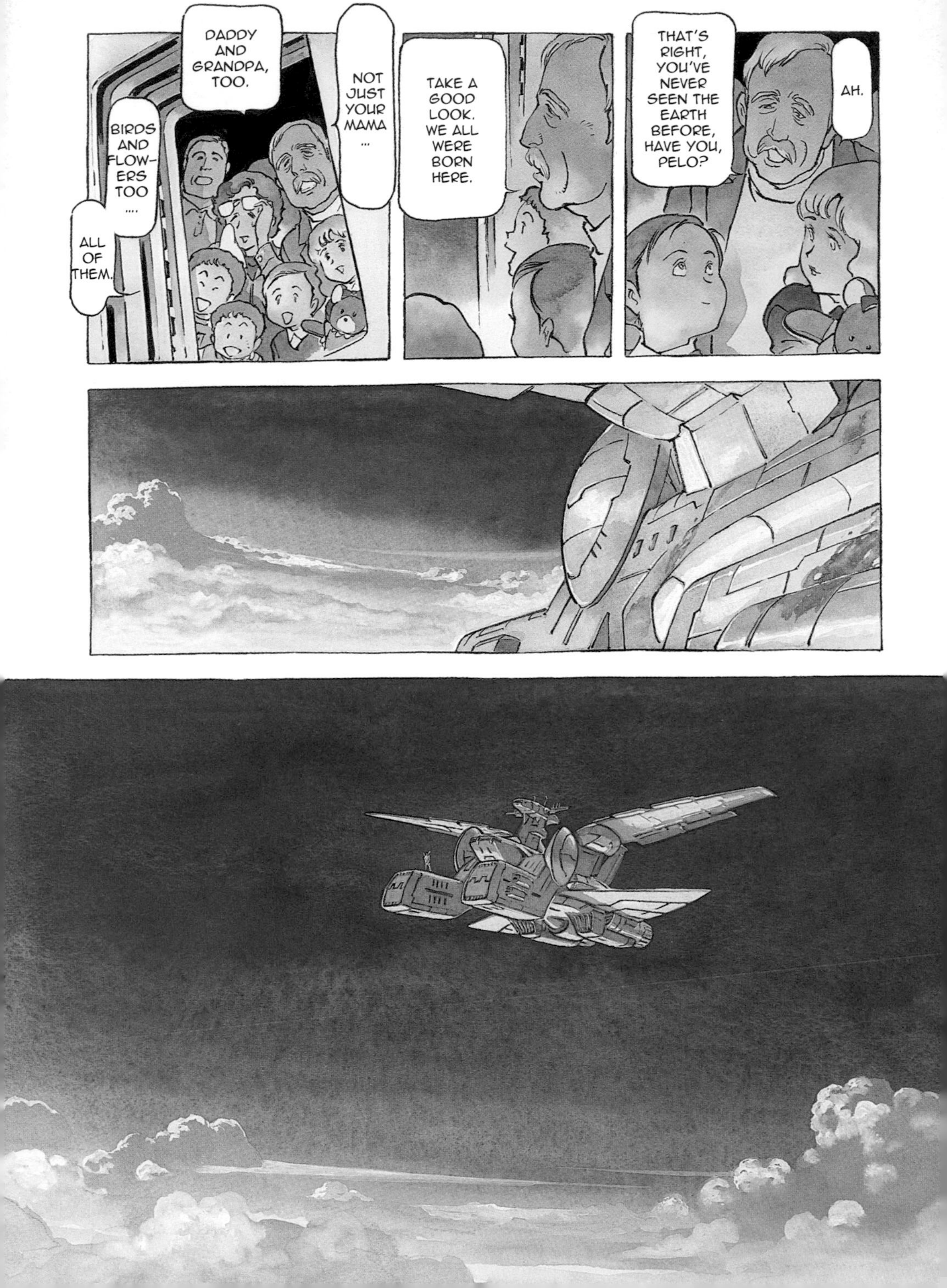
AH.
THAT'S RIGHT, YOU'VE NEVER SEEN THE EARTH BEFORE, HAVE YOU, PELO?
TAKE A GOOD LOOK. WE ALL WERE BORN HERE.
NOT JUST YOUR MAMA ...
DADDY AND GRANDPA, TOO.
BIRDS AND FLOWERS TOO ....
ALL OF THEM.

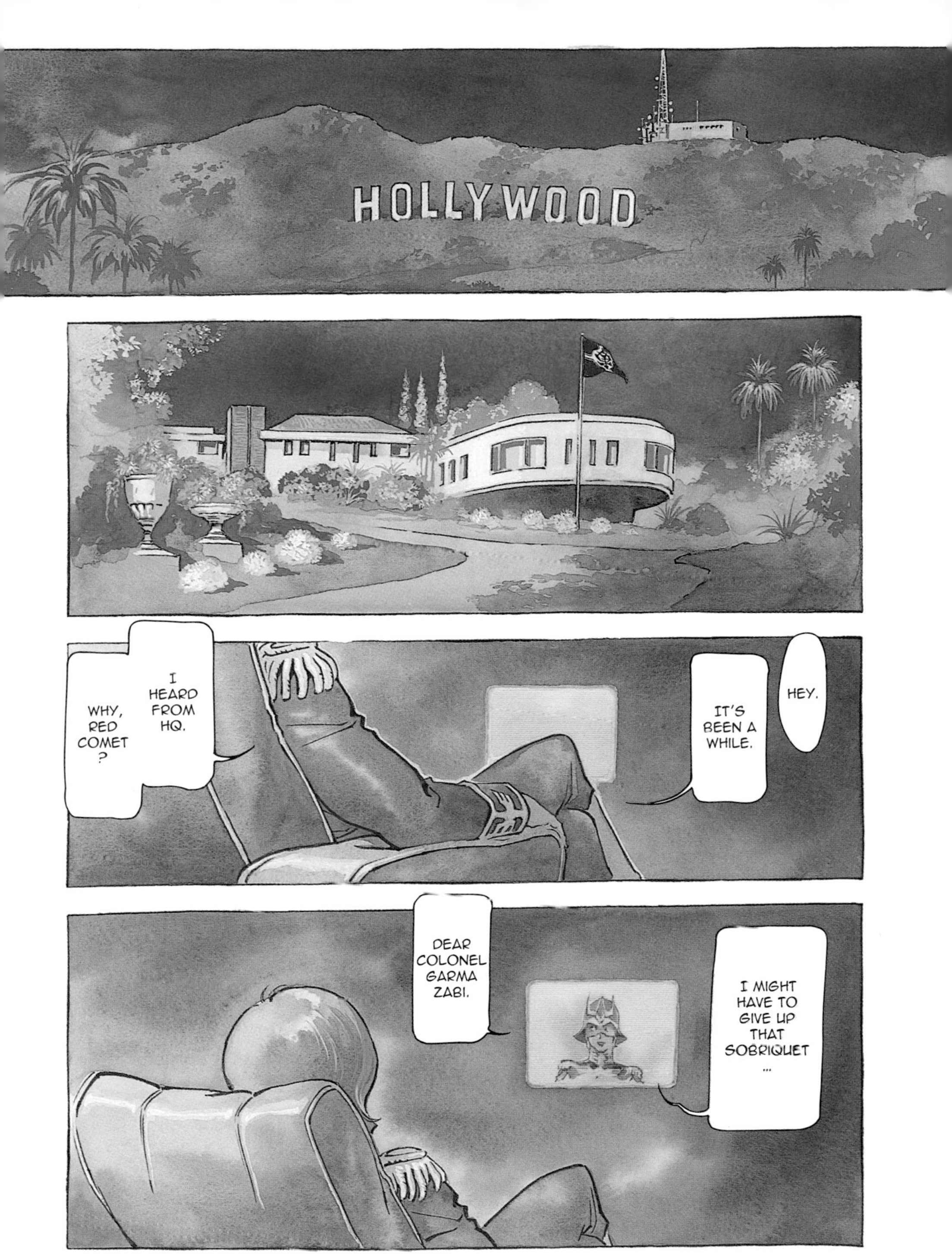
HOLLYWOOD
HEY.
IT'S BEEN A WHILE.
I HEARD FROM HQ.
WHY, RED COMET?
I MIGHT HAVE TO GIVE UP THAT SOBRIQUET ...
DEAR COLONEL GARMA ZABI.

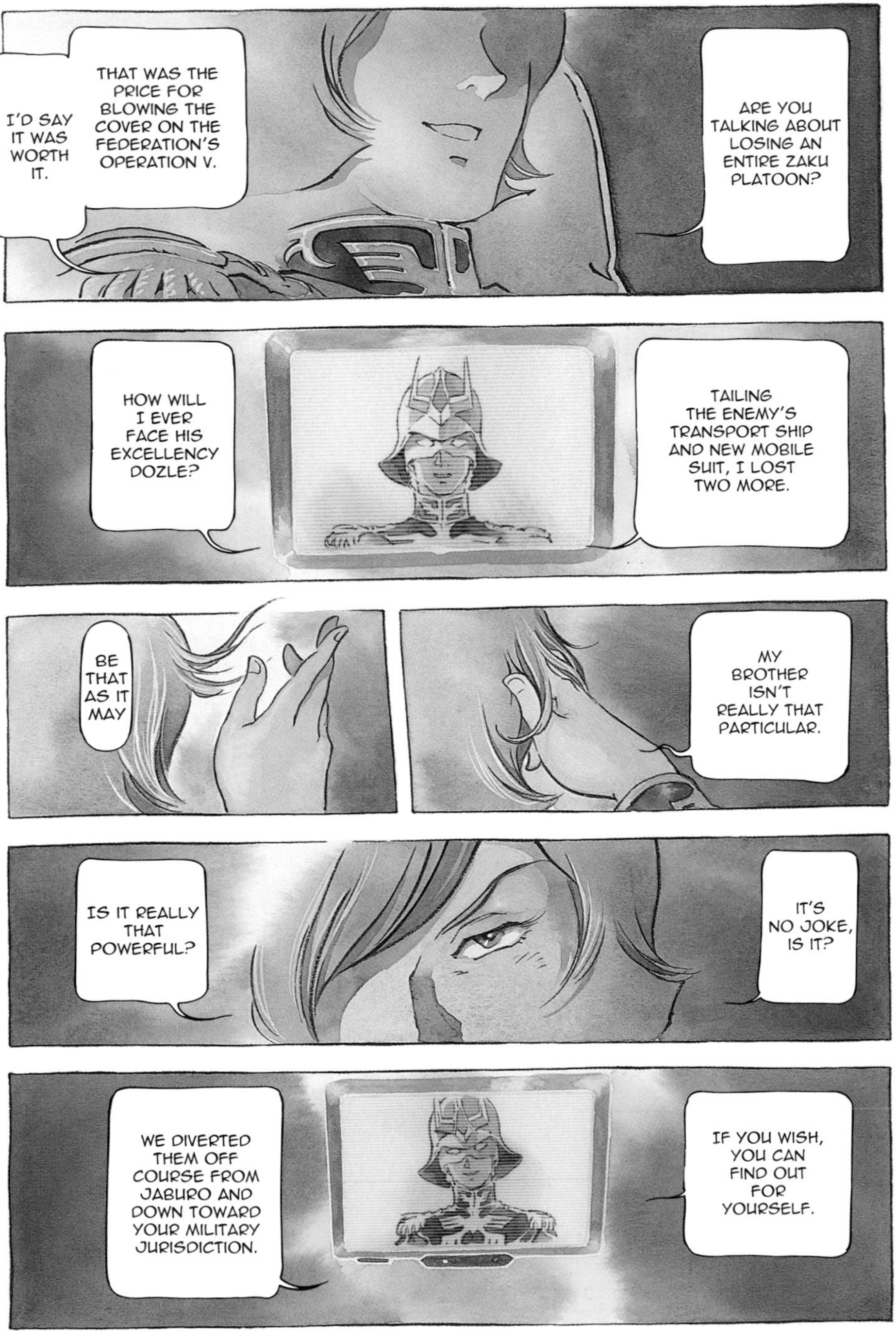
ARE YOU TALKING ABOUT LOSING AN ENTIRE ZAKU PLATOON?
THAT WAS THE PRICE FOR BLOWING THE COVER ON THE FEDERATION'S OPERATION V.
I'D SAY IT WAS WORTH IT.
TAILING THE ENEMY'S TRANSPORT SHIP AND NEW MOBILE SUIT, I LOST TWO MORE.
HOW WILL I EVER FACE HIS EXCELLENCY DOZLE?
MY BROTHER ISN'T REALLY THAT PARTICULAR.
BE THAT AS IT MAY
IT'S NO JOKE, IS IT?
IS IT REALLY THAT POWERFUL?
IF YOU WISH, YOU CAN FIND OUT FOR YOURSELF.
WE DIVERTED THEM OFF COURSE FROM JABURO AND DOWN TOWARD YOUR MILITARY JURISDICTION.

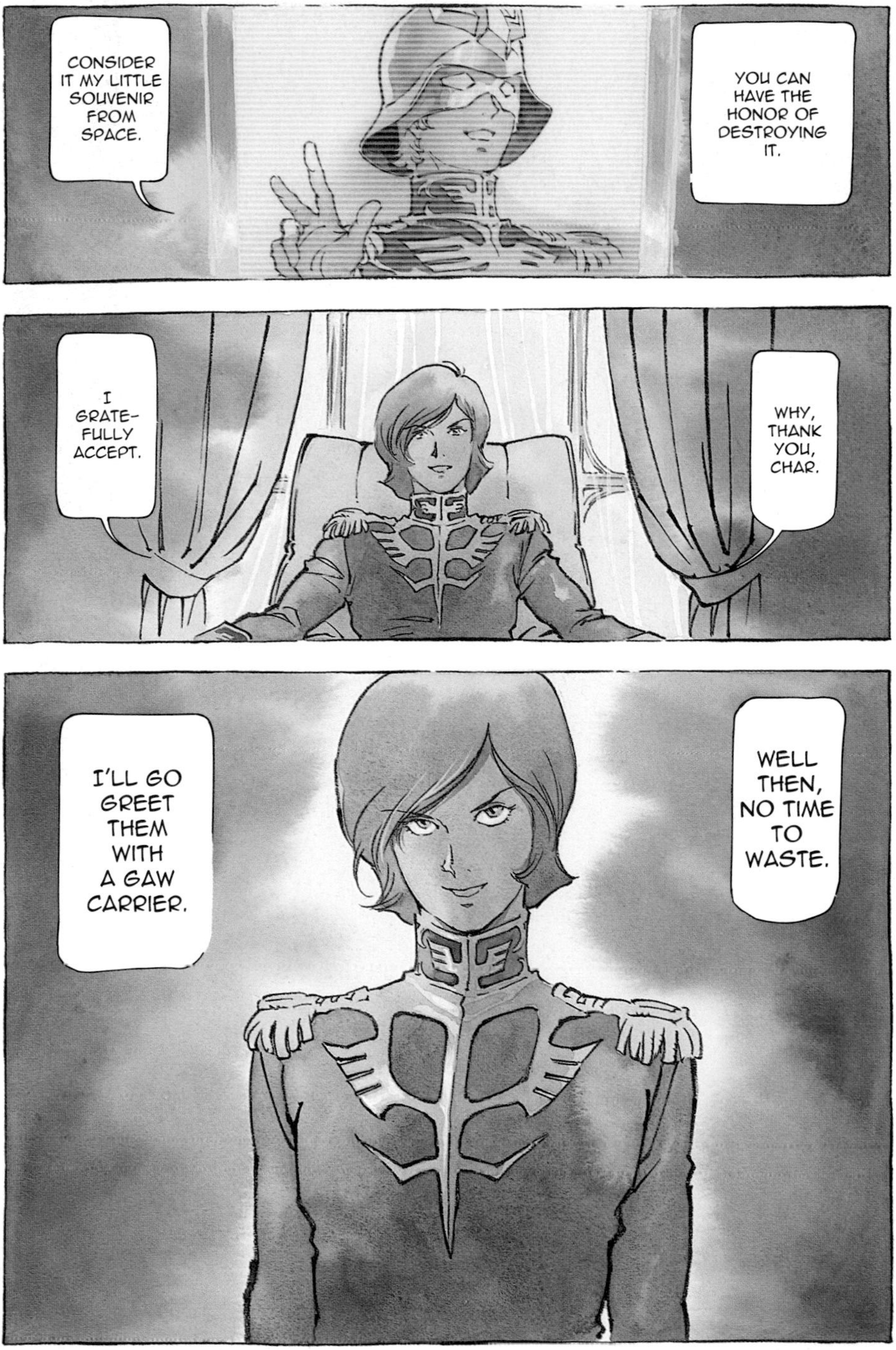
YOU CAN HAVE THE HONOR OF DESTROYING IT.
CONSIDER IT MY LITTLE SOUVENIR FROM SPACE.
WHY, THANK YOU, CHAR.
I GRATEFULLY ACCEPT.
WELL THEN, NO TIME TO WASTE.
I'LL GO GREET THEM WITH A GAW CARRIER.

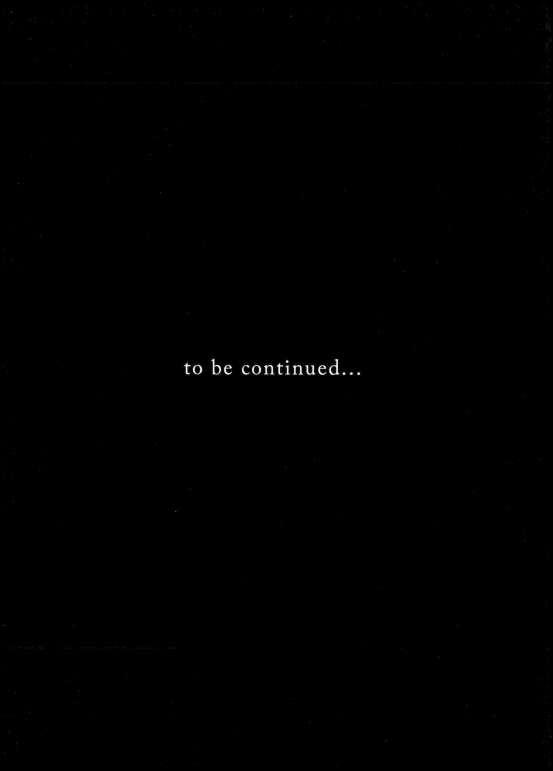

to be continued...

industry, is showing us here a true Tale through the medium of manga. I want as many people as possible to reconfirm and savor the essence and allure of Tales. I want this work's readers' receptivity to grow more fertile, more embodied.

Only Mr. Yasuhiko, I think, could have accomplished the task of reviving the Tale that is there in First *Gundam*.

I think this because I sense a certain equipoise—in that Yoshikazu Yasuhiko, the author who seconded diverging with the masses and business, who abandoned the anime industry and, as a solitary manga artist, gazed at and depicted the livelihood of individuals and state society historically, finally returns to *Gundam* after steering clear of it for over twenty years.

And I sense a certain good grace. He decides to draw *Gundam*—well-known to the masses as a premier franchise of the plastic model and anime industries—not from weariness, not as expiation, nor to return to his roots, but in earnest, as a work of his own.

That is why we are able to sense from this work a Tale that is both true and distinct from the First *Gundam* anime's.

I think that's fantastic. I thank anew that I am able to read Mr. Yasuhiko's *Gundam*.

Finally, dear reader holding this book, I urge you to pick up Mr. Yasuhiko's other works as well. I sincerely wish for you to know better what Tales are to you, to touch and feel them again.

As for me, I'll do my best so that my next project will come across as a Tale.

Hideaki Anno, *Gundam* Fan
April 10, 2005

Celebrating the Revival of *Gundam* as Tale

The world of *Gundam*, drawn once again as a Tale—that, I believe, is the greatest significance of this manga.

Of course, we also have here Mr. Yasuhiko's distinctive art, the indescribable charm woven by his gentle, delicate lines, the characters and mobile suits in particular. Yet I feel the greatest pleasure of this "Yasuhiko *Gundam*" lies in the resuscitation of a Tale lost among our memories of First *Gundam*.

It has already been twenty-five years since the broadcast of First *Gundam*.

I'm afraid the legacy of *Gundam* dwindled down to the mobile suits, in the form of plastic models as a business and military hobbyism. Even these mobile suits were summarized down to the protagonist mecha, Gundam, so that friend and foe alike were all uniformly Gundams. One could say this was inevitable: the pivotal creation that made *Gundam* a classic and drives the franchise expansion to this day is, of course, the mobile suit, represented by the RX-78 Gundam, a weapon bearing the elements of a character; and the way of the world is that characters are what ultimately remain with the audience.

It's not a bad thing. I simply find it unfortunate that the Tale that enveloped the worldview and ideas on war presented in First *Gundam* ceased to function as anything more than a device for the mobile suit fantasy.

In recent years, in the world of anime and manga too, the hollowing out of mainstream culture and the putative rise of subculture severely diluted and eroded the standing of the Tale.

Audiences have come to need a work only as an escape from reality, as a comfortable dream, judging everything on the criterion of *moe*, while creators' intellectual paucity and the jumble of trivial touches have encouraged that structure. At the same time, TV-type mass consumption, which prizes instant gratification and simplistic results, laid the impoverished grounds of contemporary Japanese entertainment, giving rise to masses that can only respond with praise for superficial details and technical proficiency; with tears, laughter, fear, or some other outpouring of simple emotions; or with identifying and particularism.

And here we are, in this stagnant state of affairs. I am stuck here myself. It's embarrassing and frustrating, and I also regret that I contributed to it.

I want it fixed. The sooner, the better.

That is why I am so glad that *Gundam*, the animation brand with the largest market in the

Toward the Birth of *THE ORIGIN*

"Yoshikazu Yasuhiko is willing to draw a manga of First *Gundam*."

It was near the end of 2000, I recall, when Sunrise proposed this sensational plan.

Mr. Yasuhiko was a grandmaster of original works as a manga artist by then. My sense was that he maintained a distance from the anime industry, my belief that he approached *Gundam*-related projects with caution. When the unexpected offer came, it was a fantastic surprise, and I remember the churn of excitement like it was yesterday.

Behind the scenes of that proposal were Sunrise's plans to expand the North American market for the *Gundam* franchise. For the linchpin of that operation, they needed a manga by Mr. Yasuhiko, but I personally tabled such concerns as secondary, overwhelmed by how badly I wanted to read it and roused by my sense of mission as an editor to obtain the manuscript for our company.

When I received the storyboards from Sunrise, they went up through the end of *Garma*, that is, the scene in which Sovereign Degwin hears of Garma's death and drops his scepter. The moment I finished reading, I had goosebumps. This was no simple rehashing of the anime version but a retelling in which the subtleties of Mr. Yasuhiko's characterization and storytelling style, honed in his historical manga, fed back into the world of *Gundam* with a brilliantly struck balance. That was the exact moment I felt certain that this work would open up new possibilities without fail.

It was Mr. Yasuhiko's request that each installment of the serialization consist of about 100 pages. To accommodate this, I immediately decided to start up an exclusive *Gundam* manga magazine. Dissenting opinions from within our firm—could we really issue a periodical based on one property?—were summarily suppressed by the success of *Gundam Ace*.

Mr. Yasuhiko's manga singlehandedly catalyzed an explosive response from fans who had reacted coolly to fervent "20th Anniversary" promotions. It segued into the subsequent "Gundam revival" and the popularity of *SEED*.

Incidentally, the audacity of naming the work fell upon me. I had "Origin" in the back of my mind as a name for the protagonist of a hero manga I wanted to see created someday, but I didn't think I'd ever get a chance to use it, and THE ORIGIN was kindly adopted as the title for the Yasuhiko *Gundam*. The fact that Mr. Yasuhiko himself liked it was, for me, the greatest joy.

Shinichiro Inoue
President and CEO, Kadokawa Shoten Publishing Co.

ancient Japan, the Roman Empire, medieval Europe, and Manchuria. No doubt this experience—obstinately, obsessively depicting societal upheaval and war from individual points of view—helped him make the valuable perspective already present in the original *Gundam* all the richer here.

The savor of an exquisite balance

As argued above, this manga exudes a strong presence far surpassing the usual level of film comics and adaptations that merely trace a screen version. With every turn of the page it grows clearer that we owe this less to Yoshikazu Yasuhiko's place among the original staff of *Gundam* than to his point of pride as a manga artist, which is having a lucid perspective and convictions.

Of course, this work has also inherited the worldview and tastes of the First *Gundam*, in whose creation the director, Yoshiyuki Tomino, played a central role. Capturing the elements that over twenty-some years have become familiar to the many fans of the animated versions, even as it deepens the saga, is exactly what makes this work moving. The unique charms of this acrobatic retelling are easy to take for granted now that the work is well known, but was it not in fact a miraculous feat of balance?

We've been blessed with the chance to read this manga in long, engrossing volumes with luxuriously large pages. Rediscovering the story's hidden depths, let us continue to relish it.

Ryusuke Hikawa
An anime critic, born in 1958 in Hyogo Prefecture, Mr. Hikawa has penned a column in the monthly *Gundam Ace* and also appeared on the NHK program *Anime Bedtime Stories.* His recent works include (as editor) *The Lorelai Surfaces.*

These characterizations give us the illusion that Char is reprising *Mobile Suit Gundam* with a more comprehensively realized persona. Such painstaking rearrangements pervade the entire work and lend a mature, full quality to *THE ORIGIN*.

A great way to enjoy this work: lose yourself in the story for your first reading, then pick it up again to discover these links and fine attention to detail.

A perspective on death engenders a view of history

While *THE ORIGIN* manages both a broad viewpoint and a profound treatment of its subjects, perhaps it strikes our chords with realness most when the "deaths of persons" are depicted. Animation—a highly public medium, a group operation with responsibilities divvied up among many—can have difficulties expressing such topics. In novels or manga, on the contrary, the writer has exclusive and intimate control, and that may be why death is something that arises in a manner that feels more essential.

As one example, we have a scene unique to *THE ORIGIN*. During the evacuation of Side 7, a man who overloaded his car so badly that it broke down threatens Fraw Bow. At Sayla's warning shot, his selfish pack backs away and is left behind, and what fate they meet after that is left unclear. When *White Base* departs, however, it's being said on the bridge that the oxygen concentration is dipping and that it's a lost cause. Precisely because this line is delivered with professional detachment, its resonance lingers and forces us to tarry on the implications.

Plain death, beyond good and evil, right and wrong, as inevitable phenomena in war, is ubiquitously depicted and sets the tone of the story.

Among named characters, the death of *White Base*'s Captain Paolo leaves a particularly strong impression. Right before his passing on Luna II, he utters significant words on generational change, one of the story's major themes. Truth be told, the face of an expired person—the nose should look a bit sunken, and so on—calls for no little artistic prowess, and Yasuhiko accomplishes this admirably, so that Paolo's life converges on the moment with a gravitas capable of underpinning the work.

The fact that Paolo once served as captain of a torpedo gunboat hints at long and varied campaigns of military suppression predating the establishment of the Principality of Zeon. A brief exchange that adds depth on the macro scale—anti-Zion measures have become so urgent that an old reservist and instructor needs to be called back into active duty—also becomes proximate when it is folded into the micro scale—the death of a person.

It cannot be emphasized enough how thoroughly this work is shot through with this multilayered perspective, namely of overlapping individual stories weaving the history of a world. Perhaps the twenty-first century, which opened with an act of terrorism, demands it.

Most crucial in the retelling of *Gundam* as a classic is such a point of view, scanning up from the individual to the whole, and forth from the past into the future. As a manga artist, Yoshikazu Yasuhiko has worked on quite a few historical pieces, set in mythical Greece,

Deeper characterizations directly enrich the story

Countless subtle strokes also flesh out the characters in this iteration to richen its appeal. Yasuhiko masterfully modifies the players while keeping intact their basic appearances and personalities. Once the characters start to breathe in the *ORIGIN* world, they gain new life and purpose, so merely copying and pasting their development from the screen would have been insufficient.

Take Amuro, the protagonist. His first scene in *Activation* gives us a startling picture of a hardcore geek: a dirty room, a computer obsession. While Amuro always had some traits of an "otaku," it was not until several years after 1979 that the stereotype entered mainstream consciousness. While his depiction in *THE ORIGIN* likely reflects this societal change, more essential to the narrative is the fact that Amuro's obsessive, obstinate side is amplified for the reader.

Because manga readily permits rereading (being planar unlike animation), links between related parts of the story are easier to tease out. As a result, the steps in Amuro's character depiction seem clearer.

In the second half of this installment, we have a serious scene showing the beginnings of a rift between Amuro, who is able to fight off Char's Zaku despite his lack of experience, and Bright, who refuses to give him any credit for his accomplishment. This confrontation leads directly to Amuro's petulant rejection of Bright's plan to attack the enemy's Papua supply ship. While this is the exact opposite of his behavior in the TV series, the development does not feel at all out of place, given the buildup of tension between the two characters and Amuro's slightly more aggressive personality in *THE ORIGIN*. Indeed, it links back to Amuro in his Side 7 room obsessively gathering information on the Gundam. Such scenes accumulate to give us a subtly different impression of the characters, but I would argue that the changes are desirable in terms of depth.

The portrayal of Amuro's rival, the immensely popular Char, has an especially positive impact on the work's overall appeal. Since the whole of the story to the last animated episode has been taken into account, traits and deeds are retrofitted to him.

The depiction of Char in a fury beneath his mask after the supply ship has been destroyed, for instance, is an unexpected reaction from the "cool villain" of the early animated episodes. Yet, when something does set off his emotions, Char, being Char, smartly moderates even anger and responds with military action without missing a beat. This modus operandi, Char's fundamental trait, is common to both the animated and manga versions.

The result is Char's daring infiltration of Luna II, which in turn leads to a major dramatic event—the brief reunion with his long-lost sister Artesia, now known as Sayla. (In the film version, they met in Side 7.) At first, he approaches Sayla as a woman he's never met before, and from his expression we get a glimpse of how he behaves toward women. Such moments create a more well-rounded, human character.

Finer worldbuilding enhances our enjoyment

What surprised the fans was the sophisticated staging, the tone of the narrative, and the expansion of the story world. Here, the keyword is *maturation*. Yoshikazu Yasuhiko's growth as a writer has imparted a deep flavor to the saga known as *Gundam*.

THE ORIGIN selects and reorders story elements from both small and big screen First *Gundam* animated properties. In addition to Yasuhiko's reconstruction of the world and reinterpretation of the characters, the art delivers a vivid real-time feeling consistent with an animator's expertise, and therein lies the special appeal of his approach to manga.

Allow me to bring up some examples. First of all, with respect to worldbuilding, he has dug into the story events and introduced additional information in order to "thicken" the setting. For instance, in *Activation* there are more details about Gundam as a prototype and the Federation Forces, with more military resource material than in the animated versions.

A representative moment: the traces of multiple mock battles indicating that the Gundam is ready to be transferred from Side 7 to *White Base*. There is even an administrative facility, as well as designated test pilots. Though never depicted in the animated versions, these background details that one surmises were there from the outset fill out the story and give it a realistic feel.

Several elements of the basic premise have also been revised. For example, in the animated versions, the Gundam, Guncannon, and Guntank were all new mobile suits developed concurrently by the Federation Forces in order to counter the Zaku. In *THE ORIGIN*, however, only the Gundam is new, while the Guntank is a land unit in use since before the advent of the Zaku and the Guncannon is an older model of mobile suit. This positioning gives a keener sense of the stages of development and the time required.

In line with these changes, there have been revisions in both side's logistics. Instead of three Zakus reconnoitering Side 7 in force, we have six, double the number, and the prototype Gundam that intercepts them has a head that differs in design from the model later piloted by Amuro. This packed a potent impact even for fans steeped in the franchise.

Back in 1979, a typical giant robot anime did not require too many details in its worldbuilding. It was quite sufficient to have military bases and civilian areas for each side and sites that turned into battlefields. In contrast, First *Gundam* submitted that people necessarily belonged to abstract immensities, to society and world, and that macroscopic entities called states perpetrated the calamity of war, within which clashes between robots occurred as a conflict of arms. *Gundam* presented a worldview where both micro and macro were manifest—it was a game-changer.

THE ORIGIN not only continues with that perspective but deepens it in a way that production at the time did not allow. Surely the medium of manga, in which one creator has comprehensive control over both the visual and storytelling aspects, is what opened up this possibility.

A Matured *Gundam* Saga

The core of the First *Gundam* visuals—Yoshikazu Yasuhiko

If you are reading this, you are most likely well aware of the impact made by the 1979 animated series *Mobile Suit Gundam* (created and produced by Yoshiyuki Tomino). Yoshikazu Yasuhiko's announcement of his great project (in the June 2001 issue of *Newtype* magazine), a manga version of that series, created an enormous stir and elicited intense anticipation among original viewers who carried the impact in their minds these past twenty-something years as well as among the many *Gundam* fans born since.

This was in no small part due to Yasuhiko's position at the core of the visual universe (excluding mechanical design and background) of the initial *Mobile Suit Gundam* series (affectionately dubbed "First *Gundam*") twenty-something years ago.

His roles in the production comprised all of the following:

1) Character design
2) Visual direction
3) Animation director
4) Cells and layout
5) Illustrator

Which is to say, Yoshikazu Yasuhiko had his hand in virtually every visual pot—from the characters' appearances to inclinations and mannerisms, from essential cinematic elements such as consistency of story space and subtle atmospheric touches to promotional illustrations. Thanks to him, the imagery of *Gundam* came together as a cohesive whole.

Of course, animation production is a joint undertaking, a crystallization of the efforts of various staff; not all of it was Yasuhiko. The mecha designs for the Gundam, Zakus and so on, for instance, were the work of Kunio Okawara. Yet, because at the time of the First *Gundam*'s production there was no such role as a mecha visual director, on film the mobile suits were characterized via Yasuhiko's delicate lines in a magnificent synergy with Okawara's designs. Even the popular plastic models, for the most part, sought to reproduce that character-like softness the mobile suits have in the films.

So it truly is quite a big deal that *Gundam*'s manga reboot came at the hand of none other than Yoshikazu Yasuhiko, the creator of its visual universe. Accordingly, our anticipation was focused on the aesthetics.

In June 2001, however, when a new magazine called *Gundam Ace* appeared boasting a serialization of *Mobile Suit Gundam: THE ORIGIN*, not only did fans find their hopes met and surpassed with regard to the visuals, they were surprised and thrilled by the emotional impact of the story as well.

Collector's Edition

Mobile Suit Gundam
THE ORIGIN

— ACTIVATION —

BONUS ESSAYS

AIZOUBAN MOBILE SUIT GUNDAM THE ORIGIN vol. 1

Translation: Melissa Tanaka

Production: Grace Lu
Hiroko Mizuno
Nicole Dochych
Daniela Yamada
Risa Cho

First published in Japan in 2005 by KADOKAWA CORPORATION, Tokyo

English translation rights arranged with KADOKAWA CORPORATION,
through Tuttle-Mori Agency, Inc., Tokyo

Translation copyright © 2013 Vertical

Published by Vertical, an imprint of Kodansha USA Publishing, LLC

Originally published in Japanese as *Kidou Senshi Gundam THE ORIGIN*
volumes 1 and 2 in 2002 and re-issued in hardcover as *Aizouban Kidou Senshi Gundam
THE ORIGIN I -Shidou-* in 2005, by Kadokawa Shoten, Co., Ltd.

Kidou Senshi Gundam THE ORIGIN first serialized in *Gundam Ace,*
Kadokawa Shoten, Co., Ltd., 2001-2011

ISBN: 978-1-935654-87-2

Manufactured in the United States of America

First Edition

Eighth Printing

Kodansha USA Publishing, LLC
451 Park Avenue South
7th Floor
New York, NY 10016
www.kodansha.us

HERE FOR THE BONUS ESSAYS? RIGHT WAY!

WANT TO READ THE MANGA? WRONG WAY!

Japanese books, including manga like this one,
are meant to be read from right to left.
So the front cover is actually the back cover, and vice versa.
To read this book, please flip it over
and start in the top right-hand corner.
Read the panels, and the bubbles in the panels,
from right to left,
then drop down to the next row and repeat.
It may make you dizzy at first, but forcing your brain to do things
backwards makes you smarter in the long run.
We swear.